TRAVELER

the caribbean

NATIONAL GEOGRAPHIC
TRAVELER

the caribbean

ports of call & beyond

Emma Stanford & Nick Hanna
photography by Matt Propert

National Geographic
Washington, D.C.

.CONTENTS

Pages 2–3: English Bay, Antigua, sparkles at twilight.
Opposite: Grenada's Annandale Falls cools visitors, island style.

TRAVELING WITH EYES OPEN

Alert travelers go with a purpose and leave with a benefit. If you travel responsibly, you can help support wildlife conservation, historic preservation, and cultural enrichment in the places you visit. You can enrich your own travel experience as well.

To be a geo-savvy traveler:

- Recognize that your presence has an impact on the places you visit.

- Spend your time and money in ways that sustain local character. (Besides, it's more interesting that way.)

- Value the destination's natural and cultural heritage.

- Respect the local customs and traditions.

- Express appreciation to local people about things you find interesting and unique to the place: its nature and scenery, music and food, historic villages and buildings.

- Vote with your wallet: Support the people who support the place, patronizing businesses that make an effort to celebrate and protect what's special there. Seek out local shops, restaurants, hotels, and inns. Use tour operators who love their home—who love taking care of it a nd showing it off. Avoid businesses that detract from the character of the place.

- Enrich yourself, taking home memories and stories to tell, knowing that you have contributed to the preservation and enhancement of the destination.

That is the type of travel now called geotourism, defined as "tourism that sustains or enhances the geographical character of a place—its environment, culture, aesthetics, heritage, and the well-being of its residents." To learn more, visit National Geographic's Center for Sustainable Destinations at *travel.nationalgeographic.com/travel/geotourism.*

the caribbean

ports of call & beyond

ABOUT THE AUTHORS & THE PHOTOGRAPHER

Emma Stanford has lived in Australia, France, and the United Kingdom and has been traveling and writing for 30 years. She has penned more than three dozen guidebooks to destinations throughout Europe and North America, compiled cruise guides to the Caribbean islands, and edited an adventure motorcycle handbook. Her globe-trotting newspaper articles have encompassed exploits as challenging and varied as rallying kit cars in the Sahara, scaling the Hindu Kush aboard a Badakshani stallion, and mountain biking through France and Spain to the pilgrim city of Santiago de Compostela. Stanford updated and wrote the new features and sidebars for the 2016 edition of this guidebook.

Nick Hanna has been a professional travel writer and photographer for nearly 30 years. He has worked as a freelance writer for numerous national and international newspapers and magazines and has written nine guidebooks, including one that covered more than 200 tropical beaches around the world. He has also co-authored a book on the conservation of coral reefs and written extensively on the marine environment and scuba diving.

Matt Propert is a freelance photographer and photo editor based in Santa Cruz, California. His work has been featured in many National Geographic books and special edition magazines. Propert has also photographed three travel books for National Geographic: *Miami & the Keys, The Caribbean,* and *Italy.* Matt is a member of Visura and is represented by Nat Geo Creative.

Charting Your Trip

A tropical paradise of picture-postcard islands anchored in turquoise seas, sugar sand beaches, teeming coral reefs, and exotic rain forest blooms, the Caribbean is the quintessential winter escape. The region's 50-plus islands and several thousand uninhabited cays, rocks, and reefs form a 2,500-mile (4,000 km) arc reaching from Cuba, 90 miles (145 km) south of Key West on the tip of Florida, to Trinidad, just 7 miles (11 km) off the coast of Venezuela.

Where to Visit

Encircling the million-square-mile (2.5 million sq km) Caribbean Sea, with the Atlantic Ocean buffeting their windward sides, the islands of the Caribbean can be roughly divided into two main geographical groups: the Greater Antilles, or Western Caribbean, ranging from Cuba around to Puerto Rico and the Virgin Islands (excluding the Bahamas, which are a separate entity); and the Lesser Antilles, or Eastern Caribbean. This latter island chain is further divided into the ex-British Leeward and Windward Islands, interspersed with the distinctly Gallic French Antilles and the Dutch Caribbean.

Variety is the spice of the Caribbean topography: It is true to say that there is no such thing as a typical Caribbean island. Each one has its own particular style shaped by a unique combination of geology, historical influences, and attitudes that can vary dramatically between neighbors separated by a few nautical miles. The best starting point for planning a Caribbean vacation is to decide on the style of break to suit you. If sightseeing is high on the agenda, then an island-hopping cruise is the ideal option and the most popular form of Caribbean travel with visitors from North America (see pp. 136–137). The Caribbean's main cruise hubs are Puerto Rico and Barbados and there are frequent departures from Miami and Fort Lauderdale.

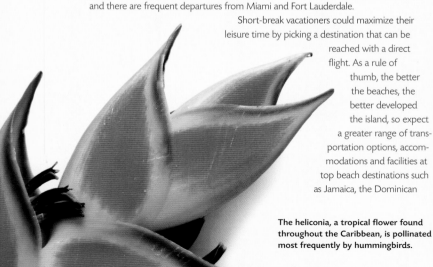

Short-break vacationers could maximize their leisure time by picking a destination that can be reached with a direct flight. As a rule of thumb, the better the beaches, the better developed the island, so expect a greater range of transportation options, accommodations and facilities at top beach destinations such as Jamaica, the Dominican

The heliconia, a tropical flower found throughout the Caribbean, is pollinated most frequently by hummingbirds.

NOT TO BE MISSED

For historic cities: the cobbled streets of Santo Domingo (Dominican Republic) or San Juan (Puerto Rico)   100, 128

For sailing: the Sir Francis Drake Channel (British Virgin Islands) or Tobago Cays (St. Vincent and the Grenadines)   166, 286

For hiking: Morne Trois Pitons National Park (Dominica) or parrot-spotting in the rain forest of St. Lucia   266, 275

For scuba diving: Saba Marine Park or the North Wall off Bonaire   184, 191

For beaches: Salt Cay's deserted North Beach (Turks and Caicos Islands)

or Shoal Bay's sugar-soft sands (Anguilla)   88, 213

For local color: Crop Over in Barbados (July–Aug.) or Carnival in Trinidad (Feb.)   301, 317

For music: Reggae Sumfest in Jamaica (July) or Santo Domingo's Merengue Festival (Dominican Republic, July–Aug.)   54, 101

For lovers of wildlife: whale-watching off the coasts of Dominica or birding in Trinidad   268, 325

For food: creole cuisine in Guadeloupe or coffee in Jamaica   25, 41

Republic, and Puerto Rico in the Western Caribbean; and the air transport hubs of Antigua, Aruba, and Barbados in the east of the region.

Where once a Caribbean vacation was a strictly horizontal affair, activity holidays now represent a significant slice of the market. Diving has become a top attraction in the Cayman Islands; in the Dutch dive spots of Bonaire, Saba, and Statia; and on Tobago. Golfers are spoiled for choice throughout the region, sailors can charter a yacht to sail the dazzling Grenadines or Virgin Island archipelagoes, and for volcano hiking, the rain forest mountains of Guadeloupe and Dominica spring immediately to mind.

Ports of Call

The historic port cities of the Caribbean act as windows on their island homes and encouragements to explore farther afield. In the Dominican Republic, the cobbled streets, elaborate cathedral, and colonial grandeur of Santo Domingo recall the days of Columbus and the riches of the Spanish Main. The bustle and buzz of the waterfront shops and malls in Charlotte Amalie, the capital of St. Thomas (USVI), or Philipsburg, Sint Maarten, or St. John's, Antigua, are not far removed from the hubbub that would have greeted traders to these mercantile hot spots several centuries ago.

Today, even if your time ashore is limited by a cruise-ship itinerary, it is usually possible to find a guided walking tour through the local tourist office or make an advance reservation with one of the operators

Online Visitor Information

All the main Caribbean islands covered in this guide have an active tourist board with a website providing reasonably up-to-date information on accommodations, sightseeing, activities, and dining. They may also offer links to local tourism operators and answers to FAQs. Some islands maintain overseas representation in North America and Europe, but this is increasingly rare and visitors are encouraged to consult websites. For contact details, see the individual island listings in Travelwise, pages 332–351, or check out the Caribbean Tourism Organization website onecaribbean.org.

When to Visit

The Caribbean region lies in the tropics, so temperatures are fairly consistent year-round, averaging 78–86°F (26–30°C) during the day and 59–64°F (15–18°C) at night on the coast. High season in the Caribbean is the generally cooler and drier period between December and April, when hotels charge their top rates, and reservations should be made well in advance for the popular Christmas and New Year's period. Humidity increases as the rainy season (June–Nov.) approaches, though showers occur throughout the year and on a daily basis in the rain forest highlands. Prices drop significantly during the summer, when there are some attractive bargains to be had.

mentioned in the main island chapters or the Sports & Activities section of this guide (see Travelwise pp. 390–400). Just an hour's stroll from the waterfront where you dock can reveal a wealth of fascinating information about an island's historic influences, architecture, culture, and food. And be sure to grab any opportunity to visit a local market piled high with all manner of colorful and exotic produce and examples of island crafts.

Exploring Beyond a Port of Call

While the port cities offer a taste of what the islands have to offer, to get a real feel for the beauty and diversity of the Caribbean, take time to explore farther afield. Cure your cabin fever rambling cliff-top fortresses like Brimstone Hill on St. Kitts, built by colonial powers to spy on their neighbors. Set out early one morning to watch the sunrise over the coffee plantations in Jamaica's Blue Mountains or sign up for a rain forest hike in the Windward Islands punctuated by the screech of parrots and the flash of brilliant plumage. There are glorious tropical gardens, elegant great houses, cacao plantations, and waterfall swimming holes to discover. Sports and activities run the gamut from golf and sportfishing to day sails, night dives, and 4WD safari adventures.

When selecting a cruise, always weigh the appeal of the shore excursions program before making a choice of cruise line. Independent travelers and cruise passengers looking for more flexibility can shop around online to find tours to suit their interests (advance bookings are strongly recommended over the peak December to March period). Licensed taxis are readily available at ports and hotels; most have special plates to identify them. Taxi rates to popular destinations are generally clearly posted at tourist disembarkation points, and unless the taxi is metered (which is rare) always agree on the price for a single journey or a tour in advance. In the French Antilles and Spanish-speaking Dominican Republic, ensure the driver can understand your instructions. The port tourist office can assist in locating an English-speaking driver. Also be sure you have an adequate supply of local currency for tips, fares, and low-cost attractions; payment on the French islands is expected in euros. Car rental is widely available, but driving can be quite challenging. Roads are frequently in poor condition and badly signposted so it's remarkably easy to get lost on your own, which is a risk probably not worth taking for cruise passengers on a tight schedule.

Choosing Your Itinerary

Caribbean cruises tend to be of the closed-loop type, which begin and end at the same point. Occasionally, a short one-way cruise might be available if it forms an early leg of a longer cruise. The most popular route covered by this guidebook is the Eastern Caribbean itinerary, which generally starts in Florida and visits three or four

Yachting, whether for sport or leisure, is popular throughout the Caribbean.

ports of call in the course of a week, including such top destinations as Puerto Rico, St. Thomas (USVI), and Sint Maarten located in the central span of the island arc. Southern Caribbean cruises are usually longer, may depart from San Juan, Puerto Rico, and extend down the island chain though the Leeward and Windward Islands, to the French and Dutch Caribbean. Western Caribbean itineraries starting in the Gulf of Mexico make calls to Grand Cayman and Jamaica.

Which Ship

There are as many cruising options in Caribbean waters as there are islands to visit, which makes choosing the perfect cruise a daunting prospect. Background reading will help narrow down the destinations best suited to your interests, such as general sightseeing, history, and shopping. The size and style of cruise ship will also inform your deci- sion (for additional tips, see pp. 136–137). Passen- gers with mobility restrictions should look for ports where disembarkation is directly from the vessel onto the pier as tendering ashore in small boats can be a challenge for anybody. Packing correctly is also important. The dress code on the Caribbean islands is generally fairly relaxed but modest (see sidebar this page). However, many cruise ships host several formal dinners during a trip and guests are required to dress accordingly. ∎

What to Wear

The dress code on most Caribbean islands is pretty relaxed. Shorts, T-shirts, and sandals should suffice for everyday wear, though wearing swimsuits off the beach is frowned upon. Fine restaurants may not permit jeans or open sandals for men. If you plan on playing a sport (golf, tennis, horseback riding) or pursuing activities such as hiking, sailing, or diving, bring appropriate gear and footwear. Hikers will find it gets cool and wet in the moun- tains. Adequate supplies of strong sunblock and mosquito repellent are essential.

History & Culture

A cannon stands guard at Brimstone
Hill Fortress in St. Kitts.
Opposite: Revelers dress in tobacco
leaves during Carnival in Gosier,
Guadeloupe.

The Caribbean Today

"A Caribbean vacation" is one of the most evocative phrases in the English language. The merest suggestion can unleash a stream of dreamy images featuring golden beaches, coconut palms, and azure seas. But however satisfying this daydream may be, it cannot beat the reality, the feel of powder-soft coral sand between your toes, the squawk and colorful flash of a parrot in the rain forest, the taste of a fresh mango plucked straight from the tree.

Caribbean Culture

Our idea of the Caribbean typically starts with the region's obvious physical attractions: the sunshine, beaches, rain forested highlands, and coral-encrusted depths. Scratch the surface, however, and you'll soon discover that the Caribbean islands are far more multilayered and interesting. Beneath the broad brushstrokes of climate and geography, there is a cornucopia of rich and varied historical and cultural influences, which add greatly to the atmosphere and attitudes of the islands and their people.

> **Language, architecture, religion, festivals, and, more significantly, the Caribbean people themselves, can trace their origins back to the days of the region's colonial rulers.**

Even today, we can't interpret island culture without understanding the colonial legacy. Language, architecture, religion, festivals, and, more significantly, the Caribbean people themselves, can trace their origins back to the days of the region's colonial rulers. Most of the people who now inhabit the Caribbean are descended from African slaves brought here to work the plantations. Certain attitudes remain ingrained centuries later, such as the courteous greetings commonly exchanged in the French islands, and the slightly formal, British influence in Barbados, where taking afternoon tea and dressing for dinner is still something of a ritual in certain circles. For all the flamboyant spectacle of Carnival and rum-fueled reggae jump-ups (impromptu dances), Caribbean islanders are essentially conservative at heart. For the most part, they are friendly, helpful, and delighted to share their local knowledge. In return, they appreciate being treated with courtesy and respect.

Sustainable Tourism

The Caribbean region has around 30 separate political entities, and a stable, albeit deeply fragmented political scene (see p. 23). Tourism is the economic mainstay, though sugar, bananas, and oil production all contribute significantly to individual national economies. Sustainable tourism has become the buzz phrase in the Caribbean lexicon these days, and considerable efforts are being made to protect natural habitats both on land and at sea. Unfortunately, coral reefs, coastal mangrove areas, and native wildlife species have already suffered significant damage from the region's rapacious development, but the growing demand for ecotourism opportunities has alerted island authorities to the importance of preserving natural resources.

The growth of ecotourism has had a notably positive effect in engaging visitors with local culture. Hiking expeditions, mountain biking tours, and other activities, as well as community tourism programs, are coaxing increasing numbers of visitors out of the hotel compound and off the cruise ship to discover the charm of the islands and their people for themselves. Such forays provide a welcome bridge between residents and travelers, and generate useful income for the local community, which in the past has seen the tourist dollar flow directly into the coffers of cruise lines and foreign hotel groups.

Taking the plunge off a pier in a small Martinique beach village

Flora & Fauna

The Caribbean's mountain ranges are cloaked in dense rain forest, which grows with explosive rapidity in the fertile volcanic soil. True rain forest is the richest natural habitat on the planet and requires an annual rainfall in excess of 70 inches (178 cm), which the Caribbean islands receive courtesy of the Atlantic trade winds. In the hothouse atmosphere beneath the rain forest canopy, dozens of ferns, creepers, and bamboo flourish at the feet of giant buttress-trunked santinay trees, as well as mahogany, gommier, and mahoe.

At higher elevations, in the montane or cloud forest, tree branches play host to a variety of bromeliads (which gain nutrients from the air) and orchids, while higher still the lichen-encrusted elfin forest opens onto grasslands frequently visited by cool, hazy drizzle and wisps of cloud.

Few mammals live in the rain forest, and indigenous species such as armadillos, opossums, and agoutis are rarely spotted. Reptiles, including tree frogs, iguanas, and dozens of species of small lizards, are a constant presence, as are winged insects such as butterflies and predatory mosquitoes. Though there are occasional sightings of nonvenomous tree snakes, the sole poisonous snake is the fer-de-lance, found only on Martinique and St. Lucia.

Bird lovers will find an aviary Eden in the Caribbean. Several species of rare indigenous parrots live in the Windward Islands, and the woodlands are also home to numerous varieties of hummingbirds, honeycreepers, tanagers, and cheeky bananaquits, which frequently leave the rain forest to feed on the brilliant tropical blooms in nearby gardens.

Many species of herons, waders, ducks, and other wetland birds gather in the coastal mangrove swamps of Jamaica and Trinidad, while flamingo colonies can be found in Bonaire and Lago Enriquillo in the Dominican Republic. Seabirds, including boobies, pelicans, magnificent frigate birds, and elegant scissor-tailed tropic birds, colonize rocky outcrops visible from the shore.

Just as the rain forest flourishes, so does the myriad variety of other plants and

Volcanic History

The Caribbean islands are poised on the brink of the Caribbean and Atlantic tectonic plates. The majority are volcanic in origin, though there are a few low-lying coral atolls such as the Cayman Islands and Anguilla, and the arid, desertlike Dutch Leewards. The oldest islands in the region lie to the north, where Jamaica, Hispaniola, and Puerto Rico were formed approximately 70 million years ago.

In the eastern Caribbean, Montserrat, Guadeloupe, Martinique, Dominica, St. Lucia, St. Vincent, and Grenada remain volcanically active with bubbling mud pools and oozing, foul-smelling sulfur pits. Off the coast of Grenada, the active submarine volcano Kick 'Em Jenny has risen to about 590 feet (180 m) below the surface.

One of the Seven Sisters waterfalls in Grenada's Grand Étang National Park

trees elsewhere on the islands. While many islanders cultivate colorful flower gardens, botanical gardens are the best place to see a whole range of eye-catching heliconias and gingers, spice trees such as nutmeg and cinnamon, and flowering trees such as the yellow- or pink-blossomed poui, scarlet poinciana, and spreading immortelle, which flowers in January and February.

Hurricanes

Though the Caribbean experiences few climatic extremes, the region is in the hurricane zone. In recent years, hurricanes have wreaked widespread destruction across the north of the region. The official hurricane season runs from June to November, though a traditional rhyme advises "June, too soon; July, stand by; September, remember; October, all over." Statistically, mid-September is the most likely time for a hurricane to pass through the Caribbean. However, cruise vessels steer well clear of the hurricane belt throughout the danger period. ∎

Cruising to Cuba

One of the first ports of call for many modern cruisers is Cuba. Located about 90 miles (145 km) from Florida, the tropical island is easily accessed by a short flight from the U.S. mainland for trips embarking in Havana, and some cruises even depart from Miami. Loosened travel restrictions have led to a surge of new American visitors eager to see a long-forbidden country, and cruise lines are stepping in to meet the demand.

Cruises around Cuba now offer the traveler a great way to get acquainted with the island.

New Regulations: Why Go Now?

As part of the landmark thaw in diplomatic relations, President Barack Obama eased travel restrictions from the U.S. to Cuba in 2015. Although ordinary sightseeing or beachgoing tourism is still illegal, Americans can travel to Cuba if the purpose of their trip falls under one of 12 categories, including educational or cultural programs, professional research, journalistic or religious activities, or visiting close relatives. Visitors must follow a full-time itinerary of activities related to their category of travel.

With a little creativity, Americans can craft a Cuba trip that fits into at least one of the categories, and many organizations and tour operators now offer "people-to-people" trips that satisfy the educational and cultural requirements. With the island opening up to foreign influence, many feel that now is the time to go and experience Cuban culture before it becomes globalized. However, the new travel laws could tighten again; be sure to check on current regulations before booking.

Why Cruise?

After being embargoed by the U.S. government for decades, Cuba simply doesn't have enough good hotels or infrastructure for a massive influx of visitors. American credit cards still aren't accepted, and don't expect to find an ATM outside Havana. Roads are rough, and it can take many hours to travel

INSIDER TIP:

For a land-based journey that offers an in-depth look at Cuban culture, see *national geographicexpeditions.com.*

—KAREN CARMICHAEL
National Geographic writer

Cuba resounds with a rich musical heritage.

between towns. Cruises offer visitors the option to circle the entire island in a week—impossible by car—with the bonus of comfortable cabins with modern amenities. Ships are also likely to have some Wi-Fi, which is virtually nonexistent throughout Cuba.

Travelers can visit diverse, out-of-the-way ports such as Antilla, Cayo Largo, and Isla de la Juventud, getting a fuller picture of the island outside Havana. Cruises often offer more flexible excursion choices than land tours (which usually follow a strict itinerary), and can even be cheaper—especially as rates for the limited number of hotel rooms in Cuba have recently skyrocketed.

Cruising Options

Most itineraries include stops in Havana and the colonial cities of Cienfuegos and Trinidad, which both feature UNESCO World Heritage sites. Popular excursions include walking tours of historic city centers, music and dance performances, visiting artisan workshops, and exploring Guanahacabibes National Park.

Cuba Cruise *(yourcubacruise.com)* offers a seven-night cruise and land itinerary, sailing on its 1,200-passenger *Celestyal Crystal* and stopping at four Cuban ports (including an overnight stay in Havana) as well as Montego Bay, Jamaica. Travelers embark in either Havana or Montego Bay. Authentic shore excursions are included.

Arcadia *(arcadiasmallshipcruises.com)* offers eight-day voyages around western Cuba on *The Panorama,* a three-masted sailing cruiser with 25 cabins. Embarking from Havana, ports of call include Cabo San Antonio and Cayo Largo. You can also cruise on *The Panorama* on trips through International Expeditions *(ietravel.com),* departing from Cienfuegos and calling at Trinidad and Maria la Gorda, before ending with several days in Havana. And U.K.-based cruise company Noble Caledonia *(noble-caledonia.co.uk)* offers deluxe cruises aboard the 110-passenger MS *Serenissima.*

U.S. firms planning Cuba cruises include Haimark *(haimarkline.com)* and Fathom *(fathom.org),* Carnival's "impact travel" line that focuses on voluntourism.

Learn About Conserving Cuban Wildlife

Both Arcadia and International Expeditions' cruises on *The Panorama* visit Cayo Largo, a small island off Cuba's southern coast. While there, travelers can meet with scientists involved in coral reef protection and visit the Sea Turtle Breeding Center, where conservationists work to preserve the loggerhead, hawksbill, and green sea turtles that annually nest on the cay's white-sand beaches.

History & Culture

Christopher Columbus first sighted the island of San Salvador in the Bahamas on October 12, 1492, and sailed into the Caribbean Sea intent on discovering a westward passage to the East Indian spice islands. The arrival of European explorers opened the book on the recorded history of the region, and the islands were named the Antilles after the legendary island of Antillia.

Pre-Columbian Caribbean

The Caribbean's first settlers, Amerindian tribes who paddled their canoes to the islands from Central America or possibly Florida, arrived thousands of years before Columbus. The Stone Age Ciboney people (or Archaic Indians) were the earliest inhabitants of the Greater Antilles islands. Archaeological digs in Cuba have uncovered Ciboney sites about 6,000 years old, while relics in Hispaniola are reckoned to be about 4,000 years old. These nomadic hunter-gatherers lived off a nourishing and varied diet of fish and shellfish, birds, iguanas, and snakes, supplemented by roots and wild fruits, and they crafted tools and utensils from stone, wood, bone, and shell.

About 300 B.C. the first Arawak migrated to the islands. They are thought to have originated in the Amazon Basin, and then they pushed north to make the sea crossing from northeastern South America (present-day Venezuela and Guyana) to the southernmost of the Lesser Antilles. Gradually they moved up the island chain, and by the time Columbus appeared on the scene, the three major Arawak groups were populating the Greater Antilles islands and Bahamas: the Taíno (Cuba, Jamaica, and Hispaniola), the Borequio or Borinquen (Puerto Rico), and the Lucayan (Bahamas).

> **After a thousand years, the Arawak's peaceful existence came to an abrupt end with the arrival of the Carib.**

The Arawak were more sophisticated than the Ciboney. They were farmers, cultivating cassava (for flour), yams, corn, beans, cacao, peanuts, tobacco, and cotton. Skilled hunters and fishermen, they were also potters capable of producing earthenware for domestic and religious purposes.

Arawak society was well organized. Villages were generally built close to the shore, and each community was presided over by a *cacique*, or village chieftain, who was responsible for both the temporal and religious life of the villagers. At the center of the village was a large open-sided *carbet* (thatched shelter) where the cacique and men held council: It was out-of-bounds to women and children except by invitation to attend special ceremonies. Unmarried men could sleep here or in a separate carbet, stringing maybe a hundred hammocks from the roof. Religion played an important part in Arawak daily life. There were gods associated with food crops, fertility, and weather, and benevolent spirits that inhabited plants and animals. Religious ceremonies included snorting trance-inducing narcotics and dancing, as well as the worship of *zemi*, simple shapes or human and animal figures made of wood, bone, or stone. Arawak believed in the afterlife and took great care with burial rituals. The dead were placed in a squatting position and were equipped with personal belongings (the wives of important chieftains were buried alive), as well as food for the journey to Coyaba, a plentiful land of nonstop dancing and feasting.

Arrival of the Carib

After a thousand years, the Arawak's peaceful existence came to an abrupt end with the arrival of the Carib. Also from South America, the warlike Carib progressed northward through the Lesser Antilles, slaughtering Arawak men and assimilating women and children into their tribes. Though the evidence is somewhat sketchy, the Carib had a reputation for cannibalism and were said to barbecue (a Carib word) their male victims, which included Europeans as they began to explore the region. The Carib were excellent marksmen with bows and arrows and fearlessly attacked Spanish sailing ships from their wooden war canoes, or *piraguas*

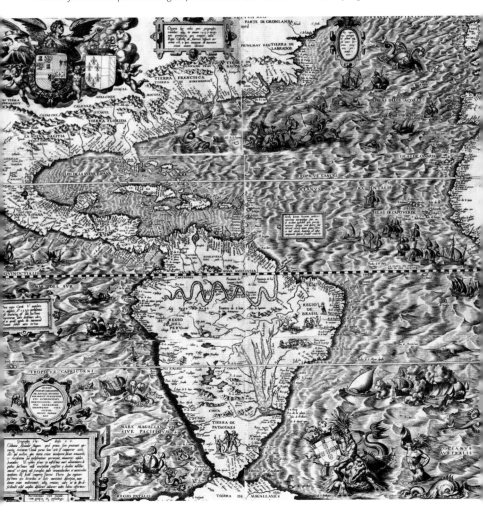

A 1562 Spanish map of the Americas

(from which the simple pirogue fishing boats still used in the Windward Islands take their name). Eventually, the Europeans pushed the Carib back into the rugged terrain of the Windward Islands, where they managed to hold out for more than 200 years. A few mixed-blood survivors still live on Dominica and St. Vincent.

European Invasion

Columbus made four voyages to the Caribbean in his attempt to discover a western route to the East Indies, stubbornly naming his finds the West Indies despite all the evidence to the contrary. On his fourth voyage, in 1502, he located the South American mainland and secured its vast mineral wealth for the Roman Catholic kings of Spain. However, he failed to make it back through the Caribbean islands; beaching his aging ships in Jamaica, he was forced to rely upon the hostile governor of Hispaniola for eventual rescue.

During the early 16th century, Spanish settlements sprang up in the Greater Antilles, first in Hispaniola, then Cuba, Jamaica, and Puerto Rico. The Arawak were enslaved, and within 50 years the indigenous population of these northern islands had been eradicated through warfare, disease, and transportation to work the mainland gold mines.

The Spanish treasure fleets making their way home to Europe acted as a magnet for pirates and privateers. Throughout the 16th and 17th centuries, French, English, and Dutch vessels lurking in the isolated cays of the Virgin Islands preyed mercilessly on heavily laden armadas. The next logical step for the interlopers was to claim colonies of their own in the region, which became easier as Spanish influence declined in Europe during the 17th century. The English and French moved in on the Lesser Antilles, commencing a 250-year struggle for dominance in the eastern Caribbean, and the Dutch cannily selected islands with a view to their strategic importance on the trading routes used by their rivals.

The *Quedagh Merchant*

Centuries after Columbus sailed the ocean blue, hired pirates, genteelly known as privateers, made a booming business out of raiding treasure-laden merchant and pirate ships. In 1698 privateer Captain Kidd captured the *Quedagh Merchant*, with its bounty of gold, silver, silk, and opium, in the Indian Ocean. Kidd made off with the loot, scuttling the ship just off tiny Catalina Island in the Dominican Republic. The *Quedagh Merchant*'s remains still lie where Kidd left them, in just 10 feet (3 m) of water, and are slated to become an underwater museum in the future.

Colonial Era

Sugarcane was introduced to the Caribbean by Dutch planters from Brazil in the 1630s (see pp. 304–305). From small-scale beginnings in Barbados, the enormously profitable trade in "white gold" triggered the rapid expansion of European colonialism in the region, and its labor-intensive cultivation brought an immediate demand for a cheap and inexhaustible workforce. Spanish settlers had imported small numbers of West African slaves to work their Caribbean plantations since the early days, but the sugar trade boosted numbers to unprecedented levels. Untold millions of Africans were sold into slavery and shipped across the Atlantic to work the sugar plantations; many thousands died en route (see pp. 250–251).

Fastest man alive: Sprinter Usain Bolt leaves Jamaica's "soon come" reputation in the dust.

By the start of the 19th century, the importance of the Caribbean sugar trade dwindled as sugar beet production in Europe rose to satisfy local demand. The planters' profits decreased, and in 1808 the antislavery movement in Britain succeeded in banning the slave trade to the colonies. This was followed in 1834 by the Emancipation Act, which outlawed the ownership of slaves. The other European nations followed suit, and the former sugar colonies fell into a decline.

As the freed slaves abandoned the plantations, major producers such as Jamaica and Trinidad imported East Indian indentured laborers, but most islands slipped quietly into the doldrums, largely forgotten by their erstwhile colonial masters.

Modern Era

The Spanish-American War of 1898 introduced U.S. influence to the region. The U.S. claimed its first territory with the capture of Puerto Rico from Spain in that year. It followed up this belated foray into Caribbean empire-building with the purchase of the U.S. Virgin Islands from Denmark in 1917. The Caribbean islands experienced the unwanted trickle-down effect of the 1930s Great Depression, which deepened the region's economic problems and heralded the rise of grassroots labor movements. These in turn spearheaded the islands' transition toward greater independence from Europe.

In 1962 Jamaica was the first British colony to achieve full independence, and Britain divested most of its colonies during the 1970s and 1980s. Several smaller islands opted

> **The Spanish-American War of 1898 introduced U.S. influence to the region. The U.S. claimed its first territory with the capture of Puerto Rico from Spain in that year.**

(continued on p. 26)

Food & Drink

Caribbean cuisine, like other aspects of Caribbean culture, reflects the region's varied heritage, blending African, Spanish, French, English, Indian, Chinese, and other influences. On a warm evening, a mellow rum or a chilled local beer can be the perfect accompaniment to a satisfying meal.

A jerk shack near Ocho Rios, Jamaica

Traditional Caribbean cooking is simple, nutritious, and filling, using plentiful local ingredients from fresh fish and seafood to a wide variety of tropical fruits and vegetables, supplemented with chicken and a little red meat. Staple foods such as rice 'n' peas (the "peas" are red kidney beans), fried plantains (a variety of banana that is inedible raw), spinachlike callaloo, starchy breadfruit, and root vegetables (yam, eddo, cassava) known as "ground provision" are found throughout the islands. Hot pepper sauce is also ubiquitous. Adventurous visitors should sample soursop, sugar and golden apples, tart tamarinds, and tiny plums. Markets are the best place to find and taste what is in season.

Guadeloupe and Martinique are renowned for creole cuisine (see sidebar opposite), while Puerto Rican specialties such as *lechón asao* (roast suckling pig), and *locrio* (a variation on paella), served in the Dominican Republic, show a distinctive Spanish influence. The Indian influence is unmistakable in Trinidad's curries and rotis (chapati envelopes filled with curried meat, seafood, or vegetables) that have now become a popular snack food in neighboring islands. Jamaican jerk is said to have been invented by runaway slaves who cooked in earth pits covered with branches.

INSIDER TIP:
More Caribbean restaurants are cropping up that offer locally grown, organic cuisine. You can find a listing of "locavore" establishments at *happycow.net*.

—LARRY PORGES
National Geographic Books author

Fresh tropical fruit at a market in Fort-de-France, Martinique

Rum & Beer

Rum has been produced in the Caribbean since the 17th century, when sugar planters first distilled a spirit from molasses. Still made throughout the region, the best quality rums traditionally come from Barbados, Jamaica, Guadeloupe, and Martinique. While most islanders prefer their rum neat, visitors are more attracted to the long list of rum cocktails available, including piña coladas (flavored with pineapple and coconut), Cuba libre (with cola), fruit daiquiris, and planters punch (the original has only lime and cane juice, but added fruit juices are popular today). There are also delicious nonalcoholic fruit punches.

Wine is not produced in the Caribbean, so it is expensive here. Local breweries, on the other hand, turn out some good lager-type beers. Particularly good are Banks from Barbados, Carib from Trinidad (with franchises on several islands), Presidente from the Dominican Republic, and Red Stripe from Jamaica.

Creole Cuisine & Dining Out

The creole cuisine of Guadeloupe and Martinique is an inspired fusion of French culinary élan, traditional African cooking, and local Caribbean ingredients. Seafood is a mainstay of creole menus and comes in a wide variety of guises, from simple *accras* (shredded salt-cod fritters) to *blaff* (a fish or shellfish stew cooked in a wine and herb court bouillon).

Other specialties include *cirique* or *étrille* (little sea crabs), *chatrou* (octopus), *lambi* (conch tenderized with lime for salads), *langouste* (lobster), *ouassous* (crayfish), and *soudrons* (clams). *Crabes farcis* are stuffed land crabs, more meaty than sea crabs, and the locals are known to feed them with dried coconut and hot peppers to improve their flavor. Try *colombo*, a curried stew of chicken or goat *(cabri)* flavored with coriander, cumin, mustard, ginger, and pepper.

Traditional accompaniments are *fruit à pain*, the rather tasteless fruit of the breadfruit tree, and *christophene*, a tropical squash served cooked or grated raw in salads.

Dining out can be expensive, but creole food is generally cheaper than French. Limited-choice menus at a fixed price *(menu touristique)* are usually good value, and service is included *(compris)*. It is de rigueur to round off a meal with a digestif from among the dozens of locally produced aged or fruit-flavored rums.

The Catholic cathedral in Roseau, Dominica. The island's diocese was established in 1850.

to remain crown colonies (now known as British overseas territories), while others have joined the British Commonwealth as independent states. The Dutch and French retain closer political ties with their colonies.

Colonial Legacy

As European colonists staked their claims to the Caribbean islands, each nation attempted in some degree to re-create a miniature home away from home in the sun. Thus, the Spanish Catholic heritage is readily apparent in the historic cities and churches of the Dominican Republic and Puerto Rico; the ex-British colonies in the Leeward and Windward Islands are rich in four-square stone Georgian architecture; the French islands retain an inimitable savoir faire combined with gastronomic flair; and in the Dutch Leewards, Curaçao's elegantly gabled buildings have been designated a World Heritage site.

Language is another long-standing legacy of the former colonial powers—English, French, Dutch, and Spanish are the dominant languages you'll hear in the region (see sidebar opposite).

The majority of Caribbean people are of African origin, and although African culture was subjugated by European customs during the colonial era, it did not disappear altogether. Freed from Old World dominance, the African heritage is now the strongest element of pan-Caribbean cultural trends. Its influence is unmistakable in music, traditional cooking, and the common animist beliefs that operate alongside traditional European religions in a very typically Caribbean compromise.

Music

Music is, so they say, the heartbeat of the Caribbean, and it is certainly hard to ignore. The strains of calypso, reggae, and soca (soul-calypso) are everywhere. Steel pan or throbbing bass dub music booms out from dollar buses, and the dance rhythms of Puerto Rican salsa, merengue from the Dominican Republic, and zouk from the French Antilles provide a catchy backdrop to the Caribbean experience.

Calypso is the grandfather of the music scene, with its origins buried way back in West African slave traditions. Forbidden to speak their native languages, slaves were, however, permitted to sing; the planters believed it helped them work faster. Yet unbeknownst to their employers, the slaves used song to keep alive the West African storytelling tradition and to pass along information and messages of protest concealed in allegorical terms. Today's calypsonians (calypso singers) are still judged not only on their music but also on the message they put across.

Calypso is the grandfather of the music scene, with its origins buried way back in West African slave traditions.

Trinidad is the home of calypso and steel-pan music, which originated in the dockyards of Port of Spain during World War II when oil drums were recycled for makeshift drums. Reggae emerged from the Kingston ghetto of Trenchtown, Jamaica, spearheaded by its most famous exponent, Bob Marley, who with his group the Wailers went on to enjoy worldwide success in the 1970s.

Live music performances in clubs and bars are easy to find throughout the islands. Music festivals are also well worth tracking down. The most famous events include Jamaica's Reggae Sumfest (July), the St. Lucia International Jazz Festival (May), and the St. Kitts Music Festival (June).

Language

English, Spanish, French, and Dutch are all spoken in the Caribbean, a legacy from colonial days. English is spoken in the lion's share of the Caribbean islands from Jamaica, the Cayman Islands, and Turks and Caicos Islands in the north, through the Virgin, Leeward, and Windward Islands (where a form of French patois is also commonly spoken on Dominica and St. Lucia), to Trinidad and Tobago. Most Spanish-speaking Puerto Ricans also speak English, but a Spanish phrase book is essential in nontourist areas of the Dominican Republic. Dutch Caribbean islanders are generally bilingual in Dutch and English. Visitors to the French Antilles should be aware that little English is spoken outside of the upscale hotels.

Carnival

Carnival is a magnificent explosion of elaborate costumes, music, singing, and dance that captures the creativity and natural exuberance of the Caribbean people. The date varies from island to island, but most carnivals take place before Lent (Feb.–March), while others celebrate the end of the sugar harvest (July–Aug.) or the anniversary of emancipation.

> **Europeans introduced Carnival to the Caribbean, marking the approach of Lent a traditional period of Christian abstinence.**

Europeans introduced Carnival to the Caribbean, marking the approach of Lent, a traditional period of Christian abstinence. This pre-Lent celebration consists of a hectic round of feasting and parties ("carnival" is derived from the Italian *carnevale*, meaning the removal of meat). After emancipation, former slaves hijacked the party season by introducing their own processions of folkloric characters, dancing, and African drumming, which, once banned by the authorities, became the core of the new Caribbean-style Carnival.

The buildup to Lenten Carnivals, such as the famous one in Trinidad (see sidebar p. 317), begins soon after Christmas, when musicians take part in the hotly contested qualifying heats, and band members and dancers participating in the main Carnival processions put the final touches on their eye-catching costumes.

Carnival begins in earnest on the Friday before Lent, and competitions held over the weekend decide the winners of the various calypso, steel-pan, and costume prizes. The main processions begin before dawn on Monday with a wild jump-up known as Jouvert (from *jour ouvert,* or daybreak, in French creole), followed by Tuesday's dazzling Mardi Gras parade. ■

A small Carnival celebration erupts in the seaside town of Grand Anse, Martinique.

Magnificent waterfalls, mountains, and fascinating historic sites matched by a vibrant cultural life

Jamaica

Barrels of coffee at the Craighton Estate in Jamaica's Blue Mountains

Jamaica

The Taíno Indians who settled Jamaica named it Xaymaca ("land of wood and water"), a description that still rings true if you venture off the tourist trail today. The island's mountainous heartland remains largely untouched, despite centuries of colonial rule beginning with the Spanish occupation of 1510. Most Jamaicans trace their ancestry to slaves brought to plantations during the 17th and 18th centuries, and lively, opinionated Jamaican culture is a vibrant fusion of African and European influences.

Under British rule the slave trade boomed, providing a labor force for the sugar plantations. Jamaica also served as a haven for pirates and buccaneers, encouraged by the British to make Kingston's Port Royal their base for harassing the Spanish fleets. Slave rebellions were a prominent feature of Jamaica's history until emancipation in 1834.

The island became a British crown colony in 1866, and during the 1890s the first tourists arrived on banana boats from North America. The Great Depression of the 1930s led to bloodshed and riots as the economy faltered, giving birth to the country's first labor union and the socialistic People's National Party (PNP) led by Norman Manley (1893–1969). Universal suffrage was granted in 1944, and in 1962 Jamaica won full independence.

Jamaica's culture is a potent brew of fierce national pride, reggae and Rastafarians, sassy attitudes, and the local dialect (known as Jamaican patois). The poverty and lack of opportunity that led to political unrest and occasional riots of the past still affect much of the island.

With more than one million visitors a year, Jamaica is one of the largest tourism draws in the Caribbean—and is currently the fastest growing cruise destination in the region. The new facility at Falmouth is capable of accommodating the world's largest cruise vessels. The main resort areas (Montego Bay, Ocho Rios, and Negril) are found in the north and west of the island, but it is well worth exploring further.

Jamaica's 4,244 square miles (10,992 sq km) embrace an enormous variety of landscapes. The island evolved from a broad arc of volcanoes rising from the seabed to form the Blue Mountains. These traverse the eastern third of the island, reaching their summit at the 7,402-foot (2,256 m) Blue Mountain Peak. The land surrounding these mountains is capped by limestone plateaus. Over the centuries, rivers have carved sinkholes, caves, and deeply rutted gullies in the limestone—most visible in the central western Cockpit Country region.

An offshore coral reef shields the white, sandy beaches of Jamaica's north shore, the island's tourist heartland. The eastern coastline,

unprotected from ocean swells, is far more rugged and dramatic. With a few exceptions, the south and west coasts are typified by volcanic black-sand beaches.

Almost half of Jamaica is under cultivation. Though agriculture now accounts for less than 10 percent of GDP, huge plantations cloak the landscape with sugarcane, bananas, cacao, coffee, rice, tobacco, and citrus fruits.

Jamaica has a population of about 2.7 million, almost one-third of whom live in the capital, Kingston. ■

NOT TO BE MISSED:

Hiking the Blue Mountains   40–41

Eating jerk pork from the stalls at Boston Bay   45

The view from Noël Coward's Firefly   47

Climbing Dunn's River Falls   49

The Bob Marley Centre & Mausoleum, Nine Mile   53

Listening to music at Greenwood Great House   56

Negril's hedonistic beaches   57–59

Rum-sampling at the Appleton Estate   66

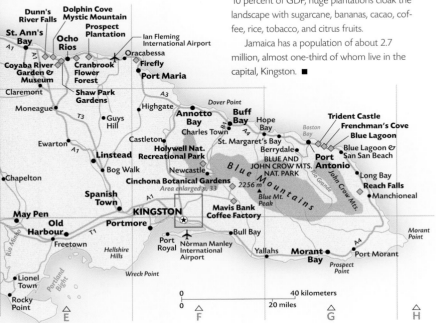

Kingston

Throbbing with energy and spirit, the dynamic capital of Jamaica is home to a population of around 800,000. The largest English-speaking city in the Caribbean, it is also one of the most important cultural and political hubs in the region.

Most visitors to Jamaica's capital stay in the New Kingston neighborhood.

Kingston

31 F2

Visitor Information

✉ 64 Knutsford Blvd.

☎ 876 929 9200

🕐 Closed Sun.–Mon.

visitjamaica.com

Kingston owes its growth to its magnificent natural harbor, the seventh largest in the world. The English recognized its strategic importance, building no fewer than five forts on the sandspit of Port Royal (see pp. 38–39) in the 17th century. When an earthquake destroyed the town of Port Royal on June 7, 1692, its inhabitants fled to Kingston, and the concentration of economic and political power in that city eventually led to the capital being transferred here from Spanish Town in 1872. The city kept on growing, and today it spreads into the foothills of the Blue Mountains.

The heart of Kingston is its downtown area, which embraces the waterfront, historic sites, and to the west some of the city's most notorious slums. In the center is the **Parade,** once a British Army parade ground. Today it reverberates with reggae as vendors of cane juice, CDs, bus tickets, and baubles ply their wares. The green heart of the Parade is **St. William Grant Park,** a leafy square with a fountain and statues of Queen Victoria, Norman Manley (see p. 30), and Alexander Bustamante (1884–1977), founder of the country's first trade union. On the north side of the Parade is the **Ward Theatre** *(tel 876 922 3213)*, an elegant building completed in 1911, which hosts performances by amateur dramatic groups as well as the National Dance Theatre Company. To the west of the Parade is the colorful **Jubilee Market,** a good place to sample some of the country's exotic fruits and vegetables.

A few minutes' stroll east from here on Duke Street is **Headquarters House,** built in 1755 by a wealthy local merchant, Thomas Hibbert. Headquarters House, with its handsome white facade and graceful fan window, has served as both a military headquarters and as home to Jamaica's legislative assembly, which met

here between 1872 and 1960. Today it houses the offices of the **Jamaica National Heritage Trust,** and you can visit the rest of the building, which includes the debating chamber and a lookout on the roof with splendid views of the mountains and the harbor. Next door stands **Gordon House** *(corner of Beeston & Duke Sts., tel 876 922 0200),* where the House of Representatives and the Senate meet. *(Entrance to the public gallery is free during debates.)*

Fronting Kingston Harbour, the waterfront area was redeveloped in the 1960s and a new shipping port was created farther west. **Ocean Boulevard** along the waterfront is lined with high-rise

Jubilee Market
- 33 A2
- Spanish Town Rd.
- Closed Sun.–Mon.

Jamaica National Heritage Trust, Headquarters House
- 33 B2
- 79 Duke St.
- 876 922 1287

jnht.com

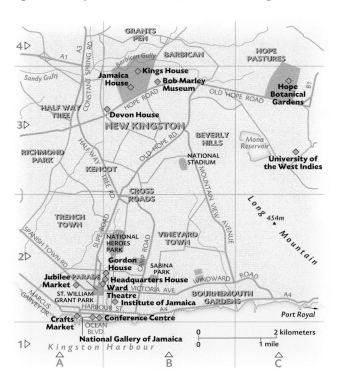

National Gallery of Jamaica
- 33 A2
- 12 Ocean Blvd.
- 876 922 1561
- Closed Sun.–Mon.
- $$

natgalja.org.jm

Institute of Jamaica
- 33 B2
- 12 East St.
- 876 922 0620
- Closed Sat.–Sun.

instituteofjamaica.org.jm

National Heroes Park
- 33 B2
- Duke St.

office buildings, shops, hotels, and apartments. About midway you'll find the bronze sculpture "Negro Aroused," a famous work by Edna Manley (1900–1987), wife of Jamaican statesman Norman Manley. It captures the spirit of the 1930s labor movement in its depiction of a bowed worker uncoiling from the chains of bondage. The original bronze is in the **National Gallery of Jamaica,** the highlight of the waterfront area. The gallery's impressive permanent collection includes numerous wood carvings (particularly noteworthy are those

INSIDER TIP:

While you're free to take pictures all around the grounds, photos aren't allowed inside Kingston's Bob Marley Museum.

—MATT PROPERT
National Geographic photographer

by Edna Manley), African-style and Rastafarian paintings, landscapes, and photography covering a variety of Jamaican themes.

Walk two blocks west to the **Crafts Market** *(Ocean Blvd., closed Sun.),* a good place to hunt for carvings, souvenirs, T-shirts, and jewelry. In the other direction on East Street is the **Institute of Jamaica,** founded in 1879 for "the encouragement of literature, science and art." The institute houses the **National Library,** which holds one of the

largest collections of historical documents in the Caribbean, as well as the **National Museum Jamaica,** which chronicles the island's history and ethnography. A harrowing collection of artifacts depicts many of the harsh realities of slavery during Jamaica's plantation era.

National Heroes Park
Poised midway between downtown and the city's uptown area, New Kingston, is National Heroes Park, a 75-acre (30 ha) open space that was once the city's racetrack. It now honors the country's national heroes, including Norman Manley and Alexander Bustamante; Sam Sharpe (1801–1832) and Paul Bogle (died 1865), both Baptist preachers involved in slave rebellions; Marcus Garvey (1887–1940), father of the Black Power movement; and Nanny, a legendary 18th-century leader of the Maroons. Norman Manley, Alexander Bustamante, and Marcus Garvey are buried here.

New Kingston
New Kingston extends from the busy crossroads of Half Way Tree Road up to Vale Royal. Wealthy merchants settled this district in the 18th century, when they fled the noise and squalor of downtown to build large residences surrounded by grazing land for their horses and cattle. Today this relatively gentrified zone hosts both businesses and residences, and most visitors to the capital choose to stay in hotels around here.

Many travelers make a pilgrimage to this part of Kingston to visit the **Bob Marley Museum,** the most popular attraction in the city. The house was a recording studio for Marley's Tuff Gong record label as well as his home from 1975 until his death from cancer in 1981. A statue of Marley with his favorite guitar and soccer ball stands at the entrance. (This is the only thing that may be photographed; cameras are prohibited elsewhere in the house.) The one-hour guided tour leads you through the grounds and house, which contains memorabilia of Marley's life, including his gold and platinum records, his favorite denim stage shirt, and several unusual guitars. There's also a re-creation of Wail'n'Soul—the shack in the poor Trenchtown area that was Marley's first house in Kingston. The tour ends with a film, screened in the room that once housed the Tuff Gong studio. The complex also has a photo gallery, restaurant, and souvenir shops.

The other big draw in New Kingston is **Devon House,** built in 1881 by Jamaica's first black millionaire, George Stiebel (1820–1896), who made his fortune in gold mining in South America. This fine Georgian-style mansion has been refurbished with four-poster beds, period chandeliers, Chippendale cabinets, and other original antiques. The courtyard, which was formerly slaves' quarters, houses an upscale craft souvenir shop, and an excellent bakery and ice cream shop. A fine dining restaurant occupies the former stables.

A statue of Bob Marley and his favorite guitar at his namesake museum

Also along Hope Road you can take a look through the gates of **Jamaica House**—the prime minister's office—which stands amid expansive lawns, manicured shrubbery, and graceful palms.

Hope Botanical Gardens, the Caribbean's largest botanical garden, stretch along the outskirts of New Kingston. Located on the former estate of Maj. Richard Hope, who arrived in Jamaica with Oliver Cromwell's army in 1655, the 200-acre (81 ha) gardens have pathways meandering between pond and lakes, greenhouses, and flowering trees and shrubs. The grounds also contain diversions to keep children amused, including the small **Hope Zoo** and a playground as well as a coconut museum, orchid house, maze, and palm avenue. The gardens are popular with Kingstonians escaping the heat of the city on weekends. ■

Bob Marley Museum
- 33 B3
- 56 Hope Rd.
- 876 927 9152
- Closed Sun.
- $$$$

bobmarleymuseum
.com

Devon House
- 33 B3
- 26 Hope Rd.
- 876 929 6602
- Guided tours: $$$

devonhousejamaica
.com

Hope Botanical Gardens
- 33 C3
- Old Hope Rd.
- 876 970 3505
- Gardens free; zoo $$$

Rastafarianism

The characteristic colors of Rastafarianism—red, black, green, and gold—are highly visible in Jamaica, adorning everything from bar fronts to bus stops and braided belts. The Rastas themselves, with their dreadlocks piled high under tall hats or knitted tams, have come to symbolize the face of Jamaica—even though for mainstream society they are still cultural rebels.

A sugarcane harvester sports Rastafarian colors: red, black, yellow, and green.

Looking to Africa

The Rastafarian movement has its roots in the teachings of the black activist Marcus Garvey (1887–1940), a national hero who prophetically advised his followers to "look to Africa, where a Black King shall be crowned." In 1930 Ras Tafari Makonnen (Ras is an honorific given to royalty, Tafari his family name) was crowned Negus of Ethiopia, taking the title Emperor Haile Selassie, King of Kings, Lord of Lords, Conquering Lion of the Tribe of Judah. The Scriptures seemed to support his claims to divinity, and Selassie was elevated to the role of the messiah who would redeem black people from suffering and white oppression.

In its early days Rastafarianism provoked considerable antagonism as it developed support in the poorer parts of Kingston, and police consistently harassed Rasta communities, which they believed were drug-crazed and planning to undermine white society. In the 1970s Rastafarianism gained a degree of respectability when the politician Norman Manley visited Haile Selassie in Ethiopia and was presented with a sacred rod, which he employed with great effect in political rallies back home. Casting himself as the people's savior, he swept to power in the 1972 elections with the support of Rastas and their allies.

Musical Breakthrough

But the real turning point for Rastafarianism came in the 1970s with the huge success of Bob Marley and the Wailers, whose music spread the word about Rasta beliefs worldwide. Reggae and Rastas became Jamaica's trendiest cultural export, but inevitably a certain commercialization set in, affecting the credibility of the movement.

The Rastafarian faith is based on the belief that Rastas are one of the lost tribes of Israel, and that eventually they will be delivered from Babylon (the corrupt white world) and returned to the promised land in Ethiopia, or Zion. Rastas let their hair grow until it mats together into dreadlocks, following the directive in Leviticus 21:5: "They shall not make baldness upon their heads, neither shall they shave off the corner of their beard, nor make cuttings in the flesh." Following the injunction not to make "cuttings in the flesh," Rastas believe in herbal bush medicine, and many are also strict vegetarians following a regime of natural and unprocessed foods, known as Ital. Salt, meat, dairy products, and alcohol are eschewed in favor of beans and vegetables.

INSIDER TIP:

Jamaican roadside restaurants marked by red, yellow, and green signs are devoted to Ital—Rastafarian cuisine—which is delicious, healthy, and cheap.

—CHARLES KULANDER
National Geographic Traveler *magazine writer*

Rastas are renowned for their copious consumption of marijuana (ganja or herb), which was introduced to Jamaica by Indian plantation workers in the late 19th century. Smoking it is a religious sacrament, as outlined in Psalms 104:14: "He causeth the grass to grow for the cattle, and the herb for the service of man." Smoking the sacred herb is believed to provide

Reggae musician Crucial Bankie performs at the St. Kitts Music Festival.

access to a higher level of spirituality and is often accompanied by recitations of prayers or poems at "reasonings," when the communal pipe or chalice is passed around the group counterclockwise.

Many latter-day Rastas don't follow all these precepts and smoke ganja whenever they wish, eat meat, drink, and allow their dreadlocks to hang loose. The 100,000 Rastas in Jamaica today are split into different sects, and many have gravitated toward the more Christian-based Ethiopian Orthodox Church. The more traditional still remain in rural communes (called camps), venturing out only to secure supplies they cannot produce themselves.

Finally, what do those vibrant Rasta colors represent? Red stands for the blood spilled in Jamaica's history, black represents the skin color of the majority of the population, gold stands for the victory over oppression, and green symbolizes the fertility of both Jamaica and Ethiopia.

Port Royal

In the 17th century Port Royal was among the wealthiest ports in the Caribbean. Built on a small island in Kingston Harbour and connected to the mainland by a causeway (the Palisadoes), it was first used by the Spanish to repair their ships. When the English captured Jamaica in 1655, they strengthened its defenses by building five forts. These combined nautical and military legacies create a powerful atmosphere in the present-day fishing village.

The inner courtyard at Fort Charles, the first fort built to protect Port Royal

Port Royal

▲ 31 F1

Visitor Information
whc.unesco.org/en /tentativelists/5430

Fort Charles

✉ Off Elizabeth Ave.

☎ 876 967 8438

$ Tours: $$

jnht.com

Traders took advantage of this safe haven, and Port Royal grew to a settlement of some 6,000 people. The wealth from trade and pirate booty turned it into one of the richest ports in the Caribbean, with fine brick houses, piped water—and innumerable brothels, gambling dens, and taverns.

The Roman Catholic Church condemned Port Royal as "the wickedest city in Christendom," and for many people it must have seemed like judgment day when a massive earthquake on June 7, 1692, sent most of the city to the watery depths, killing 2,000 people and sinking all the ships in the harbor. Most of the survivors fled to Kingston. Port Royal suffered further from a major fire in 1702 and another earthquake in 1907.

Today Port Royal is a quiet fishing village and the home base of the Jamaican Coast Guard. You can reach Port Royal by car or ferry from the Kingston waterfront (*several services daily*), and it is easily navigable on foot (*allow 2–3 hours*). Of the buildings that survive, one of the most impressive is **Fort Charles,** the first of the five forts built around the

INSIDER TIP:

Arrange a shuttle with a local fisherman at the Y-Knot Bar to Lime Cay, a spit of sand with fine snorkeling, 2 miles (3 km) offshore from Port Royal.

—CHARLES KULANDER
National Geographic Traveler
magazine writer

port and constructed from ballast bricks that arrived in the holds of British ships. The fort's embrasures still feature cannon pointing out to sea, and the small **Maritime Museum** illustrates the history of Port Royal with artifacts dredged up from the sunken city.

To one side of the fort's parade ground stands a raised wooden platform known as Nelson's Quarterdeck. The young British commander kept watch here against the threat of a French invasion fleet in 1779–1780. Between the fort and the water is **Giddy House,** a former ammunition store that now tilts at an alarming angle. Next to it is a massive gun emplacement, the **Victoria and Albert Battery,** which was also pitched earthward by the severe earthquake of 1907.

Other places of interest in Port Royal include the **Old Naval Hospital,** a stone-and-cast-iron building dating from 1819 and now in disrepair. **St. Peter's Church** is noteworthy for the tombstone in its graveyard inscribed with the remarkable tale of Frenchman Louis Galdy, who

was swallowed up by the earthquake but was then spat out into the sea by an aftershock.

The submerged portion of Port Royal, covering 33 acres (13 ha), now lies in depths of up to 40 feet (12 m). Recently, the archaeological division of the Jamaica National

---

Pirates of the Caribbean

The original pirates of the Caribbean were a most unsavory collection of ruthless maritime thugs. Their prime targets were Spanish galleons that sailed the seas heavy with New World gold. However, in peacetime anything sailing the high seas provided a potential target, regardless of the vessel's nationality.

In wartime British pirates were officially sanctioned as privateers fighting on behalf of the British Navy. One of the most notorious of these buccaneers, Henry Morgan (1635–1688), was eventually installed as Lord-Lieutenant of Jamaica. In a classic poacher turned gamekeeper maneuver, Morgan captured his former rival "Calico Jack" Rackham (so called for his preference for calico undergarments), and the infamous female pirates Anne Bonney and Mary Read. His modern-day legacy is a popular rum named in his honor.

Y-Knot Bar
 Next to Morgan's Harbour Hotel

Heritage Trust (JNHT) has undertaken a sonar search of the area and discovered a pirate ship resting on the harbor floor. There are plans afoot to develop a museum that will showcase the thousands of recovered artifacts from the city and the ship, including items such as furniture, tableware, pots and pans, tools, shoes, and a watch whose hands stopped at 11:43 a.m. on June 7, 1692, giving a precise time for the earthquake. ∎

Blue Mountains

The majestic Blue Mountains dominate the eastern third of Jamaica, rising to a height of some 7,402 feet (2,256 m) at Blue Mountain Peak. On these slopes some of the world's finest coffee is grown—sharing space with a profusion of verdant forest. In 2015 the preservation zone of Blue and John Crow Mountains National Park became a UNESCO World Heritage site.

Coffee farming on the hillsides of Craighton Estate in Jamaica's Blue Mountains

Blue & John Crow Mountains National Park

⛰ 31 G2

Visitor Information

✉ Jamaica Conservation & Development Trust (JCDT)

☎ 876 960 2849

jcdt.org.jm

Behind Kingston, the 28-mile-long (45 km) Blue Mountain range forms a cooling contrast with the sprawling metropolis below. High rainfall feeds the lush vegetation, towering trees shrouded in a green veil of epiphytic lichens, mosses and bromeliads, prolific bamboo and ferns, and more than 500 species of flowering plants. The mountains are also home to the largest butterfly species in the Americas (the giant swallow-tail, with an impressive wingspan of 6 inches/15 cm), coneys (a type of rabbit), several nonpoisonous snakes, and tree frogs. The fine native birdlife includes orioles, tanagers, and the rare streamer-tailed hummingbird (or doctor bird, whose tail feathers are thought to resemble the tailcoats once worn by doctors). **Blue and John Crow Mountains National Park** was established in 1993 to protect 193,000 acres (78,100 ha) of this area. The most accessible parts are toward the park's western end, reached via Rte. B1, which runs from Kingston to Buff Bay in the north. The **Cinchona Botanical Gardens** *(tel 876 927 1257)* were established in 1886 to provide quinine from cinchona trees. The project failed, but the rather run-down 10-acre (4 ha) grounds, clinging to the ridge at an elevation of 5,000 feet (1,525 m), contain a wide range of mature trees, shrubs, and flowering plants. A 4WD vehicle is essential to negotiate the tortuous access road, but the adventurous will be rewarded with outstanding views.

INSIDER TIP:

One of my favorite places in Jamaica is the Cinchona Botanical Gardens. The highest botanical gardens in the world, it has an inexplicable magic.

—CHARLIE BURBURY
Owner/manager, Lime Tree Farm Plantation Resort

More easily accessible is **Holywell National Recreational Park** *(tel 876 920 8278)* 2 miles (3 km) north of Newcastle, with 300 acres (121 ha) of montane forest with pine, eucalyptus, soapwood, and dogwood trees often shrouded in mist and alive with birdsong. A visitor center offers birding tours, nature trails, picnic areas, and a campsite.

EXPERIENCE:
Hiking & Biking in the Blue Mountains

Dozens of hiking trails meander across the Blue Mountains, many of which follow old mule tracks. The most spectacular is the 7-mile (11 km) Blue Mountain Trail from Mavis Bank to Blue Mountain Peak. Guides are recommended and information is available from the Jamaica Conservation & Development Trust *(tel 876 960 2849, jcdt.org.jm)*, which maintains a campsite and several basic cabins at Portland Gap 3.5 miles (5.6 km) from the summit. Bring your own food and supplies; it can be cool and wet, even in the dry season *(Dec.– April)*. Popular downhill biking tours are run by Blue Mountain Bicycle Tours *(tel 876 974 7075, bmtoursja.com, $$$$$)*, with regular pickups from main resort areas.

The verdant area is famed for its coffee, introduced to the Blue Mountains in the 18th century. The high-quality beans grown here soon commanded top prices in Europe, but setbacks from the abolition of slavery in 1834 to several destructive hurricanes took their toll on the industry. In the 1950s the government stepped in to save the plantations and established guidelines ensuring that only coffee grown between 2,000 and 5,000 feet (610–1,525 m) could use the Blue Mountain label.

At the **Mavis Bank Coffee Factory** a 40-minute tour of the government-owned plant is rounded off with a cup of the country's finest brew. In operation for more than a century, Mavis Bank is the biggest processor of Blue Mountain coffee. ∎

Mavis Bank Coffee Factory

✉ Mavis Bank, St. Andrew

☎ 876 977 8528

🕐 Closed Sat.– Sun.; guided tours

💲 $$$

bluemountaincoffee .com

Port Antonio

Port Antonio's glory days, both as a banana port and an upscale resort, appear to be well behind it, and this quiet backwater is now mostly frequented by independent travelers who use it as a base for exploring the natural attractions in the area. Behind Port Antonio's twin harbors, Portland Parish rises into the foothills of the eastern Blue Mountains and a verdant tropical landscape fed by cascading waterfalls and lazy rivers.

Port Antonio

🗺 31 G2

Visitor Information

✉ City Center Plaza

☎ 876 993 3051

Port Antonio was once Jamaica's chief banana port, immortalized in the "Banana Boat Song" (perhaps better known as "Day-O"). Its fortunes were already on the wane when Errol Flynn ran aground here in his yacht during a hurricane in 1946. He promptly purchased Navy Island out in the bay and introduced a touch of Hollywood glamour to this remote corner of the island. Today it is still possible to spot the odd celebrity, particularly musicians enjoying a break from the paparazzi while recording at the Geejam Studio at San San Beach.

Waterfront & Downtown

Down on the waterfront, the Errol Flynn Marina is the latest plan to put Port Antonio back on the map. The swish 32-slip mega-yacht facility stands alongside a small cruise-ship pier with a handful of shops, a restaurant, and a wooden promenade along the beach.

The downtown area is easy to navigate, centering on a central square and clock tower; alongside the square you'll find busy **Musgrave Market,** piled high with local produce. From here it is a short stroll up to **Titchfield Peninsula,** which bisects the two harbors. At the end of this you'll find the crumbling remains of **Fort George** *(Fort George St.),* dating back to 1791 and now part of Titchfield High School. The fort was once one of the most powerful in the region, but little remains except for a few cannon and parts of

A nature tour near Somerset Falls in Port Antonio

its 10-foot-thick (3 m) walls. This historic Georgian and Victorian residential area is scheduled for restoration. While here, you might like to look in at the venerable **DeMontevin Lodge,** an ornate colonial relic dating from 1881 that has seen better days but retains its elegant Victorian gingerbread architecture and wood-paneled interior.

INSIDER TIP:

No visit to Port Antonio would be complete without trying "da' jelly" (frozen coconut juice). You can buy some at Musgrave Market.

—CHARLES KULANDER
National Geographic Traveler
magazine writer

Port Mall & Offshore

Back in the town center turn your attention toward an unusual building on the waterfront housing **Port Mall** (*Gideon Ave.*). Conceived and built by local architect Ziggy Fahmi, this striking structure resembles a complex of town houses from different eras, ranging from Gothic to art deco via Tudor. The interior of this architectural curio contains two levels of shops.

Across from Port Mall is the redbrick **Christ Church** (*Gideon Ave.*), a fine neo-Romanesque structure built on the site of an earlier church in the mid-19th century. It has some impressive memorials dating back to the 17th century.

Just offshore from Port Antonio lies **Navy Island,** which was a ship repair yard and barracks for the British Navy in the 18th century. When the swashbuckling film star Errol Flynn bought the 60-acre (24 ha) property, he allegedly used it as a hideaway to court Hollywood starlets. Currently owned by the Port Authority, the island's lovely beaches are not open to visitors. ∎

DeMontevin Lodge

✉ 19 Fort George St.
☎ 876 993 2604

Island Boy Makes Good

As a child growing up in the diverting social whirl of Jamaica in the 1940s and '50s, Chris Blackwell found himself hanging out with Errol Flynn, Noël Coward, and Ian Fleming at parties. His glamorous and well-connected mother, Blanche, was the inspiration for Pussy Galore in *Goldfinger*, and young Blackwell scouted locations for *Dr. No* (1962), earmarking Laughing Waters Beach as the backdrop for Ursula Andress's iconic emergence from the surf. However, far from the champagne and martini set, the legendary music producer began his career supplying imported U.S. singles to island sound system shops, selling Jamaican music to London's immigrant communities from the back of his car, and founding his iconic Island Records label in 1959 at age 22. It was Blackwell who introduced the world to the homegrown talents of Bob Marley as well as acts from Roxy Music and Grace Jones to U2 (though he initially turned down "too shy" Elton John). His entrepreneurial instincts have since encompassed the prestigious Island Outpost hotel group and more recently the acclaimed 1625 Blackwell dark rum.

Around Port Antonio

The coastline east of Port Antonio embraces some of the prettiest coastal scenery in Jamaica, its rugged headlands interspersed with golden beaches and several fine hotels located next to private beaches. (Day visitors generally must pay a small charge, which also includes use of the hotel facilities.)

Young Jamaicans enjoy the surf at Boston Bay.

Frenchman's Cove

 31 G2

 Rte. A4
(5 miles/3 km E
of San Antonio)

☎ 876 993 7558

💲 $$ for visitors
not staying at
Frenchman's
Cove Hotel

Heading east from town on Rte. A4, the first major landmark is the extraordinary **Trident Castle,** a fantasy creation that is part of the neighboring Trident Hotel *(Port Antonio, tel 876 993 7000).* About a mile (1.6 km) from here you come to **Frenchman's Cove,** a gorgeous little beach framed by rocky headlands and skirted by a cool mountain stream. Another 0.75 mile (1 km) along, you will find **San San Beach** *($$),* a narrow strip fronting a broad bay with good snorkeling on the reef. From here it is an easy swim across to a beach on jewel-like Pelew Island, on the east side of the bay.

Just past San San Beach is the **Blue Lagoon** *(tel 876 993 7791).*

INSIDER TIP:

In Charles Town, 15 miles (24 km) west of Port Antonio, head to Safu Yard to catch a jam session of the Charles Town Drummers, a drum and dance group intent on preserving their Maroon culture.

—JENNIFER ALLARD
National Geographic contributor

with stands selling sizzling jerk chicken, pork, or seafood.

It is 2 miles (3 km) to the next major stopping point at **Long Bay,** a broad expanse of sand that is considered to be Jamaica's top surfing spot. A few beach bars, guesthouses, and discos have sprung up along the road to cater to independent travelers, creating a laid-back atmosphere. The beach, however, is not in the same league as the surf. Unless you're a surfer, you will find little reason to linger.

Boston Bay

🗺 31 G2

Reach Falls

🗺 31 G2

✉ 9 miles/14 km
E of San Antonio

☎ 876 993 6606

🕐 Closed
Mon.–Tues.

💲 $

Surrounded by forest foliage, the lagoon is a limestone sinkhole fed by underground streams. This scenic spot was the setting for the Brooke Shields movie *Blue Lagoon* (1980), as well as *Club Paradise* (1986), but hurricane damage has reduced the former waterside bar-restaurant to a shell. There are boat trips across the astonishingly blue-green waters, which reach a depth of 170 feet (52 m), and kayaks to rent, and visitors are free to swim independently. If you are staying nearby, avoid the crowds and visit later in the day when you'll have the place to yourself.

Along the Coast

Continue on to **Boston Bay,** a big public beach famous for its jerk cooking (see sidebar this page). This is primarily a fishing beach, but in rough weather the incoming swells can create good conditions for surfing. The main road and the beach are lined

Jerk Cooking

Jerk cooking may have originated in the 17th century with the Maroons (escaped slaves), who hunted boar in the mountains and marinated the meat in a spicy sauce. Today jerk cuisine is found all over the island and is one of Jamaica's most distinctive cooking styles. The meat (usually chicken or pork) is marinated in a special blend of spices (including peppers, cinnamon, and ginger) and then slowly grilled over a pimento wood fire. Boston Beach is the jerk aficionado mecca, although there are stalls selling jerk all around the island. Ten of the best are identified on the **Jamaica Jerk Trail** (*visitjamaica.com*).

One of the highlights of this part of the coast is lovely **Reach Falls,** accessible via a well-paved road from Manchioneal on the coast. The falls are part of the Driver River, which tumbles down from the John Crow Mountains into a series of cascades and crystal clear pools where you can swim. The entrance fee includes a guided

Inside a jerk cooking shack near Boston Bay

walk up to the falls. Although not as spectacular as Dunn's River Falls (see p. 49), there are far fewer people here, and it is a lovely spot to while away an hour or two.

Rio Grande

Extending deep inland behind Port Antonio is the Rio Grande Valley, a lush wilderness stretching below the splendor of the Blue Mountains. The main attraction here is a Rio Grande rafting trip along one of the island's largest rivers. Originally the bamboo rafts were used by local farmers to carry their bananas to Port Antonio, but when Errol Flynn arrived here, he started organizing raft races for his friends; the ride has now become one of the area's most popular attractions.

The two-hour trip from Berrydale to the coast passes through some delightfully unspoiled scenery—riverside villages, gorges, and shoals. The 30-foot-long (9 m) rafts are built from lengths of bamboo lashed together, with a seat for two at the back, and are poled along by a raft captain standing at the front. There are stops along the way for swimming and to buy snacks or drinks from vendors. ■

Rafting Logistics

If you are staying around Port Antonio, you can book the 8-mile-long (13 km) Rio Grande rafting trip through your hotel. Independent travelers will need to give some thought to the logistics of moving their car from the put-in point at Berrydale to the finishing point at Rafter's Rest. The best option is to drive to Rafter's Rest and pick up a cheap taxi ride to Berrydale. Leaving a car at Berrydale means finding an insured driver to deliver it safely to the finishing point (*tel 876 993 5778*).

Oracabessa

As you pass through this tranquil village, 15 miles (24 km) east of Ocho Rios, it is hard to imagine that celebrities once flocked to the homes of not one but two literary lions in this quiet corner of the island. While life in present-day Oracabessa revolves sedately around its daily market, in its mid-20th century heyday Winston Churchill, Hollywood film stars, and even royalty were numbered among its visitors.

More recently, resident impresario Chris Blackwell (see sidebar p. 43) has revived celebrity interest with the exclusive **GoldenEye hotel** (see Travelwise p. 354).

Oracabessa can thank two famous writers for its interesting literary heritage. The first, the English playwright Sir Noël Coward (1899–1973), built a modest house in the hills midway between Oracabessa and neighboring Port Maria in the 1950s. His home until his death, **Firefly** has been restored to look as it did when Coward lived here, with his paintings on easels in the studio, two grand pianos back to back in the music room, and the table set for lunch as it was on the day the Queen Mother visited on February 28, 1965. Coward's simple grave on the hillside, where pirate Henry Morgan once kept lookout, encompasses one of the most stupendous views on the island, taking in the Blue Mountains to the south and the dramatic northern coastline.

The Bond Connection

Oracabessa's second famous writer is Ian Fleming (1908–1964), who wrote most of the James Bond novels in **Goldeneye,** the house he built on the outskirts of town. Fleming wintered here every year from 1946 to 1964, and his guests included such notables as Graham Greene (1904–1991) and Truman Capote (1924–1984). The house now belongs to the Island Outpost hotel group and has been transformed into the GoldenEye hotel.

In Oracabessa Bay, the 007 connection continues with the

Oracabessa

⚑ 31 E3

Firefly
⚑ 31 F3
✉ Grants Pen, St. Mary
☎ 876 725 0920
$ $$$
www.firefly-jamaica.com

The view from Firefly, Noël Coward's former residence

James Bond Beach Club (tel 876 975 3663), a development with changing facilities, food outlets, water sports, and outdoor performance areas. Film buffs might recognize the headland as a backdrop to scenes from Dr. No. ∎

Ocho Rios

Situated midway along Jamaica's north shore, Ocho Rios is the country's second largest resort town after Montego Bay. The town, which lies at the intersection of the main north coast route and Rte. A3 to Kingston, is a popular getaway spot for residents of the capital. But far more visitors disembark from the massive cruise ships that moor at the western end of the bay. For those with more time, Ocho Rios has some superb hotels in quiet coves on either side of town.

For many Ocho Rios visitors, a dip in the water at Dunn's River Falls is a must.

Ocho Rios

 31 E3

Visitor Information

✉ Ocean Village Shopping Centre

☎ 876 974 7705

The Spanish who settled in this area christened it Las Chorreras, referring to the "gushing water" of Dunn's River Falls (see p. 49). The British mistook the name as Ocho Rios, or "eight rivers," even though no such rivers existed. Today the name is usually shortened to Ochi.

Despite the wide sweep of the bay and the mountain backdrop, Ocho Rios is not the most attractive of towns. Nor are there many relics of its past, save two rather forlorn cannon pointing out to sea from the surviving stone ramparts of an 18th-century British fort.

In the 19th century Ocho Rios was surrounded by plantations, principally for sugarcane and pimentos. In the 1920s an old plantation house at Shaw Park became the country's first upscale hotel, and it was soon followed by several others—but development was held back by the absence of an accessible beach. By the 1960s a cruise-ship terminal was in place, the swamps behind the town had been drained, and thousands of tons of white sand imported to create a beach.

Stop along the north shore roadside for a fresh jelly coconut or a Jamaican patty, a flaky pastry filled with meat, fish, or vegetables.

—CHRIS BLACKWELL
Hotelier & entrepreneur

Today **Turtle Beach** ($), within walking distance of the cruise-ship pier, buzzes with activity and water sports. Around and behind the beach, you'll find plenty of opportunities for dining and enjoying the varied nightlife. You can easily stroll around Ocho Rios in an hour or two. The main daytime activity is shopping, with several malls and dozens of stalls providing an outlet for all manner of handmade crafts as well as duty-free items for cruise-ship passengers. Strategically positioned almost at the foot of the cruise-ship pier, **Island Village** is a 5-acre (2 ha) themed shopping, dining, and entertainment complex developed by Island Records impresario Chris Blackwell (see sidebar p. 43). Street hagglers are forbidden within this gingerbread evocation of a Jamaican village.

The rest of Ocho Rios's attractions lie a short distance outside the town center. They are ideally placed for cruise-ship visitors on limited shore leave, so if possible you may want to time your visits to the sites at quieter moments when the cruise berths are empty or early in the morning.

Foremost among these attractions is **Dunn's River Falls.** The spectacular falls cascade down some 600 feet (183 m) of slippery rocks and ledges before spilling out onto the beach below. All day, long daisy chains of tourists wend their way up the falls, getting thoroughly drenched (bring a bathing suit). Sure-footed guides carry dozens of cameras as they lead climbers upward. The whole process is as entertaining to watch from the wooden steps running alongside the falls as it is to do.

Adjacent to Dunn's River Falls is **Dolphin Cove,** where you can swim with dolphins, sharks, and stingrays. The 5-acre (2 ha) waterfront facility lies on a natural cove and offers several interactive dolphin programs daily, shows,

Dunn's River Falls
- 🗺 31 E3
- ✉ Rte. 1A bet. St. Ann's Bay & Ocho Rios
- ☎ 876 974 4767
- 💲 $$$$

Dolphin Cove
- 🗺 31 E3

Visitor Information
- ☎ 876 974 5335
- 🕐 Reservations recommended
- 💲 $$$$$

dolphincoveja.com

EXPERIENCE: Meet the People

All too often tourism in the Caribbean creates a gulf between local people and visitors, particularly when the latter are isolated in all-exclusive properties offering little contact with the real life of the island. If you are interested in exploring Jamaica in more depth, the Jamaica Tourist Board's free **Meet the People** program can muster one of 700 local volunteer hosts, from doctors and teachers to musicians and farmers, who are prepared to welcome you into their lives. You can sign up online (tel 876 952 4425, visitjamaica.com/feel-the-vibe/people/meet-the-people-program) or ask at a local JTB office. Give a few details about yourself (job, hobbies, interests), and they will line you up with a suitable local host for the day.

One of many vendor stalls in an Ocho Rios market

Mystic Mountain

⛰ 31 E3

✉ Balmoral Rd.

☎ 876 974 3990

💲 $$$$$

**rainforestadventure
.com**

glass-bottom kayak rides, a jungle trail highlighting native birds and reptiles, and a beach grill and bar. Reservations are required in advance for the Sea Keeper-for-a-Day program, which gives participants (10 years and older) behind-the-scenes access to dolphin training and feeding areas. There's a sister facility—**Dolphin Cove Negril**—in Lucea, 45 minutes west of Montego Bay *(see map 30 B3)*. Advance tickets can be arranged through your cruise lines.

Another popular attraction is **Mystic Mountain,** a 100-acre (40 ha) swath of sensitively developed rain forest featuring four family-friendly "soft adventure" rides. Visitors can soar up the mountainside aboard the Sky-Explorer, a chairlift ride ascending 700 feet (213 m) above sea level, then return to earth via the *Cool Runnings*–style Bobsled Jamaica roller coaster. The rain forest canopy can also be admired on the Canopy Zip Line, swooping between seven high-level platforms, while the 252-foot-long (77 m) Mystic Waterslide swooshes down into an infinity pool. Various ride packages are available, and you'll find a panoramic restaurant at the top of the chairlift, plus a butterfly garden as well as craft and souvenir sellers. ∎

NEED TO KNOW

Port Logistics: Ocho Rios

The cruise pier on Ocho Rios Bay is a short taxi ride from downtown *(look for the red PPV plates; $$)* and within walking distance (less than 1 mile/1.6 km) of Turtle Beach, as well as shopping and dining opportunities at Island Village and Ocean Village Shopping Center.

Ocho Rios Highlights

Most north coast towns and attractions are easily accessible (see also Need To Know sidebars for Falmouth, p. 53, and Montego Bay, p. 56). Guided tours are advisable; or you can hire a licensed taxi (approximately $40 per hour for island tours; be sure to agree on the price in advance).

• Rose Hall Great House: 2–3 hours
• Dunn's River Falls: 3 hours
• Prospect Plantation: 3–4 hours
• Firefly: 2–3 hours
• Bob Marley Centre & Mausoleum:
  2–3 hours

Around Ocho Rios

The area around Ocho Rios offers a number of gardens, trails, and working farms that allow the visitor to appreciate and enjoy tropical plantlife.

Coyaba River Garden & Museum

Near Shaw Park Gardens (see sidebar this page), the wooden walkways of these landscaped gardens traverse well-tended beds, miniature waterfalls, and ponds. The site was once an Arawak settlement (*coyaba* means "heaven" in Arawak), and the small museum concentrates on pre-Columbian Jamaica as well as its more recent history. There is also a café-bar and craft shop. A lookout point adjoining the falls offers a panoramic view of Ocho Rios Bay.

Cranbrook Flower Forest

A green and glorious retreat from downtown Ochi, Cranbrook showcases the extraordinary beauty and diversity of tropical plantlife. Imaginatively landscaped flower gardens and emerald lawns have been carved from the woodland surrounds. There's a beautiful forest trail for walking or horseback riding along the banks of the Little River, and low-key attractions such as bird-watching, fishing, swimming, and paddling provide a relaxing way for visitors to interact with the forest. You can also bring a picnic or experience a zip line canopy tour.

Prospect Plantation

A working plantation 2 miles (3 km) east of Ocho Rios, Prospect cultivates cacao, soursops, ackees, pimentos, and limes. Take a tour around the farm in a tractor-drawn jitney (open trailer) with opportunities to stop occasionally and sample the crops.

Mud buggies, Segways, camel safaris, and horseback rides along the White River provide more active ways to tour the plantation. You can also stroll through the aviary, feed an ostrich, learn to cook a Jamaican feast or climb the nearby Dunn's River Falls (see p. 49). Tickets for tours can be obtained through cruise lines. ∎

Coyaba River Garden & Museum
- 🅰 31 E3
- ✉ Shaw Park Ridge Rd.
- ☎ 876 974 6235
- 💲 $$$

Cranbrook Flower Forest
- ✉ 18 miles (29 km) W of Ocho Rios, signed off North Coast Hwy.
- ☎ 876 770 8071
- 💲 $$$

Prospect Plantation
- 🅰 31 E3
- ✉ Rte. 3, 3 miles (5 km) east of Ocho Rios
- ☎ 876 994 1373 or 800 733 5077 (toll-free from U.S. & Canada)
- 💲 $$$$

prospectoutback adventures.com

Shaw Park Gardens

Within a few minutes' drive of Ocho Rios, in the hills high above the town, lies lovely Shaw Park Gardens (*Shaw Park Rd., tel 876 974 2723, $$$*). Once the grounds of the original Shaw Park Hotel, which burned down in 1937, the 25-acre (10 ha) gardens overflow with frangipani, bougainvillea, crotons, bamboo, and many other glorious tropical plants. A dramatic cascade drops almost vertically from the rock face, and a magnificent 80-year-old banyan tree arches its massive branches over a large pond. The lawns command superb views of the coast from 550 feet (168 m) above sea level. The site has a bar and gift shop.

Falmouth & Around

Falmouth, 23 miles (37 km) east of Montego Bay, was once one of Jamaica's busiest ports, exporting sugar from nearby plantations and boasting the island's largest and most varied collection of Georgian buildings. After more than a century in the doldrums, eclipsed by the development of neighboring "Mo' Bay," Falmouth is in the midst of a revival spearheaded by its new cruise facility and an ambitious downtown architectural regeneration program. In contrast is the country town of Nine Mile, where Jamaican legend Bob Marley grew up.

The entrance to Green Grotto Caves near Falmouth seems almost otherworldly.

Falmouth
🅰 30 C3

**Falmouth
Heritage Walks**
☎ 876 407 2245
💲 $$$$$
falmouthheritage
walks.com

The best way to explore downtown Falmouth is on foot with a guide from community-based **Falmouth Heritage Walks,** who can explain the restoration of patrician houses, public buildings, and simple artisan cottages. Specialized tour options include a visit to the Jewish Cemetery and a food tour with tastings (3 hrs). A trolley tour (1 hr) is also available from the cruise port; highlights include the Court House, Baptist Manse, Barrett House, Tharp House, William Knibb Memorial Baptist Church, and St. Peter's Anglican Church (1796).

East of Falmouth on Rte. A1 lies **Luminous Lagoon,** a shallow inlet where fresh and salt waters meet. It is host to huge concentrations of bioluminescent microorganisms (dinoflagellates). After dark, the waters of the lagoon light up with bright green phosphorescence when disturbed. Take a boat tour from Glistening Waters Restaurant & Marina (tel 876 954 3229, glisteningwaters.com).

South of Falmouth is **Good Hope Great House,** one of the

most welcoming of Jamaica's plantation houses. Built in 1755, it commanded a sugar estate of 10,000 acres (4,050 ha) manned by 3,000 slaves. Today Good Hope's 2,000-acre (810 ha) estate is home base to Chukka Adventures (see note this page).

Running through the estate is the **Martha Brae River,** which rises in Cockpit Country and reaches the sea east of Falmouth. Rafting trips start at the **Rafter's Village,** signposted from Martha Brae *(tel 876 952 0889).* Two-man rafts made of giant bamboo poles tied together and manned by a local guide glide about 3 miles (5 km) downstream for around 90 minutes through dense tropical vegetation and limpid pools.

Discovery & Runaway Bays

Midway between Falmouth and Ocho Rios, these two bayfront towns are essentially resort strips lined with all-inclusive hotels with their own beaches and beautifully manicured grounds and golf courses.

Just west of Discovery Bay, **Columbus Park** is an open-air museum with historical artifacts as well as a mural depicting Columbus's landing nearby in 1494.

Just inland *(Rte. B3),* you can visit the **Green Grotto Caves,** an impressive and extensive cave system once inhabited by Taíno Indians. During the turbulent 17th century, Spanish troops fleeing the English hid here. The 45-minute tour includes a boat ride on an underground lake.

Rte. B3 heading inland to Alexandria is the best road to take to reach the **Bob Marley Centre & Mausoleum** in his hometown of Nine Mile. Surrounded by high fences topped with characteristic flags of red, gold, and green, the compound is revered by Rastafarians. At its center is the hut where Marley was brought up, complete with the small bed he sang of in "Is This Love." Behind the hut is the meditation stone where he rested his head to sleep or contemplate.

The mausoleum itself is housed in a small chapel of Ethiopian design. There is a vegetarian restaurant on site and a gift shop. Transport/tours provided by Chukka Adventures (see margin note). ■

Good Hope Great House
🅰 30 C3
✉ Trelawny
goodhopejamaica .com

NOTE: Activity specialists Chukka Adventures *(tel 876 979 8500, chukka.com)* offer a raft of diversions from river tubing and ATV expeditions to tours of the house and estate.

Columbus Park
✉ Rte. A1
💲 $

Green Grotto Caves
🅰 30 D3
Visitor Information
☎ 876 973 2841
💲 $$$$$
greengrottocavesja .com

Bob Marley Centre & Mausoleum
🅰 30 D2
✉ Nine Mile
☎ 876 995 1763
💲 $$$

Montego Bay

Montego Bay is the country's second largest city and its biggest resort destination, offering a wider range of accommodations and amenities than anywhere else on the island. Although its beaches cannot compare with Negril, it has an attractive setting in a sweeping natural harbor backed by a fringe of gently sloping hills. Generally referred to as Mo' Bay, Jamaica's tourism capital is a good base for visiting a brace of historic great houses, golfing, and summer's Reggae Sumfest (July), which draws crowds for a weeklong celebration of Jamaican music.

The Montego Bay area is filled with inviting beaches.

Montego Bay

⛰ 30 C3

Visitor Information

✉ Cornwall Beach

☎ 876 952 4425

🕐 Closed Sun.

Reggae Sumfest

☎ 888 336 3806

reggaesumfest jamaica.com

When Christopher Columbus anchored here in 1494, he christened it El Golfo de Buen Tempo ("the bay of good weather"), but its modern name derives from the days when the Spanish hunted the wild boars that lived in the surrounding hills. They called it Manteca Bahia, the "bay of lard." The English interpreted this name as Montego Bay.

A typical waterfront sugar and banana town, Montego Bay gained international recognition as a spa in the late 19th century when a local physician, Alexander McCatty, extolled the virtues of swimming in salt water at his Sanatorium Caribee. The discovery of mineral springs at Doctor's Cave Beach marked the beginning of tourism at the resort.

Today **Doctor's Cave Beach** forms part of touristy Gloucester Avenue, known as the Hip Strip. Its beach club has good swimming and all the necessary facilities (changing rooms, lifeguards, water sports, restaurant, etc.). Nearby **Cornwall Beach** is smaller and less crowded, with snorkeling, volleyball facilities, and a café. Both beaches are open 9 a.m.–sunset daily and charge a nominal usage fee ($$). Most of the other beaches along here belong to individual hotels.

Away From the Beaches

Encircling these beaches is an extensive fringing reef that forms part of **Montego Bay Marine Park,** covering some 9 square miles (23 sq km) of coral reef, sea-grass beds, and mangroves. Snorkeling, diving, and glass-bottom boat tours are available if you want to experience the reef at closer quarters.

Around 1 mile (1.6 km) south of the Gloucester Avenue hotel zone is the downtown, a lively, typically Caribbean area. Its focal point is **Sam Sharpe Square,** named after a slave who led the Christmas Slave Rebellion in 1831 (see sidebar this page) and died on the gibbet in this square. There is a small local history museum in the Old Courthouse, and in the northwest corner you can also see the **Cage,** a lockup once used to house drunken sailors or slaves who were out past the Sunday curfew of 3 p.m. A nearby tableau

of five bronze statues, the **Sam Sharpe Memorial** depicts the rebel leader alongside fellow martyrs who shared the credit for hastening the abolition of slavery. A short walk away is the **Crafts Market** with about 200 artisan stalls *(Harbour St., 7 a.m.–7 p.m.).*

Also worth a look is the 18th-century parish church of **St. James,** a handsome white limestone building in the shape of a Greek cross. Considered to be one of Jamaica's finest churches, the building was extensively restored after an earthquake in 1957 caused considerable damage.

Doctor's Cave Beach
Visitor Information
☎ 876 952 2566
doctorscavebathing club.com

Cornwall Beach
Visitor Information
☎ 876 979 0102

Rose Hall Great House
🅰 30 C3
✉ Rose Hall
☎ 876 953 2323
💲 Day & night tours: $$$$$
rosehall.com

Christmas Slave Rebellion

Jamaica's infamous ten-day slave rebellion began around Christmas in 1831. Samuel Sharpe, a slave and Baptist preacher, originally designed the revolt as a peaceful general strike. Because the Caribbean was attuned to the abolitionist movement happening at the same time in London, the idea was to show solidarity with the cause. The strike turned violent but was quickly suppressed, and the Jamaican government responded harshly to those involved. Hundreds of slaves were killed, and Sharpe was hanged in a town square in Montego Bay as punishment for his leadership.

Great Houses

Eight miles (13 km) east of Mo' Bay is one of Jamaica's most famous plantation houses, **Rose Hall Great House.** Occupying a commanding position on the hillside with lawns sweeping

Greenwood Great House

⚠ 30 C3

✉ Greenwood (14 miles/23 km E of Montego Bay)

☎ 876 953 1077

💲 $$$$$

greenwoodgreat house.com

Scotchies Jerk Centre

✉ Falmouth Rd., Rose Hall

☎ 876 953 8041

💲 $

down toward the sea, it was built between 1770 and 1780 in the heyday of the sugar plantation era.

Local legend says that this fine Georgian house is haunted by the ghost of a wicked mistress, Annie Palmer, who ruled over it for 13 years and murdered several husbands. Supposedly a voodoo practitioner, she is said to have been strangled in her bed by one of her slave lovers: The story was fictionalized in Herbert Lisser's 1958 book, *The White Witch of Rose Hall.* The house was abandoned in the 19th century and sympathetically restored in the 1960s. Today it contains beautiful original antiques.

Farther off the beaten track, less visited, and consequently rather more evocative, **Greenwood Great House** was built for the Barrett family between 1780 and 1800. Cousins of British poet Elizabeth Barrett Browning, the cultured Barretts lived in some

INSIDER TIP:

Scotchies Jerk Centre restaurant in Montego Bay still spices its meat with a centuries-old recipe handed down by Maroons (runaway slaves).

—LARRY PORGES
National Geographic Books author

considerable style, furnishing their house with beautiful antiques and family portraits, setting the dining table with Wedgwood china, and amassing a library containing rare volumes dating back to 1697.

Another highlight of Greenwood is an extraordinary collection of antique musical instruments, some of which are played by the knowledgeable guides. There's a small bar, and the spectacular view from the veranda more than repays the effort of getting here. ∎

NEED TO KNOW

Port Logistics: Montego Bay

Montego Bay is Jamaica's premier cruise destination. The Montego Cruise Terminal's five berths lie to the west of Mo' Bay. The terminal has a visitor information booth, licensed taxi stand (look for the red PPV plates), and shops; the Freeport Shopping Center is within walking distance. Take a taxi or shuttle bus ride to reach downtown and the beaches (approximately $5). The shuttle bus service stops at the downtown craft markets, shopping and dining areas, and Doctor's Cave Beach; an unlimited-use day pass costs $15.

Montego Bay Highlights

There is plenty to see and do around Mo' Bay, but driving in Jamaica is not recommended for visitors. Cruise companies and local operators (see Travelwise p. 390) offer a full range of tours to local attractions, all best booked in advance. Golfing is another popular option. For a private tour, licensed taxis cost approximately $40 per hour; agree on the price in advance.

• Doctor's Cave Beach: 1 hour round-trip
• Rose Hall Great House: 2–3 hours
• Greenwood Great House: 2–3 hours
• Negril: half day

Negril

At Jamaica's western tip, Negril is often regarded as the island's most permissive and hedonistic resort town. The truth is perhaps somewhat more prosaic, but nonetheless Negril has traded on its laid-back, indulgent image since the genuinely decadent 1970s.

The cliffs and clear blue water at the Rockhouse Resort in Negril

Like so many others, Negril started out as a simple fishing village. Cut off from the rest of the country by swampland, it received its first trickle of visitors when the road to Montego Bay (52 miles/84 km to the east) was completed in 1965. Soon afterward its glorious 7-mile-long (11 km) beach was discovered by hippies, who descended en masse to live in simple huts beneath the coconut palms and while away their days smoking marijuana (ganja) and experiencing sunsets enhanced by readily available hallucinogenics. ("Mushroom tea" is still a specialty you can find on the beach.)

In the late 1970s one of Jamaica's first all-inclusive resorts, Hedonism II (there was no Hedonism I), opened at the eastern end of Long Bay, Negril's main beach. Tales of unlimited alcohol, nudity, and sex soon cemented Negril's reputation as a center for uninhibited bacchanalia. A building boom that began in the 1980s marked the beginning of mass tourism, inevitably quashing the

Negril
🗺 30 B2
Visitor Information
✉ Coral Seas Plaza
☎ 876 957 9314
negril.com

Picnic With a View

Negril's lighthouse stands on the western-most point of Jamaica, affording visitors a beautiful view of the cliffs and sea. It's accessible via a short walk from central Negril, and vendors sell fruit, cheese, and drinks along the road leading up to it. The open area around the lighthouse provides a perfect spot for a picnic. The keeper will give a history of the lighthouse and take visitors to the top for a few dollars.

freewheeling spirit it tried so hard to emulate. Today Negril offers a full range of upscale hotels, simple guesthouses, and frat-party-style all-inclusives.

The bay is a nonstop parade of Jet Skis, parasail boats, day-trip catamarans, glass-bottom boats, and dive boats, and you now have to be careful where you plunge into its once pristine waters. The shoreline is always busy, and beach hustlers can be a nuisance here.

For all the new elements, Negril retains a certain insouciant attitude, and the traditional ingre-dients—beach bars where reggae plays nonstop, ganja and Red Stripe beer circulating freely—are still there. It has a great reputation for live music too, and big-name bands visit the resort regularly.

Long Bay

Most of the action takes place along the sandy swath of **Long Bay,** which fronts the main strip of hotels, beach bars, discos, and vendors offering everything from aloe massages to hair braiding. To the north of Long Bay is **Bloody Bay,** a perfect crescent-shaped beach that

takes its name from the days when whales were once butch-ered in its waters. Offshore lies a small island, **Booby Cay,** named for the booby birds (sooty terns) that nest here.

Right on the main drag, **Kool Runnings Adventure Park** *(Norman Manley Blvd., tel 876 957 5400, koolrunnings.com, $$$$$)* is essentially a family water park with a handful of moderately tame activities added to the usual array of waterslides, lazy river tube rides, and the little kids' splash zone. You can now get all hot and bothered playing paintball, take a spin in a go-kart, try bungee trampolining, or head off-site for a short kayaking expe-dition in the Great Morass.

Behind the beach, Norman Manley Boulevard separates the hotels from an area of swampland known as the **Great Morass.** Jamaica's second largest wetland, this 6,000-acre (2,300 ha) refuge protects crocodiles, land crabs, and numerous species of birds, including egrets, parakeets, jaca-nas, and Jamaican euphonias.

Norman Manley Boulevard continues into Negril town; there you'll find a couple of shopping malls and a craft market in the small town center but little else to detain you.

West End

Beyond Negril is **West End,** a quieter 3-mile (5 km) stretch of coastal road along cliffs peppered with guesthouses and hotels. This area is now undergoing a resurgence in popularity as an alternative to the mass tourism that has taken hold on the beaches, and some of Negril's most imaginatively designed resorts (such as the Rockhouse and The Caves; see Travelwise p. 353) can be found here. There are no beaches, but you can reach the waters below the cliffs via stone steps, iron ladders, and diving boards.

Cliff diving is one of West End's hallmarks, particularly at Rick's Café. Every evening, bus-loads of tourists watch the sun sink beneath the horizon from this spot. West End terminates at **Negril Point,** with its historic lighthouse, built in 1894.

Not far from the lighthouse, **Barney's Hummingbird Garden** is a riot of colorful hibiscus, frangipani, lilies, and lobster claws designed to attract the island's tiny hummingbirds. Privately owned, this terrific little oasis draws emerald-breasted red-tailed streamers and mango quits resplendent in a blur of iridescent purple to come and feed from handheld bottles of sugar water.

A popular inland excursion an hour's drive from Negril is **Mayfield Falls** *(Glenbrook, Westmoreland, tel 876 610 8612, $$),* a 5-acre (2 ha) rain forest property situated in the Dolphin Head Mountains. There are 21 natural pools and two waterfall cascades to negotiate on the guided hike upriver. Be fore-warned: The trek is quite a scram-ble (bring sensible footwear and a change of clothes; you will get wet), but the sure-footed guides provide plenty of assistance and a knowledgeable commentary on local plant- and wildlife along the way. Don't forget to bring your swimwear too for a rewarding and cooling dip in one of the bathing holes. ∎

Barney's Hummingbird Garden

🄰 30 B2

✉ Hylton Lane, West End

☎ Reservations & transportation: 876 957 0732

💲 $$$$

barneyshumming birdgardenjamaica .com

A keeper still staffs Negril Point's lighthouse, which was built in 1894.

Bamboo Ave. Mountain Drive

This drive from Mandeville into the neighboring parish of St. Elizabeth passes through lovely stretches of countryside. The road is in reasonably good repair, and on a good day driving conditions are relatively easy.

Start your drive by going northeast from Mandeville following the Winston Jones Highway (Rte. A2) to Williamsfield. Here all you have to do is follow your nose and you'll end up stopping off at the aromatic **High Mountain Coffee Factory ❶**, where producers JSP roast, grind, and package some of the finest coffee in Jamaica *(tel 876 963 4211 to book tours)*.

Turn left onto Rte. B4, passing the sprawling **Kirkvine Works** alumina factory, which scoured the "red gold" from vast pits in the surrounding area.

At Shooter's Hill, home of the Picka-peppa Sauce factory (see sidebar p. 62), continue onto Rte. B6.

The stretch of road between here and **Balaclava ❷** is an idyllic farming region reminiscent of the English countryside. Sheep and cattle graze in well-tended pastures surrounded by low stone walls, presided over by towering tropical trees like the silk cotton—shrouded sentinels with a green mantle of luxuriant bromeliads and hanging lichens.

About 21 miles (34 km) from the start, the road opens to reveal a panorama of hills stretching into the distance to the south. To the north rise the higher peaks of Cockpit Country, forest-clad and almost impenetrable.

From Balaclava, Rte. B6 gently drops to the valley floor, where a good, wide road bisects the massive sugarcane fields on either side, the crops rolling off into the distance like a vast green carpet.

Two miles (3 km) beyond the ramshackle little town of Siloah is the **Appleton Estate ❸** (see p. 66). After visiting the estate, drive to the town of **Maggotty.** There is a direct shortcut to our next point of interest at YS, but check road conditions as they can be

NOT TO BE MISSED:

High Mountain Coffee Factory • Balaclava • Appleton Estate • Bamboo Avenue • YS Falls

challenging. The longer (but more reliable) route follows Rte. B6 south to Lacovia Tombstone and the junction with Rte. A2 (8 miles/13 km). Turn right and soon you find yourself driving along **Bamboo Avenue ❹**,

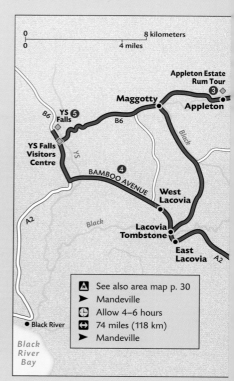

🅰 See also area map p. 30
▶ Mandeville
🕐 Allow 4–6 hours
↔ 74 miles (118 km)
▶ Mandeville

The aptly named Bamboo Avenue takes motorists through an arch of giant bamboo plants.

a 2-mile (3 km) stretch completely overshadowed by giant bamboo, which arches over the road to create a photogenic tunnel of foliage.

One mile (1.6 km) farther west, take a right signposted turn into **YS Falls** ❺ (see p. 64).

This lovely cascade is located on the up-country YS Estate cattle ranch.

From YS Falls return to Rte. A2 and turn left to head back to Mandeville. This is a big busy road, but the driving conditions are good.

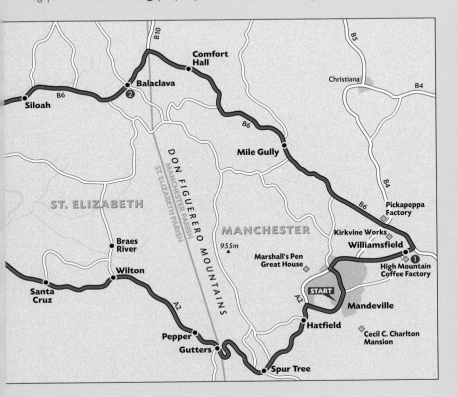

Mandeville

Jamaica's fifth largest town, Mandeville (2,000 feet/600 m above sea level), was established in the early 19th century and once served as a hill station for British soldiers recuperating from the heat of the coastal regions. The landscape around Mandeville has been shaped—and in places, marred—by large-scale bauxite mining. Yet the surrounding hills are enticingly scented with a heady aroma of chocolate, coffee, and spices.

Mandeville
△ 30 D2

**Marshall's Pen
Great House**
△ 30 D2
✉ Winston Jones
   Hwy.
☎ 876 877
   7335 (email:
   asutton@
   cwjamaica.com)
🕐 House tours
   (min. 6 people)
   and bird-
   watching by
   appt. only
💲 $$$$
jhnt.com

**Cecil C. Charlton
Mansion**
△ 30 D2
✉ George's Valley
   Rd., Huntingdon
   Summit
☎ 876 962 0585

Once the center of Jamaica's bauxite industry, Mandeville enjoys an air of prosperous tranquility that has turned it into one of the main centers for expatriate Jamaicans returning to their homeland.

The oldest buildings in the town cluster around Mandeville Square, recently renamed **Cecil Charlton Park** after a former mayor. On the south side of the square is the parish church of **St. Mark,** built in 1819. Opposite the church is the Georgian-style **courthouse,** constructed a year later next to the market, one of the biggest and busiest in the region. The venerable **Mandeville Hotel,** just to the east, was established as an officers' quarters and mess in 1875. It claims to be the oldest hotel in Jamaica; the entrance is shaded by three equally old sandbox trees. To the east is the Manchester Golf Club, one of the oldest in the Caribbean, founded in 1868. Overlooking the town center from the leafy heights of the Bloomfield district is **Bloomfield Great House &
Art Gallery** (tel 876 962 7130). This well-restored Georgian great house makes a great place to stop for lunch, and the walls are hung with local artwork.

A short distance northwest of Mandeville is **Marshall's Pen Great House.** Built in 1795, the house was once used as a "factory" for preparing coffee beans. It has since become a home furnished with antiques and artifacts, including shell and stamp collections, and antiques belonging to renowned local ornithologist Anne Hayes-Sutton. There are tours of the house and bird-watching visits of the grounds, which serve as a bird sanctuary and nature reserve.

To the south of town at Huntingdon Summit, **Cecil C. Charlton Mansion** is an interesting monument to a local self-made millionaire. ∎

Pickapeppa Sauce

The Pickapeppa factory at Shooters Hill, northeast of Mandeville, produces a world-renowned, sinus-searing spicy sauce that is found in most Jamaican households. It still tastes just like it did almost a century ago when the business was founded by Norman Nash, who made the sauce in his kitchen as a hobby. The condiment is made from natural ingredients only, including tomatoes, onions, sugar, mangoes, raisins, tamarinds, peppers, and spices, with vinegar as a preservative, and is aged in oak barrels before being shipped worldwide.

South Coast

Though Jamaica's south coast is off the main tourist trail, it repays more adventurous travelers with handsome mountain scenery, busy coastal fishing villages, hidden beauty spots, and discreet resorts tucked away in tranquil coves.

Laid-back Calabash Bay is Treasure Beach's hub.

The landscapes of Jamaica's southern parishes range from arid, cactus-strewn savannas to lush cattle pastures and vast swamplands. In the easternmost parish, St. Elizabeth, the main town is **Black River,** a peaceful port facing Black River Bay. Its main street has several colonnaded wooden houses harking back to Black River's heyday in the mid-19th century, when the town was a thriving depot for the export of logwood, used to make textile dyes. The invention of synthetic dyes killed off the logwood industry, and the town reverted to being a backwater.

Most of the activity in Black River centers on the wharf and the main street, where you'll find such faded gems as the Waterloo Guesthouse; the Invercauld Great House and Hotel with its ornate Victorian fretwork, bay windows, and gabled roofs; and the yellow-brick parish church of St. John's. Alongside the town's bridge, where the river cruise boats depart, is the Hendrick's Building, dating from 1813.

River Safaris

The majority of visitors come here for a 90-minute **boat**

Black River

🅰 30 C2

Visitor Information

✉ 2 High St.

☎ 876 965 2074

YS Estate & Falls

 30 C2

Off Rte. A2

876 997 6360

Closed Mon.

$$$$

ysfalls.com

Floyd's Pelican Bar

30 C1

Offshore bet. Black River & Treasure Beach

---

safari *(regular daily departures)* on the Black River itself, one of the few easily accessible waterways in Jamaica for spotting wildlife. The 44-mile (71 km) river, Jamaica's longest, is named for the inky black color of its waters (due to the peat moss lining the riverbed). The river is the main source for a sprawling swampland known as the Great Morass (see p. 58), which stretches across approximately 125 square miles (325 sq km) on either side of the lower reaches of the river as it descends from its source in Cockpit Country south of Montego Bay. Over its relatively short route, the Black River travels through an astonishing variety of landscapes.

The river boats navigate about 6 miles (10 km) upriver through swaths of water hyacinths and beneath the boughs of venerable mangrove trees. You're likely to see flocks of roosting cattle egrets and possibly whistling ducks, herons, ospreys, and jacanas—just some of the hundred or so species of birds that live here. The main attractions, however, are the crocodiles. Once abundant around Jamaica's coastline, their numbers are now severely depleted due to loss of habitat. Of the 300 or so survivors, about a dozen crocodiles are regularly spotted on the boat safaris. They all have names (albeit a different name depending on which boat you take!) and are used to being approached by the boats and fed scraps. Don't, however, be lulled into complacency.

YS Estate & Falls

YS Falls is 10 miles (16 km) to the north of Black River, signposted off Rte. A2. This scenic cascade lies at the heart of the 2,500-acre (1,000 ha) YS Estate, where the owners raise pedigree Red Poll cattle and Thoroughbred racehorses. The origin of the name YS has been debated for decades. One version is that it derives from the Gaelic word *wyess*, meaning "winding" or "twisting," to describe the river; another is that it comes from the original 17th-century owners, John Yates and Richard Scott.

INSIDER TIP:

Don't miss Floyd's Pelican Bar, located on stilts in the middle of the Caribbean about a quarter mile (0.4 km) off the Jamaican coast between Black River and Treasure Beach.

—MELINA BELLOWS
*Chief Education Officer,
National Geographic Partners*

The tour starts at the visitor center, where a tractor-drawn jitney takes you on the ten-minute ride across farmland to the falls. A wooden stairway leads up the highest and most spectacular waterfall, and there are caves to explore behind some of the cascades. Visitors can take a dip in the river pool, picnic at garden tables, or sign up for a zip line canopy tour. ■

More Places to Visit in the South

Jamaica's varied south offers many beaches, rivers, ponds, and savannas. Visitors can spy manatees, watch rum being produced in a centuries-old factory, or simply relax in riverine pools and laid-back fishing villages.

Grinding sugarcane the old-fashioned way at the Appleton Estate

Alligator Hole

Just beyond Gut River Pool, near Milk River Spa, is a small nature park, Alligator Hole, which is home to rare and endangered manatees. The manatees live in a maze of reeds in the river delta and come in close to the jetty to be fed. You can rent a boat at the jetty with a guide to take you out to look for them, but don't expect too much. Manatees are reclusive creatures, and the most you might see is a shadowy form gliding past underwater near the riverbank or telltale bubbles rising from the reeds as you drift by. You can also rent kayaks here.

Along the South Coast

Rearing up at the far end of Great Pedro Bay is the hulking **Great Pedro Bluff,** one of the few places in the Caribbean where a dry savanna exists in the coastal zone. Beyond here (signposted from Southfield) are the sheer cliffs and lighthouse at **Lovers' Leap,** where, legend has it, two slaves who were forbidden to be with each other leaped to their deaths. Entrance to the cliff top is through a café-restaurant complex. The view is spectacular, with the sheer bluff of the Santa Cruz Mountains dropping 1,700 feet (518 m)

Alligator Hole
▲ 30 D1

Great Pedro Bluff
▲ 30 C1

almost straight down to the ocean; the panorama extends down the coastline to Rocky Point and Clarendon in one direction, and back toward Great Pedro Bluff and Treasure Beach in the other.

Ten miles (16 km) east of Treasure Beach is the fishing village of Alligator Pond. From here a scenic drive winds 18 miles (29 km) along the south coast toward Alligator Hole (see p. 65) and Milk River Spa. This wild, unspoiled part of the country embraces dry savanna as well as the extensive swamplands of the Long Bay Morass.

Midway along is an exquisite little spot known as the **Gut River Pool.** The river flows under the road and emerges in an oasis of palm trees, bulrushes, and water lilies, with clear pools that you can jump into from the surrounding rocks: It's very popular with locals cooling off on weekends.

Appleton Estate

Three miles (5 km) east of YS Falls, beyond the small junction town of Maggotty, lies the Appleton Estate. Set amid the rolling sugarcane fields of the Black River Valley, this venerable institution is the oldest rum-producing factory in the English-speaking Caribbean, founded in 1749, and its products are among the most popular on the island. Most of the process is now mechanized, although some of the copper distillation pots are more than a century old. An aging donkey demonstrates the old-fashioned method of squeezing the juice out of the cane by turning a grinder. You can peek into the warehouse where more than 8,400 barrels of maturing rum rise up in tiers to the ceiling. The tour ends in the visitor center, where you can sample some of the assorted rums and other liquors produced here.

Treasure Beach

Some 19 miles (30 km) east of Black River by back roads, Treasure Beach is the collective name for a string of little fishing villages, beaches, coves, and rocky strands running along the seashore to the Great Pedro Bluff headland. This laid-back beach community is as close as you can get to Negril in the 1970s, albeit with slightly better communications, including a new private airfield attached to funky Jake's hotel (see Travelwise p. 354) on Calabash Bay. Calabash is Treasure Beach Central, with the greatest choice of restaurants, bars, and accommodations. ■

Gut River Pool
△ 30 D1

Appleton Estate
△ 30 C2
☎ 876 963 9215
🕐 Closed Sun.
💲 $$$$, or $$$$$ for tour with lunch

appletonestate.com

Treasure Beach
△ 30 C1

Spanish Town
△ 31 E2

Spanish Town

Jamaica's capital for more than 300 years, the south coast industrial city of Spanish Town was founded by Spanish explorers in 1523. Originally named St. Jago de la Vega, it was razed by the British and rebuilt several times, but the modern cityscape still retains fascinating relics of the European powers that shaped Jamaica. The best way to visit its former glories, including the elaborate 18th-century cathedral built over the original Spanish Catholic church, is with a guide from the Jamaica National Heritage Trust (tel 876 922 1287, jnht.com).

One of the most prosperous enclaves in the region, poised above the deepest point in the Caribbean Sea

Cayman Islands

A sea turtle glides off the Cayman coast.

Cayman Islands

The low-lying Cayman Islands are situated in the western Caribbean, some 480 miles (772 km) southwest of Miami. There are three islands in this British overseas territory, each different in character. The biggest, Grand Cayman, is the home of the capital, George Town. About 90 miles (145 km) to the northeast lie the two sister islands of Little Cayman and Cayman Brac, both comparatively undeveloped.

The tips of submarine mountains, the three islands share a similar appearance—surprisingly flat, mostly covered with dry scrub and mangrove forest. They sit on the edge of the Cayman Trench, a massive trough that drops 25,000 feet (7,620 m) into the deepest part of the Caribbean Sea. The reef walls that surround the islands plummet dramatically into the depths and attract scuba divers from all over the world. This fortuitous location coupled with vigorously implemented conservation measures has seen the Cayman Islands group develop into one of the Caribbean's top diving destinations.

The first European sighting of the islands was by Columbus on May 10, 1503, when he was blown off course on his way to Hispaniola. The explorer spotted the two smaller islands, Cayman Brac and Little Cayman. Although he didn't stop to explore, Columbus noted the enormous numbers of turtles in the surrounding waters and named the islands Las Tortugas. Over the next hundred years or so they came

to be known as Las Caymanas, from the Carib name for the saltwater crocodiles that were also abundant around the islands.

In the 16th century Dutch, French, English, and Spanish sailors stopped at these islands to replenish their freshwater supplies and capture sea turtles, a plentiful source of fresh meat for the long return sea voyage back to Europe. Even though Sir Francis Drake visited Grand Cayman in 1586 and reported that the caimans were edible, the islands remained unclaimed and uninhabited.

The Cayman Islands came under English jurisdiction in 1655, when England wrested Jamaica

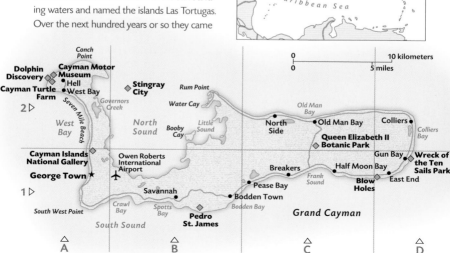

and neighboring islands from the Spanish; they were formally recognized as English territory in 1670. In the mid-1660s the first settlers arrived from Jamaica, setting up semipermanent habitations on Little Cayman and Cayman Brac to trade turtles, vegetables, water, wood, and coconuts with passing ships. Grand Cayman, which offered better protection from pirate attacks, was settled from 1700.

The Cayman Islands developed as a maritime economy. By the late 1800s up to one-third of the population was employed as merchant sailors, fishermen, or turtle catchers. The islanders rescued numerous mariners shipwrecked on the offshore reefs and salvaged lumber and cargo to build their houses and supply other needs. Over the course of time, however, a growing sense of self-sufficiency began to take hold and the islanders turned from salvage to construction. By the 1780s the

NOT TO BE MISSED:

Visiting Cayman Turtle Farm, Grand Cayman **72**

A blue iguana safari on Grand Cayman **73**

Touring Grand Cayman's Pedro St. James **74**

Diving Bloody Bay Marine Park, Little Cayman **76–77**

The seabird nesting sites in Little Cayman's Booby Pond Nature Reserve **77**

Checking out Brac Parrot Reserve, Cayman Brac **82**

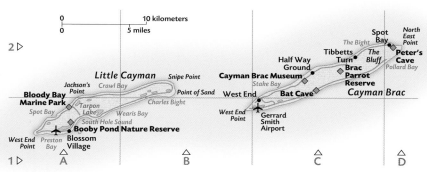

Caymanians were building their own schooners and fast becoming renowned throughout the Caribbean as master boatbuilders. Shipbuilding prospered for more than 150 years, until the launching of the last traditional Caymanian ship in January 1967.

Jointly administered with Jamaica, which gained independence from Britain in 1962, the Cayman Islands chose to remain a British overseas territory. In 1966 they introduced landmark legislation to encourage growth of the offshore banking industry, recognized today as one of the largest in the world.

The first tourists arrived on board the cruise ship *Atlantis* in 1937, and since then visitors have kept on coming in droves. Travelers to the Cayman Islands are keen to experience the islands' renowned hospitality, superb sandy beaches, and the unparalleled underwater scenery that makes them a divers' paradise. George Town is the first port of call for most, a prosperous pocket-size global banking center with U.S.-style malls and attitudes. However, head over to Grand Cayman's East End or out to the sister islands and life slows down to a much more leisurely Caribbean pace. ■

Grand Cayman

The largest of the three Cayman Islands, Grand Cayman is a modest 22 miles (35 km) east to west and 4 to 8 miles (6–13 km) across. It is easily circumnavigated in a day and is home to 96 percent of the country's population, with development concentrated along a busy west coastal fringe that gives way to the mangroves, ponds, and native woodlands of the interior.

Wary travelers can safely get up close with giant stingrays at Grand Cayman's popular Stingray City.

George Town

🅰 68 A1

Visitor Information

✉ Regatta Office Park, Windward 3, West Bay Rd.

☎ 345 949 0623

caymanislands.ky

Grand Cayman is very much an island of two halves. The tourist strip is stacked along West Bay in a glittering ribbon of hotels, condominiums, and resorts lining the glorious sandy strand of **Seven Mile Beach** (which is actually more like 5.5 miles/8.8 km long). This is also the main shopping and dining district,

and the most popular tourist attractions such as the Cayman Turtle Farm and Stingray City are also found here. For a greater insight into island life, venture to the East End, pausing at historic sites around the island's original capital, Bodden Town, and visit exotic and indigenous blue iguanas, en route to some fabulous undeveloped coastal land-marks and vistas.

George Town

The Cayman Islands' capital is primarily a business center clustered around the protective embrace of George Town

Harbour. There are close to 300 banks registered to shuffle their clients' funds through this prosperous off-shore enclave, and you can spot shoals of corporate types going about their business amid the swirling eddies of cruise passengers disembarking for a day's shopping and fun in the sun.

Downtown George Town is well served by a plethora of duty-free gift shops, jewelry stores, and restaurants. You can dip into island history and culture at the **Cayman Islands National Museum,** housed in one of the town's few remaining 19th-century structures. The two-story

building previously served as both courthouse and jail, a chapel, and a dance hall before being refitted to display permanent and changing exhibits drawn from a collection of more than 8,000 artifacts. Topics include natural history, the turtle industry, and island art.

The information center run by the **National Trust for the Cayman Islands** is worth a visit if you have time to join one of their varied guided tours or activities. Make a reservation via the website.

For a true taste of the islands, adventurous visitors can seek out **Cayman Spirits Co.,** producers of Seven Fathoms Rum, which purportedly gains its flavor from being aged seven fathoms (42 feet/ 12.8 m) under the sea.

Cayman Islands National Museum

✉ Harbour Dr., George Town

☎ 345 949 8368

🕒 Closed Sun.

💲 $$$

museum.ky

National Trust for the Cayman Islands

✉ Dart Park, 558 S. Church St., George Town

☎ 345 749 1121 for guided tours of Mission House & Mastic Trail

nationaltrust.org.ky

Cayman Spirits Co.

✉ 65 Bronze Rd., George Town

☎ 345 925 5379

🕒 Closed Sun.

💲 $$$

caymanspirits.com

EXPERIENCE: Cooking Caymanian Food

The **National Trust for the Cayman Islands** (*Dart Park, 558 S. Church St., George Town, nationaltrust.org.ky*) is a great source of information about the islands. In the shop you can pick up excellent maps and information sheets, and also sign up for activities, including cooking classes run by local chefs. The Caymanians are passionate foodies (the **Taste of Cayman** festival takes place in January; see *tasteofcayman.org*), and, on the second Wednesday of each month, the Trust offers visiting cooks the opportunity to join local experts for a lesson in preparing old Caymanian food (*tel 345 749 1121 for information & reservations, email: info@ nationaltrust.org.ky*).

Cayman Islands National Gallery

🗺 68 A1

✉ Esterly Tibbetts Hwy., West Bay

☎ 345 945 8111

🕐 Closed Sun.

nationalgallery .org.ky

Cayman Turtle Farm

🗺 68 A2

✉ 786 NW Point Rd., West Bay

☎ 345 949 3894

💲 $$$$

turtle.ky

West Bay

Fringed by the shallow azure waters of West Bay, **Seven Mile Beach** may get busy with sun worshippers, but it remains the knockout focus of the island's tourist heartland. Beach bars and water-sports concessions abound, there are excellent facilities, and

Caymanite

Caymanite is a rare, semiprecious rock that is found only in Cayman Brac and on the eastern end of Grand Cayman. A hard dolomite, this rock has a composition similar to manganese nodules found on the ocean floor. The stone's colored layers are formed by its various metallic contents, including manganese, iron, nickel, titanium, and copper among others. Polished caymanite jewelry is a popular souvenir, available in numerous jewelry stores.

good snorkeling can be found at either end of the central beach area. For divers, the main attraction farther offshore is the **U.S.S.** *Kittywake,* a 251-foot (77 m) submarine research vessel that was scuttled here in 2011 to form an artificial reef site.

Behind the beach, you'll find the **Cayman Islands National Gallery,** which has now expanded into its new home in a purpose-built arts complex designed by local architect Danny Owen, and

landscaped with native plantings. The colorful story of Caymanian art is augmented by frequently changing exhibitions. For a bird's-eye view of West Bay stretching up to North Sound, take a hike up the 75-foot (23 m) **Camana Bay Observation Tower,** in the Camana Bay resort. The funky double-helix staircase climbs up past a mosaic marinescape depicting the journey from ocean floor to the surface accompanied by details of reef corals, tropical fish, and turtles. Camana Bay is also a popular spot for shopping, dining, and catching a movie, and the resort hosts a fun farmers market on Wednesdays. This provides travelers with a good introduction to local specialties, souvenirs, and gifts to take home, from foodie treats to local crafts.

At the northern end of Seven Mile Beach, **Cayman Turtle Farm** is the island's top onshore attraction. The 23-acre site (9.3 ha) now incorporates a water park and a wide range of activities, including a saltwater snorkel lagoon with tropical fish, a 300,000-gallon (1,363,830 L) freshwater lagoon with views of the predator tank, an iguana sanctuary, and an aviary designed by the experts at Disney's Animal World.

However, it is the farm's famous green sea turtles, many thousands of them, ranging in size from cute little hatchlings that can be picked up to 600-pound (270 kg) leviathans, that draw the biggest crowds. There are shops and street entertainers, nature trails, a

The Cayman Islands National Museum is housed in a 19th-century George Town building.

wildlife rehabilitation center, and plenty of talk about conservation, but it should be noted that this is a business and the turtles are harvested for their meat. Across the street from the turtle farm, **Dolphin Discovery** is the latest addition to the Grand Cayman's tourist trail offering a choice of dolphin swim packages *(tel 866 393 5158, dolphindiscovery.com for information & advance reservations.)*.

Just up the road, the **Cayman Motor Museum** showcases an extraordinary collection of antique and luxury automobiles, motoring memorabilia, and motorbikes belonging to Norwegian millionaire Andreas Ugland. Among the treasures displayed in the state-of-the-art building are an 1886 Benz, the original

Cayman Motor Museum

- 68 A2
- 864 NW Point Rd., West Bay
- 345 947 7741
- Closed Sun.
- $$$$

caymanmotor museum.com

EXPERIENCE: Meet Blue Iguanas

The endangered Cayman blue iguana (*Cyclura lewisi*) is a rare modern phenomenon: a 21st-century conservation success story. These gentle blue giants can grow up to 5 feet (1.8 m) in length and are primarily herbivorous. Destruction of their natural habitat brought the species to the brink of extinction with numbers dwindling down to just a dozen in 2002. Today there are more than 250 "blue dragons" living on the island. To discover the methods behind this remarkable turnaround, make time to take in the Blue Iguana Recovery Program, which offers 1.5-hour, behind-the-scenes "safari" tours of its captive-breeding facility in **Queen Elizabeth II Botanic Park** (*367 Botanic Rd., tel 345 925 7599 for advance reservations, blueiguana.ky, Mon.–Fri. 11 a.m., $$$$$*).

Pedro St. James

🔺 68 B1

✉ Savannah, off coast road

☎ 345 947 3329

💲 $$$

pedrostjames.ky

Market at the Grounds

✉ Lower Valley

thegroundscayman.ky

Queen Elizabeth II Botanic Park

🔺 68 C2

✉ 367 Botanic Rd.

☎ 345 947 9462

💲 $$$

botanic-park.ky

Batmobile, and a pristine Ford Thunderbird.

A short distance inland, you can go to **Hell.** In the 1930s, so the story goes, a British commissioner shot at a bird and missed. His exclamation, "Oh, hell!" was adopted as a place-name and this small area of phytokarst rocks has been rebranded as a tourist attraction supported by sales of postcards stamped at the Hell post office and souvenir store.

Around the tip of the western peninsula, North Sound shelters Grand Cayman's eponymous **Stingray City.** Regularly dubbed the World's Best 12-foot Dive, this gentle introduction to Caribbean marine life is a must for most visitors. Groups of graceful southern stingrays gather in the sound, swooping in across the sandy seafloor looking for treats and ready to suck tidbits of squid from your fingers. When making a tour reservation, ensure the boat makes two or three stops for the most rewarding experience.

Around the Island

If time allows, it's worth renting a car to make a day trip around Grand Cayman. Road conditions are good, there are beaches aplenty for swimming and picnicking, plus a handful of low-key attractions. The first of these is **Pedro St. James,** a handsomely restored 1780s great house, built of stone using slave labor. It is the oldest surviving structure in the Cayman Islands. The interior has been immaculately furnished with period antiques, and the dining

room once served as a courtroom and home of the islands' first legislature elected in 1831. The Proclamation of Emancipation abolishing slavery was delivered from the Palladian-style staircase four years later. Make time for the excellent audiovisual presentations and a stroll in the gardens for showstopping views from Great Pedro Bluff.

INSIDER TIP:

After the Botanic Park closes, I love to circle northwest to Rum Point and sit on the jetty in the late afternoon sunshine to watch stingrays glide in and the moon rise over the water. It is pure magic.

—JOHN LAWRUS
Manager, Queen Elizabeth II Botanic Park

The around-island road continues to Bodden Town, the original island capital, where the National Trust offers tours of **Mission House,** which has been restored to depict the lifestyles of the families that once lived here. On Saturday mornings, the **Market at the Grounds** is a great place to stop off and browse the local produce and craft stalls.

Turn inland beyond the township of Breakers for **Queen Elizabeth II Botanic Park.** This

65-acre (26 ha) preserve is a treasury of colorful and exotic plantlife, native woodlands, and a lakeside wetland habitat with excellent bird-watching viewed from the woodland trail. Visitors are free to explore the landscaped gardens, where highlights include the dazzling Floral Colour Garden laid out by color, and the traditional Heritage Garden featuring a native Caymanian cottage set in a sand garden and surrounded by plants with important roles in Cayman history, such as medicinal plants and crops with economic importance. Free-roaming blue dragons, or Cayman blue iguanas, are another feature of the park (see sidebar p. 73). For an extended visit to the island interior, visitors can sign up for the National Trust's **Mastic Trail Tour,** a two-mile (3 km) guided walk through mangrove wetlands inhabited by wading birds and huge hermit crabs, pockets of savanna, and the last stand of Cayman old-growth forest undisturbed for two million years. The trailhead is by the botanic park and self-guided booklets are available.

Back on the southern shoreline near East End, if the easterly trade winds are up, stop by the **Blow Holes** for a dose of elemental drama as the ocean crashes ashore causing 20-foot-high (6 m) waterspouts to erupt through holes in the rock. Another remote and evocative place to stop is **Wreck of the Ten Sails Park,** located at Gun Bay, which commemorates a convoy of merchant vessels shipwrecked on the reef in 1794. On the North Side, the scalloped shoreline of **Old Man Bay** is riddled with secluded coves where travelers can enjoy a quiet swim. Or head on to the end of the road at **Rum Point** for beach bars and water sports on North Sound. ■

Wreck of the Ten Sails Park

 68 D1

✉ Gun Bay, East End

Little Cayman

The smallest and least developed of the Cayman islands, Little Cayman is a far cry from the commercial frenzy of Grand Cayman's Seven Mile Beach. Nine miles (15 km) long and just 1 mile (1.6 km) across at its widest point, the island is predominantly a low-lying strip of flat scrub, fringed with palm trees and sea grapes along its shoreline.

Silverside fish make way for a tarpon. Each year the silversides briefly swarm the Cayman waters.

Little Cayman
69 A1–B2

Carib and Arawak peoples may have visited the island from Cuba and Jamaica, drawn by supplies of fresh turtle, but the first permanent settlers were a ragged band of escaped slaves and shipwrecked sailors who set up a turtling station here in the 1660s. By 1900 there were still only 200 people on the island, making a living from phosphate mining, shipbuilding, and turtle catching. A hurricane destroyed most of the houses in 1932, and

the inhabitants migrated to Cayman Brac or Grand Cayman in search of work.

Isolated for decades, Little Cayman (population 150) has remained comparatively undeveloped, and it is the peace, quiet, and wilderness that now attract visitors. Diving, bird-watching, and fishing are the main activities.

The diving is superb (see Travelwise p. 390). Extending along the north shore of the island is **Bloody Bay Marine Park,** one of the Caribbean's most spectacular dive locations. The reef wall here starts in just 20 feet (6 m) of water and plunges some 6,000 feet (1,830 m) to the ocean floor. These pristine walls feature an abundance of marine life, including giant barrel and elephant ear sponges, massive elkhorn corals, lush forests of sea fans, and reef fish of all sizes. Eagle rays and turtles flip lazily past in the deep blue, and the coral canyons and crevices harbor a mass of gobies, blennies, basslets, wrasses, and many other brilliantly colored fish. Marine scientists monitor conditions from the **Little Cayman Research Centre** at Jackson Point, which can be visited by appointment (see sidebar p. 79).

Around the Island

Life ashore on Little Cayman, where lumbering iguanas enjoy right of way on the roads, can seem a little pedestrian by contrast. The island's hub is Blossom Village, sandwiched between the south coast and **Booby Pond Nature Reserve,** home to the largest colony of red-footed boobies in the Western Hemisphere. Some 20,000 of these pelagic seabirds nest on the Ramsar-designated wetlands preserve, wandering the oceans in search of food by day and returning to roost at night. The Cayman Islands' only breeding colony of magnificent frigate birds also nests here, and you'll often see them engaged in aerial battles with the boobies as they return at sundown, trying to get them to

disgorge their catch. Drop in at the neighboring **Little Cayman National Trust House** (tel 345 749 1121, nationaltrust.org.ky) for a peek through the telescopes on their viewing platform. Here you will also find local crafts, including caymanite jewelry, and a friendly café. Nearby, the **Little Cayman Museum** (tel 345 948 1033, littlecaymanmuseum.org) opens a couple of times a week tracing the island's history with exhibits and marine memorabilia.

**Booby Pond
Nature Reserve**
🅰 69 A1
✉ Outside
    Blossom Village

How Bloody Bay Got Its Name

Legend has it that Little Cayman was once settled by pirates and buccaneers who anchored their ships on the north shore and made forays out to attack passing ships. The British finally dispatched a squadron to deal with this problem by using the element of surprise. As the British vessels sailed into view, the pirates raced for their ships but were cut off and attacked as they attempted to board. The subsequent massacre gave Bloody Bay its sanguinary name.

Beyond **Tarpon Lake,** a large, brackish pond inhabited by a subspecies of tarpon deposited there by Hurricane Gilbert in 1988, the around-island road continues to East End Point Lighthouse and delectable **Point of Sand** beach with terrific views across to sister island Cayman Brac.

For fishing fanatics the main attractions are spectacular bonefishing on the flats of **South Hole Sound** and deep-sea fishing for marlin, tuna, and wahoo. ■

Coral Reefs of the Caribbean

Beneath Caribbean waters lies the complex and colorful environment of coral reefs. This mysterious, enchantingly beautiful world more than matches the terrestrial flora and fauna of the islands. It is second only to the rain forests in terms of biological diversity.

Cayman Island reefs host many of the thousand or so species of fish that live in the Caribbean.

The Coral Reef

Coral reefs have existed for 450 million years, making them among the oldest ecosystems on the planet. These remarkable structures have been built up over the centuries by tiny coral animals, or polyps, which convert sunlight and the carbon dioxide from seawater into calcium carbonate with the help of captive partners known as zooxanthellae plants that live within their tissues. The polyps use this calcium carbonate (or limestone) to build the stony structure in which they live. This symbiotic relationship functions only in warm, clear tropical waters where there is enough sunlight for the zooxanthellae to perform.

Like reefs all over the world, Caribbean reefs are subject to numerous stresses, including anchor damage, pollution, sedimentation, and coral bleaching caused by ocean warming. Marine tourism can help to preserve coral reefs, but snorkelers and divers must play their part by not touching the corals while underwater and not buying marine souvenirs.

The Caribbean is home to around 50 species of hard corals; each builds its own unique structure. Among the more familiar are the brain corals, which can grow up to 6 feet (1.8 m) across and resemble a human brain; staghorn corals, which branch out like deer antlers; elkhorn corals, which form dense patches in the surf zone; star corals, which are important reef builders; pillar corals, whose distinctive pillars can grow up to 10 feet (3 m) high; and boulder corals, which are found almost everywhere.

There are also about 20 species of soft corals, the most prominent of which are large sea fans, or gorgonians. Others include black corals, sea whips, sea plumes, and sea rods. Colorful sponges of all descriptions—delicate azure vase sponges, bloodred barrel sponges, and bright yellow tube sponges—are another important component in the dynamic reef environment, playing host to tiny invertebrates or providing hiding places for fish.

Reef Fish

The Caribbean is home to about a thousand species of fish belonging to more than 140 families. Many of them display a dazzling array of colors as they school around the reef. Among the most common are butterflyfish, particularly the four-eyed and banded butterflyfish, and angelfish, such as the magnificent queen angelfish, the yellow-and-gray French angelfish, and the black-and-yellow rock beauty. Damselfish are at home on the shallow reefs, darting out from their hiding places in the coral to graze on algae; one species of damselfish, the striped sergeant major, lays its eggs in round patches and defends them aggressively against all comers.

The wrasse family are prime scavengers on the reef, and their behavior is full of surprises. The males rule a harem of females, but should the dominant male get eaten,

Coral and sponges on a reef in Bonaire in the Dutch Caribbean

then one of the females changes sex to take his place. Closely related to the wrasses are the brightly colored parrotfish, 14 species of which live in the Caribbean. Parrotfish feed off algae on the coral rock, grinding up surprisingly large quantities of coral with their powerful jaws and then expelling it as coral sand.

EXPERIENCE:
Research the Reef

An adjunct of the nonprofit Central Caribbean Marine Institute, the **Little Cayman Research Centre's** dual mission is to promote conservation awareness through education and to carry out a year-round program of ocean field research monitoring the health of the local marine environment and its residents. Experienced divers interested in extending or enhancing their knowledge of the reef can join the **Dive With a Researcher** program, assisting the center's own reef experts in collecting and collating underwater data on a variety of projects *(information & reservations, reefresearch.org, $$$$$).*

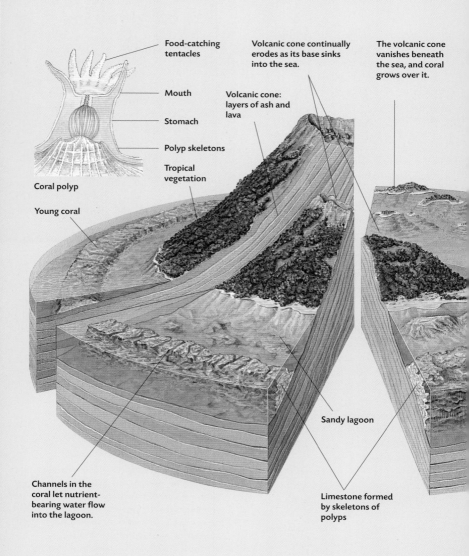

Food-catching tentacles

Mouth

Stomach

Polyp skeletons

Coral polyp

Tropical vegetation

Young coral

Volcanic cone: layers of ash and lava

Volcanic cone continually erodes as its base sinks into the sea.

The volcanic cone vanishes beneath the sea, and coral grows over it.

Channels in the coral let nutrient-bearing water flow into the lagoon.

Sandy lagoon

Limestone formed by skeletons of polyps

Predator species often seen hovering near the reef include jacks, pompano, and scads, as well as the ubiquitous snappers, of which there are 19 species. Snappers usually school facing into the current, maintaining the same position in the water column and grabbing anything that comes their way. Groupers, like snappers, are prime food fish and are therefore not as common as they once were. Groupers are impressively large and can grow up to 8 feet (2.5 m) in length and weigh more than 650 pounds (295 kg). The great barracuda usually hunts on its own, often around a chosen reef or wreck site; the three smaller species of reef barracuda are more often seen in schools.

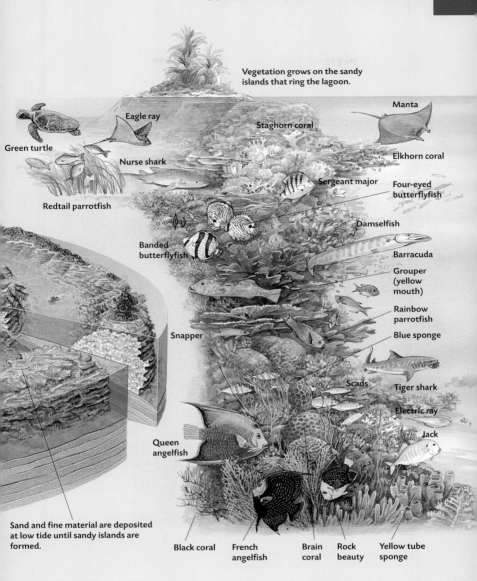

Vegetation grows on the sandy islands that ring the lagoon.

Manta

Green turtle

Eagle ray

Staghorn coral

Elkhorn coral

Nurse shark

Sergeant major

Four-eyed butterflyfish

Redtail parrotfish

Damselfish

Banded butterflyfish

Barracuda

Grouper (yellow mouth)

Rainbow parrotfish

Blue sponge

Snapper

Scads

Tiger shark

Electric ray

Jack

Queen angelfish

Sand and fine material are deposited at low tide until sandy islands are formed.

Black coral

French angelfish

Brain coral

Rock beauty

Yellow tube sponge

Sharks, Rays, & Turtles

The Caribbean has 44 recorded species of sharks, although most of these stay away from areas with people. The most common is the harmless nurse shark, often found resting on the seafloor. There are 22 species of rays, among them the southern stingray (which inhabits Grand Cayman's famous Stingray City), the majestic eagle ray, and the electric ray. Probably the most awe-inspiring ray is the Atlantic manta, also known as the devilfish or giant devil ray, but it is rare to encounter these graceful creatures. Other Caribbean residents include hawksbill and green turtles, although their numbers are now much reduced because of human predation for their meat and shells.

Cayman Brac

Although it's just 90 miles (145 km) to the northeast of Grand Cayman, Cayman Brac seems a world away from the frenetic atmosphere of the main island. Quiet, easygoing, and laid-back are some of the adjectives used to describe this little island, which is usually referred to as "the Brac."

Cayman Brac

🄰 69 C1–C2, D2

Visitor Information

✉ Department of Tourism, West End Community Park

☎ 345 948 1649

itsyourstoexplore .com

The island supports a thriving community of about 1,800 people. Residents (known as Brackers) are renowned for their hospitality and friendliness, and there's a warm welcome at the island tourist office too, which offers every visitor a free nature tour accompanied by a local guide.

The Brac is 12 miles (19 km) long and just a mile (1.6 km) wide. Its western portion is flat, whereas the eastern half is dominated by a central bluff, which rises to dramatic cliffs some 140 feet high (42 m) at the shoreline. This landmark bluff gives the island its name (*brac* is Gaelic for "bluff").

The bluff supports a wide variety of plantlife, most notably saguaro cactuses and century plants, and bird species including boobies, frigate birds, white tropic birds, herons, egrets, and bananaquits.

Other island inhabitants include a small population of endangered Cayman Brac parrots. The best place to look for them is in the **Brac Parrot Reserve,** which covers 180 acres (73 ha) of rocky woodland on the bluff. The reserve is reached by taking the main cross-island route, and turning down Major Donald Drive (also known as Lighthouse Road), toward the lighthouse at North East Point.

The island is crisscrossed with hiking trails, and you can explore limestone caves around the bluff, such as **Peter's Cave** at Spot Bay, famous as a hurricane shelter.

Offshore, the main attraction on Brac is scuba diving. The Brac is surrounded by pristine reefs teeming with fish and has around 60 registered dive sites. Of particular note is the spectacular wreck of a former Soviet warship sunk off the West End in September 1996 to become an artificial reef. Renamed the **M.V. *Captain Keith Tibbetts*** in honor of a local personality, it now lies in 55 to 110 feet (17–33 m) of water, a swimmable distance from the shore. ■

Brac Boatbuilding

The Brac's first settlers were a random assortment of pirates and refugees, including Jamaican planters, shipwrecked mariners, and adventurers. In 1833 slaves from Africa arrived on Cayman Brac and quickly established the island's reputation for boatbuilding, which remained one of its principal activities until the 1960s, when sail was superseded by motor yachts. Small, simple sailboats used for turtle catching, known as "catboats," were also built here, originally with local wood shaped by hand. The story of the Brac's early days is related in the quaint Cayman Brac Museum *(Stake Bay, tel 345 948 2622, closed Sat. p.m. & Sun., donation).*

An unspoiled natural gem, some 40 low-lying islands and cays scattered across nearly 250 square miles (650 sq km) of ocean

Turks & Caicos Islands

A Turks and Caicos beach

Turks & Caicos Islands

The Turks and Caicos Islands lie about 575 miles (926 km) southeast of Miami and consist of two island groups separated by the 22-mile-wide (35 km) Columbus Passage. To the west is the Caicos group: West Caicos, Providenciales, North Caicos, Middle Caicos, East Caicos, and South Caicos. To the east is the Turks group: Grand Turk and Salt Cay. The country's eight main islands and assorted small cays (population: 32,000) translate to just 166 square miles (430 sq km) of dry land, 80 percent of which is uninhabited.

The Turks and Caicos Islands (TCI) are more sea than land. They lie at the tail end of the Bahamas archipelago on two huge, shallow, sand-covered limestone banks that provide important habitats for marine life. Many are covered with sea-grass meadows harboring burrowing sea urchins, sea cucumbers, and mollusks. The banks are a rich fishing ground, and the 8,000-foot-deep (2,400 m) passage that divides them is popular with migrating humpback whales, rays, turtles, and dolphins. The breathtaking underwater scenery has propelled the islands into the top rank of the world's best dive destinations.

The first inhabitants of these islands were Lucayan migrating from Haiti; they arrived in the Bahamas chain around 1,200 years ago. After making landfall on Big Sand Cay or the Seal Cays, the Lucayan established themselves on the northwest corner of Grand Turk. This site, which has been extensively excavated, is the oldest known settlement in the Bahamas chain and was occupied from around A.D. 705 to 1170. Artifacts recovered include shell

beads, a mother-of-pearl pendant, a nearly complete greenstone ax, and conch-shell tools. The most important find from pre-Columbian times on Grand Turk has been a wooden paddle dating from A.D. 1100. It is now on display in the Turks & Caicos National Museum.

No one lived on the islands when the first Europeans arrived. In the 17th century Bermudians settled Grand Turk, Salt Cay, and South Caicos, using slave labor to rake the *salinas* (salt

NOT TO BE MISSED:

pans) for the salt trade. They also deforested the islands in order to speed up the evaporation process.

During the American Revolution, Loyalists fleeing the conflict set up plantations here for sisal and cotton, again using slave labor. With the abolition of slavery in 1834 the plantation system collapsed, and the Loyalists left the islands. The slaves remained and relied on subsistence farming and fishing.

The islands were under the jurisdiction of the Bahamas from the 18th century until annexed to Jamaica in 1873. After Jamaican independence in 1962, the salt industry foundered and the TCI became a British colony.

Tourism on the TCI has exploded in recent years, and the islands have garnered a reputation for a distinctive brand of laid-back luxury teamed with a strong element of eco-awareness as the local industry strives to avoid the pitfalls of overdevelopment. The capital, Cockburn Town, lies on the west coast of low-key Grand Turk, a quaint settlement of quiet streets and attractive old Bermudian-style buildings close to the modern cruise port. The main focus of tourism development in the islands is Providenciales (known as Provo), which also plays host to a thriving offshore banking sector. Opinion is still divided over the merits of certain hotel developments on Providenciales, but the TCI can still boast dozens of stunning untouched beaches and dive sites, and a choice of boutique refuges on quiet cays, so nobody needs to worry quite yet. ■

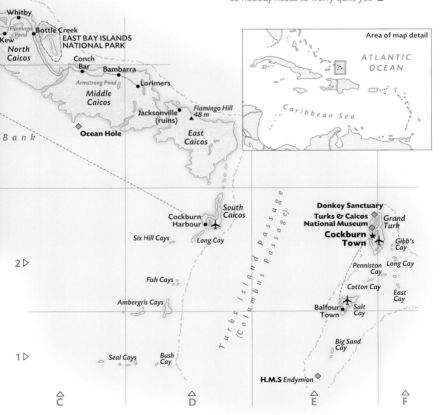

Grand Turk

Grand Turk covers only 7 square miles (18 sq km), but it is the second most populous island in the group and home to Cockburn Town, an attractive old colonial port and the seat of government. As with other islands in the Turks and Caicos, the vegetation is chiefly scrub and cactus, interspersed with flat expanses of abandoned salt pans. Wild donkeys and horses wander freely, descended from equine ancestors who once played a vital role in the salt industry.

A boy shows off a parrotfish, which are able to change their gender and coloration.

Grand Turk

⚑ 85 E2–F2

Visitor Information

✉ Front St., Cockburn Town

☎ 649 946 2321

turksandcaicos tourism.com

What Grand Turk lacks in natural beauty on land is more than made up for by the glorious, exuberant world of its coral reefs. Just a stone's throw offshore on the west side of the island, a sheer wall drops away from about 40 to 7,000 feet (12–2,134 m), providing some of the most thrilling reef diving in the Caribbean. All diving off Grand Turk is within 10 to 15 minutes of the shoreline, so operators simply pick up clients from the beach outside their hotels and whisk them straight to the dive sites.

One of the best excursions is to **Gibb's Cay,** an uninhabited island where you can hand-feed and snorkel with stingrays. From January through April, you can watch Atlantic humpback whales migrating from an observation point up by **Grand Turk Lighthouse,** which was transported piece by piece from the U.K. more than 150 years ago. Gibb's Cay is ideal for those who appreciate quirky, out-of-the-way places, friendly "belongers," as the locals are called, and a relaxed pace. You can cycle the length of the island in a couple hours.

Cockburn Town

Grand Turk's hub is Cockburn Town. Its pretty, historic heart around Duke Street and Front Street is perfect for a gentle stroll with a Heritage Walk map from the tourist board, followed by a cool drink in one of the old inns. The government offices reside in the brightly painted buildings around the small square where old cannon still face out to sea. Slightly to the north is the blue-trimmed **Odd Fellows Lodge,** one of the oldest buildings on the island. Folklore has it that the emancipation of the slaves was announced here in 1832. On Pond Street, **Her Majesty's Prison** is no longer used to incarcerate criminals and opens for inspection.

An unexpected treat is the **Turks & Caicos National Museum.** It is housed in the pre-1825 stone Guinep House, which is thought to have been built by a former shipwright, who named it after the magnificent guinep tree outside its door.

The museum's centerpiece is its extensive display on the Molasses Reef Wreck, the oldest European shipwreck so far discovered in the Caribbean. The early 16th-century Spanish caravel foundered on the rim of the Caicos Bank, and numerous items from the ship provide a fascinating time capsule of the daily life of early explorers. The upper floor of the museum is devoted to natural history, the salt trade, the Lucayan, and other aspects of the islands' history.

Continue down Front Street, past **Waterloo,** the governor's office, built as a private residence in 1815. Next is **South Base,** a former U.S. Air Force missile tracking base that had its moment of fame in 1962 when the first U.S. astronaut to orbit the Earth, John Glenn, was brought ashore here after his Mercury capsule splashed down just offshore. ∎

INSIDER TIP:

For a bird's-eye view of the islands' beauty and the contrast of ocean colors at the offshore shelf, try parasailing or take a helicopter ride.

—JUSTIN KAVANAGH
National Geographic
Travel Books editor

Turks & Caicos National Museum

⬛ 85 E2
✉ Guinep House, Front St.
☎ 649 946 2160
🕐 Closed Sat. p.m.–Sun.
💲 $$

tcmuseum.org

NEED TO KNOW

Port Logistics: Grand Turk

The Grand Turk Cruise Center *(grand turkcc.com)* occupies an 18-acre (7.2 ha) landscaped site 3 miles (5 km) south of Cockburn Town. The Center boasts one of the Caribbean's largest pools, shopping, dining, and a beach with loungers. Narrated around-island tram tours depart from the main gates; an all-day multiuse pass is a good option. Taxi fares are fixed (about $5 per person into town), and tours including snorkel/dive packages can be booked through cruise lines.

Grand Turk Highlights

• Cockburn Town: 2–3 hours
• Pillory Beach: 2 hours
• Gibb's Cay snorkel trip: 3–4 hours
• Segway tour with Oasis Divers (*oasisdivers.com*): half day
• Whale-watching *(Jan.–April)*: 3–4 hours

Islands Around Grand Turk

With few inhabitants but a wealth of history, East Caicos, Salt Cay, and South Caicos (accessed by air or ferry services from Provo) once held plantations and salt pans. Now they offer birds, whale-watching, beautiful beaches, and spectacular diving in pristine locations.

The salt ponds on Salt Cay are reminders of the industry that once supported the island.

East Caicos
🔺 85 D3
Visitor Information
☎ 649 946 2321

Salt Cay
🔺 85 E2
Visitor Information
☎ 649 946 2321

East Caicos

Covering some 18 square miles (47 sq km), East Caicos is one of the largest islands in the archipelago and the largest uninhabited island in the Caribbean. **Flamingo Hill,** on its north side, is the highest point (156 feet/48 m) in the Turks and Caicos, but most of the island consists of swamps, mangroves, and tidal mudflats.

At the beginning of the 20th century, the settlement of Jacksonville, now empty, administered a 50,000-acre (20,000 ha) sisal plantation and cattle farm. Near Jacksonville are several caves with evidence of Lucayan occupation, including petroglyphs carved on the walls.

Salt Cay

The only other inhabited island in the Turks group, Salt Cay lies 7 miles (11 km) to the south of Grand Turk. Bermudians first landed here in 1645, and salt production began in 1673, lasting until the collapse of the industry in the 1960s.

Declared a UNESCO World Heritage site, Salt Cay has a landscape dominated by reminders of its age-old industry. Miles of intricate low stone walls and canals (used to speed up evaporation) are still visible, as are numerous derelict windmills. The old salt ponds have renewed purpose as an important habitat for wading birds and ospreys. Bermudian architecture predominates in the sleepy settlement of **Balfour Town,** where Salt Cay's residents (there are fewer than 100 of them) will welcome you with open arms. There are a couple of small hotels and bars, shops, and the **White House** (*tel 649 243 9843, tours by appt. only*), which was built in the 1830s from stone ballast carried in ships' holds.

In the 19th century Salt Cay was also a major center for whaling. Nowadays the whales are more valuable alive than dead. Visitors may be lucky enough to spot migrating humpbacks from January through March.

Like Grand Turk, Salt Cay was deforested long ago, but the lack of terrestrial flora is compensated for by a flourishing underwater environment. The island has many buoyed dive sites and offers virgin diving on its reef walls with their tunnels, undercuts, and caverns. A highlight is the wreck of the **H.M.S. Endymion,** a British warship dating from 1790; it lies about 25 feet (8 m) underwater.

South Caicos

Tourists very seldom visit South Caicos, once a major commercial center for the islands, but this was not always the case. In fact, the island had the first hotel in the Turks and Caicos Islands, the Admiral's Arms Inn; it opened in the 19th century to serve the Brazilian pilots who stopped here en route between Miami and South America.

During the 19th century, South Caicos was a major player in the salt trade when the *salinas* of Grand Turk and Salt Cay could

not meet the demand for salt from the North American market. The salinas here were fed by a unique boiling hole, a subterranean passage that allowed salt water to naturally flow into the pans, where windmills pumped it into a series of reservoirs. The island exported more salt than any of its neighbors and even set up three steam-driven salt mills.

Island Donkeys

Grand Turk was once famous for its donkeys, which were found all over the island roaming the scrub, foraging in gardens, standing quietly in the shade, or even holding up traffic on the roads. They were introduced by settlers in the 17th century to haul cartloads of salt to waiting ships. By the 1800s more than 800 of the long-eared beasts resided on the island, but after the salt trade collapsed in 1964 the donkeys came to be viewed as a nuisance rather than an asset. Some were exported to islands that needed them, such as Jamaica. Many now live in a donkey sanctuary on the north shore. About 50 animals, however, still roam free.

Today South Caicos is a fishing center. **Cockburn Harbour** has one of the best anchorages in the archipelago, superb beaches (particularly Long Beach), bonefishing in the shallows of Bell Sound Native Reserve, excellent diving on the breathtaking coral walls near its eastern shoreline, and beautiful, uninhabited cays nearby (Long Cay, Ambergris Cays, Fish Cays, and Bush Cay) that can be visited on day trips. Accessible only by boat, none of the cays have any accommodations. ■

South Caicos
85 D2
Visitor Information
☎ 649 946 2321

Middle Caicos

With an area of 48 square miles (124 sq km), this is the largest island in the Turks and Caicos archipelago, linked by a drivable causeway to North Caicos (see p. 92). The 275 inhabitants of Conch Bar, Lorimers, and Bambarra depend on fishing and small-scale tourism.

Dolphins can often be found frolicking off the Turks and Caicos Islands.

Middle Caicos
 85 C3–D3

Visitor Information

✉ Front St.,
   Cockburn Town,
   Grand Turk

☎ 649 946 2321

**turksandcaicos
tourism.com**

Since the arrival of the cause-way, twin-island day-trip tours to both Middle and North Caicos have become a popular option from Providenciales and Grand Turk (see sidebar opposite). Independent travelers can rent bikes or cars to get around, but guided tours can pack more in with easy access to sites such as the caves of Conch Bar and old plantation ruins.

Middle, or Grand, Caicos was occupied by the Taíno between A.D. 750 and 1500; these early settlers called it Aniyana. **Armstrong Pond,** south of Bambarra, was an important Taíno settlement (one of 38 on the island). It features the only ceremonial ball court in the region and an arrangement of stones that may have had astrological significance for the Taíno.

Wild About Wildlife

Middle Caicos is one of the main nesting sites in the archipelago for the impressive oceangoing frigate bird, which also nests on Penniston Cay and other uninhabited islands. The pristine cays are important nesting areas for the sooty and rose-ate terns, Audubon's shearwater, and brown noddies as well. Four species of turtles (hawksbill, green, loggerhead, and leatherback) live in the surrounding waters, although local consumption of these endangered species is still common. The islands have a flourishing population of playful bottlenose dolphins, and in the winter months (January to March), majestic Atlantic humpback whales pass by on their way from cold northern seas to their breeding grounds southeast of Grand Turk. Divers often hear their haunting songs underwater.

INSIDER TIP:

The beaches of Middle Caicos are secluded and simply spectacular. To explore, arrange to have a rental car meet your ferry at the dock.

—CLARE JARDINE
Owner, Dive Provo

In the town of **Conch Bar,** on the north coast, you can explore a series of imposing limestone caves decorated with stalagmites and stalactites and home to bats and saltwater lagoons (included on island tours). Lucayan artifacts have been found here.

The island's northwest coast is characterized by dramatic limestone cliffs (unique in the archipelago) interspersed with beautiful, deserted beaches. A trail along the coastline, known as the **Crossing Place Trail,** was the main highway on the island for centuries. It runs for 12 glorious miles (19 km) through some of the most memorable scenery in the TCI, ending up at the cause-way crossing to North Caicos.

Another unusual feature is **Ocean Hole,** off the south coast of the island, which is about 1,200 feet (366 m) wide and about 200 feet (60 m) deep. This "blue hole" is thought to have been a land cave before being flooded many thousands of years ago and losing its roof. This marine sinkhole is home to bonefish, sharks, and other pelagic fish, and visitors can reach it only by boat. ∎

EXPERIENCE: Get to the Heart of the Islands

Island tour specialists **Big Blue Unlimited** (tel 649 946 5034, bigblue.tc, $$$$$) offers an excellent guided day trip to Middle and North Caicos that combines sightseeing with activities. The full-day excursion departs from Providenciales, and the fun begins with snorkeling around the Caicos Bank reefs. On North Caicos, there's a tour of Wade's Green and a home-cooked lunch with a local host, followed by flamingo-spotting. Across the causeway on Middle Caicos, a caving experience and shopping for local crafts is followed by a swim. Big Blue also leads kayaking, paddleboarding, birding, biking, and hiking trips.

North Caicos

In contrast to the aridity of most islands in the group, North Caicos is comparatively lush and is considered the garden center of the country. It has a higher rainfall (for reasons not fully understood), and its fertile soil produces abundant crops of tomatoes, corn, papayas, yams, pumpkins, limes, and avocados on farms tucked away in the interior.

North Caicos

⚑ 84–85 B4–C4

Visitor Information

✉ Front St., Cockburn Town, Grand Turk

☎ 649 946 2321

turksandcaicos tourism.com

Wade's Green Plantation

⚑ 84 B4

☎ 649 941 5710

🕐 Open Mon.–Fri.; Sat. by appt.; closed Sun.

💲 $$$

tcnationaltrust.org

Like on its sister islands Middle and East Caicos, its southern reaches consist mostly of mangrove lagoons and swamps. On the north coast, powdery sand beaches slope into a shimmering lagoon that leads out to a line of breakers crashing onto the offshore reef. Most of the 1,400-strong population lives in a handful of modest settlements. **Bottle Creek** is the commercial center, while hotels and guesthouses are found on the north coast at **Whitby.**

A popular day-trip destination and potentially next in line for tourism development, North Caicos is just a 10-minute flight from Providenciales; ferries take 30 minutes. Bicycles are a good way to get around and some rental cars are available.

Place-names echo the North Caicos idiosyncratic history: Hungry Hole (a hidden lagoon); Ready Money (a plot of land that changed hands swiftly); Pumpkin Bluff Pond; and Laughland. **Wade's Green Plantation** is the legacy of a Loyalist refugee from Florida who was granted 860 acres (340 ha) for a cotton plantation at Bellefield. By the time of his death in 1821 Wade Stubbs had nearly 400 slaves working on his plantation, now one of the best preserved ruins in the Caicos Islands from the Loyalist period.

Bird-watching is a major attraction. North Caicos has the second largest population of flamingos in the Caribbean, but depending on where they are in the extensive **Flamingo Pond Nature Reserve,** you may need binoculars. Flamingos can also be spotted at **Three Mary Cays Sanctuary,** where ospreys nest and the snorkeling is great. Indigenous rock iguanas inhabit **East Bay Island National Park.**

Protected under the international Ramsar Convention, **Caicos Nature Reserve** (see sidebar this page) supports West Indian flamingos and other waterbirds, including West Indian whistling ducks and breeding colonies of magnificent frigate birds. ∎

Caicos Nature Reserve

Stretching majestically over 210 square miles (544 sq km), the North, Grand, and East Caicos Nature Reserve is one of the Caribbean's largest protected areas. A wilderness of tidal sloughs, mangroves, mudflats, and saline ponds, this important wetland zone links the dry uplands of the islands with the turquoise coastal shallows. Submerged banks, creeks, and lagoons provide critical nursery habitat for flamingos, lobsters, conchs, turtles, and other marine species.

Providenciales (Provo)

On a cloudy day you can sometimes see a green sheen on the underside of the cloud banks over Providenciales. This unique phenomenon is caused by reflections from the shallow, dazzlingly blue inland lagoons that stretch across Chalk Sound National Park.

About 25 miles (40 km) long and 3 miles (5 km) wide, Providenciales is the most developed of the islands in terms of tourism and commerce, and is the main airport gateway to the TCI. Commonly called Provo, the island has wide sandy beaches and dramatic offshore diving sites. It makes an excellent jumping-off point for exploring farther afield.

Along the north shore, **Grace Bay'**s superb 12-mile (19 km) sweep of fine, powdery, white sand ranks among the top beaches in the Caribbean and has attracted most of Provo's hotel and condominium development. Bordering the bay is **Princess Alexandra Land and Sea National Park,** a vast area of offshore patch reefs, walls, and lagoons. There is excellent diving here and along the coast at Northwest Point.

Parks & Plantations

Sheltered behind the south coast, **Chalk Sound National Park** encompasses a huge expanse of shallow turquoise water dotted with green rocky cays, popular with a variety of bird species. In the eastern corner, Sapodilla Bay has a lovely secluded beach; on the cliffs behind the bay, shipwrecked sailors once carved their names in the rock.

Snorkelers ply the crystal clear waters off Provo.

EXPERIENCE: Go Fish

The TCI are a mecca for keen anglers. Deep-sea fishing expeditions set out from the islands in search of marlin, tuna, wahoo, and more. Closer to the shore, grouper, snapper, and jack are commonly caught, and the shallows are prime bonefish territory. Also known as "phantoms," bonefish bottom-feed on shrimp and crab. Bonefish can grow to 10 to 14 pounds (4.5–6 kg). They're notorious fighters, and once hooked can take off at speeds of up to 25 miles an hour (40 km/h).

If you want to pit your wits against local game fish, let experienced fishing guides Silver Deep (Grace Bay, tel 649 946 5612, silverdeep.com, $$$$$) or Beyond the Blue (tel 649 231 1703 or U.S. 321 795 3136, beyondtheblue.com, $$$$$) guide you to your quarry.

Providenciales

🅰 84 B3

Visitor Information

✉ Stubbs Diamond Plaza, Le Deck Rd., The Bight

☎ 649 946 4970

turksandcaicos tourism.com

Caicos Conch Farm

🅰 84 B3

✉ Heaving Dock Rd.

☎ 649 946 5330

🕐 Closed Sun.

💲 $$$

caicosconchfarm .net

Heading back toward the north coast, the ruins of **Cheshire Hall** can be seen just off the Leeward Highway. This was one of three short-lived cotton and sisal plantations started by Loyalists fleeing the American Revolution.

Blue Hills & Beyond

Of Provo's three original settlements—Five Cays, Blue Hills, and The Bight (meaning "the bay")—the most scenic is Blue Hills, a small fishing port on the north coast. Government offices and other businesses are located in the downtown, near the airport, but in general the island lacks a focal point. Shopping malls and other facilities have sprung up haphazardly along the main road, the Leeward Highway. The closest the island has to a central focus is

Turtle Cove, where you'll find hotels, a few restaurants, and a tourist office clustered around the yacht basin. At the eastern end of the island, the 6,560-yard (6,000 m), par-72 championship golf course designed by Karl Litton is one of the best in the Caribbean.

Continue on until the road runs out and you will reach the deep channel that separates Provo from adjacent Mangrove Cay. Sheltered in this natural harbor is busy **Leeward Marina,** where ferries and boat trips depart for the outer islands.

INSIDER TIP:

There are several excellent restaurants in Providenciales, but prepare for sticker shock—expect to pay double mainland U.S. prices.

—ROBERT GIROUX
Programmer, National Geographic
Global Media

Alongside the marina is **Caicos Conch Farm.** The only one of its kind in the world, this mollusk farm was set up in 1984 to develop techniques for conch harvesting (the creature is becoming endangered in the wild). An educational tour embraces the various stages the conchs move through, from the hatchery to the subsea pasture, where they grow to maturity. The conch farm exports live conchs to Florida and also sells them to local restaurants. ∎

Islands Around Providenciales

Easily reached by boat from Provo, these islands and cays are a nature lover's delight. Little Water Cay features endangered iguanas, West Caicos flamingos, and Parrot Cay a sybaritic getaway complete with diving, sailing, excursions, and a spa.

Little Water Cay

This uninhabited cay close to Provo, now a protected area under the Turks & Caicos National Trust, is popular with day-trippers who come to see its endangered rock iguanas (see sidebar p. 96). Several tour companies, including Sail Provo *(tel 649 946 4783, sailprovo.com)*, run half-day boat excursions to the island.

An isolated beach's conch shack

Parrot Cay

Originally known as Pirate Cay, this 1,300-acre (526 ha) luxury resort island was once run as a plantation. Between 1718 and 1720 it was home to the notorious pirate Anne Bonney and her lover, pirate captain "Calico Jack" Rackham. Today you are more likely to encounter A-list celebrities enjoying some downtime *(Parrot Cay Resort, tel 649 946 7788, parrotcay.com)*.

West Caicos

Isolated and uninhabited, West Caicos is renowned for its excellent diving *(visited by day boats)*. During the mid-18th century,

Little Water Cay
⚠ 84 B3

Parrot Cay
⚠ 84 B4

West Caicos
⚠ 84 A3

Island Conchs & Keeping a Clean Conscience

The beautiful, pink-lipped shellfish known as the queen conch *(Strombus gigas)* has been a staple of the Caribbean diet since long before Columbus arrived in the New World. Millions of conchs (pronounced conks) are harvested annually in the shallow waters surrounding the Bahamas, Bermuda, Florida, and the Turks and Caicos. Conch shells are often sold to tourists as souvenirs or jewelry, placed on Caribbean graves, and even used as building materials in place of bricks.

The high demand for conch and subsequent overfishing in the waters surrounding the Caicos Bank has resulted in a noticeable decline in the conch harvest, to the point that conchs are now listed as an endangered species. Some countries in the Caribbean have banned the export of queen conch shells, and tourists returning home will often find their conch shells confiscated while clearing customs. It's better to admire the living animals in their habitat and leave the shells behind.

This rock iguana may look fierce, but the species is actually gentle and shy—and endangered.

the island was used as a base by the French corsair Jean Thomas Dulaien. Later, when it had become known as Yankee Town, the island was cleared for *salinas* (salt ponds) and sisal plantations in the 1890s. Today ruins of the sisal plantations, railroad tracks, and steam engines can still be seen. At the island's center is **Lake Catherine,** a nature reserve that is home to ospreys, herons, and pink flamingos.

Diving West Caicos: West Caicos has 6 miles (10 km) of reefs along its leeward shoreline, with a reef wall that starts at about 35 to 45 feet (11–14 m) below sea level, and drops away to depths of 6,000 feet (18,000 m). The dive sites here are renowned for their enormous, colorful sponges, beautiful coral formations, black corals, and gorgonians.

Fish life includes jacks, Nassau groupers, moray eels, and French angelfish, while out in the blue there is always the chance of spotting big pelagics such as sharks, eagle and manta rays, turtles, and possibly even hammerheads or enormous whale sharks. ∎

Rock Iguanas

The rock iguana species *(Cyclura carinata)* seen on Little Water Cay is unique to these islands. This long-lived, territorial reptile mates only once a year, producing 7 to 12 eggs per clutch. Rock iguanas have disappeared from many inhabited islands due to predation by humans, cats, and dogs. About 50,000 rock iguanas remain in the Turks and Caicos, the largest population in the world, with about 2,000 on Little Water Cay and the rest on Ambergris Cays, at Fort George, and in other island reserves.

Site of the first Spanish colony in the Americas, with everything from colonial architecture to superb beaches

Dominican Republic

A stained-glass window in Santo Domingo's Catedral Basilica Santa María la Menor

Dominican Republic

Occupying the eastern two-thirds of the island of Hispaniola (the remaining third is Haiti), the Dominican Republic was home to the first European colony in the New World. It has the Caribbean's highest peak, largest lake, and biggest city. But above all it is known for its extensive white-sand beaches, about 1,000 miles (1,600 km) of them. Beyond the beach resorts, if you're adventurous, you will discover an enormously diverse country.

This fertile island was heavily populated by Taíno Indians when Columbus first arrived on its shores in 1492. He named it Isla Española (or Hispaniola) and decided it would be ideal for a colony, especially since gold deposits were also discovered.

The present-day capital, Santo Domingo, was established at the mouth of the Ozama River in 1496. During the early years of Spanish rule, the economy was fueled by gold, but by 1515 the gold had run out and the Spanish began to ignore Hispaniola in favor of the more lucrative mines of South America and the prospect of wealth in Mexico.

By the 17th century the northwestern part of the island was occupied by pirates and French buccaneers, who resisted attempts by the Spanish to drive them out. France took advantage of this to claim the western third of

the island in 1697. Over the next century Saint-Domingue, as the French portion was known, became one of the richest colonies in the Caribbean thanks to sugarcane plantations. The

NOT TO BE MISSED:

PARQUE NACIONAL HISTÓRICO Y ARQUEOLÓGICO DE LA ISABELA

4 ▷   PARQUE NACIONAL MONTE CRISTI   Monte Cristi   Villa Vásquez   La Isabela   Luperón

Dajabón   Guayubin   Mao   Esperanza

Cordille   Yaque del Norte

Sabaneta
Loma de Cabrera
Restauración

HAITI   Pedro Santana   Cordille   PARQUE NACIONAL ARMANDO BERMÚDEZ

3 ▷   PARQUE NACIONAL JOSÉ DEL CARMEN RAMÍREZ   La Ciénaga   3175m Pico Duarte

Bánica

Las Matas de Farfán   San Juan

Comendador   San Juan

Hondo Valle   El Cercado

Sierra de Neiba

La Descubierta   Neiba
Isla Cabritos
Lago Enriquillo   Yaque del Sur

2 ▷   Jimaní   Vicente Noble
Duvergé   PARQUE NACIONAL SIERRA BAHORUCO   Aeropuerto Internacional María Montez
Sierra   Cabral   Barahona
2275m   de Bahoruco

Pedernales

Cabo Rojo   Paraíso

Enriquillo

Cabo Falso   Oviedo
1 ▷   PARQUE NACIONAL JARAGUA

Isla Beata   Cabo Beata

Isla Alto Velo

△ A   △ B

eastern part of the island languished under the Spanish, whose attentions moved elsewhere.

In the 1790s Toussaint L'Ouverture (1743–1803) led a slave uprising in Saint-Domingue, which was followed by several decades of unrest. In the early 1800s, the western part of the island was ruled by Haiti, which had declared independence from Spain, but its identity was finally resolved by the creation of the Dominican Republic (D.R.) in 1844.

Since independence and the dark years under Gen. Rafael Leonidas Trujillo (1891–1961), from 1930 until 1961, the D.R. has become a stable, Spanish-speaking, Latin Caribbean democracy. The economy is based on tourism, agriculture, and mineral exports. Tourism is now the big industry, far outweighing agriculture. Farmers have been encouraged to diversify, and traditional crops, such as sugarcane, coffee, cacao, and tobacco, have been augmented by fruits and vegetables, live plants, and cut flowers. The D.R. is also the world's leading exporter of hand-rolled cigars, producing 500 million stogies annually.

The majority of visitors fly directly into the main beach resort areas around Punta Cana in the east, and Puerto Plata on the north coast. Here accommodations run the gamut from luxury spa hotels to laid-back surf camps, and the silken sands, water sports, and world-class golf are major draws. Exploring farther afield rewards the adventurous with Santo Domingo's evocative colonial district, white-water rafting in the Cordillera Central, or spectacular whale-watching off Península de Samaná. ■

Santo Domingo

The capital and chief port of the Dominican Republic, Santo Domingo is the oldest city in the New World. The city was founded by Christopher Columbus's brother Bartoloméo in 1498, after the Spanish abandoned their attempts to found a colony on the north coast. Today it is the commercial heart of the Dominican Republic and home to some three million people.

Students from nearby schools often meet in verdant Parque Colón, in Santo Domingo's colonial city.

Built on the east bank of the Río Ozama, the city was christened Nueva Isabel. The name changed to Santo Domingo when the city was moved to the west bank after a hurricane in 1502. It flourished as a port, and from here the Spanish launched major expeditions to Mexico, Puerto Rico, Cuba, and the Pacific. As the riches of the Spanish Main were revealed, Santo Domingo lost its preeminent position in the Caribbean. It suffered a further blow in 1562, when an earthquake destroyed much of the city. English privateer Sir Francis Drake (ca 1540–1596) also caused considerable damage when he attacked the port in 1586.

Despite its decline, Santo Domingo remained the political and commercial center of the country for a further 400 years before emerging restored and rejuvenated in the late 20th century as a vibrant capital city with a brace of cruise ports and an engaging atmosphere.

These days, Santo Domingo is the hub of life in the D.R., a magnet for commerce from neighboring islands, and a must-see for its beautifully restored colonial heart. The colonial city (or "La Zona" as it is commonly called) is a 12-block UNESCO

Dominican Merengue

Throughout the Dominican Republic you'll hear the sound of merengue, the national passion and the music at the heart of Carnival, local fiestas, and dances. Traditionally, this fast music has been played by a *perico ripiao* (three-man combo) performing on either a *tres* or *cuatro* (both are similar to a guitar), a *tambora* (double drum), and a *güira*. Once fashioned from a calabash gourd, the hollow güira cylinder makes a distinctive rhythmic buzzing sound when scraped.

The country's exuberant annual Merengue Festival is held between late July and early August. Most of the action takes place on Santo Domingo's Malecón, transformed into a vast open-air disco for the duration. Several days of music, hosted by popular DJs, keep your body moving in the D.R.'s most sultry dance; a "best artist" is chosen and awarded a large cash prize.

World Heritage site, and the most attractive corner of the sprawling metropolis. Though best explored on foot, there are 45-minute train tours aboard the **Chu Chu Colonial.** Official walk tour guides in khaki uniforms gather at Parque Colón; agree on a fee for the tour in advance.

The Colonial City

The historic colonial city lies on the western banks of the Río Ozama, overlooking the Don Diego cruise-ship terminal and Puerto Ozama. You should certainly allow at least a day to visit its sights; come equipped with a map and comfortable shoes (see also pp. 106–107).

Among the key historic buildings in this area is the **Fortaleza Ozama.** Built by Governor Nicolás de Ovando in 1503 on a steep bank overlooking the mouth of the Río Ozama, the fortress was Santo Domingo's principal defense from the 16th century on and was occupied by the military until the 1970s. The last fort to be built by the Spanish as they moved from north to south across the island,

it guarded the harbor throughout the colonial period. You enter via a neoclassical gateway added in 1787.

Directly ahead is the **Torre del Homenaje** (Tower of Homage), a solid structure with 7-foot-thick (2 m) walls whose clean lines and battlements give it the semblance of a medieval castle. Climb to the top of the turret to get a sense of the fort's strategic importance in guarding every major Spanish flotilla as it left the harbor for the conquest of the Americas. To one side of the tower is an 18th-century armory, beyond which can be seen the remnants of a temporary fort built before the tower was erected. The statue on the grounds is of Gonzalo Fernandez de Oviedo, the fort's governor from 1533 to 1557.

For a fascinating insight into colonial domestic life, don't miss the **Museo Alcázar de Colón.** Built between 1511 and 1516 by Diego de Colón (Columbus's son, who became the first viceroy of the New World), this impressive building has a beautiful Renaissance facade with graceful arcades and is a copy (on a slightly smaller

Santo Domingo
🗺 99 D2
Visitor Information
✉ Calle Arzobispo Meriño 157, Ciudad Colonial
☎ 809 687 8217

Fortaleza Ozama
✉ Calle Las Damas
☎ 809 686 0022
💲 $

Museo Alcázar de Colón
✉ Plaza de España
☎ 809 682 4750
🕐 Closed Mon.
💲 $

Museo de las Casas Reales

✉ Calle Las Damas
☎ 809 682 4202
🕐 Closed Mon.
💲 $

Panteón Nacional

✉ Calle Las Damas
🕐 Closed Mon.

scale) of a castle in Toledo, Spain. Most of the superb furnishings and artworks date from the 16th century and were a gift from the Spanish government when the palace was restored in the 1950s. Take time to admire the wooden ceilings, particularly the one in the entrance hall decorated with 42 sculptured animal heads—a Spanish custom to ward off evil spirits.

For an overview of the history of the Dominican Republic, you can look into the **Museo de las Casas Reales.** The collection covers the country's history from displays on the Taíno through Columbus's arrival, colonization, the plantations, and slavery. Local archaeological finds and artifacts salvaged from shipwrecked Spanish galleons are displayed alongside a highly credible reconstruction of an 18th-century pharmacy (the brightly colored ceramics are,

however, reproductions). The highlight is a collection of ancient armaments, including elaborately decorated Turkish and Moroccan muskets, Japanese samurai swords, and English crossbows. Between the court rooms is a carved elephant's tusk dating from 1552.

INSIDER TIP:

For great pictures in the colonial city, head out to the Plaza de España, just north of the Panteón Nacional, at twilight.

—RAUL TOUZON
National Geographic Traveler
magazine photographer

The **Panteón Nacional** (aka Panteón de la Patria) lies at the northern end of Calle Las Damas. Originally built in the mid-18th century as a Jesuit convent, the pantheon was used as a tobacco warehouse and, later, as a theater after the Jesuits left the island. In the 1950s Trujillo converted it into a memorial to the heroes of Dominican history; the huge chandelier suspended from the dome was a gift from the Spanish dictator General Franco. Every two hours you can see the changing of the guard.

The Mysterious Journey of Columbus's Ashes

The Faro a Colón (see p. 105) claims to hold the remains of Christopher Columbus, but is this true? When the explorer died in 1506, he was buried in Valladolid, Spain. Three years later his body was moved to Sevilla and in the 1540s sent back to Santo Domingo. His remains were then said to be shipped to Cuba when France gained control of Santo Domingo in 1795, and from there back to Sevilla in 1898. However, in 1877 renovations in the Santa María la Menor cathedral revealed a casket beneath the altar with the inscription "Almirante Cristobal Colón," and it is these ashes that now lie in state in the Faro a Colón. Whether the ashes are those of Columbus can probably never be proven.

The Modern City

The modern center of Santo Domingo extends north and west of the colonial city, down to the seafront and Avenida George Washington, usually referred to simply as **El Malecón.** This area is at its liveliest in the evenings, when Dominicans stroll or even dance to the sounds of merengue (see sidebar p. 101) blasting out from portable stereos.

In the heart of downtown is the **Plaza de la Cultura,** a large park that includes four major museums *(all closed Mon.),* the **Teatro Nacional** *(tel 809 687 3191),* and the **Biblioteca Nacional** *(tel 809 688 4086).* The best of the museums is the excellent **Museo del Hombre Dominicano,** the largest archaeological and anthropological museum in the Caribbean. It contains a wealth of material relating to pre-Columbian civilizations. The museum occupies the third and fourth floors of a large building, and the best exhibits are found on the third floor. Here you'll see the fossil remains of an extinct bear, *Megatorio,* once hunted by the prehistoric Taíno, as well as

ceremonial axes dating from 2000 B.C. Comparative displays of South American indigenous cultures place Taíno history in context. Hundreds of prehistoric pieces include necklaces and jewelry; shaped stones used to grate the staple food (yucca); dozens of examples of the three-headed god of agriculture *(Trigonolito);* heart-shaped pots with phallic necks (fertility symbols); artistically decorated conch shells that were used as trumpets for communicating across a distance; and elaborately carved stone rings whose purpose is unknown. A burial display shows skeletons in a fetal position (the Taíno believed in reincarnation, and therefore buried corpses in the fetal position so that they were ready for rebirth); one skeleton's jaws are open in a grimace of suffocation—Taíno chiefs were polygamous, and when they died their wives were buried

Plaza de la Cultura

✉ Av. Cesar Nicolas Penson, Gazcue

☎ 809 686 2472

Museo del Hombre Dominicano

✉ Plaza de la Cultura

☎ 809 687 3623

🕐 Closed Mon.

💲 $

Modern sculptures rise from the floor of the Museo de Arte Moderno.

The serene Jardín Botánico lies in northwestern Santo Domingo.

Museo de Arte Moderno
☎ 809 685 2153
🕐 Closed Mon.
💲 $

Palacio Nacional
✉ Calle Dr. Delgado
☎ 809 695 8588
🕐 By appt. only

Jardín Botánico
✉ Av. República de Colombia
☎ 809 385 2611
💲 $$
jbn.gob.do

Parque Zoológico
✉ Av. Nacional, Los Arroyos
☎ 809 378 2149
🕐 Closed Mon.
💲 $$
zoodom.gov.do

with them—alive. The fourth floor exhibits document the influences that have shaped today's culture in the Dominican Republic.

Next door is the somewhat underwhelming Museo Nacional de Historia y Geografía. Alongside a selection of Arawak artifacts, it contains a mountain of memorabilia from the Trujillo era (including the briefcase, wallet, and other items that belonged to the former dictator), and model ships relating to the Haitian-Dominican conflicts in the 19th century. The neighboring Museo de Historia Natural is equally missable.

On the other hand, the **Museo de Arte Moderno** is well worth a visit, displaying a broad range of contemporary works by both Dominican and foreign artists in the permanent collection.

Go east from the Plaza de Cultura to see the **Palacio Nacional,** an imposing neoclassical building constructed in 1947 for Rafael Trujillo. The ostentatious interior houses government offices and is open for tours.

A welcome retreat from the heat and bustle of Santo Domingo can be found on the city's northwest outskirts at the **Jardín Botánico.** Established in 1976, the gardens cover 0.75 square mile (2 sq km). A "road train" takes visitors around the broad perimeter track, but a leisurely walk will give you more chance to appreciate the tropical plants and trees. There are separate areas for orchids, water plants, bromeliads, palms, cactuses and other succulents, medicinal plants, and a wide variety of endemic Caribbean species. The Japanese garden, with its bamboo groves and ornamental ponds, is a particular highlight. Although the labeling is haphazard, these gardens are a delight.

East from the botanic gardens is the **Parque Zoológico.** Located in an unused limestone quarry landscaped with native plants and trees, the zoo covers 24 acres (9.5 ha). Most animals are in open enclosures, such as zebras, elands, and rhinos in the Great Plains area;

there are aviaries displaying parrots and macaws; and a reptile house inhabited by boas and pythons, among others. The zoo's symbol is the rare Antillean solenodon, a small, insectivorous mammal that looks a bit like a large rat.

Eastern Quarters

Across the Río Ozama, Santo Domingo's eastern quarters are the home of one of the city's most extravagant showcases, the **Faro a Colón** (Columbus Lighthouse; tel 809 591 1492), which was built as part of the 500th anniversary of Columbus's landfall in 1492. A dramatic series of caves nearby offer a natural counterpoint to the monument.

Without doubt, the hulking Faro a Colón provokes strongly divided opinions. Behind its drab and unprepossessing exterior, the interior is surprising, and worthy of a detour. At the center of the giant recumbent cross-shaped building, the marble **Tomb of Columbus** is guarded by uniformed sentries. A sarcophagus said to hold his remains was moved here from the city's cathedral on the opening day—October 6, 1992 (see sidebar p. 102). The corridors on either side of the tail of the cross contain some rather uninspiring cultural displays. One highlight, however, is an original **Maya almanac** (one of only four known) dating back to the 14th century. Another precious artifact is the original anchor of the *Santa María,* Columbus's flagship, salvaged from the north coast of Haiti, where the ship sank in 1492. Near the Faro a Colón, the **Acuario Nacional** (National Aquarium) is a popular stop with families. The shark tunnel and turtle exhibits are visitor favorites.

A few minutes' drive down Avenida de las Américas, toward Boca Chica, are a series of caves known as **Los Tres Ojos** (The Three Eyes). This spectacular series of collapsed caves contains dramatic formations and underground lakes, the last of which is reached via a rope-winched raft. Luxuriant vegetation adds a lost-world atmosphere to this unusual site—all the more striking as it's so close to a major city center. ∎

Acuario Nacional

⊠ Av. España
☎ 809 592 1509
🕐 Closed Mon.
💲 $
**acuarionacional
.gob.do**

Los Tres Ojos

⊠ Parque Los Tres Ojos, Av. de las Américas
☎ 809 788 7056
💲 $

see sidebar p. 102

NEED TO KNOW

Port Logistics: Santo Domingo

The capital boasts two fine cruise-ship terminals, one on either side of the Ozama River. On the west bank, the **Don Diego Terminal** has steps which lead directly onto Calle El Conde at the heart of the colonial city. Most cruise passengers now disembark at the new (and still expanding) **Sansoucí Terminal,** on the east bank, a five-minute taxi ride from La Zona. There are also regular shuttle services to Don Diego every 20 minutes until 5 p.m. (*$$, round -trip*). The nearest beach is Boca Chica (30 mins).

Santo Domingo Highlights

• Exploring the colonial city on foot: 2 hours
• Alcazar de Colón: 2 hours
• Shopping on Calle El Conde: 2–3 hours
• Los Tres Ojos caves: 3 hours

Colonial City Walk

The walk starts and ends in Parque Colón (Columbus Square), a busy meeting place surrounded by old stone buildings and arched walkways, with a statue of the explorer at its center. On the way you have a chance to savor the pride of Santo Domingo's colonial legacy, an ensemble of handsome buildings and monuments that mirror the country's sometimes turbulent history.

The Catedral Basilica Santa María la Menor, the Americas' oldest cathedral

On the south side of the square you will find the **Catedral Basilica Santa María la Menor ❶** *(no shorts or short skirts allowed)*. Built between 1514 and 1540, it was the first cathedral in the New World—as well as the oldest church of any description in the Caribbean. The remains of Columbus were supposedly uncovered here during restoration work in 1877 (see sidebar p. 102). The tranquil interior features a 17th-century mahogany throne as well as stained-glass windows. The cathedral was fully restored in 1992.

Palacio de Borgella ❷ flanks the east side

NOT TO BE MISSED:

Catedral Basilica Santa María la
Menor • Museo de las Casas Reales
• Monasterio de San Francisco

of the square. Built during the Haitian occupation in the mid-19th century, the building has a graceful, porticoed facade on two levels. It served as the seat of congress until 1947 and now houses administrative offices and a post office.

From here make your way to Calle El Conde, a lively pedestrian street lined with shops and cafés that bisects the heart of the colonial zone. Calle El Conde leads down toward the waterfront and Calle Las Damas, a pleasant, tree-lined street where the ladies of the court would take their evening stroll in colonial days. Most of the oldest and loveliest buildings in the colonial city are located on this street.

The Heart of the Old City

Turn right onto Calle Las Damas to visit the **Fortaleza Ozama** (see p. 101), then double back toward the north: On your right is the **Hostal Palacio Nicolás de Ovando** ❸, built in 1502 as the residence of the governor after whom it is named. This beautiful building has been restored as the five-star Sofitel Nicolás de Ovando *(53 Calle Las Damas)*. Opposite is the **Panteón Nacional** (see p. 102).

Continue on to the end of Calle Las Damas, where you'll find the imposing palace of **Casas Reales** ❹ *(corner of Calle Las Mercedes & Calle Las Damas),* which once housed the governor's office, royal court of justice (Real Audiencia), treasury, and military administration. Built in the early 16th century, it now houses the excellent **Museo de las Casas Reales** (see p. 102). Opposite is a sundial dating from 1753, on a site with fine views over the port.

Beyond here the street opens onto a large plaza. On the east side is the imposing **Museo Alcázar de Colón** (see pp. 101–102). Opposite the Alcázar, **Las Reales Atarazanas** ❺ (the royal shipyards) once housed the royal armory, customhouse, and warehouses; today the buildings are shops, restaurants, and bars.

From the plaza turn left onto La Atarazana, then Calle Isabel la Católica, to see the **Casa del Cordón** ❻ *(corner of Calle Emiliano Tejera).* Built in 1509, it was one of the first stone buildings on the island. It is named after the cord monks of the Franciscan order wore around their robes, which you can see carved over the doorway. Today it is a branch of the Banco Popular.

Follow Calle Emiliano Tejera across Calle Arzobispo Merino and then onto Calle Hostos: Here you will find the ruins of the **Monasterio de San Francisco** ❼, the first monastery in the New World. Built in the early 16th century, it was sacked by Sir Francis Drake and then further damaged by earthquakes in 1673 and 1751. Take Calle Arzobispo Merino back to Parque Colón.

- ▲ See also area map p. 99
- ► Parque Colón
- ↔ Allow 2–3 hours
- ⊕ 3 miles (5 km)
- ► Parque Colón

Southeast Coast

The southeast coast has some of the country's most spectacular white-sand beaches, lapped by the azure waters of the Caribbean and backed up by swaying palms. In recent years large, luxurious all-inclusive hotels have sprung up on many of the better beaches. Wealthy Dominicans have also built luxury villas here, an easy two- to three-hour drive from Santo Domingo.

Close to the capital city, Boca Chica's beaches draw families on weekend outings.

Boca Chica
 99 D2
Visitor Information
✉ Calle Rafael
☎ 809 523 5106

The countryside on the southeast coast is mostly flat plains in the center and south, carpeted by extensive sugarcane plantations, with a low range of mountains—the Cordillera Oriental—to the north. Much of the wealth of the major towns in the region, such as San Pedro de Macorís and La Romana, comes from the sugar industry.

The region also has its natural attractions in the form of dazzling offshore islands and the Parque Nacional del Este (see p. 111), and man-made ones,

such as the mock Italianate village, Altos de Chavón.

Heading east from Santo Domingo along the Autopista de las Américas, you pass fine stretches of coastline before arriving at the main international gateway to the island, Las Américas airport. A short distance beyond is **Boca Chica,** a beach resort on a shallow, palm-fringed bay just 5 feet (1.5 m) deep. It was one of the first areas to be developed for tourism on the island and fills up rapidly with residents from the capital on weekends and holidays.

A short distance west of town, divers flock to **Parque Nacional Submarino La Caleta,** an underwater preserve where several shipwrecks feature among the 28 dive sites on offer.

The beaches at **Juan Dolio,** 25 miles (40 km) east of Santo Domingo on Rte. 3, are a better choice, although they can also be noisy and crowded on weekends. The main beaches along here are **Embassy Beach** (a small cove popular with body surfers), **Playa Guayacanes** (calmer and more extensive), and **Playa de Juan Dolio** (also a good beach).

INSIDER TIP:

La Romana's Tabacalera de García will satisfy any aficionado's curiosity with an in-depth tour of the world's largest factory of handmade cigars.

—JENNIFER ALLARD
National Geographic contributor

One of the biggest towns on the south coast, **San Pedro de Macorís,** lies at the mouth of the Río Iguamo, 9 miles (14.5 km) east of Juan Dolio. This town was the center of the Dominican sugar industry at the turn of the 20th century, and remnants of its glory days can be seen in its houses, fire station, and the neoclassical church of **San Pedro Apostol** on the banks of the river.

San Pedro de Macorís is unusual in that it shows a marked cultural influence from the Leeward and Windward Islands. In the 19th century skilled craftsmen and builders were brought in from the smaller British islands to help build the Victorian-style wooden houses that can still be seen on Avenida Independencia. They brought with them their own dances (called *guyolas*) and music *(cainanés).* You can see both performed during the annual **Fiestas Patronales** (June).

La Romana

The provincial capital, **La Romana,** is also a sugar town, and takes its name from *la balanza romana*, the Roman scales once used to weigh the sugar exports. The town center features a bustling market, **Mercado Municipal** (*Calle Frey Juan de Utrera & Calle Dr. Teófilo Ferry*), but most visitors arriving at the international cruise terminal head straight for Casa de Campo. One excellent diversion just outside Casa de Campo is the cigarmaking **Tabacalera de Garcia,** founded by Cuban refugees in 1971.

Casa de Campo

A drop in sugar prices in the 1970s led to the development of the deserted area of scrub, east of La Romana, into a tourist complex that has since grown into the gigantic **Casa de Campo** (Country House). The biggest resort area in the region, it boasts its own international airport, with direct flights from

Juan Dolio
🅰 99 D2

San Pedro de Macorís
🅰 99 D2

La Romana
🅰 99 E2
Visitor Information
✉ Av. Libertad 7
☎ 809 550 6922

Tabacalera de García
✉ Industrial Free Zone 1, La Romana
☎ 809 556 2127
🕐 Guided tours: Tues. & Thurs. 10 a.m. by appointment (min. 24 hours ahead. Age 18+)

Casa de Campo
🅰 99 E2
casadecampo.com.do

Altos de Chavón & Museo Arqueológico Regional

⚠ 99 E2

Visitor Information

☎ 809 523 3333

casadecampo.com.do

Bayahibe

⚠ 99 E2

the U.S. Its 11 square miles (28 sq km) of grounds include three golf courses (the Pete Dye–designed Teeth of the Dog is ranked as one of the finest in the Caribbean); a 245-acre (100 ha) shooting center; an equestrian center offering lessons, trail rides, and polo; 19 swimming pools; a private beach and marina; 13 tennis courts; 20 restaurants; and much more.

EXPERIENCE: Showtime

You can take in a range of local and international music and dance performances under the stars in the scenic Altos de Chavón amphitheater. Inaugurated by Frank Sinatra in 1982, the venue has hosted world-class performers from Julio Iglesias to Sting.

Between these big-name visiting performers, local Caribbean culture meets Las Vegas in the colorful and exuberant **Kandela** music and dance spectaculars (tel 809 523 2424, $$$$$). The artists onstage encourage audience participation, offering a unique opportunity for visitors to get involved in and connect with a show that rivals any Las Vegas production for flash and glamour.

Altos de Chavón

Under the same ownership and on the same site as Casa de Campo is **Altos de Chavón.** Anyone may visit this pretty Italianate village built in the 1970s and 1980s. It is a re-creation of a 16th-century medieval village and constructed entirely from coral rock and stone, with attractive cobbled alleyways festooned with hibiscus and bougainvillea and a huge

amphitheater, which seats 5,000 people. The village overlooks the deep cleft that the Río Chavón has carved through the landscape and features several art galleries, a school of design, craft shops, a church, cafés, and restaurants. A surprising highlight is the **Museo Arqueológico Regional** (closed Mon.), which contains an excellent collection of Taíno art and ceremonial objects. Only the capital's Museo del Hombre Dominicano can rival it. The centerpiece is a rare, carved wooden idol, but the museum is also strong on finely crafted amulets, jewelry, ceremonial objects and axes, and various household items.

East of La Romana

Offshore from La Romana, uninhabited Isla Catalina has beautiful white-sand beaches, reef diving, and the underwater **Museo Vivos del Mar** (Living Museum of the Sea), which showcases the submerged remains of Captain Kidd's pirate ship, the *Cara Merchant,* shipwrecked in 1699. For information on dive trips, contact Casa de Campo (see p. 109). Excursions are also run from dive operations at Punta Cana.

The fishing village of **Bayahibe,** popular with independent travelers and divers, is about 15 miles (25 km) southeast of La Romana on Rte. 3. A couple new resorts have sprung up here, and several budget hotels are dotted among the small wooden houses and cafés in the village.

The Dominican Republic's Carnival: The Details and the Devils

In the Dominican Republic the Carnival tradition has become associated with the historic dates of February 27, 1844, when national leader Juan Pablo Duarte retook Santo Domingo from the Spanish, and August 16, 1865, when the Dominican Republic became a fully independent country. Carnival is celebrated on these dates irrespective of when Lent is observed. The days preceding Carnival are animated by street dancing, parades, and parties.

The highlights of these spectacles are the Carnival costumes of the *diablos cojuelos*, or lame devils, which chase people around the streets. They're known as *lechones* in Santiago, *cachuas* (horned devils) in Cabral, *toros* (bulls) in Montecristi, *papeluses* (paper devils) in Cotuí, *diablos de hojas de platano* (plantain leaf devils) in Barahona, and *mascaros* (masked devils) in Bonao. Each of these different forms is represented by suitably exotic decorated masks.

Bayahibe's mile-long (1.6 km) sandy beach is fringed with coconut palms and is a popular spot for catamaran tours hopping off to Isla Saona offshore.

Isla Saona forms part of **Parque Nacional del Este,** which includes the island itself as well as a stretch of coastline from Bayahibe to the Bahía de Yuma. The 53-square-mile (137 sq km) Isla Saona has only two small fishing villages—Adamanay on the southwest coast and Punta Gorda on the west coast—but hundreds of people visit the area each day, drawn to its fantastic white-sand beaches, where Christopher Columbus is said to have put ashore.

Parque Nacional del Este

▲ 99 E2

Wood carvings of macaws from Altos de Chavón

Higüey
99 E2
Visitor Information
Av. Juan XX111, Plaza El Naranjo
809 554 2672

Manatí Park Bávaro
99 E2
Plaza Bávaro
809 221 9444
$$$$$
manatipark.com

About 20 miles (32 km) northeast and inland from La Romana is the town of **Higüey**, one of the oldest on the island, founded in 1502. It holds little of interest to the visitor apart from being a major center of pilgrimage; in the heart of the town is the **Basilica de Nuestra Señora de la Merced**, a 16th-century Spanish church. Just 550 yards (500 m) to the north of this is the massive, modern **Basilica de Nuestra Señora de Altagracia**, which is dedicated to the country's patron saint. This huge concrete structure was built in the 1950s and is intended to resemble a 200-foot-high (60 m)

pair of hands praying. An annual pilgrimage is made to the site each year on January 21.

Coastal Attractions

Due east from Higüey is the **Coconut Coast**, an uninterrupted stretch of some of the most gorgeous beaches on the island, stretching from **Punta Espada** through **Punta Cana** and **Bávaro** almost all the way to **Punta Sabaneta**. Fine white sand, backed by coconut plantations, slopes off into a reef-protected lagoon that offers excellent swimming and water sports. There are scuba diving and snorkeling opportunities offshore, and arrangements can be made through the front desk at most resorts. This area has become one of the most intensively developed in the D.R., with a string of all-inclusive hotels, many with first-class facilities. Golf is a major draw, with more than a dozen top courses to choose from and many feature spectacular ocean views (see Travelwise p. 391).

Behind the beach hotels, **Manatí Park Bávaro** is a family theme park set in landscaped grounds. The park has enclosures with iguanas, parrots, vultures, butterflies, storks, an aquarium with sharks and rays, performances by parrots, dancing horses, sea lions, and dolphins. The animal and folkloric shows take place throughout the day, and there is an offshore dolphin and sea lion swim program. ∎

NEED TO KNOW

Port Logistics: La Romana/ Casa de Campo

The Dominican Republic's busiest cruise terminal offers very basic amenities. Free shuttle services whisk cruise passengers directly to the Casa de Campo resort for a day of sightseeing, shopping, and lunching at Altos de Chavón.

To venture farther afield, you can book ahead for tours of Tabacalera de Garcia (see p. 109); take a taxi to the beach at Bayahibe (20 mins) for boat trips to Isla Saona (see p. 111); or take a trip to go walking around Santo Domingo's colonial city (90 mins; see pp. 106–107).

La Romana/Casa de Campo Highlights

- Walking the colonial city: half day
- Altos de Chavón: 2 hours
- Tabacalera de Garcia tour: 1.5 hours
- Teeth of the Dog golf course at Casa de Campo: half day
- Snorkeling off Isla Saona: half day

Peninsula de Samaná

The beautiful Peninsula de Samaná juts out from the northeastern corner of the island and is bisected by the Cordillera de Samaná (Samaná Highlands). The cordillera's slopes, luxuriant with coconut palms and pines, plunge into the azure waters of the Bahía de Samaná on one side and the Caribbean on the other. Laid-back resorts and fine beaches greet travelers here.

Settlers from the Canary Islands founded the town of Santa Bárbara de Samaná in 1756. Quiet and unhurried, **Samaná** is belatedly awakening to tourism, prompted by the arrival of cruises, an expressway from Santo Domingo, and a couple small but flourishing beach resorts. It is the departure point for boat trips to view humpback whales between January and March (*tel 809 538 2494, whalesamana.com*), and also a jumping-off point for trips to the beach island of **Cayo Levantado.**

On the north coast, the relatively low-key resort of **Las Terrenas** (*map 99 D3; visitor info., Calle Libertad, tel 809 240 6141*) has a cosmopolitan vibe. Visitors will find a wide range of accommodations, water sports, restaurants, and nightlife. Altogether quieter and more remote on the east coast, **Las Galeras** (*map 99 D3*)

Whale-watching off the Peninsula rarely disappoints.

is a fishing village with a handful of small hotels.

Stretching inland from Samaná Bay, **Parque Nacional Los Haitises** is a swath of coastal mangrove wetlands interspersed with rocky limestone cays. At its heart are caves decorated with Taíno petroglyphs, and the birdlife here is truly mesmerizing. This watery hinterland can only be visited by boat or kayak trips arranged through local operators. ∎

Samaná
◭ 99 D3
Visitor Information
✉ Av. Santa Bárbara 4, Edificio Gubernamental
☎ 809 538 2332

Parque Nacional Los Haitises
Visitor Information
◭ 99 D3
☎ 809 472 4204
💲 $$

North Coast: Around Puerto Plata

The Atlantic coast of the Dominican Republic extends for some 150 miles (241 km) from the Peninsula de Samaná in the east to Monte Cristi on the Haitian border in the west. In the scenic hinterland a patchwork of cane fields lies beneath the rugged Cordillera Septentrional. The coast has some excellent beaches, but because they border the Atlantic the sea can be rougher here, and some places are more suited to bodysurfing than snorkeling.

Smaller bonefish, tarpon, and permit await anglers off the Dominican north coast.

Puerto Plata
🅜 99 C4
Visitor Information
✉ Calle José del Carmen Ariza 45
☎ 809 586 3676

Fortaleza de San Felipe
✉ End of the Malecón
☎ 809 330 8876
🕒 Closed Mon.
💲 $

The coast's main town is **Puerto Plata** (Silver Port), founded in the early 16th century beneath the dramatic outline of **Pico Isabel de Torres** (2,554 feet/779 m). Part of the mountain forms a nature reserve, the **Reserva Científica Isabel de Torres.**

Several historic Victorian homes and the attractive and very long seafront promenade, the Malecón, have benefited from the town's major regeneration program. At the town's western end,

Fortaleza de San Felipe is one of the oldest fortresses in the Caribbean, built between 1564 and 1577 to deter pirate attacks. Partially destroyed in 1659, it was rebuilt on the orders of King Philip II of Spain, after whom it is now named.

Restored in the 1970s, the fortress has neat lookout towers facing the sea and a massive keep at its center, where you'll find the small museum exhibiting the remnants of 16th-century armaments.

INSIDER TIP:

At the Reserva Científica Isabel de Torres, take the cable car up to the botanical gardens early in the morning for clear skies and the best views.

—EMMA STANFORD
National Geographic author

Puerto Plata's town square, **Parque Central,** has several turn-of-the-20th-century wooden houses with gingerbread-style fretwork on the balconies and windows. At the center of the square is a Victorian pavilion, known as **La Glorieta,** and on its southern side is the modern **Catedral de San Felipe,** built in imitation art deco style.

The town's other star attraction is the **Museo del Ambar Dominicano** (Dominican Amber Museum), just a short stroll from Parque Central. You'll find some fascinating exhibits in this well-presented museum, mostly of insects and other small creatures frozen in time since being stuck on a resinous pine tree some 50 million years ago.

Toward Haiti

Westward from Puerto Plata, the arid, cactus-strewn landscape stretches toward the Haitian border. At Cofresí, **Ocean World Adventure Park** *(map 99 C4; tel 809 291 1000, oceanworld.net, $$$$$)* is a family attraction. This sprawling waterfront complex includes a casino and marina, and offers marine shows, animal encounters, walk-through aviaries, and a rain forest exhibit.

West of **Luperón** is the site of the first European town in the New World, **La Isabela.** Founded by Columbus on his second trip to the New World in 1493, this beautiful spot is now **Parque Nacional Histórico y Arqueológico de la Isabela.**

The last town before the border is the faded Victorian port of **Monte Cristi.** Of more scenic interest is nearby **Parque Nacional Monte Cristi,** covering 204 square miles (528 sq km) of coastline and offshore islands, known collectively as the Cayos Siete Hermanos. This important sanctuary is home to alligators and several rare species of birds, such as the wood stork and the American oystercatcher. ∎

Museo del Ambar Dominicano

✉ Calle Duarte 61, Puerto Plata
☎ 809 586 2848
🕐 Closed Sun.
💲 $

ambermuseum.com

NEED TO KNOW

Port Logistics: Puerto Plata

Opened in 2015, the $85 million Amber Cove cruise facility lies on the Bay of Maimon just west of Puerto Plata. The site has two cruise berths and a transportation hub offering a fine range of shore excursions. Recreational facilities include a pool, shopping, and fine dining.

Puerto Plata Highlights

- Museo del Ambar Dominicano: 2 hours
- Ocean World Adventure Park: half day
- Parque Nacional Histórico y Arqueológico de la Isabela: 2 hours
- Iguana Mama tours: half to full day *(tel 809 654 2325 or U.S. 800 849 4720, iguanamama.com)*

Puerto Plata to Playa Grande

Some 3 miles (5 km) to the east of the docks at Puerto Plata is the resort complex of Playa Dorada, with a fringe of hotels along its sandy bay. The complex also has a first-class golf course and a commercial center with a good selection of shops, restaurants, cafés, and other facilities. Continuing east, you encounter a less built-up coastline, the lively surfers' resort of Cabarete, and Río San Juan, where Laguna Grí Grí is a highlight for many visitors.

Cabarete's lively bars and restaurants spill onto the beach.

Sosúa

🏔 99 C4

Visitor Information

✉ Calle Principal (Plaza Eric House)

☎ 809 571 3433

Cabarete

🏔 99 C4

Visitor Information

✉ Calle Principal

☎ 809 571 0972

Sosúa (17 miles/27 km east of Puerto Plata) has a big, lively beach and an extensive beach market. Most water sports, including scuba diving and snorkeling excursions, are available from operators at the beach. The town is divided into two sections. To the west of the beach is **Los Charamicos,** a fishing community. The district known as **El Batey,** where most of the hotels, restaurants, shops, and tourist facilities are located, flanks the eastern side. El Batey was settled by about 600 Jewish refugees fleeing from Nazi Germany in 1941. The settlers developed a thriving dairy industry, and although many moved away after the war, their legacy is preserved in the small museum attached to the synagogue, with several memorial plaques, and by the specialty breads sold in local bakeries.

Cabarete

Cabarete, which is 7 miles (11 km) east of Sosúa, is one of the top windsurfing resorts in the Caribbean and frequently hosts world championship events. From December through September, the trade winds generally blow at 15 to 25 knots in the afternoon, with the strongest winds from late spring through summer. The constant play of the trade winds has also brought kiteboarding to Cabarete. Even if you're not a windsurfer, you can enjoy the fine beach that stretches around the bay. Not surprisingly, Cabarete boasts the highest concentration of budget guesthouses and small hotels on the island, plus great waterfront dining and nightlife.

Cabarete is also a major center for mountain biking, horseback riding, 4WD trails, and hiking tours of the surrounding countryside, thanks to the presence of leading adventure tour operator **Iguana Mama** (tel 809 654 2325, iguanamama.com). Founded in 1993, this company offers well-organized, fully guided adventure tours that include everything from mountain biking and zip-lining to kayaking. These tours can be tailor-made to fit the needs of visitors, and the company also plows a percentage of its profits back into local environmental and educational programs. One of their most popular tours for adrenaline junkies is a guided excursion to scramble up and jump down the spectacular **27 Waterfalls of Damajagua** in the cordillera behind Puerto Plata.

Along the Coast

Some 39 miles (63 km) east of Sosúa is the small fishing village of **Río San Juan,** a picturesque jumping-off point

---

EXPERIENCE: Catching the Breeze

The Professional Windsurfers Association and the Professional Kiteboard Riders Association rank Cabarete among the world's premier destinations. **Cabarete Race Week** (June) is the high point of the year here, when the area is engulfed by a tidal wave of young, lively, international windsurfers and kiteboarders gathered for world-class competitions and equally competitive after-dark partying. Accommodations get fully booked well in advance, so make your reservations early.

---

for trips on the nearby **Laguna Grí Grí.** Boats set off from the jetty at the end of the main street, Calle Duarte, for a two-hour trip through a mangrove-lined canal that eventually opens out to the sea. The excursion continues along the coastline and enters one or two sea caves before stopping for a swim in a natural pool.

Continuing on some 7 miles (11 km) past Río San Juan, you'll come to **Playa Grande,** an impressive ribbon of sand that curves more than 0.5 mile (1 km) around a lovely bay. It's a great spot for beach walks, but swimming can be dangerous due to strong riptides.

Just past here you will come to **Parque Nacional Cabo Francés Viejo,** a protected coastal rain forest with dirt tracks leading off the road to deserted beaches and bays. Finally, there is the provincial capital of **Nagua** on the Bahía Escocesa, but it has very little to offer travelers. ∎

Rio San Juan
⊠ 99 C4

Playa Grande
⊠ 99 D4

Parque Nacional Cabo Francés Viejo
⊠ 99 D4

Santiago de los Caballeros

The second largest city in the Dominican Republic (population 750,000), Santiago de los Caballeros is the major industrial and agricultural center in the fertile Valle de Cibao. Any industrial smoke, however, can probably be linked to the main crop, tobacco; Santiago is a major producer of hand-rolled cigars and mass-produced cigarettes. The city's name derives from the 30 Spanish nobles (*caballeros*) who founded the town on Columbus's orders in 1495.

A mural in Fortaleza San Luís, just southeast of Parque Duarte, honors the women of the nation.

Santiago de los Caballeros

🅐 99 C3

Visitor Information

✉ Gobernación Provincial, Calle El Sol esq. 30 de Marzo

☎ 809 582 5885

A sprawling, prosperous metropolis, Santiago has built its fortunes on tobacco and rum. The cigarmaking process is fascinating to watch, as the skilled workers roll the leaves and bind them into the familiar tubular shape. More than 20 such factories are still in operation, and the local tourist office can provide details about tours. A popular choice for visitors

is **La Aurora Cigar World** at Tamboril (*30 mins NW of downtown*). Founded in 1903 and still owned by one of the city's leading families, the company employs 1,000 workers producing 850 million sticks a year, which are sold worldwide. From the traditional factory floor, where cigars are still rolled by hand and a reader entertains the workforce with excerpts

INSIDER TIP:

For a great souvenir of your trip, look for reproductions of indigenous Indian pottery for sale at many local Dominican shops and markets.

—ALICE SAMSON
National Geographic field researcher

from the local paper, La Aurora Cigar World tours progress into a museum arranged in a replica of the original factory building.

On the northeast corner of Santiago's central square is **Parque Duarte,** whose shady confines are alive with shoeshine boys, vendors of shaved ice, and picnicking office workers, though it is remarkably small for a city of this size. On the west side you'll find the **Centro de Recreo,** built in 1894. Inside it houses a private billiards club. The splendid facade has been painstakingly restored.

Next door to the club is the privately owned **Palacio Consistorial,** a more sober edifice from the same period. Santiago has a plethora of fine Victorian architecture, much of it built by local merchants who profited handsomely from the agricultural wealth of the Cibao Valley in the late 19th century. The style is predominantly Spanish colonial, and many of the city's buildings are attractively decorated with painted tiles, ornate wrought iron, and lacy gingerbread work.

Centro Cultural León

Allow a couple of hours to explore this exceptional cultural showcase opened in 2003 to commemorate the centenary of the E. Leon Jimenes tobacco group. The stunning purpose-built complex provides a handsome backdrop for intelligent displays exploring Dominican history and culture via Taíno pottery and carved ax heads in the anthropology section to an impressive collection of contemporary art and sculpture. Not surprisingly, the tobacco industry is highlighted; make time to check out the busy program of exhibitions and events, the café, and upscale souvenir store.

Heroes Monument

One monument you can't miss—even if only by virtue of

**La Aurora
Cigar World**
✉ Tamboril Free Zone
☎ 809 575 1903
🕐 Closed Sat.–Sun.

Centro Cultural León
✉ Av. 27 de Febrero 146, Villa Progreso
☎ 809 535 5555 or 809 582 2315
🕐 Closed Mon.
💲 $; free Tues.
centroleon.org.do

Bachata

The twangy guitar notes of *bachata* are a ubiquitous accompaniment to any journey around the country. This immensely popular musical genre evolved about five decades ago in the Dominican countryside. A Dominican equivalent of blues, it derives from traditional romantic bolero: *Bachateros* (singers) croon about broken hearts and betrayal (bachata was originally called *amargue,* bitterness). The ever evolving genre also features a more fast-paced merengue style.

Rolling handmade cigars at a factory in Santiago de los Caballeros

its commanding position above the city—is the **Monumento a los Héroes de la Restauración** on Avenida Monumental, which rises some 220 feet (67 m) from a hilltop in the center of Santiago. Made of white marble, this huge monument was constructed during the Trujillo era and honors the heroes of 1844 who helped expel the Haitians and restore self-government to the Dominican Republic (in fact, Trujillo intended it as a monument to himself).

The interior of the monument houses displays about the creation of the republic. An elevator (which is often not working) and steps take you to a platform with panoramic views over Santiago, the Valle de Cibao, and the mountains. Note the frescoes at the top of the stairs, which are by the well-known contemporary Spanish painter Vela Zanetti.

The city's main thoroughfare, **Calle del Sol,** runs from the monument down to Parque Duarte, where most of the better shops in the city are found. ∎

Cigarmaking

Cigarmaking has a long tradition in the Dominican Republic and plays an important role in the culture and economy of the country.

The prime tobacco-growing area is along the Yaque Valley, which borders the Río Yaque del Norte for some 15 miles (25 km) from the outskirts of Santiago northwest to the town of Esperanza. Despite a period of decline in the 1960s, the recent upsurge in demand for premium cigars around the world has generated a welcome boom in this area.

The Dominican Republic now produces two-thirds of the premium hand-rolled cigars sold on the world market, making it the top exporter in the region, ahead of Honduras and Cuba. Internationally known brands such as Dunhill, Partaga's, and H. Upmann are produced here.

Cordillera Central

The remote mountains of the Cordillera Central (Central Highlands) run diagonally across the western half of the Dominican Republic, culminating in the island's highest point—Pico Duarte (10,417 feet/3,175 m). There is no easy access to this wilderness area, which includes two major national parks (Parque Nacional Armando Bermúdez and Parque Nacional José del Carmen Ramírez) and the sources of some of the country's major rivers.

One of the most accessible of the hill stations is **Jarabacoa.** You can reach it on Rte. 28, winding up from the central highway (Rte. 1) through pine forests that have earned this region the title of the Dominican Alps. Here alpine-style chalets dotted about the woodlands are popular with vacationers.

Nestled in a broad valley and surrounded by the foothills of the Cordillera Central, Jarabacoa is a cool retreat with equable year-round temperatures. Many wealthy Santiago residents have weekend homes here, scattered around the outskirts of town amid fields of cultivated flowers, strawberries, pimentos, and manioc.

There is little to see in the town of Jarabacoa itself, although the charming park at its center, shaded by a magnificent tree whose branches arch over the entire square, is typical of small Dominican towns. A church, which adjoins the park, contains modern frescoes by a well-known local artist, Roberto Flores.

Jarabacoa's appeal lies mostly in its proximity to mountainous terrain, rushing rivers, and unspoiled countryside. One of the

Jarabacoa
⚑ 99 C3
Visitor Information
✉ Plaza Ramírez, Modulo 209
☎ 809 574 7287

Crossing the Río Yaque del Norte, near the village of La Ciénega, en route to Pico Duarte

Salto de Jimenoa
⚐ 99 C3

Constanza
⚐ 99 C3

most popular places to visit is the impressive **Salto de Jimenoa** (*$*) waterfall; it is easily reached via a turnoff 2.5 miles (6.5 km) from the town center on La Vega road and a 4-mile (6 km) drive along a dirt track to a hydroelectric station below the falls. The falls themselves are an easy 10- to 15-minute walk from here across a series of swinging bridges. Set in a jungle-filled, natural amphitheater, the cascade tumbles down an 80-foot-high (24 m) rock face into a huge pool where you can swim.

EXPERIENCE:
Climbing Pico Duarte

Climbing Pico Duarte, the highest mountain in the Caribbean, is usually undertaken as part of an organized trip because it's a three-day round-trip from the village of La Ciénega to the peak itself. Outfitters include Rancho Baiguate (tel 809 574 6890 or U.S. 646 727 7783, ranchobaiguate.com, $$$$) and Iguana Mama in Cabarete (tel 809 654 2325, or U.S. 800 849 4720, iguanamama.com, $$$$$).

The Río Jimenoa converges on the other side of the town with the Río Yaque del Norte at a spot 2 miles (3 km) from Jarabacoa known as the **Balneario La Confluencia,** popular with locals for weekend picnics and swimming.

The countryside around Jimenoa is perfect for exploration and adventure sports, with a network of paths and dirt tracks winding through remote hamlets and small farms. On the fringes of town (1 mile/1.6 km to the south) is the busy outward-bound

operation **Rancho Baiguate** (see sidebar this page). This multiactivity adventure center offers a wide range of things to do, including horseback riding, quad biking, mountain biking, *parapente* (descending from hills or mountaintops beneath a specially designed canopy), rafting, trekking, canyoning (rappelling into canyons), tubing, Jeep safaris, and expeditions to the top of Pico Duarte. Within a short distance of Rancho Baiguate are the **Baiguate Falls,** which can be reached on quad bikes from the ranch down several dirt tracks (journey time is around 20 to 30 minutes) and then a short walk. Here you'll find another natural swimming pool. Rafting takes place on the upper section of the Río Jimenoa, an 8-mile (13 km) ride downstream with Class III rapids. The ranch also provides accommodations and can arrange visits to a local coffee factory and excursions to watch the making of Indian bread (*casabe),* and other local activities.

Continuing southeast of Jarabacoa, Rte. 28 brings you to the town of **Constanza,** set in a high valley surrounded by the peaks of the Cordillera Central. Like Jarabacoa, it is a prime growing area for soft fruit crops such as strawberries, raspberries, peaches, pears, and apples. The town itself is very peaceful, with just a handful of restaurants and hotels, and in December and January temperatures drop below freezing. The main activities are walking and visits to the **Aguas Blancas** waterfalls, 6 miles (10 km) to the south. At 272 feet (83 m), the two-part cascade is the highest in the Caribbean and much less visited than the falls around Jarabacoa. ■

West of Santo Domingo

The southwestern corner of the D.R. is an arid region with some unusual coastal landscapes. This is an area scarcely touched by tourism, although the opening of an international airport in Barahona and a fast highway from the capital means that access is now getting easier.

La Iglesia Nuestra Señora de la Consolación, San Cristóbal

Some 15 miles (24 km) to the west of Santo Domingo is the town of **San Cristóbal.** This is where the country's first constitution was signed (on November 6, 1844), but it is better known as the birthplace of the dictator Rafael Trujillo. Trujillo built an ornate church and mausoleum to house his remains (eventually buried in France), as well as several palatial residences, including the **Castillo del Cerro,** a grandiose, six-story house on a nearby hilltop. Today it houses a police academy *(closed to the public).*

From San Cristóbal the main road (Rte. 2) leads to Baní. To the southwest is **Las Salinas,** a fishing village on the Bahía Las Calderas,

outside of which rise the largest sand dunes in the Caribbean. From Baní, Barahona is just over 60 miles (100 km) to the west.

South of Barahona

Located on the Bahía de Neiba, a three-hour drive from Santo Domingo, **Barahona** has a population of more than 80,000. Its airport, Aeropuerto María Montés (named after a Dominican actress who starred in Hollywood movies in the 1940s and 1950s), is intended to promote tourist development in this relatively remote part of the country. One of the main attractions is the coastal scenery south of Barahona. Here the Sierra de Baoruco peaks at over 6,500

San Cristóbal
⚑ 99 C2

Barahona
⚑ 98 B2
Visitor Information
✉ Av. Enriquillo
☎ 809 524 5130

Visiting Parque Nacional Jaragua

The main entrance to the park is on Highway 44, north of Oviedo. A car is necessary to explore the land-based sections of the park; local guides wait by the entrance offering two- to three-hour boat rides around the lagoon ($$$$$, by negotiation). However, to really get to grips with the park's wildlife and extraordinarily diverse terrain, consider a guided day trip with **EcoTour Baharona** (tel 809 243 1190, ecotourbarahona.com, $$$$$). Choose from a variety of minibus excursions, hikes, bike rides, and boat trips on the lakes or off to the outer islands.

Parque Nacional Jaragua

▲ 98 A1–B1

Visitor Information

☎ 809 472 1036

grupojaragua.org.do

Isla Cabritos

▲ 98 A2

feet (2,000 m) and plunges down almost to the Caribbean, where small fishing villages are interspersed with coves and inviting sandy beaches (swimming is not always possible due to surf conditions). After the fishing village of Enriquillo, the route turns inland and toward the town of Pedernales on the border with Haiti.

Natural Wonders

Parque Nacional Jaragua covers some 875 square miles (1,400 sq km) on the southwest coast of the peninsula. The park is distinguished by its dry climate, limestone formations, lagoons, and saltwater lakes. You need to be well prepared to visit this area, with its rough terrain and lack of water and decent maps (see sidebar this page). The largest protected area in the Dominican Republic, the park is known for its flamingos, sea turtle nesting sites, and critically endangered Ricord's iguanas. It includes two uninhabited offshore islands, **Isla Beata** and **Isla Alto Velo.**

Inland 36 miles (58 km) on Rte. 46 from Barahona lies **Lago Enriquillo,** a massive saltwater lake that is said to be the biggest in the region. The lowest point in the Caribbean, lying between 100 and 130 feet (30–40 m) below sea level, the lake is fed by streams from the Sierra de Neiba and the Sierra de Baoruco, but it has no outlet to the sea. Water loss is purely by evaporation, leading to a salt content in the lake three times higher than that of the Caribbean Sea. The lake is home to much wildlife, including crocodiles, rhinoceros iguanas, and flamingos.

Of the three islands in the lake, the biggest is the 5-mile-long (8 km) **Isla Cabritos** (Goat Island), the only one protected as a national park. Home to goats, the island also hosts crocodiles and many resident and migratory birds, including flamingos, clapper rails, and roseate spoonbills. The two smaller islands are known as **La Islita** and **Barbarita.** You can drive all the way around the lake, and boat tours leave from the park entrance, some 2.5 miles (4 km) to the east of the sleepy desert outpost of **La Descubierta.** (Early morning departures are best for viewing the crocodiles.)

About 0.5 mile (800 m) to the east of La Descubierta at the western end of the lake is a series of pre-Columbian petroglyphs carved into the rock face. These are marked by signs from the Carretera Enriquillo. ■

A commonwealth territory of the United States with all the benefits of stateside communications, and all the warmth of a Spanish heart

Puerto Rico

The Catedral de San Juan Bautista in Old San Juan, Puerto Rico

Puerto Rico

The most easterly of the Greater Antilles, Puerto Rico lies about 1,000 miles (1,600 km) southeast of Miami between the Virgin Islands and the island of Hispaniola. Almost rectangular in shape, it spans 112 miles (180 km) from east to west and 40 miles (65 km) from north to south. A mountain range, the Cordillera Central, runs across the center of the island, reaching its highest point at the Cerro de Punta (4,387 feet/1,338 m).

Lively and engaging, the Island of Enchantment is a happy marriage of cultural contradictions, sun-kissed beaches, lush rain forest, buzzing cities, and sedate up-country coffee *estancias*. While Puerto Rican culture is distinctly sassy and Latin American in inspiration, the island's commercial life is organized with American efficiency. You can zip from one side of the island to the other in a matter of hours along slick, four-lane highways, but turn off into the countryside and be prepared to slow down dramatically as you bounce down a potholed rural road to nowhere in particular.

Puerto Rico's interior is partially clad in dense tropical rain forest, although just one percent of the island's original forest now

remains. The central mountains are ringed by coastal plains. In the northwest the landscape is shaped by the strange hillocks and caves of limestone karst formations, while in the drier southwest the land is dominated by cactus and other drought-resistant plants.

To the native Taíno, the island was known as Boriquen, or "land of the noble lord." When

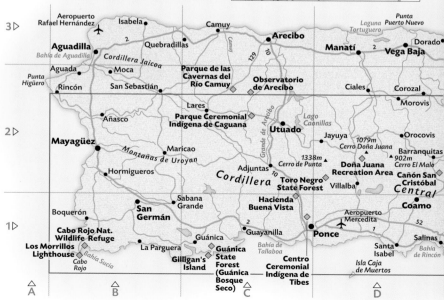

Columbus arrived here on his second voyage to the Americas in 1493, he named it San Juan Bautista. With him was Juan Ponce de Léon, who later returned to settle the island in 1508; he soon renamed it Puerto Rico, or "rich port."

The Spanish enslaved the island's 30,000 Taíno and set them to work in the gold mines; the native population was decimated. Once the gold was exhausted in the late 16th century, Spain neglected the island until 1765 when King Carlos III sent an envoy to develop the island's sugar plantations. Trade began to pick up and coffee and tobacco were also exported.

In 1897 the United States, then at war with Spain, invaded the island. Puerto Rico was ceded to the United States in December 1898, and U.S. citizenship granted to islanders in 1917. Citizens of an overseas commonwealth of the United States since 1952, the electorate rejected a proposal to induct Puerto Rico as the 51st state of the Union in 1998.

Although Spanish is the island's first language, English is ubiquitous in tourist areas and in the capital, San Juan, home to almost a third of Puerto Rico's 3.9 million residents. San Juan is a major regional transportation hub, hosting thousands of cruise passengers every day and providing air links to destinations throughout the Caribbean. Puerto Rico's many and varied landscapes and excellent road network invite exploration, and this is one of the few Caribbean islands where you shouldn't hesitate to rent a car and travel independently. ∎

NOT TO BE MISSED:

Exploring Old San Juan and the Castillo de San Felipe del Morro 129–133

Hiking in El Yunque National Forest 134

A nighttime boat trip on Mosquito Bay, Vieques 138–139

Appreciating the fine arts at the Museo de Arte de Ponce 141

Touring a working coffee estate at Hacienda Buena Vista 142

The spectacular views of La Ruta Panorámica (the Panoramic Route) 144–145

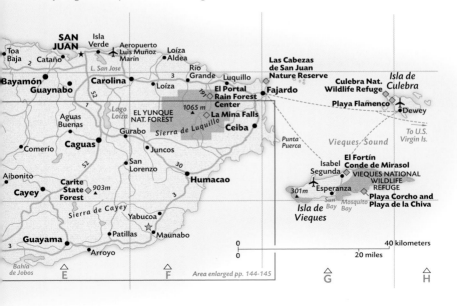

San Juan

Founded in 1510, Puerto Rico's capital city of San Juan has grown from a small town into one of the biggest metropolitan areas in the Caribbean, with a population of more than two million. The island's cultural, political, and economic center, it is also an important air and sea hub for the region. From its initial location at the entrance to the Bahía de San Juan, it has spread to the mainland, enveloped the Laguna San José, and sprouted industrial suburbs and canals.

Nighttime in Old San Juan

San Juan

📍 127 E3

Visitor Information

✉ Ochoa Building, 550 Calle Tanca

☎ 787 721 2400; 787 250 6064 (public transportation information)

If the outskirts of San Juan appear unappetizing, the center, by contrast, is a real delight. Old San Juan covers just seven blocks on a long, narrow islet at the northeast entrance to the bay; four causeways connect it to the mainland.

San Juan (New City)

Unlike Old San Juan, where everything is within walking distance, in the city proper you'll need to use public transportation, taxis, or a rental car to get around. Make the effort, though, since the rewards range from lively stretches of beachfront to bustling merchant districts and a chance to see Puerto Rico's famous Bacardí rum being made.

Within 550 yards (500 m) of the confines of Old San Juan is **El Capitolio,** a white marble building built in the 1920s as the seat of the island government (Senate and House of Representatives). A guided tour will take you inside the rotunda, where friezes depicting the country's history decorate the elaborate dome.

On the Atlantic seafront, **Condado** is a beachfront strip of high-rise resort hotels behind which are streets filled with restaurants, designer stores, fast-food outlets, and souvenir shops. This hotel strip runs along the coast as far as **Isla Verde** (6 miles/10 km), another major resort area.

Inland from Condado is the downtown district of **Santurce,** where the excellent **Museo de Arte de Puerto Rico** showcases three centuries of Puerto Rican art in an ingenious building featuring a soaring glass extension bolted onto the neoclassical former city hospital. Look out for handsome 18th-century religious works by José Campeche, and Francisco Oller's landscapes, and take time to stroll in the sculpture garden. Beyond Santurce lies the financial district of **Hato Rey,** where glass-fronted skyscrapers line the street known as the Golden Mile.

Three miles (5 km) farther south still is the suburb of Río Piedras, home to the University of Puerto Rico. Adjacent to the campus are the **Botanical Gardens** (corner of Rtes. 1 & 847, tel 787 250 4463), a tranquil retreat with walks and waterways meandering among some 200 acres (80 ha) of lush tropical vegetation.

Another attraction outside Old San Juan is the **Bacardí Rum Distillery** (Rte. 165, Cataño, tel 787 788 8400, visitcasabacardi.com), reached by a short ferry ride from Pier Two in Old San Juan. The 45-minute guided tour ($$) visits the bottling plant, a museum, and the distillery.

Old San Juan

An area of considerable charm, much of Old San Juan has been lovingly restored to its original 18th-century character. The streets are paved with cobblestones, originally brought over as ships' ballast, and lined with pastel-painted houses behind wrought-iron balconies and shuttered windows.

The old town is surrounded by more than 6 miles (10 km) of walls, 50 feet (15 m) high and 20 feet (6 m) thick, studded with small stone sentry boxes known as *garitas.* Old San Juan has two formidable forts, built to protect the city in the days when buccaneers and pirates were a constant threat.

Today the only invasion the old town faces is by cruise-ship passengers. The passenger piers lie at the very foot of the town,

El Capitolio

✉ Av. Ponce de Léon

☎ 787 721 5200 ext. 301 to reserve tours Mon.–Fri.

Museo de Arte de Puerto Rico

✉ Av. de Diego 299, Santurce

☎ 787 977 6277

🕑 Closed Mon.

💲 $$; free Wed. p.m.

mapr.org

EXPERIENCE:
Savor Puerto Rico

Puerto Rico's finest chefs and a galaxy of visiting culinary stars gather in the capital every April for the annual Saborea food and wine festival. Stalls and demonstration kitchens are set up on Escambrón Beach over a long weekend and visitors are encouraged to *saborea,* or savor, Puerto Rico. There's a fantastic variety of different foods, wines, and spirits to sample, from traditional *cocina criolla* (traditional Puerto Rican specialties) to gastronomic offerings from San Juan's leading restaurants, locally brewed beers, and the finest Puerto Rican coffee blends *(information & tickets: saborea puertorico.com, $$$$$).*

An informal serenade in the plaza fronting Old San Juan's Catedral de San Juan Bautista

San Juan National Historic Site (Castillo de San Felipe del Morro & Fuerte San Cristóbal)

✉ Calle del Morro
☎ 787 729 6960
💲 $$

nps.gov/saju

Museo Casa Blanca

✉ 1 Calle San Sebastián
☎ 787 725 1454
🕐 Closed Mon.–Tues.
💲 $

Museo de las Américas

✉ Calle Norzagaray
☎ 787 724 5052
🕐 Closed Sun. a.m. & Mon.
💲 $

museolasamericas.org

and when several berths are occupied it can seem overrun with day-trippers. Nevertheless, Old San Juan is clearly a community with a life that isn't solely defined by tourism, and locals go about their business, play dominoes in the cafés, and promenade in the evenings, much as they would anywhere else in Puerto Rico.

Old San Juan is a fascinating storehouse of island history, from the colonial fortresses and civic buildings that underpinned Spanish rule to the wealth of historical artifacts in its museums.

The most prominent feature of the old town is the massive **Castillo de San Felipe del Morro,** or El Morro as it's known. Sprawling over a rocky promontory at the northwestern tip of the old town, El Morro was begun in 1540 and gradually added to over two centuries until it achieved its present form in 1783. Built on six different

levels, the fort's interior is a fascinating complex of tunnels, labyrinths, dungeons, turrets, and ramps. A small museum traces the fort's history, and a reconstruction of an 18th-century military barracks evokes the soldiers' lives. Together with Fuerte San Cristóbal (below), El Morro forms **San Juan National Historic Site** (joint ticket available).

Although not as well known as El Morro, **Fuerte San Cristóbal** (Blvd. del Valle, tel 787 729 6777) is much bigger, covering some 27 acres (11 ha). Completed in 1678, it was designed to protect the landward side of the town and has five separate bastions linked by underground tunnels.

The downtown area has many restored historic buildings of interest. The foremost is **La Fortaleza** (Calle Recinto Oeste, tel 787 721 7000, closed Sat.–Sun.), built between 1533 and 1540 but later considerably modified. Today it houses the governor's residence and is believed to be the oldest executive residence in continuous use in the Western Hemisphere. The gardens are open to visitors on free guided tours.

Another reminder of the Spanish establishment is the **Museo Casa Blanca**, originally built as a home for Ponce de Léon in 1521. The explorer died before he could move in, and the original frame house was destroyed by a fire. Ponce de León's son-in-law built the present house in 1523, making it the oldest of about 800 Spanish colonial buildings in Old San Juan, and his descendants occupied it for some 250 years. It's now a museum of domestic life, with some fine examples of colonial furniture. It also has three lovely courtyards: the Italian courtyard, with fountains and brickwork; the classical courtyard, a wild area leading down to the sea; and the Spanish courtyard, modeled on the Alhambra in Granada, Spain.

One of the most illuminating of the old town's museums is the

INSIDER TIP:

The first Tuesday of every month in Old San Juan is known as "Noche de Galería"— it's a night of art gallery–hopping that usually includes complimentary wine.

—KATHLEEN SQUIRES
Food and travel writer

Museo de las Américas. Exhibits trace the evolution of New World cultures over the centuries, including the pre-Columbian period, and Black African heritage. The museum also exhibits popular arts and crafts. The **Museo de San Juan** is also worth visiting for its exhibitions of Puerto Rican art and an educational audiovisual presentation on the history of the city.

On a lighter note, visit the enjoyable **Museo del Niño.** It contains a wide variety of exhibits devoted to childhood, such as collections of dolls and other toys. ∎

Museo de San Juan
- ✉ 150 Calle Norzagaray
- ☎ 787 480 4547
- 🕑 Closed Mon.

Museo del Niño
- ✉ 150 Calle del Cristo
- ☎ 787 722 3791
- 🕑 Closed Mon.
- 💲 $$

museodelninopr.org

NEED TO KNOW

Port Logistics: San Juan

The downtown cruise-ship piers lie at the foot of the old town; there is a farther pier across the bay, a taxi ride away. The information kiosk on the wharf is very efficient and the old town is easily explored on foot or by free trolley, while bikes can be rented on the waterfront and Segway tours are available. The nearest beaches are Condado and Isla Verde (10–20 mins by *taxi turistico*; fares are set between $10–20). If your cruise begins or ends in San Juan, the ride to Luis Muñoz Marín International Airport takes about 20 minutes ($19).

San Juan Highlights

- Old Town San Juan: 3 hours
- El Yunque Rain Forest: half day
- Lunch from the kiosks on Luquillo Beach: 35-minute drive
- Shopping on Calle Cristo: 2 hours
- Casa Bacardí Rum Tour: 2 hours

Old San Juan Walk

This lovely walk through Old San Juan traces a roughly circular path, beginning and ending at the Plaza de Colón, one of the many elements of San Juan that play up a Columbus connection. Along the way you can appreciate the diverse components—fortresses, churches, museums, and monuments—that combine so harmoniously in this colonial district.

Fuerte San Cristóbal is the largest fort the Spanish built in the New World.

Start in the **Plaza de Colón** at the entrance to the old city, where a statue commemorates the explorer. The shady square is edged by restaurants where you can enjoy a meal or a drink before setting out. Follow Avenida Muñoz Rivera uphill to **Fuerte San Cristóbal ❶** (see p. 130). After a look at the fort, take Boulevard del Valle along the seafront. On your right you'll see a sprawling collection of closely packed houses clinging to the seashore beneath the city walls. This is the **Barrio La Perla,** originally a village that sprang up to serve the military establishment; it is now home to some 10,000 people who form a tight-knit community quite distinct from other areas of the city.

As you continue toward Calle Norzagaray and the **Museo de San Juan** (see p. 131), the **Galería Nacional ❷** is on your left, housed in the beautifully restored 16th-century Convento

NOT TO BE MISSED:

Fuerte San Cristóbal • Galería Nacional • Plazuela de la Rogativa

de los Dominicos. The convent once served as a Spanish army barracks and later as a U.S. Army HQ, but it now displays collections of Puerto Rican fine art tracing its development from the colonial period through to the mid-20th century *(tel 787 725 2670, closed Sun.–Mon., $)*. Just past here is the **Plaza del Quinto Centenario.** One of the highest points in San Juan, it was built as part of the 500th anniversary of the discovery of the New World. Its centerpiece, Totem Telúrico, is a 40-foot-high (12 m) sculpture in black granite and ceramics, referred to locally simply as "the totem" due to its tall, cylindrical shape. It's the work of Jaime Suárez, one of the country's foremost artists.

On the west side of the square is the **Museo de las Américas ❸** (see p. 131). This three-story neoclassical building has porticoed galleries overlooking the courtyard, and was formerly the military barracks. It was built in the mid-19th century and was the largest building erected in the Americas by Spanish engineers.

Continue on toward the broad expanse of park that leads across the headland to the impressive **Castillo de San Felipe del Morro ❹** (see p. 130). Then return across the park and follow the road down to the **Museo Casa Blanca ❺** (see p. 131). From the Casa Blanca take Calle San Sebastián to the Plaza de San José, in one corner of which is the **Iglesia de San José ❻**, the church of the Ponce de Léon family. A statue of the city's founding father,

Juan Ponce de León, strikes a dashing pose on the plaza. It is made from melted down cannon. The Spanish explorer was originally laid to rest here, but his ashes were moved to the Catedral de San Juan Bautista in 1971. The simple 16th-century church has a particularly ornate altarpiece, and note the attractive fresco (1550) on the far left.

Follow Calle del Cristo downhill, passing the archbishop's residence (No. 50) on your right, to reach the **Catedral de San Juan Bautista** ⑦ *(tel 787 722 0861)*, a grandiose structure topped with three cupolas. Inside, a tomb holds the remains of Ponce de León.

Turn right and walk down Caleta de San Juan, one of the prettiest streets in Old San Juan. A short detour back uphill along the city wall will bring you to the delightful **Plazuela de la Rogativa** ⑧. Here, a handsome bronze

statue depicts a torchlit procession led by the archbishop and the women of San Juan in 1797, which tricked a British naval blockade into thinking reinforcements had arrived to protect the city—the would-be invaders sailed away without attacking. The harbor views beyond are sensational. Walk back downhill to the **Puerta de San Juan** ⑨, a fortified portal dating from 1520, and once the city's main entrance. Go through the gateway and turn left, following the promenade running alongside the harbor and past **La Fortaleza** (see pp. 130–131).

Turn east past the fountain, continuing on past **Presidio de la Princesa** down Paseo de la Princesa back toward the docks. Follow Calle Recinto Sur back to the Plaza de Colón.

🅰	See also area map pp. 126–127
➤	Plaza de Colón
🕑	Allow 2–3 hours
↔	1.5–2 miles (2.5–3 km)
➤	Plaza de Colón

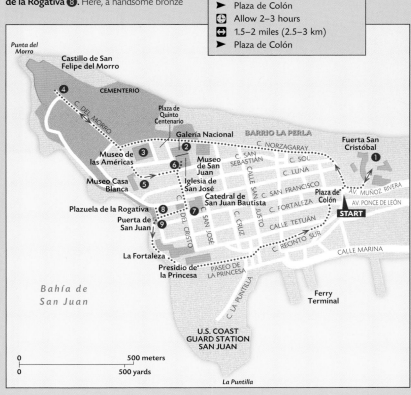

The East

Easily accessible from San Juan, the eastern end of the island is the area most frequently visited by day-trippers and has several important nature reserves, including El Yunque National Forest. This 28,000-acre (11,210 ha) tropical preserve is by far the most popular attraction in Puerto Rico, with more than a million local and foreign visitors each year.

Water plunges 85 feet (26 m) from La Coca Falls, one of many waterfalls in El Yunque.

**El Yunque
National Forest**
🅰 127 F2

**El Portal Rain
Forest Center**
🅰 127 F2
Visitor Information
☎ 787 888 1810
💲 $$
**www.fs.usda.gov
/elyunque**

The largest forested area on the island, **El Yunque National Forest** harbors many spectacular waterfalls, thousand-year-old trees, brightly colored flowering plants, and a wealth of bird species. Although much can be seen from the road, the best way to experience the forest is to set off on any of the 13 hiking trails, which cover 23 miles (37 km) of varied terrain throughout the park.

The forest is located in the Sierra de Luquillo, 25 miles

(40 km) east of San Juan. Rent a car and take Rte. 3 from the capital, and near Luquillo turn south into the mountains on Rte. 191. About 3 miles (5 km) along this road is the **El Portal Rain Forest Center.** Approached via an elevated walkway through the forest canopy, this excellent visitor center has more than 10,000 square feet (930 sq m) of exhibits. These relate to fauna such as the national emblem—the *coquí* frog—as well as the different types of forest

within the park (which include tabonuco, colorado, palm, and cloud), local geology and eco-systems, and the management of tropical forests worldwide. An educational film on El Yunque is shown every half hour, alternat-ing between Spanish (9 a.m.–4 p.m.) and English (9:30 a.m.–4:30 p.m.).

The area was sacred to the Taíno Indians, who venerated the numerous waterfalls and carved petroglyphs into the rocks along the riverbeds. It is possible that El Yunque was named for the Taíno word for a good spirit, but its more likely derivation is from the Spanish *yunque,* meaning "anvil," on account of its flat-topped mountains. In 1876 King Alfonso XII of Spain declared 12,000 acres (4,800 ha) of mountainous land in the Sierra de Luquillo as a forest reserve. After the Spanish-American War in 1898, Spanish crown lands became U.S. property, and in 1903 the area became the Luquillo Forest Reserve, making it the only tropical rain forest in the U.S. national forest system.

From El Portal the road (Rte. 191) leads up toward **La Coca Falls** (alongside the road at 5 miles/8 km), which has an 85-foot (26 m) drop. The **Yokahu Tower** (5.5 miles/9 km), one of several observa-tion towers within the park, affords magnificent views across the mountains. About 0.5 mile (1 km) past here you'll see signs for the **Big Tree Trail.** This lovely mile-long (1.6 km) route, which leads past some of the largest trees in the forest, also passes **La Mina Falls,** prob-ably the most spectacular in the park. At 7 miles (11 km) is the **Sierra Palm Information Center,** which has a picnic area and ranger service, and slightly farther on is the **Palo Colorado Information Center.** Here a trail winds up to the **Mount Britton Lookout Tower** and the peak of El Yunque itself, at 3,496 feet (1,065 m). Allow two hours for the round-trip to the summit.

INSIDER TIP:

Be sure to wear non-skid footwear when you visit El Yunque. The rocks on the rain forest footpaths can be as slippery as ice.

—CAROLINE HICKEY
National Geographic Books contributor

On the island's northeastern tip, beyond the port of Fajardo, is **Las Cabezas de San Juan Nature Reserve.** Call ahead to arrange a walk, cycle, or trolley tour of this 316-acre (128 ha) reserve, renowned for its unusual range of different ecological communities—sandy beaches, rock escarpments, coral reefs, offshore cays, dry forest, man-groves, and lagoons. A boardwalk extends to **Laguna Grande,** one of three bioluminescent lagoons on the island, and a lighthouse, **El Faro,** built in 1880, houses a nature center and an observation tower. ∎

Las Cabezas de San Juan Nature Reserve

127 G2
Rte. 987
787 722 5882
By appt. only; closed Mon.–Tues.
$$$

paralanaturaleza.org

Cruising

The Caribbean is the ultimate cruising destination, an idyllic combination of sun, sea, and varied landscapes, where it is possible to wake up every morning with a new island group on the bow and a different port at the foot of the gangplank. Christopher Columbus and Sir Francis Drake may have pioneered Caribbean cruising half a millennium ago, but today's pleasure trips are a far cry from those early missions of exploration and plunder.

St. Thomas (U.S. Virgin Islands), one of the Caribbean's most popular cruise destinations

More cruise ships ply Caribbean waters than any other place on Earth. There are more than a hundred vessels to choose from, and they vary considerably in terms of size, atmosphere, facilities, and itineraries. For first-time cruise passengers, selecting the perfect cruise can be a slightly bewildering experience, but there are ways of narrowing down the field.

Vessel Sizes

One of the first rules of cruising is that size does matter. Although no indicator of price or the vessel's position on the luxury scale, size does influence the type of cruising experience available. For instance, smaller ships catering to a maximum of 500 passengers can visit offbeat destinations inaccessible to larger vessels; they tend to allow their guests additional time ashore and to enjoy a more relaxed, intimate atmosphere. On the downside (although several smaller vessels offer a positively sybaritic degree of luxury), space is necessarily restricted.

The most common Caribbean cruising options are the midsize (500- to 1,000-passenger) and large (1,000- to 2,000-passenger) cruise ships. They fall into three main categories: luxury-class vessels appealing to a sophisticated clientele with top-notch facilities from water sports and spa treatments to gourmet cuisine and spacious accommodations; premium-class cruise ships offering good food, a high standard of service, and a broad spectrum of organized activities and entertainment; and standard-class vessels aimed at a more casual crowd with fewer facilities, simpler menus, and limited cabin space. In a class of their own are the megaships, giant floating resorts with 4,000-plus passengers and a lifestyle that revolves around shipboard activities and a wild night-life, which rather precludes much in the way of sightseeing the next day.

Shipboard Activities

The onboard activities package is a major consideration when planning a week or two afloat. Most medium to large cruise ships offer a daylong program of activities, which might include exercise classes, shore excursions, quiz competitions, cocktails to the accompaniment of a steel band, and an elaborate Las Vegas–style evening show, followed by a session in the discotheque. Mainstream vessels are all equipped with movie theaters, casinos, game rooms, and exercise facilities (worth remembering because the average cruise passenger gains around 4 pounds/2.2 kg during a weeklong cruise). All these features and up to five meals a day (excluding alcoholic drinks) are included in the price of the cruise. Families should also check that the cruise line offers adequate children's facilities. Make sure that the supervised daytime activities programs cover the right age group(s), and ask about the availability of babysitters, kids' meals, cribs, high chairs, and other vital equipment.

Itineraries & Logistics

The most popular cruise duration on the Caribbean run (excluding shorter trips to the Bahamas) is between one and two weeks. The majority of round-trip itineraries originate from the South Florida ports of Miami and Port Everglades in Fort Lauderdale, although some cruise lines operate out of San Juan, Puerto Rico. Most cruise itineraries feature a different port every day with two days at sea (sometimes three days on longer trips). High season (and high prices) is mid-December through April, but cruises are possible throughout the year and ships stay well clear of the hurricane belt from August through October. Cruises are rarely booked directly with the cruise line. For the best deals and expert advice consult a travel agent with membership in the Cruise Lines International Association (CLIA; *cruising.org*) or the National Association of Cruise-Oriented Agencies (NACOA). A wealth of cruising information is found on the Internet, too.

EXPERIENCE: Cruising With Kids

Cruise-ship vacations are not just for hon-eymooners or retirees anymore. Many cruise lines offer family-friendly activities and resort-style Kids' Clubs up to age 17.

When booking a cruise, families should check into stateroom sizes and options. In some cases, newer cruise vessels have the best family accommodations. Parents with kids who will need a nap might look for a stateroom with a balcony or separate living space.

The **Royal Caribbean** cruise line (*royalcaribbean.com*) offers many family activities, including interaction with DreamWorks Animation characters, ice-skating, and mini-golf. There's also a dining option where kids are picked up after eating dinner with their families to go to evening Adventure Ocean activities.

Norwegian Cruise Line (*ncl.com*) ships host Nickelodeon entertainment activities for little kids and a dedicated Teen Center with PlayStations, air hockey, and a video jukebox. Meanwhile, the whole family can go bowling, play basket-ball, or catch a movie.

Vieques & Culebra

Located 7 miles (11 km) off the port of Fajardo, Isla de Vieques is the largest of Puerto Rico's offshore islands, covering about 55 square miles (88 sq km). Until 2003 most of the island was owned by the U.S. Navy. Its legacy is a largely undeveloped island, with dry hills fringed by spectacular beaches, beyond which excellent snorkeling and diving abound. Tourism is on the increase and a handful of boutique hotels and hip restaurants have sprung up.

Spectacular sunsets and seascapes are common on the west coast of Vieques.

Isla de Vieques
🅰 127 G2
Visitor Information
✉ Casa Alcaldía, 449 Carlos Lebrón St., Isabel Segunda
☎ 787 741 0800
vieques-island.com

El Fortín Conde de Mirasol
🅰 127 G2
Visitor Information
☎ 787 741 1717
🕐 Closed Mon.–Tues.
💲 $

Most of the 10,000 residents of Vieques live in the main town of **Isabel Segunda,** where the ferries arrive from the mainland. The town has a fine central square (with a bust of South American revolutionary Simón Bolívar, who came here in 1816), where you'll find tourist information. On the hill above the town is a restored fort, **El Fortín Conde de Mirasol,** one of the last forts to be built by the Spanish. It now houses a museum.

The other main settlement on the island is lively **Esperanza,** on the south coast, which has a string of bars and restaurants along its seafront.

To the south of Esperanza is **Sun Bay,** one of the island's biggest and most popular beaches, with picnic and camping areas.

Vieques's best known natural attraction, **Mosquito Bay** (also known as Bio[luminescent] Bay), lies just beyond Sun Bay. This large, shallow inlet is surrounded by mangroves and is full of bioluminescent organisms (dinoflagellates), which glow eerily when disturbed by a kayak paddle, electric boat prop, or your hand dangling in the water.

The former Navy base of Camp Garcia is now part of **Vieques National Wildlife Refuge.** It is the largest wildlife refuge in the Caribbean and a good place to see nesting sea turtles, seabirds, and maybe a manatee. Some areas of the former naval site are closed to the public, but you can visit the beaches at **Bahía Corcho** (formerly Red Beach) and **Bahía de la Chiva** (Blue Beach).

Vieques can be reached either on the frequent ferries from Fajardo *(90-min crossing, tel 787 494 0934, arrive in plenty of time on weekends)* or by flying from either San Juan or Ceiba (see Travelwise p. 336). Once there, you can get around by *publicos* (shared public taxis) or a rental car *(Island Car Rental, tel 787 741 8822, islandcar rentalpr.com; Vieques Car Rental, tel 787 741 1037, viequescarrental.com).*

Isla de Culebra

Even more unspoiled than Vieques is the island of Culebra, measuring about 7 miles by 3 miles (11 by 5 km) and surrounded by a series of rocky cays and islets. The landscape is hilly, with tropical rain forest. This peaceful island is home to just 2,000 people, most of whom live in and around the main settlement, **Dewey** (known locally as Pueblo).

About 40 percent of the island forms part of **Culebra National Wildlife Refuge,** which includes 22 offshore islets and four reserves on Culebra itself. Some 40,000 sooty terns congregate on Peninsula Flamenco, the Caribbean's largest seabird nesting colony (closed to the public), and there are many nesting sites around the coast. For up-close birding, wildlife photography, and wilderness hiking, both Cayo Luis Peña and Isla Culebrita are accessible by boat. Contact the refuge for details of nighttime guided walks to watch nesting leatherback and hawksbill sea turtles.

The island's best known beach is the mile-long (1.6 km) **Playa Flamenco** on the north coast. This gorgeous stretch of white sand is best visited during the week; on weekends it fills with day-trippers. Other good beaches include **Playa Soni** and **Playa Resaca.**

You can reach Culebra from San Juan by air (see Travelwise p. 336) or by ferry from Fajardo. You can get around the island by bicycle or rental car *(Carlos Jeep Rental, tel 787 742 3514, carlosjeep rental.com; Jerry's Jeep Rental, tel 787 742 0587, jerrysjeeprental.com).*

Diving can be arranged through Culebra Divers *(tel 787 742 0803, culebradivers.com).* ■

Vieques National Wildlife Refuge
🗺 127 G2–H2
Visitor Information
✉ Vieques Office Park, Rd. 200, KM 0.04, Vieques
☎ 787 741 2138
fws.gov/caribbean /refuges

Isla de Culebra
🗺 127 G2–H2
Visitor Information
✉ City Hall, 250 Pedro Márquez St., Dewey
☎ 787 742 1033
islaculebra.com

Culebra National Wildlife Refuge
🗺 127 G2
Visitor Information
✉ Lower Camp, Rd. 250, KM 4.2, Culebra
☎ 787 742 0115
fws.gov/caribbean/ refuges

Ponce

Puerto Rico's second largest city, Ponce lies midway along the island's southern coastline. Established in 1692, the "Pearl of the South" flourished during the late 19th century when it was a major exporter of sugar and rum. The architectural gems from this period benefited from extensive renovations as part of the Columbus quincentennial celebrations in 1992; more than half of the city's 1,000 historic buildings have now been restored.

Parque de Bombas served as Ponce's firehouse for more than 100 years.

Ponce
🅰 126 C1
Visitor Information
✉ Porta Caribe
☎ 787 290 2911

Parque de Bombas
✉ Plaza Las Delicias
☎ 787 284 3338

Museo de la Historia de Ponce
✉ 51–53 Calle Isabel
☎ 787 844 7042
🕐 Closed Mon.

At the heart of the city is the aptly named **Plaza Las Delicias** (Square of Delights), where fountains and shady trees provide a cool atmosphere in which to sit and watch the Caribbean world go by. At its center is the 17th-century Spanish creole-style **Catedral de Nuestra Señora de Guadalupe** (tel 787 843 4322), while immediately behind the church is Ponce's most famous landmark, the red-and-black-striped **Parque de Bombas,** or fire station. Constructed as an agricultural

pavilion for the 1882 Ponce World Fair, the wood-clad edifice is a gem of Victorian Gothic architecture with a flourish of Moorish influence in its unusual silhouette and decoration. It became the city fire station in 1883, and served for more than a century until being refurbished as a small museum displaying antique firefighting tools and a splendid old fire engine.

City History

The story of the city is well documented in the nearby

Museo de la Historia de Ponce. An exhaustive but rewarding tour of the ten exhibition halls embraces the ecology, economy, architecture, politics, and daily life of Ponce over the centuries. Alternatively, take the narrated trolley tour from Parque de Bombas.

Calle Isabel

Ponce's finest architecture can be enjoyed on a stroll down Calle Isabel. Here you can see houses built in the four different styles for which the city is famous—classical, creole, Ponce creole, and art deco. Note the chamfered pavements on each street corner. These assisted the passage of horse-drawn carriages, allowing the wheels to ride smoothly up on a turn and avoid an uncomfortable jolt for passengers.

On the other side of Calle Isabel from the museum is the **Casa Wiechers Villaronga.** Now fully restored, this interesting building was constructed in 1911 and is notable for its many adaptations to the tropical climate—underfloor ventilation, louvered fretwork windows, stained-glass panels to filter the sunlight, and the pressed-tin ceilings that are a hallmark of Ponce architecture. One of its peculiarities is a *mirador,* an outdoor observatory on the roof, supported by columns. The dining room contains some outstanding examples of art deco furniture, ceiling lights, and glass, all of which were imported from Spain.

The city is extremely proud of its **Museo de Arte de Ponce,**

which was designed by Edward Durell Stone, the architect of the Museum of Modern Art in New York. Noted for its elegant interior, the museum claims to hold the largest collection of art in the Caribbean—more than 850 paintings, 800 sculptures, and 500 prints spanning more than five centuries of Western art. It is strong on the Pre-Raphaelites, the baroque period, and contemporary Latin American works. One of its most famous paintings is the sinuous, colorful "Flaming June," by the Pre-Raphaelite

painter Frederick, Lord Leighton. The museum also stages broad-ranging special exhibits.

Perched above the town is the **Museo Castillo Serrallés.** Built in the 1930s in Spanish revival style, the mansion was originally the home of the Serrallés family, owners of the Dom Q rum distillery. This airy, multilevel house combines Spanish and Moorish elements; the interior features

---

Take to the Hills

In the southwestern foothills of the cordillera, the charming hillside town of San Germán *(map 126 B1)* is Puerto Rico's second oldest settlement, founded in 1573. Its leafy central plazas showcase an impressive compendium of local architectural styles from handsome Spanish colonial mansions to 19th-century gingerbread villas built during the boom years of the coffee industry. The town's most popular attraction is the **Iglesia Porta Coeli,** a Dominican chapel dating from 1606, housing a museum of religious art.

Casa Wiechers Villaronga

✉ 106 Calle Reina, cnr. Méndez Vigo
☎ 787 843 3363
🕐 Closed Mon.
💲 $

Museo de Arte de Ponce

✉ 2325 Av. las Américas
☎ 787 840 1510
🕐 Closed Tues.
💲 $$

museoarteponce.org

Museo Castillo Serrallés

✉ 17 El Vigía
☎ 787 259 1774
🕐 Closed Mon.– Wed.
💲 $$$

castilloserralles.org

Centro Ceremonial Indígena de Tibes

🅐 126 C1

✉ Rte. 503

☎ 787 840 2255

🕐 Closed Mon.

💲 $$

Hacienda Buena Vista

🅐 126 C1

✉ Rte. 123, KM 16.8

☎ 787 722 5882

🕐 Closed Mon.–Tues.; reservations essential for 2-hr tours

💲 $$$$

paralanaturaleza.org

period furnishings and a beautiful inner courtyard.

The fascinating tour includes the history of the oldest rum-making family on the island, permanent and temporary exhibits, and a short film on the sugar and rum industries. The site also has a gift shop, lovely gardens, and an excellent café with views over Ponce.

Centro Ceremonial Indígena de Tibes

This intriguing Taíno site, located just outside of Ponce, is said to be the oldest cemetery in the Caribbean, with burials dating back to A.D. 700. Two dance grounds and nine ball courts have been unearthed on the 5-acre (2 ha) site, evidence of its importance as a major ceremonial center. It is assumed that there is a correlation between the positions of these constructions and solstices or equinoxes. The largest court, measuring about 110 yards (100 m), is the longest in the Caribbean; 187 skeletons have been unearthed here.

A re-creation of a Taíno village and a small museum display Indian ceremonial objects, pottery, and jewelry. The bilingual guides give informative tours about this particular site and about the pre-Columbian Taíno culture generally. Among other things, they shed light on similarities between Taíno culture and that of the Maya in Mexico.

Hacienda Buena Vista

About an hour north of Ponce, this wonderful old coffee plantation has been restored using 19th-century techniques and tools. Built in 1833, when the country's coffee production was at its peak, the whole estate is powered by an ingenious system of hydraulics. The original owners received permission to divert the Río Canas to provide power for their machinery if all the water was returned to its source—and this is how the system still works. Not a drop is wasted as the hydraulics power the depulping, husking, and polishing machines. The house has also been fully restored, with the help of old photographs and family documents,

INSIDER TIP:

If you're driving into Ponce, be sure to have a good map or GPS on hand. The roads can be baffling: There is no grid structure and everything is one way.

—MATT PROPERT
National Geographic photographer

to show how the hacienda was furnished and managed. The estate is set in a subtropical environment, home to the Puerto Rican screech owl, hummingbirds, and the mangrove cuckoo—among other noteworthy local birds. ∎

West of Ponce

The southwestern corner of the island constitutes the driest part of the country, especially in the 1,618-acre (655 ha) Guánica Bosque Seco, just outside the port of Guánica. This dry coastal forest is a UN biosphere reserve harboring some 700 plant species, 48 of which are endangered, and 16 of which exist nowhere else.

A cactus catches the late afternoon light in Guánica Bosque Seco, Puerto Rico's dry forest.

The **Guánica Bosque Seco** (Guánica Dry Forest) is also home to snakes, lizards, and endangered birds. A dozen marked trails cross the arid scrub within the park, fronted by a large double bay, **Playa de Ventenas,** popular with surfers.

Guánica itself was the beachhead for U.S. troops during the Spanish-American War. On the hill above town is an old fort, currently being restored. Between Guánica and the forest, Copamarina Beach Resort stretches along the shore opposite **Gilligan's Island,** a popular destination for divers and day-trippers. You can also take excursions from the hotel into coastal mangroves.

Farther west, **La Parguera** has grown from a fishing village into a popular resort area. It's a lively spot, particularly on weekends, and is also well known for the nearby **Bio Bay** *(tel 787 899 5891, boat tours from La Parguera).* This lagoon amid the coastal mangrove swamps is similar to Mosquito Bay on Vieques (see p. 138), although not quite as dramatic.

At the southwestern tip of the island, **Los Morrillos Lighthouse** *(tel 787 851 2999)* provides views back down the coast. Five miles (8 km) inland, wildfowl sanctuary **Cabo Rojo National Wildlife Refuge** has 12 miles (19 km) of hiking trails around Boquerón Lagoon, near the resort of Boquerón. ■

Guánica Bosque Seco
- 126 C1
- Rte. 116 to Rte. 334 and follow signs
- Closed Mon.
- 787 821 5706

Cabo Rojo National Wildlife Refuge
- 126 B1
- Rte. 301
- 787 851 7258
- Closed Sun.

fws.gov/caribbean/refuges

The Panoramic Route

Snaking its way through some of Puerto Rico's most fabulous scenery as it traverses the length of the island, La Ruta Panorámica, or the Panoramic Route, is a classic Caribbean drive. It takes at least two days, but there are several mountain *paradores* (country inns) where you can stay. Many parts of the road are extremely narrow, so drive carefully.

The route starts in the coastal town of **Maunabo,** heads inland to Yabucoa, and then crosses the Río Guayane before starting to climb into the foothills. (Note that the route throughout this drive is marked with brown signs at most junctions—but not all.) Small settlements dot the ridge along which the road runs, with valleys and ravines on either side overflowing with clumps of bamboo, tree ferns, and banana plants. After about 6 miles (10 km), the road starts to climb even more steeply. At this elevation, small coffee plantations replace the cattle pastures of the lowlands.

The route then enters **Reserva Forestal Carite ❶**, 6,000 acres (2,430 ha) of rain forest and home to 50 species of birds, several waterfalls, and a blue pool known as the Charco Azul accessible from the picnic area at KM 17.8.

If you're on this road on a weekend, detour

NOT TO BE MISSED:

Reserva Forestal Carite • Cañón San Cristóbal • Cerro Doña Juana

to Campamento Guavate (Hwy. 184) and join locals feasting on the best *lechón asado* (roast pork) served up at outdoor barbecue shacks.

The road continues along the ridgebacks of the Sierra de Cayey, bypassing the town of Cayey itself and rising again to a high point at the **Mirador Piedra Degetau ❷.** An observation tower marks this summit, which is dedicated to the memory of Don Frederico Piedra Degetau y Gonzales (1862–1914), a distinguished writer and patriot who was inspired by this panorama.

Just to the north is the town of **Aibonito ❸**, once a cool mountain retreat for the wealthy and

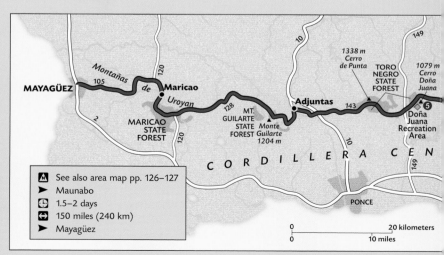

still retaining some of its grandiose homes. It is also the highest town in Puerto Rico. Beyond Aibonito **Cañón San Cristóbal** ❹ (San Cristóbal Canyon), the island's deepest gorge, plunges 700 feet (210 m) to the Río Usabon. There are some rough hiking trails into the canyon, but only experienced hikers should attempt to descend its steep slopes.

The route twists and turns along the spine of the Cordillera Central, offering stunning panoramas across to the north and south coasts. Beyond the Cerro El Malo (2,957 feet/902 m), the road enters the 7,000-acre (2,830 ha) **Reserva Forestal Toro Negro** (Toro Negro Forest Reserve; *tel 787 999 2200*), with a choice of trails, lake kayaking, and a lookout tower. This is a particularly scenic area, with the road shrouded by a leafy canopy of bamboo.

Six miles (10 km) northeast of here is the **Area de Recreativa Doña Juana** (Doña Juana Recreation Area). It's worth stopping and taking the path opposite the entrance, which leads to a huge natural swimming hole in the forest.

The route beyond the recreation area leads you upward to the **Cerro Doña Juana** ❺ at 3,538 feet (1,079 m). Take the easy footpath to the summit (no steep gradients). It takes around 90 minutes to make the round-trip. At

The picturesque harbor in the small coastal town of Maunabo

the top you can climb a small tower for a wonderful panorama of the mountains and the coastline. Beyond here you pass the **Cerro de Punta** (4,387 feet/1,338 m), the island's highest point and positively bristling with radio masts.

The road descends momentarily to the quiet little township of Adjuntas before climbing once more through the Cordillera Central, skirting the Montañas de Uroyan, and finally ending on the west coast at **Mayagüez.**

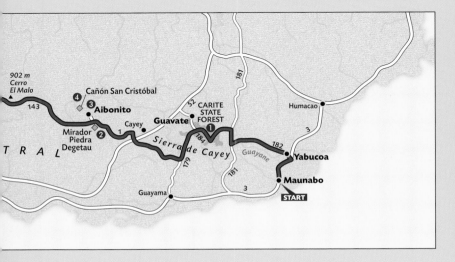

The Northwest

Northwest Puerto Rico is a limestone labyrinth laced with caves, underground rivers, and massive sinkholes. You can tour Parque de las Cavernas del Río Camuy and admire natural wonders of the subterranean world; go stargazing at the fascinating Observatorio de Arecibo; or visit the prehistoric Parque Ceremonial Indígena de Caguana.

The main entrance to Río Camuy Cave Park

Parque de las Cavernas del Río Camuy

🅰 126 C2

✉ Rte. 129,
N of Lares

☎ 787 898 3100

🕐 Closed
Mon.–Tues.

💲 $$$$

Parque de las Cavernas del Río Camuy

In the heart of the limestone karst country near Arecibo is Río Camuy Cave Park. The caves have been carved out over the centuries by the Río Camuy as it carries the rainfall off the Cordillera Central downstream to the sea. Only two other rivers in the world (the Metali in Papua New Guinea and the Reha in eastern Europe) are known to match this underground torrent.

Your guided exploration of this world of lofty caverns, mighty stalactites, and huge sinkholes begins at the visitor center, where there is a short audiovisual presentation on the cave system. You then board a motorized tram for the descent through a steep, winding ravine to the main cave, **Cueva Clara de Empalme** (Clear Cave at the Crossroads). Sunlight filters through a natural entrance to the cave. The main cavern reaches some 200 feet (60 m) at its highest point, and stalactites hang from the ceiling in various strange shapes. Five different species of bats live in the caves, as well as crickets, guavas (a kind of tarantula), and microscopic shrimp that thrive in the caves' pools. On one side of Cueva Clara is a deep cleft, at the bottom of which the Río Camuy flows.

To the east, you emerge into a vast sinkhole (a collapsed cave) more than 420 feet (128 m) deep. Lianas hang down from the uppermost cliffs, and water cascades down the sinkhole's moss-covered sides.

After Cueva Clara, the tour continues to **Sumidero Tres Pueblos** (Three Townships Sinkhole). Its 6-acre (2.5 ha) base could hold all of San Juan's El Morro fortress. In one cave at the side of this sinkhole, artifacts have been discovered that show it was once occupied by the Taíno.

The last sinkhole on the tour is the **Espiral,** which spirals downward toward the underground river. A series of 200 steps and walkways leads down to it.

Avoid crowds by visiting on weekdays. Tours are available in Spanish or English.

Parque Ceremonial Indígena de Caguana

South of the cave park, between Utuado and Lares, this pre-Columbian site dates from about A.D. 1200. Caguana is one of the largest and most important Taíno ceremonial centers in the Caribbean. In addition to the large central court here, there are ten rectangular ball courts edged by granite dolmens decorated with petroglyphs. Although permanently inhabited by very few people, the center once attracted large crowds to religious ceremonies and events.

Circled by limestone hills, the setting is impressive. The grounds contain plants such as silk cottonwood, sapodilla, palms, and cedars. A small interpretive center has displays of ceramics, carvings, and other Taíno artifacts. ■

Parque Ceremonial Indígena de Caguana
🅰 126 C2
✉ 9 miles (14.5 km) W of Utuado on Rte. 111
☎ 787 894 7325

Arecibo Observatory

As you drive through limestone karst to the south of Arecibo, a slender concrete tower becomes visible: the first indication of the extraordinary Observatorio de Arecibo (Arecibo Observatory), the world's largest radio telescope.

The enormous central dish, which covers more than 20 acres (8 ha), is surmounted by a cat's cradle of wires suspended from three concrete pylons. (If it looks familiar, it was featured in the 1995 Bond film *GoldenEye.*) Hanging like a giant spider in the middle is the receiver itself, weighing just under a thousand tons. The structure is so big that it cannot move: The planet itself has to move for it to change direction. But Arecibo has paid off handsomely. Major discoveries made here include the existence of pulsars (most of those known were mapped at Arecibo), pulsars orbited by planets, ice in Mercury's polar regions, and the rotational cycles of Venus and Mercury.

But Arecibo has also become associated with something that has more to do with *The X-Files* than radar astronomy—the search for extraterrestrial intelligence, or SETI. In 1974 the telescope transmitted a binary message into space in hopes of contacting alien civilizations.

Visitors can tour an interpretive center, the **Angel Ramos Foundation Visitor Center** (*tel 787 878 2612, naic.edu, closed Mon.–Tues., $$$*). Located at the foot of one of the giant towers supporting the telescope, the center has a viewing platform, some excellent interactive exhibits, and displays on science and astronomy.

Isla Mona

Sometimes called "the Galápagos of the Caribbean" because of its remoteness and abundance of wildlife, Isla Mona is located 46 miles (74 km) off the western coast of Puerto Rico. It is classified as a subtropical dry region, with areas of mangrove forest and superb white-sand beaches fringed by coral reefs.

Isla Mona

⛰ See inside
back cover

Just under 7 miles (11 km) long and around 4.5 miles (7 km) wide, the island was once inhabited by Taíno Indians who left behind a series of petroglyphs and rock paintings in the caves that dot the 200-foot-high (60 m) cliffs along the shore.

In the 1880s a German-born entrepreneur, Anton Mobins, was given a license to mine phosphate on Mona, and for a time about 200 people lived here as a mining community. During this brief period of commercial activity roads were built and the caves first explored. Since the mining company ceased trading in 1896, undercut by competition from Peru and the United States, Mona has been largely uninhabited.

EXPERIENCE: Isla Mona Expedition

A great way to get the best out of Isla Mona is an expedition with adventure tour operator **Acampa Nature Adventures** (tel 787 706 0695, acampa pr.com, $$$$$). You need to plan ahead and give them eight weeks' notice in order to put together a customized four-day, three-night package including transportation and supplies, gear for caving, and a range of activities you've chosen for yourself.

Splendidly isolated, Mona is renowned for its wildlife, which includes bats, seabirds, indigenous Mona rock iguanas that can measure over 3 feet (90 cm) long, and their tiny 1-inch-long (2.5 cm) cousins, *geco oriundo*. The untouched coral reefs, particularly off the eastern and western coastlines, are known for their marine life. Sea turtles are regular visitors as are humpback whales along with their young in winter.

Visiting the Island

Lying in the middle of the Mona Channel between Puerto Rico and the Dominican Republic, Mona is accessed by boat. Charter boats make the six-hour round-trip from Mayagüez and Cabo Rojo, but it's a long, rough sea passage (calmer by night) for a day trip. A better option is a camping expedition with permission from the Department of Natural and Environmental Resources *(tel 787 722 1726)*, which maintains a new visitor center with quarters for a resident biologist and rangers, or travel with an adventure tour operator (see sidebar this page). There are basic campsites on three beaches in the southwest of the island, but no shops or any other facilities, so you have to bring your food and water. ∎

A jewel-like scattering of tiny volcanic islands, rocks, and reefs embedded in a turquoise sea

Virgin Islands

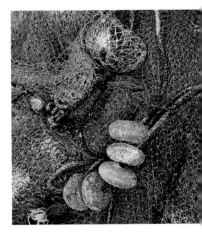

Fishing nets in Tortola

Virgin Islands

Spreading out from the Virgin Passage, 50 miles (80 km) east of Puerto Rico, the 100-plus Virgin Islands lay a ragged trail across 1,000 square miles (2,600 sq km) at the northeastern corner of the Caribbean Sea. Only a few of the greenest islands are inhabited; the rest are Robinson Crusoe islets and secretive cays once favored by pirates, rocky outcrops colonized by seabirds, and razor-sharp, wave-washed reefs.

Christopher Columbus first sailed into this nautical maze on his second voyage to the New World in 1493. Struck by their beauty (and profusion), he named the islands Las Once Mil Virgines, after the legend of St. Ursula and the 11,000 virgins (see sidebar p. 155). The tiny islands held little attraction for the major European powers, but their numerous secluded harbors and safe anchorages were a godsend for pirates, smugglers, and privateers such as Sir Francis Drake (1540–1596), who gave his name to the Sir Francis Drake Channel, one of the most picturesque maritime channels in the world.

The earliest European settlers were mid-17th-century Dutch *boucaniers,* who moved onto Tortola and raised cattle to supply passing ships with dried meat cured in smokehouses

called *boucans.* The British snatched control of the island in 1672 and laid claim to the 60 or so cays and crags at the eastern end of the archipelago, now the British Virgin Islands (BVI). Meanwhile, the Danes secured the western islands of St. Thomas (1665) and St. John (1684) and purchased St. Croix from the French in 1733. St. Thomas they transformed into a flourishing free port; St. John and St. Croix were carpeted with sugarcane. In 1917 the

Danish possessions were sold to the United States for $25 million. Today, together with 70 more rocks and reefs, they comprise the United States Virgin Islands (USVI).

Only 2 miles (3 km) separate the islands of St. John (USVI) and Tortola (BVI), but the U.S. and the British islands are light-years apart in style. St. Thomas and St. Croix are indubitably

NOT TO BE MISSED:

American, upbeat, and certainly among the most developed and prosperous islands in the region. St. John is altogether quieter and boasts an unspoiled national park, which covers two-thirds of the island.

A 40-minute ferry ride away are the relaxed British Virgin Islands, laid-back to the point of horizontal. With a population of about 25,000 compared to the 125,000 on the U.S. Virgin Islands, these islands have a more traditional rural West Indian feel. Yachting is a top attraction and many visitors simply use the islands as a jumping-off point for a sailing trip. ∎

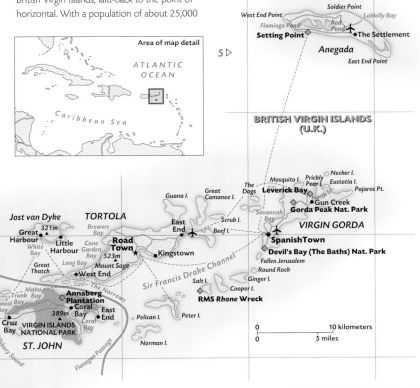

U.S. Virgin Islands

Enjoying three distinct identities, the islands of St. Thomas, St. John, and St. Croix (pronounced croy) are linked by their common history. During the colonial era, the islands were Denmark's only Caribbean possessions, and both St. Thomas and St. Croix preserve attractive Danish colonial architecture in their main waterfront towns.

The idyllic beach along St. John's Cinnamon Bay

With the emancipation of slaves on the Danish islands in 1848 and the subsequent collapse of the sugar industry, the Caribbean colonies were on the wane by the 1860s when the strategic potential of this island group first attracted U.S. interest. The need to protect the Panama Canal (opened in 1914), coupled with German naval activity in the region during World War I, finally prompted the United States to purchase the islands from Denmark and place them under the administration of the U.S. Navy. The Department of the Interior took over in 1931, and self-government was introduced in 1936, but the islanders were not permitted to elect their own governor (previously selected by the president) until 1968. Today, Charlotte Amalie on St. Thomas is the capital of the U.S. Virgin Islands, which are unincorporated territories of the United States. The islanders are U.S. citizens and taxpayers, and their 15-member legislature is represented by a nonvoting delegate in the House of Representatives in Washington, D.C.

Cosmopolitan St. Thomas is the main gateway to the islands. It is a major cruise-ship destination offering excellent duty-free shopping, fine dining and accommodations, several lovely beaches, and a few sightseeing attractions, all combining to make it an ideal choice for a short break. St. John is an easy day trip away, and for visitors in search of peace and quiet this tiny island could well be a better option. St. John is a leader in the sustainable tourism field and its national park is a major attraction. St. Croix is the least known of the USVI trio but well worth a visit. The island provides a good balance of pretty towns, shopping bargains to match St. Thomas, and more varied and interesting sightseeing opportunities. It is culturally distinct, too, celebrating a variety of musical and culinary traditions.

St. Thomas

The foundations of St. Thomas's fortunes were established in the 1670s by the traders of the Danish West India Company. The original settlement on the site of Charlotte Amalie provided a welcome watering hole for Caribbean merchants and pirates, including Edward Teach (died 1718), better known as Blackbeard. A certain raciness lingers on busy St. Thomas, as islanders offer many cruise-ship passengers their first taste of Caribbean hustle and bustle.

St. Thomas
🗺 150 B3
Visitor Information
✉ Tolbod Gade, Charlotte Amalie
☎ 340 774 8784 or 800 372 8784

visitusvi.com

Island-Hopping Excursions

There are all sorts of ways to explore the Virgin Islands. Interisland public ferries are a great (and inexpensive) way to island-hop. Frequent daily ferries link St. Thomas and St. John. The crossing takes just 15 minutes from Red Hook on the east end of St. Thomas to Cruz Bay, St. John; or 45 minutes from Charlotte Amalie *(schedules and information from Transportation Services, tel 340 776 6282)*. There are also daily ferry services from St. Thomas and St. John to Tortola, the transportation hub of the British Virgin Islands (see pp. 166–172), and less frequent direct services to Virgin Gorda and Jost van Dyke. Proof of citizenship is needed for travel between the USVI and BVI.

Day sails are yet another delightfully hassle-free way to experience the islands.

For boat trips with lunch, swimming, and snorkeling action, contact **Day Sail Fantasy** *(Red Hook, tel 340 513 3212, day sailfantasy.com),* **New Horizon Day Sails** *(Sapphire Beach, tel 340 775 1171 or 800 808 7604, newhorizons.daysails.com),* or **Simplicity Charters** *(Red Hook, tel 340 774 9348, simplicitycharters.com).*

Lastly, for something completely different and much more extravagant, **Caribbean Buzz** *(tel 340 775 7335, caribbean-buzz.com)* offers short-hop helicopter tours with amazing aerial views of St. Thomas and the closer BVI; or treat yourself to a helicopter shopping trip to St. Croix or Sint Maarten, bonefishing in Anegada (BVI), or a visit to the private island resort of Peter Island *(tel 800 346 4451, peterisland.com).*

As the town prospered, it was renamed Charlotte Amalie in honor of the Danish queen (wife of King Christian V) in 1691, and by the early 18th century its waterfront warehouses were crammed full of silks, guns, gold, and manufactured goods, which

Island Attractions: Bustling Charlotte Amalie is the hub of the 12-by-3-mile (19 by 5 km) island. Beaches, bays, and hotels hug the ragged central and eastern shorelines (the western end is largely undeveloped), and the interior rises steeply to

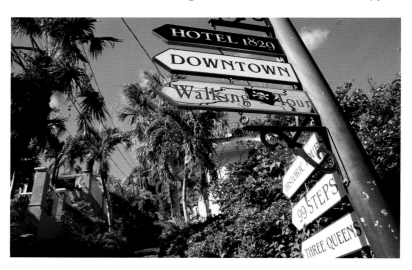

What's your pleasure? A sign points to attractions around Charlotte Amalie.

were traded for Caribbean sugar, rum, indigo, and cotton. While European conflicts were mirrored among the colonial powers of the Caribbean, St. Thomas continued to grow rich on the strength of Danish neutrality. The islanders also supplied arms to colonists fighting the American Revolution. For a time at the height of the plantation era, St. Croix eclipsed St. Thomas as the most important island in the group, and the capital was moved to Christiansted on St. Croix in 1775; it returned to Charlotte Amalie in 1871.

the 1,556-foot (474 m) peak of Crown Mountain, its ridges and crags peppered with houses and vacation homes. More than 50,000 people live here and numbers are boosted daily by thousands of cruise-ship passengers who are shepherded to mountaintop observation points and spectacular Magens Bay (see p. 159). In St. Thomas you can find diving and water sports, deep-sea fishing, and the magnificent Mahogany Run Golf Course, but the island's chief sport is undoubtedly bargain hunting in Charlotte Amalie.

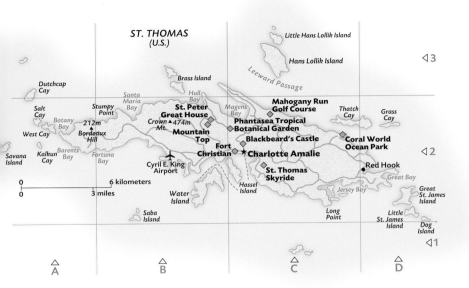

ST. THOMAS (U.S.)

Little Hans Lollik Island
Hans Lollik Island
Leeward Passage
Brass Island
Dutchcap Cay
Salt Cay
West Cay
Savana Island
Kalkun Cay
Botany Bay
Barents Bay
Bordeaux Hill
212m
Fortuna Bay
Stumpy Point
Santa Maria Bay
Hull Bay
Crown Mt. ▲ 474m
St. Peter Great House
Mountain Top
Cyril E. King Airport
Water Island
Saba Island
Magens Bay
Mahogany Run Golf Course
Phantasea Tropical Botanical Garden
Fort Christian
Blackbeard's Castle
★ Charlotte Amalie
Hassel Island
St. Thomas Skyride
Thatch Cay
Grass Cay
Coral World Ocean Park
Red Hook
Jersey Bay
Great Bay
Long Point
Little St. James Island
Great St. James Island
Dog Island

0 ____ 6 kilometers
0 ____ 3 miles

A   B   C   D

3
2
1

Charlotte Amalie: Radiating from its charming Danish colonial origins, Charlotte Amalie skirts the outline of St. Thomas Harbor and clambers up into the amphitheater of surrounding hills. In the bay, cruise ships (up to eight at a time on a busy day) lie at anchor and spill their human cargo onto the waterfront, where the merchants of Main Street await, their mercantile instincts as finely honed as the 18th-century traders whose warehouses they now occupy.

Make an exploratory foray down **Dronningens Gade** (as Main Street is also known) and its warren of narrow alleys to discover a commercial kaleidoscope every bit as dazzling and cutthroat as it must have been 250 years ago, although the barrels and bales have been replaced with designer labels and electronic gadgets.

Main Street is at the heart of Charlotte Amalie's historic district, which stretches from Rothschild Francis Market Square in the west to Emancipation Park in the east. The park is a good place to begin a walkabout, outside the recently restored **Fort Christian.** The squat bloodred fort dates

Charlotte Amalie
▲ 155 C2

The Legend of St. Ursula

The obscure and highly questionable legend of St. Ursula dates from the Dark Ages, when the Christian daughter of an English king sought to avoid marriage to a barbarian chief. Agreeing to the marriage on the condition she could undertake a visit to Rome in the company of virgins, she selected her retinue and sailed away. For three years she trained the women into a fighting force, hoping to overthrow her betrothed, but he discovered the ruse and had all 11,000 virgins massacred in the city of Cologne in Germany.

The 99 Steps

The Danes, who built stairway streets in St. Thomas in the mid-1700s, found that stair steps made the vertiginous hills of Charlotte Amalie easier to climb than steep, flat streets or switchback streets that wind and curve. The 99 Steps make up the best known example of these stairway streets in the capital. The worn brick steps are found between Government House, which holds the offices of the territorial governor, and Hotel 1829, originally built as a town house for a French sea captain. Visitors who reach the top are rewarded with fine harbor views and the statue of the Three Queens, representing the islands of St. Thomas, St. John, and St. Croix.

The bricks used to construct the steps and many local buildings were brought to the Caribbean as ballast carried from Denmark in the holds of ships.

Danish banker and merchant Hans Haagensen built a family home up here on the hill in the 1830s. Set in leafy terraced gardens, **Haagensen House** has been carefully restored and furnished with period art and antiques as one of a pair of 19th-century town house museums, together with neighboring **Villa Notman** (*Government Hill, tel 340 7746 1234, call ahead for hours, $$$*). The houses can be viewed on guided or self-guided tours. On Crystal Gade near the junction with Raadets Gade is **St. Thomas Synagogue,** flanked by palms and

INSIDER TIP:

You can find local produce, jewelry, clothing, and souvenirs at Market Square, originally the site of an 18th-century slave market.

—MARSHALL KIKER
Associate managing editor, National Geographic Books

dating from 1833. St. Thomas's first Jewish congregation consisted of refugees from Dutch Sint Eustatius, exiled for their involvement in the arms trade during the American Revolution. The adjacent small museum celebrates three centuries of Jewish worship on this site. Back on the main drag, the Jewish Pissarro family once ran

Virgin Islands Museum

 Waterfront Hwy., Fort Christian, Charlotte Amalie, St. Thomas

Skyride to Paradise Point

 Long Bay Rd., Charlotte Amalie, St. Thomas

☎ 340 774 9809

$ $$$$$

ridetheview.com

from 1672, and houses the **Virgin Islands Museum** (currently undergoing restoration). Alongside historical displays, exhibits cover bush medicine and colonial furnishings, and pride of place in the central courtyard goes to an antique, animal-powered cane crusher. From the battlements, enjoy the view down to the 19th-century **Danish barracks** near the waterfront, painted peppermint green, which now house the Virgin Islands Legislature.

Above the park is the area of **Government Hill,** crisscrossed with a grid of narrow streets and flights of steps lined with attractive private homes, public buildings, and monumental churches. Near **Government House,** a white neoclassical edifice on Kongens Gade, the **99 Steps** (actually 103; see sidebar this page) strike up toward **Blackbeard's Castle,** a stone watchtower with tremendous views.

a store at **Dronningens Gade 14,** where Impressionist artist Camille Pissarro (1830–1903) was born. The art gallery that now occupies part of the building displays some pages from the artist's sketchbook. Four blocks west, between Store Strade and Strand Gade, is the covered market at **Market Square,** which comes alive on Saturdays as farmers venture into town to sell their homegrown fruits and vegetables.

Harbor Views & Water Island: On the eastern rim of the harbor Havensight Mall fronts Charlotte Amalie's main cruise-ship berth. Across the street the **Skyride to Paradise Point** hoists glass-enclosed cable cars to an observation deck 700 feet (210 m) above sea level. The deck provides great views of the harbor, sheltered by Hassel Island in the foreground, and Water Island beyond.

On the harbor's western edge, the **Water Island** ferry *(tel 340 690 4159)* departs from Crown Bay Marina for the ten-minute

The Three Queens statue at the top of St. Thomas's 99 Steps

crossing to Phillip's Landing. Relax on Honeymoon Beach or go off-road biking with Water Island Adventures *(tel 340 626 9815)*.

Coral World Ocean Park

🅰 155 C2

✉ Coki Point, St. Thomas

☎ 340 775 1555 or 888 695 2073

💲 $$$$$

coralworldvi.com

Estate St. Peter Great House & Botanical Gardens

🅰 155 B2

✉ St. Peter Mountain Rd.

☎ 340 774 4999

💲 $$$

greathousevi.com

Around St. Thomas

There's more to St. Thomas than the sights of Charlotte Amalie. The island's hilltop gardens, marine landscapes, and beaches are well worth exploring and have particular appeal for families with children.

Coral World Ocean Park: An 80,000-gallon (363,000 L) reef tank display, 2-acre (0.8 ha) dolphin habitat, assorted marine encounter programs, predator tank, and stingray pool are among the attractions at this popular marine park on St. Thomas's northeast coast. But the real showstopper lies beneath the waves, where the picture windows of the underwater observatory resemble a darkened marine theater in the round, opening onto a 360-degree panorama of the ocean bed. A touch pool and the rescued baby turtle exhibit are big hits with kids, and there are daily talks by marine experts as well as feeding sessions at the baby shark pool. The park is adjacent to busy Coki Beach, which has a dive and snorkel center.

Glorious Gardens: Draped across the hillside 1,000 feet (305 m) above Magens Bay, the 5-acre (2 ha) **Estate St. Peter Great House & Botanical Gardens** have been laid out on the grounds of a 19th-century plantation. You can tour the gardens on wooden boardwalk trails shaded by banana plants and breadfruit trees, tall stands of lobster claw heliconias, and tropical gingers.

The great house itself has been reconstructed and furnished in contemporary style with a gallery selling eye-catching Caribbean artwork. If you fancy your views with a side order of

EXPERIENCE: Snorkeling in St. John

Snorkeling is something of a specialty in St. John. The island's numerous protected coves and shallow coastal waters make for an abundance of snorkel sites directly accessible from the beach. **Trunk Bay** in the national park even offers a 225-yard (205 m) self-guided snorkel trail with underwater signs indicating reef features. Less crowded and more colorful corals can be found farther off the beaten path at sites like **Hawknest Bay,** and **Watermelon Cay** in Leinster Bay.

St. John's snorkeling conditions are ideal for beginners, but if you're still not sure, why not try a snuba dive with **Virgin Islands Snuba Excursions** (Trunk Bay, tel 340 693 8063 or 888 294 1083, visnuba.com, $$$$$)? Snuba is a cross between snorkeling and diving with air pumped from the surface and suitable for kids from age eight on up, so it can be a fun family experience. No special equipment is required beyond a mask and fins, and participants wear a light harness attached to a scuba tank, which floats above them on a raft. The outing takes around 90 minutes, beginning with an onshore familiarization talk. The dive starts in the shallows and can reach a maximum depth of 20 feet (6 m). The maximum group size is six people; reservations are essential.

The view of St. Thomas and Charlotte Amalie from the ridge leading to Magens Bay

adrenaline, the adjacent **Tree Limin' Extreme** *(tel 340 777 9477, ziplinestthomas.com, $$$$)* offers zip line adventures and skywalks complete with dramatic panoramas across the island.

Alternatively, settle for the delicate charms of the 1,000-plus orchids sprouting in the exotic profusion of Patsy Breunlin's backyard at **Phantasea Tropical Botanical Garden** *(Bishop Dr., tel 340 774 2916, stthomasbotanicalgarden.com)*. Created over 20 years, the garden was opened to the public in 2015 and remains a glorious work in progress.

Magens Bay: Over the mountain ridge from Charlotte Amalie, St. Thomas's most famous beach lines the base of a huge rectangular bay carved out of the north coast. Magens Bay's idyllic mile-long (1. 6 km) stretch of powder-soft sand fringed with palm trees is a prime contender in any list of the world's top beaches. On weekdays there is usually plenty of room for everyone. Several beach bars and restaurants cater to the crowds.

Mountain Top: The peak of St. Peter Mountain offers superb views over Magens Bay and as far as St. John and the British Virgin Islands. This spot also claims to be the birthplace of the banana daiquiri; alcoholic and nonalcoholic versions are available at the viewing deck bar.

St. John

A 2-mile (3 km) ferry ride across Pillsbury Sound from

Magens Bay
🅰 155 C2
✉ Magens Rd., St. Thomas
💲 $

Mountain Top
🅰 155 B2
✉ Off Crown Mountain Rd., St. Thomas
☎ 340 774 2400
mountaintopvi.com

St. John
🅰 151 C3
Visitor Information
✉ Cruz Bay St. John
☎ 340 776 6450
visitusvi.com

St. Thomas, St. John is the unspoiled gem of the USVI. Two-thirds of it is Virgin Islands National Park, created with the help of Laurance Rockefeller, who donated the first tract of

cane machetes massacred settlers and managed to hold the Danish garrison for nine months. The uprising was eventually quashed with the assistance of French troops, and the last rebels are

St. John's Maho Bay

land in 1956 (a cunning ploy preventing anybody else building near his Caneel Bay resort), and much of the remaining third is untouched. Dense woodlands carpet the rolling hills of the interior, while sandy bays punctuate the irregular coastline.

During the colonial era, St. John was planted with sugarcane and cotton. One of the Caribbean's most successful slave revolts was staged on the island in 1733, when slaves armed with

believed to have leaped to their deaths from Mary's Point on the north coast. Things have been very quiet since, and the population of 5,000 mainly consists of newcomers from down island and American expatriates lured by the serenity.

Cruz Bay & Around the Island: Most visitors arrive in St. John at the **Cruz Bay ferry dock,** to be greeted by a coterie of taxi drivers and an engaging huddle of shops and restaurants set back from the waterfront. Over the hill south of town is **Great Cruz Bay,** the island's busiest resort area. But most set off on their around-island tour by taking the North Shore Road out of Cruz Bay, past the attractive Mongoose Junction

INSIDER TIP:

The historic Taíno rock carvings at Petroglyph Pool, found off the Reef Bay Trail, are well worth the hike.

—JUSTIN KAVANAGH
*National Geographic
Travel Books editor*

mall, housed in a local plantation-style stone complex, and the informative **Virgin Islands National Park visitor center** *(tel 340 776 6201, nps.gov/viis).*

St. John's best beaches are found around the rim of the north coast from Honeymoon Beach on Caneel Bay, through Hawksnest Bay, famously gorgeous **Trunk Bay,** and Cinnamon Bay (backed by a campground) to Maho Bay. Beyond Maho, a side road heads off to **Annaberg Plantation** *(tel 340 776 6201),* where a self-guided tour leads visitors around the foundations of slave cabins, the old windmill, boiling room, and storehouse.

North Shore Road then meets Centerline Road, which returns to Cruz Bay along a twisting mountain route with superb views across

to Sir Francis Drake Channel. Its eastern arm continues to the quiet village of Coral Bay, St. John's original settlement.

Straddling the island around three 1,000-foot (300 m) peaks, culminating in Bordeaux Mountain (1,277 feet/389 m), the land-based portion of **Virgin Islands National Park** is a subtropical tangle of forest greenery that has swallowed up all but the merest traces of the hundred-plus plantation estates that once carpeted the landscape. The visitor center provides a helpful introduction with maps, historical and natural history displays, and an activities program. A relief model graphically illustrates St. John's rugged terrain and details the park's 20-plus trails. These vary from short walks around Cruz Bay to more challenging hikes such as the **Reef Bay Trail,** which descends to the south coast from Centerline Road.

Accessible Nature Trails in Virgin Islands National Park

An inspired initiative in VI National Park has seen the introduction of accessible trails, allowing wheelchair users, stroller pushers, and those less "sure of foot" to enjoy St. John's backcountry. A 610-foot (185 m) ramp now winds through the sugar factory ruins at Cinnamon Bay, and there is another accessible trail at Francis Bay.

St. Croix

⚐ 151 C1–E1

Visitor Information

✉ 321 King St., Christiansted

☎ 340 772 0357

visitusvi.com

NOTE: The **Annaly Bay Trail,** on the north coast of western St. Croix, is approximately 2 miles (3 km) in length. Ask the guard at the Carambola Beach Resort & Spa *(Kings Hill, tel 340 778 3800)* for directions to the trailhead. Bring plenty of water and wear sensible shoes.

A smart way to avoid the strenuous return trip on this route is to take the Park Service guided tour (check schedules). Walkers are bused to the trailhead for the 2.5-mile (4 km) downhill hike through wet and dry forest to the Reef Bay sugar mill ruins. The trail detours to a petroglyph site decorated with rock carvings attributed to Arawak Indians. Take time to swim and snorkel before the boat trip back to Cruz Bay.

The park's 5,650-acre (2,287 ha) **marine preserve** offers excellent snorkeling in the clear waters off the north coast beaches (see sidebar p. 158) and the less accessible south coast around Saltpond and Lameshur Bays. Parrotfish, angelfish, tangs, grunts, rays, snappers, jacks, and tarpon are frequent visitors to the reef areas and shallow sandy bays. One reason for the wealth of marine life is the mangrove nurseries where fish and marine species breed in the safe, nutrient-rich waters of the coastal swamp. The **Francis Bay Trail,** just next to Maho Bay, has a boardwalk section leading out into the

INSIDER TIP:

A dip in the Annaly Bay tide pools on the north coast is worth the trek across rocky (and occasionally muddy) terrain from the Carambola Beach Resort & Spa.

—MARSHALL KIKER
Associate managing editor, National Geographic Books

mangroves where herons, Western Indian whistling ducks, pintails, teal, sandpipers, and other waterbirds come to feed.

St. Croix

The largest of the USVI at 84 square miles (217 sq km), St. Croix lies 40 miles (64 km) to the south of St. Thomas and the main body of the Virgin Islands. A former sugar island with mountains in the west and flat, fertile agricultural plains in the center, St. Croix takes its history seriously. The **St. Croix Heritage Trail,** a self-guided

---

EXPERIENCE: A Crystal Clear Kayak Trip

Now here's a great idea: a totally see-through kayak. Father and son watersport fanatics Craig and Bryce Scott of **Sea Thru Kayaks VI** *(tel 340 244 8696, seathrukayaksvi.com, $$$$$)* have rustled up a fleet of sleek, totally transparent two-person kayaks molded from tough polycarbonate (the same material used for fighter jet canopies) for paddling expeditions around St. Croix's coastal lagoons and reefs. Setting off from the beach at Cane Bay for an exploration of the coral-encrusted barrier reef, there's a chance of spotting sea turtles and dolphins, while among the mangrove nurseries of Altoona Lagoon, schools of juvenile fish dart beneath your feet and iguanas bask on the shore. The nighttime Creepy Crawly Critter Hunt is a blast as kayaks equipped with lamps scoot above lionfish, lobsters, crab, and shrimp, or experience the magical glitter of bioluminescent organisms shimmering in the dark waters of Salt River.

driving tour, lists 200 sites of historic and cultural interest, including the Cruzan Rum Distillery (see sidebar p. 164).

Columbus made landfall at Salt River Bay on the north shore in 1493. He beat a hasty retreat on encountering the belligerent Carib but claimed the island for Spain and named it Santa Cruz ("holy cross"). Claimed by France in 1650, the island's name was translated to St. Croix, and it stuck when the Danes purchased the island in 1733.

The capital of St. Croix is Christiansted, a delightful little Danish-style town with a miniature fortress and shops tucked into a clutch of 18th- and 19th-century arcaded buildings. The island's main sightseeing attractions lie off Centerline Road, heading west, although there are lovely drives along North Shore Road (Rte. 80) and on Mahogany Road (Rte. 76) through the rain forest.

On the west coast, Frederiksted (see p. 165) is where the cruise ships dock. It is another pretty town, splendidly renovated in 1998 to celebrate the 150th anniversary of the abolition of slavery in the Danish colonies. Denmark was the first nation to abolish the slave trade, in 1803, although King Frederik VIII made no move toward emancipation until 1848, when he issued an edict stating that all slaves would be freed in 1859. The slaves on St. Croix and St. John rose up in revolt at the news, and the Danish governor, Peter von Scholten, taking the law into his own hands, declared the slaves free on July 3, 1848, at Fort Frederik.

Christiansted: St. Croix's pint-size capital was laid out around a calm, reef-sheltered bay in 1733 and named in honor of the King of Denmark, Christian VI.

Christiansted National Historic Site

▲ 164 C1

Visitor Information

☎ 340 773 1460

$ $$

nps.gov/chri

Along a covered stairway in St. Croix

Overlooking the waterfront in **Christiansted National Historic Site,** spick-and-span **Fort Christiansvaern** looks like a child's toy carved out of yellow marzipan. It was built between 1738 and 1749, and its

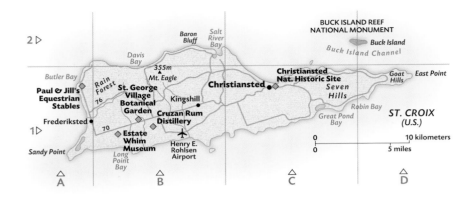

St. Croix Archaeology Museum

✉ 6 Company St., Christiansted, St. Croix

☎ 340 277 4072

🕐 Open Sat. 10 a.m.–2 p.m. or by request

stcroixarchaeology.org

battlements are still guarded by neatly blacked cannon, which have never been fired in anger; there are historical displays on the upper level.

Around the small park in front of the fort are the **Old Danish Customs House** dating from 1751; the 19th-century **Scale House,** where ships' cargoes were inspected and weighed; the 1735 **Steeple Building,** a former Lutheran church housing a small museum; and the original **West Indies & Guinea Company Warehouse,** where slave auctions were once held in the courtyard. A short walk west down Company Street stands the 1832 **Apothecary Hall,** now restored to display pre-Columbian artifacts found on the island. The **St. Croix Archaeology Museum** traces human habitation on St. Croix back more than 5,000 years before the arrival of Columbus. Ax heads, pottery, beads, and tools are among the finds.

One block to the north on King Street, **Government House** occupies two fine 18th-century town houses converted into a fitting residence for Peter von Scholten in the 1830s.

Between King Street and the bay is the **Kings Wharf open-air mall**—a pleasant place to shop or find a café table in the sun before taking a stroll up Strand Street, past boutiques and shops squirreled away beneath picturesque, creeper-clad arcades.

Around St. Croix

St. Croix's history, from pre-Columbian to colonial, can

Cruzan Rum Distillery

Cruzan Rum Distillery (*Rte. 64, off Centerline Rd., tel 340 692 2280, cruzanrum.com, closed Sat.–Sun., $$*) is the largest rum producer in the Virgin Islands and a popular side trip. Eight generations of the Nethropp family have perfected their rum-making skills on St. Croix, and although state-of-the-art practices have crept into the modern production line, rum aficionados will be delighted to see that dark rums are still aged in the traditional charred oak barrels essential to their smooth, aromatic taste. Visits to the factory start with a video presentation and guided tour, followed by tastings of rums in tropical cocktails or enjoyed straight up over ice.

be discovered at attractions along the route between Christiansted and Frederiksted. Snorkelers will want to head to Buck Island.

Buck Island Reef National Monument: Located 5 miles (8 km) off Christiansted (about an hour's sail), uninhabited Buck Island is renowned for its excellent reef snorkeling and diving. Here corals grow to 30 feet (9 m) tall, and the reefs are home to a rich selection of marine life. On land visitors will find walking trails, sandy beaches, and picnic facilities.

Frederiksted: A 30-minute drive west of Christiansted, this sleepy little town is startled into life every year when the winter cruise ships arrive. Bloodred 1752 **Fort Frederik** (closed Sat.–Sun.) was named for King Frederik V. Governor von Scholten announced the slave emancipation in the courtyard, and several rooms contain island history and cultural displays. The town's center is worth exploring for its pretty Victorian ginger-bread houses and the trim row of arcaded waterfront buildings alongside the arts center. North of town, a sandy beach extends to the old Sprat Hall Plantation.

St. George Village Botanical Garden: This 17-acre (6.8 ha) spread of lawned gardens and colorful plantings is set amid the ruins of a 19th-century sugar planta-tion, which was laid out over the site of a pre-Columbian Amerindian settlement dating back to about A.D. 100. The marked trail is lined with more than 1,500 native and exotic botanical species, and the site has a rain forest section as well as a cactus garden. Some of the plantation's ruins have been restored.

Estate Whim Museum

St. Croix's Danish colonial past is on display at this restored 18th-century great house. The interior is kept remarkably cool by 3-foot-thick (90 cm) stone walls and an air moat, while the rooms are furnished with antique mahogany pieces, including a splendid four-poster bed with typical pineapple carv-ings, the Caribbean symbol for hospitality. On the grounds are the remains of the old sugar mill. ∎

Buck Island Reef National Monument

🗺 164 C2–D2

Visitor Information

☎ 340 773 1460

💲 $$$$$ (Boat access from downtown Christiansted or Green Cay Marina)

nps.gov/buis

St. George Village Botanical Garden

🗺 164 B1

✉ Centerline Rd., St. Croix

☎ 340 692 2874

💲 $$

sgvbg.org

Estate Whim Museum

🗺 164 B1

✉ 52 Estate Whim, Frederiksted, St. Croix

☎ 340 772 0598

🕐 Closed Sun.

💲 $$$

stcroixlandmarks.com

NEED TO KNOW

Port Logistics: Frederiksted

Cruise vessels berth on Frederiksted's downtown waterfront, close to the information center and taxi ranks. Cruise lines may offer a cross-island shuttle to Christiansted. A 30-minute taxi ride costs $25 for two people; a three-hour around-island tour for four costs $100–125.

Frederiksted Highlights

- Christiansted sightseeing & shopping: 3 hours
- Estate Whim Museum: 2 hours
- Cruzan Rum Distillery: 1.5 hours
- Buck Island: day trip

British Virgin Islands

Known locally as Nature's Little Secrets, these rugged small islands with amoebic outlines are scalloped into sheltered coves and bays. Once a haven for pirates and smugglers, the British Virgin Islands (BVI) now offer an escapist paradise for sailors and a surprising choice of luxurious resorts for vacationers. Part of the charm of the BVI, however, is to savor them as the islanders do—island-hopping by ferry, snorkeling, or having a quiet drink in a harborside bar.

Massive boulders tower above visitors at The Baths on Virgin Gorda.

Most of the islands and islets of the BVI group, from the verdant heights of Tortola and Virgin Gorda to the rocky jumble of Fallen Jerusalem, are arranged in two irregular lines flanking the 3-mile-wide (5 km) Sir Francis Drake Channel. Only 15 of the 60 or so volcanic outcrops are inhabited, including Anegada, the group's only coral island.

It took some time for the British to show a proper interest in their Virgin Island colonies and clear them of the piratical likes of Blackbeard, Henry Morgan (1635–1688), and Jost van Dyke (who has an island named after him). In the heyday of the 18th-century plantation era, settlers imported African slaves to plant and tend cotton and sugarcane on the challenging terrain, but their efforts were only moderately successful, and many planters sailed away, abandoning their slaves before emancipation in the 1830s. In order to survive, the freed slaves turned to small-scale farming. The BVI muddled along as part of the Leeward Islands federation of British colonies until independence. They toyed with the idea of political union with the USVI but opted to become a crown colony of Britain.

The BVI remain charmingly sleepy and friendlier than their better developed neighbors. But tourism and the financial services sector have brought increased prosperity, and a mini-construction boom is under way.

Tortola

Tortola was named for its turtle doves, which still outnumber the island's 28,000 inhabitants. It is the largest island in the BVI, measuring just 11 miles (18 km) east to west and 3 miles (5 km) north to south. To cross from the capital Road Town on the south coast to the beaches in the north, you have to tackle the central island ridge, where Mount Sage peaks at 1,716 feet (523 m), the highest point in the Virgin Islands archipelago.

Most visitors use Tortola as a springboard for yacht charters and visits to the outer islands. However, it is a relaxing place to stay for a few days, soak up the sun, hop aboard a couple of ferries, and generally unwind.

A handful of streets running parallel to the reclaimed waterfront, **Road Town** is the administrative and commercial center of the BVI. The harbor is usually a lively spot, with ferries coming and going and yachts checking in and out of the busy marinas, and there's a significant added bustle when a moderate-size cruise ship drops off passengers for an island tour and a bit of shopping.

There is no need to allocate much sightseeing time to the town itself, although one very pleasant stop is the small **J.R. O'Neal Botanic Gardens.** A short walk from the town center, the lush palm-tree-shaded oasis

Tortola

🅰 151 C3–D3

Visitor Information

✉ BVI Tourist Board, Ferry Building, Road Town

☎ 284 494 3134

bvitourism.com

J.R. O'Neal Botanic Gardens

🅰 167 C2

✉ Botanic Rd., Road Town, Tortola

☎ 284 494 4557

🕐 Closed Sun.

💲 Donation

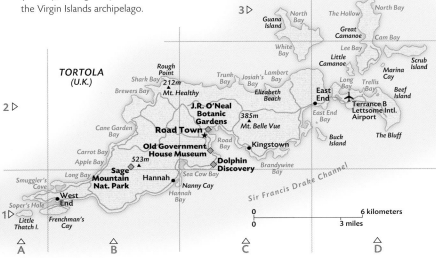

Old Government House Museum

✉ Waterfront Dr., Road Town, Tortola

☎ 284 494 4091

🕐 Closed Sun.

💲 $$

of indigenous and exotic tropical plants is arranged around a water lily pond, orchid house, and pergola walk. Nearby, the **Old Government House Museum** offers tours of its formally furnished rooms and colorful BVI stamp collections laid out in the former governor's residence. Another possible detour is the **Lower Estate Sugar Works Museum** *(Station Ave., closed Sat.–Sun.),* housed in a collection of wood-framed buildings dating from the 1780s. Exhibits include Amerindian relics and articles salvaged from the wreck of the R.M.S. *Rhone* (see p. 172). Around the western arm of the waterfront, the historic ruins of **Fort Burt** afford sweeping harbor views, and the ubiquitous **Dolphin Discovery** experience at Prospect Reef is a popular option with cruise visitors.

Around the Island: Tortola's hotels and best beaches are strung out along the north

INSIDER TIP:

Soper's Hole on Tortola's West End is a delight. Wander about the marina on Frenchman's Cay, a strip of pastel-colored boutiques and cafés.

—OLIVIA STREN
National Geographic writer

coast. Starting in the west, secluded **Smuggler's Cove** is recommended for snorkeling and reached by a bumpy unpaved road from Long Bay. **Long Bay** itself is a mile-long (1.6 km) strip of blond sand backed by palm trees and a hotel. **Apple Bay** is the surfers' favorite and home to Bomba's Surfside Shack, a great beach bar notorious for its full-moon parties. **Carrot Bay** has a couple of bars and a waterfront restaurant. Curving **Cane Garden Bay** is the island's best equipped beach, with windsurfing, waterskiing, and boating opportunities as well as beach bars, restaurants, and a few hotels. **Brewers Bay** is recommended for snorkeling when the sea is quiet; the sandy beaches at **Trunk Bay, Josiah's Bay, Lambert Bay,** and **Elizabeth Beach** are good for swimming. Attached to Tortola by a causeway is **Beef Island,** with fine beaches at **Trellis Bay** and **Long Bay.**

In the center of Tortola is 92-acre (37 ha) **Sage Mountain**

Flamingo Restoration

At one time, many colonies of pink flamingos called Anegada home. But by the late 20th century, the flamingo population had been wiped out after humans rounded up and consumed the young birds.

In 1992 the Conservation Agency hatched a plan to reintroduce flamingos to Anegada. They airlifted 22 young birds from Bermuda and released them into the island's natural habitat, where the long-legged birds find a haven from storms and raise their offspring, born from a single egg. The new flamingos quickly began forming their own colony, and hundreds of flamingos now live on Anegada.

EXPERIENCE: Charter a Yacht

The Caribbean was surely created as a paradise for boaters. Its clear skies, calm blue seas, and arrestingly beautiful islands have seduced sailors since Columbus. Right at its heart lies Tortola, undisputed capital of Caribbean yachting, whose mountainous central spine is serendipitously positioned to form a wind barrier between the Atlantic and the Sir Francis Drake Channel.

This pint-size sailing center boasts the greatest concentration of bareboat charter vessels in the world, yet it is still possible to set sail from Road Town or the West End, quickly lose the crowds, and discover your own private paradise amid the dozens of islands and islets scattered nearby. This exceptional wealth of anchorages and the ever changing scenery make for an idyllic sailing holiday.

A team relaxes during the Mount Gay Rum yacht race.

Crewed Charters

Crewed charters offer all sorts of advantages, from complete relaxation and an itinerary tailored to your requirements to an experienced captain and a chef. The charter company will discuss your vacation needs in advance, including food preferences and the sort of activities (snorkeling, water sports, beaches) you have in mind. The type of vessel can be determined by the accommodation your party requires (number of cabins, bathrooms). Most crewed charters are multihulled (catamaran or trimaran) vessels, which provide more space and are suited to families and groups. They are also more stable, and the smoother ride is worth considering if seasickness is a concern. You can treat your crewed vessel as a chauffeured limo, taking the helm occasionally, or select a charter that includes sailing instruction to prepare yourself to go it alone next time.

Bareboat Charters

If a bareboat charter appeals, the good news is that you don't have to be a seasoned navigator to captain your own boat. The charter company will check on previous boating experience (type of craft, conditions) and will give you a sail test. Less experienced sailors can opt to hire a captain for a couple of days to relearn the ropes before going solo. The plus side of bareboat chartering is independence and flexibility, as well as privacy. However, you need to consider provisioning (food, fuel, etc.), which is not included in charter rates except by prior arrangement.

Charter Operators

Dozens of yacht charter operations are based in Tortola alone. For an overview of what's available there and elsewhere around the islands, and what to consider before booking, two very useful websites are run by the **Virgin Islands Charter Yacht League** (vicl.org) and **BVI Charter Yacht Society** (bvicrewedyachts.com).

For a full list of marinas, moorings, anchorages, and entry ports to be found throughout the islands, consult the BVI Tourism website (bvitourism.com).

Some of the Caribbean's larger charter operators are **Bareboats BVI** (bareboats bvi.com), **BVI Yacht Charters** (bviyachtcharters.com), **The Moorings** (moorings.com), and **Sunsail** (sunsail.com).

Sage Mountain National Park

⛰ 167 B2

✉ Ridge Rd.

☎ 284 494 2069

💲 $$

Anegada

⛰ 151 E5

Cooper Island

⛰ 151 D3

Jost Van Dyke

⛰ 151 C4

National Park, which was established in 1964 to protect the remnants of the native forest that once covered the whole of Tortola. The park's **Rainforest Trail** features many typical rain forest plants, such as giant elephant ear vines, tree ferns, bromeliads, and philodendrons flourishing beneath an umbrella of 100-foot-high (30 m) bulletwood trees and buttress-trunked ficus. The **Mahogany Forest Trail** leads off the main path up through white cedar, West Indian and broadleaf mahogany plantations.

Ferries for the island of Jost van Dyke and the U.S. Virgin Islands depart from **Soper's Hole** harbor in Tortola's West End. Across the bay on Frenchman's Cay is the **Soper's Hole Marina,** which packs in private yachts and charter boats like sardines. On the dock, cute clapboard buildings house a few shops and restaurants.

More Places to Visit in the British Virgin Islands

Ferries and airplanes can take you around the smaller islands of the BVI to destinations for diving, hiking, and enjoying a drink on the beach.

Anegada: North of Virgin Gorda—flights and ferries depart from Tortola—lies Anegada, the second largest of the BVI at 15 square miles (39 sq km). Its name means "the drowned one" in Spanish, as the island barely reaches 28 feet (8.5 m) above sea level. Anegada's main attraction is its offshore coral reefs, with their superb diving. The island has a small hotel with its own dive facilities, a couple of guesthouses, bar-restaurants, campgrounds, and food stores.

Cooper Island: Cooper Island's dinghy dock and bar-restaurant attract boaters sailing the Sir Francis Drake Channel. Those who linger will find a good beach, dive shop, and the unpretentious Cooper Island Beach Club with cottages on Manchioneel Bay.

Jost van Dyke: A 4-mile (6.5 km) ferry hop across from Tortola's West End is the

---

NEED TO KNOW

Port Logistics: Road Town

Cruise passengers arriving in Tortola generally tender directly to Road Town's downtown waterfront, near the tourist office and Virgin Gorda ferry dock; only smaller vessels can berth at Wickham's Cay, a short walk away. Taxis are readily available, but there are no set rates.

A ten-minute ride to Cane Garden Bay costs about $25; a two-hour tour around $150 for four people. Independent travelers can travel to Virgin Gorda by ferry (30 mins); but an organized shore excursion with transportation can be a better deal.

Road Town Highlights

You can spend your entire port of call time at any one of these destinations, but here are some suggested times to help with your planning. Note, these do not allow for travel time to and from and/or waiting in line:

• J.R. O'Neal Botanic Gardens: 1 hour
• Sage Mountain National Park: 2 hours
• Snorkel trip to R.M.S. Rhone (off Salt Island): half day

laid-back island of Jost van Dyke. Local legend claims van Dyke was a 17th-century Dutch pirate, one of many who rampaged around the islands at the time.

Jost van Dyke boasts several magnificent white-sand beaches, although few visitors bother to venture beyond **Great Harbour,** where the ferry docks. Here there is a simple inn, a watersports concession, and a couple of beach bars. **Foxy's,** at the east end of the beach, is the epicenter of one of the Caribbean's most excessive New Year's parties.

Norman Island: Uninhabited, save for a handful of goats, Norman Island is reputed to have been the setting for Robert Louis Stevenson's *Treasure Island.* Snorkeling is good around **The Indians**

(four jagged pinnacles accessible by yacht). Hungry explorers can refuel at the **Pirates Bight** *(tel 284 443 1305)* bar and grill on the beach, or **The Willy T** *(tel 284 340 8603),* a floating restaurant popular with the yachting crowd.

Peter Island: Just across the Sir Francis Drake Channel from Tortola is the exclusive **Peter Island Resort.** Even if you are not staying there, you can sample the luxury lifestyle on a day trip from Road Town by ferry.

Salt Island: Salt Island's three salt ponds once supplied passing ships with their vital salt rations, and in an appropriate variation of the traditional peppercorn (nominal) rent system, the islanders used to pay an

Norman Island
▲ 151 D3

Peter Island
▲ 151 D3

Salt Island
▲ 151 D3

A marina on Anegada Island, the second largest of the British Virgin Islands

Virgin Gorda

◭ 151 E3–E4

Visitor Information

✉ Virgin Gorda Yacht Harbour

☎ 284 495 5181
or
From U.S.
800 835 8530

bvitourism.com

NOTE: Getting to **The Baths** To the south of Spanish Town is the island's chief sightseeing attraction, The Baths, a bizarre jumble of monumental boulders piled along the shore. From the drop-off point (accessible by shared taxis from the dockside), a path leads 350 yards (320 m) downhill to the beach and the boulders. Turn left here and enter the caves for a ten-minute scramble up and down the giant rocks and across slapping, bubbling tidal pools to secluded Devil's Beach, which girdles an idyllic snorkeling spot.

annual tax of one bag of salt to the British monarch. Now the island is chiefly known for the wreck of the R.M.S. *Rhone,* one of the best wreck diving sites in the Caribbean. The British royal mail ship went down with 300

INSIDER TIP:

The Baths on Virgin Gorda are a must-see—visitors should hike the Devil's Bay Trail, which winds under, around, and over huge granite boulders.

—LYNNE CAMPBELL
Owner, Carefree Yacht Charters

of its crew during a hurricane in 1867, and it lies in 30 to 80 feet (9–24 m) of water on the reefs south of the island. Other notable local dive sites are **Blonde Rock** and **Painted Walls** to the west.

Virgin Gorda

Christopher Columbus coined Virgin Gorda's unflattering sobriquet, the "fat virgin." From the low and rock-strewn southern end, the island bulges up to a height of 1,359 feet (414 m) at **Gorda Peak** and is supposed to resemble a pregnant woman lying on her back. Most of Virgin Gorda's 3,500 inhabitants live in **Spanish Town** (often referred to as The Valley), a meandering collection of old West Indian houses and more modern concrete villas on the southwest coast. Ferry passengers from Tortola disembark here, and there is also a small marina and an airstrip.

Heading north from The Valley, the landscape becomes greener and more hilly. The road passes twin crescents of powdery white-sand beach edging along **Savannah Bay** on the west coast, and then it climbs toward **Gorda Peak National Park.** There are hiking trails striking up to the mini-mountaintop signposted from the roadside; the steep climb takes about 45 minutes, round-trip.

The views from the mountain road are fantastic, stretching down the Sir Francis Drake Channel to the south and across the North Sound, a spectacular turquoise bay hemmed in by Mosquito and Prickly Pear Islands. When the road divides, the northern spur leads on to **Leverick Bay;** the other ends at **Gun Creek,** where small motorboats shuttle guests out to the Bitter End and Biras Creek resorts. ∎

NEED TO KNOW

Port Logistics: Virgin Gorda

Cruise visitors tender into either the island's main settlement, Spanish Town (a short public shuttle ride from The Baths), or into Gun Creek or Leverick Bay in the North Sound. Definitely consider a shore excursion to get around, or team up for a two-hour shared taxi tour ($150).

Virgin Gorda Highlights

• The Baths: 1 hour
• View from Virgin Gorda Peak: 1 hour
• Snorkeling at Spring Bay Beach: 3 hours

Two distinctive island clusters: one amid the northerly Leeward Islands and the other poised off the coast of Venezuela

Dutch Caribbean

You never know what you'll see during the colorful revelry of Carnival in Aruba.

Dutch Caribbean

More than 500 miles (800 km) separate the two very distinct groups of islands that make up the Dutch Caribbean (formerly the Netherlands Antilles). To the north are Sint Maarten, Sint Eustatius, and Saba, and to the south lie Aruba, Bonaire, and Curaçao (referred to as the ABCs). The northern group is known as the Dutch Windward Islands, although their closest neighbors are the British and former British Leeward Islands.

The confusing terms date from the days of sail, when they described an island's geographical location in relation to its home country's preferred outbound and inbound Caribbean trading routes. The ABCs, lying within plain view (on a clear day) of South America, are the Dutch Leewards. Although the Dutch are credited with introducing the sugar industry to the region, they didn't choose their possessions with an eye to sugar growing but as trading posts. Hence, they took control of arid, mountainous Sint Maarten, two tiny volcanic blips known as Sint Eustatius (shortened to Statia in local parlance) and Saba, and the ABCs, three low, wind-blasted, cactus-strewn islets close to South America and the Dutch colonies in Brazil. Before long the calculated gamble paid off, and the islands of Sint Eustatius and Curaçao boasted two of the richest mercantile ports during the 17th and 18th centuries.

Like other Caribbean islands, the Dutch possessions changed hands on several occasions. In an unusually pragmatic arrangement, the island of Sint Maarten/St.-Martin was divided between Dutch and French colonists in 1648. Dutch Sint Maarten and French St.-Martin continue to occupy the 37-square-mile (96 sq km) island, the smallest in the world shared by two sovereign states.

The Dutch secured the six Netherlands Antilles islands under the Treaty of Paris in 1816, but by then the sugar boom was over and by the mid-19th century the Caribbean trade had dried up. The discovery of oil in South America brought renewed prosperity to the ABCs in the 1920s, when North American and European oil companies built vast refineries on Aruba and Curaçao. The capital of Curaçao, Willemstad, became the administrative capital of the Netherlands Antilles and seat of the Staten (parliament), which was granted autonomy within the Kingdom of the Netherlands in 1954.

The collapse of the local oil industry in the mid-1980s was a time of major upheaval for the ABCs and forced the islands to rely on tourism. Aruba's festering resentment at Curaçao's domination in the Staten hardened into demands for independence, and the island was granted autonomy in 1986. When the Netherlands Antilles was dissolved in 2010, Sint Maarten and Curaçao devolved into constituent states within the Kingdom of the Netherlands (similar to Aruba). Bonaire, Saba, and Sint Eustatius chose to retain closer political ties and became "special municipalities."

NOT TO BE MISSED:

Aruba is now the tourism leader in the Dutch Leewards. Its hotel-lined shores, casinos, and busy cruise-ship terminal are the envy of the Curaçaoans, whose tourist industry is taking longer to develop. Quiet Bonaire has built up a reputation as one of the world's top diving destinations. Meanwhile, 500 miles (800 km) to the north, tourism is also the mainstay of the Dutch Windward Islands. Sint Maarten flourishes as a duty-free enclave in the old Dutch West India Company tradition. Sint Eustatius and Saba maintain a more low-key approach. With few beaches, their rustic charm endears them to visitors in search of peace and quiet. ■

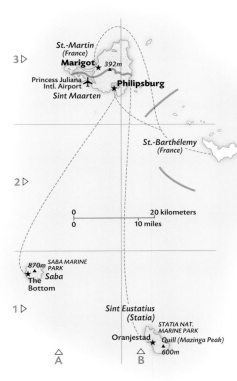

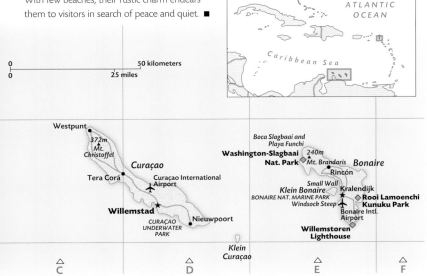

Sint Maarten/St.-Martin

Sint Maarten/St.-Martin, one of the smaller islands in the region at just 37 square miles (96 sq km), celebrated 350 years of dual nationality in 1998. The French occupy the slightly larger northern portion. Although there are no border controls between the two sides of the island, local people are proud of their separate identities. This is particularly noticeable in French St.-Martin, which cultivates a distinctive Gallic air.

Fort Louis overlooks Marigot's harbor on the French side of the island.

Philipsburg

🅰 175 A3, 177 C1

Visitor Information

✉ Wathey Sq.
    cruise facility
    & Captain
    Hodge Wharf

☎ 721 542 2337

st-martin.org

According to local legend, the division of the island was settled by a Frenchman and a Dutchman who set out to walk around the island in opposite directions, the former armed with a bottle of brandy, the latter with a bottle of gin. The Frenchman, refreshed by brandy, fared better and when the dividing line was drawn up, the French had secured a territory of 21 square miles (54 sq km), the Dutch only 16 square miles (41 sq km).

In spite of its diminutive proportions, Sint Maarten/St.-Martin attracts more than a million visitors a year. The Dutch capital of Philipsburg is the major gateway. This top Caribbean cruise-ship destination and duty-free port is well stocked with shopping bargains. The island is also famed for its beautiful beaches, which encircle the steep, scrub-covered hinterland. Most of the development is on the west coast between Philipsburg and the French capital, Marigot (St.-Martin), where hotels and time-share apartments jostle for space around the Simson Baai Lagoon. You can travel between the two island capitals on minibuses.

Philipsburg

Squeezed onto a narrow sandbar between Grand Bay and the landlocked expanses of Great Salt Pond, Philipsburg unfurls along four long, parallel streets linked by alleys known as *steeges*. The heart of town is **de Ruyterplein,** or Wathey Square, where day-trippers arrive by boat from the cruise ships anchored in the bay. At the top of the square is the restored 19th-century **courthouse,** which has a carved pineapple topknot. To either side of this, Front Street stretches off in a rich seam of duty-free shops, boutiques, and galleries. Follow the narrow steege down the right-hand side of the courthouse to a street market offering T-shirts and Haitian carvings.

Back on Front Street, head east and look for the entrance to the **Sint Maarten Museum** on an unnamed steege. Laid out on the second floor, the tiny museum is a mine of local information. Geological displays include a relief map illustrating how the island was once linked to neighboring St.-Barthélemy (St. Barts) and Anguilla. Check out the colonial artifacts, old musket balls, and other relics salvaged from the 1801 wreck of the frigate H.M.S. *Proselyte.*

Beyond the museum the steege ends at the sandy bayfront, a short walk from **Bobby's Marina,** with its popular restaurants, daily ferries to Marigot, and boat trips to St. Barts and Saba. Minibuses depart for the French capital of Marigot from Back Street (one block behind Front Street).

Around Sint Maarten

The only sightseeing attraction on the Dutch side is **Sint Maarten Park,** a family-friendly

Sint Maarten Museum

- ✉ 7 Front St.
- ☎ 721 542 4917
- 🕐 Closed Sat.–Sun.

museumsintmaarten .org

Sint Maarten Park

- 🗺 177 C2
- ✉ Arch Rd., Madame Estate
- ☎ 721 543 2030
- 💲 $$$

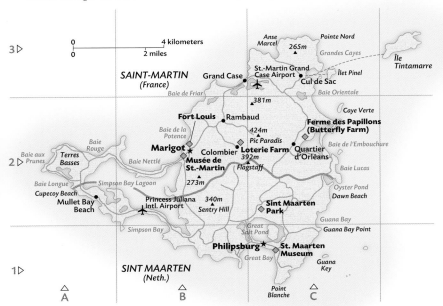

COURTHOUSE

Philipsburg's 19th-century courthouse

Marigot

⬛ 177 B2

Visitor Information

✉ Rte. de Sandy Ground

☎ 590 87 57 21

st-martin.org

zoological garden on the far side of Great Salt Pond. Caribbean birds are displayed in walk-through aviaries, and there's a small but interesting selection of South American reptiles and mammals such as capybaras.

Beyond Philipsburg, Sint Maarten's chief lure is the beach. On the south side is **Simson Bay Beach,** which has good swimming and windsurfing, although it does lie in the flight path for Princess

Juliana Airport. Head northwest along the coast for **Mullet Bay Beach,** which has water-sports concessions. For something quieter, try **Cupecoy Beach,** which is backed by low cliffs; nude bathing is permitted at the northern end. Heading east from Philipsburg, just before the border with St.-Martin, a track leads right off the main road for lovely **Dawn Beach,** a fine place to spend the day sunning, snorkeling, and lunching at a local restaurant.

Farther afield, a day trip to the ultra-chic neighboring island of St. Barts (see pp. 244–246) is a favorite pastime with visitors ready for a change of scene. A day-return boat service *(Tues.–Sat.)* makes the 45-minute crossing from Pelican Marina in Philipsburg *(tel 721 544 2640),* or you can travel independently by water taxi.

Marigot

The unmistakably French capital of St.-Martin appears to have been plucked straight from the Côte d'Azur and grafted onto a Caribbean island. This is café-and-croissant country, where the sidewalk terraces blossom with bright umbrellas. The town center is

NEED TO KNOW

Port Logistics: Philipsburg

The **A.C. Wathey** cruise facility lies a 20-minute walk or short water taxi ride from the downtown waterfront and information kiosk at Wathey Square. Taxis are readily available, and popular destinations and tours are displayed with prices on boards. Renting a car is an option for exploring the tiny island

and its beaches, but allow plenty of time for the return journey as swing bridges can cause long traffic delays.

Philipsburg Highlights

• Marigot: 3 hours
• Sint Maarten Museum: 1 hour
• Loterie Farm: half day
• Ferme des Papillons: 3 hours

laid out between the twin poles of the waterfront and **Marina Port La Royale.** A craft market lines the waterfront, and the old warehouses along the boulevard de France now serve as restaurants and cafés.

The ruins of 18th-century **Fort Louis** survey the scene from the heights above the harbor, where the frequent daily ferry service to Anguilla (*tel 264 497 2231*) and boat trips to St. Barts (*tel 0590 87 10 68*) depart from the pier.

A grid of shopping streets leads back to rue de Hollande and the minibus pickup/drop-off points for Philipsburg and Grand Case. To the west are the yacht-filled slips of the marina, edged by a collection of cafés and boutiques.

The exemplary **Musée de Saint-Martin** is well worth seeking out for its Amerindian section and exhibits detailing island history, geology, and marine life.

Around St.-Martin

The French side offers a further range of fine beaches (and topless bathing), starting with the alluring mile-long (1.6 km) expanse of **Baie Longue** on the southern tip of the Simson Baai Lagoon peninsula. Around the corner is **Baie aux Prunes,** popular with surfers and snorkelers; **Baie Rouge,** where beachgoers can rent sun loungers and umbrellas or swim around the point to a secluded cove; and hotel-lined **Baie Nettlé,** which is good for water sports.

North of Marigot is **Grand Case,** its one pretty, sandy street lined with some of the island's best restaurants. Boats bob at anchor farther east in the harbor fronting **Anse Marcel,** which has safe swimming for children and water-sports concessions. Off the east coast are glorious bayside beaches on **Îlet Pinel,** accessible by ferry from Cul de Sac, and undeveloped **Île Tintamarre.** On the mainland is **Baie Orientale,** with fine restaurants and shops.

Located in the lee of **Pic Paradis**—at 1,390 feet (424 m) the island's highest peak—**Loterie Farm** is a secluded private forest reserve. Old mountainside slave trails have been restored for hikers. There's also a range of treetop zip line adventures and the Ti-Tarzan obstacle challenge for little kids; a beautiful spring-fed pool/bar area with cabanas for rental; plus a tempting café and restaurant. Another detour leads to the **Ferme des Papillons** (Butterfly Farm) at Baie de l'Embouchure. Hundreds of butterflies flutter about the gardens and miniature waterfalls inside a huge climate-controlled sphere. It's best to arrive early in the day when the chrysalises hatch. ∎

Musée de Saint-Martin
- 177 B2
- 7 rue Fichot
- 0690 56 78 92
- Closed Sat.–Sun.
- $

museesaintmartin
.e-monsite.com

Loterie Farm
- 177 B2
- Colombier
- 590 87 86 16
- Closed Mon.
- $$$$$. Guides available—arrange 24 hours in advance

loteriefarm.com

Ferme des Papillons
- 177 C2
- Rte. du Galion
- 590 87 31 21
- $$$

thebutterflyfarm
.com

Sint Eustatius

A sleepy Caribbean backwater some 35 miles (56 km) south of Sint Maarten, Sint Eustatius is the undeveloped Rip van Winkle of the Dutch Windwards, dozing quietly in the lee of its imposing volcanic cone, the Quill. Better known as Statia (pronounced STAY-sha), the island attracts a handful of curious visitors, day-trippers from Sint Maarten, and a motley crew of American and European expatriates who revel in the absence of chic resorts, shopping malls, discos, and other manifestations of mass tourism.

Quill/Boven National Park became the Netherlands Antilles' first national park in 1998.

There are no decent beaches on Sint Eustatius, but therein lies the island's quirky charm. Instead, Statia's glittering past looms large from the history books, out of all proportion to its modest physical dimensions. The island is just 2 miles (3 km) wide and only 5 miles (8 km) long from its hilly northern tip through the low central plain to the southern slopes of the Quill. The 3,000 islanders live in the capital, Oranjestad, on the central west coast.

Savvy traders from the Dutch West India Company set up shop in Oranjestad in 1636 and developed the port into such a phenomenally successful mercantile center and slave market that Statia was nicknamed the "Golden Rock." Merchant vessels flying every conceivable national flag crowded the harbor, and as business expanded, land was reclaimed to build additional warehouses. On November 16, 1776, the cannon of Fort Oranje fired an 11-gun salute in reply to the merchant ship *Andrew Doria,* an American colonial brig flying the Stars and Stripes, and unwittingly Holland became the first nation to

INSIDER TIP:

If heading out to hike the Quill, be sure to wear layers. The crater's volcanic interior can be steamy, especially in contrast with the cool of the mount's summit.

—LARRY PORGES
National Geographic Books author

recognize the United States of America. This act earned the tiny island the sobriquet "America's Childhood Friend." In 1781, in retaliation, a British naval expedition under Adm. George Brydges Rodney (1718–1792) descended on Statia, taking possession of all the ships and goods in the port.

Statia never recovered, and her beachless shores have hampered the tourist industry. Today the island is quietly developing a reputation as the new Saba for attracting divers in search of pristine dive sites. With good walks around the Quill (Mazinga Peak) and incredibly friendly local people, the island makes an interesting offbeat escape for visitors with an open mind, and a no-frills, no-problem attitude.

Oranjestad

A small cliff separates the villagelike island capital into two distinctive parts. Hurricanes and Admiral Rodney's handiwork have all but destroyed the Lower Town around the harbor, so everybody lives in

the **Upper Town,** perched on the cliff top guarded by 17th-century **Fort Oranje.** The **St. Eustatius Historical Foundation Museum** is housed in a restored 18th-century brick home occupied by Rodney during his stay. Here pre-Columbian artifacts, blue glass trading beads used during the slave era,

A Jewish Heritage

In the 17th century, in an effort to improve the economies of their Caribbean holdings, the Dutch began offering grants to European Jews to encourage immigration to Sint Eustatius. Spanish, Portuguese, and eastern European Jews accepted the offer, and Jewish communities grew and became an integral part of Statia's mercantile success for the next century. When the British attacked Statia in the 18th century, the Jews were expelled. As the ruins of Honen Dalim Synagogue attest, the island's Jewish community never recovered. Today the synagogue is being rebuilt as a testament to the Jews' contributions to Sint Eustatius.

and porcelain from the Nanking cargo salvaged from the *South China Sea,* which foundered in 1752 en route to Statia, can be seen alongside rooms furnished in colonial style.

The town has several historic ruins, including the **Honen Dalim Synagogue,** the second oldest temple in the Western Hemisphere, dating from 1742 (see sidebar this page). The building fell into disrepair after Rodney took the Jewish community's money and then deported its inhabitants.

Sint Eustatius

🅰 175 B1

Visitor Information

✉ Fort Oranjestraat

☎ 599 318 2433

statiatourism.com

St. Eustatius Historical Foundation Museum

✉ Wilhelminaweg, Oranjestad

☎ 599 318 2288

🕐 Closed Sat.–Sun.

💲 $$

steustatiushistory .org

Around the Island

A trek up **Mazinga Peak** (the Quill) is a must during any visit to Sint Eustatius. Permits *($$)* and guides are available through the STENAPA Office at Gallows Bay *(tel 599 318 288, statiapark .org)*. Several routes go to the lip of the crater; the most direct follows a moderately steep path and takes about 45 minutes. Beneath the Quill's high point (1,968 feet/ 600 m), the 550-foot-deep (168 m) crater is carpeted with lush vegetation. On the southwest coast are the ruins of **Fort de Windt,** which afford views across to St. Kitts. Around to the southeast, the **Miriam C. Schmidt Botanical Garden** *(tel 599 318 2884)* flourishes on the slopes of the Quill. Volunteers have created a series of tranquil areas showcasing native plant species and rarities, a local-style kitchen garden, a bird observation trail, and the Lookout Garden with magnificent views of St. Kitts across the channel, where migrating humpback whales may be seen in winter *(Jan.–March)*.

Continuing on up the Quill's eastern flanks, the **Lynch Plantation Museum** *(tel 599 318 2338, by appt. only)* makes an intriguing detour. Here, the Berkel family's collections of period furnishings, tools, domestic utensils, and personal items offer a unique through-the-keyhole glimpse of life on Statia almost a century ago.

Beaches & Diving

Statia does have a couple of beaches, but with grayish volcanic sand. Close to the Lower Town is **Oranje Beach,** popular with locals, and **Crooks Castle** is farther south. Because of dangerous currents, swimming is not safe in the bays on the Atlantic coast. Statia's incredible underwater landscape— even more dramatic than its textbook-perfect volcano—is protected by **Statia National Marine Park** *(statiapark.org)*. There are 30-plus sites ranging from coral reefs and canyons to the ***Supermarket*** wreck site, where rare flying fish occasionally pay a flying visit. The site is composed of two shipwrecks around a section of reef. The easily accessed **City Wall** site, just outside the harbor, was the original sea wall for the old Lower Town warehouse district. ■

The view from Fort de Windt

Saba

From a distance, tiny Saba (pronounced SAY-ba) rises out of the sea like a witch's hat from its 5-square-mile (13 sq km) base. On closer inspection, the dramatic outline of Mount Scenery (2,909 feet/870 m) doesn't stand alone but among a supporting cast of lesser peaks and ridges that make up the impressively rugged, green interior. The cliffs that edge the island drop away beneath the waves into an underwater world no less fantastically sheer and rated one of the top dive destinations in the Caribbean.

The famous stairs leading down to Saba's Ladder Bay

Life on Saba moves at a sedate pace. The 1,800 Sabans live in attractive villages where little white cottages with uniform red roofs perch precariously one above the other on steep hillsides. The capital of the island is the town of The Bottom, but most travelers head up the twisting route known simply as The Road (see sidebar p. 185) to visit the steeply canted, upland village of Windwardside.

Columbus sighted Saba in 1493, but it took a shipwreck to land the first Europeans on the island more than a century later. Dutch colonists from Sint Eustatius founded the first permanent settlement in the 1640s. In 1665 the infamous Welsh pirate Henry Morgan (1635–1688) captured Saba and banished all non-English speakers during his short stay. Thereafter the almost impregnable island changed hands by treaty

Saba

 175 A1

Visitor Information

✉ Windwardside

☎ 599 416 2231

sabatourism.com

rather than invasion, supported a few small sugar plantations, and lived very quietly.

Around the Island

Saba's capital, **The Bottom,** lies in a sloping valley and probably takes its name from the Dutch word *botte* (bowl). Among the traditional gingerbread-fringed clapboard homes are small businesses, shops, and bars.

To the south for about a mile (1.6 km), The Road wriggles steeply down to **Fort Bay,** the main port. A leg-trembling flight of 500-plus steps descends to the harbor on **Ladder Bay.** In pre-Road days this was the only route on and off the island, and everything from a box of nails to a tin bathtub had to be carried up on somebody's back.

Tucked into the lee of Mount Scenery, with fine views down to the coast, **Windwardside** clings tenaciously to the slopes, its neat

INSIDER TIP:

Seek out the historic path to an old pirate hideout at Mary's Point, off Well's Bay Road north of The Bottom. The village ruins take you back to the time of the buccaneers.

—KAI WULF

Parks manager, Saba Conservation Foundation

cottages linked by a cat's cradle of narrow alleys. Two historic Saban cottages have been transformed into appealing small museums. The **Harry L. Johnson Museum** and the **Dutch Museum Saba** (*museum-saba.com*) both illustrate a slice of local domestic and seafaring history through period furnishings, paintings, antique china, and needlework.

EXPERIENCE: Dive Saba Marine Park

Established in 1987 to protect Saba's pristine marine environment, **Saba Marine Park** (*The Bottom, tel 599 416 3295, sabapark.org/marine_park*) rings the small island. The marine park is divided into commercial and recreational zones: Most of the dive sites are marked by permanent buoys off the west coast.

The astonishing diversity of the park's underwater landscapes is matched by vibrant marine life. Excellent visibility ranges upward from 125 feet (38 m) in winter. Varied, challenging diving is ensured by elkhorn forests; giant boulders encrusted with sponges; soft and hard corals; submerged pinnacles that attract

big groupers, jacks, and rays; and walls dropping to depths of 1,000 feet (305 m) within half a mile (800 m) of the shore. Green and hawksbill turtles feed in the protected waters.

The park is partially funded by the small fee (\$\$) paid for each dive. Further information about dives can be obtained from Saba Marine Park or by contacting local dive operators such as the **Saba Deep Dive Center** (*tel 599 416 3347 or 866 416 3347 from U.S., sabadeep.com, \$\$\$\$\$*); **Saba Divers** (*tel 599 416 2740, sabadivers.com, \$\$\$\$\$*); and **Sea Saba Advanced Dive Center** (*tel 599 416 2246, seasaba.com, \$\$\$\$\$*).

A small cluster of homes on the mountain slope above Windwardside

Although diving is Saba's chief draw, hiking **Mount Scenery** is an excellent land-based diversion. The 1,064-step path to the summit passes through secondary rain forest to a gnarled and stunted world of elfin woodland carpeted with mosses and ferns and is often wreathed in mist. The **Saba Trail Shop** *(tel 599 416 2630, sabapark .org)* in Windwardside has details of other trails and local guide services.

From Windwardside, The Road continues its serpentine way for just under a mile (1.6 km) to the settlement of **Hell's Gate** and on to the airport at Flat Point. From Flat Point, hike the steep crags down from the breathtaking heights of the forest to the tide pools below. In calm seas the pools fill with still, crystal clear water and ocean wildlife—sea urchins, kaleidoscopic-colored fish, and abundant sea flora. ∎

The Road

A minor miracle of engineering and a monument to Saban stubbornness, The Road traverses Saba from Fort Bay in the southwest to Flat Point in the northeast. When the Sabans first investigated the possibility of a road to augment the old footpaths and donkey tracks in the 1930s, Dutch civil engineers said it couldn't be done. Josephus Hassell's response was to sign up for a correspondence course in civil engineering, and utilizing his newly acquired knowledge, work began at Fort Bay in 1938. The Road reached The Bottom five years later, crept into Windwardside in 1951, and eventually arrived in Flat Point after carving a 19-mile (31 km) corkscrew passage across the island.

Curaçao

Curaçao has the greatest landmass of the Dutch Leewards group, anchored a short hop from the South American mainland. This historic trading center boasts diverse multicultural influences and the ethnic mix of the islanders is as beguiling as Curaçao's beaches and limpid blue waters. It seems fitting that the island should also be known for its vividly colored liqueurs.

A colonial-era government building in Willemstad

Curaçao

📍 175 C1–D1

Visitor Information

✉ Pietermaai 19, Willemstad

☎ 5999 434 8200

curacao.com

The chief Dutch possession in the Caribbean since the 17th century, Curaçao measures 38 miles (61 km) by 9 miles (14.5 km) and lies just 35 miles (56 km) off the coast of Venezuela. Curaçao's rocky shoreline, with its cliffs and coves, is indented with fingernail slivers of white-sand beach and is lapped by staggeringly blue waters. Inland, giant cactuses lord it over the rugged *cunucu,* a scrub-covered landscape that receives less than 23 inches (580 mm) of rain a year.

The Spanish landed on Curaçao in 1499 and dubbed it the Isla de los Gigantes ("island of giants") for the tall, seafaring Caquetio people there. These were soon shipped off to work in the gold mines of Hispaniola, and the ABCs were declared *islas inútiles* (useless islands). In 1634 the Dutch West India Company spotted the potential of Sint Annabaai, Curaçao's huge natural harbor, the largest in the region and one of the largest in the world. The company ejected a handful of Spanish settlers, fortified the harbor entrance, and constructed Willemstad within sturdy defensive walls.

Under the Dutch, Curaçao grew wealthy. Willemstad's

duty-free port handled goods from sugar to gold bullion; it also developed into the Caribbean's busiest slave market. A few plantations were established on the island but failed due to the arid climate and infertile soil. Their legacy is a collection of Dutch colonial *landhuizen* (plantation houses) in the rolling hinterland.

The Dutch didn't abolish slavery until 1863, and Curaçao idled along until 1918, when construction of the world's largest oil refinery refueled the island's prosperity. Workers poured in from around the Caribbean, the Americas, and beyond, creating the multiracial society that distinguishes the island and is perfectly illustrated by Papiamento, the colorful (and incomprehensible to

outsiders) local dialect (see sidebar p. 196). The current population of 145,000 is concentrated around Willemstad and the southwestern beaches, where Curaçao's rather belated tourism boom is focused. However, the unspoiled northern part of the island draws visitors to Christoffel National Park (see p. 190). This area is very quiet, with just a few small hotels, restaurants, and dive shops on the shore backed by acres of green gray cunucu backcountry.

EXPERIENCE: Taste Curaçao Cocktails

For some, the name Curaçao brings to mind the bottles of vivid blue, red, orange, and green liqueurs that lurk behind cocktail bars the world over. This is where they originate, courtesy of the bitter Laraha orange. The sun-dried peels of this inedible fruit, which was introduced by the Spanish, are distilled with water and sugar to form a clear liqueur that is then colored with flavorless additives. The **Senior Curaçao Liqueur Distillery** *(Elias R.A. Morena Blvd., Saliña, tel 5999 461 3526, closed Sat.–Sun.)* has a Willemstad showroom in the 19th-century **Landhuis Chobolobo.**

EXPERIENCE: Go Wild in the Wilderness

Getting out and about in the *cunucu* is a must, and several adventure tour operators offer hiking, mountain biking, and ATV experiences. To experience Christoffel National Park, **Yellow Jeep Safaris** *(tel 5999 462 6262, jeep-safaris.com, $$$$$)* takes you off the beaten path to explore the rugged north coast and the heart of the park with a stop at Brua Cave, a former refuge for escaped slaves. Guided mountain bike excursions are led by **WannaBike Curaçao** *(tel 5999 527 3720, wannabike.com, $$$$$)*. Cyclists need to be reasonably fit; bikes, helmets, and water bottles are provided. Pilot your own ATV

for a guided scramble around the sights and into the backcountry with **Eric's ATV Adventures** *(tel 5999 461 0071, curacao -atv.com, $$$$$)*. Or how about an ostrich safari? North of Willemstad, off the road to Santa Catharina, Curaçao's very own **Ostrich Farm** *(Groot St. Joris, tel 5999 747 2777, curacaoostrichfarm.com, $$$$)* invites visitors to get up close and personal with African ostriches. After a guided driving tour, there are opportunities to weigh a giant ostrich egg, tuck into an ostrich burger at the Zambezi Restaurant, and even "ride" a full-grown ostrich for a memorable vacation snapshot.

Fortkerk Museum

🅰 187 C1
✉ Fort Amsterdam, Gouvernementsplein
☎ 5999 461 1139
🕐 Closed Sat.–Sun.
💲 $

fortchurchcuracao .com

Mikvé Israël-Emanuel Synagogue & Jewish Museum

✉ Hanchi Snoa 29
☎ 5999 461 1067
🕐 Closed Sat.–Sun.
💲 $$$

snoa.com

Maritime Museum

✉ Van der Brandhofstraat 7
☎ 5999 465 2327
🕐 Closed Sun.–Mon.
💲 $$

curacaomaritime.com

Willemstad

A little pocket of the Caribbean that will be forever Amsterdam, Willemstad's **Handelskade** waterfront is charming. Dutch gables and terra-cotta roof tiles adorn buildings painted pastel pink and pistachio, with a dash of citrus yellow here and curlicue white stucco plasterwork there. Though modern structures now outnumber historic buildings, the effect is still startlingly attractive and beloved of the scores of visitors who arrive by cruise ship to plunder the capital's duty-free stores and explore its beautifully preserved streets. Willemstad is, not surprisingly, a UNESCO World Heritage site.

The city is divided by the Sint Annabaai channel, which leads into Schottegat Harbor. On the west side is the **Otrabanda quarter,** where the cruise ships dock; to the east Handelskade fronts the central **Punda district,**

where the main shops and sights are found. One of the Punda's most popular attractions is the busy daily **Mercado Flotante** (Floating Market). Located around the corner from Handelskade, on the watery cul-de-sac of Waaigat, Venezuelan schooners line the **Sha Caprileskade** waterfront and goods spill out onto colorful market stalls arranged with fresh fruit and vegetables grown on the South American mainland.

A tour of historic Willemstad should begin on the waterfront along Handelskade at **Fort Amsterdam,** the former Dutch West India Company headquarters, now occupied by government offices. There's free access to the courtyard and the 1769 fort church, which houses the small **Fortkerk Museum,** with its displays of antique silverware and maps. The church once doubled as a sail loft, and its rainwater cisterns were built of the tiny yellow and red bricks—used in many

buildings around town—shipped from Holland as ballast.

Several years before Fortkerk was completed, Willemstad's Jewish community had begun to worship in the **Mikvé Israël-Emanuel Synagogue,** the oldest synagogue in continuous use in the Americas. Portuguese Jews arrived in Curaçao in the 1650s and founded the first synagogue in 1674; Mikvé Israël was dedicated in 1732. Located in the heart of the Punda, the synagogue occupies an attractive courtyard complex alongside a museum displaying religious artifacts and memorabilia.

The old Jewish residential district of **Scharloo,** across Waaigat, is slowly being restored. In a reclaimed 18th-century waterfront mansion, the **Maritime Museum** displays collections of model ships, maps, and miniatures and offers ferry tours of the harbor. **Scharlooweg,** one block behind the waterfront, is lined with some of Willemstad's best preserved 18th- to 19th-century town houses.

The Otrabanda district is reached by crossing the **Koningin Emmabrug** (Queen Emma Bridge) from Handelskade. The impressive swinging pontoon bridge was designed by U.S. consul Leonard B. Smith and installed in 1888. (A free ferry takes travelers across the river whenever the bridge is opened to allow ships through.) Otrabanda is home to the cruise-ship terminal and the **Riffort,** a 19th-century fort that guards one side of the harbor. Also here is the excellent **Museum**

Fresh produce for sale at the Punda's Mercado Flotante

Kurá Hulanda, part of a beautifully restored complex of Dutch colonial buildings, which houses one of the largest collections of African art and artifacts in the Caribbean. Exhibits range from art treasures of the West African empires to the re-created hold of a transatlantic slave ship.

One mile (1.6 km) north of the city center is the **Curaçao Museum,** located in a former seamen's hospital. The museum exhibits monumental colonial furniture, pre-Columbian relics, and works by local artists. ∎

Museum Kurá Hulanda

✉ Klipstraat 9
☎ 5999 434 7765
🕐 Closed Sun.
💲 $$$

kurahulanda.com

Curaçao Museum

🅰 187 C1
✉ Van Leeuwenhoekstraat
☎ 5999 462 3873
🕐 Closed Sun.–Mon.

thecuracaomuseum.com

NEED TO KNOW
Port Logistics: Willemstad

Be sure to catch the view of the Willemstad waterfront as you berth at Otrobanda: It's a 10-minute stroll into Handelskade, the central historic district. Taxis (with fixed rates to destinations around the island) and maps are available at the terminal.

Willemstad Highlights

• Downtown Willemstad: 2–3 hours
• Museum Kurá Hulanda : 2 hours
• Curaçao Sea Aquarium & Beach: half/full day
• Dive excursion: half/full day

Around Curaçao

A national park at the island's northern tip combines natural and colonial history in one hikable location. Fans of sea life can view it in tanks or from the beach at the Curaçao Sea Aquarium.

Christoffel National Park

🅰 187 B3

✉ Savonet

☎ 5999 864 0363

💲 $$$

christoffelpark.org

Curaçao Sea Aquarium

🅰 187 C1

☎ Bapor Kibra, SE of Willemstad

☎ 5999 461 6666

💲 $$$$$

curacao-sea-aquarium.com

Hato Caves

🅰 187 C2

✉ Rooseveltweg

☎ 5999 868 0379

💲 $$

Christoffel National Park

The 4,650-acre (1,880 ha) Christoffel National Park, in the north of the island, is composed of three former plantations on the slopes of **Mount Christoffel** (1,220 feet/372 m), the highest point in the Dutch Leeward Islands.

The park center provides information on island geology, flora, and fauna, and it is the starting point for a network of hiking and driving trails that strike off into the *cunucu* or down to the wave-lashed cliffs at **Playa Grandi.** There are fascinating guided walks daily *(call for reservations),* and special evening walks offer a chance to spot the rare Curaçaoan deer, a subspecies of the North American white-tailed deer introduced to the island in pre-Columbian times.

Guides can also be arranged for safari tours, private hikes, and bird-watching expeditions, and make time for a visit to the new **Landhuis Savonet Museum.**

Curaçao Sea Aquarium

A marine life showcase with family appeal, the Sea Aquarium offers outdoor lagoons for sea lions and sharks, tanks housing toothsome eels and tropical fish, touch tanks, and various shows. More unusual aspects are an underwater observatory anchored to the shore and the "open-water-system" that keeps the tanks and enclosures constantly refreshed with pumped seawater. A range of encounter activities includes shark feeding and the Dolphin Academy *(reservations required).*

The adjacent **Sea Aquarium Beach** is one of the island's best, providing access to the 12-mile-long (19 km) **Curaçao Underwater Park,** a magnet for snorkelers and divers.

Hato Caves

Curaçao's past and present almost collide at these 200,000-year-old caves near the airport. Hollowed beneath sea level and adorned with limestone stalactites and stalagmites, the caves were once visited by Caiqueto Indians and runaway slaves. Today long-nosed fruit bats roost here. ∎

Landhuizen

About 300 country estates had spread across the island's interior by the early 19th century. Most had a modest Dutch colonial *landhuis* (plantation house) for the owner's family. A handful have been restored and opened for visits including **Landhuis Brievengat, Landhuis Jan Kok,** and **Landhuis Kenepa. Landhuis Papaya,** which is painted bloodred (the rarer of the two traditional Curaçaoan color schemes), and **Landhuis Daniel** are on the Westpunt road outside Willemstad. The latter is now a bar-restaurant and a simple hotel with a good restaurant *(tel 5999 864 8400).*

Bonaire

Shaped like a distorted boomerang and lying 30 miles (48 km) east of Curaçao, Bonaire is a diver's paradise—and that's official, according to the legend adorning local car license plates. Along the sheltered leeward coast of the island and around the offshore islet of Klein (Little) Bonaire, more than 80 dive sites give access to some of the most spectacular and varied marine landscapes in the entire Caribbean.

Bonaire is a derivation of the Arawak word *bojnaj,* meaning "low country." During the 1700s, Dutch settlers introduced slaves to harvest the salt pans in the island's flat southern portion and raised cattle on the scrub-covered backcountry to supply the colony of Curaçao.

Activity on the island stuttered to an almost complete halt with the abolition of slavery in 1863, until Bonaire's salt industry was revived in the 1960s. The decade also saw the first divers venturing to the out-of-the-way island, and Bonaire's special brand of low-key, dive-oriented tourism was born. Although the news about Bonaire's spectacular underwater world is out, the island is still quiet and definitely casual. Nondivers can find fantastic snorkeling from walk-in sites directly off the shore, as well as hiking, mountain biking, horseback riding, and bird-watching.

The modest capital of Bonaire is **Kralendijk** ("coral dike"), a small town of yellow and gold Dutch Caribbean buildings, restaurants, and hotels facing the rounded outline of Klein Bonaire. From Kralendijk a road circles the southern portion of the island, passing the glittering white salt stacks awaiting shipment from the solar saltworks, which conceal flamingo

Snorkeling in Bonaire

nesting grounds at Pekelmeer. The **Willemstoren Lighthouse** overlooks the rocky tip of the island, and on the west coast a handful of abandoned **slave huts** pay silent witness to Bonaire's dark past. East of the capital there's an interesting detour to **Rooi Lamoenchi Kunuku Park** *(tel 599 717 8489, by appt. only, $$).* Call ahead for a personal tour of this restored plantation homestead and gardens set amid aloe vera fields and cactus-strewn *cunucu.* There is also an old dam where waterbirds such as herons, egrets, and ducks gather.

Northwest of Kralendijk is Bonaire's oldest settlement, the sleepy inland village of **Rincón,** on the road to the national park. A short distance away on the Atlantic

Bonaire

🄰 175 E1

Visitor Information

✉ Kaya Grandi 2, Kralendijk

☎ 599 717 8322

tourismbonaire.com
bonairehelpdesk.com

NOTE: Bonaire's natural resources are partially supported by tariffs levied on park visitors. All snorkelers and swimmers pay a Nature Fee *($$$),* which is valid for a year. Divers can pay a one-day Nature Fee *($$$)* or a full year's Nature Fee *($$$$$);* the latter includes admission to Washington-Slagbaai National Park. Fees can be paid at dive shops and park offices.

EXPERIENCE:
Get a Fish-Eye View

Photos are a great way to relive vacation high spots, but it's a lot harder if the most memorable experiences (and mind-blowing vistas) occur underwater. Cue Tim Peters of **Fish-Eye Photo** (*Kaya Gobernador N. Debrot 18A, tel 599 717 4571, fisheyephoto.com, $$$$$*), a studio photographer turned scuba instructor turned underwater photographer. He runs underwater photography courses in Bonaire Marine Park. Half- and one-day courses aimed at beginners, two- or three-day advanced courses, and PADI digital underwater photographer (DUP) tuition combine underwater practicalities with camera skills. Participants can use their own cameras (SLR or digital), or borrow equipment for free.

Washington-Slagbaai National Park

🅰 175 E1
☎ 599 717 8444
💲 $$$$$

washingtonpark bonaire.org

Bonaire Marine Park

🅰 175 E1
☎ 599 717 8444
💲 Non-dive $$$; dive $$$$$

bmp.org

coast, at **Boca Onima,** Caquetio Indians left their marks scribbled in red dye on cave walls.

To the north of Rincón, and covering the northwestern portion of the island, is **Washington-Slagbaai National Park.** This 13,500-acre (5,463 ha) tract of land occupying one-fifth of the island has operated as a wildlife preserve since the 1960s. It is crisscrossed by 4WD trails and hiking paths, one of which scales Mount Brandaris (784 feet/240 m). The park is home to most of Bonaire's 190 bird species, including parrots, hummingbirds, and a flamingo colony on the Goto-meer lagoon. Several snorkel and dive sites lie off the leeward coast, such as **Boca Slagbaai** (Slaughter Bay) and **Playa Funchi.** The park's beaches are protected sea turtle nesting sites.

The island is surrounded by **Bonaire Marine Park,** a rigorously safeguarded conservation zone covering around 700 acres (280 ha). Designated a marine preserve in 1971, the park rings the island and extends from the shore to the 200-foot-deep (60 m) contour through shallow, sloping terraces of fringe reefs to the drop-off. More than 80 species of corals have been identified, including elkhorn, staghorn, and leaf corals, and the reefs are patrolled by a dazzling array of electric blue tangs, angelfish, parrotfish, grunts, and sea horses. These delights are accessible to snorkelers, too. Simply locate one of the yellow stone dive markers and wade out. Top snorkeling sites include **Windsock Steep,** on the east coast; the beaches in Washington-Slagbaai National Park; and **Small Wall,** off the west coast and best accessed on a snorkel cruise. ∎

NEED TO KNOW
Port Logistics: Kralendijk

Tenders bring cruise passengers into downtown Kralendijk, close to the shops, restaurants, and marina for snorkel and dive cruise departures. Stop by the tourist office for a map. Water taxis nip across to the beach on Klein Bonaire (no facilities), or take a fixed rate taxi island tour.

Kralendijk Highlights

- Snorkel cruise, departing from the marina: half/full day
- Rooi Lamoenchi Kunuku Park (call ahead for personal tour appointment; see p. 191): 2–3 hours
- Washington-Slagbaai National Park: half/full day

Aruba

Fifteen miles (24 km) as the pelican flies off the coast of Venezuela, diminutive Aruba—just 20 miles by 6 miles (32 by 10 km)—has created the blueprint for successful tourism development in the region. The island's silky, blond beaches, top-notch hotels and casinos, water sports and activities programs, and five-star shopping and dining opportunities all add up to one of the Caribbean's hottest vacation destinations. *Bon bini*—or welcome, as they say around here!

Unwisely dismissed as an *isla inútil* (useless island) by its Spanish discoverers, Aruba was eventually used for ranching and developed something of a reputation for horse breeding. In 1824 gold was discovered, prompting a small-scale gold rush, but the mining became unprofitable and ceased altogether in 1914. Remains of the old mines and smelting works can be seen around Balashi and Bushiribana. Aloe vera plantations sprouted in the early 1900s, but oil refineries built in the mid-1920s made the island's fortunes, caused a population explosion, and gave Aruba one of the highest standards of living in the Caribbean region.

Arubans still live comfortably and the island experience is generally hassle-free. Visitors enjoy North American standards of service, and most islanders speak fluent English and Spanish as well as Papiamento (see sidebar p. 196). The islanders' Amerindian heritage is reflected in their looks, though there are now more than 40 nationalities bubbling within the Aruban melting pot.

Oranjestad

The island capital, Oranjestad was named in honor of the

A fishing boat off the coast of Aruba

Dutch ruling family, the House of Orange. The town is a mixture of old Dutch Caribbean buildings and modern pastiches that house shops and busy malls stretching back from the immaculate mile-long (1.6 km) waterfront boulevard. The oldest building on the island is **Fort Zoutman,** constructed on the waterfront in 1796. Now a short distance inland due to land reclamation, it still affords a good view over the yacht harbor. The Willem III Tower was added to the fort in 1868, doubling as a lighthouse and the island's first public clock. A small museum displays modest

Aruba
🗺 174 A2–B2
Visitor Information
✉ L.G. Smith Blvd. 172, Eagle Beach
☎ 297 582 3777 or 1800 TO ARUBA
aruba.com

Fort Zoutman Historical Museum
🗺 194 A2
✉ Zoutmanstraat 6, Oranjestad
☎ 297 582 6099
🕐 Closed Sat.–Sun.
💲 $$

National Archaeological Museum Aruba

✉ Schlepstraat 42, Oranjestad

☎ 297 582 8979

🕐 Closed Mon.

namaruba.org

Balashi Brewery

✉ L.G. Smith Blvd. & Hwy. 4 (south), Barcadera

☎ 297 592 2544

🕐 Closed Sat.–Sun.

💲 $$$

collections of Spanish and Dutch Colonial artifacts. Every Tuesday evening year-round, the **Bon Bini Festival,** an entertaining folkloric show featuring local crafts, food stalls, music, and dancing, takes place in the fort precincts.

Set several blocks back from the waterfront, the **National Archaeological Museum Aruba** is well worth seeking out for its surroundings alone. Amerindian tools, pottery, and 2,000-year-old skeletons unearthed from around the island are among the treasures displayed in the old Ecury Complex, a former family compound comprising a restored 1920s mansion and contemporary wing grafted onto an original 1870s *cunucu* home. And if all this culture is working up a thirst, the **Balashi Brewery,** purveyors of fine local beer, offer factory tours followed by a tasting and a beer garden serving food. ∎

NEED TO KNOW

Port Logistics: Oranjestad

The cruise facility is just a few minutes' walk from Oranjestad's main shopping and dining district, also served by a free downtown trolley service. Taxis are non-metered but rates are clearly posted (around $10–15 for the 10- to 15-minute ride to Eagle or Palm Beach).

Oranjestad Highlights

• Oranjestad walking tour and shopping: 2–3 hours

• Lazing on Eagle Beach

• Water sports on Palm Beach: half day

• Snorkel tour from Renaissance Marina: half day

• 4WD trip to Mount Jamanota: half day

Around Aruba

Beaches at the north and south ends of Aruba provide plenty of sandy options for visitors. Desertlike scenery and ancient rock paintings mark the island's interior.

The Hooiberg mountain dominates Aruba's landscape; its name translates to "haystack."

Aruba's Beaches

Northwest of Oranjestad, Aruba's twin tourist poles are the magnificent sandy sweeps of **Eagle Beach** (the "low-rise strip") and **Palm Beach** (the "high-rise strip"). Both are busy and hotel-lined, with watersports concessions. Behind Palm Beach, the gardens of **Butterfly Farm** provide visitors with a spectacular natural kaleidoscope of floral and winged beauty.

Two smaller, less crowded beaches lie farther to the north—**Malmok Beach** is a windsurfers' favorite. **Arashi Beach** is close by the landmark California Lighthouse, which offers the traveler great views and handy café.

There's another clutch of beaches at the southeastern end of the island beyond Sint Nicolaas, Aruba's largest town. **Grapefield Beach** is a quiet spot, but the sea is rougher here and there are no facilities. **Baby Beach** is aptly named for its calm, shallow bay, and swimmers will enjoy **Rodger's Beach** despite the presence of the refinery in the background. Around the tip of the island are the breezy strands of **Bachelor's Beach** and **Boca Grandi,** while an adventurous 4WD ride through Arikok National Park is rewarded by towering sand dunes, rocky cliffs, and thundering seas at **Boca Prins,** near the Fontein Cave.

Aruba's Beaches
🗺 194

Butterfly Farm
✉ J. Irausquin Blvd. (opposite Divi Resort)
☎ 297 586 3656
💲 $$$$
thebutterflyfarm .com

Alto Vista Chapel
▲ 194 B3

Arikok National Park
▲ 194 B2
Visitor Information
☎ 297 585 1234
arubanationalpark
.org

Ayo
▲ 194 B2

Aruba Ostrich Farm
▲ 194 B2
✉ Matividiri 57, Paradera
☎ 297 585 9630
$ $$$
arubaostrichfarm
.com

Hooiberg
▲ 194 B2

Alto Vista Chapel

On the remote northwest coast, this tiny mustard-colored chapel was built on the site of an 18th-century Spanish chapel, hedged by cactuses and sea.

Arikok National Park

A short drive but light years away from Aruba's urbanized west coast beach strip, this sprawling park occupies around 20 percent of the island's interior and east coast. Here cactus-studded hillsides, twisted *divi-divi* trees, great swords of aloe, limestone plateaus, sand dunes, and vast boulders illustrate Aruban nature in the raw. Some 20 miles (32 km) of walking trails wind across the dusty terrain to sites such as **Cunucu Arikok,** a century-old adobe farmhouse. Free, ranger-led tours depart from the visitor center, or adventurous hikers can explore several caves set in the eastern corner of the park, including the **Fontein Cave,** decorated with ancient rock paintings. Other trails scale the relative heights of Jamanota (615 feet/188 m),

Aruba's highest point, and access the beaches on the east coast *(swimming not advisable).*

Ayo Rock Formations

Inland, around the village of **Ayo,** giant boulders litter the dusty *cunucu,* and there are Amerindian rock paintings in nearby caves. These smooth boulders, and those at **Casibari,** are a geological anomaly unrelated to the rest of the island's natural habitat.

Aruba Ostrich Farm

The world's heaviest bird has a brain the size of a walnut and can outrun a leopard, but mostly it just wants to eat tidbits from your hand. A favorite with kids, this tour bus stalwart delivers everything you ever wanted to know about ostriches and more.

The Hooiberg

The Hooiberg (548 feet/167 m) is a local landmark located at the center of the island. Steps lead to the hill's top, which does look a bit like its Dutch name suggests—a haystack. The view stretches from coast to coast. ■

Papiamento

The mother tongue of the Dutch Leewards, Papiamento (from the Spanish *papia,* meaning "talk" or "babble") emerged from the pidgin speech of early colonists and their African slaves. Dutch merchants, Portuguese Jews, Spanish missionaries, South American traders, and local Indians all added to the vocabulary. The language is now spoken throughout the region, with slight island variations, and taught in schools. Islanders will be hugely entertained if you try a few words.

Welcome	*Bon bini*
Good morning	*Bon dia*
Good afternoon	*Bon tardi*
Good evening	*Bon nochi*
How are you?	*Con ta bai?*
I am fine	*Mi ta bon*
Goodbye	*Aye*
Thank you very much	*Masha danki*
Beautiful	*Bunita*
Very good	*Hopi bon*

Between the Virgin Islands and the Windwards, six isles renowned for their laid-back charm

Leeward Islands

A sandy stretch of Friars Bay, St. Kitts

Leeward Islands

The six English-speaking Leeward Islands head up the chain of the Lesser Antilles, mingling with the Dutch Windward Islands and the French possessions of St.-Martin and St.-Barthélemy (St. Barts). Antigua is the main gateway to this corner of the Caribbean, and it has been since the British established their chief Caribbean naval base here in the 18th century. Even now, the British influence lingers on throughout the region.

The main European influence on the Leeward Islands might be British, but indigenous Caribbean culture is here, too, in the exuberant local carnivals, reggae, rasta, and the studied art of relaxation. There are beaches galore, water sports, and hiking, plus accommodations ranging from family-friendly resorts to state-of-the-art spas to gorgeous plantation hotel retreats.

England's first successful Caribbean colony was St. Kitts, settled in 1623. Nevis followed in 1628, and a decade later Antigua and Montserrat were added to a growing portfolio of Caribbean possessions. At first, English and French settlers agreed to share St. Kitts, banding together to rid the island of inhospitable Carib people. Once the Carib were defeated, the good neighbors soon fell out. And so began the battle for control of the eastern Caribbean islands, which would continue into the 19th century and cause the demise of the sugar industry.

While Antigua was systematically stripped of its native forest to make way for sugar plantations—and settlers did their best to plant cane wherever the topography allowed on St. Kitts, Nevis, and Montserrat—barren, low-lying Anguilla became a nest of pirates and smugglers. Slaves brought to the island by prospective planters were soon turned loose to scratch a living from the thin, sandy soil; they developed a local reputation for carpentry and boatbuilding. This early self-reliance fostered the Anguillans' fiercely independent spirit, typified by the bizarre circumstances of the Anguillan "revolution" (actually a reactionary desire to remain British and avoid independence as a satellite of St. Kitts) in the late 1960s.

> ## NOT TO BE MISSED:
>
> **Historic Nelson's Dockyard, Antigua 205–206**
>
> **Bird-watching at Barbuda's Frigate Bird Sanctuary 211**
>
> **Taking to the water at Shoal Bay, Anguilla 213–214**
>
> **The outlook from Brimstone Hill Fortress, St. Kitts 219**
>
> **The panoramic views of an active volcano at the Montserrat Volcano Observatory 226**

Slavery was abolished throughout the British Caribbean in 1834, although a term of forced "apprenticeship" legally bound former slaves to their masters for a further period of years. In the end European sugar beets undermined the Caribbean trade to emancipate the slaves for good in the late 1830s. The islands sank into an impoverished backwater status, administered under the presidency of the Leeward Islands until 1967, when associated statehood brought a degree of autonomy. The twin-island nation of Antigua and Barbuda achieved independence in 1981, followed by St. Kitts and Nevis in 1983. Anguilla and Montserrat elected to remain British crown colonies.

Sugar continued to be grown in Antigua until the 1970s and still provides a modest income for St. Kitts, but for more than a century the Leeward Islands' precarious economies had been almost entirely dependent on remittances—money sent by islanders working overseas. In the last 70 years tourism has gradually injected new life into the region, and the top beach islands of Antigua and Anguilla, in particular, have seen considerable hotel development.

Although the Leewards share a common background, each island enjoys its own identity. For the ultimate laid-back Caribbean beach vacation, it would be hard to beat Anguilla, which focuses all the attention on its fabulous white-sand strands and superluxurious resorts. Very quiet and relatively undiscovered, Barbuda boasts a selection of delectable and often deserted beaches, where the only crowds are propelled by fins and inhabit magical coral reefs.

Antigua is altogether a more lively choice. In addition to claiming a beach for every day of the year (a wild but forgivable exaggeration), the island's historical sites make for interesting excursions, and friendly pubs provide live reggae and impromptu jump-ups at night. Lush St. Kitts and tiny Nevis combine colonial history with romantic plantation retreats and some fine upland hiking and riding country. St. Kitt's is definitely angling to expand its tourism infrastructure in the near future. Meanwhile, pint-size and once lush and lovely Montserrat suffered a major setback to its quietly developing nature-tourism industry when the Soufrière Hills volcano erupted in 1995. However, the enterprising islanders have reopened for business and now welcome volcano-watching visitors. ■

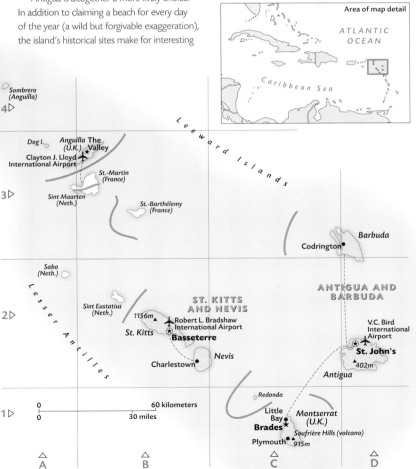

Antigua

At 108 square miles (280 sq km), Antigua (pronounced An-TEE-gah) is the largest of the Leeward Islands. Its irregular coastline, resembling a ragged Rorschach inkblot, incorporates hundreds of scalloped inlets and bays. The locals boast there are 365 beaches to choose from, many of them secluded coves backed by sea grape trees and accessible only by boat.

The harbor view from Antigua's Shirley Heights

Antigua

🗺 199 D2

Visitor Information

✉ ABC Financial Centre, High St., St. John's

☎ 268 562 7600

antigua-barbuda.org

visitantiguabarbuda .com

The interior of the island is rolling and dry. The lush carpet of sugarcane has disappeared and has been replaced by yellow-gray scrubland dotted with the shells of abandoned windmills. Small country villages provide brief bursts of color and greenery, painted wooden cottages and modern villas with flower gardens straggle along the roadside, and tethered goats and cattle graze in the dust. Antigua's coastal heights are topped with the remains of British ramparts; the most interesting is Shirley Heights (see sidebar p. 204), in Nelson's Dockyard National Park, overlooking the confines of English Harbour.

The first human traces on Antigua date back to the Stone Age Ciboney people, who migrated from South America to settle the

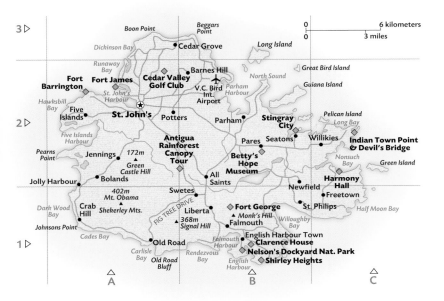

island around 3000 B.C. Peaceable Arawak arrived on the scene about A.D. 100, and raiding parties of Windward Island Carib were moving up the island chain by the time Columbus sighted the island on his second voyage in 1493. He named it Santa Maria de la Antigua after a miraculous statue of the Virgin in Seville Cathedral. The Spanish and French showed little interest in the island, discouraged by its shortage of freshwater, but English colonists from St. Kitts established a base in 1632. Sugar was introduced in the 1650s, and by the height of the 18th-century plantation era, Antigua had more than 200 cane-crushing windmills, with African slaves forming 93 percent of the population.

Antigua's protected harbors (an important consideration in the Caribbean hurricane belt) and strategic position at the apex of a rough triangle between the major-league sugar colonies of Barbados and Jamaica made the island a natural choice for Britain's chief naval and military base in the Leewards. Fortresses sprang up along the coast, with the main defenses concentrated in the south around English and Falmouth Harbours. Britain's enemies gave the whole island a wide berth.

After British emancipation of the slaves in 1834, Antigua's fate mirrored that of other colonial possessions. The dockyard was closed, many plantations failed, and the islanders slipped into an unremitting pattern of subsistence agriculture. They were consequently largely ignored by Britain.

Appalling working conditions inspired the first organized labor movement in 1939. It gained strength during World War II, which heralded an influx of U.S.

servicemen sent to man military bases on the island. The postwar Labour Party, under Vere C. Bird, led Antigua and the sister island of Barbuda to self-governing associated statehood in 1967 and full independence in 1981.

Antigua and Barbuda's combined population numbers around 93,000, of which some 85 percent are of African descent. The capital of the twin-island nation is St. John's, a bustling port city and cruise-ship destination on the west coast. Antigua has several diversions for the inquisitive traveler. Renting a car is the best way to explore. Nelson's Dockyard National Park (see pp. 205–206) showcases the finest surviving Georgian naval complex in the world, while the history of the island's sugar industry is explained at the restored Betty's

INSIDER TIP:

Save a Saturday morning to shop for artisan crafts and local foods at the farmers market on Market Street in southern St. John's.

—LARRY PORGES
National Geographic Books author

Hope Museum (see p. 208) in the center of the island.

A favorite out-of-the-way detour on the southeast coast is a trip to Harmony Hall (see p. 209), a charming old sugar mill complex housing an arts-and-crafts gallery and an excellent Italian restaurant.

Tourists are generally welcomed wherever they go, and for a surefire conversational gambit

EXPERIENCE: Enjoy an Antiguan Ecotour

For those interested in wandering off the beaten path, ecotourism provides a conservation-centered way to see Antigua untouched by tourist crowds. A variety of companies offer guided, educational tours that explore protected landscapes and ecosystems.

Local ecotour companies include **Antigua Nature Tours** (*Seatons, tel 268 720 1761, antiguanaturetours.com, $$$$$*), located on Mercers Creek Bay on the eastern shore of Antigua. Start your day by discovering sanctuaries that provide a home to indigenous monkeys, parrots, brown pelicans, and assorted regional wildlife. From there, take a speedboat ride to the company's kayak dock where you will paddle among red mangrove-riddled inlets to North Sound Marine

Park, a haven of Antiguan flora and fauna delights. After exploring the waterways, move on to Great Bird Island for snorkeling among brain coral and shoals of blue tang, sea cucumbers, and upside-down jellyfish. Finish with a hike through coconut tree high-rises, stomping ground to an abundance of tropical birds, or settle in for a sun-soaked rest and a rum punch on the pink sands.

Other ecotour operators include **Adventure Antigua** (*Dickinson Bay, St. John's, tel 268 726 6355, adventure antigua .com, $$$$$*), run by former competitive kitesurfer Eli Fuller. For an around-island Jeep safari or a combination of safari and kayaking, contact **Tropical Adventures Antigua** (*Lower Redcliffe St., St. John's, tel 286 480 1225, tropicalad.com, $$$$$*).

try cricket or sailing, the islanders' twin passions. To capture Antiguans at their most spontaneous, join in the regattas and riotous partying that accompany the annual Antigua Sailing Week at the end of the December-to-April yachting season (see sidebar p. 207). For a more modest hint of the local atmosphere, the Sunday afternoon jump-ups (impromptu dances) at Shirley Heights are entertaining rum-and-reggae-soaked affairs.

St. John's & Around

St. John's is an appealing West Indian town sloping gently back from the downtown waterfront in an orderly pattern of streets and narrow alleys laid out in 1702. Old wooden buildings with drooping balconies cluster on the hill below the cathedral and its landmark silver cupolas. Charmingly timeworn, they appear anchored together for support by a web of telephone wires above the road.

The sidewalks of St. John's are always crowded. More often than not during the winter high season, armies of day-tripping cruise passengers pile ashore intent on plundering the duty-free stores in the modern **Heritage Quay** mall at the foot of the pier.

The compact waterfront district remains the focal point of town. Next to Heritage Quay, there's a covered market full of souvenir stalls, and on its far side is **Redcliffe Quay,** a pretty shopping street lined with restored wood and stone town houses and warehouses now occupied by

The Cathedral of St. John the Divine opened its doors in 1847; it has withstood a massive earthquake and hurricanes.

boutiques, galleries, and restaurants. The area behind the quay was once part of a large barracoon, or dockside slave-holding compound, before emancipation.

It's a short walk up Long Street to the **Museum of Antigua & Barbuda,** housed in the neo-classical Old Court House, built in 1750 from stone quarried on Antigua's offshore islets. The fusty,

Museum of Antigua & Barbuda

⊠   Corner of Long & Market Sts., St. John's

☎   268 462 4930

🕒   Closed Sun.

💲   Donation

antiguamuseums.net

old-fashioned layout conceals an informative introduction to the islands' history and geology. The archaeological finds are particularly interesting and include Stone Age Ciboney tools, an Arawak ax with a special hole designed to allow tree spirits to escape, and a collection of *zemi,* small stone or carved bone objects that were believed to attract benevolent powers.

At the top of the hill is the **Cathedral of St. John the Divine,** flanked by its twin towers and currently undergoing restoration. Constructed on the site of a previous stone church

Exploring Shirley Heights

The military abandoned Shirley Heights in the 1850s, and since then many of its buildings have simply disappeared behind a screen of scrub. But signposts and footpaths still lead to an assortment of crumbling barracks and batteries, water cisterns, powder magazines, and the Military Cemetery, where the numerous victims of tropical fevers were laid to rest. The signal station at the highest point of the complex (490 feet/149 m) used flags to send messages to Fort George at Monk's Hill, above Falmouth, which were then relayed across a chain of hilltop signal stations to St. John's.

demolished by an earthquake in 1843, the cathedral has a cool, lofty interior clad in pitch pine to protect it against hurricane and earthquake damage. Take a little time to inspect the grand memorial plaques bedecked with coats of arms and flowery inscriptions.

The entrance to St. John's Harbour is overlooked by the

INSIDER TIP:

Try to time your visit to Shirley Heights with sunrise or sunset. The view is spectacular during those times of day.

—MATT PROPERT
National Geographic photographer

ruins of two historic forts with good views. On the north side, reached by Fort Road, is **Fort James,** which was founded in 1706 shortly after the death of King James II. Continuing up the coast, there are a few hotels lining the beach at **Runaway Bay.** Just around a small headland is Antigua's most developed pocket of shoreline—**Dickenson Bay.** This is no Miami Beach high-rise strip but a mile-long (1.6 km) swath of fine, powdery white sand that turns the water a translucent opal. The beach is backed by just a handful of low-rise hotels set in landscaped gardens. A good spot for active beachgoers, Dickenson Bay has several water-sports concessions.

On the south side of St. John's Harbour is 17th-century **Fort Barrington,** one of Antigua's earliest (and most active) fortresses. From the ruins there are views across to the neighboring islands of St. Kitts and Nevis on a clear day.

Several of Antigua's best beaches are tucked into the bays and coves of the southwest coast. Out on the peninsula, near Fort Barrington, are **Deep Bay, Galley Bay,** and the assorted coves and hotel beaches of **Hawksbill**

A relic of bygone days along the road through Nelson's Dockyard

Bay, so named for the hawksbill turtle–shaped rock they overlook. The **Jolly Harbour** complex incorporates a busy marina, shops, and hotels, as well as a beach on Lignumvitae Bay. Farther south, **Dark Wood Bay** has a lovely strip of sand with a beach bar, and glorious views across to neighboring Montserrat. Busy on weekends, it is almost deserted on weekdays.

Nelson's Dockyard National Park

The national park covers some 12 square miles (31 sq km) on the south coast around Falmouth Harbour, the original capital site of Antigua. A popular yachting center on its own sheltered bay, Falmouth is divided by a narrow isthmus from the virtually landlocked confines of English Harbour. English Harbour served as the British Royal Navy's eastern Caribbean headquarters during the 17th and 18th centuries.

Shirley Heights is the best place to begin a visit to the park. The sprawling 18th-century military complex was named for General Sir Thomas Shirley, governor of the Leeward Islands between 1781 and 1791. It occupies a commanding position on the high ground above the dockyard, which is reached by a well-signed road from English Harbour. Make an initial stop at the **Dow Hill Interpretation Centre,** where a 15-minute multimedia presentation covers Antiguan history and culture from the Carib to cricket. The road continues to wind uphill, past the elegant stone colonnade of the officers' quarters, now open to the sky and studded with cactuses, until it reaches **Shirley Heights Lookout.** From here, eagle-eyed sentries could see all the way south across the water to

Nelson's Dockyard National Park

🏛 201 B1

Visitor Information

☎ 268 481 5021

💲 $$

nationalparks antigua.com

Horatio Nelson

England's naval hero spent a miserable posting in Antigua between 1784 and 1787. As captain of the 28-gun frigate H.M.S. *Boreas*, and head of the Squadron of the Leeward Islands, the youthful Nelson was dispatched to enforce the unpopular Navigation Act, which banned planters and merchants from trading with the newly independent United States of America. At times his mission so incensed the islanders that he was afraid to put into shore and took refuge on Nevis, where he met and married the wealthy and well-connected young widow Fanny Nisbet. "Woefully pinched by mosquitoes," the miserable Nelson felt so ill when he left for England that he ordered a barrel of rum be taken on board to preserve his body for a home burial if he died during the voyage.

(1758–1805). He was plain Captain Nelson in 1784, when he and his shipmates aboard H.M.S. *Boreas* arrived in the Leeward Islands for a three-year tour of duty. The dockyard was decommissioned in 1889 and fell into disrepair until the 1960s, when it was restored, renamed, and opened as a national park. It is a delightful place for a stroll, guided by a series of signs that identify the various stores and workshop buildings. You can take a guided tour from the entrance gate.

Sights include the **Admiral's Inn,** housed in a former pitch and tar store, with the coral rock pillars of a sail loft in the gardens. Note the rounded water cisterns flanking the brick walls of the charming **Copper & Lumber Store Hotel,** and visit the **Dockyard Museum,** laid out in the Admiral's House, which dates from 1855. There's a short walk out to **Fort Berkeley,** the dockyard's first line of defense, built on a rocky spit of land in 1704. The path starts by the dinghy dock in the marina, and there are grand views back across the harbor basin to waterfront **Clarence House.** ■

the French island of Guadeloupe, giving the British plenty of advance warning in the event of an attack. The French were never foolhardy enough to attempt it. (See also sidebar p. 204.)

Down at sea level is **Nelson's Dockyard,** which was considered a hardship posting and "an infernal hole" by its famous namesake, Admiral Lord Horatio Nelson

NEED TO KNOW
Port Logistics: St. John's

Passengers disembark directly into the downtown shopping district from the Heritage and Nevis Street Piers, close to the tourist information kiosk and ground transportation. Some vessels dock at the Deep Water Harbour (a 10- to 15-minute taxi ride away), which is slated for development, but currently offers no facilities.

Ask taxi drivers for rate cards and fix a price for your whole trip in advance (Nelson's Dockyard 30 mins/$30 one way).

St. John's Highlights
• Nelson's Dockyard: 3 hours
• Dickenson Bay Beach: 2 hours
• Lunch at Harmony Hall: 3 hours
• Antigua Rain Forest Canopy Tour: 3 hours

EXPERIENCE: Share in a Passion for Sailing

"Sail fast, live slow," they say in Antigua, and there are many opportunities to do just that on this sail-obsessed island. Constant trade winds, sparkling seas, and a picture-perfect coastline dotted with dozens of secluded beaches and coves, many of which are only accessible by boat, make for terrific sailing whether the object is a relaxing day sail or deadly serious competitive racing.

Antigua's main sailing hubs are English Harbour and Falmouth Harbour on the south coast, and Jolly Harbour in the west. Day sail options with a barbecue lunch are readily available from the likes of **Treasure Island Cruises** *(tel 268 461 8875, treasureislandcruises.ag, $$$$$)* and **Wadadli Cats** *(tel 268 462 4792, wadadlicats .com, $$$$$)*. Both operators offer a choice of snorkel trips to Cades Reef or family favorite Great Bird Island (popular with children).

For a longer day's sailing, a complete circumnavigation of the island is a 60-mile (96 km) trip with lunch and snorkel stops en route. **Tropical Adventures Antigua** *(tel 268 480 1225, tropicalad.com, $$$$$)* sails to Barbuda for the day; and **Miramar Sailing** *(tel 268 721 3456, miramarsailing.com, $$$$$)* offers training courses, private day sails, and charters.

If you have a little bit of time and some sailing experience you can go it alone. Yacht charter companies can supply vessels of all sizes, bareboat and crewed, by the day, week, or longer. Contact longtime Caribbean charter experts **Nicholson Yacht Charters** *(tel 268 782 1101 or U.S. 409 849 0344, nicholson charters.com, $$$$$)*, or rent a dinghy from **Sunsail** *(tel 268 460 2615 or 888 350 3568, sunsail.com, $$$$$)*.

If all that relaxed cruising seems a bit tame, then consider visiting during **Antigua Sailing Week** *(sailingweek .com)*, a five-day celebration of international world-class yachting held at the end of April. In this week, more than 100 vessels ranging from 32-foot (10 m) family cruisers to 100-foot (30 m) state-of-the-art racing machines battle it out for a place at the prize-giving ceremony in historic Nelson's Dockyard.

A sailing crew catches the Caribbean wind.

Around Antigua

The eastern half of Antigua contains a number of interesting destinations for a day trip or longer. The ruins of old sugar plantations, where slavery built prosperity for a few, still stand in several locations, while the Atlantic surf breaks on the islands' northeastern point.

One of the two windmills on the Betty's Hope sugarcane plantation still functions today.

Betty's Hope Museum
- 🅰 201 B2
- ✉ SE of Pares
- ☎ 268 462 1469
- 🕐 Closed Sun.– Mon.

Fig Tree Drive
- 🅰 201 A1–B1
- ✉ St. Mary's Parish

Betty's Hope Museum

Antigua's pioneer plantation, Betty's Hope was established during the 1650s. For 250 years this was one of the island's most prosperous estates. Today acacia bushes and tamarind trees have swallowed up the cane fields, but one of two windmills has been restored. Refitted with wooden sails and cane-crushing machinery, it is the only working sugar mill in the Caribbean.

Inside the small **visitor center** are exhibits explaining sugar processing and the work of the slave gangs; Betty's Hope employed about 310 West African slaves. There are also maps and drawings relating to the history

of the plantation as well as a detailed scale model of the now demolished great house, complete with smartly dressed white settlers strolling in the great house gardens. In reality, most plantation owners preferred to live in Europe and leave their overseas estates in the hands of managers.

Fig Tree Drive

A rare pocket of lush natural vegetation in the southwest of the island, Fig Tree Drive runs 5 miles (8 km) from the inland village of Swetes down to Old Road, on the coast at Carlisle Bay. For a bird's-eye view of the treetops, check out **Antigua Rain Forest Canopy Tours** (*tel 268 562 6363*, antiguarainforest.com). The exhilarating combination of bridges, trails, and zip lines provides a roller-coaster forest ride. To the west is **Mount Obama** (1,319 feet/402 m), Antigua's highest point, rising above the Shekerley Mountains.

INSIDER TIP:

Rendezvous Bay's beach, on the south coast just west of Falmouth Harbour, is the most beautiful and unspoiled in Antigua.

—FEONA BAILEY
Manager, Catamaran Hotel, Falmouth

Fort George

An easy hiking expedition for history buffs, Fort George perches on the modest heights of Monk's Hill, behind Falmouth Harbour. To reach the fort, turn off the main road at the village of **Liberta** (one of the first settlements founded by freed slaves) in the direction of Table Hill Gordon. The mile-long (1.6 km) marked track is on the right, navigable by 4WD vehicles or on foot. The fort, which dates from 1689, was intended as a stronghold for livestock, women, and children if Falmouth was attacked. Sections of the high defensive walls, powder magazines, and cannon emplacements have survived around the 8-acre (3 ha) site.

Harmony Hall

A delightful spot on the east coast, Harmony Hall is worth a detour. The former great house of the Brown's Bay Mill sugar estate has been transformed into a gallery of Caribbean arts and crafts and a six-room B&B inn. The old windmill houses a bar overlooking Nonsuch Bay, and there is a restaurant serving lunch and afternoon tea. A short drive (3 miles/5 km) southeast, beyond Freetown, is the alluring curve of **Half Moon Bay,** popular with swimmers, sunbathers, and bodysurfers.

Indian Town Point & Devil's Bridge

Way out at the northeast tip of the island, a side road leads off 1 mile (1.6 km) to Indian Town Point and the site of Devil's Bridge. On a blustery day the Atlantic surf crashes against the coastline, where it blasts through blowholes in the rock. Archaeologists have made excavations in the Indian Town Point area, which was declared a national park in the 1950s. A short drive to the north is sandy **Long Bay.**

Stingray City

A low-key version of the Cayman Islands' eponymous tourist attraction, **Stingray City** is both fun and educational. After a short boat ride out to a platform where you can stand in shallow water, staff provide a wealth of stingray facts as inquisitive southern rays glide up for a friendly look and a tidbit or two. ∎

Fort George
- 201 B1
- Monk's Hill, near Liberta

Harmony Hall
- 201 C2
- Brown's Bay (N of Freetown)
- 268 460 4120
- Closed June–Oct.

harmonyhallantigua.com

Indian Town Point & Devil's Bridge
- 201 C2
- E of Willikies

Stingray City
- 201 B2
- Seatons
- 268 562 7297
- $$$$$

stingraycityantigua.com

Barbuda

A 28-mile (45 km) boat ride or puddle-jumper flight from Antigua, Barbuda bakes quietly in the sun and takes things very, very easy. The 14-by-8-mile (22.5 by 13 km) coral atoll is almost two-thirds the size of its more developed, upbeat sister, Antigua, but there are just 1,600 islanders, who live mainly by fishing, farming, and a little low-key tourism.

The magnificent frigate bird is the national bird of Barbuda and Antigua.

Barbuda
A 199 C3–D3
Visitor Information
antigua-barbuda.org
barbudaful.net

Barbuda's top attractions are mind-blowing, pinkish white-sand beaches and superb snorkeling. Any visit comes with a caveat: Accommodations are limited to a brace of small luxury beach hotel retreats or guesthouses in Codrington. You may want to consider a day trip. In addition to air services and the daily Barbuda Express ferry from Antigua (see Travelwise p. 343), day sail cruises are an option.

Barbuda's only settlement is **Codrington,** a handful of streets leading back from the saltwater lagoon. Both were named for Christopher Codrington, a 17th-century governor-general of the

Leeward Islands who leased the whole island from the British crown in 1691. (It remained in the family's hands until 1872.) Poor soil and an annual rainfall of only about 38 inches (965 mm) meant sugar cultivation was impossible on Barbuda, but Codrington introduced deer, wild boar, and guinea fowl for hunting, raised cattle, and grew provisions to supply his five Antiguan estates.

Barbuda is almost completely ringed by breathtaking beaches. One magnificent 14-mile (22.5 km) stretch starts at the southerly tip of **Cocoa Point** and sweeps up the west coast, past the landmark 18th-century **Martello Tower** to

Palmetto Point, where it takes a sharp turn around the headland and continues on up the outer arm of **Codrington Lagoon.**

In the south, there's excellent snorkeling around **Gravenor Bay** and the 2-mile-long (3 km) **Palaster Reef,** a protected marine reserve off Cocoa Point. Goat Reef, in the north, is renowned for its wreck diving. As yet, Barbuda has no organized dive operation, so divers will need to bring all their equipment, except for tanks, which can be rented or filled in Codrington. Local fishing boats are available for charter.

Be sure to take a boat trip out into the mangrove-lined **Frigate Bird Sanctuary** at the north end of Codrington Lagoon (see note this page). This is the largest nesting colony of magnificent frigate birds in the world, with an estimated 2,500 pairs. The glossy black birds have an 8-foot (2.5 m) wingspan and can soar at altitudes of 2,000 feet (600 m). In the mating season *(Aug.–Nov.),* male birds try to attract a female by puffing out their scarlet neck pouches like a huge balloon, trembling their

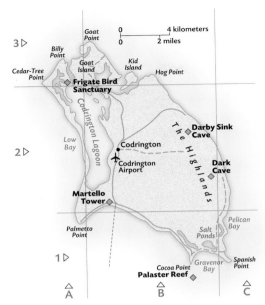

outstretched wings, and emitting a strange drumming sound. Their ungainly, pure white young are born in winter *(Dec.–Feb.).* More than 400 other bird species have been identified in the area.

East of Codrington, **Dark Cave** and **Darby Sink Cave** harbor rare blind shrimp and surprising touches of greenery. ■

NOTE: Authorized bird-watching trips through **Frigate Bird Sanctuary** can be arranged through the national park office *(tel 268 460 0217).* Visits are also included in day tours from Antigua.

Redonda: Royalty, Peers, & Bird Droppings

An uninhabited volcanic rock 30 miles (48 km) southwest of Antigua, Redonda is the third territory of Antigua and Barbuda. It has a rather bizarre recent history. In the mid-19th century some enterprising souls recognized there was money to be made from Redonda's guano deposits.

Thousands of tons of bird droppings were shipped off the island for use as fertilizer. Subsequently, Britain annexed

Redonda to its Leeward Island possessions. But an Irishman from Montserrat proclaimed himself King of Redonda, and the title has since passed to a succession of colorful (nonresident) literary types who have generously created Redondan peers out of any famous people who attract their attention, from Welsh writer and poet Dylan Thomas to filmmaker Pedro Almodóvar and architect Frank Gehry.

Anguilla

Long before a wealth of superb sandy beaches was considered an attraction, Spanish explorers took one look at the flat, desiccated, and most northerly of the Leeward Islands, christened it Anguilla (pronounced An-gwil-lah), meaning "eel," and sailed on in search of richer, greener, and more promising territories. Only 16 miles (25 km) long and 3 miles (5 km) wide at its broadest point, present-day Anguilla's fortunes are founded on its 33 dazzling white beaches with sand so fine and deep that you have to wade rather than walk along them.

A quiet moment on Shoal Bay, one of Anguilla's liveliest beaches

Anguilla
  199 A3–B3

Visitor Information

✉ The Valley

☎ 264 497 2759
  or U.S. 800 553
  4939

🕐 Closed Sat.–Sun.

ivisitanguilla.com

Forget rain forest hikes, historic forts, casinos, and duty-free shopping (although commercialized Sint Maarten/St.-Martin is only a 20-minute ferry ride away), and prepare to get horizontal. Anguilla has been neatly summed up in a one-line T-shirt slogan: "Life's a beach, and then you dine." And you can dine spectacularly well on Anguilla. The island may be lacking somewhat in the general interest department, but it does boast a selection of the Caribbean's most luxurious spas and architecturally striking hotels, with dining opportunities to match, several on the shore in earshot of gently lapping waves.

This alluring combination draws an impressively star-studded A-list crowd.

To work up an appetite, wind-assisted water sports are available, and Anguilla boasts six marine parks, nine wreck dives, and terrific snorkeling. Most of the larger hotels have tennis courts and fitness centers, and the Greg Norman–designed CuisinArt Golf Course is a spectacular oceanfront affair. Rental bikes (available from hotels) are a great way to explore.

INSIDER TIP:

Rum lovers should be sure to try one of the several varieties of the local Anguillan tipple— Pyrat rum, a blend of elixirs fused with up to nine aged and fla- vored spirits.

—JENNIFER ALLARD
National Geographic contributor

The Valley

Exploring Anguilla takes a day, but most visitors enjoy a change of scene, even if it's just swap-ping one beach for another. In the middle of the island is The Valley, the capital and adminis-trative center. The settlement has no real focus, but there are some attractive shingled and shuttered traditional houses in jaunty poster-paint colors.

Set back from the main street is the **Anguilla National Museum** *(closed Sat.–Sun.,*

EXPERIENCE:
H Is for Heritage

To encourage visitors to explore the island, the Anguilla tourist office produces a self-guided tour map, which is also available from hotel reception desks. Called "H Is for Heritage," it describes some ten historic and interesting sites dotted around the island. For a more in-depth understand-ing of local history and culture, join an Anguilla Culture Tour run by **Anguilla Access** *(tel 264 772 9827, anguillaaccess .com, $$$$$),* which proudly claims that no two tours are the same. There are twice-daily departures (with hotel pickups) and the route might include visits to an island broommaker, caves decorated with ancient Arawak petroglyphs, local boatbuilders, and a Rastafarian community, ending up at a beach bar for a barbecue.

---

donation), which presents chang-ing exhibits on local themes and is home to the **Anguilla National Trust** *(tel 264 497 5297, email: axanat@anguillanet.com).* The trust organizes walks and tours that include visits to Amerindian sites, bird-watching spots, and hawksbill turtle nesting grounds in summer. Near the airport is the 1787 **Wallblake House,** an annex of the museum and the island's only surviving plantation house, complete with its old stable block and bakery *(tours Mon., Wed., Fri. 10 a.m.–2 p.m., $$).*

Around the Island

Northeast of The Valley lies **Shoal Bay,** the island's liveliest beach, a broad belt of ankle-deep sand with a handful of beach bars, hotels, and water-sports concessions renting out

St. Gerard's Church fronts Wallblake House, the island's only surviving plantation house.

snorkeling gear, windsurfing equipment, and dinghies.

Five miles (8 km) farther east by road, opposite the fishing village of Island Harbour, is gorgeous **Scilly Cay,** a tiny offshore islet with a palm-thatched restaurant and good snorkeling. If it's too far to swim, wave for the water taxi.

In the southeast corner of the island, seek out the **Heritage Collection** *(East End at Pond Ground, tel 264 497 4092, closed Sun.),* a fascinating privately owned museum. The bulk of the exhibits are devoted to the revolution (see sidebar this page), with a detailed account of the proceedings and some entertaining photographs. There are also pieces of Amerindian pottery decorated with pelican heads and antique kitchen implements made out of coral.

You'll find other attractions to the west of The Valley. The island's deepwater port is located on the north coast at **Sandy Ground,** balanced on a curved spit of sand dividing the old salt pans from the ocean. The old salt factory is now a restaurant, and a ferry provides regular service to **Sandy Island,** another offshore beach and snorkeling spot. Continuing west, several hotels and good restaurants are gathered in the **Mead's Bay** and **Barnes Bay** area.

On the south coast, the futuristic apartments of Covecastles preside over **Lower Shoal Bay;** the Cap Juluca resort fronts **Maunday's Bay;** and Anguilla's longest beach, **Rendezvous Bay,** stretches out in a curving ribbon of dunes facing St.-Martin. ∎

"The Eel That Squealed"

Laid-back Anguilla seems the last place on Earth to harbor revolutionary tendencies, but in the late 1960s it became the first British colony to stage a successful revolution *against* independence. In 1967, faced with the prospect of an unwanted union with St. Kitts and Nevis, the Anguillans rounded up and deported a detachment of Kittitian policemen, rolled an antique cannon onto the beach, and appealed to Britain for continued colonial status. Embarrassingly out of touch, the British government dispatched armed paratroopers to reestablish order two years later. They were greeted by cheering Anguillans waving Union Jacks and singing "God Save the Queen." The fiasco was dubbed Britain's Bay of Piglets. For an entertaining account of the whole saga, pick up a copy of Donald E. Westlake's *Under an English Heaven,* available on the island.

St. Kitts

The twin-island nation of St. Kitts and Nevis is located near the northern tip of a 500-mile-long (800 km) arc of volcanic peaks that stretches from Saba to Grenada along a curving submarine fault between the Atlantic Ocean and the Caribbean Sea. St. Kitts is the larger of the two islands at 68 square miles (176 sq km), with three distinct mountain ranges squeezed into its lush, green tadpole-shaped body. A spine of dry, rugged hills forms the tail, which trails southeast toward Nevis.

Honoring a former island estate owner, Basseterre's Berkeley Monument includes a clock and drinking fountain.

St. Kitts's main resort area, Frigate Bay, lies at the top of the tail section, close to the bustling island capital of Basseterre (see p. 217). The island's best beaches flank the isthmus as it reaches south to The Narrows, the channel dividing St. Kitts from neighboring Nevis. To the north, the green-clad lower slopes of the ranges rise to a peak at Mount Liamuiga (3,792 feet/1,156 m), and a single perimeter road hugs the coast, linking quiet rural villages.

The Amerindian name for St. Kitts was Liamuiga (meaning "fertile land"), but when Christopher Columbus sailed by in 1493, he named it St. Christopher after his own patron saint and the patron saint of travelers. Just over a century later, British colonists, led by Sir Thomas Warner (1575–1649), settled on St. Kitts and set about cultivating tobacco. Having defeated the resident Carib population at Bloody Point in 1626, they ousted French colonists from the southern portion of the island,

St. Kitts

⚑ 199 B2

Visitor Information

✉ Pelican Mall, Bay Rd., Basseterre

☎ 869 465 4040

stkittstourism.kn

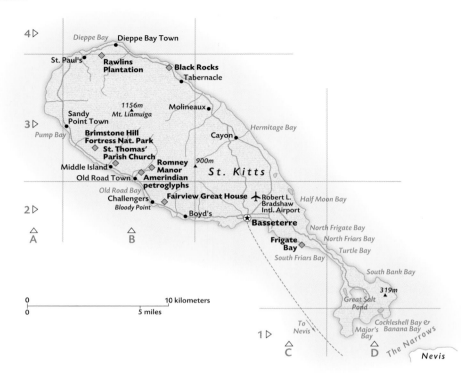

4 ▷

Dieppe Bay   Dieppe Bay Town

St. Paul's   Rawlins
              Plantation   Black Rocks
                            Tabernacle

              1156m   Molineaux
Sandy   Mt. Liamuiga
Point Town

3 ▷   Hermitage Bay
Pump Bay   Brimstone Hill
            Fortress Nat. Park   Cayon
            St. Thomas'
            Parish Church
Middle Island   Romney   900m
Old Road Town   Manor
                 Amerindian   St. Kitts
                 petroglyphs
Old Road Bay
            Challengers   Fairview Great House   Robert L.   Half Moon Bay
            Bloody Point   Bradshaw
                                                    Intl. Airport
                            Boyd's
2 ▷   Basseterre
                                                    North Frigate Bay
△   △   Frigate   North Friars Bay
A   B   Bay   Turtle Bay
                            South Friars Bay
                                                    South Bank Bay

0   319m
0   10 kilometers
        5 miles   Great Salt
                                   Pond
                                                    Cockleshell Bay &
                                          To   Banana Bay
                                   Major's   Bay
1 ▷   Bay
                                                    The Narrows
                            △   △
                            C   D
                                                    Nevis

around Basseterre, anglicized the island's Spanish name, and St. Kitts became known as the Mother Colony of the West Indies.

Naturally, the French refused to give up easily. The island and neighboring Nevis were important sugar producers, and St. Kitts, or parts of it, changed hands regularly despite the vast fortress built by the British at Brimstone Hill (see p. 219), grandly but inaccurately touted as the "Gibraltar of the West Indies." Britain finally secured sovereignty of the islands under the Treaty of Versailles in 1783. When the sugar bubble burst half a century later, the high-living plantocracy quit the islands in droves, and St. Kitts and Nevis shared the same dismal fate as other Caribbean sugar islands.

As Britain prepared to divest itself of its Leeward Island territories in the 1960s, plans were drawn up for a new tri-island state comprising St. Kitts, Nevis, and Anguilla. The Anguillans rejected the proposal, fearing domination by larger and more populous St. Kitts (see sidebar p. 214). Despite similar reservations, Nevis entered into the state of St. Kitts and Nevis in 1983.

Basseterre is the focus of island life, with its boisterous street life and markets, restaurants tucked away in pretty stone courtyards, and harborfront cruise-ship pier. The island's tourist heartland is concentrated in the southeast peninsula, where several upscale resorts have opened recently as part of an ambitious growth plan.

There are plans afoot to develop a major entertainment venue. Beyond the town and the beach, rain forest hikes are popular. It takes a full day to hike the round-trip up to Mount Liamuiga's crater lip, but local companies offer less strenuous options, as well as Jeep safaris to ruined plantation houses and sugar mills.

Basseterre

Originally settled by the French, as its name implies, Basseterre ("low ground") skirts a broad bay at the foot of the Southeast Range. The British moved their capital here from Old Road in 1727, but most of the attractive skirt-and-blouse buildings (so called for their stone ground floors and wooden uppers) postdate the major fire of 1867.

The heart of town is arranged around the twin poles of **The Circus**—where the traffic makes its way around a fancy Victorian clock tower, public seating area, and meeting place—and **Independence Square.** The grassy square (a former slave market) has a gaudily painted fountain, a few palms, and a single poinciana, the national tree, which sports brilliant red blooms in summer. On the east side of the square the Roman Catholic church dates from 1670 but has been reconstructed several times. Behind a row of metal railings on the south side of the square stands the handsome **Old Georgian House.**

The Basseterre waterfront has undergone a major face-lift, spearheaded by the **Port Zante** cruise-ship pier facility, though the adjacent shopping and dining development is taking time to live up to expectations. Meanwhile, the Old Treasury Building has been restored to house assorted island artifacts gathered in the **National Museum.** Follow Bay Road west, past fishing boats and old warehouse buildings, for ferry services to Nevis, which depart from behind the bus station.

EXPERIENCE: Go Ape

Beat the island's green vervet monkeys at their own game with a rain forest **Sky Safari** at the Wingfield Estate *(Old Road Village, tel 869 466 4259, skysafaristkitts .com, $$$$$)*. After a familiarization session on the trainer zip line, the sky's the limit for four further rides. The Boss, a 1,350-foot-long (411 m), 250-foot-high (76 m) flight through the forest canopy, skims over the Valley of the Giants. Back on terra firma, there are guided walks and the ruins of the former estate sugar plantation to explore.

Brimstone Hill Fortress & the North

A circumnavigation of northern St. Kitts makes a good day trip, with several historic sites, fine scenery, and a choice of plantation house lunch stops. You can hop aboard the **St. Kitts Scenic Railway** *(tel 869 465 7263, stkittsscenicrailway.com)* and follow the old sugar train route, or rent a car and take the coast road northwest from Basseterre out along the Caribbean shore.

First stop, some 3 miles (2 km) beyond the capital, is **Fairview Great House,** the historic former French military commander's

Basseterre
◪ 216 C2

National Museum
✉ Bay Rd., Basseterre
☎ 869 465 5584
🕐 Closed Sat. p.m. & Sun.
🔖 $$

Fairview Great House
◪ 216 B2
Visitor Information
☎ 869 465 3141

Brimstone Hill Fortress once had walls that were 7 feet (2 m) thick.

Romney Manor
🅰 216 B3
✉ Old Road Town
☎ 869 465 6253
**caribellebatikstkitts
.com**

residence with glorious views across to Nevis. The 300-year-old property has been recently restored with a handsome dining room furnished with a huge mahogany dining table, hurricane lamps, and elegant antique silver tableware. The separate kitchen building has its old volcanic stone and brick oven, and there are 2 acres (0.8 ha) of landscaped gardens to enjoy as well as a restaurant *(tel 869 465 3021, nirvanafairview .com)*. The gift shop sells Fairview's homemade chutneys and jams.

South (0.25 mile/0.4 km) of the village of Challengers is **Bloody Point,** the scene of the last pitched battle between St. Kitts's European settlers and Carib Indians. At **Old Road Town,** the first British settlement and island capital for a century, **Amerindian petroglyphs** are carved into a boulder on the side road leading up to **Romney Manor.** The partially rebuilt 17th-century manor houses the textile workshops of Caribelle Batik.

At Middle Island the tomb of Sir Thomas Warner lies in

Monkey Business

The French legacy of St. Kitts extends beyond a few place-names, such as Basseterre and the quiet former sugar port of Dieppe Bay. The poinciana tree, with its flamboyant red blooms, is named after the first French governor of the island, Philippe de Poincy. The French also introduced green vervet monkeys, which were kept as pets. An estimated 50,000 descendants of the original monkeys are now living in colonies in the mountains. They feed off insects, berries, and fruit, and during summer (when food in the forest is more limited) they make forays to pillage small-scale farms on the edge of villages, where they are considered pests.

the overgrown graveyard of **St. Thomas' Parish Church.** Beyond the village the hulking volcanic outcrop of **Brimstone Hill** looms ahead with commanding views across to the Dutch Windward Islands of Sint Eustatius and Saba.

A UNESCO World Heritage site, the colossal **Brimstone Hill Fortress National Park** covers a 37-acre (15 ha) site 800 feet (240 m) above the coast. Built from blackened volcanic stone beginning in 1690, the "Gibraltar of the West Indies" was considered impregnable until 8,000 French troops laid siege to it in 1782. It took a month of bombardment to destroy every building and breach the 7-foot-thick (2 m) walls, forcing the 1,000-strong garrison of defenders to surrender. The British regained control in 1794 and rebuilt the fortifications, crowned by **Fort George Citadel,** which once again bristles with cannon.

As the main road rounds the north end of the island, it runs through the village of St. Paul's and past a bumpy track leading up to the lovely **Rawlins Plantation.**

Continuing down the east coast, make a stop at **Black Rocks,** jagged volcanic formations created by lava from Mount Liamuiga.

Frigate Bay & the South

Just south of Basseterre lies **Frigate Bay,** St. Kitts's hotel enclave, with an 18-hole golf course and beaches on both sides of the isthmus. The broad, sandy beach on the more sheltered (southern) Caribbean coast is the island's busiest with a choice of bars and restaurants. On the

Atlantic side of the peninsula the water is rougher, but there's good bodysurfing and the swimming is safe. Swimming isn't recommended at **North Friars Bay,** however, which has dangerous currents, but its opposite number, **South Friars Bay,** is sandwiched between palm trees and glassy calm water.

A 10-mile (15 km) highway roller-coasters down to the southern tip of the island, rounding the old salt ponds where several species of wading birds can be spotted and egrets balance on the backs of cattle by the roadside.

Facing Nevis across The Narrows are the small, undeveloped beaches on **Major's Bay** and **Banana Bay.** Busier **Cockleshell Bay** and **Turtle Bay** each boast lively bar-restaurants, snorkeling off the beach, and water sports, including sailing, diving, and sailboard and kayak rental. ■

Brimstone Hill Fortress National Park

🗺 216 B3

✉ Brimstone Hill

☎ 869 465 2609

💲 $$$

brimstonehillfortress .org

Frigate Bay

🗺 216 C2

NEED TO KNOW

Port Logistics: Basseterre

The Port Zante pier lies just a couple minutes' stroll from the heart of Basseterre and the tourist office. Fixed-rate taxi fares are posted for Brimstone Hill and the beaches; an around-island tour (3–4 hours) costs about $100. Ferries to Nevis (30- to 45-minute crossing) depart from the waterfront; check daily timetables carefully.

Basseterre Highlights

• Brimstone Hill Fortress National Park: 2 hours
• Romney Manor: 1 hour
• Plantation house lunch: 2–3 hours
• Cockleshell Bay: half day

Nevis

Divided from St. Kitts by a 2-mile-wide (3 km) channel known as The Narrows, Nevis rears up precipitously to an imposing volcanic cone. Columbus named the island Nuestra Señora de las Nieves ("our lady of the snows") in a rather fanciful allusion to the almost permanently cloud-capped heights of Nevis Peak (3,232 feet/985 m); his poetic name was later mangled by British settlers to less romantic but more serviceable Nevis (pronounced NEE-viss).

Nevis Peak is nearly always shrouded in clouds.

Nevis

🗺 199 B2

Visitor Information

✉ Main St., Charlestown

☎ 869 469 7550

nevisisland.com

Colonists established a toehold on the island in 1627, and by the mid-18th century the planters of Nevis were so prosperous and fashionable that the pint-size island was hailed as the "queen of the Caribees," renowned for its grand plantation houses, fabulous parties, and the spa in Charlestown's Bath Hotel. Nevis was not immune to the French raiding parties that targeted St. Kitts, and it suffered several attacks. African slaves captured from the famed and highly profitable slave market on Nevis were regarded as an additional prize and were shipped away to work the sugarcane fields of Guadeloupe and Martinique. A century and a half after the abolition of slavery, Nevis accepted independence from Britain as part of the Federation of St. Kitts and Nevis.

The smaller (36 square miles/93 sq km) and quieter partner in the two-island coalition, Nevis retains vestiges of its rich colonial past in a clutch of gracious plantation house hotels and the sturdy stone buildings of the main settlement, Charlestown.

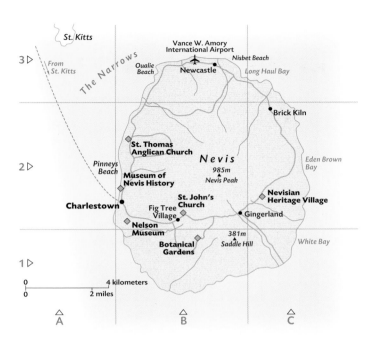

St. Kitts

From St. Kitts

The Narrows

Vance W. Amory International Airport

Oualie Beach

Newcastle

Nisbet Beach

Long Haul Bay

Brick Kiln

St. Thomas Anglican Church

Pinneys Beach

Museum of Nevis History

Nevis

985m Nevis Peak

Eden Brown Bay

Charlestown

St. John's Church

Fig Tree Village

Nevisian Heritage Village

Gingerland

Nelson Museum

Botanical Gardens

381m Saddle Hill

White Bay

0   4 kilometers
0   2 miles

A   B   C

In recent years the Nevisian economy, boosted by offshore tax status, has outstripped that of St. Kitts, and traditional interisland rivalries have been further exacerbated by what the Nevisians feel is undue Kittitian interference in their affairs. The question of secession has been openly discussed in the assembly.

The 10,000 Nevisians are among the most hospitable hosts in the Caribbean region, and the island's unhurried pace and gentle charm are soothing antidotes to world-weariness. Tourism Nevis-style is relatively upscale but determinedly low-key. Nevis has no casinos or air-conditioned malls, not even a major historical site, although Lord Nelson got married on the island, with a future king of England in attendance. Instead, guests at most of the plantation hotels have to journey to the beaches on the Caribbean (west) coast, work up an appetite horseback riding or

Alexander Hamilton

Born on Nevis on January 11, 1757, Alexander Hamilton served as aide-de-camp to Gen. George Washington during the American Revolution. He was nicknamed "the little lion" on account of his relatively diminutive stature (5 feet 7 inches/170 cm) and ferocious temper, which, it was said, turned his blue eyes to black when he was angry. Hamilton trained as a lawyer, and Washington appointed him the first secretary of the treasury. He died in a duel with Vice President Aaron Burr (1756–1836), his political rival, in 1804.

Museum of Nevis History

🔺 221 B2

✉ Low St., Charlestown

☎ 869 469 5786

🕐 Closed Sat. p.m. & Sun.

💲 $$

hiking in the rain forest, and make an around-island tour that takes all of half a day.

Charlestown

Located two-thirds of the way down the Caribbean west coast, Charlestown is the capital of Nevis and the liveliest spot on the island. Founded about 1660 and named in honor of King Charles II in 1671, the town straggles along the main island

St. Kitts unload passengers and provisions onto the dock.

At the north end of Main Street is the **Museum of Nevis History,** housed in Alexander Hamilton House, birthplace of the American statesman (1757–1804) whose image graces the U.S. ten-dollar bill (see sidebar p. 221). The one-room museum's collections cover island history and culture, from Amerindian pottery sherds to independence.

Net casting at Pinneys Beach

road to its hub, a grassy triangle that doubles as a meeting place and minibus depot a short walk from the pier. Traditional two-story stone and wood colonial buildings with balconies and gingerbread trim line the street, and a selection of shops, cafés, and small businesses has moved into the alleys leading down to the rejuvenated waterfront, where ferries from

An early European visitor to Nevis was Captain John Smith and a party of 144 Englishmen. They spent six days on Nevis in 1607 en route to found the colony at Jamestown, Virginia. The group were revived by a dip in the hot spring that would later feature as the centerpiece of the 18th-century **Bath Hotel** at the southern end of town. Today the hotel buildings are being restored, and visitors can once again take a dip in the steaming waters.

Just up from the hotel is the **Nelson Museum,** which examines the life and times of the great English naval hero. Horatio Nelson married local girl Fanny Nisbet at the Montpelier Estate in 1787, during an uncomfortable posting to Antigua (see sidebar p. 206). Exhibits include a plate from the wedding feast, a portion of the Union Jack flag under which Nelson stood when fatally wounded at the Battle of Trafalgar in 1805, and items from the mountain of memorabilia commissioned to commemorate his death.

Around the Island

Just north of Charlestown, parallel to the coast road, **Pinneys Beach** unfurls in a 4-mile (6.5 km) reel of golden sand backed by palm trees. Along the way North you'll pass **St. Thomas Anglican Church.** Founded in 1643, it is believed to be the oldest congregation on the island. Farther north, **Oualie Beach** has good snorkeling and water sports. Beyond the airport is **Newcastle Pottery,** set in a small roadside workshop, where handmade bowls, candleholders, and jugs are fashioned from local red clay. As the road circles around to the rougher Atlantic coast, there is more reef snorkeling off the white coral sands of **Nisbet Beach.**

Four of Nevis's five plantation house hotels nestle beneath **Nevis Peak,** overlooking the south coast between Gingerland and Fig Tree Village. Along the way, you can dip into island culture and building styles at **Fothergill's Nevisian Heritage Village,** and enjoy a stroll and refreshments at the 5-acre (2 ha) **Botanical Gardens of Nevis,** which offer plenty to interest the plant lover, from the fragrant rose and vine gardens to a rain forest conservatory, lily pools, and shady orchid terraces. Nelson and Fanny Nisbet's marriage at Montpelier Estate is recorded in a copy of the register on display at **St. John's Church** in Fig Tree, on the road back to Charlestown. ■

Nelson Museum
- 221 B2
- Bath Rd., Charlestown
- 869 469 0408
- Closed Sat. p.m. & Sun.
- $$

Botanical Gardens of Nevis
- 221 B1
- Montpelier Estate, St. John's Parish
- 869 469 3509
- Closed Sun.
- $$$

botanicalgarden nevis.com

NEED TO KNOW
Port Logistics: Charlestown

Tenders ferry cruise passengers to the downtown ferry pier near visitor information in tiny Charlestown. There are taxis waiting on Main Street for around-island tours (3 hours for around $100) and trips to the beach and to plantation house hotels. It's a 5-minute ride ($10) or 15-minute walk to Pinneys Beach.

Charlestown Highlights

- Exploring Charlestown: 1–2 hours
- Botanical Gardens of Nevis: 2 hours
- Plantation House Lunch: 3 hours

Montserrat

The most southerly outpost of the Leeward Island group, Montserrat was long regarded as a haven of tranquility. A real slice of the old Caribbean with a smattering of beaches and hotels, it has a lush, mountainous interior that invites exploration. The island's peaceful idyll was shattered by the devastating eruption of the Soufrière Hills volcano in 1995.

Montserrat's Tar River Valley before it was devastated by the Soufrière Hills volcano in the 1990s

Montserrat

🏔 199 C1

Visitor Information

✉ Montserrat Tourist Board, Little Bay

☎ 664 491 2230

visitmontserrat.com

Montserrat is part of the volcanic Windward Island chain poised on the rim of the Atlantic and Caribbean tectonic plates. It was named by Columbus for the famous Montserrat Abbey near Barcelona, Spain, and settled in the 17th century by Irish Catholics seeking refuge from Protestant persecution on St. Kitts. This Irish connection earned Montserrat its nickname, "the emerald isle." Today the islanders celebrate St. Patrick's Day as a national holiday (see sidebar p. 226), in addition to the Queen's birthday in recognition of the island's status as a British overseas territory.

Apart from the occasional high-profile visitor, such as Stevie Wonder or Sir Paul McCartney recording at Sir George Martin's renowned Air Studios, life was a gentle round of fishing, farming, and a little low-key tourism until Montserrat's quiet repose was shaken by ominous grumblings from the volcano in the summer of 1995. All the major Windwards have an active volcano, usually called a *soufrière,* from the French for "sulfur." These tend to bubble along harmlessly, producing hot springs and boiling mud pools (notably on Dominica and St. Lucia), but as the tectonic plates grind together far beneath Montserrat, magma escaped from the earth's core and the soufrière erupted, raining ash, rocks, and lava over the southern portion of the island. The area was evacuated to a safe zone established in the northern third of the territory. Increased volcanic activity in 1997 saw the abandoned capital, **Plymouth,** destroyed and the island's population diminished from 10,000 to 4,000, with many former residents unable to return. At the present time volcanologists are unable to predict an end to the soufrière's intermittent activities.

This has not stopped the optimistic and engagingly friendly Montserratians from reinventing their island as a tourist destination with a difference. Forget your classic Caribbean beach holiday and visit Montserrat for a right up close volcano-watching experience, which might feature spectacular dome collapses, massive ash clouds, and glowing nighttime lava flows. The extraordinary, postapocalyptic landscape of the exclusion zone has become a surprising tourist draw, viewed from lookout points

The domino games outside Montserrat's rum shops provide an entertaining window into the island's colorful local culture.

—CAROLINE HICKEY
National Geographic Books contributor

in the surrounding hills and boat tours along the coast. Plymouth has been touted as a "modern-day Pompeii." An unexpected benefit of the 2-mile (3 km) marine exclusion zone around the island has been the creation of an underwater reserve replete with pristine dive sites, abundant marine life, and some new and spectacular submarine landscaping formed by pyroclastic flow from the volcano.

Montserrat's new capital is taking shape at **Little Bay,** on the northwest coast just beyond Brades. Here the **National Museum of Montserrat** doubles as the headquarters of

National Museum of Montserrat/ Montserrat National Trust

✉ Montserrat Tourist Board, Little Bay

☎ 664 491 3086

🕐 Closed Sat.–Sun.

💲 $$

montserratnational trust.ms

EXPERIENCE: Take a Day Trip to the Emerald Isle

All transportation services to Montserrat depart from neighboring Antigua *(for flights and ferry information, see Travelwise p. 343).* Tour operators on both islands offer day-trip tours with volcano viewing, lunch, and maybe a beach or snorkeling opportunity. For details, contact **Carib World Travel** *(Antigua, tel 268 480 2999 or U.S. 410 878 7761, carib-world.com, $$$$$);* **Jenny Tours** *(Antigua, tel 268 722 8188, jennytours.webs .com, $$$$$);* or **Scriber's Adventure Tours**

(Montserrat, tel 664 491 3412, scribersadven tures.com, $$$$$). For an unforgettable sailing experience, Antigua-based **Ondeck Ocean Racing** *(tel 268 562 6696, ondeck sailing.com, $$$$$)* can take you on an eight- to nine-hour round-trip voyage aboard a sleek Farr 65 ocean-racing yacht out of Falmouth Harbour. The day trip leaves time for only an hour on Montserrat, so an overnight stop is recommended. Tailor-made island tours can be arranged.

The Soufrière Hills volcano is still active. The chance to spot ash clouds or glowing lava is now part of the island's draw.

the **Montserrat National Trust,** an excellent source of information. Changing exhibits illustrate different facets of island life, from history and culture to wildlife, and there are evocative images of pre-eruption Montserrat. This is the place to pick up hiking maps and arrange island tours, bird-watching trips, guides for expeditions into the hills, and

visits to the exclusion zone when conditions permit.

Not to be missed is a visit to the **Montserrat Volcano Observatory** (MVO; *tel 664 491 5647, www.mvo .ms, closed Fri.–Sun., $$$*), housed in a striking state-of-the-art facility with panoramic views of its objective. The MVO monitors the Soufrière Hills site constantly, posting real-time webcam images on its website. At the Interpretation Centre, visitors are treated to a documentary film of the eruption, interactive displays, and exhibits. Other excellent vantage points for volcano-watching are **Garibaldi Hill** (where the MVO sites its webcam) with sweeping views over Plymouth; and the purpose-built **Jack Boy Hill** viewing platform with a telescope, picnic area, and short trail.

Mid-island, the **Centre Hills** are beguiling hiking country. The rain forest is rich in tropical bird- and plantlife and home to the Montserrat oriole, rare forest thrushes, hummingbirds, tree frogs, and the half-snake, half-lizard galliwasp. The terrain can be quite challenging, especially after heavy rain, and hikers are advised to take a guide (*contact the Montserrat National Trust*). The **Blackwood Allen Trail** is a favorite expedition, as is the hike up through banana plantations to **The Cot,** a former summer cottage 1,000 feet (305 m) above sea level.

Montserrat has one white-sand beach, **Rendezvous Bay,** accessible by boat from Little Bay. The rest are volcanic silver-gray, and those on the west coast, such as **Woodlands, Lime Kiln Bay,** and tiny **Bunkam Bay,** are among the best and safest for swimming. ■

Irish Heritage

Montserrat's affinity with distant Ireland is stamped into every visiting passport in the shape of a shamrock. The national flag features the legendary Irish figure of Erin with her harp alongside the British Union Jack, and the national dish, goat water, is supposed to be based on a traditional Irish stew. St. Patrick's Day in Montserrat is in reality St. Patrick's Week, celebrated on and around March 17, and it is a double celebration for it also marks a slave uprising on the island in 1768. Islanders let their hair down with an explosion of live music, feasting, dancing, masquerade processions, and special events. Be sure to wear something green!

The vibrant creole culture of Guadeloupe and Martinique and the sybaritic, European chic of St.-Barthélemy

French Antilles

The Pitons du Carbet rain forest

French Antilles

At the heart of the French Caribbean are two of the largest islands in the Lesser Antilles (after Trinidad), Guadeloupe and Martinique, exuding a zesty creole atmosphere that permeates every aspect of daily life. Some 150 miles (240 km) away, among the Dutch islands and former British colonies of the Leewards, the smaller French territory of St.-Barthélemy (St. Barts) mimics the lifestyle of *la métropole*, as mainland France is known.

The first French colony in the Caribbean was founded on St. Kitts in 1624, the year after an English settlement was established on the island. A decade later, ambitious French colonists expanded their horizons and bravely tackled the Cannibal Isles, gaining a foothold on both Guadeloupe and Martinique between 1635 and 1636. The introduction of sugar cultivation in the latter part of the 17th century heralded *l'age d'or blanc* (the age of white gold) and the expansion of French influence down the eastern Caribbean chain and north to St.-Domingue (present-day Haiti). As slave ships unloaded their human cargo to work the vast tracts of sugarcane, sizable fortunes flowed into the planters' coffers, and the town of St.-Pierre on Martinique developed into one of the most prosperous and fashionable cities in the West Indies.

Things did not always run smoothly, of course. Britain challenged France's authority at every turn and by a combination of treaties and brute force occupied virtually every French Caribbean territory during the 18th century. France did her best to return the compliment.

Ironically, the supporters of the ancien régime of Martinique actually called the old enemy in to assist when the French Revolution decreed the abolition of slavery. The British ruled the island for 20 years without liberating the slaves. Napoleon (whose wife came from a family of Martiniquais planters) reintroduced slavery in 1802, causing widespread chaos and slave rebellions in Haiti and Guadeloupe. The law was not repealed until 1848, when the plantations turned to East Indian indentured laborers to replace the freed slaves.

Unlike the British islands, which were gently but firmly urged down the road to independence in the 20th century, France has bound her Caribbean territories more closely. Guadeloupe and Martinique have been integrated into the republic's political mainstream as semiautonomous overseas *régions*. The islanders have the same rights as their mainland counterparts and elect representatives to the Assemblée Nationale in Paris, vote in French elections, and enjoy the benefits of substantial government subsidies that have elevated local standards of living way above average for the region.

Dramatic volcanic eruptions raised Guadeloupe and Martinique from the seabed, and both islands boast beautiful mountain ranges choked with rain forest greenery and encircled by cane

NOT TO BE MISSED:

Driving the Route de la Traversée, Guadeloupe   240–241

Boat trips from Guadeloupe to Les Saintes & Marie-Galante   242–243

Café society (and croissants) in Gustavia, St.-Barthélemy   246

Walking along the white-sand beach of Anse de Grande Saline, St.-Barthélemy   246

The tropical plants of Jardin de Balata, Martinique   256

Viewing the mementos of devastation at the Musée Vulcanologique, St.-Pierre, Martinique   256

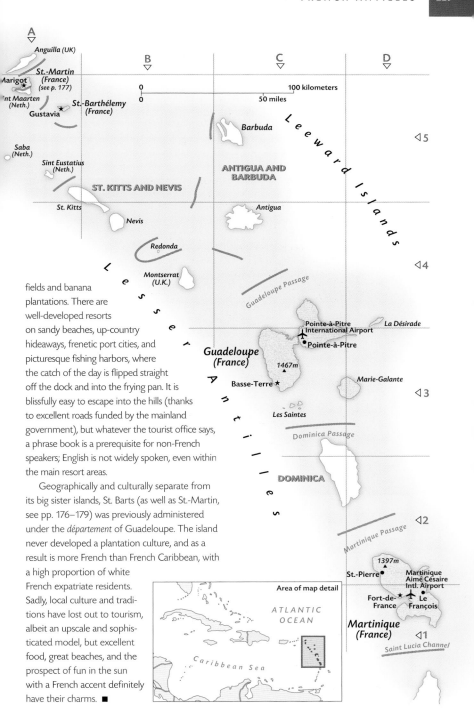

A △

Anguilla (UK)

St.-Martin
(France)
(see p. 177)

Marigot ★

'nt Maarten
(Neth.)

Saba
(Neth.)

Gustavia ★ St.-Barthélemy
(France)

Sint Eustatius
(Neth.)

B △

0 _____ 100 kilometers
0 _____ 50 miles

Barbuda

Leeward Islands

C △

ANTIGUA AND
BARBUDA

ST. KITTS AND NEVIS

St. Kitts

Nevis

Redonda

Antigua

Montserrat
(U.K.)

Lesser

fields and banana
plantations. There are
well-developed resorts
on sandy beaches, up-country
hideaways, frenetic port cities, and
picturesque fishing harbors, where
the catch of the day is flipped straight
off the dock and into the frying pan. It is
blissfully easy to escape into the hills (thanks
to excellent roads funded by the mainland
government), but whatever the tourist office says,
a phrase book is a prerequisite for non-French
speakers; English is not widely spoken, even within
the main resort areas.

Geographically and culturally separate from
its big sister islands, St. Barts (as well as St.-Martin,
see pp. 176–179) was previously administered
under the *département* of Guadeloupe. The island
never developed a plantation culture, and as a
result is more French than French Caribbean, with
a high proportion of white
French expatriate residents.
Sadly, local culture and traditions have lost out to tourism,
albeit an upscale and sophisticated model, but excellent
food, great beaches, and the
prospect of fun in the sun
with a French accent definitely
have their charms. ■

D △

5 ◁

La Désirade

4 ◁

Guadeloupe Passage

Pointe-à-Pitre
International Airport
Pointe-à-Pitre

*Guadeloupe
(France)*   1467m ▲

Basse-Terre ★

Les Saintes

Marie-Galante

3 ◁

Dominica Passage

DOMINICA

Antilles

Martinique Passage

2 ◁

1397m
▲

St.-Pierre ●   Martinique
Aimé Césaire
Intl. Airport

Fort-de- ★   Le
France   François

*Martinique
(France)*   1 ◁

Saint Lucia Channel

Area of map detail

ATLANTIC
OCEAN

Caribbean Sea

Guadeloupe

Shaped like a butterfly with mismatched wings, Guadeloupe is in fact two islands crowded together by seismic upheavals and linked by a bridge over the Rivière Salée (Salt River). The western wing is Basse-Terre, marked by verdant and volcanic peaks, and the eastern is Grande-Terre, a rolling, dry limestone plateau fringed by beaches. Making up the Guadeloupean archipelago are the islands of La Désirade, Marie-Galante, and the eight tiny islets of Les Saintes.

Drums beat out the rhythms of Carnival in Guadeloupe.

Guadeloupe

🅰 229 C3

Visitor Information

✉ 5 Square de la Banque, Pointe-à-Pitre

☎ 0590 82 09 30

guadeloupe-islands .com

Perhaps inspired by the dozens of streams and waterfalls that tumble down Basse-Terre's rainforested flanks, the Carib people called the island Karukera ("island of beautiful waters"). Christopher Columbus sailed past in 1493 and rechristened it Santa Maria de Guadalupe de Extremadura in honor of a famous Spanish monastery. A century and a half later the

French colonized Guadeloupe with indentured settlers who worked for three years to pay off their sea passage. Unaccustomed to tropical conditions, they farmed with limited success until a four-year British occupation (1759–1763) turned the plantations around. The slow start meant Guadeloupe was administered from more successful Martinique and was forced to trade through the commercial port of St.-Pierre, whose merchants paid artificially low prices for Guadeloupean sugar. As news of the French Revolution traveled across the Atlantic in 1789, it found the unhappy Guadeloupeans ripe for change.

Guadeloupe's settlers embraced the revolutionary regime with enthusiasm. Bands of armed *patriotes* (supporters of the revolution) overthrew the planters and installed a revolutionary government led by Victor Hugues (1770–1826). They erected the mandatory guillotine in Pointe-à-Pitre, where more than 300 enemies of the revolution lost their

heads. The slaves were freed in 1794, but their freedom was short-lived. The old regime regained control, and slavery was bloodily reestablished; many former slaves preferred death to submission. The British came and went a couple more times before France secured the colony for good in 1815. The Guadeloupeans' independent cast of mind remains a force to be reckoned with today. There are occasional calls for independence from *la métropole,* but French cash is a powerful incentive to remain under the old colonial umbrella, particularly in view of the massive grants made available to help the island rebuild in the wake of hurricane damage.

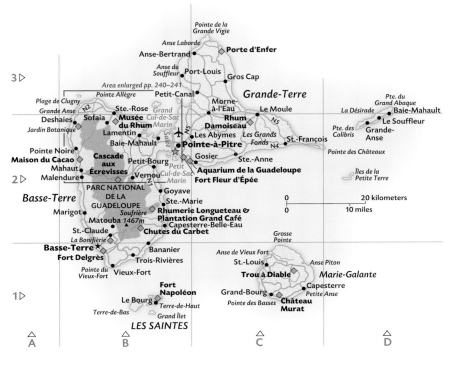

INSIDER TIP:

Creole street food heaven is a paper cone of crispy, fried *accras* (seasoned fish balls fried in batter) dipped in searing hot sauce.

—EMMA STANFORD
National Geographic author

Guadeloupe encompasses 530 square miles (1,372 sq km) and has a population of about 470,000. The contrasting island wings possess two equally diverse main cities. On the southwest coast of Basse-Terre is Basse-Terre town (see pp. 238–239), the modest administrative capital tucked in the lee of the Soufrière volcano. A string of small towns and villages, linked by an around-island ring road, circle the coast of Guadeloupe's west wing. Only one route, La Traversée, scales the central mountain range, clambering up into Parc National de la Guadeloupe (see sidebar p. 239), a magnificent natural preserve with some of the best—and most challenging—hiking in the Caribbean.

In the southwest corner of Grande-Terre is Guadeloupe's biggest and busiest city—the sprawling commercial center and cruise-ship port of Pointe-à-Pitre (see opposite). No great beauty, it has a frenetic pace at odds with the usual leisurely Caribbean tempo, but it's fun to explore the local markets, and ferries for the

Guadeloupe's Route de Traversée offers one of the Caribbean's most appealing drives.

Creole Costume

Brightly checkered madras cotton is a ubiquitous feature of Guadeloupe, Martinique, and the French-speaking Windward Islands, which include Dominica and St. Lucia. Souvenir shops are piled high with madras table linens, costumed dollies, and, of course, traditional creole costumes perfect for the dressing-up box back home.

Madras cotton was introduced to the islands by indentured laborers from the Indian subcontinent in the late 1800s. Colorful and cheap, it was enthusiastically adopted by former slaves whose drab clothing had been limited to cast-off canvas and even rough grain sacks. Renowned for their Gallic style, women fashioned the simple cotton fabric into elaborate robes worn to celebrate feast days and holidays.

The five-piece costume consists of a white blouse trimmed with lace and ribbons, a madras cotton skirt worn over flouncy petticoats, and a foulard scarf thrown over the shoulder and secured in the waistband, all topped by a significant silk head scarf. The scarf is a work of art in itself with a variable number of points *(bouts)*, which signal the wearer's intentions:

Tête à un bout (one point)—
my heart is for the taking
Tête à deux bouts (two points)—
my heart is taken
Tête à trois bouts (three points)—
my heart is spoken for, but . . .

---

offshore islands leave from the waterfront. Dotted east along the coast from Pointe-à-Pitre are the seaside resort towns of Gosier, Ste.-Anne, and St.-François. Gosier is the most developed, with a wall of large, modern hotels fronting the shore and packed beaches. Ste.-Anne and St.-François have retained more of their local character. Here it is sometimes possible to catch a game of *boules* in progress on one of the dusty, tree-shaded squares before dining out stylishly *à la française* at an excellent (although not inexpensive) fish restaurant along the promenade.

Pointe-à-Pitre

A teeming metropolis by day, Pointe-à-Pitre lies on a sheltered bay at the southern end of the Rivière Salée. Although the city dates from the 17th century,

hurricanes, earthquakes, and fires have taken their toll, and modern concrete structures outnumber the few remaining colonial buildings.

With the sunlight blotted out by tall, thin buildings, downtown Pointe-à-Pitre is a maelstrom of traffic and pedestrians fighting for space on the narrow streets. At times it appears that there are more cars on the sidewalk than pedestrians, and jaywalking is obligatory. (Avoid driving in the downtown area at all costs.)

The focus of the old town is **La Darse,** the bustling waterfront area, with its ferry dock and jumble of street vendors' stalls selling everything from T-shirts and wood carvings to fresh produce and piping hot *accras.* Behind the dockside hubbub is **Place de la Victoire,** with its fringe of old colonial houses, their balconies full

Pointe-à-Pitre

▲ 231 B2

Visitor Information

✉ 5 Square de la Banque, Pointe-à-Pitre

☎ 0590 82 09 30

guadeloupe-islands .com

Musée Schoelcher

- ✉ 24 rue Peynier
- ☎ 0590 82 08 04
- 🕐 Closed Sat.–Sun.
- 💲 $

of flowers. Several sidewalk cafés provide a restful view of the city's green heart, planted with palm, mango, and African tulip trees.

Plunge into the grid of busy side streets west of the gardens to the **Cathédrale St.-Pierre et St.-Paul,** Place Gourbeyre. Nicknamed *la cathédrale de fer* (iron cathedral) for its elaborate ironwork, the building was constructed in the early 19th century and has some fine stained glass.

Rue Frébault, the city's main shopping street, is lined with boutiques and stores full of French

fashions and European imports. On the corner of Frébault and rue Peynier is the **Marché Couvert** (Covered Market), providing a boisterous slice of island life. Its maze of stalls is piled high with fruits and vegetables, bags of ground spices, and bunches of vanilla pods presided over by garrulous female vendors who giggle and haggle in a machine-gun patter of incomprehensible creole.

West along rue Peynier is the **Musée Schoelcher,** devoted to the life and times of 19th-century abolitionist Victor Schoelcher (1804–1893), a leading light in the French antislavery movement. When emancipation finally reached the French Caribbean in 1848, Schoelcher was elected a deputy of Guadeloupe. The museum occupies a pretty pink town house with wrought-iron decorations and a double staircase leading up to the entrance. Exhibits range from plantation-era artifacts and Schoelcher's campaigning pamphlets to African carved ivories, model ships, and other curios. The statue in front of the building depicts the revolutionary leader Victor Hugues.

NEED TO KNOW
Port Logistics: Pointe-à-Pitre

A short stroll from the central shopping district, the downtown cruise terminal has Wi-Fi and shopping, and the helpful information staff can assist with finding English-speaking taxi drivers for island tours (taxis have meters). Guadeloupe's roads are good, so you might consider renting a car in advance, but limit your driving in busy Pointe-à-Pitre itself. Buses are a cheap and reasonably efficient way to get to the beaches at Gosier (20 mins) and Ste.-Anne (35 mins), but beware of very heavy traffic later in the afternoons. Don't forget you will need euro currency.

Pointe-à-Pitre Highlights

You can spend your entire port of call time at any one of these destinations, but here are some suggested times to help with your planning. Note, these do not allow for travel time to and from:

- Explore Pointe-à-Pitre's shops & markets: 2–3 hours
- Visit Parc National de la Guadeloupe: half/full day
- Relax on Plage Caravelle, Grande-Terre: half day

The Renaissance Theater in Pointe-à-Pitre

Around Grande-Terre

Though Grande-Terre's southern beaches act as a magnet for tourists, most of the island is undeveloped, a rural backwater where rolling limestone hills, known as Les Grands Fonds, shelter a smattering of small farming hamlets, and the sugarcane harvest is still transported to the mill by ox-drawn carts.

Between Pointe-à-Pitre and Gosier is **Bas-du-Fort's** busy marina, the largest in the Caribbean. It's a good place to stop off and sample the nautical atmosphere from a sunny café or to dine out in one of the many restaurants. Next to the marina is the **Aquarium de la Guadeloupe.** A showcase for tropical fish, it also has a mangrove section and a huge shark tank with a walk-through Plexiglas tunnel.

On a headland above Bas-du-Fort are the 18th-century coral rock ruins of **Fort Fleur d'Epée,** laid out on a hilltop site shaded by flamboyant red-flowering trees.

Across Grande Baie is the seaside town of **Gosier,** Guadeloupe's chief resort, taking its name from the brown pelican, a familiar sight throughout the Caribbean. The old town has been swamped by an avalanche of hotels, restaurants, cafés, and discos spilling downhill to the shore and stretching for miles along the narrow sandy beaches. Hotels and concessions are well equipped for water sports, and small boats make the short voyage out to the tiny offshore pimple of **Îlet du Gosier,** where there's a lighthouse and another public beach (clothing optional).

Midway along the coast is **Ste.-Anne,** where long, sandy Caravelle beach offers water-sports activities and a Club Med resort to the west of town. Nearby is

Aquarium de la Guadeloupe
- 231 B2
- ✉ Place Créole-Marina
- ☎ 0590 90 92 38
- 💲 $$$

aquariumdela guadeloupe.com

Fort Fleur d'Epée
- 231 B2
- **Visitor Information**
- ☎ 0590 90 94 61

Gosier
- 231 C2

Ste.-Anne
- 231 C2

Club Med
✉ Quart Caravelle, Ste.-Anne
☎ 0590 85 49 50

clubmed.us

St.-François
⬛ 231 C2

Rhum Damoiseau
⬛ 231 C2
✉ Rte. D101, on the road from Le Moule to Les Abymes
☎ 0590 23 55 55
🕐 Open for visits. Call for hours & admission fee

damoiseau.fr

Ste.-Anne Plage, a lovely strip of fine white sand on a turquoise bay. It can get crowded, but plus points for families include shady trees, a row of café-restaurants across the street, and carts selling hot, sweet crêpes and ice cream.

St.-François has a salty tang, with fishermen constructing traditional hexagonal fish traps on the

INSIDER TIP:

Club Med at Ste.-Anne's Caravelle beach offers day passes to nonguests for the use of its beach and water-sports equipment, as well as lunch and drinks.

—JENNIFER ALLARD
National Geographic contributor

waterfront. The closest beach is **Plage des Raisins Clair,** but to the east of town is a 7-mile (11 km) road, lined with beaches along the southern shore. **Plage Tarare,** on the north side, is a nudist haunt. At the tip of the headland is **Pointe des Châteaux,** with its own small beach cove where surfers ride the powerful Atlantic waves that have hollowed caves from the soft limestone. A rocky path scales the cliffs to an orientation table with blustery views to the outer islands and peaks of Basse-Terre.

From St.-François, Rte. N5 runs north to **Le Moule,** once the capital of Guadeloupe and another surfers' hangout. On a back road west of town is **Rhum Damoiseau,** the only rum distillery on Grande-Terre.

A country road continues up to the northern tip of the island, past a viewpoint at **Porte**

Beachgoers in the calm waters near Ste.-Anne

EXPERIENCE: Explore Nature Preserved

Caught between Guadeloupe's twin island butterfly wings, **Réserve Naturelle du Grand Cul-de-Sac Marin** (*guadeloupe-parc national.fr/?Le-Grand-Cul-de-Sac-Marin*), is an annex of Parc National de la Guadeloupe (see sidebar p. 239). Its 9,000-acre (3,600 ha) territory encompasses mangrove swamps, mudflats, wetland prairies, coastal forest, and an adjacent marine preserve renowned for its rich and rare biodiversity. Researchers at the park study estuaries, coral reefs, river fauna, mangrove ecosystems, and more. The foreshore is a prime feeding ground for both salt- and freshwater waterfowl and wading birds, such as egrets and kingfishers.

For a closer look at the preserve, take a sea kayak tour with TamTam Pagaie (*Ste.-Rose, Basse-Terre, tel 0590 28 13 85, guadeloupe-kayak.com, $$$$$*). Half-day, full-day, and overnight guided camping trips explore the mangrove-lined bay and deserted islets where you stop off to go snorkeling.

d'Enfer (Gate of Hell), before reaching **Pointe de la Grande Vigie** (Grand Lookout), where French sentries once scanned the horizon for signs of British activity on Antigua.

Beach stops on the west coast include **Anse Laborde** (just north of Anse-Bertrand) and **Anse du Souffleur** (at Port-Louis). In the center of the island is **Morne-à-l'Eau,** famous for its classic French Caribbean cemetery.

Around Southern Basse-Terre

Viewed from the sunny beaches of Grande-Terre, the towering, luxuriantly green bulk of neighboring Basse-Terre appears to brood like some giant leviathan beneath a blanket of clouds. About two-thirds of the island is the unspoiled Parc National de la Guadeloupe (see sidebar p. 239) with *traces* (walking trails) ranging from short, muddy scrambles to waterfall beauty spots to serious long-distance hikes across the ridgeline or up

to the Soufrière volcano. A fast modern road (Rte. N1) whisks you down the east coast from Pointe-à-Pitre to the capital of Basse-Terre town in less than an hour, although there are several minor detours en route.

Inland from Petit-Bourg, the botanic gardens at **Domaine de Valombreuse** are laid out in the foothills. There are more than 1,000 species of plants, trails, birdlife, and a children's play area. Just south of **Ste.-Marie,** a small coastal town where Christopher Columbus is thought to have encountered his first Carib in 1493, there are signs off the main road to the **Rhumerie Longueteau** distillery and Plantation Grand Café, a banana plantation. Cane fields surround the modern Longueteau estate house and its tiny, old-fashioned steam mill. Informal tours operate year-round, but the mill is only working (and interesting) during the January-to-July harvest season. After your visit, you can sample straight rums and potent

Domaine de Valombreuse
✉ Cabout
☎ 0590 95 50 50
$ $$

valombreuse.com

Rhumerie Longueteau
Ⓜ 231 B2

Visitor Information
☎ 0590 86 07 91
🕐 Closed Sat. p.m. & Sun.; Dec.– April open Sun. a.m.

rhumlongueteau.fr

Plantation Grand Café

🏛 231 B2

Visitor Information

☎ 0590 86 33 06
🕐 Closed Sat.–Sun.
💲 $$

homemade rums spiked with tropical fruits.

Just up the road is the **Plantation Grand Café,** which celebrates the not-so-humble banana. A banana garden displays varieties from around the world—little plump pink velutinas from

Although the path continues on to the two upper falls, the most popular access point is another side road about a mile (1.6 km) farther along Rte. N1, which takes a scenic route up to a parking area and collection of roadside barbecue stalls. It's a 20-minute uphill

One of the many beautiful waterfalls on Basse-Terre

Chutes du Carbet

🏛 231 B2

Basse-Terre

🏛 231 B1

Visitor Information

✉ Maison du Port, off blvd. du Général de Gaulle
☎ 0590 81 24 83

India and crocodile's fingers from Indonesia, among others. The 30-minute tours rattle around the plantation in open-sided trucks.

On the southern edge of the town of Capesterre-Belle-Eau a side road leads up to the trailhead for the third and least spectacular of the **Chutes du Carbet,** a series of three waterfalls in the national park fed by the Rivière Grand Carbe, which originates on Soufrière. The third fall is a mere 65 feet (20 m) high, but it's a peaceful 45-minute trek into the rain forest beneath giant mahogany, gommier, and *bois rouge* trees.

hike to the popular 360-foot-high (110 m) second fall. It takes two hours to reach the 410-foot-high (125 m) top fall and three hours to ascend to Soufrière.

Basse-Terre Town

At the southwestern tip of the island is Basse-Terre town, which offers little to detain the dedicated sightseer, although it has a bustling provincial charm. Across the street from its French-style, palm-lined seafront esplanade, stalls display succulent fruits and vegetables. A tight grid of shopping streets squeezes in between the Hôtel de Ville and the gray stone Catholic cathedral. To the south, **Fort Delgrès** stands guard over the harbor and houses a small history museum as well as the **Maison du Volcan,** with displays charting the origins of volcanoes and the history of Soufrière.

Behind the busy city center residential suburbs spread up the hillsides to St.-Claude, where a few old creole houses still cling tenaciously to the slopes. Well worth a stop here is the very tantalizing **La Bonifièrie,** a restored 18th-century estate complex with a coffee mill, a gourmet chocolate factory, and an excellent on-site café. Chocolate and coffee in a tropical setting: What more could a traveler ask for?

Above St.-Claude, Rte. D11 strikes on up through the encroaching rain forest, narrowing as it climbs toward **Savane à**

Mulets, 1,000 feet (305 m) below the volcano's summit. From here the round-trip hike to the summit takes around two and a half hours along a well-marked trail past lava flows and boulders. The climb is generally accompanied by a steady drizzle and cool winds, so bring appropriate clothing. At the summit, not one crater but a chain of reeking, sulfur-spewing pits are staggered along the fault line.

To complete a tour of southern Basse-Terre, the slow west coast road (Rte. N2) parallels the shore, through Vieux-Habitants, where the **Musée du Café** (*tel 0509 98 54 96*) delves into the history of coffee on a working plantation. At **Mahaut** the Route de la Traversée (see pp. 240–241) crosses the park back to the east coast for Pointe-à-Pitre. If you're in a hurry, however, it's quicker to return along the east coast. ■

Fort Delgrès
🗺 231 B1
Visitor Information
☎ 0590 81 37 48

La Bonifièrie
🗺 231 B2
✉ Section Morin, St.-Claude
☎ 0590 80 06 05
🕐 Closed Mon.
💲 $$

Parc National de la Guadeloupe

A UNESCO-designated biosphere reserve covering 74,000 acres (30,000 ha) of central southern Basse-Terre, the national park cloaks the cloud-shrouded bulk of Soufrière (4,813 feet/1,467 m), rising to the highest point in the Lesser Antilles.

Venturing into the virgin, green heart of the park, where Soufrière's flanks course with rivers and waterfalls, is not recommended for the fainthearted. Conditions are frequently wet, muddy, and chilly, so hikers should come prepared with rain gear and sturdy boots.

Dozens of trails crisscross the mountainsides, ranging from a gentle stroll from a parking lot on the Route de la Traversée (see pp. 240–241) to extended

treks that require a considerable degree of fitness, the correct equipment, and an experienced guide. The main access points to the park's trail network are along the Route de la Traversée and to the south around Soufrière.

The park headquarters at **Habitation Beausoleil** (*Montéran 97120, St.-Claude, tel 0590 41 55 55, guadeloupe-parcnational .fr*) is an excellent source of information, providing trail guides graded by difficulty. Guided hikes and rain forest experiences such as canyoning can be arranged through **Vert Intense** (*tel 0590 99 34 73, vert-intense.com, $$$$$*) and **Les Heures Saines** (*tel 0590 98 86 63, heures-saines .gp, $$$$$*).

A Drive Around Northern Basse-Terre

This clockwise circuit of northern Basse-Terre begins with a spectacular rain forest drive along the Route de la Traversée before looping around the top half of the island. You can experience a variety of suggested diversions along the way, from a glass-bottom boat trip to museums of cacao, wood, and rum.

From **Pointe-à-Pitre** ❶ (see pp. 233–234), follow signs for Basse-Terre west across the Rivière Salée and south on the fast Rte. N1 to the exit for La Traversée (Rte. D23). The cross-island road skims west through cane fields before ascending into the rain forest, where it enters Parc National de la Guadeloupe (see sidebar p. 239).

Just inside the park boundary is the pretty **Cascade aux Écrevisses** ❷ (Crayfish Falls),

a popular picnic spot at the foot of a scenic waterfall edged by dripping mosses and creepers. Beneath the forest canopy it's hard to resist scrambling around on the boulders that litter the stream like giant stepping-stones.

Just over a mile (1.6 km) farther, **Maison de la Forêt** provides an excellent introduction to the 74,000-acre (29,950 ha) park with exhibits covering geology, flora, and fauna (only in French). Hiking maps are available with details of the well-maintained, 190-mile (306 km)

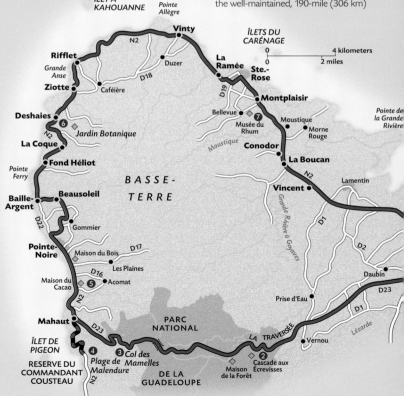

NOT TO BE MISSED:

Maison de la Forêt • Jardin Botanique • Musée du Rhum

trail network within the park, and there are several round-trip walks from the *maison*.

One of the park's more challenging hikes is the **Trace des Crêtes,** which follows the mountain ridge above the west coast and crosses La Traversée at the **Col des Mamelles** (1,922 feet/586 m), a mountain pass between twin volcanic peaks. This is the highest point on the road, with fantastic views of the park on a clear day, although the vista is frequently obscured by cloud and rain (the annual rainfall here is about 250 inches/6,350 mm).

After the hairpin descent to the coast at **Mahaut,** there's an optional short (3 miles/5 km) detour south to **Plage de Malendure** , where glass-bottom boat trips depart for the marine preserve surrounding tiny Îlet de Pigeon. **Reserve du Commandant Cousteau** honors oceanographer Jacques Cousteau (1910–1997). The coral reef site is rather crowded with divers and pleasure boats these days, but the visibility on a clear

day (averaging 100 feet/30 m) ensures there's always something interesting to see. *(For details of dive operators, see Travelwise p. 396. Advance reservations advised.)*

One and a half miles (2.5 km) north of Mahaut on Rte. N2 you will come across **Maison du Cacao** *(tel 0590 98 25 23, $$$),* which delves into the history, cultivation, and processing of cacao beans, introduced to Guadeloupe by the Arawaks. Blocks of 100 percent natural cocoa are on sale.

The drive continues through the attractive fishing village of **Deshaies** , overlooking the broad curve of Grande Anse, one of Guadeloupe's finest beaches. This 2-mile-long (3 km) sweep of rosy gold sand is backed by palm trees, and there's a choice of snack bars and creole-style café-restaurants serving traditional seafood specials and salads if it's time for a lunch break. Deshaies' other star turn is the magnificent **Jardin Botanique** *(tel 0590 28 43 02, closed Mon., $$$$, jardin-botanique.com),* a shady oasis of palms, dramatic stands of tropical gingers and lobster claws, and veritable floral cascades of bougainvillea and eye-catching blue jade vine. Winding trails allow visitors to explore the 10-acre (4 ha) site, which features lagoons, a flock of flamingos, parrot aviary, and café.

Continue along the road (Rte. N2) as it rounds the northern tip of the island and continues on to **Ste.-Rose;** follow the signs for the **Musée du Rhum** *(tel 0590 28 70 04, musee-du-rhum.fr, closed Sun.)* at nearby Bellevue. Exhaustive signboards and displays examine every last detail of three centuries of rum-making in the Caribbean, and the museum contains a variety of antique artifacts, such as an enormous cane juice vat hewn out of a single tree trunk. The interesting insect gallery displays some 5,000 butterflies, beetles, and bugs from around the world. After watching a short film (some showings in English), you can take a tour of the adjacent Distillerie Reimonenq.

Back on the main road (Rte. N2), it's a swift run back to Pointe-à-Pitre.

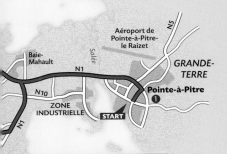

See also area map p. 231
► Pointe-à-Pitre
🕐 A full day with stops
🔁 58 miles/93 km
► Pointe-à-Pitre

The Guadeloupean Archipelago

The Guadeloupean archipelago forms a graceful southerly arc separating Guadeloupe from Dominica. These small islands complement the busier pace of Guadeloupe with tranquil backdrops of humble fishing villages and rolling sugarcane farms guarded by windmills.

A hat seller models her goods in Grand-Bourg on Marie-Galante.

La Désirade
231 D2

Marie-Galante
231 C1
Visitor Information
✉ rue du Fort, Grand-Bourg
☎ 0590 97 56 51

ot-mariegalante.com

La Désirade

An arid, flat-topped table mountain 6 miles (10 km) off Pointe des Châteaux (the eastern tip of Guadeloupe), La Désirade signaled the end of a long Atlantic crossing for Columbus, hence the name "desired one." Only 8 miles (13 km) long and 1 mile (1.6 km) wide, the island is a 145-million-year-old geological anomaly; jewelry made from its colored stones makes an unusual souvenir. The main settlement is **Beauséjour,** where the ferry docks on the sheltered southern shore; farther up the coast, past the golden sands of **Grande-Anse** and **Le Souffleur,** you can see the ruins of an old leper colony at **Baie-Mahault.** Visitors

can also enjoy panoramic walks, free-range iguanas, and boat trips to the sea turtle nesting reserve on Petite-Terre.

Daily ferry services *(Le Colibri, tel 0690 35 79 47; Babou One, tel 0690 26 60 69)* depart from St.-François in Guadeloupe (one hour). There are a few basic lodgings on the island, and locals offer B&Bs.

Marie-Galante

Twenty miles (32 km) south of Grande-Terre is the flat limestone island of Marie-Galante, settled in 1648. Old windmills dot the sugarcane fields, still harvested for the island's famous rums.

Grand-Bourg is Marie-Galante's main settlement. South of town is the 18th-century

Habitation Murat (*tel 0590 97 94 41, closed Sat.–Sun.*) plantation house, which has a windmill and a museum. Along the bottom of the island there is good swimming at **Petite Anse,** and water sports at **Pointe de la Feuillère,** near Capesterre. Inland, a maze of country lanes burrows through tunnels of sugarcane; several rum distilleries offer tours and tastings. The best of these is the award-winning eco-distillery **Domaine Bellevue** (*tel 0590 97 26 50, closed p.m.*). Another tourist stop is **Trou à Diable** (Devil's Hole), an underground cavern that requires a flashlight and sturdy footwear to explore.

Fine beaches span the northwest coast between Vieux Fort and the fishing village of **St.-Louis.** Daily ferry services (*L'Express des Îles, tel 0590 91 11 05, express-des-iles.com or Brudey, tel 0590 90 04 48*) to Grand-Bourg and St.-Louis leave from Pointe-à-Pitre (one hour); flights are available (15 minutes). Cars and scooters can be rented from Automoto Location (*St.-Louis, tel 0590 97 19 42, automoto-location.com*).

Les Saintes

Only two of these tiny, volcanic islets 7 miles (11 km) south of Basse-Terre are inhabited. The quieter and less visited is **Terre-de-Bas,** a sleepy former plantation island with a couple of good beaches, one hotel, and rooms to rent. **Terre-de-Haut,** on the other hand, greets the daily invasion of day-trippers with the restaurants and boutiques of **Le Bourg.** A fishing

Battle of the Saints

One of the most famous naval battles of the 18th century, the Battle of the Saints was the decisive factor in determining British supremacy in the Caribbean. In the spring of 1782 the French fleet was in Martinique, readying itself for an invasion of Jamaica calculated to destroy British credibility in the region. The preparations were being monitored by Adm. George Rodney (1718–1792) of the Royal Navy from his base on Pigeon Island, St. Lucia. On April 7, under Adm. François de Grasse, 33 French ships of the line set sail; Rodney gave chase, meeting the French off Les Saintes on the morning of April 12. In a surprise maneuver, which owed more to the weather than design, Rodney broke the French line in not one but three places and carried the day. The tactic was later employed by Admiral Nelson at Trafalgar.

port, Le Bourg is set on a magnificent bay sheltered by **Îlet à Cabrit** (Goat Island). Nowhere on the island is more than a 30-minute walk from Le Bourg, but it's a stiff uphill climb to **Fort Napoléon** (*tel 0690 61 01 51, closed p.m., $$*). The fortress houses a museum of local history, with a section devoted to the Battle of the Saints (see sidebar this page).

Terre-de-Haut's best beach is **Plage Pont Pierre,** in the east. Two quieter beaches are **Petite Anse Pain de Sucre,** west of Le Bourg, and **Anse du Figuier,** on the south coast. Daily ferry services (*L'Express des Îles, tel 0590 91 11 05, or Brudey, tel 0590 90 04 48*) run to Terre-de-Haut and Terre-de-Bas from Pointe-à-Pitre (one hour) and Trois-Rivières (30 minutes). There are daily sailings between Le Bourg and Terre-de-Bas, and flights from Guadeloupe. ■

Les Saintes
⬛ 231 B1

St.-Barthélemy

Known as Manhattan-sur-Mer to the cognoscenti, St.-Barthélemy is the epitome of French Caribbean chic and arguably the most exclusive and expensive speck of volcanic rock in the region, give or take a private island or two. This is the winter playground of the super-rich and super-casual, where the shops overflow with Chanel and champagne, but dressing for dinner is frowned upon.

Cactuses contrast with the bright blue waters of Baie de St.-Jean in St. Barthélemy.

St.-Barthélemy

🅐 229 A5

Visitor Information

✉ Quai du Général de Gaulle, Gustavia

☎ 0590 27 87 27

saintbarth-tourisme .com

One of the first things to strike visitors to St. Barts (or Saint-Barth in French) is the paucity of black faces; almost all 9,000 permanent inhabitants are white, affluent, and of French descent. French culture defines every detail, from the humble baguette to the rarefied heights of gourmet cuisine, from designer labels to traditional *calèche* bonnets, the old-fashioned women's hats (now rarely seen except on holidays) that recall St. Barts's colonists from Normandy and Brittany.

St. Barts was not born with a silver spoon in its mouth. The 8-square-mile (21 sq km) island was named San Bartolomé for Columbus's brother and colonized by 60 French settlers from St. Kitts in 1648. The first colony was wiped out by a Carib raiding party, but the strategic position of St. Barts amid the English

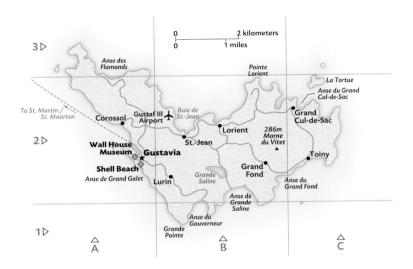

3▷

Anse des
Flamands

Pointe
Lorient

La Tortue

Anse du Grand
Cul-de-Sac

To St. Martin /
St. Maarten

Corossol   Gustaf III   Baie de
Airport   St.-Jean

Grand
Cul-de-Sac

2▷

Wall House
Museum   Gustavia

St.-Jean

Lorient

286m
Morne
du Vitet ▲

Toiny

Shell Beach
Anse de Grand Galet   Lurin

Grande
Saline

Grand
Fond

Anse du
Grand Fond

Anse de
Grande
Saline

1▷

△
A

Anse du
Gouverneur

Grande
Pointe

△
B

△
C

0 ——— 2 kilometers
0 ——— 1 miles

Leeward Island colonies prompted a second attempt by Protestant Huguenots in 1674. While other islands planted cotton and cane, St. Barts's stock in trade was piracy. Buccaneers frequently took refuge in its convenient coves.

In 1784 French king Louis XVI exchanged St. Barts for trading rights in the Baltic, and the island became Swedish for a century.

The Swedes declared their sole Caribbean possession a free port, and for a while it profited handsomely, trading with the newly independent United States of America. When business tailed off, the island was sold back to France in 1878 and subsided into obscurity until quietly reemerging as a stylish jet-set hideaway during the 1980s.

Racing Stripes

Yachting is not just a sport in St. Barts; it's a passion driven by the constant trade winds and sensational scenery. The island's sporting calendar is jam-packed with regattas and races starting in November with the prestigious St. Barth CataCup. One of the region's top sailing events, it attracts a world-class field of racing catamarans to Baie de St.-Jean. New Year's is an excuse for a waterborne around-the-island parade, featuring a host of multicolored sails. In March hundreds of craft big and small gather for the Bucket Regatta and three days of friendly races and onshore partying. The season draws to a close in April, but not before the weeklong Les Voiles de Saint-Barth. Les Voiles (The Sails) is staged over six days. It pitches maxi yachts, racing yachts, and multihulls against each other over a series of stunning courses around the outer islands.

Gustavia

△ 245 A2

Wall House Museum

△ 245 A2
✉ La Pointe
☎ 0590 29 71 55
🕐 Closed Sun.
💲 $

Le Sélect

✉ rue du Centenaire
☎ 0590 27 86 87

Gustavia

Postcard-pretty Gustavia was named in honor of the Swedish king Gustav III and hems in three sides of its sheltered harbor, guarded by four hilltop forts. During the height of the winter season, splendiferous gin palaces line the docks, berthed sleek-cheek-by-elegant-jowl, and the boutiques, jewelers, and terrace cafés of the tiny town center are packed with serious shoppers and gawking day-trippers from Sint Maarten. The pointy roofed Swedish belfry is a local landmark. On the western side of the harbor is the **Wall House Museum,** which provides a quick roundup of local history and customs in a former waterfront warehouse. Its collections include Amerindian votive objects, colonial documents, and stiff-sided calèche bonnets, also known as *quichenottes* (kiss-me-nots), once regarded as a woman's best defense against amorous

INSIDER TIP:

In Gustavia, check out Le Sélect, the hangout that inspired Jimmy Buffet's song "Cheeseburger in Paradise."

—BARBARA NOE
National Geographic Books writer

Englishmen and Swedes. The closest beach is **Shell Beach,** a ten-minute walk south of town at **Anse de Grand Galet.**

St. Barts peaks at less than 1,000 feet (305 m), but its tightly packed folds of perpendicular green hills make it seem much taller, while lovingly cultivated gardens create an impression of tropical lushness. The 18 small villages dotted about the island are linked by narrow roads that crawl doggedly up into the hills and then plummet back to the coast. At the bottom of a vertiginous descent north of Gustavia is the charming fishing village of **Corossol.**

On the north coast is St. Barts's chief tourist hub, **St.-Jean,** where hotels, restaurants, and shops have sprung up along the roadside facing a glorious bay and busy beach. A road circles the east end of the island, past the beach at Anse du Grand Cul-de-Sac and around **Morne du Vitet** (938 feet/286 m). The two best beaches are on the south coast: **Anse de Grande Saline,** reached via St.-Jean, and **Anse du Gouverneur,** south of Lurin. Both are undeveloped, with deep white sand and terrific views of distant Saba, Sint Eustatius, and St. Kitts. ∎

NEED TO KNOW
Port Logistics: Gustavia

Cruise visitors are tendered into the heart of Gustavia's waterfront shopping and dining district, close to the excellent information bureau. Taxis await on the dockside; fares are based on driving time (10 mins to St.-Jean/20 mins to Anse de Grand Saline). However, it's fun to rent a small car for the day, pick up a gourmet picnic, and find the perfect beach.

Gustavia Highlights

• Window shopping in Gustavia: 2 hours
• St.-Jean's shops & beach: 3–4 hours
• Anse de Grand Saline: half day

Martinique

Martinique is one of the most beautiful of all the Caribbean islands. The Amerindians called it Madinina, the "island of flowers," and Martinique is still celebrated for its glorious gardens and rampant rain forest, as well as its lovely people, fine beaches, and distinctive creole culture. Measuring 50 miles (80 km) long and 22 miles (35.5 km) wide, it is flanked by the Windward Islands of Dominica to the north and St. Lucia to the south.

Martinique's colorful Carnival culture on display during a celebration in Grande Anse d'Arlet

Northern Martinique is tall and explosively green, swathed in dense rain forest that swoops down from the heights of Mont Pelée, the island's only active volcano, through the lesser but still impressive peaks of the Pitons du Carbet, and the *mornes,* to a fringe of banana plantations clinging to the lower slopes. The central plain, stretching east from Fort-de-France, the island's capital on the west coast, is Martinique's sugarcane belt. The south of the island is characterized by dry, hilly folds that back a scattered collection of beaches and small coastal resorts.

Columbus may have spotted Martinica, as he called it, on his second voyage, but he definitely stopped off here on his fourth expedition in 1502. He waxed lyrical about the beauty of the island and the Carib women who greeted his arrival with cries

Martinique

229 D1–D2

Visitor Information

✉ 76 rue Lazare Carnot, Fort-de-France

☎ 0596 60 27 73

tourismefdf.com

of "Madinina." It is uncertain whether Martinica is a corruption of Madinina or maybe a homage to St. Martin. The Carib were still in possession of the island when French settlers first came ashore near Le Carbet on the west coast in 1635. After a quarter of a century of violent skirmishes, a treaty ceded the Atlantic-facing east coast to the Carib, but before long the French had the whole island to themselves and proceeded to carpet it with sugarcane.

Martinique's administrative capital was established at Fort Royal (present-day Fort-de-France) in 1681, but the real focus of the island was St.-Pierre, a gracious harbor city at the foot of Mont Pelée, which became the hub of French trade and culture in the region. The British captured the island in 1762 but returned it a year later (along with Guadeloupe) in exchange for Dominica, Grenada, St. Vincent, and Tobago, plus French territories in Senegal and North America. The extent of the French concessions reflected the importance they

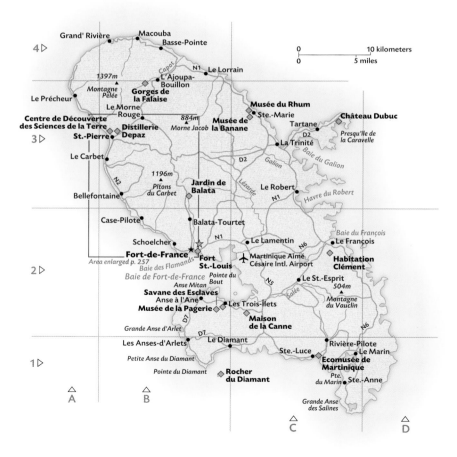

INSIDER TIP:

Martinique is a place where you'll want time to stand still: Allow yourself three or four days for a really good look around the island.

—JUSTIN KAVANAGH
*National Geographic
Travel Books editor*

attached to their Caribbean possessions. In 1793 the French Revolution arrived in Martinique, and initially the republicans carried the day. But within a year the planters had restored the old regime, with the help of the British.

Although relatively stable, Martinique witnessed several slave uprisings before the abolition of slavery in 1848 and the subsequent decline in wealth and importance of the sugar economy. Yet the most devastating day in the island's history occurred 54 years later, on May 8, 1902, when Mont Pelée erupted, destroying the city of St.-Pierre and killing all but one of its 30,000 inhabitants.

While life has returned to St.-Pierre in a small way, it remains a shadow of its former self. In contrast, Fort-de-France has boomed. A big and bustling port city with approximately 100,000 inhabitants, the capital is gobbling up the wooded hillsides behind the Baie des Flamands and spreading eastward to the industrial quarter of Le Lamentin and the airport. Facing the city from across the broad mouth of the Baie

de Fort-de-France are the well-developed hotel strip of Pointe du Bout and quieter Anse à l'Ane. The island's other two leading resort areas are the yachting center of Le Marin and Ste.-Anne, found down on the southeast peninsula close to Grande Anse des Salines, Martinique's best beach.

The Atlantic shore is rough and rocky, with another peninsula, Presqu'île de la Caravelle, about halfway up the coast, home to a few small hotels, sugar mill ruins, and a nature reserve.

Take a Ferry

Ferries are a good way to cross from Fort-de-France to beach resorts across the bay. Frequent, inexpensive ferry services are run by several companies including Vedettes Tropicales *(tel 0596 63 06 46, vedettes-tropicales.com, $$)* **from the waterfront near Fort St.-Louis to Les Trois-Îlets, Pointe du Bout, Anse Mitan, and Anse à l'Ane. Ferries operate from around 6 a.m. until about 6 or 7 p.m. (reduced services on weekends and holidays) to Pointe du Bout; the crossing takes 20 minutes.**

The rain forest luxuriance of the north is dominated by the cloud-capped bulk of simmering Mont Pelée. It's not a particularly interesting volcano to climb, but there are several pretty walks out of the village of L'Ajoupa-Bouillon and a memorable drive north through the Pitons du Carbet from Fort-de-France (see pp. 256–257). Although distances are modest and the roads good, leave plenty of time to explore.

(continued on p. 252)

Slavery

Sugar and slavery, twin bastions of the West Indian colonial era, arrived in the New World with Columbus. Spanish conquistadores created the first Caribbean slaves when they put Amerindians to work on the plantations of Hispaniola (in the present-day Dominican Republic). It took less than 20 years to decimate the population through disease and ill-treatment, prompting the Spanish to import African slaves to Hispaniola as early as 1511.

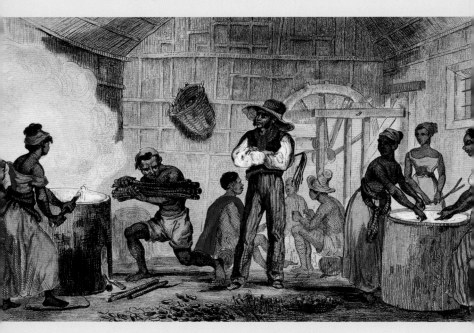

An engraving of slaves in the midst of preparing manioc flour in the Antilles

The Triangular Trade

Portuguese merchants introduced the first African slaves to Europe in the 1450s as exotic ornaments for the court. Domestic slavery of captured enemies was accepted practice among the tribes of the West African coast, and local traders were keen to exchange slaves for European manufactured goods such as textiles, glass, and weapons. The colonization of South America added a new dimension to this modest two-way traffic, bringing a steady trickle of African slaves across the Atlantic during the 16th century.

At first the British and French West Indian colonies relied on European laborers, but a combination of unaccustomed heat and tropical diseases killed as many as three out of four white settlers within two years of their arrival. When the sugar boom in the mid-1700s unleashed an urgent requirement for plentiful, cheap labor better prepared for the climate and backbreaking plantation work, the "triangular trade" was born. Ships from Europe headed to Africa where manufactured goods paid for African slaves. The slaves then embarked on the infamous Middle Passage to the New World, where the living cargo was exchanged for raw materials such as sugar, tobacco, cotton, and rum bound for Europe.

The Middle Passage

For the terrified slaves destined for the New World, their ordeal often began months ahead of transportation. Slavers selected their cargo from the vast barracoons (slave forts) that dotted the West African coast from Cape Verde to the Bight of Biafra, journeying from port to port until their vessels were filled to capacity. In preparation for the five- to eight-week voyage, food and water were taken on board and the cargo holds were subdivided into "slave decks," wooden shelves often no more than 2.5 feet (0.75 m) apart, where the slaves were packed in lying flat, the males shackled together left leg to right leg and wrist to wrist. Sickness, disease, and despair were rampant on the slave ships: One in eight slaves died on the Middle Passage. The survivors were oiled up to make them look healthier and auctioned off to the highest bidder in the slave markets of Curaçao, Nevis, Martinique, and Sint Eustatius, or on the wharf where the ship came into land.

It has been estimated that more than four million African slaves survived the journey to the West Indian colonies. British slave traders alone imported 2.5 million live slaves between 1690 and 1807, and the French added at least another million. By the 1750s black slaves already represented 90 percent of the population on sugar-growing islands, though the proportion was much lower in the Bahamas, Cayman Islands, and Netherlands Antilles where plantations were impractical. The dramatic imbalance between black and white meant the planters lived in constant fear of slave rebellions and ruled their private fiefdoms with rods of iron. Ferocious slave drivers, armed with whips, disciplined the slave gangs in the fields, and savage penalties were meted out for acts of disobedience or theft.

Rebellion & Emancipation

Despite the planters' best efforts to suppress their workforce, there were slave rebellions throughout the colonies in the 18th century. Most lasted no more than a couple weeks or months before being ruthlessly crushed, though a successful revolt in the French colony of St.-Domingue led to the creation of the black Republic of Haiti in 1804. In the 1780s European intellectuals who had long opposed slavery on moral grounds were joined by churchmen, and the combined pressure of forceful pamphleteering campaigns and sermons caused widespread antislavery sentiment. The British outlawed the slave trade to their colonies in 1808, and decreed the abolition of slavery in 1834. Sweden (1846), France and Denmark (1848), and Holland (1863) followed suit, while the Spanish held out until 1873 in Puerto Rico.

Working Patterns

West Indian planters devised two basic work regimes, the harshest of which was the "gang system" preferred on sugar estates. Slaves were divided into groups according to their strength, with the strongest first gang allocated the hardest manual tasks. Youths and old people in the second gang undertook lighter work, and the children in the third gang weeded and tidied. The gangs worked 10 to 12 hours a day, six days a week, and up to 18 hours during the harvest. The more liberal "task system" adopted on smaller farms and by slaves working as skilled craftsmen involved specific tasks that had to be completed in a given time. Slaves were then free to work their vegetable plots or undertake other jobs.

Fort-de-France

⬛ 248 B2

Visitor Information

tourismefdf.com

Musée Départemental d'Archéologie et de Préhistoire

✉ 9 rue de la Liberté, Fort-de-France

☎ 0596 71 57 05

🕐 Closed Mon. a.m., Sat. p.m., & Sun.

💲 $

Fort-de-France

A vibrant and attractive city, Fort-de-France enjoys a splendid position on the Caribbean coast, set against a backdrop of dark green hills. Its compact heart is inviting and easy to explore on foot, with a busy shopping district and narrow streets of flat-fronted buildings adorned with elaborate ironwork balconies.

The original settlement grew up around **Fort St.-Louis,** founded by the French in 1639. The sturdy fortress has been considerably extended and sits on a headland jutting out into the water, where it guards the **Baie des Flamands** waterfront to the west and the yacht harbor to the east. There is always plenty of activity down on the wharf, where cruise-ship passengers arrive, ferries depart for the beaches across the **Baie de Fort-de-France** (see sidebar p. 249), and kids dive off the piers just for fun.

Across the street from the wharf is a colorful craft and souvenir market, which lays out its wares on the edge of **La Savane.** These 12-acre (4.5 ha) gardens are shaded by magnificent royal palms, and it's a pleasant place to take a stroll and admire the flowers or sit on a park bench and watch the world go by. Overlooking the gardens from rue de la Liberté is the **Musée Départemental d'Archéologie et de Préhistoire,** where you can find displays of pottery and other Amerindian artifacts, as well as exhibits on slavery and

The Bibliothèque Schoelcher was shipped from France to Martinique after the 1889 Paris Exhibition.

Fort-de-France has a lively and colorful downtown area. Be sure to try a warm *pain au chocolat* at one of the Parisian-style cafés.

—MATT PROPERT
National Geographic photographer

colonial life illustrated with the help of period furnishings, crafts, and clothing.

Continue along the west side of the gardens to the fabulously eccentric **Bibliothèque Schoelcher,** a library named in honor of the great French abolitionist Victor Schoelcher and housed in an exotic Byzantine–Romanesque art nouveau structure designed for the 1889 Paris Exhibition. When the show was over, the building was taken to pieces, shipped to Martinique, and reconstructed. Opposite the library is a headless statue of the empress Joséphine (1763–1814). Once the pride of her Martiniquais compatriots, the empress was removed from her position at the center of La Savane and beheaded in 1991, after a guidebook revealed her role in encouraging Napoleon to reintroduce slavery in 1802.

For further insights into Martiniquais customs and traditions, take a detour to the **Musée Régional d'Histoire et d'Ethnographie,** housed in a pretty 19th-century creole villa and handsomely furnished in bourgeois period style.

Across the street from the library is rue Victor Sévère, which marks the top end of the main shopping district, bounded by rue de la Liberté, rue Victor Hugo, and rue de la République. The **Préfecture** is the first of several imposing colonial government buildings along this fine street. At the heart of the grid, among the fashionable boutiques, tempting patisseries, and stores filled with French luxury goods, stands the **Cathédrale de St.-Louis** on rue Victor Schoelcher. The distinctive brown-and-cream building, with its clock tower, steeple, and fancy ironwork, was erected on the foundations of six former churches in 1878. ∎

Bibliothèque Schoelcher

✉ Corner of rue de la Liberté & rue Perrinon, Fort-de-France
☎ 0596 55 68 30
🕐 Closed Mon. a.m., Sat. p.m., & Sun.

Musée Régional d'Histoire et d'Ethnographie

✉ 10 blvd. Général-de-Gaulle, Fort-de-France
☎ 0596 72 81 87
🕐 Closed Tues. a.m., Sat. p.m., & Sun.
💲 $$

NEED TO KNOW
Port Logistics: Fort-de-France

Downtown Pointe Simon is the most convenient cruise terminal, a short walk from shops and ferries *(vedettes)* to the Pointe du Bout beaches across the bay. The Tourelles terminal is a 20-minute walk (5 min/10 euros/$11 taxi ride) from the city center. Helpful, English-speaking information staff are available to arrange taxi tours, and cruise-line tours will circumnavigate the language barrier.

Fort-de-France Highlights

You can spend your entire port of call time at any one of these destinations, but here are some suggested times to help with your planning.

- St.-Pierre: half/full day
- Jardin de Balata: 2 hours
- Habitation Clément: half day
- Anse Mitan for snorkeling and lunch: half day

Around Southern Martinique

Visible across the bay from Fort-de-France, Martinique's most developed tourist enclave is the promontory of Pointe du Bout and the adjacent beach at Anse Mitan. This vacation center has a lively concentration of hotels, restaurants, beaches, and water-sports concessions frequented by day-tripping cruise passengers who hop across from the city by ferry.

Beach sunset near the town of Les Trois-Îlets

Les Trois-Îlets

🗺 248 B2

Visitor Information

✉ Place Gabriel Hayot

☎ 0596 68 47 63

Musée de la Pagerie

🗺 248 B2

✉ Les Trois-Îlets

☎ 0596 68 38 34

🕐 Closed Mon. & Sat. p.m.

💲 $$

Waterfront **Les Trois-Îlets** is an attractive little seaside village. A Saturday market is held on the square in front of the church where Napoleon's future empress was christened Marie-Rose Joséphine Tascher de la Pagerie in the summer of 1763. Just outside the village is the former family estate, where the **Musée de la Pagerie,** is laid out in a simple stone cottage among the ruins of the sugar mill. A few personal possessions of the empress, including letters from the emperor, are on display.

On the main road (Rte. D7) east of the village is the informative **Maison de la Canne.** Exhibits cover the history of the early plantations and the slave trade amid a welter of antique paraphernalia, models, and bilingual signboards. Across the road, down a bumpy track in the Quartier La Ferme district, **Savane des Esclaves** *(tel 0596 68 33 91, $$)* is a re-created slave village with simple thatched huts, kitchen, and medicinal gardens depicting the conditions *Neg marrons* (runaway slaves) would have lived under in the early 1800s.

Heading counterclockwise around the coast from Les Trois-Îlets, you reach the narrow sandy beach at **Anse à l'Ane** and its popular beach bars. The lovely village of **Les Anses-d'Arlets** has several dark-sand beaches nearby, including the tiny black-sand strip of **Petit Anse du Diamant,** where dozens of traditional fishing boats ride the gentle swell in the bay. Around the headland there's a fine view of the **Rocher du Diamant,** an offshore islet shaped like a giant brioche with a slice carved out of it. In 1804 British troops from St. Lucia captured the rock to harass French shipping. It was "commissioned" into the British navy, armed with cannon, and nicknamed H.M.S. *Diamond Rock.* The British garrison held out for 18 months, hoisting provisions ashore from visiting ships until a concerted French bombardment forced the occupiers to withdraw.

East of Ste.-Luce, across the Rivière Pilote, is the **Ecomusée de Martinique,** providing a detailed and fascinating account of island history. The excellent sections on Amerindian society and culture are accompanied by artifacts, models, and a list of common words derived from Amerindian languages, such as alligator, barbecue, and tobacco.

Continuing eastward, visit the yachting center of **Le Marin** at the foot of a deep, sheltered bay behind its packed marina. On the waterfront you can choose from a clutch of seafood restaurants serving up the catch of the day, accompanied by the creak of rigging in the breeze. Around the bay is the **Pointe du Marin** headland, with its crescent of sandy beach fringed by palms; a hillside Calvary dominates the

approach to the pretty resort town of **Ste.-Anne.** South of Ste.-Anne, the road passes the dry, sunbaked peninsula and salt ponds to **Grande Anse des Salines,** a curve of blond sand, where palms, sea grape trees, and Australian pines provide a shady retreat. Here you'll find snack wagons, vendors selling pineapple, and restaurants.

From Le Marin, Rte. N6 cuts across to the east coast town of **Le François.** In the rolling countryside just south of town is the old **Habitation Clément** sugar estate, which opens its doors to the public. Rum hasn't been distilled here since 1988, but the fully equipped distillery is on display, as are the *chais* (storehouses) where barrels of Rhum Clément mature in oak imported from France. The

highlight of the visit is the lovely 19th-century plantation house. In the dining room, carved colonial furniture is enhanced by oil lamps and antique silver. Upstairs, be sure to see the embroidered coverlets on the four-poster beds. ■

Maison de la Canne

- 🗺 248 B2
- ✉ Les Trois-Îlets
- ☎ 0596 68 32 04
- 🕐 Closed Mon.
- 💲 $

Ecomusée de Martinique

- 🗺 248 C1
- ✉ Anse Figuier
- ☎ 0596 62 79 14
- 🕐 Closed Mon.
- 💲 $

Habitation Clément

- 🗺 248 C2
- ✉ Le François (2 miles/3 km from St.-François on Rte. D18)
- ☎ 0596 54 75 51
- 💲 $$

habitation-clement .fr

A Drive Through the Pitons du Carbet to St.-Pierre

The first leg of this tour follows the historic inland trail to St.-Pierre, the Route de la Trace, carved through the highlands in the 17th century. Martinique's tropical profusion is on display in the Jardin de Balata and in the untamed rain forest, while the grim but compelling story of St.-Pierre unfurls among century-old ruins.

From **Fort-de-France's** ❶ (see pp. 252–253) inner city ring road, boulevard Général-de-Gaulle, Rte. N3 follows the Rivière Madame north (toward Le Morne Rouge) and then climbs into the hillside suburbs. Stop off at the church of **Sacré Coeur** ❷ for a tremendous view over the capital. The domed "Montmartre Martiniquais" was erected in 1923 as a memorial to the dead of World War I.

The air is noticeably cooler as the road winds up to the **Jardin de Balata** ❸ *(Rte. de Balata, tel 0596 64 48 73)*, a gorgeous tropical garden laid out around a creole home some 1,475 feet (450 m) above the coast. Meandering paths trail through flaming red-and-pink torch ginger, orchids, and spice bushes gathered in the shade cast by palms and flamboyant trees. The road begins to twist and turn in earnest as it passes through the *pitons* (peaks) flanked by soft banks of ferns and huge rain forest trees dangling twisted lianas.

NOT TO BE MISSED:

Jardin de Balata • St.-Pierre
• Distillerie Depaz

At the town of **Deux Choux** take Rte. D1 8 miles (13 km) west to **St.-Pierre** ❹ and the Caribbean coast, passing through the banana plantations. (See sidebar this page for a possible detour.) Overlooking a handsome bay in the shadow of Mont Pelée, St.-Pierre was once a thriving colonial city renowned for the wealth of its merchants and the elegance of its buildings. In the spring of 1902, after centuries of inactivity, Mont Pelée rumbled. On May 7, a mere 1,000 Pierrotins packed their bags and headed for Fort-de-France. A little before 8 a.m. on May 8, Mont Pelée erupted, sending a giant cloud of burning ash and poisonous gases into the sky. The pyroclastic flow, reaching temperatures of over 3700°F (2040°C), swept down over the town and caused the sea to boil.

Today the **Cyparis Express** tourist train *(place des Ruines du Figuier, tel 0596 55 50 92, cyparisexpress.com)*, named for the only survivor, makes a narrated (in French) circuit, or visitors can roam freely around the shell of the old theater, inspect the cell where Cyparis was sheltered, and visit the cathedral rebuilt behind its surviving facade. The **Musée Vulcanologique** *(rue Victor Hugo, tel 0596 78 15 16)* displays photographs of the old city, melted glass bottles, and other curios. Two attractions north of the town center are the **Centre de Découverte des Sciences de la Terre** *(Quartier la Galère, tel 0596 52 82 42,*

St.-Pierre on Film

An interesting detour is a visit to the **Maison Régionale des Volcans** *(tel 0596 52 45 45, closed Sat. p.m. & Mon. a.m.)* in Le Morne Rouge. As well as information (in French) on volcanism, this small museum on the main street shows a 45-minute video compiled from footage of St.-Pierre before and after the 1902 eruption (English version on request). The black-and-white images illustrate the grandeur of the former "Paris of the Antilles" and the aftermath of the cataclysmic eruption.

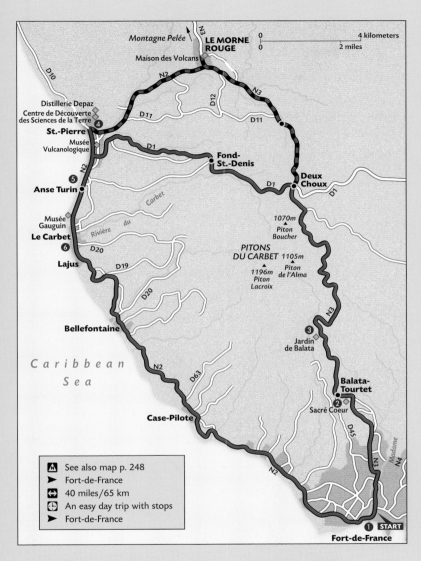

Montagne Pelée
LE MORNE ROUGE
Maison des Volcans
Distillerie Depaz
Centre de Découverte
des Sciences de la Terre
St.-Pierre
Musée
Vulcanologique
Anse Turin
Musée
Gauguin
Le Carbet
Lajus
Bellefontaine

**Fond-
St.-Denis**
**Deux
Choux**

Carbet
Rivière du

PITONS
DU CARBET
1196m
Piton
Lacroix
1105m
Piton
de l'Alma
1070m
Piton
Boucher

Jardin
de Balata

**Balata-
Tourtet**
Sacré Coeur

Case-Pilote

*Caribbean
Sea*

0   4 kilometers
0   2 miles

See also map p. 248
Fort-de-France
40 miles/65 km
An easy day trip with stops
Fort-de-France

1 START
Fort-de-France

cdst.e-monsite.com, closed Mon., $$), a high-tech earth sciences center featuring a fascinating film about the Mont Pelée eruption. Nearby, there are rum tastings and tours at **Distillerie Depaz** (tel 0596 78 1314, depaz.fr, closed Sun.).

Take the Rte. N2 coast road a couple miles (3 km) south of St.-Pierre to **Anse Turin 5**, which once played host to French painter Paul Gauguin (1848–1903). The **Musée Gauguin** (tel 0596 78 22 66, $) covers his stay.

Rte. N2 hugs the scenic coast back to Fort-de-France, passing the village of **Le Carbet 6**, where the founder of St.-Pierre, Pierre Belain d'Esnambuc, landed with a hundred Norman colonists to claim Martinique for France in 1635.

The North & Northeast

The verdant northern and northeastern regions of Martinique provide luxuriant rain forest scenery and glimpses into the island's agricultural mainstays: sugar, rum, and bananas.

L'Ajoupa-Bouillon
◪ 248 B4

**Caravelle
Peninsula
(Presqu'île de
la Caravelle)**
◪ 248 C3

Ste.-Marie
◪ 248 C3

L'Ajoupa-Bouillon

This self-proclaimed *ville florale* boasts roadside banks of wild begonias, massed crotons, and shrimp plants. The village is the starting point for walks to the **Gorges de la Falaise** (tel 0596 53 36 53). The 30-minute trail starts just west of town, and local guides lead the way into the jungle-clad ravine down a series of deep-cut steps to a swimming hole fed by a waterfall. Wear sensible footwear and take a swimsuit for a cooling dip before tackling the return trip.

Ti'Punch

The standard Caribbean rum punch is fairly sweet and flavored with tropical fruit juice. On the French islands, however, be sure to try *ti'punch* (one measure of cane syrup to three or four measures of white *rhum agricole*) served in a short glass. Fruit punch is called *un planteur* and mixed in a long glass.

Caravelle Peninsula

From the main road follow signs for **Tartane** (Rte. D2), a small resort on the north coast of this wooded peninsula. At the end of the road a section of rough track leads to the ruins of 17th-century **Château Dubuc** (tel 0596 58 09 00, $$), which crown a rise overlooking a protected bay and the foundations of an old sugar mill. A quirky little museum houses old belt buckles, broken bottles, and clay pipe stems unearthed around the estate. From the parking lot, footpaths strike off into a natural reserve and to the cliffs and coves lining the shore.

Ste.-Marie

Martinique is known for its rum and bananas. The **Musée de la Banane** (Rte. de Bézaudin, tel 0596 76 27 09, $$$) sits at the heart of a working banana plantation. Check out the history of the banana and amazing banana trivia (Germans devour more than 33 pounds/ 15 kg of bananas per person per year). Stroll along the banana walk and visit the packing houses on weekdays.

The **Musée du Rhum** (tel 0596 69 30 02, closed Sat.–Sun.) also believes in transporting visitors to the business end of its operations with guided tours of the **Distillerie Saint-James** during the sugar cane harvest (March–June). The museum with its collections of antique tools and memorabilia is located in the old plantation house, and you can also take a 20-minute tourist train ride ($$) out into the surrounding cane fields and banana plantations. ∎

The lofty and richly forested islands of Dominica, St. Lucia, St. Vincent, and Grenada

Windward Islands

Nutmeg and mace are major agricultural products of Grenada.

Windward Islands

The majestic quartet of Windward Islands tapers off toward the tail end of the Lesser Antilles, rising sheer from the Atlantic surf on one side and the gentle wavelets of the Caribbean Sea on the other. The islands are the mere tips of a volcanic mountain range that has sprouted where the Atlantic and Caribbean tectonic plates collide. Three of the four main Windward Islands have an active *soufrière*, a sulfurous volcanic vent liable to erupt every hundred years or so (Grenada, the exception, has bubbling hot springs).

Tall enough to create their own microclimates by trapping the winds off the Atlantic and converting them to rain clouds, the Windwards are fantastically fertile. Islanders grow bananas, coconuts, and spices for export, and farmers have their work cut out for them trying to keep the encroaching sea of green at bay.

Today Dominica, St. Lucia, St. Vincent (with its chain of islands known as the Grenadines), and Grenada are independent nations, but their long association dates back to the days of sail when they fell to the windward side of the English colonial trading routes between Europe and the Caribbean. Later the term was adopted by the 19th-century British administrators who governed the islands as a group distinct from British colonies in the Leeward Islands.

The earliest inhabitants of the Windward Islands were the Arawak, farmers and fishermen whose peaceful reign ended abruptly with the arrival of warlike Carib people (also known as Kalinago in Dominica today) in about A.D. 1000. Spanish explorers gave the "Cannibal Isles" a wide berth, and they became the focus of Carib resistance in the region until the mid-17th century, when the sugar trade spurred French and English colonists into action. Initially the two most topographically challenging islands, Dominica and St. Vincent, were left to the Carib, who were joined by escaped African slaves. But a century later, white settlers had forced Dominica's few remaining Carib into exile on the Atlantic coast; on St. Vincent mixed-race Carib took refuge in the hills and continued a dogged resistance until the early 19th century.

Throughout the plantation era, Europe's conflicts were mirrored in the Caribbean arena, where Britain and France squabbled over the Windwards incessantly and won, lost, and regained territories with bewildering frequency. The islands inherited a confused legacy of French and English place-names, as well as the French-influenced creole patois that is still widely spoken in Dominica and St. Lucia, although the islands have been officially English-speaking for 200 years. When slavery was abolished in 1834, former slaves turned to the land and carved small-scale farms out of the rich soil. The islands slid into an agricultural backwater administered by a British governor based in Grenada. Several attempts to federate the British Caribbean territories came to nothing, and eventually the individual Windward Islands were granted self-government in the 1960s and full independence in the late 1970s. They are now members of the British Commonwealth.

Part of the Windward Islands' appeal is the coexistence of tourism and traditional island life. This is particularly true on Dominica, where vast tracts of primal rain forest and uplands remain in pristine condition, and fishing and farming still underpin the local economy. Also unspoiled and underappreciated, St. Vincent is another rain forest wilderness and tropical market garden, but it is generally consigned to the role of stepping-stone for yachtsmen heading for the Grenadines.

The Grenadines are a yachting paradise, an alluring chain of minuscule islands with great beaches, some uninhabited, some harboring exclusive resorts. Others, such as pretty Bequia, fall somewhere between the two. To the south is charming Grenada. Easygoing and friendly, the Spice Island is overloaded with natural beauties and ringed by sandy beaches, spice plantations, and pretty villages. St. Lucia is the most developed of the Windwards, but even here it's easy to escape the resort beaches of the northwest and take a trip to the mountains, where villages nestle amid tropical flowers and vegetable plots on the edge of the forest. ■

Area of map detail

ATLANTIC OCEAN

Caribbean Sea

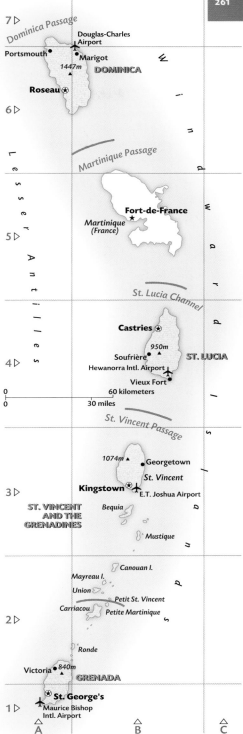

Dominica

Dominica (pronounced dom-in-ᴇᴇ-ka) was known to the Carib as Wai'tukubuli ("tall is her body"). From a 29-by-16-mile (47 by 26 km) base, the soaring interior peaks at Morne Diablotin (4,747 feet/1,447 m) within 5 miles (8 km) of the coast, and the jagged mountains of the central north-south spine average more than 3,000 feet (900 m). Dominica is home to one of the world's last untouched rain forests, 300-plus rivers, and almost as many waterfalls.

Boats line up near the fishing village of Scotts Head in Dominica.

Dominica

🗺 261 A6–B6

Visitor Information

✉ Discover Dominica Authority, first floor, Financial Centre, Roseau

☎ 767 448 2045

discoverdominica .com

Despite its undoubted beauty, Dominica is one of the Caribbean's least developed islands with a population of about 71,000. Most people still struggle to make a living from the land, and local infrastructure and several communities took a tough battering from Tropical Storm Erika in August 2015. Farming and fishing, augmented by traditional crafts, sustain one of the world's last surviving Carib, or Kalinago, communities, living on the Carib Territory in the northeast. With few beaches (and those that exist tend toward narrow strips of gray volcanic sand), tourism is still in its infancy here. Dominica offers fairly low-key accommodations, and facilities are mostly modest and unsophisticated, though several delightful rustic retreats have sprung up in stunning (albeit remote) locations and there is talk of the island's first upscale resort being developed on Cabrits Bay. On the plus side, Dominica is a rare Caribbean eco-haven for adventurous travelers keen to hike, dive, and explore without the usual tourist distractions. A highlight is the 125-mile (200 km) Wai'tukubuli National Trail, the first long-distance hiking route of its kind in the region, which traverses the island from end to end in 14 stages.

Dominica lies between the French islands of Guadeloupe and Martinique. (It is not to be confused with the Dominican Republic in the Greater Antilles; see pp. 97–124.) Christopher Columbus sailed around Wai'tukubuli's northern tip on his second voyage to the New World in November 1493. It was a Sunday, so he christened his find Dominica and noted in his logbook that the island was "remarkable for the beauty of its mountains . . . and must be seen to be believed." French colonists laid claim to Dominica in the 1750s but ceded it to Britain under the Treaty of Paris in 1763. Despite a century of French raids, slave rebellions, and isolated attacks by bands of marauding Maroons (escaped slaves who hid in the near-impenetrable mountains), the British remained more or less in control. From the mid-19th century Dominica was administered with the Leeward Islands until 1939, when it was transferred to the Windward Islands. Independence arrived in 1978, and two years later the Dominicans elected the Caribbean's first female prime minister, Dame Eugenia Charles.

The capital of the island, Roseau (see p. 264), is a small weather-beaten town and cruise-ship stopover with about 14,000 inhabitants. It lies at the mouth of the Roseau River on the southwest coast. Inland along the river are the popular Trafalgar Falls (see

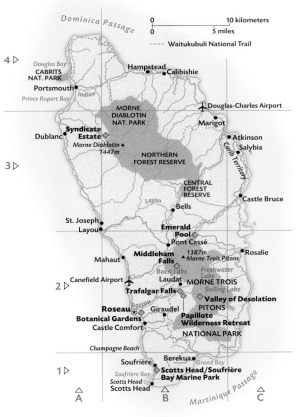

p. 265). The nearby village of Laudat is a drop-off point for hikes in Morne Trois Pitons National Park (see pp. 266–267). South of Roseau there are several hotels and dive outfits on the water at Castle Comfort, and a narrow road hugs the shore to the southern tip of the island, home to Scotts Head/Soufrière Bay Marine Park (see p. 269).

On the northwest coast, Dominica's second largest settlement is Portsmouth. Above the coast, endangered sisserou and

Roseau

⚑ 263 B2

Dominica Museum

✉ Dame Eugenia Charles Blvd., Roseau

☎ 767 448 2401

🕐 Closed Sat. p.m. & Sun. in the low season

💲 $$

jaco parrots are protected in **Morne Diablotin National Park** on the slopes of Morne Diablotin, and a road crosses over to the Atlantic coast, past good swimming beaches at **Hampstead** and **Hodges Bay.** There are a couple of beach bars, restaurants, and guesthouses at laid-back **Calibishie.** South of Melville Hall Airport, the Transinsular Road carves a splendid route to Roseau through the Central Forest

INSIDER TIP:

You will find several pristine hot springs at the base of the Trafalgar Falls.

—BARBARA A. NOE
National Geographic Books writer

Reserve and the pretty mountain village of Bells. The drive takes 90 minutes and affords grand views of cloudy peaks and the rain forest. Remaining on the windward side, the coastal road runs through Carib Territory, passing roadside stalls selling basketwork, to Castle Bruce and an alternative route back to the capital via the waterfall at Emerald Pool (see p. 267).

Roseau & the Roseau Valley

Dominica's capital, which moved to Roseau (pronounced row-so) from Portsmouth in the late 18th century, is laid out in a neat grid between the banks of the Roseau River and Fort Young. Roseau has a certain dilapidated charm, with its motley collection of stone

colonial buildings. Several historic gingerbread houses are being restored, and the run-down bayfront has been smartened up with a couple new developments. The town center is easy to explore on foot, and there are several small galleries, cafés, and craft shops around Cork Street.

Roseau's most animated corner is the local **produce market,** which spills out from the shade of its tin roof and onto the sidewalk at the river end of the waterfront.

The hub of colonial Roseau was the Old Market Place on **Dawbiney Square,** off King George V Street. Slave auctions were once held in the small cobbled, tree-shaded plaza, now annexed by a café and souvenir stalls. On one side of the square, facing the waterfront and downtown cruise-ship berth, is the **Dominica Museum,** which provides a good overview of island history and culture. Among the exhibits are Carib tools and a thatched *carbet* (hut), a section on Dominican writers, including Jean Rhys, and a series of 18th-century prints by Agostino Brunias, an Italian-born artist employed by Dominica's first British governor, Sir William Young.

Sir William's name lives on at **Fort Young,** a short walk away along the seafront. Now a hotel, the fort was constructed of blackened volcanic stone in 1775. It retains few reminders of its military heyday, except for a couple fancy brass cannon and workmanlike snipers' embrasures in the walls of the dining room.

Opposite the fort is the **Anglican church,** which contains memorial tablets eulogizing 19th-century British colonial officials, and stained-glass windows behind the altar. The **Roman Catholic cathedral,** on Turkey Lane, is in rather better shape, built of dark river rocks between 1800 and 1916. To the east are the green expanses of the **Botanical Gardens** *(map 263 B2; off King George V St.),* stretching over a 40-acre (16 ha) former cane field on the lower slopes of Morne Bruce. Teams play cricket in the grassy park, and an aviary houses indigenous sisserou and jaco parrots. Among the botanical exhibits are flowering cannonball trees with their strange waxy blooms, teaks, flamboyants, and cassia trees. The Division of Forestry, Wildlife and Parks office *(tel 767 266 3817)* located here is a good source for information on hiking in the national parks, passes, maps, and experienced guides.

The **Trafalgar Falls** are located about 5 miles (8 km) east of town at the head of the Roseau Valley. *(map 263 B2; take King George V St. out of central Roseau, in the direction of Laudat, and follow signs).* Carving

One of the major cascades at Trafalgar Falls

an imposing cleft deep into the green buttress of the Morne Trois Pitons highlands, the valley walls swoosh up to either side of the road. The bumpy track runs out near the **Papillote Wilderness Retreat** *(map 263 B2, tel 767 448 2287, papillote.dm),* a delightful small hotel and restaurant set in pretty gardens, where guides offer their services. From here it's a steep 10- to 15-minute hike to the twin waterfalls, known as "mother" and "father." The father fall on the left is warm, while the mother is cold, and they plummet down the 200-foot (60 m)

NEED TO KNOW

Port Logistics: Roseau

Roseau's downtown cruise-ship berth is right across from the tourist information center and museum. Dominica's roads are rough and badly signed, so exploring beyond Roseau is best done on an organized tour, or agree on a price in advance for a taxi tour (around $30–40 per hour).

Roseau Highlights

- The "hot and cold taps" of Trafalgar Falls & Papillote Wilderness Retreat: 2 hours
- Snorkeling off Champagne Beach: 2–3 hours
- Guided hike to Middleham Falls: half day

Morne Trois Pitons National Park

🅰 263 B2

Visitor Information

✉ Forestry Division, Roseau

☎ 767 266 3817 ext. 3431

💲 National park passes: $, one-site pass; $$$, one-week pass

cliff face in a roar of tumbling water and spray to a pool below. Beneath the viewing platform are paths leading to swimming areas.

Morne Trois Pitons National Park

Most of Dominica's best known natural attractions are found in this 17,000-acre (6,880 ha) national park, a UNESCO World Heritage site, stretching south of Morne Trois Pitons (4,550 feet/1,387 m). Sprinkled with mountain lakes, hissing volcanic fumaroles, sulfur springs, and an annual rainfall of almost 300 inches (7,600 mm), this is superb (if rather damp) upland hiking country. Together with Morne Diablotin National Park, the central highlands showcase the many different faces of the rain forest, from the grandeur of 100-foot-tall (30 m) secondary forest to stunted, high-altitude elfin woodlands, and a treasury of island plantlife that includes some 74 species of orchids and 22 kinds of fern.

Dominican wildlife is fairly difficult to spot, but there are occasional sightings of agoutis, iguanas, and five nonvenomous snakes, including the elusive boa constrictor. More than 170 bird species have been identified.

The easiest starting point for explorations in the park is the village of **Laudat,** east of Roseau. Within the national park, **Freshwater Lake,** 2,500 feet (760 m) above sea level, is accessible by car, and **Boeri Lake,** cupped in a volcanic crater, is an attractive 40-minute walk farther on.

The park's best known and most challenging hike is the trail to **Boiling Lake,** a 200-foot-wide (60 m) flooded volcanic fumarole that bubbles and steams at 180°F to 200°F (82–93°C). It's best to

Hanging out in Roseau, Dominica, at the end of a school day

engage a qualified guide before undertaking the strenuous seven- to eight-hour round-trip trek. Local guides wait at the trailhead, or you can hire one through a reputable guide company. En route to Boiling Lake, the trail crosses the **Valley of Desolation,** a suitably hellish landscape cluttered with huge boulders, where the fumes from sulfur springs and pools of bubbling gray mud have killed off all but the hardiest plants.

At the western edge of the park are the **Middleham Trails** *(3 hours round-trip),* which strike out from Cochrane or Laudat for the dramatic 500-foot-high (150 m) **Middleham Falls** via the **Stinking Hole bat caves.**

A challenging four- to five-hour round-trip trail from Pont Cassé tackles **Morne Trois Pitons** itself, climbing into the eerily quiet world of elfin forest frosted with lichens and wrapped in mosses and mist.

A few miles farther east, outside the park and just off the Castle Bruce road, is **Emerald Pool.** The small swimming hole is fed by a waterfall and set in a fern-flanked rain forest grotto beneath lianas and elephant ears.

Morne Diablotin National Park & Northern Forest Reserve

Larger than neighboring Morne Trois Pitons National Park, this 22,000-acre (8,900 ha) forested preserve *(map 263 B3, tel 767 448 2733)* on the slopes of Morne Diablotin was established in 2000 as a refuge for Dominica's two endemic parrot

---

EXPERIENCE:
Join the Community

Eleven small communities scattered around the island offer a warm welcome and unique insight into Dominican life through **Community Tourism Dominica** *(tel 767 266 3005, communitytourism.dm),* a grassroots initiative. Take to the hills with **Bellevue Organic Farmers** and learn about growing spices and medicinal herbs, or sign up for a day of garden tours, flower arranging, and creole cooking in Eggleston, the "flower basket of Dominica." Other entertaining and unusual day tour options include kayaking and tubing on the **Layou River** *($$$$$)*; paddling your own canoe down mangrove waterways as featured in one of the *Pirates of the Caribbean* films; and an eccentric, 100 percent natural spa experience in the steaming mud pools and mineral springs of **Wotten Waven.**

---

species: sisserou and jaco. The green-and-brown sisserou is Dominica's national bird and the rarer of the two. Captive breeding programs have helped swell numbers in the wild to approximately 350. There are many more of the more colorful jaco, or red-necked parrots.

A road from Dublanc, south of Portsmouth, climbs to the park entrance at **Syndicate Estate.** At this former citrus and banana plantation 1,800 feet (550 m) above sea level, a short trail provides excellent opportunities for birdwatching. The best way to ensure you see the full range of birds around the park is to take a tour.

A guide is also highly recommended for a strenuous six- to seven-hour round-trip ascent of **Morne Diablotin.**

Around Dominica

Dominica's Carib Territory provides a rare glimpse into pre-colonial culture, while birders and divers will enjoy parks at either end of the island.

Carib Territory: Established in 1903, the 3,700-acre (1,500 ha) Carib Territory encompasses eight small villages along the Atlantic coast between Atkinson and Castle Bruce. Some 2,200 Kalinago (formerly Carib) people live in the territory, descendants of Amerindian migrants who paddled dugout canoes across from the Amazon Basin.

Modern Carib have abandoned traditional thatched huts in favor of more comfortable wooden creole homes balanced on stilts overlooking the sea. Basket-weaving is a local specialty on display at roadside stalls alongside model boats and other wood carvings. At **St. Marie of the Caribs Catholic Church** in Salybia there is an altar carved in the shape of a dugout canoe.

A few ancient ceremonies and traditions such as boatbuilding survive, and you can see traditional dancing, crafts, and practices in action during a 45-minute guided tour of **Kalinago Barana Autê** (Carib Cultural Village by the Sea; *tel 767 445 7979, kalinagobaranaaute.com, $$$*) on the Atlantic coast near Salybia. Farther down the coast, south of Sineku, a petrified natural lava flow called the **Escalier Tête de Chien** (Snake's Staircase) tumbles down the cliffs to the sea.

Portsmouth & Cabrits National Park: Portsmouth, the island capital until malarial mosquitoes in the nearby swamps sent the British scurrying down to Roseau, is a scruffy little town

---

EXPERIENCE: Go Whale-Watching

Though Dominica's dive credentials are now well established, a lesser-known fact is that the island is the only country in the world where whales can be spotted year-round; around 90 percent of whale-watching trips make a successful sighting. Twenty-two recorded species of cetacean are found in Dominican waters, but the prize is a clear view of a sperm whale. These marine leviathans come to breed and calve in the deep, sheltered bays off the west coast during winter *(Nov.–March)*, when there is also a good chance of sighting humpback, pilot, pygmy, and false killer whales. Acrobatic bottlenose, spinner, and spotted dolphins provide plenty of entertainment while visitors scan the horizon for the whales' telltale water spouts.

During summer *(late March–Oct.)*, the Dominican wildlife nursery moves ashore to the beaches, where huge female leatherback turtles lumber out of the water to lay their eggs.

Nighttime turtle excursions can be arranged through the **Dominica Sea Turtle Conservation Organization** *(sea turtle hotline tel 767 616 8684, domsetco .org, $$)*. Whale-watching expeditions with the Anchorage Hotel's **Whale Watch & Dive Centre** *(tel 767 448 2638, anchoragehotel.dm, $$$$$)* and **Dive Dominica** *(tel 767 448 2188, www.divedominica .com, $$$$$)* depart from **Castle Comfort.**

of 5,000 souls set on the yachts-man's haven Prince Rupert Bay.

On the southern edge of town take a boat trip on **Indian River,** paddling upstream through a tunnel of swamp ferns, bwa mang trees, and anthuriums. Herons and egrets stalk the shallows.

Just over a mile (1.6 km) north is **Cabrits National Park** *(map 263 A4),* occupying the forested peninsula at the top of the bay and extending into wetlands areas and a marine preserve totaling more than 1,300 acres (900 ha). In 1765 the British founded **Fort Shirley** to defend the harbor. Its remains, linked by footpaths, litter the hillside. Some of the old vol-canic stone and redbrick buildings have been overtaken by jungle, but several others have been partially restored, and the former **Powder Magazine** houses a small museum. The driving force behind the restoration has been local historian and author Dr. Lennox Honychurch, whose website *(lennoxhonychurch.com)* is a mine of information on local and Caribbean history and culture.

Black-sand beaches fringe Prince Rupert Bay, with several hotels and a dive shop at **Picard Beach.** The best snorkeling and coral reef and wall diving sites are located in **Douglas Bay,** north of Cabrits Peninsula.

Scotts Head & the South

A half-hour drive from Roseau around the curve of Soufrière Bay, the narrow finger of Scotts Head peninsula juts out from the Caribbean coast at the southern tip of the island. From

A makeshift fish market in the village of Soufrière

the ruins of **Fort Cashacrou,** the view stretches off to Martinique 20 miles (32 km) to the south and back up the Dominican coast to the mountains.

Beneath the waters of the bay is a submerged volcanic caldera a mile (1.6 km) across and almost 1,000 feet (305 m) deep, forming the centerpiece of **Scotts Head/ Soufrière Bay Marine Park,** Dominica's top dive site. Around the crater rim lava pinnacles and reef sites are frequented by a kalei-doscope of marine species. Corals and forests of sponges stud the walls of dramatic drop-offs. One site with real appeal for snorkelers is **Champagne,** which forms a cloud of tiny bubbles released from a vol-canic vent in the seabed.

The nearby fishing village of **Soufrière** is named for hot sulfur springs reached by a winding road into the hills. You can also get there by the Tête Morne road above Ber-ekua, on the shore at Grand Bay. ■

Scotts Head/ Soufrière Bay Marine Park

🔼 263 B1

Soufrière

🔼 263 B1

St. Lucia

Lavishly adorned with dense green rain forest, landmark peaks rising sheer from the sea, golden beaches, rare parrots, and a profusion of vivid tropical flowers, St. Lucia is a first-rate Caribbean beauty. The 27-by-14-mile (43 by 23 km) island is shaped like a pear and lies between Martinique to the north and St. Vincent in the south.

St. Lucia (pronounced LOO-sha) is the most developed and populous of the Windward Islands. Nevertheless, the entire central portion of the island is mountainous forest ringed by

The town of Soufrière is dwarfed by the famous Pitons ("peaks") that tower above it.

rolling acres of banana plantations, sugarcane, and coconut groves. Small fishing villages dot the coast, mountain hamlets cling perilously to absurdly verdant valleys, and most telltale signs of tourist development have been tucked neatly into the northwestern corner of the island above the capital, Castries (see pp. 272–273), home to more than a third of St. Lucia's 170,000 inhabitants.

Christopher Columbus may have set foot on St. Lucia on his fourth voyage to the New World in 1502, but the island's earliest recorded European resident was one François Le Clerc, a 16th-century French pirate who established a base on Pigeon Island and attacked passing Spanish galleons. Also known as Jambe de Bois for his wooden leg, Le Clerc appears to have survived the attentions of the island's resident Carib people, who had already dispatched two attempted British settlements before the French finally established a colonial toehold in 1651.

St. Lucia was one of the most hotly contested plantation islands in the eastern Caribbean, nicknamed "the fair Helen of the West Indies" for all the ships launched in the battle for her favors. Strategically placed next to the flourishing French sugar

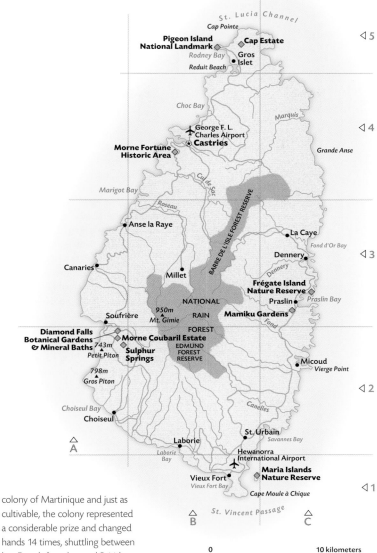

St. Lucia Channel
Cap Pointe
**Pigeon Island
National Landmark** ◇   **Cap Estate** ◇
Rodney Bay   Gros
● Islet
Reduit Beach

Choc Bay
Marquis

✈ George F. L.
Charles Airport
☉ **Castries**   Grande Anse
**Morne Fortune
Historic Area** ◇

Marigot Bay
Cul de Sac
Roseau
BARRE DE L'ISLE FOREST RESERVE
● Anse la Raye
● La Caye
Fond d'Or Bay
Dennery ●   ◁ 3
Dennery
Canaries ●   **NATIONAL**
Millet ●   **Frégate Island
Nature Reserve** ◇
950m   **RAIN**   Praslin ●   Praslin Bay
Soufrière ●   ▲   **Mamiku Gardens** ◇
Mt. Gimie
FOREST
**Diamond Falls
Botanical Gardens**   743m   ◇ **Morne Coubaril Estate**   **EDMUND
FOREST
RESERVE**
& Mineral Baths   ▲
Petit Piton   **Sulphur
Springs**
798m   ● **Micoud**
▲   Vierge Point
Gros Piton
◁ 2
Choiseul Bay   Canelles
● **Choiseul**
△
A   ● **Laborie**   **St. Urbain** ●   Savannes Bay
Laborie
Bay   Hewanorra
International Airport
✈
Vieux Fort ●   **Maria Islands
Nature Reserve** ◇
Vieux Fort Bay   Cape Moule à Chique   ◁ 1
△   St. Vincent Passage   △
B   **C**

0 ———————————— 10 kilometers
0 ———————————— 5 miles

◁ 5
◁ 4

colony of Martinique and just as cultivable, the colony represented a considerable prize and changed hands 14 times, shuttling between her French founders and British usurpers. The British finally gained the upper hand after a fierce battle culminating on the slopes of Morne Fortune (see p. 273) above Castries in 1796, although French revolutionaries continued a guerrilla war from hideouts in the mountains for some time afterward. St. Lucia was secured by

Britain under the Treaty of Paris in 1814. The island, which became independent in 1979, remains part of the British Commonwealth.

Despite a century and a half of British occupation, St. Lucia displays her Gallic heritage at every turn. French place-names are

St. Lucia

🅰 261 B4

Visitor Information

✉ Sureline Bldg.,
Vide Bouteille,
Castries

☎ 758 452 4094

stlucianow.com

Castries

 271 B4

Visitor Information

✉ La Place
Carenage &
booth at Pointe
Seraphine

☎ 758 452 7577

more common than English, and the local patois is based on creole. Creole cooking, creole architecture with its fancy gingerbread trimmings, and a lingering fondness for the checkered madras fabrics, more usually seen on the French islands, conspire to make St. Lucia stand out from her Windward Island neighbors. St. Lucians are spontaneous and party loving. The island's summertime Carnival is a riot of costumes, music, and food. The Friday-night jump-up

---

Views of the Pitons

Heading south from Castries, drivers have their work cut out on the stretch of serpentine road that drops briefly to sea level at Canaries, a small fishing community, before carving a path up through the rain forest and emerging above Soufrière. This is one of the best views of the Pitons, with Petit Piton (2,461 feet/743 m) in the foreground and Gros Piton (2,619 feet/798 m) 1.5 miles (2.5 km) behind.

---

street party at Gros Islet (see p. 274) is an institution that has inspired Anse la Raye's Friday seafood cookout and Dennery's Saturday-night Fish Fiesta, enjoyed by locals and visitors alike. Musical events are scheduled throughout the year, including a world-class summer jazz festival, and any number of fêtes, sailing regattas, and impromptu jump-ups.

African traditions also maintain a hold on the local imagination. Although the majority of the population is Roman Catholic (a French legacy), St. Lucia has a rich folkloric culture. Evil spirits are banished by

the beating of drums, and houses are made safe by magical wreaths of thorny acacia and special herbs.

Although St. Lucia's traditional tourist heartland is the northwest, around the popular yachting center of Rodney Bay, most of the island's attractions are found south of Castries along the Caribbean coast and in the rain forest highlands. There has also been a recent flurry of luxury hotel developments, and a number of elegant spa resorts have opened their doors around Marigot, Soufrière, and even on the previously uncharted Atlantic coast.

Near the town of Soufrière are the Pitons ("peaks"), St. Lucia's most famous landmarks, which are depicted on the national flag. A brace of lofty volcanic plugs, they soar dramatically from the shore, upstaging the island's tallest peak, Mount Gimie (3,118 feet/950 m) a few miles inland. Close by are a number of attractions, including the Soufrière district itself, which makes a good base for exploring, hiking, or diving, or simply enjoying the low-key atmosphere.

Castries

St. Lucia's unremarkable capital lies at the foot of a sheltered inlet encircled by steep, forested hills. Castries was founded in the 1760s and named for the French Minister of the Marine, the Maréchal de Castries, who would have appreciated the well-protected natural harbor. The city has a bad habit of burning down, and most of its uninspiring concrete architecture dates from the last conflagration, in 1948. St. Lucia is a regular feature on cruise-ship itineraries, and as the giant liners enter the harbor, they pass the old French battery at Vigie (Lookout) Point before berthing at the modern Pointe Seraphine cruise complex or right up against the downtown waterfront.

Set back from the waterfront is **Jeremie Street,** a bustle of market stalls, traffic, and pedestrians. T-shirt sellers and souvenir stalls perch on the dockside. Across the street the old covered market building has been hijacked by wood carvings, basketware, and beach bag vendors, while the produce market is still the place to find a healthy dash of local color among the piles of citrus fruits and bananas, squashlike christophene, yams, gingerroots, and hot peppers.

A couple of blocks inland, past the Parliament and Court House on Laborie Street, lies the 19th-century **Cathedral of the Immaculate Conception.** The interior is painted from floor to ceiling with murals depicting biblical figures, African clerics, and pineapple motifs (the traditional Caribbean symbol for hospitality). Next to the cathedral, **Derek Walcott Square** honors the Nobel Prize–winning St. Lucian poet and playwright. There's a massive samaan tree on the square and a few old-style West Indian buildings around the edge.

Running south from the city center, Government House Road labors up Morne Fortune (pronounced for-TU-nay), past the governor-general's residence, and on to the **Morne Fortune Historic Area** at the top of the hill. In 1796 British soldiers of the 27th Inniskilling Regiment spent two days fighting their way to the summit of the morne, forcing the French to surrender. Their bravery is commemorated by the Inniskilling Memorial on the grounds of **Fort Charlotte,** where old military buildings have been restored and made into a college.

Rodney Bay & the North

From Castries the main road north swings alongside the

NEED TO KNOW

Port Logistics: Castries

The Pointe Seraphine cruise and duty-free shopping complex is a five-minute cab or water taxi ride ($5 per person) across the harbor from La Place Carenage, the alternative cruise-ship berth on the downtown waterfront. Both offer visitor information services and taxi ranks. Half- or full-day sail and snorkel tours are a great way to sightsee; for a five- to six-hour taxi tour, budget about $85 per person.

Castries Highlights

- **Pigeon Island National Landmark & Rodney Bay: half day**
- **Soufrière & Diamond Falls Botanical Gardens & Mineral Baths: half day**
- **Morne Coubaril Estate: add 1 hour**
- **Snorkel at Anse Chastanet: add 2 hours**

In the waterfront village of Gros Islet

Pigeon Island National Landmark

🅰 271 B5

✉ Pigeon Point

☎ 758 452 5005

💲 $$

local airport, which is edged by 2-mile-long (3 km) **Vigie Beach,** and on past the Gablewoods Mall and Choc Bay hotel enclave to Rodney Bay, St. Lucia's busiest resort area. On the southern side of the bay, hotels line the soft white sands of **Reduit Beach.** At the head of the beach a narrow channel gives access to the yacht harbor and Rodney Bay Marina. This bustling Caribbean sailing center is bordered to the north by the waterfront village of **Gros Islet,** home

to the famous Friday-night jump-up.

The north shore of Rodney Bay curves around to **Pigeon Island,** the *gros islet* (big island) that gave the neighboring village its name. The former pirate lair of notorious Capitaine Jambe de Bois is now **Pigeon Island National Landmark,** linked to the mainland by a sandy causeway. In 1778 Adm. George Rodney of the British Royal Navy set up a naval base in Gros Islet Bay (later renamed in his honor) and established a lookout post on the island. According to one story, the sentries on hilltop Fort Rodney used carrier pigeons to report sightings of passing vessels and developments on the French island of Martinique, clearly visible 20 miles (32 km) to the north. (A more prosaic explanation attributes the name to the quantities of red-necked pigeons that congregated here before the native forest was stripped away.) The ruins of Fort Rodney still afford spectacular views north to Martinique, and south down the serried peaks of St. Lucia's mountainous interior to

---

EXPERIENCE:
Zip Through the Forest

If you'd like to experience the rain forest but haven't brought your hiking boots, **Rain Forest Adventures St. Lucia** *(east of Castries at Chassin, tel 758 458 5151 or U.S./ Canada 866 759 8726, rainforestadventure .com, $$$$$)* can hoist you up into the canopy for either a gentle two-hour circuit on the aerial tramway or a zip line tour. Naturalists comment on the forest and its wildlife as the tramway's open gondolas travel through the treetops. Hiking trails and birding tours are also available.

the Pitons. A botanical trail meanders around the 40-acre (16 ha) island, where you can explore old military ruins, such as barracks, powder magazines, and a sunken musket redoubt.

The restored 1824 Officers' Quarters has an interpretive center with exhibits tracing Admiral Rodney's famous victory at the Battle of the Saints in 1782 (see sidebar p. 243). Look for the tavern under the arches of the cellars and bring towels and a suit for a swim.

INSIDER TIP:

Heritage Tours of St. Lucia *(tel 758 458-1454, heritagetoursstlucia.org, $$$$$)* **offers active and cultural introductions to local life.**

—PETER GWIN
National Geographic
magazine writer

To the east of Rodney Bay, the exclusive **Cap Estate** quarter occupies the hilly northern tip of the island. There are several stunning private houses, a golf course, and a handful of luxurious resorts featuring upscale restaurants with exquisite sea views.

South to Soufrière

There are two ways to explore the sights of southern St. Lucia, and visitors staying in the north of the island should reckon on a full day to visit the Soufrière area sights with a stop for lunch. A hassle-free option is to take a

Rain Forest Birds

Of the 43 or so bird species that inhabit the St. Lucian rain forest, 33 are endemic, such as the rare white-breasted thrasher, St. Lucia oriole, St. Lucia wren, and the endangered St. Lucian parrot. Conservation measures established in the 1970s brought this last species back from the edge of extinction. Known as the jacquot locally, the 16- to 18-inch-tall (40–45 cm) parrot is one of the most colorful inhabitants of the rain forest. It has a green back, blue head, red throat patch, and flashes of yellow and red under its wings.

A good way to find the parrots is to look for a stand of towering santinay trees, where they like to nest and feed on the small pink fruits. Their raucous screech is another telltale sign.

day sail from Castries or Rodney Bay, which includes a land tour of the attractions around Soufrière. Or you can rent a car and tackle the beautiful switchback road down the Caribbean coast, with the option of continuing around the island on a tour from the capital.

The road south to Soufrière starts from Morne Fortune, south of Castries, and swoops downhill into the banana plantations and cane fields of the Cul de Sac Valley. Across the ridge at the end of the valley, there is a turn on the right to **Marigot Bay,** an idyllic little hurricane hole surrounded by steep wooded hills, where Rex Harrison talked to the animals during the filming of *Doctor Dolittle* in 1967.

The bay has been transformed from a sleepy yachting backwater into the idyllic setting for one of St. Lucia's newer and most luxurious

Soufrière

🗺 271 A3

Visitor Information

✉ Bay St.

☎ 758 459 7419

hotel and villa resorts, with an upscale marina village complete with shopping and dining opportunities. A regular ferry shuttles across the mouth of the bay to the beach opposite.

A short run farther south is **Anse la Raye** (Skate Bay; named after the fish once caught here), a picturesque West Indian fishing village. Its narrow streets are lined with sun-bleached wooden cottages, and down on the waterfront you'll see a few fishing boats hollowed out of gommier trees. On Friday evenings, the village comes alive as crowds gather for the fish feast (from 6:30 p.m.).

Framed by Mount Gimie and the Pitons, and ranged along sheltered Soufrière Bay, **Soufrière** was St. Lucia's first capital, founded by the French in 1746. The thriving 18th-century port was transformed into a hotbed of revolutionary zeal during the French Revolution and renamed La Convention. A guillotine was erected on the market square. Soufrière's fortunes waned when the British chose Castries as their new capital, and the town subsided into a gentle decline, relying on its fishing fleet to keep afloat.

Today Elizabeth Square remains the focal point of town, though the only threat posed here these days comes from overenthusiastic street traders. There are a few surviving traditional creole houses with gingerbread trim, and the market building has been brightened up with colorful friezes. Cruise liners disgorge their passengers onto the wharf for a flying visit to the south of the island. Chief among the sightseeing stops are the Soufrière Estate, home to the Diamond Falls Botanical Gardens; and the pungent sulfur springs fed by the town's namesake Soufrière volcano (see opposite). ■

EXPERIENCE: Hike the Hills of the Rain Forest

A number of trails carve their way through St. Lucia's 19,000-acre (7,700 ha) **National Rain Forest.** From the lush lower slopes, some hikes strike up into areas of cloud forest and elfin woodland with fabulous views and bird-spotting opportunities. Permission to hike in the rain forest must be obtained from the Forest and Lands Department (tel 758 468 5649), which provides information and guides.

The short guided walking tour through **Barre de l'Isle Forest Reserve** makes a good introduction to St. Lucia's unspoiled hinterland. Accessed from the Castries-Dennery road, the reserve spans the island's spine, affording peerless sea views over both coasts. A more challenging option is **Edmund Forest Reserve** above Soufrière or the vertiginous scramble up the Pitons.

Just off the southern tip of St. Lucia, the uninhabited **Maria Islands Nature Reserve** is home to endemic lizards, seabirds, and the kuowes, a rare but harmless snake. Guided excursions can be arranged through the **National Trust** (tel 758 454 5014, slunatrust.org).

On the Atlantic coast, near Praslin, a clifftop trail overlooks **Frégate Island Nature Reserve,** where soaring frigate birds, known as *scisseux* (scissors) for their distinctive tail feathers, descend to their nesting grounds from May to July (binoculars are an advantage).

Around Soufrière

A drive around to St. Lucia's Atlantic coast combines plantation visits and botanical gardens with fine views and birding. At the *soufrière*'s crater, an olfactory experience awaits.

To the Atlantic Coast

Not far beyond Soufrière, the around-island route exchanges its border of lush green forest for open countryside. At Choiseul Bay, the village lines a crescent of sand where fishing boats unload at the waterfront market.

The town of **Vieux Fort** crouches at the neck of Cape Moule à Chique, St. Lucia's most southerly point, facing St. Vincent in the distance. Off the east coast

INSIDER TIP:

The historic Fond Doux Estate is an eco-friendly cacao planta-tion, complete with holiday cottages and a restaurant.

—JUSTIN KAVANAGH
*National Geographic
Travel Books editor*

is **Maria Islands Nature Reserve** (see sidebar opposite), harboring seabirds and several endemic wildlife species. On the outskirts of Vieux Fort, **Mankote Magrove Swamp** is a rewarding bird-watching area with several short trails and a viewing tower.

The relatively swift return route to Castries passes the hamlet of Micoud, the **Mamiku Gardens,** near Praslin *(tel 758 455 3729)* with their lovely woodland trails

and ocean views, and an observation point overlooking **Frégate Island Nature Reserve** (see sidebar opposite). At the banana town of Dennery, the road heads inland, crossing the Barre de l'Isle Ridge on its journey back to the island capital.

Diamond Falls Botanical Gardens & Mineral Baths

Set in the hills above Soufrière, these lovely botanical gardens display a glorious profusion of tropical plants and trees crowding narrow pathways. The mineral baths were built for French troops on the orders of Louis XVI.

Sulphur Springs Park

As you can drive to within yards of the soufrière's sinister and smelly volcanic vent, it has been billed as "the world's only drive-in volcano." At the heart of the 7-acre (3 ha) crater, pools of boiling mud belch in the moonscape.

Morne Coubaril Estate

Established in 1713, the 250-acre (101 ha) Morne Coubaril Estate is still producing cacao and coconuts. During a 30-minute visit, visitors learn how copra, coconuts, sugarcane, cacao, and cassava were processed over a century ago. The estate also operates a zip line experience and horse-riding trails *($$$$$)*. ∎

Diamond Falls Botanical Gardens & Mineral Baths

🅰 271 A2
✉ E of Soufrière
☎ 758 459 7565
💲 $$

diamondstlucia.com

Sulphur Springs Park

🅰 271 A2
✉ SE of Soufrière
☎ 758 459 5500
💲 $

Morne Coubaril Estate

🅰 271 A2
✉ S of Soufrière
☎ 758 459 7340; reservations 758 712 5805
💲 $$$

stluciaziplining.com

Fond Doux Estate

✉ Fond Doux (S of Soufrière)
☎ 758 459 7545

fonddouxestate.com

St. Vincent & the Grenadines

St. Vincent heads up the chain of the Grenadine Islands like an emerald green kite with a 75-mile-long (120 km) tail trailing down toward Grenada. At 18 by 11 miles (29 by 18 km), it's the smallest and probably the least discovered of the Windward Islands, with a slumbering volcano and a nearly impenetrable jungle heart where generations of Carib once hid out. This jungle kept the Europeans at bay for more than two centuries.

A secluded beach on Bequia in the Grenadines

St. Vincent

 261 B3

Visitor Information

✉ NIS Building, Upper Bay St., Kingstown

☎ 784 456 6222

discoversvg.com

St. Vincent

St. Vincent is still relatively overlooked today, outshone by the golden beaches and yachting havens of the Grenadines (see pp. 284–287) and the more widely publicized attractions of St. Lucia and Barbados. But while St. Vincent is no classic Caribbean idyll, all palm-fringed sands and rum punches (although the latter *can* be found), it does offer a quiet backwater charm,

a miraculously undeveloped hinterland, and several hotels with discreet appeal for less hidebound travelers.

Successive waves of Ciboney, Arawak, and Carib settlers paddled their way from South America to Hairoun, as they called St. Vincent before Europeans added it to the New World map. But the island's rugged terrain and the prospect of ending up at the sharp end of a Carib barbecue curtailed further

INSIDER TIP:

If you like scuba diving and photographing tiny, weird-looking marine critters, St. Vincent and the Grenadines is for you. A macro lens is a must.

—BILL TEWES

Professional diver/photographer

investigation, and St. Vincent became a refuge for Carib people forced from other islands. They were joined by escaped African slaves, some the survivors of shipwrecks off the coast, while others set sail on rafts from Barbados and were blown to St. Vincent by the westerly trade winds. Mixed Afro-Carib/Black Carib soon outnumbered the original Yellow Carib and started to take their lands. In retaliation the Yellow Carib allowed the French to establish a small colony in 1719. The Black Carib took to the hills to continue their resistance, surviving the First Carib War, initiated by a British invasion in 1763—a Caribbean extension of Britain and France's long-running European conflicts.

The French snatched the island back with embarrassing ease in 1779. When the challengers sailed in for the attack, the entire British garrison was away working the governor's plantation in the north of the island, and no one could locate the key to the gun battery. With the British reinstated by the Treaty of Versailles in 1783, the French switched allegiance to the Black Carib and

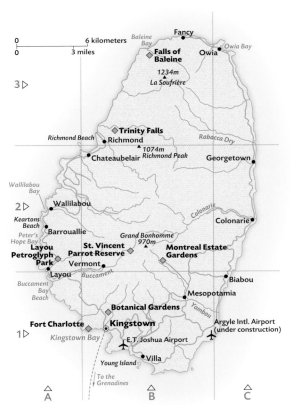

backed the uprising that became known as the Second Carib War, or Brigands' War, lasting from 1795 to 1797. British plantations and settlements were torched and planters fed through the cane-crushing gear of their own sugar mills until the army regained control. The surviving 5,000 Black Carib were deported to British Honduras (present-day Belize). The last Yellow Carib retreated to the far north of St. Vincent, where their descendants still live today. The wars over, St. Vincent settled down to a quiet agrarian existence, growing a little sugar, Sea Island cotton, and arrowroot.

Kingstown

⚑ 279 B1

Visitor Information

✉ Cruise Ship Terminal

☎ 784 457 1592

The island was granted independence from Britain in 1979, and it remains a member of the British Commonwealth.

Agriculture is still a mainstay of St. Vincent's economy, and the island is rampantly fertile. There's no escaping the evidence, from the stranglehold of its creeper-clad rain forest peaks to the vegetable plots and tropical fruit orchards clinging to steep-sided valleys. Jagged mountains rip the underbellies of lowering gray rain clouds, so it always appears to be raining somewhere on the island. Regular dustings of volcanic fertilizer from La Soufrière, one of the Caribbean's most active volcanoes, further enrich the crumbling red earth. They say you could plant a pencil here, and it would take root.

The capital of St. Vincent and the Grenadines is Kingstown on the south coast of St. Vincent, a 20-minute drive from the main tourist enclave at Villa. A busy working port, Kingstown is a transportation hub for the Grenadines and is served by regular ferries and small island-hopper aircraft. It's also a good place to begin any exploration of the island. Look to the west coast for quiet volcanic sand beaches and secluded coves accessible only by boat. Yachting is a major attraction, and day sails can be combined with diving and snorkeling. Hikers can plan some great days out around La Soufrière and the Buccament River Valley, where the raucous and rare St. Vincent parrot makes its home.

Kingstown: Hemmed in by a crown of steep, wooded ridges, the capital of St. Vincent and the Grenadines hugs the mile-long (1.6 km) curve of Kingstown Bay and pushes back up the hillside. Down on the waterfront there's a lively bustle of cargo ships, ferries, and fishing boats, while the cruise facility and yachting complex sits smartly at the eastern end of the harbor. Behind the docks is Kingstown's pocket-size downtown district, which still has a few bumpy, old-fashioned cobbled streets and rows of

---

EXPERIENCE: Go Local, Know Local

On St. Vincent you can undertake short walks easily without a guide, but local knowledge adds greatly to the rain forest experience, and guides are recommended for volcano hikes. If you plan to tackle La Soufrière, the **Richmond Vale Diving and Hiking Center** (tel 784 458 2255, richmondvalehiking.com) provides experienced guides. The strenuous five- to six-hour return trip is rewarded with majestic views over the caldera on a clear day. Wear sturdy boots, pack insect repellent, and be prepared for rain. Hiking trips can also be organized through **Sailor's Wilderness Tours** (tel 784 457 1721, sailorswildernesstours.com, $$$$$), and cycle enthusiasts can explore the challenging terrain on mountain bike tours (three hours to a full day). Local tour specialists **Bamboo Adventures** (tel 784 570 8000, booksvgnow.com) can arrange hiking and sailing trips, build-your-own-drum workshops, homestays, and nightlife tours. (See also Travelwise p. 399.)

arcaded shops sheltering the sidewalk from the sun and occasional cloudburst.

Heading west on Halifax Street, take a detour down Hillsboro Street (by the Cenotaph) to investigate the **produce market.** The busiest days are Friday and Saturday, when farmers venture into town from all around the island. On the opposite side of Halifax Street, iron railings fence in the imposing gray stone **Law Courts,** where the St. Vincent Parliament meets. Pastel-painted **St. George's Anglican Cathedral,** founded in 1820, is just a little farther on. The interior of the church has an unusual stained-glass window depicting a red-robed angel. Supposedly commissioned by Queen Victoria to celebrate the birth of her first grandson, it was destined for St. Paul's Cathedral in London. But the monarch preferred her angels white, so the homeless window was presented to St. George's by the dean of St. Paul's. Among the many memorial plaques set in the walls of the cathedral, one commemorates Maj. Alexander Leith, a British war hero, who killed the Carib leader Chatoyer in a fencing duel on Dorsetshire Hill in 1795.

Across from the cathedral is Kingstown's most bizarre architectural monument, the 19th-century **St. Mary's Roman Catholic Church.** A riot of conflicting styles with a playful assortment of turrets, towers, pinnacles, and twisted barley-sugar columns, it was designed by a Belgian priest who drew his inspiration from pictures of famous European cathedrals.

The harbor at Kingstown in St. Vincent

Visitors with an interest in island history should stop at the **Carnegie Building** (headquarters of the St. Vincent and the Grenadines National Trust), where a small but fascinating collection of Amerindian artifacts is displayed.

On top of Berkshire Hill, at the western end of town, stands **Fort Charlotte,** which affords magnificent views down the Grenadines from its aerie 600 feet (180 m) above the bay. Named

SVG National Trust

✉ Carnegie Building, Heritage Square
☎ 784 451 2921
🕐 Closed Sat.–Sun.
💲 $$

svgnationaltrust.org

Fort Charlotte

✉ 10-min drive W of Kingstown

Botanical Gardens

- ⬛ 279 B1
- ✉ Off Leeward Hwy.
- ☎ 784 457 1003
- 💲 $$ for a guide

Villa

- ⬛ 279 B1

for George III's queen, the sprawling 1806 fortress never fired a shot in anger.

Kingstown's pride and joy are the **Botanical Gardens** set in the hills above the town center. The gardens, founded in 1763, are the oldest of their kind in the Western Hemisphere and originally operated as a distant adjunct of Kew Gardens in London. The region's first breadfruit trees, introduced from the South Pacific to provide cheap, nutritious food for slaves working on the Caribbean plantations, arrived here aboard the H.M.S. *Bounty*. At first the slaves refused to touch the bland,

NEED TO KNOW

Port Logistics: Kingstown

A few minutes' walk from central Bay Street, the Cruise Ship Complex has a small mall and taxi stand. Prearranged tours are the best way to explore farther afield or agree on a price for taxi tours (around $30 per hour or $5 for a run up to the Botanical Gardens). Ferries for Bequia (1 hr) depart from the neighboring pier.

Kingstown Highlights

- Kingstown & Botanical Gardens with lunch in Villa: half day
- Montreal Estate Gardens: 3 hours
- Day-sail to Falls of Baleine
- La Soufrière Hike: full day with guide

alien fruit, but now the breadfruit's starchy flesh is a staple vegetable dish throughout the Caribbean.

Guides loiter near the entrance waiting to conduct tours, and their services certainly liven up a visit. They know all the good stories, such as how the traveler's palm tree automatically aligns itself east-west and contains a reservoir of water for the lost and thirsty adventurer.

There's no need to search for the aviary; the piercing screech of the St. Vincent parrot *(Amazona guildingii)* is guide enough. Predominantly yellow-gold with a glorious lilac head, these parrots are part of a successful captive-breeding program.

Villa & the East Coast:

Most visitors will embark on their explorations from hotels in the small town of Villa, southeast along the coast from Kingstown. It makes an ideal starting point for touring the east coast of St. Vincent, along with its adjacent—and highly productive—agricultural highlands.

Facing Villa's narrow sand beaches is the **Young Island resort,** which you can reach by water taxi from the waterfront. According to legend, the island was a gift from a Carib chief to Sir William Young, a British governor of St. Vincent who had presented the local leader with a horse. Behind Young Island are the ruins of **Fort Duvernette,** hugging another rocky islet. A staircase carved into the cliff leads to the 200-foot (60 m) summit, from which there are fine views.

North of Villa via the Vigie Highway, a panoramic vista extends over Kingstown to the Grenadines and inland to the misty mountains from a lookout point on the knife-edge ridge of **Ayri Hill.** The road continues to

St. Vincent is covered in lush greenery, due to its rich volcanic soils and its warm, rainy climate.

the fertile Marriaqua (or Mesopotamia) Valley, where much of the island's fresh produce is grown. A side road leads up to the gorgeous **Montreal Estate Gardens,** set in a circlet of cloudy peaks scoured by waterfalls. Giant orchids and tulip trees shade tropical flowers on terraces built of river rocks.

The Yambou River flows down from the village of Mesopotamia, past rocks carved with Arawak petroglyphs, and through the Yambou Gorge toward the Atlantic coast. Here the Windward Highway wriggles along the shore to Georgetown, through banana and coconut plantations, and continues around to the north of the island, dominated by the impressive bulk of La Soufrière volcano (4,048 feet/1,234 m).

At **Rabacca Dry River,** just north of Georgetown, a 4WD track strikes up to the trailhead for the 3.5-mile (5.5 km) four-hour round-trip hike up the east side of La Soufrière. It's a rewarding walk to the mile-wide (1.6 km) crater rim and back. A more challenging route sets out from Chateaubelair on the Caribbean side, and the two can be combined if you're in the mood for a really strenuous expedition (see sidebar p. 280).

The West Coast & Falls of Baleine:

The Leeward Highway clambers north out of Kingstown and begins a roller-coaster journey past a series of small fishing villages to the beaches around Barrouallie and Richmond. Beyond these coastal attractions are a series of diverting stops, ranging from archaeological artifacts to exotic wildlife and scenery on a grand scale.

About 5 miles (8 km) from Kingstown, as the highway runs through the Buccament River

Montreal Estate Gardens

- ▲ 279 B2
- ✉ N of Mesopotamia
- ☎ 784 458 1198
- 🕐 Closed Sept.– Nov. & Sat.–Sun.
- 💲 $$

Layou Petroglyph Park

- 🗺 279 A2
- ✉ 800 m off Leeward Hwy., N of Layou
- ☎ 784 454 8686
- 💲 $

svgnationaltrust .org

The Grenadines

- 🗺 261 B2

Yachting Information

- ✉ Customs & Excise Dept., Kingstown, St. Vincent
- ☎ 784 456 1083

customs.gov.vc

Valley, a side road leads to the **Vermont Nature Trails.** The connecting trails are well marked and easy to follow, making a 2-mile (3 km) rain forest loop between the 1,000- to 2,000-foot (300 to 600 m) levels of Grand Bonhomme Mountain in the 10,870-acre (4,440 ha) **St. Vincent Parrot Reserve** (map 279 B2). One path follows the Dalaway River, which supplies 45 percent of St. Vincent's drinking water, and heads on through an area of Caribbean pine trees dripping with epiphytes. It continues into the rain forest proper, where giant buttressed santinay trees are a favorite parrot habitat. It's usually easiest to spot them in the late afternoon at the **Parrot Lookout,** perched on the edge of a wooded valley. Also keep an eye out for the brilliantly colored hooded tanagers found only on St. Vincent and Grenada, several species of hummingbirds, and broad-winged and black hawks.

Palm Island & Petit St. Vincent

The Grenadine Islands make idyllic miniature resorts. In addition to Young Island, off the south coast of St. Vincent, there are two more pint-size hideaways in the southern Grenadines. A mile off Union Island is Palm Island (*palmislandresort grenadines.com*), which changed its name from Prune Island after owners John and Mary Caldwell planted coconut palms in their laid-back resort. Three miles farther south is Petit St. Vincent (*map 285 B1, petitstvincent.com*), better known as PSV, and another paradise for sailors.

The highway drops down to the coast near **Buccament Bay Beach,** a strip of white (imported) sand fronting a luxurious villa resort. Just beyond Layou, look for the turning to **Layou Petroglyph Park,** where 1,300-year-old Arawak petroglyphs adorn a 20-foot (6 m) rock. **Peter's Hope Bay** and **Keartons Beach,** lying on either side of the fishing village of Barrouallie, are good spots for a dip in the Caribbean Sea. Scenes from the *Pirates of the Caribbean* franchise were filmed in lovely **Wallilabou Bay.** There's another fine beach near **Richmond** at the end of the highway. A popular excursion from here is the 45-minute hike to **Trinity Falls** (*map 279 B3*), which you can reach from a trail several miles north of town. The lovely rain forest walk emerges at a swimming hole fed by the waterfall.

At the north end of the island, accessible only by boat, are the **Falls of Baleine** (*map 279 B3*), tumbling down from La Soufrière in a 60-foot (18 m) cascade to a rock pool. A day-sail trip to the falls makes a great day out with fine views along the coast, lunch, snorkeling, and a dip in the pool beneath the cascade. (For day-sail details, see Travelwise p. 399.)

The Grenadines

An irregular chain of 30-plus tiny islands and cays interspersed with a host of lesser sandbars and reefs, the Grenadines trail off from St. Vincent for about 75 miles (120 km) toward Grenada and the Grenadian Grenadine Islands of Carriacou and Petit Martinique (see pp. 295–296).

Fewer than a quarter of the islands are inhabited (part of their charm for yachtsmen), and while some welcome no-frills sailors and divers, others have been transformed into tiny oases of barefoot luxury (see sidebar opposite).

It's not essential to be a yachtsman to see the Grenadines by boat. The M.V. *Barracuda* mail boat *(tel 784 455 9835)* sails down island from St. Vincent to Canouan, Mayreau, and Union Islands on Mondays and Thursdays, returning Tuesdays and Fridays, and makes a round-trip on Saturday. The M.V. *Gem Star (tel 784 526 1158)* makes a down-island run Tuesdays and Fridays, returning the following day. The St. Vincent–Bequia crossing is made several times a day by the *Admiral Express (tel 784 458 3348)* and the *Bequia Express (tel 784 457 3539)*. A speedier, though pricier, option for services throughout the Grenadines is the M.V. *Jaden Sun Fast Ferry (tel 784 451 2192, jadeninc.com)*.

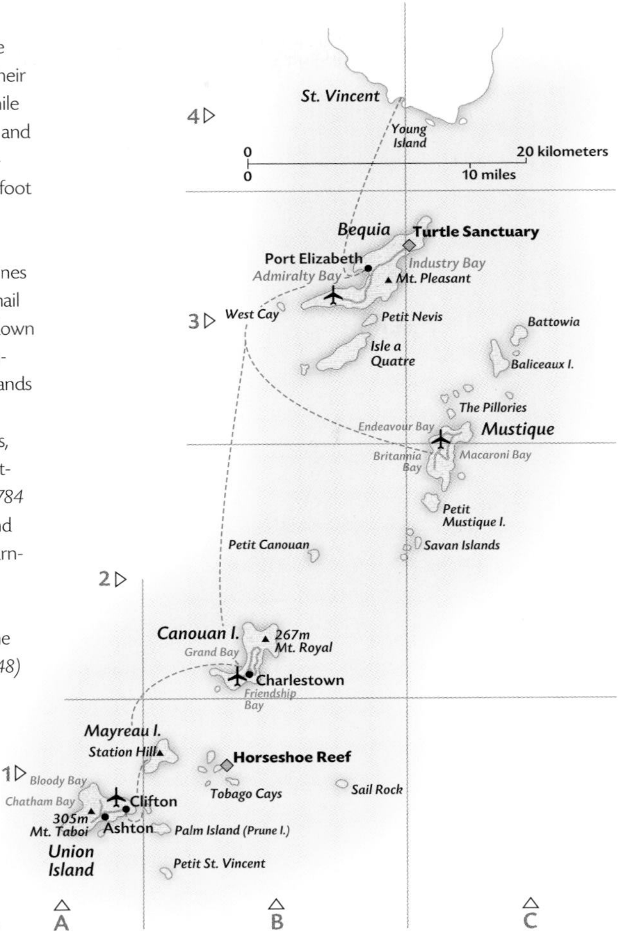

Bequia: An hour's ferry ride from St. Vincent is Bequia (beck-way), the largest of the St. Vincent Grenadines at 6 square miles (15 sq km). The quaint settlement of **Port Elizabeth** fringes Admiralty Bay, where the ferry docks within a stone's throw of shops and eateries overlooked by the 18th-century Hamilton Battery. Water taxis shuttle around to the palm-backed sands of **Princess Margaret Beach** and **Lower Bay.**

You can tour the island on foot or by taxi, or rent a scooter

for a fun trip up to **Mount Pleasant,** with its view south to the tip of Grenada. Down on the windward side there's safe swimming and snorkeling at **Industry Bay,** and it's worth continuing along the shore to the **Old Hegg Turtle Sanctuary** *(tel 784 458 3245, turtles .bequia.net)* at the end of the path leading to Park Beach. Here, Orton "Brother" King rears rescued hawksbill turtles.

Bequia
🗺 285 B3
Visitor Information
✉ Port Elizabeth
☎ 784 458 3286
bequiatourism.com

A boat taxi driver waits for a fare at Port Elizabeth on Bequia.

Canouan Island: Midway down the Grenadines, dry and hilly Canouan Island (pronounced CAN-oo-ahn; *map 285 B2*) has beautiful sandy beaches around the port of **Charlestown** in the curve of Grand Bay. A popular yachting center, the island also harbors the ultra-luxurious Canouan Resort *(tel 784 458 8000, canouan.com).*

Mayreau Island: Two fabulous beaches flank the 1.5-square-mile (4 sq km) scrubby island of Mayreau (pronounced MY-row; *map 285 B1*). It's a steep climb from the makeshift dock to the village on **Station Hill** (population about 250). A couple of bar-restaurants cater to yachtsmen,

and there are a few rooms to rent. **Salt Whistle Bay,** a silken sandbar on the tip of the island, is a favorite anchorage with passing yachtsmen. Snorkelers flit lazily around the calm, crystal clear water on one side of the beach, while Atlantic surf rolls in on the other.

Tobago Cays: The five low-lying, uninhabited islands of Tobago Cays *(map 285 B1)* lie east of Mayreau in shimmering turquoise waters protected by the gentle curve of **Horseshoe Reef.** For snorkelers, these are the crown jewels of the Grenadines, set in shallow lagoons where you can feast your eyes on the dazzling tropical fish nursery beneath and swim with

INSIDER TIP:

Friendly St. Vincentians love "limin'," local-speak for hanging out and having a chat over a cold beer.

—JENNIFER ALLARD
National Geographic contributor

giant turtles, feel sugar-soft sand between your toes, and generally live the dream. It's no wonder location scouts for the *Pirates of the Caribbean* franchise chose to shoot here, though the series's star, Johnny Depp, was ferried back to St. Vincent's Young Island resort to sleep. **Tobago Cays Marine Park** is accessible only by boat, but it's a popular spot, and there are usually several day-sail boats and visiting yachts at anchor.

Mustique: The chic Caribbean hideaway of Mustique *(map 285 C2–C3)* offers money-no-object accommodations in 60 or so private villas, a 20-room hotel, and an upscale boutique hotel *(mustique-island.com).*

Yachts gather in **Britannia Bay,** and day-trippers are permitted ashore (no ferry service) to sample the gleaming white sands of **Macaroni Bay** or enjoy a drink at Basil's Bar. There are good walks around the 1,350-acre (546 ha) island and more swimming and snorkeling at secluded **Gallicaux Bay** and the hotel beach at **Endeavour Bay.**

Union Island: While not the most alluring Grenadine, Union is certainly visually arresting, with a range of peaks culminating in Mount Taboi (999 feet/305 m), the island chain's highest point. It's a busy transportation hub, with a lively yacht harbor and a couple of hotels at **Clifton,** the main town.

The best beaches are **Chatham Bay** on the west coast and **Bloody Bay** to the north, both accessible only on foot or by boat. ∎

**Tobago Cays
Marine Park**
Visitor Information
✉ Clifton, Union Island
☎ 784 485 8191
tobagocays.org

Union Island
🄰 285 A1
Visitor Information
✉ Clifton
☎ 784 485 8082
unionisland.com

Critter Capital of the World

Some tourist destinations might cringe at the moniker "critter capital of the world," but for St. Vincent it's a ringing endorsement that the island's spectacular coral reefs are in terrific shape, and they are justly proud of the accolade. *Scuba Diving* magazine voted St. Vincent the "world's #1 small animal destination" with a perfect score of 100 for its extraordinary wealth of teensy marine critters. You need sharp eyes to spot the southern teardrop crab—no bigger than a penny—pea crabs, snapping shrimp, anemone shrimp, delicate sea stars, baby sea horses, expertly camouflaged sea slugs, and shy octopuses. There are darting, agile beauties like the neon pink and orange fairy basslet, endearingly pug-ugly spotted scorpionfish, and pop-eyed frogfish.

The best critter dive sites are usually close to the leeward shore, where the dense volcanic granite sand settles quickly when disturbed, so visibility is excellent. Keen photographers should arm themselves with a macro lens and seek out local critter expert and photographer Bill Tewes of **Dive St. Vincent** *(tel 784 457 4948, divestvincent.com, $$$$$).*

Grenada

Typically green and mountainous, Grenada is the southernmost of the Windward Islands, only 100 miles (160 km) or so from the coast of South America. Its smaller sister islands, Carriacou and Petite Martinique, are part of the Grenadines chain, which stretches north to St. Vincent. Grenada is wrapped in rain forest and sprinkled with sandy beaches. Visitors can hike and dive, swim in waterfalls, stock up on spices from stalls run by pipe-chewing old women, and generally relax on one of the friendliest small islands (21 by 12 miles/34 by 19 km) in the region.

The port of St. George's was named for England's King George III.

Grenada

 261 A1–A2

Visitor Information

✉ Burns Point
(S side of the Carenage),
St. George's

☎ 473 440 2001
or 473 440 2279

puregrenada.com

Christened Concepción by Columbus in 1498, Grenada (pronounced gren-AY-dah) was renamed by Spanish sailors homesick for the hills of southern Spain. French settlers from Martinique purchased the island from indigenous Carib for a handful of beads and tools in 1650, but the peace was short-lived and the last Carib are said to have jumped to their deaths from the cliffs at La Morne des

Sauteurs (Leapers' Hill) in 1651 (see p. 294). The French and English fought for control of the plantation island until it was ceded to Britain in 1783. During the French Revolution, Grenada was the scene of a bloody slave revolt led by Julien Fédon, a French planter, from his isolated coffee and cacao estate at Belvidere. Arms were smuggled in from Guadeloupe, and the rebels overran most of the island, slaughtering British settlers, including the governor, during the 15-month insurrection. When the British finally regained control in June 1796, Fédon disappeared and the plantations were in ruins.

Grenada was rescued from the doldrums by the introduction of nutmeg in the 1830s. Popular legend has it that a doctor from the East Indies arrived with a couple nutmeg trees in his baggage and jazzed up the local rum punch with a dusting of grated nutmeg. Grenada's nutmeg industry took

off in the 1850s, and other spices were introduced. Thus the West Indies finally achieved a spice island by default, 400 years after Columbus had set out to find one.

Grenada took full independence from Britain in 1974, but freed from colonial restraints, local politics became increasingly fraught, culminating in the murder of Prime Minister Maurice Bishop in 1983. Order was swiftly restored by a joint U.S.–Eastern Caribbean "friendly invasion."

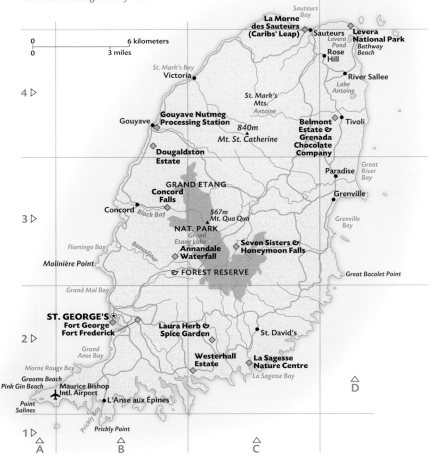

St. George's
🌋 289 B2

Putting the episode behind them, the Grenadians set about building up a low-key but very successful tourist infrastructure with a range of hotels concentrated in the south of the island, good roads and communications,

St. George's

There's no better introduction to Grenada than sailing into St. George's Harbour. It is one of the most picturesque ports in the Caribbean, nestled within the steep-sided walls of an extinct

Grenadian Spices

Grenada is an olfactory banquet of spices, redolent with the pungent tang of nutmeg, cloves, and sweet woody cinnamon. Nutmeg is the island's most important spice and easy to find by the roadside and in the hills. The nutmeg tree (*Myristica fragrans*) produces an apricot-like yellow fruit that splits when ripe to reveal a brown shell covered with a waxy red web of mace. The fruit is used to make preserves, the mace is processed

as a separate spice, the inedible shell is recycled as a path-building material, and the inner kernel is the spice used in cooking and pharmaceuticals.

Like the nutmeg tree, cinnamon trees were imported from the East Indies. The bark is used as a food flavoring. Allspice (*Pimenta officinale*) originated in Jamaica. As its name implies, it tastes like nutmeg, cinnamon, and cloves all rolled into the one tiny unripe fruit.

and the national pride and joy, a cricket stadium. On September 7, 2004, disaster struck when Grenada met the full force of Hurricane Ivan, which caused almost a billion U.S. dollars of damage. The islanders began to rebuild immediately. Within a year almost 80 percent of the island was back up and running.

The Grenadians are easygoing and welcoming hosts. There is much to see and do, and the island enjoys a high percentage of repeat visitors. Sweet-smelling nutmeg and cacao estates beckon, as do the craft shops and galleries of St. George's. There are secluded beaches, nature trails, fine gardens, and captivating dive sites including a spooky underwater sculpture park peopled by 55 life-size figures standing sentry on the **Molinière Reef.**

volcanic crater and guarded by a battery of old fortresses. St. George's was founded by the French but renamed in honor of England's King George III, and there are numerous examples of Georgian colonial architecture among the church steeples and neat rows of red-roofed homes that cling to the precipitous hillsides like contour lines.

A sharp ridge divides St. George's into two parts, which are linked by a Victorian tunnel bored through the rock in 1895. On the harbor side the horseshoe-shaped **Carenage** hugs the waterfront, edged by shops and restaurants. It is named for the wharves where ships were once careened (tipped on their sides to have their hulls cleaned), now a bustle of cargo boats, ferries, and fishing sloops from nearby Carriacou.

INSIDER TIP:

If you head out very early to the underwater sculpture park at Molinière Reef, the sun illuminates all the bright colors of the corals and sponges on the statues' faces.

—JASON DECAIRES TAYLOR
Underwater sculptor &
photographer

In the shadow of the ridge is the **Grenada National Museum,** housed in former French barracks dating from 1704. Island history and culture are explored in an assortment of Amerindian finds, colonial knickknacks, and a detailed, well-balanced account of the 1983 intervention.

Close to the museum is the 350-foot-long (107 m) **Sendall Tunnel,** which burrows beneath the ridge to the seafront **Esplanade** on the bay side of St. George's. Protecting the town from the headland at the harbor mouth is **Fort George,** with its great views over the town from the 18th-century battlements.

A block back from the cruise-ship terminal and minibus depot on the bayfront is the **market square,** best visited on a Saturday morning. Women in head scarves and bright cotton dresses preside over a carpet of fresh fruit, vegetables, and spices spread out on the sidewalk as they banter from the shady recesses of large, striped umbrellas.

A strenuous climb up Market Hill leads to **Church Street,** where several of St. George's finest Georgian buildings once perched on the hillside. In 2004 Hurricane Ivan caused major damage to historic **York House,** seat of the Grenadian Parliament and Supreme Court, and also to **St. George's Anglican Church,** built in 1825. More than a decade later both buildings remain in ruins, open to the sky. Market Hill continues up to a busy junction orchestrated by a white-gloved traffic officer. Lucas Street heads past **Government House,** the governor-general's official residence guarded by pith-helmeted sentries, to tumbledown **Fort Matthew** and the rather better preserved remains of **Fort Frederick.**

Grenada National Museum
- ✉ Monckton St. (off Long St.)
- ☎ 473 440 3725
- 🕐 Closed Sat. p.m. & Sun.
- 💲 $

Fort George
- 🅰 289 B2
- ✉ Church St.

NEED TO KNOW
Port Logistics: St. George's
Most cruise passengers arrive at the downtown Melville Street Cruise Terminal by the Esplanade Mall, a short taxi ride ($5) from the alternative disembarkation pier on the Carenage. Taxis are readily available (rates clearly displayed), or consider a day pass for the mini train if you're staying in town (free entry to sights). A taxi to Grand Anse Beach costs around $15, less (and more fun) by water taxi, cheaper still by local minibus. Island tours are recommended (4–6 hours).

St. George's Highlights
- Grand Anse Beach: half day
- Snorkel tour or Molinière Reef dive: half day
- Belmont Estate & Grenada Chocolate Co.: half day
- Grand Étang National Park: 2–3 hours

**Laura Herb &
Spice Garden**

▲ 289 C2

✉ Perdmontemps,
St. David's

☎ 473 443 2604

🕐 Closed Sat.–Sun.

💲 $

Grand Anse & the South Coast

Lying just over 2 miles (3 km) south of St. George's is Grand Anse, Grenada's main tourist enclave. A clutch of low-rise hotels lines the 2-mile (3 km) stretch of white-sand beach facing the Caribbean Sea. The swimming is safe, and water-sports concessions rent wind-surfers, dinghies, and kayaks. Waterskiing and parasailing are also available, and dive operators arrange trips to the reef sites off Molinière Point just north of St. George's, the Kick 'Em Jenny submarine volcano, and the scuttled wreck of the cruise ship *Bianca C.*

West of Grand Anse, en route to the very tip of the island at Point Salines, is **Morne Rouge Beach,** set in a quiet cove. There are sandy crescents at **Dr. Grooms Beach, Magazine Beach,** and

the deliciously named **Pink Gin Beach,** which nestles beneath an exclusive spa hotel. Tucked into the rocks at the end of **Tamarind Beach** is a great bar-restaurant with kayak rentals and snorkel-ing. On the southern shore of the peninsula a handful of hotels, apartments, and homes inhabit the secluded coves of **Prickly Bay** and the narrow strip of sand beach at **L'Anse aux Épines.**

As the main road heads east from St. George's and the beaches, it swiftly runs into the countryside and cane fields growing at the foot of steep, forested hills. You could drop in at **Laura Herb & Spice Garden,** on the road to Windsor Castle, where top-quality herbs and spices are grown and packaged for export. To the south is **Westerhall Estate** *(St. David, tel 473 443 5477, westerhallrums.com),* where they will provide an impromptu tour on weekdays. Though rum is no

The New Black Gold

For centuries many of the Caribbean islands' up-country estates, planted on rich, volcanic soil, have cultivated small quanti-ties of coffee for domestic consumption. (The exception being Jamaica, whose fine, flavorsome Blue Mountain coffee beans are exported around the world.) Recently on the Windward Islands, cacao has emerged as a niche crop. Chocoholic visi-tors to Grenada can get a taste of heaven at the **Belmont Estate** *(Tivoli, tel 473 442 9524, belmontestate.net, closed Sat.),* a 400-year-old plantation in the St. Patrick's district 20 miles (32 km) northeast of St. George's. The beans cultivated here are known as Trinitario, developed in Trinidad, with a low yield but sensational taste.

Estate tours follow the cocoa-making process from the orchard to the drying rack. There is a small museum, and the creole lunch buffet served in the planta-tion house is not to be missed.

At this stage the beans are ready for transportation to the nearby **Grenada Chocolate Company** *(Hermitage, tel 473 442 0050, grenadachocolate.com, closed Sat.–Sun.),* an engagingly eccentric but highly successful eco-friendly operation established in 1999. Here, the beans are roasted, ground, mixed, and molded into rich, dark chocolate bars, or packaged in the form of cocoa powder. The company's award-winning wares are sold around the island and exported overseas.

A tour guide explains old-fashioned nutmeg processing—Grenada is one of the world's top producers of the spice.

longer distilled here, the factory blends fine Westerhall rums, and a few pieces of antique plantation machinery can still be seen dotted around the grassy lawns. A small museum of local memorabilia displays distilling equipment, and oddities including a World War I Maxim machine gun.

Midway along the south coast, look for signs to **La Sagesse Nature Centre.** Follow the bumpy track to the beach, past a carefully tended checkerboard of vegetable gardens. The nature center is rather less official than it sounds. In reality it is a charming guesthouse and alfresco restaurant arranged around a little pink plantation house on a lovely beach.

Around Northern & Central Grenada

A clockwise circuit of northern Grenada, returning to St. George's via the central highlands, reveals a landscape of rich diversity from sea-level mangrove swamps to rain forest mountains, and scenes from island life in spice plantations, a nutmeg factory, and charming creole villages.

Heading north of St. George's, the main road hugs the twisting coastline, edged by cliffs and the Caribbean Sea. At Concord, follow signs inland for **Concord Falls** up into the hills through spice plantations and cacao walks (cacao tree groves) to the lowest of the three falls. It's an energetic 30-minute climb to the second fall and one and a half hours to the upper fall; but the rewards make the effort well worthwhile as both falls have inviting swimming holes. The hike (4.5 hours) may be continued all the way to Grand Étang (see sidebar p. 294).

Gouyave Nutmeg Processing Station

🔼 289 B4

✉️ Gouyave

☎️ 473 444 8337

🕐 Closed Sat.–Sun.

💲 $

Grand Étang National Park

🔼 289 C3

Visitor Information

✉️ Grand Étang

☎️ 473 440 6160

💲 $

Back on the main road just south of the fishing village of Gouyave, look for the **Dougaldston Estate** on the right. In a sweet-smelling clapboard barn learn how nutmeg and other spices are still processed in the old-fashioned way. In Gouyave (French for "guava"), you'll find the **Gouyave Nutmeg Processing Station,** which welcomes visitors interested in sniffing around its working plant, stuffed full with sacks of nutmeg kernels.

Beyond Gouyave the around-island road circles the St. Mark's Mountains and **Mount St.**

Hiking in Grand Étang National Park

Grenada's best hiking opportunities lie within this national park in the central highlands. The **Mount Qua Qua Trail** is a moderately energetic, three-hour round-trip from the park visitor center through elfin woodlands to the rocky summit of Mount Qua Qua. For a more challenging hike, take the **Concord Trail,** which continues from Mount Qua Qua for another three hours to Concord Falls. Other popular hiking destinations include **Honeymoon Falls** and **Seven Sisters Waterfalls,** both of which are best tackled with a guide. Contact **Henry's Yacht Services & Tours** (tel 473 444 5313, henrysafari.com, $$$$$), who also lead an adventurous five- to six-hour hike to the jungle cave hideout of 18th-century rebel leader Julien Fédon.

Catherine (2,757 feet/840 m), Grenada's highest peak. The clifftop known as **La Morne des Sauteurs** (Leapers' Hill), on the north coast, is where in 1651 the island's last Carib

threw themselves to their deaths (see p. 288).

On the virgin northeast coast is **Levera National Park** (map 289 D5), with its mangrove swamp and fine stretch of golden sand where leatherback turtles come ashore to lay their eggs in summer (April–June). The swimming is safer, however, at nearby **Bathway Beach.** Bird-watching is good around **Levera Pond,** a wildfowl breeding and feeding ground where scarlet ibis are occasionally spotted. Nearby are the **River Sallee Boiling Springs,** which represent Grenada's token volcanic activity.

The main road runs inland above the Atlantic coast, passing through the pretty country villages of Mount Rose, Tivoli, and Paradise. From **Grenville,** Grenada's second largest town, the cross-island road climbs into the rain forest and **Grand Étang National Park & Forest Reserve.** Natural history displays at the park center detail local geology, flora, and fauna, and a 15-minute nature trail offers fine views off to the coast and a chance of spotting mona monkeys, introduced from Africa more than 300 years ago. Across the road a path leads you to Grand Étang (Big Pond), a crater lake encircled by a 90-minute hike. The trailhead for longer hikes to Mount Qua Qua and Concord Falls can be found just a short distance west of the park center.

On the road back to St. George's, **Annandale Waterfalls** is a popular beauty spot with a swimming hole hemmed in by greenery and fed by the dramatic 30-foot (9 m) cascade. ■

Carriacou

The largest Grenadine island, 23 miles (37 km) north of Grenada, is a laid-back destination where visitors can get a close-up view of the craft of boatbuilding, appreciate imaginative local art, or simply enjoy the fine snorkeling and secluded white-sand beaches.

A Carriacouan tends to his goats.

A 90-minute fast ferry ride from St. George's, Carriacou (pronounced CARRI-ah-COO) is the largest of the Grenadines (8 by 5 miles/13 by 8 km), with a population of about 6,000.

The island is hilly and dry, still largely undeveloped, and fringed by white sand. It takes its name from the Carib word for "land of reefs," and there's excellent snorkeling and diving to be enjoyed offshore. Carriacou was once planted with cotton and sugar, but when the plantations died out in the 19th century, the islanders turned to fishing, boat-building, and smuggling.

INSIDER TIP:

During school vacations, you may come across makeshift roadside boatbuilding schools offered to youngsters by the Ministry of Culture.

—LARRY PORGES
National Geographic Books author

Accessed from Grenada by daily air and ferry services, the tiny capital, **Hillsborough,** is built on a curving bay. Close by are several waterfront restaurants and

Carriacou

🄰 261 B2

Visitor Information

✉ Main St.,
Hillsborough

☎ 473 443 7948

A cottage in the coastal village of Windward. The island of Petite Martinique rises offshore.

the small **Carriacou Museum** *(Paterson St., closed Sat.–Sun.).* Its collections of Amerindian and colonial relics are laid out in a former cotton ginnery. There is also a collection of charming naïve-style paintings by local artist Canute Calliste (1914–2005). Calliste's lively and often humorous island subjects—boatbuilders, Carnival-goers, fishing boats, and his trademark mermaids—became highly collectible overseas. Beyond Hillsborough, a whistle-stop tour of the island's high spots takes little more than an hour, but to enjoy a

more in-depth experience such as a guided hike, a boat trip in a traditional Carriacou sloop, or a snorkel excursion to Tobago Cays, contact **Simply Carriacou** *(tel 473 443 2029, simplycarriacou.com).* Traveling up the west coast, **Anse la Roche** has a secluded beach, while at the highest point of the island (956 feet/291 m), **High North Nature Reserve** commands dazzling views that stretch south to Grenada and north up the Grenadine Islands chain toward St. Vincent. At ground level, hikers may spot the odd land turtle, iguanas, and soldier crabs. Over on the east coast, the village of **Windward** is a good place to watch the local boatbuilders in action, working the white island-grown cedar wood.

South of Hillsborough, the well named **Paradise Beach** boasts a fine sweep of white sand with a beach bar facing Sandy Island. A water taxi will ferry you out there for a few hours snorkeling and sunning, Robinson Crusoe–style. On the southwest shore is **Tyrrel Bay,** a popular yacht anchorage with a modest restaurant row. For details of dive operators, see Travelwise p. 398. ■

Petite Martinique

The tiny island of Petite Martinique is a volcanic cone lying 2.5 miles (4 km) off the northeast coast of Carriacou. Ferries from Hillsborough make the 20-minute crossing a couple times daily during the week, less frequently on weekends. Petite (pronounced PETT-y) Martinique is pretty much a closed community of 900 or so islanders who live in and around the sole town of Paradise. Most make their living from fishing and boatbuilding, and tourist facilities are limited to a guesthouse or two. There are some fine beaches on the leeward side and excellent snorkeling, but apart from a taxi tour along the 2-mile-long (3 km) main road, there is little else to do unless you visit during the surprisingly energetic pre-Lenten Carnival.

Exquisite beaches, sophisticated lodgings, and a wealth of things to see and do in the gateway to the West Indies

Barbados

A palm-studded beach at Bathsheba in Barbados

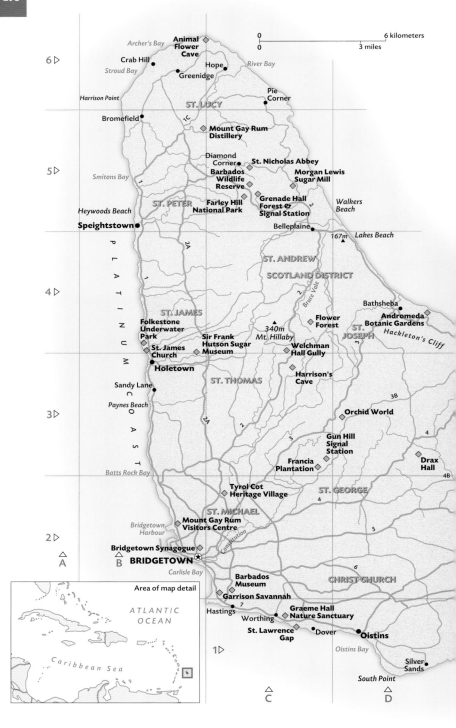

Archer's Bay

Animal Flower Cave

Crab Hill

Hope

6 ▷

Stroud Bay

Greenidge

River Bay

Pie Corner

Harrison Point

Bromefield

ST. LUCY

1C

Mount Gay Rum Distillery

Diamond Corner

St. Nicholas Abbey

5 ▷

Smitons Bay

Barbados Wildlife Reserve

Morgan Lewis Sugar Mill

1

ST. PETER

Farley Hill National Park

Grenade Hall Forest & Signal Station

Walkers Beach

Heywoods Beach

Speightstown

Belleplaine

167m

Lakes Beach

2

2A

ST. ANDREW

P L A T I N U M   C O A S T

SCOTLAND DISTRICT

1

4 ▷

2

Bruce Vale

Bathsheba

Flower Forest

Andromeda Botanic Gardens

ST. JAMES

Folkestone Underwater Park

340m
Mt. Hillaby

ST. JOSEPH

Hackleton's Cliff

3

St. James Church

Sir Frank Hutson Sugar Museum

Welchman Hall Gully

Holetown

ST. THOMAS

Harrison's Cave

Sandy Lane

Paynes Beach

3B

3 ▷

2A

2

Orchid World

4

3

Gun Hill Signal Station

Drax Hall

Batts Rock Bay

Francia Plantation

4B

Tyrol Cot Heritage Village

ST. GEORGE

4

ST. MICHAEL

Mount Gay Rum Visitors Centre

Bridgetown Harbour

5

Constitution

2 ▷

△
A

Bridgetown Synagogue

△
B

BRIDGETOWN ★

6

CHRIST CHURCH

Carlisle Bay

Barbados Museum

Garrison Savannah

Hastings

7

Graeme Hall Nature Sanctuary

Worthing

St. Lawrence Gap

Dover

Oistins

1 ▷

Oistins Bay

Silver Sands

South Point

△
C

△
D

0   6 kilometers
0   3 miles

Area of map detail

ATLANTIC OCEAN

Caribbean Sea

Barbados

Barbados lies 100 miles (160 km) east of the Windward Islands, surrounded by the Atlantic Ocean. Unlike its volcanic neighbors, the island is an undulating limestone massif. Its coral rock underpinnings are responsible for the famous Platinum Coast beaches, the island's upscale tourist heartland. The more informal (and affordable) side of Barbados is the south coast resort area, with a string of equally appealing destinations.

The British ruled Barbados for 340 uninterrupted years before independence and left an indelible, slightly formal imprint on this former sugar colony. There's considerable pride in the Barbados Parliament and more than a touch of Little England in the local passion for cricket, the ritual of afternoon tea, and the practice of dressing for dinner in some quarters.

Barbados takes its name from the huge, native bearded fig tree, also known as a banyan, which drops a curtain of aerial roots to the ground. Portuguese explorers called them *barbados* (bearded ones). Although Amerindian settlers discovered the island almost 4,000 years ago, it was uninhabited when English colonists landed near the site of Holetown on the west coast in 1627. Dutch settlers played a significant part in developing the early plantations, and they introduced sugarcane from Brazil in 1637. As the colony prospered, indentured laborers were shipped out from Britain, but they struggled with the climate, and soon African slaves were brought in to swell the plantation workforce. With the abolition of slavery in 1834, the sugar industry lurched

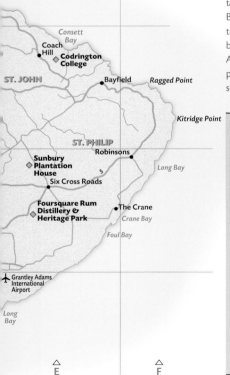

NOT TO BE MISSED:

Delving into island history at the Barbados Museum, Bridgetown **303**

Afternoon tea at St. Philip's Sunbury Plantation House **306–307**

Walking through blooming tropical plants in St. Joseph's Flower Forest **307**

Viewing the cliff-clinging Andromeda Botanic Gardens, St. Joseph **308**

The elegant colonial atmosphere of St. Nicholas Abbey in St. Peter **308**

Spotting monkeys at the Barbados Wildlife Reserve in St. Peter **310** from virtual failure to moderate success, and Barbados eventually achieved independence from Britain.

The colonial heart of the island is Bridgetown, together with the old British military headquarters just south of the city at Garrison Savannah. Barbados is a gift for history buffs, who will have a field day perusing handsome examples of traditional Georgian architecture and visiting historic Holetown (the original British settlement), restored plantation houses, and any number of picturesque sugar mill ruins.

Beyond the sprawling capital city, and the resort areas to either side, Barbados's

A typical day in Worthing, one of Barbados's resort towns

INSIDER TIP:

When blacks weren't allowed to play in the whites-only tennis clubs of the 1930s, they came up with their own street game: road tennis. Bajans play it across the island on Sunday afternoons.

—CHARLES KULANDER
National Geographic Traveler *magazine writer*

landscape is remarkably rural. The island is divided into 11 parishes (Christ Church and 10 more named after saints), which are frequently given as an address rather than the name of the nearest village. Sugarcane fields and pockets of woodland roll back from the leeward coast, and dozens of tiny (and spectacularly unsigned) country roads burrow into the interior. Renting a car is a great way to explore, but it's very easy to get lost, so leave plenty of time, relax, and enjoy the mystery tour. For less intrepid travelers, ground operators offer all manner of sightseeing excursions, or you can arrange a taxi tour with a clued-up local driver.

To the northeast, Mount Hillaby (1,089 feet/340 m) is the highest point on the island, and the 1,000-foot (300 m) crest of Hackleton's Cliff is poised dramatically over the Atlantic on the windward coast. This exhilarating, surf-dashed shore is in complete contrast to the silky smooth resort beaches of the eastern coast, and it is where Bajans come to relax. The atmosphere is low-key with little sign of development, though visitors looking for peace and quiet will find several small guesthouses and B&Bs. The damper climate on this side of the island has encouraged the creation of several sensational gardens clinging to the hillsides perched above the ocean.

Because of its height, Mount Hillaby provides one of the best scenic lookouts in Barbados, especially to the east, west, and north coasts of the island. ∎

Bridgetown

Bridgetown, the island's energetic capital city, is an important Caribbean business center and home to about 100,000 residents. The heart of the city lies on the Careenage, a narrow inner harbor at the mouth of Constitution River, where an English expedition discovered an Amerindian bridge in 1625. A handful of waterfront cafés makes the Careenage wharf area a pleasant place to take a break and watch the world go by.

The bustling Careenage, complete with waterfront cafés, in Bridgetown

On the north bank of the inlet is **National Heroes Square,** the old colonial heart of the city. Here the mellow complex of coral rock public buildings contains the House of Assembly, the seat of the Barbados Parliament where the island's legislators meet. Although the buildings date only from the 19th century, the historic assembly was first established in 1639.

Crop Over—Carnival Bajan-Style

The Bajan summer Carnival *(July–Aug.)* dates back to the late 1700s, when Barbados was the world's largest sugar producer and plantation owners permitted their slave laborers to celebrate the end of harvest. Animals were slaughtered, special breads and pots of peas and rice were prepared, all washed down with "swank," a sweet rum mix that fueled a night of singing and dancing. Today preparations begin far in advance with magnificent costumes sewn (in some cases constructed), dance routines practiced, and calypso acts honed for months prior to the event *(check schedules on websites such as* ncf.bb *or* funbarbados.com*)*.

Bridgetown

 298 B2

Visitor Information

✉ Bridgetown Harbour

☎ 246 427 2623

🕐 Closed Sat.–Sun.

visitbarbados.org

Bridgetown Synagogue

✉ Magazine Ln.

🕐 Closed Sat.–Sun.

💲 $

Barbados Museum

▲ 298 C2

✉ St. Ann's Garrison, St. Michael

☎ 246 427 0201

🕐 Closed Sun. a.m.

💲 $$

barbmuse.org.bb

A short walk eastward on St. Michael's Row leads you to **St. Michael's Cathedral,** which has been rebuilt several times (most recently in 1831) on the site of the original church, founded in 1625. George Washington (1732–1799) is said to have worshipped in one of its former incarnations in 1751, during his only trip outside what is now the U.S.A., and his half brother, Lawrence, stayed at Bush Hill House in Garrison Savannah (see below).

West of National Heroes is **Broad Street,** the city's main shopping and business district. Among modern offices and department stores are a number of fine old colonial buildings dressed up with fancy ironwork balconies. A few blocks away, off Magazine Lane, is the ice-cream pink-and-white **Bridgetown Synagogue.** The first synagogue on the island was established by Jewish immigrants from Brazil and consecrated in 1654. Bridgetown's prosperous Jewish community acted as financial agents and export brokers for the fledgling colony, and it grew considerably in the mid-17th century, when the British islands offered freedom of religious practices under the direction of Oliver Cromwell (1599–1658). Largely destroyed by a hurricane in 1831, the present synagogue was reconsecrated in 1833, but many tombs in the cemetery date back much further.

From the city center the Princess Alice Highway heads west to **Bridgetown Harbour** and the cruise-ship complex.

To the south, across the Careenage via the Chamberlain Bridge, Bay Street follows the curve of Carlisle Bay into the **Bayville** district, where a few pretty 19th-century town houses with gingerbread trimmings have survived on quiet back streets shaded by palm and mango trees.

A mile (1.6 km) beyond Bridgetown is **Garrison Savannah,** once a British parade ground. This now doubles as a jogging track and a racecourse where the Barbados Turf Club hosts weekend races *(tel 246 626 3980, barbadosturfclub.org).*

INSIDER TIP:

At sunrise on race days, grooms from Garrison Savannah's racetrack bathe their horses in the ocean at Pebbles Beach.

—MATT PROPERT
National Geographic photographer

Nearby are several 19th-century buildings, including the **Main Guard** (aka the Savannah Club), the former barracks and ramparts of 17th-century **Fort Charles,** and **St. Ann's Fort,** founded in 1704 but never completed. Also here is George Washington's lodgings in the former Bush Hill House, which has been restored by the Barbados National Trust and is now known as **George Washington House** *(tel 246 228 5461, closed Sun., $$$).* The kitchens and reception rooms have been furnished in period style; a museum of Bajan memorabilia is upstairs.

Barbados Museum

The old military prison near Garrison Savannah houses the excellent Barbados Museum. A tour begins with an overview of the island's natural history and early Amerindian inhabitants accompanied by archaeological finds and copious background notes.

In the plantation-era section, the **Aall Gallery** displays rare antique maps, including a second edition of Richard Ligon's original map of Barbados, published in 1657. It depicts the island still partially covered in native forest, with plantations blocked neatly along the leeward coast and wild boars rampaging about the interior. Prisoners once broke stones in the museum's lower courtyard and lived in cells around the leafy upper courtyard, now occupied by a series of rooms furnished in 19th-century style.

The **Chancellor Gallery** houses a small, interesting selection of local military memorabilia. A fascinating collection of 17th- and 18th-century engravings is a highlight in the **Cunard Gallery.** Fine island views and studies of plantation great houses compete for attention with the colorful portraits of fashionable planters, dandies, dancers, and Rachel Pringle, Barbados's most famous 18th-century madame. ■

Cool runnings: A stable hand prepares his horse for race day.

NEED TO KNOW

Port Logistics: Bridgetown

A mile (1.6 km) west of the city center ($5 by taxi), Bridgetown's busy cruise terminal offers the full complement of communications, dining, tourist information, and duty-free shopping opportunities. Taxi tours are based on an hourly rate (about $40), and it's easy to arrange a return ride if you stop off at a main beach; the closest beaches to the harbor are on Carlisle Bay.

Bridgetown Highlights

- Garrison Savannah & Barbados Museum: 1–2 hours
- Sunbury Plantation House: 2–3 hours
- Snorkeling off Paynes Beach: 2–3 hours
- Bajan buffet lunch

Sugar

At the height of the 17th- to 18th-century sugar era, Barbados was one of the most powerful islands in the Caribbean. For two centuries sugar was the backbone of the West Indies, the "white gold" that lined the planters' coffers, shaped the foreign policy of distant European countries, and instigated the largest forced transportation of human beings in history.

Sugarcane stalks can grow to a height of 20 feet (6 m), making the harvest an arduous task.

Sugar Arrives in the New World

The Spanish conquest of the New World in the 16th century was fueled by South and Central American gold and precious gems. Lacking the mineral wealth of the mainland, the success of the West Indian colonies founded in the early 17th century depended on finding a profitable crop that could not be grown in Europe, and that would survive the vagaries of transatlantic transportation. Cotton, indigo, and coffee were early contenders, but tobacco proved the most profitable option until new plantations in Virginia flooded the market with better quality tobacco, leaving the Caribbean settlers searching for an alternative.

Sugarcane was among a selection of experimental crops brought to the Spanish colony of Hispaniola by Christopher Columbus in 1493. Although the cane flourished, it was more than a century before Dutch planters from Brazil reintroduced sugarcane and their vital expertise to Barbados in the 1630s. By this time the new fashion for coffee and chocolate drinking in Europe provided a burgeoning home market, and the success of the first sugar crops ignited a planting frenzy that carpeted Barbados with cane by the 1650s.

Cultivation & Processing

Compared with tobacco, which could be grown profitably on small holdings, sugar required larger plantations and extensive capital outlay for buildings and processing equipment. The labor force on the islands was also insufficient, so slaves were imported from West Africa to work the cane fields.

To prepare the land for sugar cultivation, the planter's first task was to clear native vegetation and divide his estate into large fields arranged around the central mill and processing facility. A crop grown from cane tops planted in well-prepared earth could be harvested after 18 months; but the Dutch perfected *ratooning*, a less expensive and faster method of propagation using shoots grown on cane roots left in the ground after the previous harvest and ripe for harvesting within a year.

Slaves cut the crop by hand—brutally hot, backbreaking labor—during the dry season (Jan.–May) and carried it to the mill, which could be powered by wind, water, animal, or slave labor. Here the cane was crushed by rollers, the bagasse (trash) removed for fuel, and the cane juice diverted into a series of copper boiling pans. Lime water was added to assist clarification, and as the boiling syrup progressed through pans of ever decreasing size and increased temperature, it was skimmed to remove impurities. From the final pan, liquid sugar was poured into wooden cooling troughs where it separated into *muscovado* sugar crystals and molasses. The molasses was then drained off and distilled to make rum, and the semi-refined sugar was packed into hogsheads (large wooden barrels) to await shipment overseas.

INSIDER TIP:

Descendants of Irish and English "Redlegs"—white slaves who worked the sugar plantations—still live off the land in the hills of eastern Barbados.

—LARRY PORGES
National Geographic Books author

Boom & Bust

At the beginning of the 18th century, the lucrative spoils of the booming Caribbean sugar trade were shared between Britain and France, and trade was at the core of a century of bitter rivalry between the two countries. Peace treaties inevitably involved the transfer of colonial powers to the victors.

Peace with France in 1814 brought Britain a handful of former French West Indian colonies and a glut of sugar accompanied by a dramatic reduction in profits. Across the Channel, the French turned to sugar beets, grown in Europe as a vegetable since Roman times, and a far cheaper and easier way of producing sugar since the discovery of a viable method of sugar extraction in 1812. The widespread cultivation of sugar beets in Europe, coupled with the emancipation of the slave workforce, spelled the end of the sugar industry in the smaller West Indian colonies in the 1840s. Only the big producers such as Barbados, Jamaica, and Trinidad survived by importing indentured labor from overseas.

The Origins of Sugar

The recorded history of sugar begins in India, though how sugarcane reached the subcontinent from its probable origins in Polynesia is unknown. Discovered by Persian invaders circa 510 B.C., sugarcane and the secret of "honey without bees" traveled to the Middle East. A few centuries later, the ancient Greeks and Romans prized it as a luxury and a medicine, and during the Middle Ages small quantities of sugarcane were cultivated around the Mediterranean region. It was still regarded as a rare and expensive alternative to honey when Crusaders returning from Syria introduced the "new spice" to England in 1099.

Plantation Houses & Gardens

The colonial heritage of Barbados comes alive in its wonderful plantation houses and lush tropical gardens. Plantation owners built gracious residences to reflect their exalted social standing. In doing so, they achieved a refinement that matched that of the sugar that underpinned their wealth, while fine gardens reinforced the notion of living in an island paradise.

The Sunbury Plantation House was built in the 1660s.

Sunbury Plantation House

🅰 299 E2
✉ St. Philip
☎ 246 423 6270
💲 $$

barbadosgreathouse .com

The Southern Heartland

The rolling countryside of southern Barbados cuts a swath eastward from Bridgetown and north of Grantley Adams Airport. The atmosphere here is redolent of two Barbadian mainstays: sugar processing and rum. Set back from the coast amid the undulating green carpet of cane fields that provided its wealth for centuries, the 350-year-old **Sunbury Plantation House** was a private home

until the 1980s. This historic great house still retains charmingly homey touches such as fresh-cut flowers and potted plants dotted among the traditional Barbadian mahogany furniture and collections of antique china, glass, and silver. The bedrooms upstairs are open for inspection, with Victorian clothes laid out on capacious four-poster beds. The old yam cellar has been turned into a carriage museum and repository of old-fashioned agricultural and domestic implements. The Courtyard Restaurant in the garden serves lunch and afternoon tea. If the idea of a hurricane-lamp-lit dinner in the main house appeals, call and make a reservation for the five-course Plantation Dinner.

A short distance to the west, **Drax Hall** is one of the oldest houses in the region, dating from the mid-17th century. It is occasionally opened to the public under the Barbados National Trust's Open House Programme (see sidebar this page).

Highland Sites

The central highlands of Barbados lie just to the east of the Platinum Coast. The terrain here was too hilly for large-scale plantations, so the landscape feels more unspoiled.

The first garden you come to is **Welchman Hall Gully,** located about 5 miles (8 km) due east from Holetown along the west coast. Originally laid out as a botanical walk in the 1860s, this fabulously lush mile-long (1.6 km) wooded gorge was created by the collapse of a limestone chamber in part of the Harrison's Cave underground cavern network (see p. 311). Around the fantastical pinnacles and limestone rock formations, more than 200 species of exotic plants and flowers flourish in the cool shade of giant forest trees and stands of bamboo. Ferns and trailing lianas add to the jungle-like atmosphere, and you might hear vervet monkeys crashing about in the treetops in the early morning or late afternoon.

Another haven of exuberant tropical plantlife, the 50-acre (20 ha) **Flower Forest** lies just 2 miles (3 km) northeast of Welchman Hall Gully. It occupies a commanding position in the Scotland district with views across a ruffle of hills to the wide blue Atlantic. In the woodlands, steep paths zigzag down through a forest of gingers, lobster claw heliconias, Chinese hat plants, and red hot cat's tails to a grassy lookout. A leisurely inspection of the orchid collection provides a welcome break on the trek back.

If orchids are your thing, then don't miss **Orchid World,** near Gun Hill. More than 30,000 orchids are gathered here in a dazzling display. Paths traverse the 6.5-acre (2.6 ha) landscaped gardens and there are five orchid houses to explore.

The views from nearby Gun Hill Signal Station (see p. 311) reach all the way to the coast. Just

Welchman Hall Gully
- ▲ 298 C3
- ✉ Welchman Hall, St. Thomas
- ☎ 246 438 6671
- 💲 $$$

welchmanhallgully barbados.com

Flower Forest
- ▲ 298 C4
- ✉ St. Joseph
- ☎ 246 433 8152
- 💲 $$$

flowerforest barbados.com

Orchid World
- ✉ Groves, St. George
- ☎ 246 433 0306
- 💲 $$$

(see p. 311)

Barbados Open House

Barbados's rich architectural history runs the gamut of styles from Jacobean gems and imposing contemporary mansions to wooden chattel houses. Most of these architectural treasures remain in private hands. The popular annual Open House Programme *(Jan.–April)* encourages owners to open their homes for a few hours once a year. In recent times access has been given to the prime minister's official residence as well as to a couple of stunning modern residences in exclusive Sandy Lane. Contact the **Barbados National Trust** *(Wildey House, Wildey, St. Michael, tel 246 426 2421, barbadosnationaltrust.org, $$$$$).*

Andromeda Botanic Gardens

△ 298 D4

✉ Bathsheba, St. Joseph

☎ 246 433 9384

$ $$$

andromedabarbados .com

St. Nicholas Abbey

△ 298 C5

✉ Cherry Tree Hill, St. Peter

☎ 246 422 8725

🕐 Closed Sat.

$ $$$$$

stnicholasabbey.com

down the hill, the handsome early 20th-century great house, Francia Plantation, is now a private school.

Northeast Coast

The rolling uplands of the interior end abruptly in a series of dramatic coastal cliffs in the east. Although relatively unpopulated, the northeast coast of Barbados has a pair of memorable sites.

The first is **Andromeda Botanic Gardens,** lying some 4 miles (6.5 km) east of Flower Forest. World-renowned for a fabulous collection of indigenous and exotic tropical flowers, these lovely gardens cling to the cliffs above the Atlantic coast like their namesake heroine in Greek mythology. The 6-acre (2.5 ha) gardens were established privately by Mrs. Iris Bannochie in 1954 and arranged in outdoor "rooms," where orchids, heliconias, hibiscus, and clouds of bougainvillea abound alongside fragrant bowers, water

Flowers bloom at the Andromeda Botanic Gardens.

INSIDER TIP:

Learn to recognize the poisonous machineel trees (many are marked with a red X)—even just standing under one in the rain can cause blistered skin.

—CHARLES KULANDER
National Geographic Traveler
magazine writer

lily ponds, and shady corners planted with ferns and striking ornamental foliage.

A shore road runs northward along the rocky eastern coast of Barbados, where there are few settlements but extensive beaches. Some 9 miles (14.5 km) north from Andromeda Botanic Gardens is **St. Nicholas Abbey.** A rare example of Jacobean architecture in the Caribbean, the "abbey" rejoices in a splendid gabled facade dating from around 1650–1660, although the building never had any religious connections. Recently, the property has undergone an impeccable restoration. The elegant, paneled reception rooms have been filled with antique furnishings, Wedgwood china, and exquisite glassware. Visitors are free to wander in the beautiful gardens, drop into the café, discover an avenue of 250-year-old mahogany trees, and explore leafy gullies. The estate is once more making fine rum and a steam mill operates several times a week during the reaping season *(Feb.–May).* ■

South Coast

Around the southwest tip of Barbados from Garrison Savannah, the main coastal highway runs into Christ Church parish and the island's busiest resort area.

Between Hastings and Worthing on the south coast

Hastings, Worthing, and **Dover** back the best of the lovely south coast beaches, while the St. Lawrence Gap is a veritable restaurant row enjoying the best nightlife on the island. By day the action moves to water sports on the beach. A little-known escape from the crowds at Worthing, **Graeme Hall Bird Sanctuary** has a swamp boardwalk lookout on the island's largest expanse of inland water.

Beyond **Oistins,** a fishing center with a popular Friday-night fish fry, is lively **Silver Sands Beach,** a favorite with windsurfers and kiteboarders. Farther east you'll find secluded beach coves at Foul Bay, Crane Bay (renowned for its pink sands), and Long Bay.

The interior of the south coast also has its share of attractions,

including the unashamedly touristy **Heritage Park & Foursquare Rum Distillery** at Six Cross Roads. The south coast runs out at Ragged Point, where the rocks beneath East Point Lighthouse are lashed by the Atlantic. ∎

Heritage Park & Foursquare Rum Distillery

🅰 299 E2

✉ Foursquare Plantation, St. Philip

☎ 246 420 1977

Rum Punch

On the French islands the blending and aging of rums is a serious business; the top producers even date their premium products to create vintages like wines. Rum punch was the planters' favorite tipple and was once a good way of transforming some of the rougher local brews into a palatable drink. The traditional recipe for rum punch calls for one measure of sour (lemon or lime), two of sweet (cane juice), three of strong (rum), and four of weak (water).

Around Barbados

There's no excuse for boredom on Barbados, where dozens of fascinating sites, natural and historical, are scattered about the island. From local architecture at Tyrol Cot Heritage Village to the legacy of sugar and rum to agoutis and anemones, it's all within a short drive.

The 700-foot-high (213 m) perch of Gun Hill Signal Station

Animal Flower Cave
- 298 B6
- St. Lucy
- 246 439 8797
- $$

Barbados Wildlife Reserve & Grenade Hall Signal Station & Forest
- 298 C5
- Farley Hill, St. Peter
- 246 422 8826
- $$$

Codrington College
- 299 E3
- St. John
- 246 423 1140
- $

Animal Flower Cave

At the northern tip of the island, dozens of multicolored sea anemones flower in the rock pools of this subterranean cave hollowed out of the cliffs by wave action. Visitors can swim around with a guide, watch the "animal flowers" waving their tiny tentacles, and take a dip in one of the larger pools.

Barbados Wildlife Reserve & Grenade Hall Signal Station & Forest

The first of three attractions conveniently grouped in the same location, the Barbados Wildlife Reserve is a miniature animal kingdom set in a 4-acre (1.5 ha) pocket of mahogany forest. Vervet monkeys, shy Brocket deer, porcupines, and agoutis (tropical rodents) wander freely in the woodlands and provide real wildlife spotting opportunities that delight children. The reserve has an iguana sanctuary decorated with orchids, a walk-through aviary, and a secure caiman pool, as well as a caged python.

Across the parking lot is the Grenade Hall Signal Station, one of half a dozen towers built in the early 1800s to keep a watch on slaves working on the plantations.

Nature trails in the adjacent Grenade Hall Forest offer a glimpse of how Barbados would have appeared to the first settlers.

Nearby, **Farley Hill National Park** is a favorite picnic spot on the grounds of a ruined plantation house with an arboretum.

Codrington College

A magnificent avenue of slender cabbage palms flanks the driveway leading to the imposing facade of this Anglican

INSIDER TIP:

At Grantley Adams International Airport, don't miss the Barbados Concorde Experience (barbadosconcorde.com).

—PETER GWIN
National Geographic
magazine writer

theological college. The college, founded in 1743, was financed by a bequest from Christopher Codrington (1668–1710), a onetime governor-general of the Leeward Islands whose family was among the earliest settlers on Barbados. Access is limited, but visitors can view the outside of the Principal's Lodge (the original 17th-century estate house where Codrington was raised), stroll around the gardens that lead down to Consett Bay, and take a turn around the pretty water lily pond. Codrington Woods offers a short nature trail through mature woodland, where native silk cotton, ironwood, whitewood, and imposing mahogany trees flourish.

Gun Hill Signal Station

A strategic position 700 feet (213 m) above sea level gives this 1818 signal station unparalleled views across the island and off to the Atlantic. The site was first used as a lookout in 1697 and later became a convalescent station on account of the comfortably cool breezes. At the foot of the hill is the whitewashed Military Lion, carved from a single piece of rock by a convalescent British officer.

Harrison's Cave

The island's top sightseeing attraction is a miniature trolley ride around a subterranean cave carved out of the coral limestone by underground rivers. Passengers don hard hats and set off on a nearly mile-long (1.6 km) ride through a series

---

EXPERIENCE:
Submarine Views

Scuba diving is one way of seeing marine life up close, but if you don't want to get your hair wet, take an Atlantis Submarines tour *(tel 246 436 8929, barbados.atlantissubmarines.com, $$$$$).* **There's a short boat ride from the dock to the dive site, where the 48-passenger minisub awaits. The submarine excursion lasts around 45 minutes and reaches depths of around 150 feet (46 m) with clear views of a coral reef and a shipwreck site. Nighttime dives are also available.**

---

of spooky, theatrically lit caverns festooned with dripping stalactites, rimstones, flowstones, and a spiky forest of stalagmites. The speleothems (cave formations) take approximately a hundred years to grow a single cubic inch of solid calcite, but eventually the stalactites and stalagmites can join up to create impressive pillars. There is also an underground lake fed by a 40-foot (12 m) cascade. The cave lies at one end of the Welchman Hall Gully botanic walk (see p. 307).

Morgan Lewis Sugar Mill

Hundreds of sugar mills once dotted the Barbadian landscape, and their crumbling ruins are a common sight along the roads of the sugarcane belt today. The 250-year-old Morgan Lewis Mill was the last old-style mill to close when it ceased operations in 1944. Placed on the List of 100 Most Endangered Sites in the World by the World Monuments Fund (1996), its weathered

---

Gun Hill Signal Station

🅰 298 C3
✉ Gun Hill, St. George
☎ 246 429 1358
🕐 Closed Sun.
💲 $$

Harrison's Cave

🅰 298 C3
✉ Welchman Hall, St. Thomas
☎ 246 417 3700
💲 $$$$$
harrisonscave.com

Morgan Lewis Sugar Mill

🅰 298 C5
✉ Cherry Tree Hill, St. Andrew
☎ 246 422 7429
💲 $$

Brightly painted shops in Holetown's Chattel Village

in the little coral rock St. James' Church, founded in 1629. Many of the island's most elegant hotels and private houses are located here. You can explore **Paynes Bay,** a lively stretch of beach, with beach bars and water-sports concessions.

Just north of Holetown there's snorkeling in **Folkestone Underwater Park** (*map 298 B4; tel 246 422 2314*) as well as an aquarium and marine museum. Farther north along the coast is another busy strip at **Heywoods Beach,** north of Speightstown.

Mount Gay Rum Visitors Centre

🏔 298 B2

✉ Spring Garden Hwy., St. Michael

☎ 246 227 8800

🕐 Tours every 30 min (closed Sat. –Sun.)

💲 $$$

mountgayrum.com

Portvale Sugar Factory

🏔 298 B4

✉ St. James (Off Hwy. 2A)

☎ 246 425 1941

🕐 Closed Sun.

💲 Museum $$, including factory tour $$$

Tyrol Cot Heritage Village

🏔 298 C2

✉ Codrington Hill, St. Michael

☎ 246 424 2074

🕐 Closed Sat.–Sun.

💲 $$$

stone cone is the largest surviving windmill in the Caribbean. All its working parts are intact (demonstrations Dec.–April). Climb up to the sail compartment for fine views of the Scotland district.

Mount Gay Rum Visitors Centre

Rum has been produced on Barbados since the 1640s. The Mount Gay distillery (established 1703) is in the north of the island at St. Lucy, but here at the visitor center near Bridgetown Harbour the aging, blending, and bottling processes are on display, followed by tastings at the end of the tour.

Platinum Coast

The focus of the famed Platinum Coast is **Holetown** (*map 298 B3; 7 miles/11 km N of Bridgetown on Rte. 1*), where English settlers first disembarked in 1627 and established a small village they called Jamestown after King James I. The original name (it was changed to Holetown after a tidal hole close to the beach) is still preserved

Portvale Sugar Factory

Visits to Barbados's only working sugar factory can be a bit hit or miss. The spring harvest season (*Feb.–May*) is the best time to visit, when tours plunge into the sweet and steamy atmosphere of the factory floor.

The dusty but informative **Sir Frank Hutson Sugar Machinery Museum,** adjacent to the factory, traces the history of the industry.

Tyrol Cot Heritage Village

A single-story stone house painted a jaunty white and orange, Tyrol Cot, built in 1854, was the home of former prime minister Sir Grantley Adams (1898–1971). It is furnished with many family pieces, handcrafted mahogany furniture, paintings, and photographs.

In the gardens the Heritage Village illustrates how the local architectural style developed from a basic slave hut to its gingerbread-trimmed chattel house descendants. The cottages now house artisans' workshops, and craftwork is on sale. ∎

Twin islands with different paces: the rhythms of steel pan and calypso on Trinidad, and the more relaxed beats of Tobago

Trinidad & Tobago

A boy fishes with a hand line off the north coast of Tobago.

Trinidad

A twin-island nation at the southern extent of the Lesser Antilles, Trinidad and Tobago
make an odd couple. Boisterous, multicultural Trinidad is the larger of the two and home
to the capital, Port of Spain. At 50 by 38 miles (80 by 61 km), it's also the largest of the
eastern Caribbean islands, a chunk of South America severed from the Venezuelan coast.
Trinidad's industrialized economy has shunned tourism until recently. Tobago, a more
typical West Indian escapist haven, offers one of the warmest welcomes in the region.

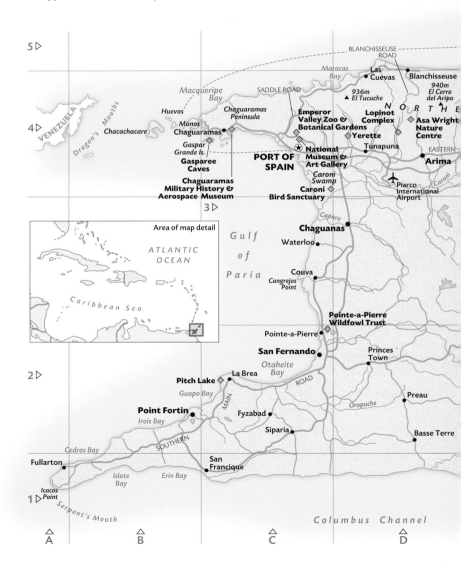

The Iere ("land of hummingbirds") of the Arawak was rechristened Trinidad ("trinity") by Christopher Columbus, who sighted three peaks in the southeast of the island on his third voyage to the New World in 1498. Although the island was claimed for Spain, its Amerindian inhabitants kept settlers at bay until 1592, when the Spanish established a toehold, grew a little tobacco, and kept watch over their treasure fleets.

French planters introduced sugar and cacao plantations in the 18th century, but Britain snatched the island in 1797, taking possession of neighboring Tobago in 1814.

Trinidad's plantations foundered after emancipation in 1838, but the island found the solution by bringing in East Indian indentured laborers. Many stayed after their five-year term, and their descendants now number more than 35 percent of the island's unusually diverse population of about 1.3 million. Another 40 percent of Trinidadians can trace their roots back to Africa, while the remaining 25 percent are of European, Chinese, Middle Eastern, South American extraction, and mixed heritage.

World War II brought Americans to 225 bases around the island. At about this time the first stirrings of steel-pan music were heard in the "panyards" of Port of Spain, as musical Trinidadians recycled old oil drums as musical instruments.

Trinidad and Tobago gained independence from Britain in 1962 and became a republic within the Commonwealth in 1976. Trinidad's oil wealth insulated the island from the tourism development that swept through other islands in the 1960s and '70s, but the 1980s oil slump changed attitudes. Trinidad's tourist industry is still rudimentary (beach hotels are a novelty), but ecotourism is the island's trump card. ■

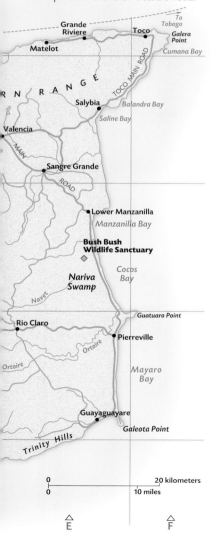

NOT TO BE MISSED:

The all-out festivities of Carnival in Trinidad **317**

The mating dance of the manakin at Asa Wright Nature Centre, Trinidad **321**

Turtle-watching at Grande Riviere and Matelot Beach, Trinidad **324**

Rain forest hikes in the Tobago Forest Reserve **329**

Diving (and limin') in Charlotteville, Tobago **330**

Port of Spain

Trinidad's frenetic capital city, Port of Spain, reflects the island's multicultural heritage. Its teeming streets overflow with shoppers and market stalls, while pompous British colonial architecture rubs shoulders with Muslim mosques, West Indian gingerbread houses, and more modern concrete office buildings.

A busy shopping street in Port of Spain, Trinidad's capital since 1757

Port of Spain

 314 C4

Visitor Information

✉ Trinidad &
Tobago Tourism
Development
Company,
Maritime
Centre, 29 Tenth
Ave., Barataria;
also at Piarco
Airport

☎ 868 638 7962

**gotrinidadandtobago
.com**

Port of Spain's main thorough-fare is **Frederick Street,** which links Brian Lara Promenade with the grassy expanse of Queen's Park Savannah. The southern end of Frederick Street resembles an East Asian bazaar, with Indian fabric shops spilling out onto the sidewalk.

Midway up the street is **Woodford Square,** a small park bisected by paths where locals meet to "lime" (hang out and chat) on benches under the trees. The entire west side is flanked by the imposing bulk of the **Red House,** seat of the Trinidad and Tobago Parliament. On the south side is the mellow stone **Trinity Cathedral,** dating from the early 19th century. It's worth a visit for its soaring wooden ceiling and patchwork of stained glass (entrance on Queen Street).

A 15-minute walk north on Frederick Street takes you to the **National Museum & Art Gallery.** There's a colorful section on the famous Carnival, complete with sequined-and-plumed costumes, elaborate masks, and a photo montage of Carnival kings and queens. Among the art on display, look for Jackie Hinkson's colorful depictions of Port of Spain in the 1940s.

Frederick Street ends at **Queen's Park Savannah,** a large open space proudly hailed by Trinidadians as the "largest traffic circle in the world." The Savannah plays a central role in the Carnival festivities and doubles as a sports field during the rest of the year, but do not walk here at night.

On the northwest side are seven grand old colonial mansions built in various styles around 1900. They have been nicknamed the **Magnificent Seven,** although several are now looking very tired.

To the north is **Emperor Valley Zoo** (Queen's Park Savannah, tel 868 622 3530, $$), which showcases many South American mammals, from capybaras and tapirs to the giant Brazilian otter. Here you can find deer, agoutis, and tree porcupines from Trinidad's forests, and aviaries for wetland birds.

Next door to the zoo are the **Botanical Gardens,** laid out in the 1820s by Sir Ralph Woodford and shaded by magnificent tropical trees. At the far side of the gardens is the President's House, an L-shaped British colonial affair.

Southwest of the Savannah is the **Woodbrook district,** noted for its gingerbread houses and its good choice of restaurants. Farther west, **Western Main Road** leads into the St. James district, known as the "city that never sleeps," thanks to its nightlife, bars, ice-cream parlors, and street vendors selling rotis (Indian-style bread pockets stuffed with chicken, meat, or vegetables). ■

Carnival

Trinidad's famous Carnival originated in the late 18th century with French Catholic settlers, who marked the approach of Lent with elaborate feasts and masquerades. The buildup to Carnival begins in the New Year with calypso and panorama (steel band) competitions around the island. The main event kicks off in Port of Spain the Friday before Lent. For calypsonians, the big night is Dimanche Gras (Sunday), while the main parade, J'Ouvert, hits the streets at 4 a.m. on Monday (it's not called "daybreak," or *j'ouvert,* for nothing!). Carnival culminates on Shrove Tuesday as the Parade of Bands gathers on Queen's Park Savannah. Anyone can join in Carnival (or "play mas"), whether it's just dancing in the street or signing up with a mas camp and renting a fabulous Carnival costume. The tourist office carries details and a countdown to Carnival on its website (gotrinidadandtobago.com).

National Museum & Art Gallery

- ✉ 117 Frederick St.
- ☎ 868 623 5941
- 🕐 Closed Sun. a.m. & Mon.

nmag.gov.tt

NEED TO KNOW

Port Logistics: Port of Spain

A port of call on longer Caribbean cruise itineraries, the King's Wharf Cruise Complex is right on the downtown waterfront alongside the business district. Here, red-shirted visitor guides can assist with maps, taxis, and other information. The city's Restaurant Row is Ariapita Avenue in Woodbrook; the nearest beach, Maracas Bay, is an hour away (round-trip taxi for four about $100).

Port of Spain Highlights

- City tour with lunch on Ariapita Avenue: half day
- Maracas Bay: 4–6 hours
- Asa Wright Nature Centre: half to full day with lunch

Cricket in the Caribbean

Cricket occupies a unique position in the Caribbean region. In many countries, particularly former British colonies such as Jamaica, Barbados, Antigua, and Trinidad, the sport is followed with a passion that verges on the religious. But more important, it is one of the very few successful cooperative endeavors in a region where most other attempts at integration have failed.

A cricket batsman plays a shot during a match in Barbados.

19th-Century Origins

The story of the development of West Indian cricket is a fascinating one, and it says much about the importance of the sport in the region that one of the best accounts of its development, *A History of West Indian Cricket* (1988), should have been written by no less a person than Michael Manley, former prime minister of Jamaica.

When cricket was introduced by the British, it was mostly played by army officers and plantation owners, but in the sweltering heat they preferred to bat rather than bowl (pitch), and it was the slaves and sons of slaves who were drafted in to bowl for them. After emancipation a network of cricket clubs sprang up, and it soon became clear that the descendants of the former slaves were incredibly good at the sport.

The first English team toured the West Indies in 1895, and in 1897 the first All–West Indies team was picked to play against another visiting English team. The first tour of England by a West Indies team took place in 1900, but the great turning point came in the 1920s, when the West Indies were granted Test status—that is, the right to compete on the international cricket circuit.

The West Indian team soon gained a reputation for stylish and exuberant playing, bringing a free-flowing athleticism and sense of humor to the game and earning them the nickname of the "calypso cricketers."

During the 1930s West Indian cricket was dominated by the presence of George Headley, judged to be the greatest West Indian batsman ever and globally among the six best of all time. He has a unique place in Caribbean history in that he personified black excellence in a white-dominated sport, a symbol of self-worth for the adoring crowds. In 1954 another cricketing legend and arguably the game's greatest all-rounder, Sir Garfield "Gary" Sobers, made his debut for the West Indies aged just 16. Over the next 20 years Barbados-born Sobers helped steer his interisland Caribbean team to the highest level of international Test cricket.

The Golden Age & Later Challenges

The golden age of Caribbean cricket, however, was yet to come. This was the decade, from 1976 to 1986, when the West Indies dominated the cricketing world. Out of 17 Test matches they won 15, drew 1, and lost 1—a remarkable record of victories in any sport. West Indian batsmen and bowlers such as Viv Richards (from Antigua), Clive Lloyd (Guyana), and Michael Holding (Jamaica) achieved a level of preeminence that was so great that opposing sides were almost beaten before the game began, so formidable was their reputation.

Since then, the West Indies team has struggled to find its footing in a cricketing world dominated by England, India, and the Southern Hemisphere nations.

Commentators hope that this malaise will pass, and that the region will continue to produce naturally gifted, world-class cricketers. But others worry that chronic underinvestment in infrastructure and grassroots training, mismanagement and a lack of cohesion at board level, and the ascent of popular alternative sports will eclipse Caribbean cricket. Soccer, basketball, and track and field disciplines, inspired by the likes of Olympic gold medal winners Usain Bolt (Jamaica) and Kirani James (Grenada), are becoming increasingly popular among younger generations. Baseball has long been the national sport of Cuba, the Dominican Republic, and Puerto Rico, with many Dominicans and Puerto Ricans going on to play major league baseball—and earning big money—in the United States.

Nonetheless, on many Caribbean islands an impromptu game of cricket will spring up anywhere that youngsters can find a few sticks to act as stumps and a tennis ball to practice with, be it on the beach or the back streets. The aspirations and hopes of generations have become embedded in a game that symbolizes a rare sense of unity among Caribbean peoples and it is to be hoped that this sense of common purpose and natural optimism has a 21st-century future.

EXPERIENCE: Catch a Match

Whether you are a die-hard cricket fan or just along for the Caribbean-flavored fun of the sport, catching a match is easy. Short T20 matches (one innings per team limited to 20 overs) are a good introduction to the game. They last about three hours; Test matches can run over five days! Most Caribbean islands have a sports complex that puts on seasonal games at reasonable prices.

In Trinidad, **Queen's Park Oval** (94 Tragarete Rd., Port of Spain, tel 868 622 3787, qpcc.com) is one of the many official venues of the West Indies team, and fans can call ahead to arrange guided tours of its Cricket Heritage Museum. The locally dubbed "mecca of cricket," Barbados's **Kensington Oval** in Bridgetown (Fontabelle, tel 246 274 1200, kensingtonoval .org) is another Test venue. **Sir Vivian Richards Stadium** in Antigua (North Sound, tel 268 81 9200) hosts local, regional, and international matches.

For an insider's tour of cricket history in the islands, call the **West Indies Cricket Heritage Centre** (Spice Basket, Beaulieu, St. George, tel 473 437 9000, windiescricket heritage.com, $).

Around the North

Trinidad's flora, fauna, and waterfront life can be viewed via a scenic looping drive around the northern third of the island. Bird-watchers in particular will find much to enjoy at the Asa Wright Nature Centre and at the Caroni Bird Sanctuary, home to spectacular scarlet ibis. History buffs can explore Trinidad's contributions to World War II in Chaguaramas.

At the Asa Wright Nature Centre, visitors can see hundreds of species of plants, insects, and birds.

The mountains of the Northern Range stretch across the north of Trinidad, dividing the coast from the central plain. This is where you'll find the island's two highest peaks, **El Cerro del Aripo** (3,083 feet/940 m) and **El Tucuche** (3,075 feet/936 m). The range is cloaked in a lush tangle of rain forest that is home to many of Trinidad's 430 bird species, 630 species of butterflies, and 2,300 varieties of flowering plants. Two roads cross the mountains: the **Saddle Road,** which links Port of Spain and the beach at Maracas Bay;

and the **Blanchisseuse Road** from Arima, which can also be accessed from Lopinot. The roads form the basis of a good circular day tour out of Port of Spain, heading counterclockwise to Arima, then up to the Asa Wright Nature Centre, north to Blanchisseuse, and along the coast to Maracas before returning over the Saddle Road.

West from Port of Spain is the **Chaguaramas Peninsula** *(map 314 C4),* Port of Spain's busy weekend playground on the Gulf of Paria. The beaches are not particularly enticing, though there's a man-made sandy strand at **Chagville,** and **Macqueripe Beach** on the north coast has been spruced up with hiking and biking trails. More appealing is a boat trip out to the islands off the tip of the peninsula, colonized by vacation homes and a popular stop-off with sailors.

Asa Wright Nature Centre

A visit to the Asa Wright Nature Center provides an unmissable chance to sample Trinidad's myriad and colorful bird- and plantlife; more than 170 bird species have been recorded in the Arima Valley, where the nature center sits at 1,200 feet (365 m) above sea level, hemmed in by the rain forest.

A series of trails explores the 200-acre (80 ha) estate, and guided walks provide a window on the rain forest, where leaf-cutter ants share the paths and blue morpho butterflies flutter past like elegant turquoise magic carpets. The mating dance of the white-bearded manakin makes an entertaining sideshow, accompanied by what sounds like a salvo of Chinese firecrackers as the male birds snap their wings with a loud popping noise. For a comfortable seat overlooking the main event, settle down on the veranda at the lodge to watch hummingbirds, honeycreepers, tanagers, and trogons drop in to snack on sugar water or fresh fruits.

Guests staying a minimum of three nights at the center qualify for a visit to the world's most accessible colony of oilbirds. Known as guacharo ("one who wails" in Amerindian), this cave-dwelling bird feeds its young on oily fruits such as palm, camphor, and laurels. Guacharos were prized for their fat, which was used for cooking and fueling oil lamps. They are now a protected species.

Bring sensible footwear because the trails can be muddy and slippery, a bathing suit for a dip in the swimming hole, and adequate mosquito repellent.

Caroni Bird Sanctuary

This 40-acre (16 ha) wetlands preserve in the Caroni Swamp is renowned for the evening flight of the scarlet ibis returning

Asa Wright Nature Centre

🅰 314 D4

✉ Arima Valley

☎ 868 667 4655

🕐 Guided tours and lunch daily, by reservation only, 10:30 a.m. & 1:30 p.m.

💲 $$$

asawright.org

Caroni Bird Sanctuary

🅰 314 C4

✉ Uriah Butler Hwy.

💲 $$$

G.I. Memories

A 20-minute drive west of Port of Spain, the **Chaguaramas Military History & Aviation Museum** (map 314 C4; Western Main Rd., Chaguaramas, tel 868 634 4391, closed Sun., $$) is sure to appeal to military history enthusiasts. Leave plenty of time to ramble around the extensive collections of military hardware and memorabilia, much of which relates to the U.S. forces stationed here during World War II. There are also displays devoted to conflicts dating back to the native Amerindians and Spanish conquistadores, and Trinidad's short-lived coup by Muslim extremists in 1990.

---

to mangrove roosts just before sunset. Flat-bottom boat tours leave from the dock (follow the signs from the highway) at about 4 p.m., puttering through tree-lined waterways to the heart of the swamp (see sidebar p. 325). Along the way you can

Lopinot Complex

A twisting scenic route leads up into the Northern Range, passing through small villages with burgeoning gardens and flapping Hindu prayer flags, to the settlement of Lopinot, founded by French cacao planter Charles Joseph, Comte de Lopinot, in 1806. The count's simple wooden estate house contains a one-room museum surrounded by magnificent saaman trees, and there's a cacao barn and old slave quarters.

Lopinot is one of the main centers of *parang*, the Spanish-based traditional music of Christmas in Trinidad. Introduced from Venezuela, parang is played on tiny, four-stringed *cuatro* guitars.

Lopinot Complex
 314 D4
✉ Lopinot Valley

spot caimans, four-eyed fish, mangrove roots festooned with oysters, maybe even a silky anteater, and 186 species of birds, from the not-so-common common potoo (a nocturnal bird that is devilishly difficult to spot) to the egrets, herons, and scampering willets feeding on the mudbanks among a lunatic orchestra of fiddler crabs sawing away with their outsize pincers.

About 10,000 scarlet ibis inhabit the sanctuary, nesting between March and September. Ibis chicks don't achieve their brilliant red-orange adult plumage for two to three years. Scarlet ibis are now protected from hunters, who once prized the feathers for Carnival costumes.

About half an hour before sunset the ibis begin to knife through the sky, iridescent red darts congregating in the dark mangrove greenery until it blazes like a Christmas tree caught in the last rays of the sun.

Gasparee Caves

A group of five small islands lies off the tip of the Chaguaramas Peninsula, colonized by vacation

INSIDER TIP:

Just east of Maracas Bay is Blanchisseuse, a small fishing village where the days revolve around the tides and the fish. Seeing locals living their daily routine provides real insight into West Indian culture.

—JENNIFER ALLARD
National Geographic contributor

homes. A 15-minute boat ride from the mainland, **Gaspar Grande Island** is renowned for its natural limestone cave system. It's also a popular picnic spot, and you can ramble around its old military fortifications. Inexpensive water taxis depart from several of the marinas along Western Main Road (20 minutes from Port of Spain). Permission to visit the caves must be obtained from the Chaguaramas Development Authority *(tel 868 634 4227).*

Maracas Bay & the Northwest Coast

Protected by steep wooded headlands and a stately border of palm trees, Maracas Bay *(map 314 D4)* is Trinidad's most popular beach and attracts the crowds on weekends. This is the place to sample traditional shark-and-bake, a fish sandwich spiced with hot pepper—and—tamarind sauce, served up from palm-thatched vendors' stalls.

Northeast Coast

The rugged and windswept northeast coast lies well off the beaten path but richly rewards any visitor who ventures up here. Take the Toco Main Road north up the island's eastern shore, passing the safe swimming beach at **Salybia;** bodysurfers prefer to congregate at **Balandra Bay.** At Toco, make a right to **Galera Point Lighthouse** for stupendous,

A secluded beach near the fishing village of Blanchisseuse

Five miles (8 km) east of Maracas there's another curve of fine white sand at **Las Cuevas,** which takes its name from the caves (*cuevas* in Spanish) along the shore. Vacation homes dot the coast road from there to the fishing village of **Blanchisseuse.** Neighboring **Damier Beach** is a favorite destination for windsurfers.

blustery views across to neighboring Tobago from Trinidad's most easterly point.

The laid-back fishing village of **Grande Riviere,** on the north shore, has a few low-key hotels, guesthouses, and restaurants. In season (March–Aug.), with a permit, you can watch turtles nesting on the beach (see sidebar p. 324). ■

Around the East & South

A journey around Trinidad's eastern and southern coasts takes you to a number of good beaches and wildlife-viewing sites, including the fine Pointe-à-Pierre Wildfowl Trust. In the southwest, the vast reservoir of bitumen known as Pitch Lake is an inky curiosity.

Bush Bush Wildlife Sanctuary
315 E3

The Eastern Main Road from the town of Arima cuts across to Trinidad's Atlantic coast and a long palm-fringed sandy shore stretching down to the southeast tip of the island at Galeota Point. There are good beaches at **Manzanilla Bay** (named for the green, poisonous machineel trees behind the beach), **Cocos Bay,** and **Mayaro Bay.**

Inland is the 3,840-acre (1,554 ha) **Nariva Swamp,** home to a fantastic variety of wildlife. The best way to explore the wilderness is on a kayak tour that includes **Bush Bush Wildlife**

Sanctuary. For advance reservations, contact an accredited tour operator (see sidebar opposite).

On the west coast, just north of Trinidad's second largest city and oil center San Fernando, is the **Pointe-à-Pierre Wildfowl Trust** (map 314 C2; call ahead, tel 868 658 4200 ext. 2512, $, papwildfowltrust.org). Bizarrely located in the shadow of a vast (and smelly) refinery, the trust's wetlands and forest trails provide remarkable bird-watching opportunities.

Pitch Lake

Around Otaheite Bay from San Fernando is Pitch Lake at La Brea (map 314 C2), one of Trinidad's most famous (but least exciting) sights. Probably the world's largest natural bitumen reservoir, the 100-acre (40 ha) "lake" looks like a massive parking lot, although predatory guides aim to liven up a visit with a fund of anecdotes (fix a fee in advance). The gloopy black tar was used to caulk the hulls of conquistadores' galleons and to pave the streets of Paris and London, as well as those of Port of Spain, where it was also used as fuel for 19th-century streetlamps until residents complained about the fumes. A small museum (tel 868 651 1232) outlines the lake's history. ∎

Turtle Watch

Endangered leatherback turtles lay their eggs on the beaches of eastern and northern Trinidad during the March-to-August breeding season. To see them, take the Toco Main Road, found beyond Arima and Valencia, which reaches the turtle beaches at Matura Bay and then rounds the tip of the island to the beautiful, undeveloped north coast beaches at Grande Riviere and Matelot. (It is about a two-hour drive from Port of Spain to Toco.) The turtle beaches are strictly monitored, and permits are required from the Forestry Department (tel 868 668 2518), which issues a limited number per day. Local guides can be arranged through **Nature Seekers** (Matura, tel 868 668-7337, natureseekers.org, donation) and the **Nature Tour Guides Association** (Grande Riviere, tel 868 469 1288).

EXPERIENCE: Birding in Trinidad

The first thrill was a green honeycreeper, followed by a ravenous flock of pushy little banana-quits. A jaunty red cap and flash of yellow breast announced the fleeting visit of a ruby topaz hummingbird, to be replaced by a common or garden (for the Asa Wright Nature Centre) mot mot. Breakfast time at the bird tables, 1,200 feet (365 m) up in the Arima Valley, is a smorgasbord of tropical fruit for the star attractions and the dawn of another magical day in the rain forest for onlookers gathered on the veranda, binoculars and birding guides at the ready.

The Arawak didn't call Trinidad the "land of the hummingbird" for nothing. Sixteen different species of these tiny jewel-like creatures flit through the island's woodlands and gardens. In total some 433 different bird species flourish in and around Trinidad's notably diverse natural habitats, which range from rain forest and littoral woodland to mudflats and mangrove swamplands. Many more visit regularly as both Trinidad and Tobago lie at a migratory crossing point.

Birding Sites

A former cacao and coffee estate high in the lush Northern Range, the **Asa Wright Nature Centre** (see p. 321) is legendary in tropical bird-watching circles. The New York Zoological Society established a research station here in 1949, and enthusiasts continue to be dazzled by the forest's birdlife.

A few miles west along the Northern Range, the **Pax Guest House** (Tunapuna, tel 868 662 4084, paxguesthouse .com) makes an excellent base for woodland hikes, and the gardens attract trogons, tanagers, and the tufted coquette, a glorious little hummingbird the size

of a large moth and the third smallest bird in the world.

On the slopes of the Maracas Valley, Dr. Theo Ferguson's garden, **Yerette** (reservations, tel 868 663 2623, email hello@yerette .com), is an enchanting hummingbird haven.

Less than an hour's drive from Port of Spain, **Caroni Swamp's** (see pp. 321–322) dense tangle of mangrove waterways is navigable only by boat. The rich, silty waters support numerous waterfowl and wading birds, including Trinidad's national bird, the scarlet ibis. The ideal time to visit is late afternoon, when the ibis return to roost. Make boat trip reservations with Caroni expert Winston Nanan of **Nanan's Tour Operators** (tel 868 645 1305, nananeco tours.com, $$$$$).

Farther south down the west coast, 120 bird species have been recorded at the **Pointe-à-Pierre Wildfowl Trust** (see opposite). Its lakes are popular with whistling ducks, cormorants, and gallinules, among others. The Ramsar-accredited **Nariva Swamp,** on the Atlantic coast, is Trinidad's largest freshwater wetlands area, interspersed with littoral forest, mangroves, and flooded

A male green honeycreeper in Trinidad's Northern Range

marshlands. **Limeland Tours** (tel 868 668 1356, limeland -tours.com, $$$$$) leads kayak expeditions into the swamp, where caimans and manatees may be seen and hawks, kites, and ospreys wheel overhead.

Bush Bush Wildlife Sanctuary is a haven for red-bellied macaws, Amazonian parrots, manakins, and cascaras, as well as red howler monkeys and anacondas.

Wherever you go bird-watching in Trinidad, mosquito repellent and binoculars are essential, while a copy of Richard ffrench's illustrated A Guide to the Birds of Trinidad and Tobago is an excellent investment.

Tobago

Trinidad's little sister island, Tobago, also broke away from South America (several million years ago in this case), but in look and feel it's more similar to the Windward Islands in the north. Just over 20 miles (32 km) from the hustle and bustle of Trinidad, Tobago is a mountainous green oasis of charm and calm, where the Trinidadians come to relax and the Tobagonians take pride in their easygoing hospitality and unspoiled natural surroundings.

Playing reggae in the village of Charlotteville

Tobago

 327

Visitor Information

✉ Crown Point (opposite airport)

☎ 868 639 0509

gotrinidadandtobago.com

It's probable that Christopher Columbus sighted Tobago when he discovered Trinidad in 1498. He called it Bellaforma ("beautiful form"), although the original Amerindian name (derived from the word for "tobacco") has stuck. The Dutch, English, and French all laid claim to the island, which changed hands more than 20 times and developed into one of the richest sugar islands in the region. Secured by the British in 1814 and administered with the Windward Island group, Tobago found that its fortunes waned after emancipation in the 1830s. It was declared bankrupt in 1888 and appended to neighboring Trinidad. After a century as an impoverished rural backwater, Tobago now has a small but flourishing tourist industry, concentrated on the northwest coast

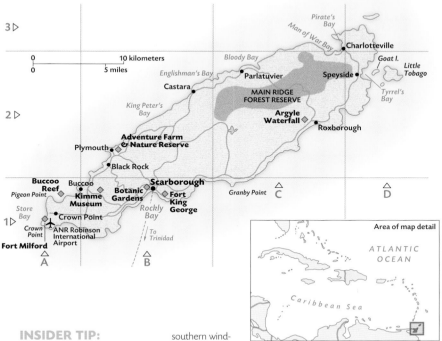

3 ▷

Pirate's
Bay

Man of War Bay

Charlotteville

0   10 kilometers
0   5 miles

Bloody Bay

Goat I.

Little
Tobago

Englishman's Bay

Parlatuvier

Speyside ●

Castara ●

Tyrrel's
Bay

**MAIN RIDGE
FOREST RESERVE**

King Peter's
Bay

2 ▷

**Argyle
Waterfall** ◇

**Adventure Farm
& Nature Reserve**

Roxborough ●

Plymouth ●◇

● **Black Rock**

**Buccoo
Reef**   Buccoo

Scarborough

Pigeon Point ◇   ● ◇

**Kimme
Museum**   **Botanic
Gardens** ◇   ◇ **Fort
King
George**

Granby Point

△
C

△
D

Store
Bay

Rockly
Bay

1 ▷

Crown Point ●

Crown
Point   **ANR Robinson
International
Airport**

To
Trinidad

Fort Milford △

△
A

△
B

Area of map detail

**ATLANTIC
OCEAN**

Caribbean Sea

The cooperative tradition of "Len' Hand" is alive and well on Tobago. If you see villagers hauling nets to the beach, go ahead and lend a hand.

—CHARLES KULANDER
National Geographic Traveler
magazine writer

between A.N.R. Robinson International Airport and Plymouth.

For a mere strip of an island at 20 miles by 5.5 miles (32 by 9 km), Tobago packs a punch. A central spine of mountains rises in the east and falls sharply through the rain forest to the broad bays of the southern windward coast and sheltered north shore. Here at the eastern end of the island, wooden pirogues from the villages of Speyside and Charlotteville ferry scuba enthusiasts out to Tobago's famous coral reefs. Enriched by nutrients swept along on the Guiana Current from Venezuela's Orinoco River, the reef sites boast 44 species of corals, including the world's biggest brain coral (12 feet by 16 feet/3.5 m by 5 m), a colony of giant manta rays, and occasional visitations by black-tipped, hammerhead, and huge plankton-eating whale sharks. The western end of the island is flat and covered in coconut palms, with stunning white-sand beaches created by offshore reefs. ■

Around the Island

Tobago is an ideal island to explore if you don't want to feel pressured to pack too much into a single excursion. The island's compact size ensures that no single trip is too long, and the laid-back atmosphere encourages you to linger along the way, pausing to admire the view, stop for a swim, or chat with local fishermen mending their nets on the shore.

Scarborough

The majority of the 62,000 Tobagonians live in the island's west end and in the pint-size capital of Scarborough *(map 327 B1; visitor information, Dept. of Tourism, 12 Sangster Hill, tel 868 639 2125, visittobago.gov.tt),* founded in 1769 on the south coast.

This unpretentious town climbs steeply from Rockly Bay into a circlet of hills overlooked by **Fort George.** The Lower Town is a melee of fish sellers and noisy market stalls. Take a break from the town's hustle and bustle in the charming **Botanic Gardens** *(Greenside St.),* once part of a sugar estate, where the grassy slopes are planted with poinciana and poui trees, spreading Indian almonds, a mango grove, and a huge silk cotton tree.

You will find Scarborough's few remaining colonial buildings in the Upper Town. On the way up to Fort George, look for **Gun Bridge,** with its black metal railings made out of old rifle barrels. The fort dates from the 1780s and affords a commanding view along the southeastern coast. The **Tobago Museum** *(84 Fort St., tel 868 639 3970, closed Sat.–Sun.)* is next door and worth a visit. It has a marvelous collection of Amerindian finds, including tools, religious objects, and pottery adorned with animal motifs.

One of Crown Point settlement's beautiful beaches

INSIDER TIP:

If you're heading to Charlotteville on the northern coast, be sure to take the walk over the headland to Pirate's Bay, one of the most scenic and secluded beaches on the island.

—HEATHER BRADY
National Geographic contributor

Crown Point

The Crown Point settlement occupies the western tip of Tobago, with the airport and a handful of hotels and guesthouses set on Store Bay. Behind the scrap of beach, where fishing boats are drawn up on the sand, is a clutch of stands selling crafts and souvenirs, bars, and snack shops. On Sandy Point you will find the low coral rock battlements of 18th-century

Fort Milford, facing Pigeon Point, a classic Caribbean beach bordered by leaning palms. Offshore is **Buccoo Reef,** Tobago's most visited underwater attraction, besieged by the glass-bottom boat crowds.

Around the Northern Coast

Beach hotels dot the road to **Plymouth** *(map 327 B2),* where the ruins of Fort James are still guarded by antique cannon. Make a detour to see the hummingbirds at **Adventure Farm & Nature Reserve** *(Arnos Vale Rd., tel 868 639 2839, closed Sat.–Sun., $$).* The drive through the hills behind the coast to **Parlatuvier** is charming, and you'll find fine secluded beaches down dirt tracks at King Peter's Bay, Englishman's Bay, and Bloody Bay before the road cuts up into the rain forest (see sidebar this page) and down to the Atlantic coast at **Roxborough.**

Fort Milford
🗺 327 A1

EXPERIENCE: Hiking in the Tobago Forest Reserve

Tobago's eastern highlands are cloaked in fabulously unspoiled rain forest. **Main Ridge Forest Reserve** was established back in 1764 in order to protect a tract of native forest from rapacious sugar planters. It is the Western Hemisphere's oldest legally protected forest, so perhaps with this degree of preservation it is not surprising that there are very few established trails that can be followed without a guide.

An exception is the 2-mile (3 km) **Gilpin Trace,** which makes a loop off the Roxborough-Parlatuvier cross-island

road. If you park at the trailhead, the trace loops off the road down to the Hut and it's a simple hike back up.

Otherwise you can hike into the heart of the reserve with an experienced guide from **Harris' Jungle Tours** *(tel 868 639 0513, harris-jungle-tours.com, $$$$$)* or Peter Cox of **Tobago Nature Tours** *(tel 868 751 5822, tobagonaturetours.com, $$$$$).* Cox also offers night safaris in the rain forest, when armadillos, opossums, bats, owls, and other beasties that go bump, screech, and howl in the night come out.

Overlooking Man of War Bay on Tobago's northern coast

Just short of Roxborough, a side road leads to **Argyle Waterfall** *(map 327 C2)*. From the parking area in an old cacao plantation, it's a shady 15-minute walk upriver to the falls, which bounce down a series of ledges on the cliff face to a swimming hole.

Speyside and Charlotteville flank the northeastern end of Tobago. Speyside borders Tyrrel's Bay along the Atlantic coast, overlooking the islets of Little Tobago and Goat Island. **Little Tobago** *(map 327 D2)* is a seabird sanctuary and a breeding ground for frigate birds, boobies, and tropic birds. Boat trips run from the jetty, where dive operators and glass-bottom boats depart with visitors for the offshore reefs.

Charlotteville, on the Caribbean side, is a sleepy fishing village and dive center on the broad expanse of **Man of War Bay.** Here, old wooden houses nestle beneath giant breadfruit trees, and the stone seawall is shaded by sea grape trees. A 15-minute walk to the east of the village takes you to **Pirate's Bay,** a fine beach. ■

Tobago Homage

A Tobago resident for more than 30 years, German-born sculptor Luise Kimme (1939–2013) drew inspiration directly from the island and its people. Her life-size Tobagonian figures were carved from whole tree trunks or cast in bronze, and she created the **Kimme Museum** *(tel 868 639 0257, open Sun. 10 a.m. –2 p.m. or by appt., $)* to display her work in the hills above the Mount Irvine Hotel. Kimme's murals decorate the Castle, a fanciful terra-cotta and white stucco studio (which bears more than a passing resemblance to a Hindu temple). You can see more of her work in the Church of Transfiguration at Black Rock.

Travelwise

The Caribbean's trade winds make for favorable sailing passages.

TRAVELWISE

GENERAL INFORMATION

Airlines

Although price is a factor in your choice of airline, check also on the number of stops (flights to smaller islands often include one stop at a hub destination) and frequency of flights. No-frills airlines usually have a limited number of flights.

Major airlines:
American Airlines, tel 800/433-7300, aa.com; JetBlue, tel 800/538-2583, jetblue.com; United Airlines, tel 800/538-2929, united.com; US Airways, tel 800/428-4322, usairways.com
Smaller airlines: Cape Air, tel 800/227-3247, capeair.com; Caribbean Airlines, tel 800/920-4225, caribbean-airlines.com; LIAT, tel 866/549-5428 or 268/480-5601, liat.com; Seaborne Airlines, tel 866/359-8784, seaborneairlines.com; Spirit Air, tel 801/401-2222, spirit.com; and Winair, tel 866/466-0410, fly-winair.sx

Climate

Temperatures average 77°–86°F (25°–30°C) year-round. Northeasterly trade winds are fairly constant and provide some respite from the heat and humidity. The higher the latitude, the cooler the temperature, especially from November to January. May to October is the wettest period, and the hurricane season is July to October. The Weather Channel gives up-to-date forecasts at weather.com.

Driving

Driving regulations in the Caribbean vary, so consult the Getting Around section for each island. As a rule, current and former British dependencies drive on the left-hand side; French and Dutch on the right. Some islands require you to have a temporary visitor license (or local license). These are generally available from rental companies, or you should contact the local police station or tourist office. The state of main roads is good, although local roads can be poor. Be sure to take a road map with you.

Electricity

On most islands 110 and 120 volts AC supply is used, and outlets are identical to those in the United States. On the French and Dutch islands, and those with a British background, you may need an adapter for U.S. appliances. When making a reservation, ask your hotel which voltage is used. Most hotels will have adapters for guests to use.

Festivals & Events

These are listed by island in this section. Contact local tourist offices and websites for more detailed festival information.

Insurance

A comprehensive travel insurance policy is a useful precaution and will include cancellation, interruption, default, trip delay, and full medical coverage.

Safety

The main crime concern for travelers in the Caribbean region is theft, and the best safeguard is common sense. Be vigilant in crowds and at the airport, and thefts from rental cars are not uncommon, so leave nothing behind. When you are carrying documents or significant amounts of cash, keep them close, preferably in a money belt. Credit cards are widely accepted and easy to cancel if they go missing. Women traveling alone will encounter plenty of chat-up banter, but a firm "No, thanks" or "I'm married" disarms predators. It is very unwise to visit a deserted beach alone.

Time Zones

Most islands are on Atlantic standard time (AST), which is eastern standard time (EST) plus one hour (GMT -4). AST is not affected by daylight saving time (DST). Jamaica and the Cayman Islands are on EST with no daylight saving, and the Turks and Caicos Islands are on EST with daylight saving.

Tipping

Rules for tipping vary widely in the Caribbean, so check your bill for a service charge. If no service charge is included in the bill, leave a tip of 10 to 15 percent. Tipping can be an important source of income.

Travelers With Disabilities

The Caribbean travel industry is becoming more aware of the needs of travelers with disabilities, but the region can prove quite a challenging destination for those with mobility problems. One area where compliance with ADA (Americans with Disabilities Act) regulations is vastly improved is the cruise sector, with wheelchair-accessible cabins and facilities for assisted embarkation/disembarkation. The U.S. Virgin Islands and Puerto Rico are also well-served destinations. When making reservations, ask specific questions concerning your needs and give airlines plenty of advance warning. Better still, consult a specialist agency such as Connie George Travel Associates (tel

610/532-0989 or 888/532-0989, cgta.com, email info@cgta.com).

JAMAICA

PLANNING YOUR TRIP

Arrival/Departure

Visitors heading for Montego Bay, Ocho Rios, Negril, and other resorts on the north coast arrive at Sangster International Airport, 2 miles (3 km) east of Montego Bay. For Kingston and Port Antonio, use Norman Manley International Airport, 10.5 miles (17 km) from Kingston. Small aircraft can access Ian Fleming International Airport 8 miles (14 km) east of Ocho Rios.

Air Jamaica, now owned by Caribbean Airlines, tel 800/523-5585, caribbean-airlines.com, as well as American Airlines, Delta, JetBlue, US Airways, and Air Canada provide service from gateways such as New York, Boston, Chicago, Miami, Atlanta, Houston, and Toronto. Numerous charter airlines also fly from the United States and Canada. Regional services are provided by Cayman Airways and Caribbean Airlines. There are also small domestic airstrips in Negril, Port Antonio, and Tinson Pen (near the center of Kingston). They are served by Airlink Express Shuttles, tel 876/940-6600, intlairlink.net.

Airport departure tax is US$20 (most airlines include it in the cost of the ticket).

Entry Requirements

A valid passport is required, along with onward or return ticket.

Festivals & Events

January Accompong Maroon Festival; Jamaica Jazz and Blues Festival (Montego Bay)
February Bob Marley Week
March–April Carnival

celebrations in Kingston, Montego Bay, and Ocho Rios
May Calabash International Literary Festival
June Ocho Rios International Jazz Festival
July Reggae Sumfest (Montego Bay), Portland Jerk Festival
October International Marlin Tournament (Port Antonio)

National holidays include New Year's Day (Jan. 1), Ash Wednesday, Good Friday, Easter Monday, Labor Day (4th Mon. in May), Emancipation Day (Aug. 1), Independence Day (Aug. 6), National Heroes Day (3rd Mon. in Oct.), Christmas Day (Dec. 25), and Boxing Day (Dec. 26).

GETTING AROUND

Car Rental

Major companies include Avis, tel 876/952-0762, avis.com; Budget, tel 876/924-8762, budgetjamaica.com; Island Car Rentals, tel 876/929-5875, islandcarrentals.com; and Hertz, tel 876/979-0438, hertz.com. To rent a car you must be 25 years old with a valid driver's license and major credit card. Driving on Jamaican roads is on the left.

Although major roads are generally good, you may encounter stray goats, dogs, chickens, erratic cyclists, pedestrians—and potholes. At intersections, traffic coming from the right has priority, but don't rely on this. Always use your horn when passing, in case the driver in front suddenly swerves to avoid a pothole. There are few good signs, and you can rely on only major towns and resorts being shown. In towns, watch out for No Entry signs, which are often below hood level.

Public Transportation

Local bus timetables are erratic, and the buses are overcrowded.

Minibuses travel on many of the same routes and may be slightly quicker, but are equally overcrowded. Fares are inexpensive. Buses or minibuses can be flagged down along the roadside.

Taxis are widely available and most are unmetered: Agree on a fare before setting off (ask at your hotel for advice). Licensed taxis display red PPV (Public Passenger Vehicle) plates; avoid unlicensed cabs. Route taxis (or shared taxis) ply set routes around large towns or between popular destinations. The Jamaican Union of Travellers Association (JUTA) operates a fleet of tourist buses and taxis, and is often contracted for ground transfers.

PRACTICAL ADVICE

Emergencies

All emergencies, ambulance and fire: tel 911
Police: tel 119

Telephones

The area code is 876.

Tourist Information

Kingston: 64 Knutsford Blvd., tel 876/929-9200, fax 876/929-9375, visitjamaica.com

U.S. & Canada Offices

Florida: 5201 Blue Lagoon Dr., Ste. 670, Miami, FL 33126, tel 305/665-0557 or 800/526-2422, fax 305/666-7239
Toronto: 303 Eglington Ave. E., Ste. 200, Toronto, ON M4P IL3, tel 416/482-7850 or 800/465-2624, fax 416/482-1730.

CAYMAN ISLANDS

PLANNING YOUR TRIP

Arrival/Departure

Owen Roberts International Airport on Grand Cayman is the main point of entry, with direct flights every day from Miami. The national flag carrier is Cayman Airways, which has direct flights from Miami, Tampa, New York (JFK), Chicago, Havana (Cuba), and Kingston and Montego Bay (Jamaica).

Other carriers include American Airlines, Delta, and US Airways, with departures from Atlanta, Charlotte, Chicago, Detroit, Philadelphia, New York, Miami, and Tampa. Air Canada has a nonstop service from Toronto.

Cayman Airways and Cayman Express provide daily small aircraft services to the sister islands of Cayman Brac and Little Cayman. Charter operator Island Air, tel 345/949-5252, islandair.ky, can also provide flights to both islands from Grand Cayman.

Entry Requirements

All visitors including U.S. citizens require a valid passport and onward or return ticket.

Festivals & Events

January Taste of Cayman Food & Wine Festival; Cayman Cookout (Ritz Carlton Hotel)
April Cayman Batabano Carnival
November Pirates Week
December Jazz Fest

National holidays include New Year's Day (Jan. 1), Ash Wednesday (Feb. or March), Good Friday, Easter Monday (March or April), Discovery Day (mid-May), Queen's Birthday (mid-June), Constitution Day (1st Mon. in July), Christmas Day (Dec. 25), and Boxing Day (Dec. 26).

GETTING AROUND
Car Rental

Rental companies (or the police station) will issue a temporary driving permit (US$7.50) on production of a valid driver's license. Reputable companies include Avis, tel 345/949-2468, aviscayman.com; Budget Rent-A-Car, tel 345/949-5605, budget cayman.com; Dollar Rent-A-Car, tel 345/949-4790, dollar.com; and Thrifty Car Rental, tel 345/949-6640, thrifty.com.

Driving in the Cayman Islands is on the left. Speed limits of between 20 and 50 miles an hour (30–80 km/h) are strictly enforced. Seat belts are required. Avoid driving into George Town at rush hour.

On Little Cayman, hotels provide free bicycles for guests, and this is just about all you need to explore the western end of the island. Rental cars are available from McLaughlin Rentals, tel 345/948-1000, in Blossom Village if you want to reach the more remote beaches on the eastern end of the island. Hotels may also offer a drop-off/pickup service to Point of Sands.

On Cayman Brac, CB Rent-A-Car, tel 345/948-2424, cbrentacar .com, and B & S Motor Ventures, tel 345/948-1646, bandsmv.com, rent cars and vans.

Public Transportation

Grand Cayman: Minibus services operate from a terminal by the Public Library in downtown George Town. Routes include a service to Seven Mile Beach. Taxis are available from the airport, all resorts, and the taxi stand by the cruise-ship dock in George Town.

Little Cayman and Cayman Brac have no bus services, but taxis are available for transfers or sightseeing tours.

PRACTICAL ADVICE
Emergencies
Grand Cayman
Police, fire, ambulance: tel 911
Royal Cayman Islands Police: tel 345/949-4222. George Town Hospital: tel 345/949-8600.

Little Cayman
Emergency: tel 911
Police: tel 345/926-0639
Clinic: tel 345/948-0072
Cayman Brac
Emergency: tel 911
Hospital: tel 345/948-2243

Telephones
The area code is 345.

Tourist Information
Cayman Islands Department of Tourism, Regatta Office Park, Windward 3, West Bay Rd., P.O. Box 67 GT, George Town, Grand Cayman, tel 345/949-0623, fax 345/949-4053, caymanislands.ky

U.S. & Canada Offices
New York: Empire State Building, 350 Fifth Ave., Ste. 2720, New York, NY 10118, tel 212/889-9009 or 1-877/4CAYMAN
Toronto: 2 Bloor St. West, Ste. 700, Toronto, ON M4W 3R1, 416/485-1550 or 800/263-5805

■ TURKS & CAICOS

PLANNING YOUR TRIP
Arrival/Departure

There are international airports on Providenciales and Grand Turk. Providenciales is the main international gateway, served by daily flights from Miami by American Airlines. There are also scheduled services from Atlanta, Boston, Charlotte, New York, Philadelphia, Montreal, and Toronto, and regular services to Jamaica, Haiti, the Dominican Republic, Puerto Rico, and the Bahamas. Interisland services are provided by InterCaribbean Airways, tel 649/946-4999, intercaribbean.com.

Departure tax is US$20 (included in cost of international tickets).

Entry Requirements

Visitors require a valid passport and onward or return ticket.

Festivals & Events

January Junkaroo Jump-up (Jan. 1, most islands)
May Big South Regatta Festival (last weekend; in South Caicos)
June Heineken Game Fishing Tournament (Grand Turk)
July Summer Festival (Providenciales)
November Turks & Caicos Conch Festival (Providenciales)

National holidays include New Year's Day (Jan. 1), Good Friday, Easter Monday, Commonwealth Day (spring), National Heroes Day (end of May), Queen's Birthday (mid-June), Emancipation Day (1st Mon. in Aug.), National Youth Day (late Sept.), Columbus Day (October), International Human Rights Day (Oct. 25), Christmas Day (Dec. 25), and Boxing Day (Dec. 26).

GETTING AROUND
Car Rental

Rental agencies on Providenciales include Avis, tel 649/946-4705; Budget, tel 649/946-4079; and Tropical Auto Rental, tel 649/946-5300, tropicalautorentaltci.com. Foreign driver's licenses are valid; driving in Turks and Caicos is on the left-hand side of the road.

Public Transportation

Taxis are widely available and can be hired for island tours (agree on a price in advance). A daily ferry service runs between Providenciales and North Caicos; contact TCI Ferry, Walkin Marina, Leeward, Providenciales, tel 649/946-5406, tciferry.com. A ferry also runs from Grand Turk to Salt Cay (1 hour) three times a week; contact Salt Cay Ferry, tel 649/241-1009.

PRACTICAL ADVICE
Emergencies

Call either 999 or 911.

Telephones

The area code is 649.

Tourist Information

Grand Turk: Turks & Caicos Islands Tourist Board, Front St., Grand Turk, tel 649/946-2321, fax 649/946-2733, turksand caicostourism.com
Providenciales: Stubbs Diamond Plaza, tel 649/946-4970, fax 649/941-5494

U.S. & Canada Offices
New York: 225 W. 35th St., Ste. 1200, New York, NY 10001, tel 646/375-8830 or 800/241-0824.
Toronto: 340 Sheppard Ave. E., Ste. 100, Toronto, ON M2N 3B4, tel 416/642-9771 or 866/413-8875

■ DOMINICAN REPUBLIC

PLANNING YOUR TRIP
Arrival/Departure

The main international gateway is Las Américas International Airport, 18 miles (29 km) to the east of Santo Domingo, which receives frequent scheduled services from North America. American Airlines, Delta, JetBlue, Spirit, and United Airlines are among the many airlines offering flights either direct to the Dominican Republic or one-stop services via Miami or San Juan, Puerto Rico. In addition to Santo Domingo, there are international airports at Barahona (María Montez), Puerto Plata (Gregorio Luperón), Punta Cana, La Romana/Casa de Campo, Samaná, and Santiago. Domestic flights and ground transportation services are operated by Dominican Air Shuttles, tel 809/931-4073, dominicanshuttles.com.
Departure tax is US$20, but is included in the ticket price.

Entry Requirements

Visitors require a full valid passport and a tourist card. Tourist cards can be purchased on arrival (US$10, cash only, valid for 30 days) or online beforehand, and the receipt should be kept safely and shown on departure.

Festivals & Events

January The festival of the patron saint of the Dominican people, Our Lady of Altagracia, is celebrated with all-night vigils, family visits, and singing and dancing.
July Merengue Festival (Santo Domingo)
November Jazz Festival (Cabarete)

National holidays include New Year's Day, Epiphany (Jan. 6), the birthday of Juan P. Duarte (Jan. 26), Independence Day (Feb. 27), Good Friday, Labor Day (May 1), Restoration Day (Aug. 16), Columbus Day (Oct. 12), and Christmas Day (Dec. 25).
Each town also celebrates its own particular saint's day with a *fiesta patronal*.

GETTING AROUND
Car Rental

Santo Domingo offices: Avis, tel 809/535-7191; Budget, tel 809/566-6666; Hertz, tel 809/221-5333; National-Alamo, tel 809/562-1444. A valid driver's license or international driver's license is required, as well as a credit card and passport. Driving in the Dominican Republic is on the right; speed limits are 50–62 miles an hour (80–100 km/h) on highways, 25 miles an hour (40 km/h) in cities, unless otherwise indicated.

Public Transportation

Taxis are available in all tourist areas, at hotels, and at the airports. They are generally cream-colored or yellow and marked Taxi Turístico. Look for taxi tariff information boards and always agree on a price before setting off.

The country has a widespread network of public buses, with the better ones featuring air-conditioning and onboard snacks and videos on long-distance routes; it is advisable to reserve seats in advance. On lesser routes, privately operated minibuses known as *guaguas* operate between towns and villages, stopping to pick up or drop off passengers frequently.

PRACTICAL ADVICE
Emergencies
Police, fire, ambulance: tel 911 Cestur (Specialist Touristic Security Corp.), tel 809/222-2123, can assist tourists in dealing with local police.

Telephones
The area code is 809.

Tourist Information
Santo Domingo: Ministry of Tourism, Av. Gregorio Luperón, cnr. Cayetano Germosen, tel 809/221-4660, fax 809/682-3806, godominicanrepublic.com

U.S. & Canada Offices
Chicago: 180 N. LaSalle St., Ste. 3757, Chicago, IL 60601, tel 312/981-0325
Miami: 848 Brickell Ave., Ste. 747, Miami, FL 33131, tel 305/358-2899 or 888/358-9594, fax 305/358-4185
New York: 136 E. 57th St., Ste. 805, New York, NY 10022, tel 212/588-1012 or 888/374-6361, fax 212/588-1015
Montreal: 2055 Peel St., Ste. 550, Montreal, QC H3A 1V4, tel 514/499-1918 or 800/563-1611, fax 514/499-1393
Toronto: 26 Wellington St. East, Ste. 201, Toronto, ON M5E 1S2, tel 416/361-2126 or 888/494-5050, fax 416/361-2130

■ PUERTO RICO

PLANNING YOUR TRIP
Arrival/Departure
The main gateway is San Juan's Luis Muñoz Marín International Airport. Most U.S. airlines offer direct flights to Puerto Rico from gateway cities across North America. The dominant carriers are American Airlines, with nonstop flights from Miami, Chicago, Dallas, and New York; and JetBlue from Boston, Fort Lauderdale, Chicago, Hartford, Washington, D.C., New York, and Tampa. Regular scheduled services also depart from Atlanta, Philadelphia, and Washington, D.C., among others. There are frequent short-hop services to destinations throughout the region with local carriers including Seaborne Airlines and LIAT. Many shorter flights, including services to the islands of Vieques and Culebra, depart from Ribas Dominicci Airport in San Juan's Isla Grande district, which is more centrally located than the international airport.

Entry Requirements
Currently there is no requirement for U.S. citizens to present a passport on reentry to the mainland U.S. from Puerto Rico. However, check updated travel news on travel.state.gov. Other visitors will need to present a valid passport, visa, and onward or return ticket in compliance with standard U.S. immigration procedures on arrival in Puerto Rico.

Festivals & Events
March/April Pre-Lenten Carnival parties, parades, and music throughout the island. Ponce hosts one of the most colorful celebrations.
April Saborea Food & Wine Festival, Escambrón Beach, San Juan
May Heineken Jazz Festival
June Celebrations of St. John the Baptist (June 23)
December The Christmas season starts early in December and lasts through Three Kings Day (Jan. 6).

National holidays include all U.S. holidays as well as nine local holidays honoring local leaders or events of the island's history.

GETTING AROUND
Car Rental
Avis, tel 787/253-5927, 800/331-1212; Budget, tel 787/791-0600, 800/527-0700; Dollar, tel 787/253-7074; and Thrifty, tel 787/253-2525. Local rental companies can offer better value; try Charlie Car Rental, tel 787/728-2418, charliecars.com; Vias, tel 787/ 791-4120, viascarrental.com; or Target, tel 787/728-1447 or 800/934-6457, targetrentacar.com.

Public Transportation
All taxis are metered, except when they are chartered for long-distance rides. In San Juan, *taxis turísticos* (white, with a logo on the door) operate with fixed rates between the airport, ports, and tourist areas. City buses are a good way to get around San Juan.

There are no scheduled bus services between cities, although you can catch shared taxis (known as *publicos,* they have yellow number plates with the letters P or PD at the end) that run to most parts of the island.

PRACTICAL ADVICE

Emergencies

Police, fire, and ambulance:
tel 911
Medical emergencies:
tel 787/754-2550
Tourist Zone Police (Condado):
tel 787/343-2020

Telephones

The area code is 787.

Tourist Information

San Juan: Ochoa Building, 550
Calle Tanca, Old San Juan, tel
787/721-2400 or 800/866-7827,
fax 787/722-6238; Luis Muñoz
Marín International Airport, tel
787/791-1014; seepuertorico.com

U.S. Office
New York: Puerto Rico Tourism
Company, 135 W. 50th St., 22nd
fl., New York, NY 10020, tel
212/586-6262, fax 212/586-1212

■ VIRGIN ISLANDS

U.S. VIRGIN ISLANDS

Entry Requirements

U.S. citizens do not require a
passport to visit the USVI, but will
need to provide proof of identity
and a photo ID upon departure.

Telephones

The area code is 340.

National Holidays

These include New Year's Day
(Jan. 1), Martin Luther King
Jr. Day (3rd Mon. in Jan.),
President's Day (3rd Mon. in
Feb.), Transfer Day (March 31),
Good Friday, Easter Monday,
USVI Emancipation Day (July 3),
Independence Day (July 4),
Labor Day (1st Mon. in Sept.),
Columbus Day (2nd Mon.
in Oct.), Thanksgiving Day
(4th Thurs. in Nov.), Christmas

Day (Dec. 25), and Boxing Day
(Dec. 26).

ST. CROIX

PLANNING YOUR TRIP

Arrival/Departure

Nonstop flights to St. Croix are
available through American Airlines (from Miami and Baltimore)
and Delta (from Atlanta). Seaborne Airlines, tel 787/946-7800
or 866/359-8784, seaborne
airlines.com, has daily services
between St. Croix and St. Thomas,
as does Cape Air, tel 508/771-
6944 or 800/227-3247, capeair
.com, with services between
St. Thomas, St. Croix, and
Puerto Rico. A fast ferry service
(90 mins) links St. Croix with
St. Thomas daily except Wednesday, tel 340/775-7292.

Festivals & Events

December–January The month-
long Crucian Christmas Festival
culminates in the Three Kings
Day parade (Jan. 6).
May St. Croix Ironman
July Emancipation Day
celebrations
September Grand Crucian Quadrille. For a glimpse of the island's
heritage catch a performance by
Crucian quadrille dancers.

GETTING AROUND

Car Rental

Avis, tel 340/778-9355; Budget
Rent a Car, tel 888/264-8894,
budgetstcroix.com; Judi of Croix,
tel 340/773-2123 or 877/903-
2123, judiofcroix.com; and
Olympic Rent-a-Car, tel 340/
718-3000 or 888/878-4227,
olympicstcroix.com, all arrange
airport and hotel pickups and
delivery. U.S. driver's licenses are
valid on the island; driving is on
the left in St. Croix.

Public Transportation

Taxis are readily available at the
airport and hotels or from taxi
stands on King Street and at
Market Square in Christiansted,
or by Fort Frederik in Frederiksted. Taxis are not metered, but
are instead regulated by an official tariff carried by drivers. Check
the fare in advance. Taxi vans
offer cut-price transfers from the
airport to island hotels. The bus
service between Christiansted
and Frederiksted costs just a dollar (departures every two hours
5:30 a.m.–9 p.m. Mon.–Sat.).

PRACTICAL ADVICE

Emergencies

Police, fire, and ambulance: tel 911
Governor Juan F. Luis Hospital &
Medical Center, tel 340/778-6311,
has a 24-hour emergency room.
Hotels have access to a 24-hour
duty doctor, and the Department of Tourism Helpline is tel
340/772-0357.

Tourist Information

Christiansted: 321 King St., Ste. 7,
VI 00840, tel 340/772-0357, fax
340/772-5074, visitusvi.com

U.S. Office
Miami: 18495 S. Dixie Hwy., Ste.
160, Miami, FL 33157-6817, tel
305/442-7200 or 800/372-8784,
email Jacqueline Hodge-Jackson,
jacqueline.hodge@dot.vi.gov

ST. THOMAS & ST. JOHN

PLANNING YOUR TRIP

Arrival/Departure

The major U.S. airlines provide
daily direct flights to St. Thomas,
and there are connections from
numerous U.S. cities via Puerto
Rico on American Airlines.
St. John does not have an airport,
but it is a short ferry ride from St.
Thomas. Regular services depart

from St. Thomas, either from Charlotte Amalie (45 minutes) or Red Hook (20 minutes), throughout the day. The Westin and Caneel Bay hotels provide a private boat service for guests.

Festivals & Events

March St. John Blues Festival
March–April International Rolex Regatta (4th weekend in March, St. Thomas), including long-distance Pillsbury Sound race
April Virgin Islands Carnival (St. Thomas)
June St. John Festival (month-long event)
August Open/Atlantic Blue Marlin Tournament

GETTING AROUND
Car Rental

Avis, tel 340/774-1468, and Budget, tel 340/776-5774. Local operators, including Dependable, tel 340/774-2253 or 800/522-3076, dependablecar.com, on St. Thomas, and St. John Car Rental, tel/fax 340/776-6103, stjohncarrental.com, on St. John, can offer more competitive rates. U.S. driver's licenses are valid on the islands, but unlike in the United States, mainland driving is on the left on St. John.

Public Transportation

There is a local bus service on St. Thomas. On St. John, a regular bus shuttles between the ferry dock at Cruz Bay and Coral Bay on the east coast throughout the day. Taxis are readily available from St. Thomas's Airport and St. John's Cruz Bay ferry dock, as well as from hotels and taxi stands in tourist areas. They are not metered but regulated by an official tariff carried by drivers. Check the fare in advance. Taxi vans offer cut-price transfers from St. Thomas Airport to hotels around the island.

PRACTICAL ADVICE
Emergencies

Police, fire, and ambulance: tel 911. Roy Schneider Hospital, tel 340/776-8311, has a 24-hour emergency room. There are clinics in St. John, but medical emergencies will be transferred to St. Thomas. Hotels have access to a 24-hour duty doctor.

Tourist Information

Charlotte Amalie: U.S. Virgin Island Department of Tourism, P.O. Box 6400, St. Thomas, USVI 00804, tel 340/774-8784, fax 340/774-4390, visitusvi.com

U.S. Office
See St. Croix, p. 337.

BRITISH VIRGIN ISLANDS

PLANNING YOUR TRIP
Arrival/Departure

There are no direct flights to the British Virgin Islands from North America, but American Airlines and several local providers, including Air Sunshine, Cape Air, and Seaborne, offer frequent short-hop service from Puerto Rico and St. Thomas, USVI, to Tortola. Local airlines also offer flights to Virgin Gorda and Anegada. Air links are also available from Antigua and Sint Maarten. With the exception of Anegada, the main BVIs are linked to each other, and St. Thomas and St. John in the USVI, by regular, inexpensive ferry services. Ferries depart from Tortola to Anegada three times a week from Road Town. Schedules are available at bviwelcome.com/ferries.php.

Departure tax is US$20 for air travelers, US$15 for those leaving by sea, except cruise passengers (US$7).

Entry Requirements

Visitors are required to produce a valid passport, together with a return or onward ticket. A passport may not be necessary for U.S. citizens on day trips from the USVI, but check current U.S. reentry requirements before departure.

Festivals & Events

April–May BVI Spring Regatta, a weeklong festival of sailing, races, and parties based on Nanny Cay, Tortola
May BVI Music Fest Local and international musicians gather on the beach at Cane Garden Bay, Tortola.
June–July HIHO windsurfing championships and regatta
August BVI Festival (Tortola, 1st Mon., Tues., & Wed.)
December Foxy's famous New Year's Party (Jost van Dyke's Great Harbour, Dec. 31)

National holidays include New Year's Day, Commonwealth Day (2nd Mon. in March), Good Friday, Easter Monday, Whit Monday (May), Queen's Birthday (2nd Mon. in June), Territory Day (July 1), St. Ursula's Day (Oct. 21), Prince Charles's Birthday (Nov. 14), Christmas Day (Dec. 25), and Boxing Day (Dec. 26).

GETTING AROUND
Car Rental

On Tortola, Avis, tel 284/494-3322, avis.com; Hertz, tel 284/495-6600, hertz.com; and International Car Rentals, tel 284/494-4715, internationalcarrentalsbvi.com, offer rental cars and 4WD vehicles.

On Virgin Gorda, contact L & S Jeep Rental, tel 284/495-5297, landsjeeprental.com, or Mahogany, tel 284/495-5469, mahoganycar rentalsbvi.com.

On Anegada, try Anegada Reef Hotel, tel 284/495-8002, anegada reef.com, or DW Jeep Rentals, tel

284/495-9677. Foreign driver's licenses are valid up to 30 days. Roads can be rough, and 4WD vehicles are preferable for negotiating bumpy tracks to the beach. Driving in the British Virgin Islands is on the left.

Public Transportation
On Tortola, an irregular bus service operates out of Road Town to destinations along the south coast, but taxis are a more reliable alternative. There are taxi stands at the airport and at ferry terminals.

There are frequent ferry services daily from Tortola to Virgin Gorda, Jost van Dyke, and the U.S. Virgin Islands of St. John and St. Thomas. Ferries also link Tortola and Anegada, and Virgin Gorda with St. Thomas/St. John several times a week.

PRACTICAL ADVICE
Emergencies
Police, fire, and ambulance: tel 999 or 911. Peebles Hospital: Road Town, Tortola, tel 284/494-3497. Hotels can assist with locating a duty doctor. Serious medical emergencies are airlifted to St. Thomas, USVI, or San Juan, Puerto Rico.

Telephones
The area code is 284.

Tourist Information
Tortola: BVI Tourist Board, Ferry Terminal, P.O. Box 134, Road Town, tel 284/494-3134, fax 284/494-3866, bvitourism.com. There is also a bureau in the Virgin Gorda Yacht Harbour, tel 284/495-5181, fax 284/495-6517.

U.S. Office
New York: BVI Tourist Board, 1270 Broadway, Ste. 705, New York, NY 10001,

tel 212/696-0400 or 800/835-8530, fax 212/563-2263

■ DUTCH CARIBBEAN

Entry Requirements
For all islands in the group, U.S. citizens are required to produce a valid passport, together with a return or onward ticket. On the Dutch/French island of Sint Maarten/St.-Martin, there are no passport controls between the two halves of the island.

National Holidays
These include New Year's Day, Good Friday, Easter Monday, Queen's Birthday (April 30), Labor Day (May 1), Ascension Day (May), Christmas Day (Dec. 25), and Boxing Day (Dec. 26). St.-Martin only: Whit Monday and All Saints Day (Nov. 1).

ARUBA

PLANNING YOUR TRIP
Arrival/Departure
Aruba's Queen Beatrix International Airport is served by direct daily flights from Miami with American Airlines, and from Atlanta and New York with Delta. Other scheduled services include JetBlue from Boston and New York; United Airlines flies from Chicago; US Airways from Charlotte and Philadelphia. There are charter flights from many other U.S. cities. Local carrier Insel Air, tel 5999/737-0444, fly-inselair.com, offers scheduled services to Miami.

Departure tax is US$36.75 for the U.S.; US$33.50 elsewhere, except Bonaire (US$9).

Festivals & Events
January New Year celebrations
January–February Carnival

Monday (early Jan.)
June Windsurfing Festival
October Aruba Music Festival
December Sint Nicolas's (Santa Claus) Birthday (Dec. 5)

GETTING AROUND
Car Rental
Avis, tel 297/582-5496, avis.com; Budget, tel 297/582-8600, budget.com; Econo Car Rental, tel 877/461-9913, econoaruba.com; and Value Car Rental, tel 297/586-4188, valuearuba.com, have offices at the airport and other useful tourist locations. Foreign driver's licenses held for a minimum of two years are valid here; driving is on the right in Aruba.

Public Transportation
Aruba has an inexpensive and reliable bus service that links the hotel areas with Oranjestad (every 15 minutes 5:45 a.m.–6 p.m.; every 40 minutes until 11:30 p.m.), the airport, and San Nicolas; private minibus services offer greater flexibility. Taxis are easy to find at the airport or hotel, or call the Oranjestad depot, tel 297/582-2116.

PRACTICAL ADVICE
Emergencies
All emergencies: tel 911. Police: tel 100. Oranjestad Hospital: tel 297/527-4000. All hotels have a doctor on-call 24 hours.

Telephones
The country code is 297.

Tourist Information
On the island, contact the Aruba Tourism Authority, L.G. Smith Blvd., Eagle Beach, tel 297/582-3777, fax 297/583-4702, aruba.com.

U.S. Office
New Jersey: Aruba Tourism Authority, 400 Plaza Dr., Ste. 101, Secaucus, NJ 07094, tel

201/558-1110 or 800/TO-ARUBA, fax 201/558-4768

BONAIRE

PLANNING YOUR TRIP
Arrival/Departure
Delta operates several weekly nonstop flights from Atlanta to Bonaire's Flamingo Airport, and United flies nonstop from Newark and Houston. Direct flights into Curaçao and Aruba connect with local carriers Insel Air, tel 5999/737-0444, fly-inselair.com, and Divi Divi Air, tel 5999/717-2121, flydivi.com.

Departure tax is US$39 (or US$5.75 to Aruba or Curaçao).

Festivals & Events
February Carnival
April Rincon Day
September Bonaire Day (Sept. 6)
October Annual Sailing Regatta

GETTING AROUND
Car Rental
Avis, tel 599/717-5795, avis.com; Budget, tel 599/717-4700, budget.com; and Hertz, tel 599/717-7221, hertz.com, all have offices at the airport. Local operators include Caribe Car Rental, tel 599/717-6050, caribebonaire.com, and Island Car Rental Bonaire, tel 599/717-2100, islandcarrental bonaire.com.

Foreign driver's licenses are valid. Driving is on the right on Bonaire.

Public Transportation
Taxis are available at the airport and can be booked through hotels, or call Taxi Despatch, tel 599/717-8100. Rates are fixed.

PRACTICAL ADVICE
Emergencies
Police, fire, and ambulance, tel 911.

St. Francisco Hospital in Kralendijk, tel 599/717-8900, has a decompression chamber.

Telephones
The country code is 599.

Tourist Information
Bonaire: Kaya Grandi 2, Kralendijk, tel 599/717-8322, fax 599/717-8408, tourism bonaire.com

U.S. Office
New York: Tourism Corporation Bonaire, c/o Adams Unlimited, 80 Broad St., Ste. 3202, New York, NY 10004, tel 212/956-5910, fax 212/956-5913

CURAÇAO

PLANNING YOUR TRIP
Arrival/Departure
Curaçao International Airport receives daily direct flights from Miami with American Airlines and Curaçao-based Insel Air, tel 5999/737-0444, fly-inselair.com, which also offers a service from Charlotte. There are regular interisland shuttles from Aruba and Bonaire, and services from San Juan, Puerto Rico, Kingston, Jamaica, and Sint Maarten.

Departure tax is US$39 for international flights, or US$20 for trips to Aruba and Sint Maarten, and US$10 for Bonaire.

Festivals & Events
February/March Carnival
March Springtime fishing tournaments
April Celebration of the Queen's Birthday (April 30); Sailing Regatta
July Flag Day (July 2)
August Salsa Festival
October Jazz Festival

GETTING AROUND
Car Rental
Avis, tel 5999/461-1255, avis .com; Budget, tel 5999/868-3466, budget.com; National, tel 5999/869-4433, national.com; and Sixt, tel 5999/461-3089, sixt .com. Foreign driver's licenses are valid and driving is on the right on Curaçao

Public Transportation
Inexpensive public buses provide a limited service over main routes around the island from Willemstad. Taxi tariffs are fixed.

PRACTICAL ADVICE
Emergencies
Police and fire: 911. Ambulance: 912. Tourism police: 5999/735-0044. St. Elisabeth Hospital, Willemstad, tel 5999/462-4900. Emergencies: tel 910

Telephones
The country code is 5999.

Tourist Information
Willemstad: Curaçao Tourist Board, P.O. Box 3266, Pietermaai 19, tel 5999/434-8200, fax 5999/461-5017, curacao.com

U.S. Office
Miami: 80 S.W. 8th St., Ste. 2000, Miami, FL 33130, tel 305/423-7156 or 800/328-7222

SABA

PLANNING YOUR TRIP
Arrival/Departure
There are no direct flights from the United States, but Winair, tel 721/545-4237 or U.S./Canada 866/466-0410, fly-winair.sx, makes the 15-minute hop from Sint Maarten to Juancho E. Yrausquin Airport several times a day. Saba-based high-speed ferry

Dawn II, tel 599/416-2299, sabactransport.com, runs between Saba's Fort Bay and Dock Maarten in Sint Maarten Tues., Thurs., and Sat.; while Sint Maarten–based *The Edge,* tel 721/544-2640, stmaarten-activities.com, runs to Fort Bay from Pelican Marina in Sint Maarten Wed., Fri., and Sun. Crossings take 75–90 minutes.

Departure tax is US$10.

Festivals & Events
April Celebration of the Queen's Birthday (April 30)
July–August Carnival
December Saba Day Festivities (1st weekend Dec.)

GETTING AROUND
Car Rental
To explore the island independently, contact Morgan Car Rental, Breadline Plaza, tel 599/416-2881, email info@icssaba.com.

Public Transportation
Taxis are available at the airport or can be booked through hotels.

PRACTICAL ADVICE
Emergencies
All emergencies: 911. Police: tel 599/416-3237. Medical Centre, The Bottom: tel 599/416-3288. Medical emergencies are generally flown to Sint Maarten.

Telephones
The country code is 599.

Tourist Information
Windwardside: Saba Tourist Office, P.O. Box 527, tel 599/416-2231, fax 599/416-2350, saba tourism.com

SINT EUSTATIUS

PLANNING YOUR TRIP
Arrival/Departure
There are no direct flights from the U.S., but Winair, fly-winair.sx, operates several daily island-hopper services into F. D. Roosevelt Airport from Sint Maarten; the flight takes less than 20 minutes. Departure tax is US$15.

Festivals & Events
April Celebration of the Queen's Birthday (April 30)
July Carnival
October Antillean Day (Oct. 21)
November Statia/America Day (Nov. 16)

GETTING AROUND
Car Rental
Browns, tel 599/318-2266, and Reddy Car Rental, tel 599/318-5453, are two local rental operators. Foreign licenses are valid in Statia; driving here is on the right.

Public Transportation
With no buses on Statia, most visitors tend to walk or cycle. Taxis are available at the airport and can be ordered at hotels.

PRACTICAL ADVICE
Emergencies
Police: tel 911. Fire: tel 912. Ambulance: tel 913. Queen Beatrix Medical Center: tel 599/318-2211. Medical emergencies are generally flown to Sint Maarten.

Telephones
The area code is 599.

Tourist Information
Oranjestad: Sint Eustatius Tourism Development Foundation, Fort Oranje, 3 Fort Oranjestraat, tel/fax 599/318-2433, statiatourism.com

SINT MAARTEN/ ST.-MARTIN

PLANNING YOUR TRIP
Arrival/Departure
Princess Juliana Airport in Sint Maarten is the main island gateway. American Airlines flies direct from New York and Miami and provides connections from other North American cities via Puerto Rico. Delta, JetBlue, and US Airways all offer services originating in the United States.

Regional carriers Caribbean Airlines, LIAT, and Winair provide air links to the Leeward Islands, Saba, Statia, St Barts, Tortola (BVI), and Puerto Rico. Insel Air, fly-inselair .com, flies to Curaçao; while Air Antilles Express, flyairantilles. com and Air Caraïbes, aircaraibes. com serve the French Antilles with smaller planes departing from St.-Martin's L'Espérance-Grand Case regional airport. St.-Barth Commuter (stbarthcommuter.com) flies several times daily to St.-Barthélémy from both Princess Juliana and Grand Case airports.

Departure tax is US$30 for international flights or US$10 for trips within the Dutch Caribbean.

Festivals & Events
January Epiphany (Jan. 6, St.-Martin)
February/March Carnival (St.-Martin)
March Heineken Regatta
April Queen's Birthday celebrations (Sint Maarten, April 30), Carnival (Sint Maarten)
June June Fest cultural events
July Bastille Day (St.-Martin, July 14); Schoelcher Day, marked with boat races in Grand Case (St.-Martin, July 21)
November Discovery Day (Nov. 11)

GETTING AROUND
Car Rental
Avis, tel 721/545-2847, avis.com; Francine's Rentals, tel 721/545-2316; and Hertz, tel 721/545-4541, hertz.com, operate out of Princess Juliana Airport with local offices in St.-Martin. Foreign driver's licenses are valid on the island, and driving on St.-Martin is on the right.

Public Transportation
Frequent and inexpensive mini-bus services shuttle between Philipsburg and Marigot with connections to Grand Case. Taxis are plentiful (rates are fixed in US$).

PRACTICAL ADVICE
Emergencies
Sint Maarten Emergencies: tel 911. Ambulance: tel 912. Doctors on call: tel 5111. Hospital: tel 721/543-1111.
St.-Martin Police: tel 17. Fire: tel 18. SAMU (medical emergencies): 15. Hospital: tel 590/52 25 52

Telephones
The country code for French St.-Martin is 590; while Sint Maarten is a member of the North American Numbering Plan with an assigned area code of 721. To call from the Dutch side to the French side of the island is an international call. To call St.-Martin from the U.S., dial the international access code (011) + the country and area codes (590 590) + the local number; to call Sint Maarten from the U.S. dial area code 721 + the local number. For calls within Sint Maarten, dial the seven-digit local number; for calls from the Dutch to the French side, dial 011 590 590 + the 6-digit local number. For calls within St.-Martin, dial the 10-digit number beginning 0590 for landlines or 0690 for cells; for calls from the French

side to the Dutch side, dial 001 + 721 + the local number.

Tourist Information
Sint Maarten
Philipsburg: W.G. Buncamper Rd. 33, tel 721/542-2337, fax 721/542-2734, vacationst maarten.com. Information kiosk by the Philipsburg pier.

St.-Martin
Marigot: Office de Tourisme de St.-Martin, Rte. de Sandy Ground, Marigot, 97150 St.-Martin, tel 0590/87 57 21, fax 0590/87 56 43, stmartinisland.org

◼ LEEWARD ISLANDS

Entry Requirements
For all islands in the group, U.S. citizens are required to produce a valid passport, together with a return or onward ticket.

National Holidays
Holidays common to all islands include New Year's Day (Jan. 1), Good Friday, Easter Monday, Labor Day (1st Mon. in May), Christmas Day (Dec. 25), and Boxing Day (Dec. 26).

ANGUILLA

PLANNING YOUR TRIP
Arrival/Departure
There are no direct flights from the U.S. to Anguilla's Clayton J. Lloyd International Airport. The closest international gateways are Sint Maarten, Puerto Rico, Antigua, and St. Kitts. Anguilla Air Services (anguillaairservices.com) operates seven-minute puddle-jumper flights between Anguilla and Sint Maarten/St.-Martin two to three times a day. Cape Air (capeair.com) and Seaborne

(seaborneairlines.com) both provide regular services from Puerto Rico, and interisland services to various Virgin Island destinations. LIAT (liat.com) flies from Antigua.

A frequent (every 30–45 minutes 7:30 a.m.–7 p.m.) and inexpensive 25-minute ferry service operates between Blowing Point, Anguilla, and Marigot, St.-Martin; find info at ivisitanguilla.com. Ferry services are also available to Princess Juliana Airport, Sint Maarten.

Departure tax is US$20 at the airport, or US$5 for the ferry crossing to St.-Martin.

Festivals & Events
March Moonsplash Music Festival
April Festival del Mar
May Anguilla Day
June Celebration of the Queen's Birthday
August Carnival
November Tranquility Jazz Festival

National holidays include Anguilla Day (May 30), Whit Monday, and Constitution Day (Aug. 6).

GETTING AROUND
Car Rental
Andy's Car Rentals, tel 264/584-7010, andyrentals.com; Avis, tel 264/497-2642, avis.com; Island Car Rentals, tel 264/497-2723, islandcar.ai; and Triple K/Hertz, tel 264/497-2934, hertz.com. Visitors must purchase a temporary license (US$20) in addition to presenting a valid overseas permit. Driving on Anguilla is on the left.

Public Transportation
There is limited public bus service on Anguilla. Fixed-rate taxis are available at the airport, tel 264/497-5054, and ferry dock, tel 264/497-6089, or can be arranged through the hotel.

PRACTICAL ADVICE

Emergencies

All emergencies: tel 911. Princess Alexandra Hospital, Stoney Ground: tel 264/497-2551. Serious medical cases are airlifted to Puerto Rico.

Telephones

The area code is 264.

Tourist information

The Valley: Anguilla Tourist Board, Coronation Ave., tel 264/497-2759 or 800/553-4939, fax 264/497-2710, ivisitanguilla.com

U.S. & Canada Offices

New York: PM Group, 301 E. 57th St., 4th fl., New York, NY 10022, tel 212/490-2098 or 800/553-4939
Ontario: SRM Marketing, Ste. 156, 2186 Mountain Grove, Burlington, ON L7P 4X4, tel 905/689-3695 or 866/348-7447, fax 905/689-1026

ANTIGUA & BARBUDA

PLANNING YOUR TRIP

Arrival/Departure

Several carriers serve Antigua's V. C. Bird International Airport direct from the United States, including American Airlines out of New York, Miami, and Charlotte, Delta from Atlanta, and AirCanada from Montreal and Toronto. Antigua is also the hub for local carrier LIAT, liat.com, which offers frequent connections to other islands.

Barbuda is served daily by SVG Air, tel 268/562-8033, svgair.com, from Antigua (15 mins flight time); and the Barbuda Express ferry, tel 268/560-7989, barbuda express.com, providing a 90-minute power catamaran service and day-trip tours.

Departure tax from Antigua is US$28; there is no tax payable and no immigration requirements for trips between Antigua and Barbuda, but bring your passport for identification.

Festivals & Events

April Antigua Sailing Week; Antigua & Barbuda International Kite Festival
July Carnival

National holidays include Good Friday, Easter Monday, Labor Day (1st Mon. in May), and Independence Day (Nov. 1).

GETTING AROUND

Car Rental

Avis, tel 268/462-2840, avis.com; Dollar Rent-A-Car, tel 268/462-0362; and Hertz, tel 268/481-4440, hertz.com, are found at Antigua's airport and other locations around the island. Visitors have to purchase a temporary driver's permit (US$20) in addition to presenting a valid overseas license. Driving is on the left in Antigua and Barbuda.

Public Transportation

Antigua has an irregular daytime bus service geared to commuters heading into St. John's from around the island. Buses leave only when they are full; fares are inexpensive.

Taxis, bookable from the hotel, are not metered, but government fixed rates apply. Agree on the fee in advance. There is no public transportation on Barbuda.

PRACTICAL ADVICE

Emergencies

All emergencies: tel 911. Police headquarters in St. John's: tel 268/462-0125. Mount St. John's Hospital: Queen Elizabeth Hwy., St. John's, tel 268/462-2700. Serious cases are airlifted to

Puerto Rico or Miami. Most hotels are served by a 24-hour duty doctor.

Telephones

The area code for Antigua and Barbuda is 268.

Tourist Information

St. John's: Antigua and Barbuda Department of Tourism, ACB Financial Centre, 3rd fl., High St., St. John's, tel 268/562-7600, fax 268/562-7602, visitantigua barbuda.com.

U.S. & Canada Offices

New York: 305 E. 47th St., Ste. 6A, New York, NY 10017, tel 212/541-4118 or 888/268-4227
Toronto: 60 St. Claire Ave. East, Ste. 601, Toronto ON M4T 1N5, tel 416/961-3085, fax 416/961-7218

MONTSERRAT

PLANNING YOUR TRIP

Arrival/Departure

Access to Montserrat is via the neighboring island of Antigua. There are regular short-hop flights (15–20 mins) into John A. Osborne Airport with Fly Montserrat (flymontserrat.com) and SVG Air (montserrat-flights.com). Ferry services are also available (crossings a minimum 90 mins); check schedules with the Montserrat Tourist Board (tel 664/491-2230, visitmontserrat.com). For further details see also sidebar p. 225.

Departure tax is EC$55 (approx. US$21) or EC$10 (US$3) for day trips.

Festivals & Events

March St Patrick's Week celebrations. See sidebar p. 226
July Calabash Festival
December–New Year's Day Carnival

GETTING AROUND
Car Rental
Gage's Car Rental, St. John's, tel 664/493-5821, gagescar rental.com; Montserrat Enterprises, Old Towne, tel 664/491-2431, montserratenterprises .com; and Tip Top Enterprise tel 664/496-1842, tiptopcar rentals.com, all rent out cars and Jeeps. There is one main road which runs along the coast and into the hills but ends short of the exclusion zone; be sure to respect the marked boundaries of the zone. Visitors require a temporary driver's license (approx. US$20) available from any police station and at the immigration office just outside the airport.

Public Transportation
Taxis and minibuses have green license plates starting with an H. They can be hailed anywhere (there are no fixed routes). Taxis are unmetered and rates are fixed. Most drivers make knowledgeable guides and offer set fees for tours depending on duration.

PRACTICAL ADVICE
Emergencies
Police: tel 999. Fire: tel 911. Operator assistance: tel 411. Minor emergencies can be dealt with at the Glendon Hospital, St. John's: tel 664/491-2552; air ambulance services fly to Antigua.

Telephones
The country code is 664.

Tourist Information
Brades: Montserrat Tourism Division, E.K. Osbourne Bldg., Little Bay, tel 664/491-4700, visitmontserrat.com

ST. KITTS & NEVIS

PLANNING YOUR TRIP
Arrival/Departure
American Airlines offers direct flights from Miami, and flies from New York and Charlotte, to St. Kitts's Robert L. Bradshaw International Airport. Delta flies direct from Atlanta. There are no direct flights from North America to Nevis's Vance W. Armory Airport, but both islands are easily accessed via regional gateways including Puerto Rico with Cape Air (capeair.com) and Seaborne (seaborneairlines.com); Antigua with LIAT (liat.com); and Nevis is linked to Sint Maarten with Winair (fly-winair.sx). Regular inexpensive ferries run several times a day between island capitals Basseterre and Charlestown (crossings take 45 minutes). Water taxis depart on demand.

Departure tax is US$22 from St. Kitts and from Nevis.

Festivals & Events
June St. Kitts Music Festival
August Culturama, around Emancipation Day (1st Mon. in Aug., Nevis)
September Heritage Festival on Independence Day (Sept. 19, St. Kitts and Nevis)
December–January National Carnival kicks off on Dec. 26 and lasts into the New Year (St. Kitts).

National holidays include Whit Monday, Queen's Birthday (2nd Sat. in June), and National Heroes Day (Sept. 16).

GETTING AROUND
Car Rental
Car and Jeep rentals are available through Avis, avis.com: St. Kitts, tel 869/465-6507; and local operator Thrifty/TDC Rentals (tdclimited.com):

St. Kitts, tel 869/465-2991; Nevis, tel 869/469-5430. Both operators also offer a useful exchange rental arrangement between St. Kitts and Nevis if you are keen to explore the twin islands. Visitors must obtain a temporary driver's permit (US$25) in addition to presenting a valid foreign license. Driving on St. Kitts and Nevis is on the left.

Public Transportation
Inexpensive minibus services leave the ferry dock in Basseterre, and from Main Street Charlestown when they are full or the driver is ready. Taxis are readily available and fares are fixed by the government.

PRACTICAL ADVICE
Emergencies
Police and ambulance: tel 911. Fire: tel 333 St. Kitts; or 469-3444 Nevis. For medical problems, hotels can call for a doctor. Joseph N. France Hospital in Basseterre, tel 869/465-2551, and Alexandra Hospital in Nevis, tel 869/469-5473, treat minor casualties. Serious medical emergencies are sent to Puerto Rico.

Telephones
The area code is 869.

Tourist Information
St. Kitts: St. Kitts Tourism Authority, Pelican Mall, Bay Rd., Basseterre, tel 869/465-4040, fax 869/465-8794, stkittstourism.kn
Nevis: Nevis Tourism Authority, P.O. Box 184, Main St., Charlestown, tel 869/ 469-7550, fax 869/469-7551, nevisisland.com

St. Kitts U.S. & Canada Offices
New York: 350 Fifth Ave., 59th fl., New York, NY 10118, tel 914/949-2164 or 800/582-6208
Toronto: 133 Richmond St. West,

Ste. 311, ON M5H 2L3, tel 416/368-6707 or 888/395-4887, fax 416/368-3934

Nevis Telephone Inquiries:
U.S.: tel 407/287-5204
Canada: tel 403/770-6697

■ FRENCH ANTILLES

National Holidays

Holidays common to all islands include New Year's Day (Jan. 1), Shrove Tuesday, Ash Wednesday, Good Friday, Easter Monday, Labor Day (May 1), Victory Day 1945 (May 8), Ascension Day (May), Abolition of Slavery Day (May 22), Whit Monday, Bastille Day (July 14), Feast of the Assumption (Aug. 15), All Saints Day (Nov. 1), All Souls Day (Nov. 2), and Christmas Day (Dec. 25).

GUADELOUPE

PLANNING YOUR TRIP

Arrival/Departure

Pôle Caraïbes Airport lies just north of Pointe-à-Pitre, convenient for Gosier and other Grande-Terre coastal resorts. Air France (tel U.S. 800/237-2747, airfrance.com) offers a direct daily service to Guadeloupe from Miami; Norwegian Airlines (tel U.S. 800/357-4159, norwegian .com) flies direct from New York (JFK), Boston, and Baltimore several times a week; and there is also a direct service from Miami with American Airlines. Air Canada provides a nonstop service from Montreal. The island is well served by connections from regional island air hubs, such as Puerto Rico (see p. 336) by local carriers LIAT (liat.com) and Seaborne (seaborneairlines.com). LIAT also flies from Antigua (see p. 343), and Air Caraibes (aircaraibes.com) provides services from

St.-Martin (see p. 341), and short-hop flights on to the islands of the Guadeloupean archipelago.

Inexpensive daily ferry services link Guadeloupe with Martinique (3 hrs 45 mins) and the islands of the archipelago. Ferries to Dominica and St. Lucia operate several times a week. For schedule information, contact L'Express des Îles, tel 0825/35 90 00, express -des-iles.com. Crossings can be rough; travelers might prefer a short plane ride.

Entry Requirements

Visitors will need to produce a passport and a return or onward ticket. Check visa requirements.

Festivals & Events

January Carnival preparations begin early in the New Year and culminate in a giant three-day event running up to Ash Wednesday.
July Creole Arts Festival (Ste.-Anne)
August Fête des Cuisinières, a gastronomic showcase

GETTING AROUND

Car Rental

Avis, tel 0590/21 13 54, avis .com; Budget, tel 0590/21 13 49, budget-guadeloupe.com; Europcar, tel 0590/21 13 52, europcar.com, are among the rental agencies. Scooter rentals are also widely available. Overseas driver's licenses are valid for 20 days in Guadeloupe; driving is on the right.

Public Transportation

Public buses serve most destinations around the island and operate from early morning until 6–7 p.m. There is a useful service along the south coast of Grande-Terre to Pointe-à-Pitre with drop-off and pickup points near the ferry terminal on La Darse.

Carry small change for the fare. To stop the bus, shout *"arrêt"* or press a buzzer.

Taxi rates are fixed; agree on the price in advance. Travelers should look for the "Friendly Taxi" logo on drivers' uniforms and vehicles at the harbor and airport.

PRACTICAL ADVICE

Emergencies

Police: tel 17. Fire: tel 18. Ambulance: tel 15 or SAMU 0590/89 11 00. There are hospitals in all major towns, and duty doctors can be summoned by hotels.

Telephones

The country code is 590. Guadeloupean local telephone numbers have ten digits. Landline numbers begin 0590; cell phones begin 0690. To make calls within Guadeloupe and to the other French Caribbean islands, dial the full ten digits. To call Guadeloupe from the U.S., dial 011 590 590 plus the remaining six-digit number. To call the U.S. from Guadeloupe, dial 00 1 followed by the area code and telephone number. Calls made from phone boxes require a pre-paid *télécarte*.

Tourist Information

Pointe-à-Pitre: Comité du Tourisme des Îles de Guadeloupe, 5 Square de la Banque, 97166, tel 0590/82 09 30, fax 0590/ 83 89 22, guadeloupe-islands.com

U.S. Office
New York: Atout France, 825 3rd Ave., 29th fl., New York, NY 10022-7519, tel 212/745-0989, fax 212/838-7855, guadeloupe -islands.com

ST.-BARTHÉLEMY

PLANNING YOUR TRIP

Arrival/Departure

St. Barts's Gustave III Airport can only take small STOL (short take-off and landing) aircraft, so the easiest access to St. Barts is from Sint Maarten (see p. 341), which is well served by direct flights from North America, and only a ten-minute hop away. St. Barth Commuter, stbarthcommuter .com, and Winair, fly-winair.sx, offer frequent daily services from Sint Maarten/St.-Martin, and there are Winair connections to many other destinations in the Eastern Caribbean.

Express ferries make the sea crossing daily from Sint Maarten/ (45 minutes)/St. Martin (75 minutes). For services from Simson Baai, contact The Edge, tel 721/544-2640, stmaarten -activities.com. From Philipsburg, contact Great Bay Express, tel 721/542-0032, greatbayferry .com; from Marigot, contact Voyager, tel 0590/87 10 68, voy12 .com. Voyager also has departures from Oyster Pond. The trip can be quite rough, however fine the weather. Catamaran trips are slower but smoother.

Entry Requirements

Visitors will need to produce a passport and a return or onward ticket. Check visa requirements.

Festivals & Events

January Festival de Musique
March–May Sailing regatta season
April Festival du Cinéma Caraïbe
July Deep Sea Fishing Tournament
December New Year's Eve Regatta

GETTING AROUND

Car Rental

Avis, tel 0590/27 71 43; Budget, tel 0590/27 66 30; and Hertz, tel 0590/27 71 14. Motorbikes and scooters can be rented through Barth'loc, tel 0590/27 52 81, and Chez Béranger, tel 0590/27 89 00, among others. Foreign driver's licenses are valid; driving is on the right on St.-Barthélemy. There are two gas stations on the island, at St. Jean and Lorient. Both are closed on Sundays and some weekday afternoons, but fuel can be obtained using a credit card.

Public Transportation

There is no public bus service on the island. Taxis are available from the airport, and the taxi stand on Quai du Général de Gaulle in Gustavia, tel 0590/27 66 31. There is a flat rate for rides up to five minutes, and it goes up every three minutes thereafter.

PRACTICAL ADVICE

Emergencies

Police: tel 17. Ambulance and fire: tel 18. The Hôpital de Bruyn in Gustavia, tel 0590/27 60 35, can handle most casualties and hotels can help locate the duty doctor. Serious medical emergencies are taken to Sint Maarten or Puerto Rico.

Telephones

The country code is 590. When making a local call or calling from another French Antillean island, dial 0590 and the six-digit number. When calling from the U.S., dial 011 590 590 and the remaining six-digit number.

Tourist Information

Gustavia: Office du Tourisme, Quai du Général de Gaulle, 97133, tel 0590/27 87 27, fax 0590/27 74 47, saintbarth -tourisme.com.

U.S. Office

See Guadeloupe, p. 345.

MARTINIQUE

PLANNING YOUR TRIP

Arrival/Departure

American Airlines has daily direct flights from Miami to Martinique's Aimé Césaire Airport, at Lamentin, outside Fort-de-France. Norwegian Air recently began nonstop flights from New York, Boston, and Baltimore. There are direct flights from Montreal with Air Canada, and interisland services with Seaborne (seaborne airlines.com) and Air Caraïbes (aircaraibes.com) from Puerto Rico, providing connections to a wide variety of U.S. gateways. Local carriers, including LIAT (liat .com), serve other regional hubs such as Antigua (see p. 343), Barbados (see p. 350), and Sint Maarten (see p. 341).

Inexpensive ferry services link Martinique to Guadeloupe (4.5 hours); Dominica (2 hours); and St. Lucia (1 hour 30 minutes). For schedules, contact the Fort-de-France interisland ferry terminal, tel 0596/59 00 00. Crossings can be rough, so travelers might prefer a short-hop plane ride.

Entry Requirements

Visitors will need to produce a passport and a return or onward ticket. Check visa requirements. No departure tax.

Festivals & Events

January Pre-Carnival activities kick off in January and climax on Ash Wednesday.
April Martinique Food Show
July Fort-de-France Cultural Festival
August La Yole Rond (around-island boat race)
December Winter Music Festival

GETTING AROUND
Car Rental
Avis, tel 0596/42 11 00, avis.com; Budget, tel 0596/42 04 04, budget.com; Europcar, tel 0596/42 42 42; and Jumbo Car, tel 0596/42 22 22. Overseas driver's licenses are valid for 20 days and driving on Martinique is on the right.

Public Transportation
Public buses from Fort-de-France operate from early morning until around 7 p.m. They stop at designated bus stops; to get off shout "*arrêt*." Ferries from Fort-de-France serve several local beaches and Ste.-Anne. Taxi rates are fixed; agree on the price in advance.

PRACTICAL ADVICE
Emergencies
Police: tel 17. Fire: tel 18. Medical emergencies and ambulance: tel 15 or SOS Médecins (24-hour doctor service), tel 0596/63 33 33. There are well-equipped hospitals and local clinics. Hotels or the tourist office can help locate an English-speaking doctor.

Telephones
The country code is 596. Martiniquais telephone numbers have ten digits beginning 0596, or 0696 for cell phones. When making a local call or calling from another French Antillean island, dial 0596 and the six-digit number. When calling from the U.S., dial 011 596 596 and the number. To the U.S., dial 001, followed by the area code and number.

Tourist Information
Fort-de-France: Comité Martiniquais du Tourisme, Le Beaupré, Pointe de Jaham, 97233 Schoelcher, tel 0596/61 61 77, fax 0596/61 22 72, martinique.org

U.S. & Canada Offices
New York: CMT USA, 825 3rd Ave., 29th fl., New York, NY 10022-7519, tel 212/838-6887, fax 212/838-7855, us.martinique.org
Montreal: 1800 McGill College, Ste. 1010, Montreal, QC H3A 3J6, tel 514/844-8566, fax 514/844-8901

■ WINDWARD ISLANDS

National Holidays
Holidays for the group include New Year's Day, Good Friday, Easter Monday, Whit Monday, Labor Day (1st Mon. in May), May Day, Dominica (May 1), Christmas Day (Dec. 25), and Boxing Day (Dec. 26).

DOMINICA

PLANNING YOUR TRIP
Arrival/Departure
There are no direct flights to Dominica from the U.S. mainland, but Seaborne (seaborneairlines.com) has a daily service from Puerto Rico (see p. 336) to Dominica's Douglas-Charles Airport, located in Melville Hall in the north of the island (1 hour from Roseau). Local carrier LIAT, liat.com, provides services from regional transportation hubs including Antigua (see p. 343), Barbados (see p. 350), and Puerto Rico. Some smaller planes use Canefield Airport, just outside Roseau.

Dominica can also be reached by high-speed ferries from Guadeloupe (2–2.5 hours) and Martinique (2 hours); contact L'Express des Îles in Roseau, tel 767/448-2181 or 767/255-1125, express-des-iles.com. The crossing can be rough.

Entry Requirements
U.S. visitors require a passport and a return or onward ticket.
Departure tax is US$23.

Festivals & Events
February–March Carnival (Mon. & Tues. before Lent)
July Dive Fest
October World Creole Music Festival
November Independence Day (Nov. 3)

Other holidays include 1st Mon. in Aug. and Community Day of Service (Nov. 4).

GETTING AROUND
Car Rental
Island Car Rentals, tel 767/255-6844, islandcar.dm; Road Runner, tel 767/275-5337, roadrunner carrental.com; and Valley Rent-A-Car, tel 767/275-1310, valley rentacar.com. Drivers will need a temporary visitor's permit (US$12) in addition to their valid overseas license. Driving on Dominica is on the left.

Public Transportation
Irregular but frequent minibus services cover all the major island destinations from Roseau. Taxis (identified by the letters H, HA, or HB on their license plates) are readily available from the airports and Roseau by day, or make an arrangement with your hotel. Reserve a taxi in advance for evening excursions. Government rates apply.

PRACTICAL ADVICE
Emergencies
Police, fire, and emergencies: tel 999. Princess Margaret Hospital in Roseau, tel 767/448-2231, and Portsmouth Hospital, tel 767/445-5237, are the main medical facilities. Princess Margaret Hospital

has a decompression facility. Serious medical emergencies are dispatched to Puerto Rico. Hotels can assist in locating a duty doctor.

Telephones
The area code is 767.

Tourist Information
Roseau: Discover Dominica Authority, Financial Centre Bldg., P.O. Box 293, Commonwealth of Dominica, tel 767/448-2045, dominica.dm
U.S. & Canada Inquiries: tel 866/522-4057, email dominicany@dominica.dm

GRENADA, CARRIACOU, & PETITE MARTINIQUE

PLANNING YOUR TRIP
Arrival/Departure
Grenada's Maurice Bishop International Airport receives direct flights from New York and Atlanta with Delta, from New York with JetBlue, daily direct services from Miami with American Airlines, and Caribbean Airlines offers one-stop flights via its Port of Spain hub in Trinidad from Miami, New York, Orlando, and Toronto. Air Canada flies from Toronto daily direct to Barbados for onward connections, and direct to Grenada over the winter months. Regional carrier LIAT (liat.com) provides regular services from Puerto Rico, connecting to numerous North American departure points and links to other island gateways such as Antigua (see p. 343), Barbados (see p. 350), St. Vincent (see p. 349), and Trinidad (see p. 351).

Lauriston Airport on Carriacou is served by daily island-hopper flights from Grenada with SVG

Air, svgair.com. The islands are also connected by a weekday round-trip ferry service with Osprey Lines, tel 473/440-8126, ospreylines.com, which operates a reduced service on weekends.

Petite Martinique can be reached by water taxi from Windward, on the northeast coast of Carriacou.

Entry Requirements
Visitors will be required to produce a passport together with a return or onward ticket.

Departure tax from Grenada is included in air and cruise ticket prices.

Festivals & Events
February–March Carriacou Carnival (held before beginning of Lent); weeklong St. Patrick's Day celebration (Sauteurs, Grenada)
June Fisherman's Birthday in Gouyave (end June)
July–August Carriacou Regatta; Grenada Carnival (St. George's)
December Carriacou Parang Festival

National holidays include Independence Day (Feb. 7), Corpus Christi (June), Emancipation Day (1st Mon. & Tues. in Aug.), and Thanksgiving Day (Oct. 25).

GETTING AROUND
Car Rental
David's Sun Car Rental, tel 473/444-3399, davidscars.com, and Ye&R Car Rental, tel 473/444-4448, carrentalgrenada.com, operate in Grenada. For rentals in Carriacou, contact Sunkey's Auto Rentals, tel 473/443-8382, email sunkeywp@yahoo.com, or Wayne's Auto Rentals, tel 473/443-6120, email waynes autorentals@yahoo.com. Drivers will require a temporary local driver's permit (EC$60, about US$22) plus a valid overseas license. Driving is on the left.

Public Transportation
Private minibuses (dollar buses) cover virtually every corner of Grenada and Carriacou on an unscheduled though frequent basis from early morning until early evening. Visitors can flag them down and be squeezed in by the "put-man" who also collects the money. Rap hard on the roof to get off.

Taxis are available from the airport and main taxi stand on the Carenage in St. George's, by the ferry dock in Hillsborough, or make arrangements with your hotel. Always agree on the price in advance.

For interisland ferry information, see Arrival/Departure.

PRACTICAL ADVICE
Emergencies
Police and fire: tel 911. Ambulance, St. George's: tel 473/440-2113. St. George's Hospital in Grenada, tel 473/440-2050, can cope with most sicknesses, though serious medical emergencies may be transferred to Puerto Rico. Hotels can contact the duty doctor. On Carriacou, contact Princess Royal Hospital, tel 473/443-7400, or the ambulance, tel 774.

Telephones
The area code for Grenada, Carriacou, and Petite Martinique is 473.

Tourist Information
Grenada: Grenada Board of Tourism, P.O. Box 293, St. George's, tel 473/440-2279, fax 473/440-6637, grenadagrenadines.com
Carriacou: Main St., Hillsborough, tel 473/443-7948, fax 473/443-6127

U.S. & Canada Offices
New York: Grenada Tourism Authority, 800 2nd Ave.,

Ste. 400K, New York, NY 10017, tel 917/929-7892; inquiries tel 561/948-6925, email cnoel@ grenadagrenadines.com
Toronto: 90 Eglington Ave. East, Ste. 605, Toronto, ON M4P 2Y3, tel 416/995-1581, email canada@puregrenada.com

ST. LUCIA

PLANNING YOUR TRIP
Arrival/Departure
Hewanorra Airport on the island's south coast is St. Lucia's chief gateway for international jet flights, served by direct flights from North America by American Airlines from Miami and Charlotte, JetBlue from New York and Boston, and AirCanada from Montreal and Toronto. It is a 90-minute transfer to hotels in the north of the island. Smaller planes serve George Charles Airport at Vigie/Castries, including daily services with local carrier LIAT (liat.com) from Puerto Rico, and frequent services from local transportation hubs such as Antigua (see p. 343) and Barbados (see p. 350).

High-speed ferry services link St. Lucia with Martinique (1 hour 30 minutes), Dominica, and Guadeloupe. For information, contact Cox & Co., Castries, tel 758/456-5000, agents for L'Express des Îles, express-des-iles.com.

Entry Requirements
Visitors are required to produce a passport and return or onward ticket. The departure tax of US$26 is included in air and cruise tickets.

Festivals & Events
May St. Lucia Jazz Festival (Pigeon Island & Castries)
July Carnival
September–October St. Lucia Billfishing Tournament (all

welcome); Jounen Kweyol Entenasyonnal (International Creole Day)
November–December Atlantic Rally for Cruisers (Rodney Bay Marina)

National holidays include Independence Day (Feb. 22), Corpus Christi (June), Emancipation Day (1st Mon. in Aug.), Thanksgiving Day (Oct. 4), and National Day (Dec. 13).

GETTING AROUND
Car Rental
Avis, tel 758/452-2700, avis stlucia.com; Budget, tel 758/452-9887, budgetstlucia.com; Hertz, tel 758/ 452-0680; and West Coast Jeeps, tel 758/459-5457, westcoastjeeps.com. A temporary visitor's permit (US$20) is required plus a valid overseas license. Driving on St. Lucia is on the left.

Public Transportation
Frequent and inexpensive minibus services run between Castries, Rodney Bay, and the north until about 10 p.m. (later on Fri. for visitors to the Gros Islet jump-up party). Less frequent services to Soufrière and the south depart from Bridge St.

Taxi rates are fixed by the government; always agree on the fare in advance.

PRACTICAL ADVICE
Emergencies
Police, fire, and ambulance: tel 911. St. Lucia's main hospitals are the Victoria Hospital in Castries, tel 758/452-2421, and St. Jude's in Vieux Fort, tel 758/454-6041. All hotels have a resident or on-call doctor.

Telephones
The area code is 758.

Tourist Information
Castries: St. Lucia Tourist Board, Sureline Building, Vide Bouteille, P.O. Box 221, Castries, tel 758/452-4094, fax 758/453-1121, stlucia.org

U.S. & Canada Offices
New York: St. Lucia Tourist Board, 800 2nd Ave., Ste. 910, New York, NY 10017, tel 212/867-2950 or 800/456-3984, fax 212/867-2795, email stluciatourism@ aol.com
Toronto: 60 St. Clair Ave. East, Ste. 909, Toronto, ON M4T 1N5, tel 416/392-4242 or 800/869-0377, email sltbcanada@aol.com

ST. VINCENT & THE GRENADINES

PLANNING YOUR TRIP
Arrival/Departure
There are no direct flights to St. Vincent and the Grenadines from the U.S. mainland. There are easy connections from the neighboring islands of Barbados, Grenada, and St. Lucia, as well as Puerto Rico, Martinique, and Trinidad. Local carriers include LIAT, liat.com, and SVG Air, svgair.com. St. Vincent's E.T. Joshua Airport, outside the capital city of Kingstown, is a transportation hub for the Grenadine islands, with onward flights to Bequia, Canouan, Mustique, and Union Island. The islands can also be reached by scheduled boat services originating from Kingstown, St. Vincent (see p. 285).

Entry Requirements
Visitors will be required to produce a passport and a return or onward ticket.
Departure tax is US$18.

Festivals & Events

March–April Bequia Easter Regatta
June–July Carnival or Vincy Mas (Kingstown, St. Vincent)
December Nine Mornings marks the nine-day run-up to Christmas with arts and crafts, parades, carol singers, and nighttime jump-ups.

National holidays include St. Vincent and the Grenadines Day (Jan. 22), Caricom Day (July 5), Emancipation Day (Aug. 2), and Independence Day (Oct. 27).

GETTING AROUND
Car Rental

On St. Vincent, Avis, tel 784/456-6861, avis.com, has an office at the airport; Ben's Auto Rental, tel 784/456-4026; David's Auto Clinic, tel 784/456-4026, and Rent and Drive, tel 784/457-5601, rentand drive@vincysurf.com, will pick up from the airport. A temporary driving permit costs around US$25. You can find rental cars on the Grenadines, too. Driving is on the left.

Public Transportation

Private minibuses (known as dollar buses) ply St. Vincent's south coast route between Kingstown and Villa/Calliaqua throughout the day, less frequently in the evening. To hail a bus anywhere along the route, point down at the road; to get off, rap on the roof or shout "driver, stop" over the music. East coast bus services to Georgetown and on to Fancy, and west coast services to Richmond depart from the waterfront depot in Kingstown. Taxis are available from the airport, downtown Kingstown, and through hotels. Fares are fixed by the government.

PRACTICAL ADVICE
Emergencies

Police, fire, coast guard: tel 911. Police headquarters: tel 784/457-1211. Milton Cato Memorial Hospital, Kingstown: tel 784/456-1185. Medical emergencies can be air-lifted to Barbados or Puerto Rico. Hotels will contact a duty doctor.

Telephones

The area code for St. Vincent and the Grenadines is 784.

Tourist Information

Kingstown: St. Vincent and the Grenadines Tourism Authority, P.O. Box 834, NIS Bldg., Upper Bay St., tel 784/457-1502, fax 784/451-2425, discoversvg.com

U.S. & Canada Offices
New York: 801 2nd Ave., 4th fl., New York, NY 10017, tel 212/687-4981 or 800/729-1726, fax 212/949-5946
Toronto: 55 Town Centre Ct., Ste. 624, ON M1P 4X4, tel 416/630-9292 or 866/421-4452, fax 416/630-9291

■ BARBADOS

PLANNING YOUR TRIP
Arrival/Departure

Barbados has good air connections with North America. American Airlines flies direct from New York, Dallas/Fort Worth, and Miami to Grantley Adams International Airport; American also provides daily services from Puerto Rico. US Airways has flights from Charlotte; Caribbean Airlines flies from Miami, New York, and Toronto. LIAT, liat.com, and other local airlines provide a network of inter-Caribbean links with the Leeward and Windward Islands, the French Antilles, Sint Maarten, and Trinidad and Tobago.

Entry Requirements

U.S. visitors require a passport or proof of citizenship and photo ID, plus a return or onward ticket.

Festivals & Events

January Barbados Jazz Festival
February Holetown Festival, a weeklong celebration of the first settlers
July–August Crop Over Festival, the Bajan Carnival

National holidays include New Year's Day, Good Friday, Easter Monday, Labor Day (May 1), Whit Monday, Emancipation Day (July 31), U.N. Day (Oct. 6), Christmas Day (Dec. 25), and Boxing Day (Dec. 26).

GETTING AROUND
Car Rental

Local operators include Coconut Car Rentals, tel 246/437-0297, coconutcars.com; Courtesy Rent-A-Car, tel 246/431-4160, courtesy rentacar.com; Stoutes Car Rental, tel 246/416-4456, stoutescar.com; and Top Class, tel 246/228-7368, topclassrentals.com. In addition to a valid overseas license, drivers must purchase a temporary visitor's driving license (US$5). Driving in Barbados is on the left.

Public Transportation

Regular and inexpensive public buses and minibuses serve the coastal regions and Bridgetown from early morning until around midnight. Taxis are not metered, so agree on a price in advance.

PRACTICAL ADVICE
Emergencies

Police: tel 211. Fire: tel 311. Ambulance: tel 511. Queen Elizabeth Hospital, Bridgetown North: tel 246/436-6450. Hotels can contact a duty doctor.

Telephones
The area code is 246.

Tourist Information
Bridgetown: Barbados Tourism Authority, P.O. Box 242, Prescod Blvd., tel 246/427-2623, fax 246/426-4080, visitbarbados.org

U.S. & Canada Offices
New York: Barbados Tourism Marketing Inc., 820 2nd Ave., 5th fl., New York, NY 10017, tel 212/551-4350 or 800/221-9831, fax 212/573-9850
Toronto: 105 Adelaide St. West, Ste. 1010, ON M5H 1P9, tel 416/214-9880 or 888/BARBA DOS, fax 416/214-9882

■ TRINIDAD & TOBAGO

PLANNING YOUR TRIP
Arrival/Departure
There are direct flights to Trinidad's Piarco Airport, about 30 miles (48 km) east of Port of Spain, with American Airlines from Miami; Caribbean Airlines, caribbean-airlines.com, from Miami, New York, and Toronto; and with United from Houston. LIAT, liat.com, also offers connections from Antigua, Barbados, Jamaica, and Sint Maarten. There are no direct flights to Tobago's ANR Robinson International Airport (formerly Crown Point) from North America. Most visitors fly to Trinidad and hop to Tobago on the frequent Caribbean Airlines air bridge service (25 minutes) between the two islands.

Ferry services also provide an inexpensive but slow sea bridge between the islands (2.5 hours). Contact the Port Authority of Trinidad and Tobago, www.patnt.com.

Departure tax is included in air and cruise ticket prices.

Festivals & Events
January–March Preparations for the famous Trinidad Carnival
March Phagwa (Hindu New Year)
June Muslim Hosay, a three-day event tied to the Islamic calendar
July Tobago Heritage Festival
August Steelband Week (Trinidad)
September Tobago Festival
October–November Divali (Hindu Festival of Light)

National holidays include New Year's Day, Good Friday, Easter Monday, Labor Day (June 19), Emancipation Day (Aug. 1), Independence Day (Aug. 31), Christmas Day (Dec. 25), and Boxing Day (Dec. 26).

GETTING AROUND
Car Rental
Rental cars can be picked up from Trinidad's Piarco Airport from Avis, tel 868/669-0905, avis.com, and Budget, tel 868/669-1635, budget.com. Rental operators with representation at both Piarco and at ANR Robinson include Kalloo's, tel 868/669-5673 (Trinidad) or 868/780-2886 (Tobago), kalloos.com, and Thrifty, tel 868/669-0602 (Trinidad) or 868/639-8507 (Tobago), thrifty.com.

U.S. and Canadian driver's licenses are valid on the islands. Driving in Trinidad and Tobago is on the left. Gas stations are sparse, so fill up before leaving.

Public Transportation
Inexpensive public buses cover most destinations on Trinidad from the main depot at South Quay in Port of Spain. Tickets have to be purchased in advance.

Private minibuses, known as maxi-taxis, are faster. The maxis are color coded by destination: yellow stripes for Port of Spain area; red for the east; green for the south. Taxis are readily available from the airport (fixed fares to Port of Spain and other popular destinations).

Tobago has public and private bus systems. Public buses depart from Sangster's Hill, Scarborough, for Crown Point and other destinations. Maxi-taxis (minibuses with a blue stripe) are often a better option and can be flagged down along any roadside.

Taxis, designated by the letter H on their license plates, wait at the airport and some of the busier hotels. There are fixed rates from the airport to hotels.

PRACTICAL ADVICE
Emergencies
Police: tel 999. Fire: tel 990. Ambulance: tel 811. Port of Spain General Hospital: tel 868/623-2951. In Tobago, minor casualties are handled by Scarborough Hospital, tel 868/639-2551. Emergencies may be airlifted to Trinidad.

Telephones
The area code for Trinidad and Tobago is 868.

Tourist Information
Port of Spain: Trinidad and Tobago Tourism Development Company, Level 1, Maritime Centre, 29 10th Ave., Barataria, tel 868/675-7034, fax 868/635-7377, gotrinidadandtobago.com

U.S. & Canada Offices
Coral Gables: Cheryl Andrews Marketing, 331 Almeria Ave., FL 33134, tel 305/444-4033, fax 305/447-0415
Toronto: 130 Spadina Ave., Ste. 606, ON M5V 2L4, tel 416/561-8243, fax 416/323-9746

Hotels & Restaurants

Accommodations in the Caribbean are generally very expensive, but cheaper options are available. Prices drop dramatically in the low season, but you will be taking more chances with the weather. All-inclusive resorts can offer good value, although it can be too easy to stay in the resort and not explore the islands.

Rewarding dining experiences can range from jerk chicken to top-class French cuisine. Restaurants are informal and seating arrangements and closing times are flexible. Call ahead to check.

Hotels and restaurants in this section have been organized by region, then price, then in alphabetical order.

■ JAMAICA

KINGSTON & THE BLUE MOUNTAINS

SOMETHING SPECIAL

▦ STRAWBERRY HILL
▥ $$$
IRISH TOWN
TEL 876/944-8400 OR
800/232-4972
strawberryhillhotel.com
Perched 3,000 feet (900 m) above Kingston in the Blue Mountains with fabulous views over the city, Strawberry Hill is an award-winning property owned by the Island Outpost hotel group. The pretty colonial-style villas have private verandas, kitchens, hand-crafted plantation furniture, four-poster mahogany beds with mosquito nets, and louvered windows. The hotel also has a spa, multimedia center, and the excellent **Strawberry Hill Restaurant & Bar** renowned for its "new Jamaican" cuisine and superb Sunday brunch.
🛈 12 villas 🏊 🛜 Free
🚭 All major cards

▦ LIME TREE FARM
$$
TOWER HILL, MAVIS BANK
TEL 876/446-0230
limetreefarm.com
You don't have to move farther than the veranda to go bird-watching at this delightful Blue Mountain hideaway on a working coffee farm. Spacious cottages with fabulous views, wonderfully hospitable staff, delicious locally grown food (full board inclusive), and nature walks and hikes. A trained masseuse is at hand, and a yoga area is available.
🛈 4 🅿 🛜 Free in restaurant

▦ SPANISH COURT
$$
1 ST. LUCIA AVENUE, KINGSTON 5
TEL 876/926-0000
spanishcourthotel.com
Conveniently located in New Kingston, close to shops, restaurants, and businesses, this is a good stopover option. Comfortable rooms; outside seating area. Friendly, helpful staff.
🛈 121 rooms & suites
🅿 🍴 🛒 🏊 📺 🛜 Free
🚭 All major cards

▥ GLORIA'S RENDEZVOUS
$$
1 HIGH STREET, PORT ROYAL
TEL 876/967-8066
Sidewalk dining at its most basic, but don't miss out on scrumptious fresh seafood specials, including jerk lobster and garlic shrimp, washed down with chilled Red Stripe.
🚭 MC, V

▥ REDBONES BLUES CAFE
$$
1 ARGYLE ROAD, KINGSTON 10
TEL 876/978-8262
redbonesbluescafe.com
Laid-back and funky bar-restaurant-night spot with lashings of atmosphere; generous fresh Jamaican food, grills, and pasta served with a side order of jazz.
🚭 All major cards

▥ CAFE BLUE
$
IRISH TOWN, ST. ANDREW
TEL 876/944-8918
jamaicacafeblue.com
You know you'll find a great cup of coffee at Cafe Blue here in the home of Jamaican Blue Mountain coffee, or at one of the Cafe Blue outlets in Kingston and Mo'Bay. You can also enjoy a generously filled savory bagel or croissant, a stack of pancakes, fluffy muffins, or yummy freshly baked cakes.
🚭 All major cards

▦ Hotel 🛈 No. of guest rooms ▥ Restaurant 🕐 Open/Closed Hours 🅿 Parking 🚭 Nonsmoking

MONTEGO BAY

🏨 HALF MOON GOLF, TENNIS & BEACH CLUB
$$$$–$$$$$

ROSE HALL
TEL 800/438-7241 OR
888/830-5974
halfmoon.rockresorts.com
Seven miles (11 km) east of Mo'Bay, this huge colonial-style resort is set on more than 400 acres (162 ha) and offers a range of rooms, suites, and villas. Activities include an 18-hole golf course, tennis, horseback riding, and water sports.
🛈 197 plus 33 villas 🏢 🏊 🏋 🛜 Free 🗺 All major cards

🏨 ROUND HILL HOTEL & VILLAS
$$$$

P.O. BOX 64, MONTEGO BAY
TEL 876/956-7050 OR
800/972-2159
roundhill.com
One of Jamaica's finest traditional resorts, perched on a promontory 10 miles (16 km) west of Mo'Bay. Timeless style; impeccable service. The villas all have kitchens and housekeepers to prepare your breakfast, and many have pools.
🛈 36 plus 27 villas 🏊 🏋 🛜 Free 🗺 All major cards

🏨 IBEROSTAR GRAND HOTEL ROSE HALL
$$$

NORTH COAST HWY. (8 MILES/13 KM E OF MONTEGO BAY)
TEL 876/680-0000
iberostar.com
Attractive all-inclusive resort property ranged along the beachfront just east of Mo'Bay. Family friendly and perfect for sporty types with a wide range of water sports, diving, tennis, golf (complimentary round with a 3-4 night stay), choice of dining, shops, and a spa.
🛈 366 rooms & suites

🅿 🏢 🏊 🛜 🏋 🛜 Free 🗺 All major cards

🍽 SEAGRAPE TERRACE
$$$$

HALF MOON GOLF, TENNIS & BEACH CLUB, ROSE HALL
TEL 876/953-2211
Poised on the beachfront, the alfresco Seagrape is perfectly positioned for sunset drinks before hundreds of fairy lights are switched on. The long menu features grills; among the seafood options, the lobster is worth a special mention. Reservations required.
🗺 All major cards

🍽 PORK PIT
$

27 GLOUCESTER AVENUE
TEL 876/940-3008
The local jerk stop on the Hip Strip. Be warned, the full, fiery, high-octane Jamaican recipe is served with no concessions to delicate tourist taste buds. Delicious nonetheless and a bargain. Sidewalk tables and takeout.
🗺 MC, V

NEGRIL

SOMETHING SPECIAL

🏨 THE CAVES
$$$$

LIGHTHOUSE ROAD, WEST END
TEL 876/957-0270 OR 800/688-7678
islandoutpost.com
Set above the honeycomb cliffs of Negril's West End, this beautiful property features handcrafted thatched and wood cottages nestled in tropical gardens. A series of steps lead down to sundecks and hidden grottoes at sea level. All rooms have CD players and king- or queen-size beds, and there's an Aveda spa treatment center.
🛈 13 cottages 🏊 🗺 All major cards

🏨 TENSING PEN
$$–$$$

WEST END ROAD
TEL 876/957-0387
tensingpen.com
A collection of stylish, individually designed bamboo and wood cottages set in lovely cliff-top gardens. A superb West End retreat.
🛜 Free at front desk 🗺 All major cards

🏨 ROCKHOUSE HOTEL
$–$$

WEST END ROAD
TEL 876/957-4373
rockhousehotel.com
The resort's thatched-roof, beehive huts over-look Pristine Cove on West End's foreshore. Connected by wooden walkways, the huts have four-poster beds and ceiling fans. There is a stunning pool on the shore. Children must be over 12.
🛈 34 🏢 🏊 🛜 Free 🗺 All major cards

🍽 LE VENDÔME
$$$$

CHARELA INN, NEGRIL BEACH
TEL 876/957-4648
charela.com/restaurant
Pretty and popular terraced dining room serving light pizza/pasta/salad lunches. In the evening the culinary bar is set higher with an à la carte and five-course gourmet menu of French cuisine with a Jamaican twist. Live entertainment.
🗺 All major cards

🍽 NORMA'S
$$–$$$

SEA SPLASH HOTEL, NORMAN MANLEY BLVD.
TEL 876/957-4041
seasplash.com/normas-restaurant.html
Lovely setting on a raised deck overlooking the beach and a menu that delivers an often surprising and always delicious take on traditional local fare.
🗺 All major cards

🛗 Elevator 🏢 Air-conditioning 🏊 Indoor pool 🏊 Outdoor pool 🏋 Health club 🛜 Wi-Fi 🗺 Credit cards

RICK'S CAFE
$$
WEST END ROAD
TEL 876/957-0380
rickscafejamaica.com
A Negril institution, with a lively terrace restaurant. Specialties include seafood pasta dishes, broiled lobster, and enticing desserts.
All major cards

OCHO RIOS/ORACABESSA

SOMETHING SPECIAL

GOLDENEYE
$$$$$
ORACABESSA
TEL 876/622-9007
OR 800/688-7678
goldeneye.com
This makeover of Bond author Ian Fleming's holiday home is a masterpiece. Luxurious, discreet, and chic, GoldenEye's villas and beach cottages combine the best of local (jalousies and outdoor bathrooms) and contemporary design. Fabulous food, private beaches, water sports, kids' stuff, and activities from riding to deep-sea fishing by arrangement.
4 villas, 11 cottages, 6 suites Free
All major cards

HIBISCUS LODGE
$
83–85 MAIN STREET
TEL 876/974-2676
hibiscusjamaica.com
Small, friendly hotel set in pretty gardens on the cliff side with pool and tennis courts. Pleasant rooms and the fine **Almond Tree** restaurant.
26 Free
All major cards

EVITA'S
$$–$$$
EDEN BOWER ROAD
TEL 876/974-2333
evitasjamaica.com
Set on the hillside above town, this cheerful Italian-owned restaurant serves homemade pasta (with a Jamaican twist), salads, soups, and a wide range of desserts in an elegant setting overlooking the bay.
All major cards

SCOTCHIES TOO
$
NORTH COAST HIGHWAY., DRAX HALL
TEL 876/794-9457
A ten-minute drive west of Ochi, this outpost of the original Scotchies in Mo'Bay is worth finding. Succulent jerk chicken threaded on bamboo skewers, sides of sweet dumpling-like festival and roast breadfruit, lashings of house hot sauce, cold beers, and tables in tin-roofed gazebos dotted about the garden.
MC, V

PORT ANTONIO

MOCKINGBIRD HILL
$$$$
SAN SAN
TEL 876/993-7267
hotelmockingbirdhill.com
Charming and comfortable little eco-resort in the hills above San San. The light, airy rooms feature bamboo furniture, ocean-view balconies, and works by the artist-owner.
10 Free
All major cards

MILLE FLEURS
$$$
HOTEL MOCKINGBIRD HILL, SAN SAN
TEL 876/993-7134
Almost every dish at Mille Fleurs is homemade from top-quality local ingredients, stylishly presented, and an absolute treat. Savor the catch of the day with chili, mango and lime salsa, slow-cooked lamb, home-baked breads, plus creative and delicious vegetarian and even vegan dishes, plus sea views from the terrace to top it all.
All major cards

SOUTH COAST

JAKE'S
$–$$
TREASURE BEACH, CALABASH BAY, ST. ELIZABETH
TEL 876/965-3000
OR 877/526-2428
jakeshotel.com
Funny collection of rooms and cottages designed in a mix of Jamaican, Mexican, and Catalan styles. Cooled by sea breezes and ceiling fans, the cottages have private outdoor showers, no phones or television. Spa, buzzy bar, excellent restaurant.
50 rooms incl. cottages & villas Free in common areas & some rooms
All major cards

JACK SPRAT
$$
CALABASH BAY, TREASURE BEACH
TEL 876/965-3583
OR 876/564-8983
Colorful tin-roofed diner with a woodsy interior and shady terrace tables right on the beach. Blackboard menu featuring pizzas and seafood (lobster a specialty) served with disks of delicious fried bammy (cassava bread soaked in coconut milk). Live music.
All major cards

LITTLE OCHIE
$–$$
ALLIGATOR POND
TEL 876/610-6566
littleochie.com
You can hop aboard a water taxi from Treasure Beach to reach this rustic huddle of palm-thatched huts on the beach. Local fish and seafood baked, curried, stewed, or grilled over pimento wood fires and finished with a big

squeeze of lime juice. If fish isn't your thing, check out the jerk pork or juicy spit-roasted chicken.

■ CAYMAN ISLANDS

CAYMAN BRAC

▦ BRAC REEF BEACH RESORT
$$
WEST END
TEL 345/948-1323
OR 800/594-0843
bracreef.com
Relaxing and friendly property on the white-sand shore. All rooms feature balcony or patio. The hotel has a good beach and a full-service dive shop, tennis, and spa.
ⓘ 40 🔲 🔳 🔽 📶 Free 🔳 All major cards

▦ BRAC CARIBBEAN & CARIB SANDS BEACH RESORT
$
195 SOUTH SIDE ROAD WEST
TEL 345/948-1121
OR 866/843-2722
caribsands.com
Bright, spacious and good value one-, two-, three-, and four-bedroom condos in a brace of beachfront properties with snorkeling on the doorstep and transportation to Reef Divers down the road. The poolside restaurant-bar gets especially lively on weekends.
ⓘ 65 🔲 🔳 🔳 🔽 🔳 MC, V

▦ WALTON'S MANGO MANOR
$
STAKE BAY
TEL/FAX 345/948-0518
Quaint B&B in an old house with beach access, and fruit trees and parrots in the garden. Five spotlessly clean rooms and a two-bed villa ($$).
ⓘ 7 🔳 🔳 🔳 D, MC, V

GRAND CAYMAN

▦ CARIBBEAN CLUB
$$$$$
871 WEST BAY ROAD,
SEVEN MILE BEACH
TEL 345/623-4500 OR
800/941-1126
caribclub.com
Über-luxurious boutique condominium hotel with 37 three-bedroom, three-bathroom beachfront suites and villas. Each spacious apartment is fitted with the latest technology. Infinity pool, nanny service, concierge.
ⓘ 37 🅿 🔳 🔳 🔽 📶 Free 🔳 All major cards

SOMETHING SPECIAL

▦ RITZ-CARLTON GRAND CAYMAN
$$$$–$$$$$
SEVEN MILE BEACH
TEL 345/943-9000
ritzcarlton.com
This fabulous beachfront behemoth has set a new gold standard for luxury in the region. Facilities include La Prairie Spa, a Nick Bollettieri tennis school, a Greg Norman–designed golf course, and gourmet cuisine.
ⓘ 365 rooms & suites + 24 condos 🔳 🔳 🔳 📶 Free 🔳 All major cards

▦ WESTIN GRAND CAYMAN SEVEN MILE BEACH RESORT & SPA
$$$$
WEST BAY ROAD,
SEVEN MILE BEACH
TEL 345/945-3800
OR 800/WESTIN-1
westingrandcayman.com
One of the smarter resorts along Seven Mile Beach and a great choice for families. Kid programs (ages 4–12), water sports, diving. Round-the-clock room service and swim-up bar.
ⓘ 343 🔳 🔳 🔳 🔽 📶 Free 🔳 All major cards

▦ SUNSET HOUSE
$$–$$$
S. CHURCH STREET,
GEORGE TOWN
TEL 345/949-7111
OR 800/854-4767
sunsethouse.com
A popular choice for dedicated divers, Sunset has a fully equipped dive school, underwater photo tuition, and good shore diving. Deluxe rooms have ocean views.
ⓘ 60 🔳 🔳 📶 Free in some areas 🔳 All major cards

▦ COBALT COAST
$$
18-A SEA FAN DRIVE, WEST BAY
TEL 345/946-5656
OR 888/946-5656
cobaltcoast.com
Designed in the style of a Caribbean great house, this comfortable, welcoming hotel is well away from the bustle of Seven Mile Beach and has a 120-foot (37 m) jetty with access to great shore diving.
ⓘ 22 🔳 📶 Free in some areas & some rooms 🔳 All major cards

▦ WYNDHAM REEF RESORT
$$
2221 EAST END, COLLIERS BAY
TEL 345/947-3100
OR 888/232-0541
thereef.com
Good value beachfront resort, 20 miles (32 km) from George Town at the quieter east end of the island. Generous condo-size suites ideal for families. Close to first-rate diving and snorkeling.
ⓘ 152 🔳 🔳 🔳 🔳 📶 Free in public areas 🔳 All major cards

▦ TURTLE NEST INN
$–$$
BODDEN TOWN
TEL 345/947-8665
turtlenestinn.net
Spacious and attractive units in a friendly and intimate seaside

inn 10 miles (16 km) from George Town. Patios/verandas with barbecues; good snorkeling off a quiet sandy beach.

[i] 18 apartments & condos 🏊 ⛱ 📶 Free 🚭 All major cards

🍽 LIGHTHOUSE RESTAURANT
$$$–$$$$
BREAKERS, EAST END
TEL 345/947-2047
lighthouse.ky
A Cayman landmark for the last 30 years. Very popular and romantic with a nautical theme and terrace overlooking the seashore. Caribbean-Italian specialties include pasta, fish, and mixed seafood grills.
🚭 All major cards

🍽 CRACKED CONCH
$$$
NORTHWEST POINT ROAD, WEST BAY
TEL 345/945-5217
crackedconch.com.ky
A long-standing institution, serving distinctly upscale Caribbean cuisine: signature conch chowder, jerk-seasoned tuna. Caribbean Sunday brunch. Patio dining and mellow tiki bar overlooking the ironshore.
🕐 Closed L Jun.–Nov.
🚭 All major cards

🍽 CIMBOCO
$–$$
MARQUEE PLAZA, SEVEN MILE BEACH
TEL 345/947-2782
cimboco.com
Jaunty island-style Caribbean café with an open kitchen and wood-burning oven. Home-baked breads and pizzas, pasta salads, jerk grills, and posher nosh such as banana leaf roasted snapper followed by epic homemade desserts. Great weekend brunches.
🚭 All major cards

LITTLE CAYMAN

🏨 SOUTHERN CROSS CLUB
$$$$–$$$$$
SOUTH HOLE SOUND
TEL 345/948-1099 OR 800/899-2582
southerncrossclub.com
Luxurious chalets spaced out across a white sandy beach; excellent food and service; sportfishing, kayaks, and a dive center.
[i] 14 chalets & 1 cottage 🏊 ⛱ 📶 Free in clubhouse 🚭 AE, MC, V

🏨 PIRATES POINT RESORT
🍽 $$$–$$$$
PRESTON BAY
TEL 345/948-1010
piratespointresort.com
Perennial favorite with simple but charming bungalows set on a small beach. Gladys Howard's cuisine is legendary (non-residents book in advance). Fully equipped dive operation run by experienced staff.
[i] 11 🏊 ⛱ 📺 📶 Free in clubhouse 🚭 All major cards

🏨 LITTLE CAYMAN BEACH RESORT
$$$
BLOSSOM VILLAGE
TEL 345/948-1033 OR 800/327-3835
littlecayman.com
Modern resort with good facilities set out around a small pool with funky underwater lighting. Tennis, spa, water sports, and dive center.
[i] 40 🏊 ⛱ 📺 📶 Free in some rooms 🚭 AE, MC, V

🍽 HUNGRY IGUANA
$$
SOUTH HOLE SOUND
TEL 345/948-0007 OR 877/322-9626
hungryiguana.com
Next door to the airport at Paradise Villas, the restaurant/

sports bar is a popular meeting place with ocean views. Local and international cuisine.
🕐 Closed Aug.–Oct.
🚭 D, MC, V

■ TURKS & CAICOS

GRAND TURK

🏨 OSPREY BEACH HOTEL
$$
DUKE STREET, COCKBURN TOWN
TEL 649/946-2666
ospreybeachhotel.com
Attractive beachfront rooms/suites with cool, crisp decor and patio/balcony; some four-posters (atrium rooms face inner courtyard). Bar, restaurant, scuba packages.
[i] 37 ⛱ 📶 Free in some rooms 🚭 All major cards

🏨 ISLAND HOUSE
$–$$
COCKBURN TOWN
TEL 649/232-1439
islandhouse.tc
A few minutes outside town, overlooking North Creek, this comfy and quiet complex features spacious and well-equipped suites. Transportation required.
[i] 8 🏊 ⛱ 📶 Free 🚭 All major cards

🏨 SALT RAKER INN
🍽 $
DUKE STREET, COCKBURN TOWN
TEL 649/946-2260
saltrakerinn.com
Dating from the 1840s, this charming old inn (once a Bermudian shipwright's home) has a hospitable atmosphere; good restaurant, **The Secret Garden;** and lovely shady garden.
[i] 13 🏊 📶 Free in restaurant 🚭 MC, V

🍽 BIRDCAGE RESTAURANT
$$–$$$

OSPREY BEACH HOTEL,
DUKE STREET, COCKBURN TOWN
TEL 649/946-2666
Salads and fish sandwiches for
lunch; classic steaks and seafood
for dinner, but the real key to
its success is the twice-weekly
barbecue nights (Wed. & Sun.).
Great atmosphere, live music.
MC, V

THE SANDBAR
$$
DUKE STREET, COCKBURN TOWN
TEL 649/946-1111
Popular hangout for sundown-
ers. Tasty, no-nonsense menu
of fish sandwiches, cracked
conch, quesadillas, and burgers
served on the deck overlooking
the beach.
MC, V

MIDDLE CAICOS

BLUE HORIZON RESORT
$$
CONCH BAR
TEL 649/946-6141
bhresort.com
Unpretentious beachfront
cottages and villas sporting
bright blue tin roofs. Kitchens,
screened porches, bicycles
available. Spectacular views,
but quite remote.
5 cottages + 3 villas Free
MC, V

NORTH CAICOS

PELICAN BEACH HOTEL
$–$$
WHITBY
TEL 649/946-7112
pelicanbeach.tc
This was the first locally owned
hotel on the island and has a
friendly, laid-back atmosphere.
Very quiet; no phones. Rooms
are showing their age but are
charming nonetheless.
14 Free in public
areas & some rooms
All major cards

**HOLLYWOOD BEACH
SUITES**
$
HOLLYWOOD BEACH DRIVE,
WHITBY
TEL 649/231-1020 OR
U.S./CANADA 800/551-2256
hollywoodbeachsuites.com
Thoughtfully equipped one-
bed suites in a truly stunning
beachfront location a short
walk/bike ride from restaurants
and grocery stores. Free bikes
and kayaks, home-cooked
meals by arrangement.
4 suites P Free
MC, V

PROVIDENCIALES

**GRACE BAY CLUB
& VILLAS**
$$$$$
GRACE BAY ROAD
TEL 649/946-5050
OR 800/946-5757
gracebayclub.com
Intimate, all-suites hotel
with excellent resort facilities
featuring stylishly equipped
ocean-facing accommodations
with kitchens and terraces (no
children under 12 in hotel).
Families can opt for the villa
complex equipped with health
club, spa, and kids' club.
59 suites Free
All major cards

**GANSEVOORT TURKS +
CAICOS**
$$$$–$$$$$
LOWER BIGHT ROAD, GRACE BAY
TEL 649/941-7555
OR 888/844-5986
gansevoortturksandcaicos
.com
Set slightly apart from Grace
Bay's hotel strip, this upscale
boutique resort is long on style
and substance. Sleek urban
chic married to a cool cream
and blue palette, infinity pool,
luxurious spa, and bistro-bar.
91 (incl. 4 penthouse suites)
P Free
All major cards

SIBONNÉ BEACH HOTEL
$–$$
GRACE BAY
TEL 649/946-5547
OR 800/528-1905
sibonne.com
Small, casual, and right on the
beach, Sibonné is the oldest
property on the bay, but one
of the friendliest. Good value
courtyard and fine ocean-view
rooms (plus airy one-bedroom
apartment), bar and veranda
dining in the **Bay Bistro**. Close
to diving and amenities.
30 Free
All major cards

COCO BISTRO
$$$$–$$$$$
GRACE BAY ROAD
TEL 649/946-5369
cocobistro.tc
Canopied beneath the fronds
of the island's largest palm
tree grove, this superior bistro
serves elegantly crafted dishes
full of island flavors. Sample
homemade conch ravioli,
lobster thermidor, or shrimp
curry with coconut rice and
banana chutney. Impeccable
service, reservations required.
Closed L, Mon.
All major cards

SOMETHING SPECIAL

**INFINITI RESTAURANT
& RAW BAR**
$$$$–$$$$$
GRACE BAY CLUB
TEL 649/946-5050
Provo's only gourmet beachfront dining experience simply
oozes island chic and ambience.
Romantic lounge areas with
fire pits, fabulous cocktails, live
music and a menu full of temptations such as tamarind roast
salmon, chicken with lemon
quinoa, molten chocolate cake,
super-fresh ceviche, and killer
liquid desserts from the raw
bar. Dinner only.
All major cards

Elevator Air-conditioning Indoor pool Outdoor pool Health club Wi-Fi Credit cards

🍴 CAICOS CAFÉ
$$$
GRACE BAY ROAD, GRACE BAY
TEL 649/946-5278
Pretty West Indian cottage with a shady terrace ideal for a romantic evening. Perfectly grilled steaks, lobster and shrimp from the barbecue, French-Mediterranean specialties, and an impressive wine list.
🕐 Closed Sun. 🔲 AE, MC, V

🍴 DA CONCH SHACK
$–$$
BLUE HILLS BEACH
TEL 649/946-8877
daconchshack.com
The best fresh conch in the islands. Conch every which way from spiced to salad via cracked and fritters, plus chilled rum punch in an eye-catching beachside shack. Good for escapists.
🔲 All major cards

SALT CAY

🍴 PORTER'S ISLAND THYME
$$–$$$
TEL 649/946-6977
islandthyme.tc
Start the day with homemade cinnamon-dusted doughnuts; snap up a zesty chicken sandwich for lunch; and head back for cocktails and delicious Caribbean-Asian fusion cuisine at dinnertime. Fun island hangout with accommodations in oceanfront cottages.
🔲 MC, V

■ DOMINICAN REPUBLIC

CENTRAL HIGHLANDS

🏨 RANCHO BAIGUATE
$–$$
JARABACOA
TEL 809/574-6890 OR U.S./CANADA 646/727-7783
ranchobaiguate.com

The country's only dedicated adventure-sports center, set on extensive grounds bordered by the Baiguate and Jimenoa Rivers just outside Jarabacoa. Activities include trekking, mountain biking, quad-biking, canyoning, paragliding, rafting, plus expeditions to Pico Duarte. The center has a large pool, restaurant, and bar. Accommodations (including dorms) are clean and simple, and will appeal to those seeking peace and quiet.
🛈 27 🔲 🔲 All major cards

NORTH COAST

CABARETE

🏨 NATURA CABANA
$–$$
PLAYA PERLA MARINA
TEL 809/571-1507
naturacabana.com
Eco-sensitive, upscale Robinson Crusoe thatched-roof cabanas and rustic stone bungalows shaded by palms and almond trees on the beachfront just outside Cabarete. Take a yoga class, relax with a spa therapy. Family-run and kid friendly; healthy eating.
🛈 11 🔲 🛜 Free 🔲 All major cards

🏨 VELERO BEACH RESORT
$
CALLE DE PUNTA 1
TEL 809/571-9727
velerobeach.com
Separated from the waterfront by palm-shaded lawns, this is a pleasantly quiet corner in easy walking distance of shops, supermarkets, and the main beach area. Suites/condos with fridges or decent kitchenettes, all day bar-restaurant, family friendly.
🛈 50 rooms & suites 🅿️ 🔲 🔲 📺 🛜 Free 🔲 All major cards

PUERTO PLATA

🏨 CASA COLONIAL BEACH & SPA
$$$–$$$$$
PLAYA DORADA
TEL 809/320-3232 OR 866/376-7831
casacolonialhotel.com
A delectable boutique hotel, impeccably tasteful from the rooftop infinity pool to the wine cellar via spacious suites with Roman tubs in the bathroom, Asian-Mediterranean cuisine, and a Bagua spa.
🛈 50 🅿️ 🔲 🔲 🛜 Free 🔲 All major cards

🏨 BLUE BAY VILLAS DORADAS
$$$
CALLE PRINCIPAL 538, PLAYA DORADA
TEL 809/320-3000
bluebayvillasdoradas.com
Relaxing adults-only all-inclusive with a great beachfront location adjacent to the Playa Dorada golf course. Simple, stylish rooms; attractive

and well-maintained grounds; excellent food and service; plus tennis, spa, and entertainment.

🛈 245 P 🅲 🔼 📶 Free in lobby 🅢 All major cards

🏨 GRAN VENTANA BEACH RESORT
$$–$$$

PLAYA DORADA

TEL 809/320-2111

OR 866/376-7831

granventanahotel.com

Family-friendly all-inclusive option with a kids' club and activities galore, ranging from merengue classes to beach volleyball and evening shows. The property is arranged as three low-rise "villages" with distinct family and quiet areas. Charming staff, good food.

🛈 506 rooms & suites

P 🅲 🔼 📶 🅢 All major cards

🍴 THE BEACH CLUB AT SEA HORSE RANCH
$$–$$$

CABARETE-SOSÙA HWY. 5

TEL 809/571-4995

sea-horse-ranch.com

From an airy, palm-thatched rotunda perched on a low bluff above the shore, the Beach Club's panoramic ocean views alone are worth the trek to the exclusive Sea Horse Ranch villa community. Fortunately, there's a great menu, too, running the gamut from Italian filet mignon with porcini or pasta and pizza to fresh, zingy Asian and Middle Eastern salads.

🕐 Closed Mon.

🅢 All major cards

🍴 MARES RESTAURANT
$$

FRANCISCO J. PEYNADO 6A

TEL 809/261-3330

maresrestaurant.com

Tucked away in an unassuming house, this gastronomic hideaway is a revelation. A pretty garden terrace, small pool, and twinkly lights accompany chef Rafael Vasquez's esoteric

cuisine. Full of personal touches, it spans the globe from seared scallop and pumpkin risotto via meltingly slow-cooked rack of lamb to a Dominican take on sushi.

🕐 Closed L & Mon.

🅢 All major cards

PENINSULA DE SAMANÁ

🏨 VILLA SERENA
$

LAS GALERAS

TEL 809/538-0000

villaserena.com

Pretty colonial-style villa hotel set in tropical gardens by the beach. Spacious rooms with generous verandas and sea views, some four-posters. Conservatory restaurant, spa treatments, yoga, excursions by arrangement, free kayaks and bikes.

🛈 21 P 🅲 🔼 📶 Free

🅢 All major cards

🍴 MI CORAZON
$$$–$$$$

CALLE DUARTE 7, LAS TERRENAS

TEL 829/655-0401 (English) OR 809/240-5329 (Spanish)

micorazon.com

Traditional town house on the main street with an upstairs dining room arranged around a galleried courtyard open to the stars. Great mojitos from the bar, ambitious international cuisine with local and Asian touches, patisseries from the street-level bakery.

🕐 Closed L, Mon. mid-Oct.– April, & Sun.–Mon. May– mid-Oct.

SANTO DOMINGO

🏨 HOSTAL NICOLAS DE OVANDO MGALLERY
$$$–$$$$$

CALLE LAS DAMAS

TEL 809/685-9955

mgallery.com

A luxurious landmark hotel carved out of a historic

16th-century residence in the heart of the colonial city. The elegant conversion is a chic modern take on colonial style with high ceilings, exposed stonework, and spacious bedrooms featuring minimalist four-posters and rattan furniture. Fine dining, cigar club.

🛈 104 P 🅲 🔼 🎽 📶 Free

🅢 All major cards

🏨 RENAISSANCE JARAGUA HOTEL & CASINO
$$–$$$

AV. GEORGE WASHINGTON 367

TEL 809/221-2222

renaissance-hotels.marriott.com

On the Malecón, this well-managed and recently renovated hotel ticks all the boxes. Tennis facilities, free-form pool, choice of bars and dining.

🛈 300 🛗 🅲 🔼 🎽 📶 Free

🅢 All major cards

🏨 HOTEL DOÑA ELVIRA
🍴 $

PADRE BILLINI 207

TEL 809/221-7415

dona-elvira.com

Behind a discreet street entrance, this lovingly restored, beamed and tiled 16th-century colonial mansion B&B is a haven. Simple rooms, comfy beds, charming pool patio.

🛈 15 🔼 📶 Free 🅢 All major cards

🍴 MESÓN DE BARI
$$$$

EUGENIA MARIA DE HOSTOS 302

TEL 809/687-4091

Reservations are advisable for this memorable artist's haunt. Top-notch cocina criolla from mouthwatering crab empanadas to superb grilled chicken. Artwork on every wall, family friendly, and great service.

🅢 All major cards

🍴 VESUVIO MALECON
$$$$
AV. GEORGE WASHINGTON 521
TEL 809/221-1954
vesuvio.com.do
Vesuvio specializes in gourmet seafood and Italian dishes.
🅢 All major cards

🍴 EL MESÓN DE LA CAVA
$$$
AV. MIRADOR DEL SUR 1
TEL 809/533-2818
elmesondelacava.com
Funky restaurant set in a natural cave 50 feet (15 m) belowground and reached via a spiral staircase. Renowned for steaks and seafood. Live music in the evening.
🅢 All major cards

🍴 EL CONUCO
$–$$
CALLE CASIMIRO DE MOYA 152
TEL 809/686-0129
elconuco.com.do
Highly atmospheric restaurant with a country theme. The food is excellent, and at lunchtime there is a popular buffet. When the waiters and waitresses are finished serving they perform a song-and-dance routine. Touristy but fun.
🅢 All major cards

SOUTHEAST COAST

🏨 CASA DE CAMPO
$$$$$
LA ROMANA
TEL 809/523-3333
casadecampo.com.do
Easily accessible from its own international airport a five-minute ride from check-in, Casa de Campo claims to be the Caribbean's most complete resort. Accommodations include luxury villas and spacious rooms. Its three championship golf courses are world famous; it also offers a shooting center, polo stables, its own beach and marina, dive shop, 20 restaurants, and 13 tennis courts.

ⓘ 247 rooms & suites + 60 villas 🅢 🅢 🅢 🅢 🅢 Free
🅢 All major cards

🏨 IBEROSTAR BÁVARO
$$$
PLAYA BÁVARO, HIGÜEY
TEL 809/221-6500
OR 888/923-2722
iberostar.com
Spacious and comfortable all-inclusive resort on a good stretch of Punta Cana's beach. Diving, golf, water sports.
ⓘ 596 🅢 🅢 🅢 🅢 Free
🅢 All major cards

🏨 WESTIN PUNTACANA RESORT & CLUB
$$–$$$$
PLAYA BLANCA, PUNTACANA
TEL 809/959-2222
westinpuntacana.com
A new beachfront resort hotel within a vast Puntacana estate, which incorporates an international airport. Panoramic ocean view rooms/suites, kids' club, golf, tennis, walking trails, water sports, sportfishing.
ⓘ 200 rooms & suites 🅟
🅢 🅢 🅢 🅢 🅢 Charge
🅢 All major cards

🍴 PLAYA BLANCA
$$
PUNTACANA RESORT & CLUB, PLAYA BLANCA
TEL 809/595-2714 EXT. 2234
Shaded by rustling palm trees right on the beach, this is a great place for Dominican-style tapas and a cold beer, a prawn and green papaya salad, or fine grills and local seafood served up in rustic cast-iron dishes.
🅢 All major cards

■ PUERTO RICO

CENTRAL HIGHLANDS

🏨 CASA GRANDE
🍴 MOUNTAIN RETREAT
$

RTE. 612, KM 0.3, UTUADO
TEL 787/894-3939
hotelcasagrande.com
Set high up in the mountains of the Cordillera Central, with stunning views across an unspoiled valley, this peaceful, small hotel has simple rooms equipped with balcony and hammock. Once a coffee plantation, the house is surrounded by tropical gardens, and there are several hiking trails in the surrounding hills. It also has its own restaurant.
ⓘ 21 🅢 🅢 All major cards

CULEBRA

🏨 CLUB SEABOURNE
🍴 **$$–$$$**
RTE. 252, PLAYA SARDINAS II
TEL 787/742-3169
clubseabourne.com
Charming boutique hotel with simple but chic rooms and villas tucked into a tree-shaded hillside above Fulladoza Bay. Wooden floors, pastel colors, and natural fabrics. Private dock, water sports, and a good Nuevo Latino restaurant on the screened porch.
ⓘ 12 🅟 🅢 🅢 🅢 🅢 Free in lobby 🅢 All major cards

DORADO

🏨 EMBASSY SUITES BY HILTON DORADO DEL MAR
$$–$$$
201 DORADO DEL MAR BLVD.
TEL 787/796-6125
embassysuites3.hilton.com
Two-room suites fronting Dorado Beach 25 miles (40 km) from San Juan, this is a good location and an excellent family option. Guests have access to water sports, tennis, spa, shopping, and restaurants with ocean views.
ⓘ 174 🅟 🅢 🅢 🅢 🅢 Free in lobby 🅢 All major cards

FAJARDO

⊞ EL CONQUISTADOR RESORT
$$$–$$$$$
AV. EL CONQUISTADOR
TEL 787/863-1000 OR
888/543-1282
elconresort.com
This huge complex occupies a commanding position above the point where the Atlantic and Caribbean meet. Fabulous ocean views and lush landscaping; bright, spacious rooms with a splash of crisp color; also Las Casitas, one-, two-, and three-bedroom villas. There is no beach, but the hotel boasts its own offshore island, with regular shuttle service from the on-site marina. There is a water park with speed slides and a lazy river, tennis, horseback riding, and the 18-hole Arthur Hills championship golf course. The resort has more than 20 restaurants.
🛈 765 rooms & suites + 235 villas 🛗 ❄ 🏊 🏋
📶 Free 🖪 All major cards

GUANICA

⊞ COPAMARINA BEACH RESORT
$$–$$$
KM 6.5, RTE. 333, CANA GORDA
TEL 787/821-0505
OR 800/468-4553
copamarina.com
On 20 acres (8 ha) of lawned gardens at the water's edge, this resort offers water sports, diving, tennis, mountain biking, and ecotours in the neighboring Guánica Biosphere Reserve. The hotel has two pools, two restaurants, a spa, and a fitness center. The comfortable rooms are decorated in bright tropical colors and equipped with all amenities.
🛈 106 ❄ 🏊 🏋 📶 Free
🖪 All major cards

PONCE

⊞ PONCE PLAZA HOTEL & CASINO
$
CALLE REINA (AT UNION)
TEL 787/813-5050
ponceplazahotelandcasino.com
Dating from 1882, this jaunty canary yellow small independent hotel is centrally located on a leafy square. Colonial-style suites and rooms in a contemporary annex, cozy coffee bar, good restaurant and pool seating in a courtyard, helpful advice from the front desk staff.
🛈 69 rooms & suites 🅿 🏊
🏋 📶 Free 🖪 All major cards

🍽 PITO'S SEAFOOD
$$$
LAS CUCHARAS
TEL 787/841-4977
pitosseafoodpr.com
With a large terrace overlooking the ocean just outside Ponce, Pito's is a great place for a long, indulgent lunch. Specialties include plantain stuffed with shrimp and lobster, stuffed clams, grilled mahimahi, and red snapper in creole sauce.
🖪 All major cards

RINCÓN

SOMETHING SPECIAL

⊞ HORNED DORSET PRIMAVERA
$$$$$
KM 3, ROAD 429
TEL 787/823-4030
OR 800/633-1857
horneddorset.net
Undoubtedly the island's most chic and exclusive hotel, this hacienda-style resort is impeccably run and caters to a discerning clientele seeking absolute tranquility and relaxation—there are no TVs or radios, and there's a yoga pavilion in the lovely gardens. The luxurious split-level villa suites, furnished with antiques and a hint of Moroccan elegance, are immaculate. Superb food is served in two restaurants, including gourmet **Restaurant Aaron** (see below).
🛈 15 ❄ 🏊 🏋 📶 Free
🖪 All major cards

🍽 RESTAURANT AARON
$$$$
KM 3, ROAD 429
TEL 787/823-4030
One of the island's top restaurants outside the capital, Restaurant Aaron's sophisticated setting and imaginative cuisine have won it many admirers. Dishes include shrimp and fennel bisque, grilled tuna with mango salad, and grilled marlin with fresh herbs and lemon.
🕐 Closed L & Mon.–Wed. off-season 🖪 All major cards

RIO GRANDE

⊞ WYNDHAM GRAND RIO MAR BEACH RESORT & SPA
$$$–$$$$$
6000 RIO MAR BLVD.
TEL 787/888-6000
OR 887/636-0636
wyndhamriomar.com
Well-run property on its own beach, handy for El Yunque National Forest. The hotel's impressive range of facilities includes a spa and fitness center, tennis center, restaurants, casino, shops, a full range of water sports, and swimming pools. The 481-acre (195 ha) complex also includes two world-class golf courses (the River Course and the Ocean Course).
🛈 600 rooms & 72 suites
🛗 ❄ 🏊 🏋 📶 Free
🖪 All major cards

🍽 PALIO AT THE WYNDHAM GRAND RIO MAR
$$$$
6000 RIO MAR BLVD.
TEL 787/888-6000

🛗 Elevator ❄ Air-conditioning 🏊 Indoor pool 🏊 Outdoor pool 🏋 Health club 📶 Wi-Fi 🖪 Credit cards

The resort's top restaurant offers a wonderfully tempting array of dishes styled with Italian flair. Specialties include fish baked in a banana leaf, with tomatoes, fresh peppers, and onions.

🚳 All major cards

SAN JUAN

🏨 HOTEL EL CONVENTO
$$–$$$$

100 CALLE CRISTO, OLD SAN JUAN
TEL 787/723-9020
elconvento.com

This small, deluxe hotel occupies the top floors of a historic building (once a convent) in the heart of the old town; the inner courtyard features cafés, restaurants, galleries, and shops. All rooms have views over San Juan and the sea. Access to beach club at sister hotel on Isla Verde.

🛏 58 rooms & suites
🔁 🅢 🚲 🍽 📶 Free
🚳 All major cards

🏨 GALLERY INN
$–$$$

NORZAGARAY 204,
OLD SAN JUAN
TEL 787/722-1808
OR 866/572-2783
thegalleryinn.com

Charming and idiosyncratic hostelry in an old rambling building, with great views over the venerable colonial city.

🛏 22 rooms & suites
📶 Free in public areas
🅢 🚳 All major cards

🍴 PIKAYO
$$$$

CONRAD PLAZA HILTON, 999
ASHFORD AVE., CONDADO
TEL 787/721-6194

Chef Wilo Benet is an established star in the island's culinary world, and his restaurant is one of the most celebrated in the city. His imaginative take on *criolla* cuisine and perfectionist attitude ensure a steady stream

of repeat customers to this stylish, contemporary restaurant.

🕐 Closed L 🚳 All major cards

🍴 MARMALADE
$$$

CALLE FORTALEZA 317,
OLD SAN JUAN
TEL 787/724-3969
marmaladepr.com

Cool lighting and a '60s vibe to the orange decor provide a stylish backdrop for chef Peter Schintler's sensational take on Latino cuisine. Signature white bean soup with truffles, decadent desserts (don't miss the beignets), and wonderful service.

🕐 Closed L 🚳 All major cards

🍴 PAMELA'S CARIBBEAN CUISINE
$$$

NUMERO UNO GUESTHOUSE,
CALLE SANTA ANA 1,
OCEAN PARK
TEL 787/726-5010

On the beach with indoor and outdoor dining, Pamela's has a relaxed atmosphere with first-class service that matches the culinary creations emerging from chef Esteban Torres's kitchen. Fresh seafood is the mainstay, accompanied by an extensive wine list and some delectable desserts.

🚳 All major cards

🍴 DRAGONFLY
$$

364 CALLE FORTALEZA,
OLD SAN JUAN
TEL 787/977-3886
dragonflysanjuan.com

In the heart of the hip SOFO (South Fortaleza) sector of Old San Juan, Dragonfly is a popular eatery with a difference, offering Latin-Asian cuisine dishes such as pork and amarillo dumplings and Peking duck nachos.

🕐 Closed L 🚳 AE, MC, V

🍴 CASA CORTÉS CHOCOBAR
$

CALLE SAN FANCISCO 210,
OLD SAN JUAN
TEL 787/722-0499
casacortespr.com

A retro-styled chocoholic pit stop that displays the Cortés family's heritage on its walls. Enjoy churros with dipping chocolate and frozen chocolate drinks; chocolate even sneaks into savory toasties and entrées.

🕐 Closed D & Mon. 🚳 MC, V

VIEQUES

🏨 W RETREAT & SPA
🍴 $$$$$

RTE. 200, KM 3.2
TEL 787/741-4100
wvieques.com

Fabulous beachfront retreat long on style (think Sean Connery–era Bond with a contemporary twist) and mood with stunning pools, palm trees, fire pits, and tree swing seats. Private beaches, a spa, tennis, diving, kayaks, and upscale Puerto Rican–inspired dining at the **Sorcé**.

🛏 176 rooms & suites
🅿 🅢 🚲 🍽 📶 Free
🚳 All major cards

🍴 CARAMBOLA
$$$

INN ON THE BLUE HORIZON,
RTE. 996, ESPERANZA
TEL 787/741-3318

Pretty island-style dining room extending onto a terrace under the stars. A good mix of local seafood (ceviche, grills) alongside house-smoked pork ribs and delicious chicken *pinchos* flavored with tamarind and cilantro.

🚳 All major cards

■ VIRGIN ISLANDS

U.S. VIRGIN ISLANDS

ST. CROIX

🏨 THE BUCCANEER
$$$–$$$$
GALLOWS BAY
TEL 340/712-2100
OR 800/255-3881
thebuccaneer.com
Luxurious family-run resort with secluded beaches, water sports, golf, tennis, kids' club, and eco-packages. Spacious accommodations (all with private balconies) in the attractive hilltop main building or nearer the beach; also family villas and deluxe suites.
🛈 138 P ⬆ 🏊 🏋 🎛 Free 🅰 All major cards

🏨 RENAISSANCE ST. CROIX CARAMBOLA BEACH RESORT & SPA
$$$
KINGSHILL
TEL 340/778-3800
OR 888/503-8760
renaissance-hotels.marriott.com
Elegant former Rockresort spread across 28 beachfront acres (12 ha) with a Trent Jones–designed golf course and excellent sports facilities. Generous suite-style rooms with screened porches and fully equipped kitchenettes.
🛈 157 P 🏊 🏋 🎛 Free 🅰 All major cards

🏨 MOUNT VICTORY CAMP ECO-LODGE
$
CREQUE DAM ROAD, P.O. BOX 1456, FREDERIKSTED
TEL 340/201-7983
mtvictorycamp.com
Small, friendly eco-camp in a valley enfolded in the green hills west of Frederiksted. Four bungalows (sleeping up to six) and one apartment are fashioned from local hardwoods.

All have kitchenette, linen, cold water. Hot water bathhouse. Campsites available.
🛈 5 units P 🎛 Free at Pavillion 🅰 No credit cards

🏨 THE WAVES AT CANE BAY
$
CANE BAY
TEL 340/718-1815
thewavescanebay.com
Airy and comfortable studios and a villa on the waterfront a couple of minutes' walk from the beach. Low-key and friendly; good snorkeling and diving; on-site restaurant.
🛈 11 studios, 1 villa P
🛎 Some rooms 🏊 🅰 All major cards

🍴 THE BLUE MOON
$$$
17 STRAND STREET, FREDERIKSTED
TEL 340/772-2222
thebluemoonstcroix.com
Bistro cum jazz spot (live music Fri. night & Sun. brunch) facing the waterfront with a garden patio and eclectic menu—Cajun shrimp, Luna Pie (cheese and vegetable phyllo pastry parcel), and hot, hot, hot creole chicken.
🕐 Closed Mon.
🅰 All major cards

🍴 RUM RUNNERS
$$–$$$
HOTEL CARAVELLE, BOARDWALK, CHRISTIANSTED
TEL 340/773-6585
rumrunnersstcroix.com
Location, location, location is a clue to Rum Runners' success. This local favorite enjoys a wonderful harborfront position in the center of town and serves up a pretty good burger, too. Ribs, steaks, pick-your-own lobster salad.
🅰 All major cards

🍴 SAVANT
$$–$$$
4C HOSPITAL STREET, CHRISTIANSTED
TEL 340/713-8666
savantstx.com
A pretty, twinkly garden patio setting for an eclectic menu featuring the likes of chicken lollipops with crispy wonton and spicy dressing, signature goat cheese–stuffed filet, and a zingy Cruzian lime pie. Good cocktails, pleasant service.
🕐 Closed L & Sun.
🅰 All major cards

🍴 OFF THE WALL
$–$$
NORTH SHORE (RTE. 80), CANE BAY
TEL 340/718-4771
otwstx.com
An all-day beach bar and restaurant that can offer anything from eggs Benedict for breakfast to spectacular sunsets and a hammock for a postprandial nap. Burgers, pizzas, nachos, and seafood, plus jazz on weekends.
🅰 All major cards

🍴 PIER 69
$
CUSTOM HOUSE STREET, FREDERIKSTED
TEL 340/772-0069
A block back from the waterfront, this is the spot for great barbecue. Grab a courtyard table, check out the daily specials (pulled pork, tenderloin, burgers and lashings of epic bbq sauce). Homemade breads and don't miss the cheesecake.
🅰 MC, V

🍴 POLLY'S AT THE PIER
$
3 STRAND STREET, FREDERIKSTED
TEL 340/719-9434
The cognoscenti pile in for the cinnamon buns and breakfast waffles early in the day. Later

you'll find hungry divers chomping their way through gourmet grilled cheese sandwiches, quesadillas, and Asian chicken wraps. This cheery eatery is located in a typical island cottage opposite the pier.

🕐 Closed D 🗖 MC, V

ST. JOHN

SOMETHING SPECIAL

🏨 **CANEEL BAY RESORT**
$$$$$
CANEEL BAY
TEL 340/776-6111
OR 888/ROSEWOOD
caneelbay.com
Classic Laurance Rockefeller–built luxury resort on a stunning 170-acre (68 ha) peninsula site with seven beaches. Rooms in two-story blocks or stone-walled cottages strung along the shore (no phone, TV, or air-conditioning); tennis, water sports, children's activities.

🛈 166 🅿 🏊 🎾 🛜 Free
🗖 All major cards

🏨 **GALLOWS POINT RESORT**
$$$$–$$$$$
CRUZ BAY
TEL 340/776-6434
OR 800/323-7229
gallowspointresort.com
Very comfortable rental suites (individually decorated) in two-story units amid gardens, five minutes' walk from Cruz Bay town. Swimming and snorkeling from the shore.

🛈 50 🅿 🍴 🏊 🛜 Free
🗖 All major cards

🏨 **CONCORDIA ECO-RESORT**
$
CONCORDIA
TEL 340/693-5855
OR 800/392-9004
concordiaeco-resort.com
Tranquil and remote surrounded by national park

forest, Concordia's eco-tents and woodsy units cling to the hillside above Salt Pond Bay. The basic facilities are more than compensated for by the glorious views, trails, yoga, snorkeling in the bay, and a seasonal restaurant.

🛈 18 studios & condos + 25 tents 🅿 🛜 Free in some rooms
🗖 MC, V

🍴 **FISH TRAP**
$$$$
RAINTREE COURT, CRUZ BAY
TEL 340/693-9994
thefishtrap.com
Locals recommend this casual alfresco restaurant for its fresh fish specialties, grilled steaks, pasta dishes, and diet-breaking homemade desserts.

🕐 Closed L & Mon.
🗖 All major cards

🍴 **ASOLARE**
$$$–$$$$
NORTH SHORE ROAD
TEL 340/779-4747
asolarestjohn.com
Gorgeous views overlooking Cruz Bay and St. Thomas, and a dynamic fusion of Asian and Pacific Rim cuisine make this one of St. John's hottest dining experiences. There are a few classical French dishes among the Thai beef salads and specialty seafood dishes. Reservations advised.

🕐 Closed L 🗖 All major cards

🍴 **SWEET PLANTAINS**
$$$
16119 LITTLE PLANTATION, CORAL BAY
TEL 340/777-4653
sweetplantains-stjohn.com
Tasty Caribbean/creole cooking and rum samplers served up in a colorful dining room opening on to a courtyard by the waterfront. Meaty Cuban-style *ropa vieja* stews, great seafood, not-to-be-missed curry nights, and rich desserts.

🗖 All major cards

PRICES

HOTELS
An indication of the cost of a double room in the high season is given by **$** signs.

$$$$$	Over $750
$$$$	$500–$750
$$$	$350–$500
$$	$200–$350
$	Under $200

RESTAURANTS
An indication of the cost of a three-course meal without drinks is given by **$** signs.

$$$$$	Over $100
$$$$	$75–$100
$$$	$55–$75
$$	$35–$55
$	Under $35

🍴 **MORGAN'S MANGO**
$$
CRUZ BAY
TEL 340/693-8141
Lively dinner spot and bar with a lamp-lit wooden deck opposite the national park dock. International influences range from the Caribbean and South America to Asia; also a long cocktail menu and live music on Thursdays.

🕐 Closed L 🗖 All major cards

ST. THOMAS

🏨 **RITZ-CARLTON**
$$$$$
6900 GREAT BAY
TEL 340/775-3333
OR 800/542-8680
ritzcarlton.com
Sybaritic luxury in elegant faux-Italianate surroundings with gardens and tinkling fountains. All the balconied rooms have sea views. Excellent facilities include fine dining, tennis, boat trips, water sports, and a beach.

🛈 180 🅿 🍴 🏊 🎾 🛜 Free
🗖 All major cards

🏨 BOLONGO BAY BEACH RESORT

$$-$$$

7150 BOLONGO BAY

TEL 340/775-1800

OR 800/524-4746

bolongobay.com

Lively family-run beach resort property offering water-sports facilities, tennis, beach volleyball, and basketball courts.

🛈 65 🅿 🅱 🌊 🎽 📶 Free 🅲 All major cards

🏨 POINT PLEASANT RESORT

$$-$$$

ESTATE SMITH BAY

TEL 888/619-4010

pointpleasantresort.com

Spacious suites in a series of red-roofed villas spread across the hillside (kitchens, cable, balconies). Snorkeling from the beach, dive package, tennis, trails through 15 acres (6 ha) of tropical greenery.

🛈 80 suites 🅿 🅱 🌊 📶 Free 🅲 All major cards

🏨 SECRET HARBOUR BEACH RESORT

$$-$$$

6280 ESTATE NAZARETH

TEL 340/775-6550

OR 800/524-2250

secretharbourvi.com

Spacious studios and one- and two-bedroom housekeeping condos with tropical decor. Palm-lined beach, water-sports center, tennis.

🛈 69 🅿 🅱 🌊 📶 Free 🅲 All major cards

🏨 VILLA SANTANA

$

2602 BJERGE GARD 2D,

DENMARK HILL,

CHARLOTTE AMALIE

TEL 340/776-1311

villasantana.com

A steep climb from town, this historic small estate enjoys stunning views over the harbor. Six attractive villa rooms with

kitchens set in the lawned gardens, some with patio/terrace, bare rock walls, and antiques.

🛈 6 🅿 🌊 🅲 MC, V

🍽 BANANA TREE GRILLE

$$$$-$$$$$

BLUEBEARD'S CASTLE, 1331

ESTATE TAAMBURG,

CHARLOTTE AMALIE

TEL 340/776-4050

bananatreegrille.com

Perched atop Bluebeard's Hill, a top spot for sunset cocktails and captivating views over the harbor at dusk. The well-crafted and stylishly presented menu starts with the likes of chef's ravioli of the day and crab cakes with citrus aioli before steak house and seafood classics, followed by luscious desserts.

🕐 Closed L & Mon. 🅲 All major cards

🍽 OLD STONE FARM HOUSE

$$$$

MAHOGANY RUN GOLF COURSE

TEL 340/777-6277

oldstonefarmhouse.com

Fine dining amid the 200-year-old brick arches of a former sugar estate building. Sample a light garden vegetable strudel, Caribbean crab cakes, flash grilled tuna, or pan-seared potato-crusted pork loin with Calvados brandy sauce.

🕐 Closed L & Mon. 🅲 All major cards

🍽 GRANDE CRU

$$$-$$$$

YACHT HAVEN GRANDE

TEL 340/774-7263

grandecruvi.com

Grande Cru's veranda sits right over the water in this mega-yacht marina. Excellent burgers, club sandwiches, tapas, and charcuterie platters are among the lunchtime offerings. Chef's pasta and cracked pepper shrimp recommended in the evenings; long wine list.

🅲 All major cards

🍽 CUZZIN'S CARIBBEAN RESTAURANT & BAR

$-$$

7 BACK STREET,

CHARLOTTE AMALIE

TEL 340/777-4711

cuzzinsvi.com

Delicious local cooking in an attractive downtown brick dining room decorated with Carnival props and local art. Mutton stew, curried chicken, shrimp creole, and a host of tasty local side dishes.

🕐 Closed Sun. & D Tues. 🅲 All major cards

🍽 DUFFY'S LOVE SHACK

$-$$

RED HOOK PLAZA,

EAST END

TEL 340/779-2080

duffysloveshack.com

It's loud, it's fun—that applies to the decor, the waitstaff, the music, and the outrageous cocktails. Classic burgers and wings, plus coconut-smoked New York Strip and tamarind-honey ribs.

🅲 No credit cards

BRITISH VIRGIN ISLANDS

ANEGADA

🏨 ANEGADA REEF HOTEL

$$

SETTING POINT

TEL 284/495-8002

anegadareef.com

Total quiet in simple, charming rooms (oceanfront or garden), with three meals a day. Fishing and diving from the hotel boat, Jeep rentals.

🛈 20 🅿 🅱 📶 Free in restaurant 🅲 All major cards

TORTOLA

🏨 FRENCHMANS HOTEL

$$$-$$$$

FRENCHMANS CAY, WEST END

TEL 284/494-8811

frenchmansbvi.com

Tropical hideaway on a

---

secluded peninsula near Soper's Hole Marina. Attractive one- and two-bedroom cottages set on a hillside above the beach. Gorgeous views from swing seats on the veranda; tennis, kayaks, and snorkel gear. Good food in the clubhouse (breakfast included).

🛈 9 cottages 🅿 🚭 🛜 Free 🚭 All major cards

🏨 LONG BAY BEACH CLUB
$$$–$$$$
LONG BAY
TEL 284/495-4252
OR 866/237-3491
longbay.com
Very comfortable and well-equipped rooms and beachview suites on the hillside, and rustic waterfront cabanas perched on stilts. All boast generous decks, terraces, or balconies. Open-air restaurant, fine dining twice weekly, tennis, water sports.

🛈 72 🅿 🚭 🛜 Free
🚭 All major cards

SOMETHING SPECIAL

🏨 SCRUB ISLAND RESORT, SPA & MARINA
$$$$
VIA TORTOLA
TEL 284/394-3440
scrubisland.com
Guests are met with cocktails on the dock at this hideaway island property, a ten-minute boat ride from Trellis Bay. Deluxe rooms, well-equipped suites, fabulous pool, and lots to do. Island and boat tours with picnics, kayaks, paddleboards, golf carts to reach the best beach. Engaging staff.

🛈 61 rooms & suites + 7 villas
🚭 🚿 🍴 🛜 Free 🚭 All major cards

🏨 SUGAR MILL HOTEL
🍴 $$$–$$$$
APPLE BAY
TEL 284/495-4355
sugarmillhotel.com
Quiet hideaway attached to a

notable restaurant of the same name (see below). There are comfortable modern rooms and family suites, a two-bedroom villa, and two simple rooms in a wooden cottage set in rampant garden foliage.

🛈 23 🅿 🚭 Some rooms
🚿 🛜 Free 🚭 All major cards

🍴 BRANDYWINE ESTATE RESTAURANT
$$$–$$$$
BRANDYWINE BAY
TEL 284/495-2301
brandywinerestaurant.com
Tortola's most elegant dining room, with a terrace overlooking the Sir Francis Drake Channel. Florentine specialties grilled over charcoal, homemade pasta and sauces with fresh garden herbs, and plenty of Italian wines.

🕐 Closed L & Tues. (Mon.–Tues. in summer) 🚭 All major cards

🍴 THE DOVE
$$$
67 MAIN STREET, ROAD TOWN
TEL 284/494-0313
thedovebvi.com
You have to fight the locals for a table at this traditional West Indian gingerbread house. Small, creative menu of French/Asian-inspired dishes (dainty dumplings, softshell crab, Thai curries) and perfectly cooked steaks; sublime sorbets, chocolate soufflé. Upstairs, the more affordable BarFly serves drinks and tapas with a side of jazz.

🕐 Closed L & Sun.–Mon.
🚭 All major cards

🍴 SUGAR MILL
$$$
APPLE BAY
TEL 284/495-4355
sugarmillhotel.com
Lovely evening setting in the former boiling house of an old sugar mill; lunch is served in the bar. Cookbook writers Jinx and Jefferson Morgan offer a small but delicious daily menu:

Caribbean sweet potato soup with gingered shrimp, tropical game hen with orange curry butter, and garden vegetables.

🕐 Closed L 🚭 All major cards

🍴 QUITO'S GAZEBO
$–$$
CANE GARDEN BAY
TEL 284/495-4837
Bar-restaurant with a covered deck overhanging the beach. Burgers and sandwiches, fettuccine Alfredo, or grilled kingfish followed by homemade brownies or pecan pie. Quito himself leads the live music on Fri. and Sat. nights.

🚭 All major cards

VIRGIN GORDA

🏨 BITTER END YACHT CLUB
$$$$–$$$$$
NORTH SOUND
TEL 284/494-2746
OR 800/872-2392
beyc.com
Friendly yacht-club ambience, excellent sailing school, and a selection of kayaks, windsurfers, dinghies, and yachts. Hillside villas (good for families) or romantic thatched huts on stilts with wooden decks.

🛈 85 🚭 🚿 🛜 Free in restaurant 🚭 All major cards

🏨 ROSEWOOD LITTLE DIX BAY
$$$$–$$$$$
LITTLE DIX BAY
TEL 284/852-5500
OR 888/767-3966
littledixbay.com
Sister to Caneel Bay on St. John (USVI), casually elegant Little Dix bears the inimitable Rockefeller stamp. Hexagonal and stilted rooms catch the breeze, though air-conditioning (and phone) is an option here. Hiking, tennis, water sports, boat trips, children's program.

🛈 98, plus 4 villas 🅿 🚿
🍴 🛜 Free 🚭 All major cards

🏨 LEVERICK BAY HOTEL
$
LEVERICK BAY
TEL 284/495-7421
OR 800/848-7081
leverickbay.com
Brightly painted villas with sea views and amazingly afford-able rates for hotel rooms and one- and two-bedroom suites with kitchen. Tennis, spa, water sports, and dive shop.
🛏 18 🅿 ❄ 🏊 📶 Free
💳 All major cards

🍴 THE RESTAURANT AT LEVERICK BAY
$$–$$$
LEVERICK BAY MARINA
TEL 284/495-7154
Located at the top of the island, the beach bar makes a useful lunchtime pit stop serving salads, burgers, and pasta. In the evening, the terrace offers more sophisticated dining with lovely views over North Sound and a classic menu of steak, seafood, and rack of lamb.
💳 All major cards

🍴 TOP OF THE BATHS
$$
THE BATHS
TEL 284/495-5497
topofthebaths.com
A terrific position above The Baths augments the eclectic menu with views over the Sir Francis Drake Channel. Break-fast omelets and pancakes; lunchtime sandwiches, sushi, burgers, grills, jerk dishes; coconut rum cake.
🕐 Closed D 💳 All major cards

■ DUTCH CARIBBEAN

ARUBA

🏨 HYATT REGENCY ARUBA RESORT & CASINO
$$$$–$$$$$

J.E. IRAUSQUIN BLVD. 85,
PALM BEACH
TEL 297/586-1234 OR
800/554-9288
aruba.hyatt.com
Luxurious resort complex on 12 acres (5 ha) of beachfront. Attractive, well-equipped rooms and suites; spectacular pool area, tennis, golf, water sports, and Camp Hyatt offering kids' activities.
🛏 357 🅿 ❄ 🏊 📶 Free
💳 All major cards

🏨 AMSTERDAM MANOR BEACH RESORT
$$$–$$$$
J.E. IRAUSQUIN BLVD. 252,
EAGLE BEACH
TEL 297/527-1100 OR
800/969-2310
amsterdammanor.com
Pretty Dutch colonial-style all-suite resort. Studios and two-bedroom apartments with kitchens and sea views across from the beach. On-site mini market; water sports nearby.
🛏 72 🅿 ❄ 🏊 📶 Free
💳 All major cards

🏨 PLAYA LINDA BEACH RESORT
$$$–$$$$
J.E. IRAUSQUIN BLVD. 87,
PALM BEACH
TEL 297/586-1000
OR 800/992-2015
playalinda.com
Fully equipped one- and two-bedroom condos and three-bedroom town houses in a smart beachfront develop-ment. Tennis, water sports, shopping, and kids' programs.
🛏 214 🅿 ❄ 🏊 📶 Free
💳 All major cards

🍴 DRIFTWOOD
$$$–$$$$
KLIPSTRAAT 12, ORANJESTAD
TEL 297/583-2515
driftwoodaruba.com
Rugged, woodsy dining room with a seafood menu, much of it sourced by the owner's

fishing charter business. Great fish soup, catch of the day, lob-ster, garlic shrimp, and home-made *pan bati* (corn bread) to sop up the juices.
🕐 Closed L & Sun.
💳 All major cards

🍴 PAPIAMENTO
$$$–$$$$
WASHINGTON 61,
NOORD
TEL 297/594-5504
papiamentoaruba.com
Utterly charming family res-taurant set in the gardens of a 126-year-old manor house. The Ellis parents occupy the front of the house, while the children cook award-winning seafood, steaks, and special healthy and vegetarian dishes.
🕐 Closed L & Mon.
💳 All major cards

🍴 CUBA'S COOKIN'
$$$
RENAISSANCE MARKETPLACE,
L.G. SMITH BLVD. 30,
ORANJESTAD
TEL 297/588-0627
cubascookin.com
Cocktails, live music, Cuban art, and a menu of classic Cuban and Nuevo Latino favorites served up in a re-created 1960s Havana-style bar-restaurant. Generous Cuban sandwiches at lunchtime; try succulent roast pork, fried chicken, or Cuban steaks for dinner.
🕐 Closed Sun. in low season
💳 All major cards

🍴 GASPARITO
$$$
GASPARITO 3, NOORD
TEL 297/586-7044
OR 297/594-2550
gasparito.com
Combination restaurant and Aruban art gallery specializing in local cuisine and global dishes. Try creole fish soup, cheese-stuffed *keshi yena* chicken, barracuda ravioli, shrimp in coconut milk and

brandy, or a typical *stoba* (stew) with *funchi* (corn polenta).

🕐 Closed L & Sun.
🏧 All major cards

BONAIRE

🏨 HARBOUR VILLAGE BEACH CLUB
$$$–$$$$
KAYA GOB. N. DEBROT 73
TEL 599/717-7500
OR 800/424-0004
harbourvillage.com
Bonaire's top hotel boasts a palm-fringed beach and attractive rooms or housekeeping condos in Mediterranean-style villas. Also tennis, diving, a full-service marina, and shopping.
🛏 40 rooms + 20 suites
🅿️ 🚭 🌊 📶 Free
🏧 All major cards

🏨 CAPTAIN DON'S HABITAT
$$$
KAYA GOB. N. DEBROT 103
TEL 599/717-8290
OR 800/327-6709
habitatbonaire.com
Captain Don's is Bonaire's dive supremo, and his Habitat offers casual, comfortable suites, villas, and two-bedroom cottages, plus diving, water sports, and a minuscule beach.
🛏 93 🅿️ 🚭 🌊 📶 Free
🏧 All major cards

🏨 DIVI FLAMINGO BEACH RESORT
$–$$
J. A. ABRAHAM BLVD. 40
TEL 599/717-8285
OR 800/367-3484
diviflamingo.com
Low-rise hotel and a clutch of brightly painted studio suites set in waterfront gardens. A friendly atmosphere, tennis, a casino, and entertainment. Dive programs include special facilities for the disabled.
🛏 129 🅿️ 🚭 🌊 📶 Free
🏧 All major cards

🏨 SAND DOLLAR CONDOMINIUM RESORT
$–$$
KAYA GOB. N. DEBROT 79
TEL 599/717-8738
OR 800/288-4773
sanddollarbonaire.com
Studio, one-, two-, and three-bedroom individually furnished apartments with full kitchens and balconies overlooking the waterfront. Top-rated dive operation, tennis, grocery store, and wide-ranging activities.
🛏 50 🅿️ 🚭 🌊 📶 Free
🏧 All major cards

🍽 LA GUERNICA
$$$
KAYA BONAIRE 4C,
KRALENDIJK
TEL 599/717-5022
laguernica.com
Fine boardwalk location overlooking the harbor with a terrace and distinctly laid-back dining room with a tapas menu. Also good seafood, some Japanese dishes.
🏧 All major cards

🍽 PATAGONIA ARGENTINEAN STEAKHOUSE
$$$
KAYA GRANDI 52, KRALENDIJK
TEL 599/717-7725
Lively grill in the harborfront lighthouse. Gargantuan portions—the mixed grill could comfortably feed a small family on steak, ribs, chicken, pork loin, sausages, and seafood.
🕐 Closed Mon. & L Sat.–Sun.
🏧 D, MC, V

🍽 BISTRO DE PARIS & ZAZU BAR
$$–$$$
HARBOUR VILLAGE MARINA
TEL 599/717-7070
bistrodeparis.com
French bistro cuisine bursting with flavors, from the bouillabaisse and cognac-flambéed

shrimp to classic tarte tatin. Equally enjoyable is the bar menu featuring crêpes, burgers, and charcuterie served on the deck overlooking the marina.
🕐 Closed Sun. & L Sat.

🍽 MONA LISA BAR & RESTAURANT
$$–$$$$
KAYA GRANDI 15, KRALENDIJK
TEL 599/717-8718
This popular off-waterfront bar-diner serves excellent French-Dutch-international fare. Memorable tuna sashimi, beautifully cooked catch of the day, and classics from steak to schnitzel. Killer desserts, good wine list; open late.
🕐 Closed L & Sat.–Sun.
🏧 All major cards

CURAÇAO

🏨 BAOASE LUXURY RESORT
$$$$–$$$$$
WINTERSWIJKSTRAAT 2
TEL 5999/461-1799
OR U.S./CANADA 888/409-3506
baoase.com
Romantic Asian-inspired small resort featuring delectable ocean-view private suites and one- to three-bedroom villas with private pools and fully equipped kitchens. Exceptional service includes beach butlers, spa treatments, and an in-house tour guide.
🛏 23 suites & villas 🅿️ 🚭 🌊
🍽 📶 Free 🏧 All major cards

🏨 AVILA BEACH HOTEL
$$$–$$$$
PENSTRAAT 130–134,
WILLEMSTAD
TEL 5999/461-4377
OR 800/747-8162
avilahotel.com
The heart of this attractive waterfront complex is a charming historic hotel, a former governor's residence, now flanked by tasteful modern wings. The newest, the

---

🏨 Hotel 🛏 No. of guest rooms 🍽 Restaurant 🕐 Open/Closed Hours 🅿️ Parking 🚭 Nonsmoking

Octagon Wing, boasts a spa and pool.

[i] 165 [P] [A/C] [pool] [health] [wifi] Free [cards] All major cards

CURAÇAO MARRIOTT BEACH RESORT & EMERALD CASINO
$$–$$$$
PISCADERA BAAI
TEL 5999/736-8800
OR 800/223-6388
curacaomarriott.com
Elegant and very upscale resort with a contemporary colonial-style motif. Very comfortable accommodations with balcony or terrace set in landscaped gardens. Excellent water-sports facilities and dive shop, tennis, kids' program, full casino.

[i] 247 [P] [A/C] [pool] [health] [wifi] Free [cards] All major cards

ALL WEST APARTMENTS & DIVING
$
PLAYA PISKADO, WESTPUNT
TEL 5999/461-2310
allwestcuracao.com
Simple, bright, and attractive studios and apartments (sleep four) with kitchenettes, balconies/terraces, and sea views. Quiet location; dive packages and PADI courses.

[i] 7 [P] [wifi] Free [cards] All major cards

SOMETHING SPECIAL

BISTRO LE CLOCHARD
$$$$$
RIFFORT, WILLEMSTAD
TEL 5999/462-5666
bistroleclochard.com
Cozy dining room in the former fortress jail with a waterfront terrace. Delectable Swiss-French cuisine includes fondues, beef and shrimp cooked on a heated stone slab brought to the table, and rich chocolate desserts.

[cards] All major cards

GOUVERNEUR DE ROUVILLE
$$$
DE ROUVILLEWEG 9, OTROBANDA
TEL 5999/462-5999
de-gouverneur.com
There are great views over Annabaai from the terrace of the historic house named for an 18th-century Dutch governor. The menu ranges from salads, steak, or smoked snapper sandwiches at lunch to local dishes such as *sop'i piska* (fish soup), meaty *stoba* (stew), pasta, and grills.

[cards] All major cards

JAANCHIE'S
$$–$$$
WESTPUNT 15
TEL 5999/864-0126
Great spot for a lazy lunch. Outdoor tables shaded by greenery. Seafood and local dishes such as goat stew, or iguana for the adventurous.

[clock] Closed D [cards] All major cards

DANIEL
$$
WEG NAAR WESTPUNT
TEL 5999/864-8400
landhuisdaniel.com
Great setting on the shady, breeze-cooled veranda of a historic plantation house hotel set back from the sea. The imaginative menu is full of unusual ideas. Seasonal local game dishes, French-Italian-Mediterranean influences, and organic produce from the kitchen garden.

[cards] All major cards

SABA

QUEEN'S GARDENS RESORT
$$
TROY HILL
TEL 599/416-3494
queensaba.com
Growing out of the rain forest

hillside with glorious sea views framed by twin peaks from every balcony, deck, and the pool terrace, this a tranquil retreat for the grown-ups. Pared-down Saban chic in the spacious suites; lovely restaurant; honeymoon, diving and foodie packages.

[i] 12 suites [P] [service] On request [pool] [health] [wifi] Free [cards] All major cards

JULIANA'S
$–$$
WINDWARDSIDE
TEL 599/416-2269
OR 866/783-3319
julianas-hotel.com
A cute and cozy small hotel set in gardens bursting with colorful tropical plants. There are studio-style rooms with balconies and three adorable one- or two-bedroom Saban cottages, all simply but comfortably decorated.

[i] 12 [P] [pool] [wifi] Free [cards] All major cards

BRIGADOON
$$–$$$
WINDWARDSIDE
TEL 599/416-2380
The dining area is hemmed in by trellises, and the menu is long on seafood. Try the local bouillabaisse-style fish soup, shrimp creole, or fresh lobster.

[clock] Closed L & Tues. [cards] All major cards

SCOUT'S PLACE
$$
WINDWARDSIDE
TEL 599/416-2740
scoutsplace.com
A country inn with rooms and a local institution just above the village. The lively bar is a popular hangout, and the veranda restaurant serves plenty of fresh seafood and local dishes.

[cards] MC, V

[elevator] Elevator [A/C] Air-conditioning [indoor pool] Indoor pool [outdoor pool] Outdoor pool [health club] Health club [wifi] Wi-Fi [cards] Credit cards

SINT EUSTATIUS

🏨 OLD GIN HOUSE
$$
ORANJE BAAI
TEL 599/318-2319
OR 800/634-4907
oldginhouse.com
This historic inn is one of
the island's most appealing
addresses. Colonial-style rooms
with tiled floors and dark
wood furnishings overlook a
pool. Good restaurant; also
a grill and four ocean-facing
rooms over the road.
🚪 20 🅿 🅂 ⛴ 🛜 Free
🚫 All major cards

🍴 BLUE BEAD BAR
& RESTAURANT
$$–$$$
GALLOWS BAY
TEL 599/318-2873
Popular with locals and visi-
tors, this is the place to settle
in for sunset drinks and a bar
snack. Fresh catch of the day,
coconut shrimp, and other
seafood specials, plus good
pizzas, pasta, and burgers.
🕐 Closed Tues.
🚫 No credit cards

SINT MAARTEN

🏨 DIVI LITTLE BAY
BEACH RESORT
$$$
LITTLE BAY,
PHILIPSBURG
TEL 721/542-2333
OR 800/367-3484
diviresorts.com
An appealing jumble of red
roofs, whitewashed buildings,
and palm trees balanced on a
narrow peninsula just outside
Philipsburg. Good-value rooms
and suites in cool pastel shades
with wooden latticework.
Water sports, tennis, diving,
spa, and children's programs.
🚪 300 🅿 🅂 ⛴ 🛜 🛜 Free
🚫 All major cards

🏨 MARY'S BOON BEACH
PLANTATION
$$–$$$
117 SIMSON BAAI ROAD
TEL 721/545-7000
OR 800/497-5834
marysboon.com
Relaxed, friendly inn on a
3-mile (5 km) stretch of white-
sand beach close to shops and
restaurants. Colorful studios
and suites with Indonesian
furnishings. Charming staff.
Restaurant, honor bar.
🚪 37 🅿 🅂 ⛴ 🛜 Free in
most rooms 🚫 All major cards

🏨 PASANGGRAHAN
ROYAL GUESTHOUSE
$–$$
19 FRONT ST., PHILIPSBURG
TEL 721/542-3588
pasanhotel.net
Bayfront, 19th-century former
governor's residence where
Queen Wilhelmina once stayed.
The old-fashioned charm
extends to afternoon tea. Quiet,
central location; refurbished
rooms with colonial-style
furnishings and balconies.
🚪 30 🅂 🛜 Free
🚫 All major cards

🍴 ANTOINE
$$$
119 FRONT ST., PHILIPSBURG
TEL 721/542-2964
antoinerestaurant.com
Pretty blue-and-white terrace
dining room with a view across
the bay. Classical French menu
featuring chilled vichyssoise,
red snapper with sauce beurre
blanc, veal Dijonnaise, plus a
few Italian pasta dishes.
🚫 All major cards

🍴 THE GREENHOUSE
$$
BOBBY'S MARINA,
PHILIPSBURG
TEL 721/542-2941
thegreenhouserestaurant.com
A restaurant, bar, and night-
club rolled into one, this island
institution has been packing

them in since 1986. Happy
hour is a 150-minute marathon
complete with reduced price
appetizers. The official menu
offers steak, ribs, lobster, and
fresh Caribbean fish.
🚫 All major cards

🍴 ZEE BEST
$
PLAZA DEL LAGO, SIMSON BAAI
TEL 721/544-2477
zeebestrestaurant.com
Certainly zee best breakfast
you can find in Simson Baai.
Divine flaky almond croissants, apple turnovers, Danish
pastries. Generously stuffed
baguettes, chicken salad wraps,
and Zee pizzas for lunch.
🚫 No credit cards

ST.-MARTIN

SOMETHING SPECIAL

🏨 BELMOND LA
🍴 SAMANNA
$$$$$
BAIE LONGUE
TEL 590/87 64 00
OR 800/957-6128
belmond.com
Gorgeous superluxurious
enclave with a Moorish-
Mediterranean theme
set in tropical gardens
above the beach. Elegant
accommodations in rooms,
suites, and villas. Gourmet
restaurant, superb service,
tennis, and water sports.
🚪 82 🅿 🅂 ⛴ 🛟 🛜 Free
🚫 All major cards

🏨 LE PETIT HOTEL
$$$$–$$$$$
BLVD. DE GRAND CASE 248,
GRAND CASE
TEL 590/29 09 65
lepetithotel.com
Intimate and romantic boutique hotel in a stucco villa right
on the beachfront restaurant
row. Spacious studios and suites
with a sleek, contemporary

look, dark wood Balinese furnishings, and ocean-facing balconies. Helpful staff.
(i) 10 **P** **S** 🛜 Free
S All major cards

🏨 CAPTAIN OLIVER'S HOTEL
$$
OYSTER POND
TEL 590/87 40 26
captainolivershotel.com
Comfortable efficiency bungalows decorated in pastel shades and set on landscaped grounds beside a lagoon. The complex includes a marina, dive shop, and bar frequented by yachting types. Water taxi service to Dawn Beach.
(i) 50 **P** **S** 🛟 🛜 Free
S All major cards

🍴 LE PRESSOIR
$$$–$$$$
BLVD. DE GRAND CASE 30, GRAND CASE
TEL 590/87 76 62
lepressoir-sxm.com
A local institution set in a pretty 19th-century creole cottage across the street from its namesake antique salt press. Seriously good seafood such as lobster ravioli (there's a dedicated lobster menu) and Dover sole with a warm hint of turmeric. Fine wines and smiling service. Reservations.
🕐 Closed L year-round & Sun. in low season
S All major cards

🍴 LE TASTEVIN
$$$–$$$$
BLVD. DE GRAND CASE 86, GRAND CASE
TEL 590/87 55 45
letastevin-restaurant.com
Delicious French Caribbean fusion fare and attentive service in a casual/elegant setting overlooking the beach. Begin with prawns with mint and ginger; entrées might include duck breast smoked in Chinese tea or Moroccan-style lamb;

memorable crème brûlée. Reservations advised.
S All major cards

🍴 BISTRO NU
$$–$$$
ALLÉE DE L'ANCIENNE GEÔLE, MARIGOT
TEL 590/87 97 09
bistronu.com
Cozy dining room tucked away in an alley off rue de Hollande. Generous French creole brasserie-style cuisine (snails, *steak-frites*) and very popular.
🕐 Closed Sun. **S** MC, V

🍴 LA BELLE EPOQUE
$$–$$$
MARINA ROYALE, MARIGOT
TEL 590/87 87 70
Tables spill out onto a deck overlooking the marina and a long brasserie-style menu ranges from tasty salads and pizzas and pastas to creole Colombo chicken, duck, and grills. Luscious profiteroles and sorbets for dessert; plenty to enjoy from the wine list too.
S MC, V

◼ LEEWARD ISLANDS

ANGUILLA

🏨 CAP JULUCA
$$$$$
MAUNDAY'S BAY
TEL 264/497-6666
OR 888/858-5822
capjuluca.com
Gorgeous Moorish-style oasis set on a curving white-sand beach surrounded by lush gardens. Huge rooms decorated in restful beige and white, monumental double tubs in the suites, a tented restaurant, babysitting, and top-notch sports facilities.
(i) 79 rooms/suites + 6 pool villas **P** **S** 🛟 🍽 🛜 Free
S All major cards

🏨 CUISINART GOLF RESORT & SPA
$$$$$
RENDEZVOUS BAY
TEL 264/498-2000
OR 800/943-3210
cuisinartresort.com
Dazzling white beachfront accommodations trimmed with blue echo sand and sky. Light and spacious rooms, lovely villas, and a raft of activities: water sports, tennis, gym, Greg Norman–designed 18-hole golf course, and spa. A hydroponic farm supplies the restaurants with fresh vegetables and salad leaves.
(i) 100 rooms + 6 villas **P** **S** 🛟 🍽 🛜 Free
S All major cards

🏨 ANGUILLA GREAT HOUSE BEACH RESORT
$$
RENDEZVOUS BAY
TEL 264/497-6061
OR 800/583-9247
Friendly, unpretentious spot on a fabulous beach. Simple, spacious gingerbread cottages with tin roofs, shutters, and mahogany furnishings. Beach bar and restaurant.
(i) 35 **P** **S** Some 🛟 🛜 Free
S All major cards

🍴 BLANCHARDS
$$$$$
MEAD'S BAY
TEL 264/497-6100
blanchardsrestaurant.com
Candlelit tropical elegance on Mead's Bay. Melinda Blanchard's cuisine incorporates New American and Asian flavors with specialties such as lemon-glazed lobster dumplings and Japanese-inspired tuna fillet. Award-winning wine list. Reservations advised.
🕐 Closed L & Sun., also Mon. in low season
S All major cards

🍽 MANGO'S SEASIDE GRILL

$$$–$$$$

BARNES BAY

TEL 264/497-6479

mangosseasidegrill.com

Casual beachfront setting with a canvas awning over the wooden deck. Homemade bread, "famous" Barnes Bay lobster cakes, sesame-crusted snapper fillet marinated in soy, mouthwatering cakes and pies, and an extensive wine list.

🕐 Closed Tues.

🚫 All major cards

🍽 TASTY'S

$$–$$$

SOUTH HILL

TEL 264/497-2737

tastysrestaurant.com

Malliouhana-trained chef Dale Carty's upscale diner combines great island cuisine with a distinctly funky paint job. Traditional Johnny cakes for breakfast, knockout lobster salad for lunch, and delicious dinners.

🕐 Closed Thurs.

🚫 All major cards

🍽 JACQUIE'S RIPPLES

$$

SANDY GROUND

TEL 264/497-3380

A cozy indoor dining room and tables on the veranda (reserve ahead). The broad-ranging menu features grilled fish, Thai salads, pasta, crispy coconut chicken, and the like. The bar gets buzzy in the evening.

🚫 D, MC, V

ANTIGUA

🏨 CURTAIN BLUFF

🍽 $$$$$

MORRIS BAY

TEL 268/462-8400

OR 888/289-9898

curtainbluff.com

Antigua's most famous and elegant hotel perched on a steep bluff winding down to the beach. Excellent all-inclusive sports facilities and gourmet dining on the terrace or casual on the beach.

🛈 72 🅿 �.. 🏐 🛜 Free

🚫 All major cards

🏨 HAWKSBILL BY REX RESORTS

$$$$

FIVE ISLANDS

TEL 268/462-0301

rexresorts.com

Bright, comfy rooms and cottage-style accommodations along the shore (access to four beaches, including one "clothing optional"). Deluxe club cottages for romantics; beach cottages with connecting doors for families. Water sports, tennis, kids' activities.

🛈 99 🅿 🚭 🚭 🛜 Charge

🚫 All major cards

🏨 ADMIRAL'S INN & GUNPOWDER SUITES

$$–$$$

ENGLISH HARBOUR

TEL 268/460-1027

admiralsantigua.com

Charming historic inn and waterfront garden in Nelson's Dockyard. Renovated rooms with antique furnishings in both the main building and an annex, a handsome loft suite, dining, spa, and boat shuttle to the beach.

🛈 23 rooms & suites 🅿

🚭 Some rooms 🛜 Free

🚫 All major cards

🏨 SIBONEY BEACH CLUB

$$–$$$

DICKENSON BAY

TEL 268/462-0806

OR 800/533-0234

siboneybeachantigua.com

Delightful small property at the quiet end of Antigua's busiest beach. Twelve one-bedroom suites with kitchenettes and balconies overlooking tropical gardens. The restaurant is a big plus (see **Coconut Grove**, below). Water sports nearby.

🛈 12 🅿 🚭 🚭 🛜 Free

🚫 All major cards

🏨 CATAMARAN HOTEL

$–$$

FALMOUTH HARBOUR

TEL 268/460-1036

Friendly, intimate, and right on the bayfront, the plantation-style "Cat Club" really does feel clubby. Helpful staff can organize activities or lend you a dinghy to pop across to English Harbour. Spick-and-span rooms with views, some with broad verandas and well-equipped kitchenettes. Family friendly.

🛈 14 rooms & suites 🅿 🚭

🚭 🛜 Free 🚫 All major cards

🍽 LA BUSSOLA

$$$–$$$$

RUNAWAY BAY

TEL 268/562-1546

labussolarestaurant.net

Persevere down the bumpy track for a warm Mediterranean welcome and excellent Italian cuisine on the bay. Classic dishes with a modern twist from fresh pasta to scene-stealing lobster; the beachfront setting is delightful.

🕐 Closed Tues.

🚫 All major cards

🍽 COCONUT GROVE

$$$

SIBONEY BEACH CLUB,

DICKENSON BAY

TEL 268/462-1538

coconutgroveantigua.com

Romantic lantern-lit beach-front setting with smoochy music. Offerings include fresh swordfish and salmon carpaccio, seared mahimahi with Antiguan herbs, and Jamaican jerk chicken with banana-guava marmalade. Good wine and brandy list.

🚫 All major cards

BOOM
$$–$$$
ADMIRAL'S INN,
ENGLISH HARBOUR
TEL 268/460-1027
A short boat shuttle across from the inn, this is the place to settle in for a long, lazy afternoon of good food, magnificent views, and soaking up the sun. Menu offerings include salads, steak sandwiches, fish cakes, and more substantial mahimahi on risotto. After lunch hammocks or a lounger by the infinity pool await.
🕐 Closed D year-round & Mon.–Wed. off season
🚫 All major cards

PAPA ZOUK
$$–$$$
HILDA DAVIS DRIVE, GAMBLES
TEL 268/464-6044
OR 268/464-0795
Take a taxi to this eccentric little creole-style bar-restaurant in a residential quarter north of St. John's. The blackboard sign reads "fish 'n' rum" and that's exactly what you get: More than 200 rums behind the bar, and the seafood specials (bouillabaisse, grilled snapper, lobster, shrimp) are simple and perfectly cooked.
🕐 Closed L & Sun.
🚫 No credit cards

BIG BANANA PIZZAS IN PARADISE
$$
REDCLIFFE QUAY, ST. JOHN'S
TEL 268/480-6985
A handy refueling stop in an old brick warehouse in the shopping district. Pizzas, sub sandwiches, salads, espressos, cappuccinos, and cold drinks.
🕐 Closed Sun.
🚫 All major cards

CATHERINE'S CAFÉ PLAGE
$$
PIGEON POINT BEACH,
FALMOUTH HARBOUR
TEL 268/460-5050
Upscale French café by the waterfront, all white wood, wicker, and louvered jalousies, with views of passing yachts through the trees. Relax with a *ti'punch* or a glass of rosé (from the exclusively French wine list) and share a platter of delicious tapas or dive into creative salads, warm lobster sandwiches, and divine desserts served with Gallic flair.
🕐 Closed Tues., D Sat.–Mon. & Thurs. (except high season), & May–mid-Nov. 🚫 MC, V

RUSSELL'S
$$
FORT JAMES
TEL 268/462-5479
Fabulous views over St. John's Harbour are reason enough to seek out this welcoming spot. Sunsets are a specialty, and a predominantly seafood menu includes steamed cockles in white wine, conch fritters, and grilled lobster. Traditional Antiguan lunch buffet on Sat.; reggae band on Fri.
🕐 Closed Mon. L & Sun.
🚫 MC, V

MONTSERRAT

GINGERBREAD HILL
$
ST. PETER'S
TEL 664/491-5812
gingerbreadhill.com
Up in the hills with superlative views to the ocean, this little eco-retreat run by the hands-on Lea family is a find. Simple self-catering accommodations set in lush gardens and citrus orchards; car rental, mountain bikes, diving packages, and volcano tours.
ℹ️ 5 rooms/cottages
🅿️ 🛜 Free 🚫 No credit cards

OLVESTON HOUSE
$
OLVESTON
TEL 664/491-5210
olvestonhouse.com
Once occupied by Beatles producer Sir George Martin, this attractive guesthouse boasts a pool with views, spacious and comfy rooms, and a broad wraparound veranda for lolling in the shade. The popular restaurant serves fine Anglo-Caribbean cuisine.
ℹ️ 6 🔶 Some rooms
🅿️ 🛁 🛜 Free in lobby & bar
🚫 MC, V

PONTS BEACH VIEW
$–$$
LITTLE BAY BEACH
TEL 664/496-7788
Laid-back local spot hemmed in by explosive tropical greenery and the deep, blue sea. Plastic chairs, buoys hanging from the rafters and generous island cooking. Seafood specials, popular Sunday barbecue.
🕐 Closed Mon. & some D in off season

ST. KITTS

SOMETHING SPECIAL

KITTITIAN HILL
$$$$$
ST. PAUL'S
TEL 869/465-7388
OR U.S. 855/846-3951
kittitianhill.com
Something extraordinary is taking shape at the old Belle Mont Farm plantation on the slopes of Mount Liamuiga: a world-class, sustainable, luxury resort embracing the farm-to-table ethos, built and serviced by Kittitians. The first phase of 84 pretty shingled guesthouses opened in 2014/15; the organic farm, restaurant, and nine holes of golf are up and running; further accommodations, a spa, beach club, and culinary and arts programs are slated. Watch this space.
ℹ️ 84 suites 🅿️ 🔶 🛁 🏋️
🛜 Free 🚫 All major cards

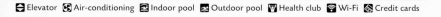
🔽 Elevator 🔶 Air-conditioning 🛁 Indoor pool 🏊 Outdoor pool 🏋️ Health club 🛜 Wi-Fi 🚫 Credit cards

🏨 OTTLEY'S PLANTATION INN
$$–$$$$
OTTLEY'S
TEL 869/465-7234
OR 800/772-3039
ottleys.com
Splendid 18th-century plantation great house set in gardens surrounded by cane fields. Huge, pretty rooms in the main house with its antique furnishings and breezy verandas, plus two- or three-bedroom cottages on the grounds. Spa, **Royal Palm** restaurant (see this page), beach shuttle.
ⓘ 23 🅿 🚭 🏊 🛜 Free
🚭 All major cards

🏨 ST. KITTS MARRIOT RESORT & THE ROYAL BEACH CASINO
$$–$$$
858 FRIGATE BAY ROAD, FRIGATE BAY
TEL 869/466-1200
OR US/CANADA 800/223-6388
marriott.com
Large family-friendly Atlantic side resort with lots of activities, a spa, 18 holes of golf, and beach cabanas. Spacious ocean-view suites. Dining in the main seafood and steak restaurants is pricey; meal plans available.
ⓘ 393 🅿 🚭 🏊 🛜 Free
🚭 All major cards

🏨 TIMOTHY BEACH RESORT
$–$$
FRIGATE BAY
TEL 869/465-8597
timothybeach.com
The only property on the Caribbean beachfront in Frigate Bay. Good value accommodations, all with balconies or patios. Versatile layout, excellent for groups/families. On-site restaurant, shops and tennis nearby.
ⓘ 60 🅿 🚭 🏊 🛜 Free
🚭 All major cards

🍴 ROYAL PALM
$$–$$$$
OTTLEY'S PLANTATION INN, OTTLEY'S
TEL 869/465-7234
A wonderful way to enjoy a taste of the gracious plantation hotel experience on an around-island tour. Arrive in time for a preprandial walk around the grounds, and then relax in the terraced restaurant overlooking manicured lawns to the sea. Lunch options include club sandwiches, grilled fish tacos, and sublime tropical fruit sorbets; notable Sunday brunch buffet. More refined classical fare in the candlelit evenings.
🚭 All major cards

🍴 FISHERMAN'S WHARF
$$–$$$
FORTLANDS, BASSETERRE
TEL 869/465-2754
fishermanswharfstkitts.com
Something of an island institution with sweeping views of the harbor from a big wooden deck. Steak and seafood cooked on an open charcoal grill, good and spicy jerk chicken, lobster, excellent chowder. Live music on weekends.
🕐 Closed Sun. & L
🚭 All major cards

🍴 BALLAHOO
$
THE CIRCUS, BASSETERRE
TEL 869/465-4197
Popular downtown spot. Tuna melt subs, sandwiches, and burgers for lunch; hot chili shrimp, mahimahi steaks with basil-mustard butter, and vegetarian options in the evening.
🕐 Closed Sun.
🚭 All major cards

NEVIS

🏨 FOUR SEASONS RESORT NEVIS
$$$$$
PINNEYS BEACH
TEL 869/469-1111
OR 800/819-5053
fourseasons.com/nevis
Luxurious property in a terrific position on Nevis's main beach. Large rooms and suites with oversize baths and private patios by the waterfront or golf course. Sports packages, children's facilities, polished service.
ⓘ 196 rooms & suites, 42 villas & cottages 🅿 🚭 🏊 🛜
🛜 Free 🚭 All major cards

🏨🍴 MONTPELIER PLANTATION INN
$$$–$$$$$
FIGTREE
TEL 869/469-3462
montpeliernevis.com
Glorious old stone plantation house on a former sugar estate. Airy, elegant rooms in cottages set in the 10-acre (4 ha) landscaped grounds. Meals served in the main building English country house–style. Tennis, beach shuttle.
ⓘ 19 rooms + 3 villas 🅿 🏊
🛜 Free 🚭 All major cards

SOMETHING SPECIAL

🏨 HERMITAGE
$$–$$$
GINGERLAND
TEL 869/469-3477
OR 800/682-4025
hermitagenevis.com
Enchanting plantation inn with rooms in gingerbread cottages dotted about the flower-filled gardens of the oldest wooden house in the Caribbean (circa 1680–1740). Romantic four-posters, hammocks on the veranda, horseback riding, peace and quiet.
ⓘ 17 🅿 🏊 🛜 Free
🚭 All major cards

🏨🍴 GOLDEN ROCK INN
$$–$$$
GINGERLAND
TEL 869/469-3346
goldenrocknevis.com

🏨 Hotel ⓘ No. of guest rooms 🍴 Restaurant 🕐 Open/Closed Hours 🅿 Parking 🚭 Nonsmoking

Artists Helen and Brice Marden have brought vision and a bold palette to this old sugar estate on the slopes of Nevis Peak. Magnificent garden and sea views from stone terraces, delicious curried chicken and mango salad, jerk pork with plantain chips, and a signature lobster salad sandwich. Reservations; the inn has 11 rooms.
🔒 All major cards

🏨 OUALIE BEACH RESORT
$$
OUALIE BEACH
TEL 869/469-9735
OR 800/682-5431
oualiebeach.com
Small and informal beachfront property with well-priced rooms and studios in wooden cottages; screened porches overlook the beach. PADI diving and adventure packages, mountain bikes.
🛏 32 🅿 🔆 🛜 Free
🔒 All major cards

🍴 SPICE MILL
$$–$$$
COCKLESHELL BEACH
TEL 869/765-6706
spicemillrestaurant.com
Bang on the beach with a big breezy deck, showstopping views of Nevis Peak, and a menu drawing inspiration from around the globe. Good local ingredients with zing such as mussels in a ginger tomato broth, spicy jerk, or lush crab cakes. Creative island decor too—spot the dugout canoe bar and hanging crayfish trap lanterns.
🕐 Closed Thurs. off season
🔒 All major cards

🍴 DOUBLE DEUCE
$$
PINNEYS BEACH
TEL 869/469-2222
doubledeucenevis.com
Classic beach bar-restaurant with a difference: Chef Mark Roberts knows his seafood.

Expect perfectly barbecued catch of the day, grilled lobster, garlicky jumbo shrimp, fish soup with tania fritters, juicy steaks, and ice-cold beers. Karaoke Thursday night.
🕐 Closed Mon.
🔒 No credit cards

■ FRENCH ANTILLES

GUADELOUPE

🏨 LA TOUBANA
$$–$$$
STE.-ANNE, GRANDE-TERRE
TEL 590/88 25 78
toubana.com
Lovely sea views and quaint one- and two-bedroom cottages *(toubanas)* with kitchenettes on the hill leading down to a small beach cove with water sports. Tennis; some evening entertainment.
🛏 32 bungalows + 12 suites
🅿 🌊 🛜 Free
🔒 All major cards

🏨 JARDIN MALANGA
$$
LES TROIS RIVIÈRES, BASSE-TERRE
TEL 590/92 67 57
jardinmalanga.com
Fabulous hillside setting with views of the Îles des Saintes from the deck of this low-key hideaway. Minimalist chic rooms in 1920s plantation house or superb cottages.
🛏 9 🅿 🔆 🌊
🔒 All major cards

🏨 LE TOULOULOU
🍴 **$$**
PETITE-ANSE, CAPESTERRE-MARIE-GALANTE
TEL 0590/97 32 63
letoulolou.com
Right on the beach, this island institution serves fresh seafood and excellent *ti'punch,* as well as local specialty *bébélé,* an offal stew. Live music, an after-dinner disco, and also five simple beach bungalows.

🕐 Closed Sun. D & Mon.
🔒 MC, V

🏨 HÔTEL AMAUDO
$–$$
ANSE À LA BARQUE, ST.-FRANÇOIS, GRANDE-TERRE
TEL 590/88 87 00
amaudo.fr
There's a warm welcome at this pretty gingerbread-trimmed B&B with enviable clifftop views and infinity pool. Simple cottagey rooms, delicious fresh fruit and croissants for breakfast. Steep path down to sandy beach; car recommended.
🛏 10 units 🅿 🔆 🌊
🛜 Free 🔒 MC, V

🏨 AUBERGE LES PETITS
🍴 SAINTS AUX ANARCADIERS
$
TERRE-DE-HAUT, LES SAINTES
TEL 590/99 50 99
www.petitssaints.com
Pretty creole home overflowing with antiques and collectibles. Comfortable rooms five minutes from the town center; good restaurant.
🛏 11 🛜 Free in lobby
🔒 All major cards

🏨 VILLA LE RAYON VERT
$
FERRY, DESHAIES, BASSE-TERRE
TEL 590/24 12 04
villa-rayon-vert.com
Pared-back and restful B&B rooms leading out onto a shared rustic chic terrace, all terra-cotta tiles, natural wood, and billowing cream drapes. Peaceful hillside gardens with sea views, charming multilingual hosts, wonderful home-cooked dinners on request.
🛏 4 🅿 🔆 🌊 🛜 Free
🔒 MC, V

🍴 LA VIEILLE TOUR
$$$
AUBERGE DE LA VIEILLE TOUR
GOSIER, GRANDE-TERRE

TEL 590/84 23 23
Elegant hotel dining room with sea views (reserve a window seat) and a classic French creole menu. Crayfish tartare, fresh fish with lobster butter, and magnificent desserts. Good value prix fixe menus; reservations advised.
🅢 All major cards

🍴 IGUANE CAFÉ
$$–$$$
RTE. DE LA POINTE DES CHÂTEAUX, ST-FRANÇOIS, GRANDE-TERRE
TEL 590/88 61 37
iguane-cafe.fr
Chic-rustic eatery on the beach road serving a creative menu strong on local ingredients. Marble of foie gras and lobster with dark rum and shellfish aspic, crispy saffron conch and christophene gratin, five-spice fish.
🕑 Closed Tues. & L (except Sun.) 🅢 All major cards

🍴 LA PORTE DES INDES
$$–$$$
DEVARIEUX, ST-FRANÇOIS, GRANDE-TERRE
TEL 590/21 30 87
Connoisseurs of Indian cuisine cannot praise this delightful *temple de la gastronomie* highly enough. A statue of the elephant god Ganesh presides over the dining pavilion and a classic and creative Indian menu. Excellent wine list.
🕑 Closed L Tues.–Sat., Sun. D, & Mon. 🅢 V

🍴 LE ROCHER DE MALENDURE
$$–$$$
LE ROCHER DE MALENDURE-PIEGEON, BOUILLANTE
TEL 590/98 70 84
le-rocher-de-malendure.restaurant-guadeloupe.org
A collection of blue-and-white dining terraces clinging to the rocky cliffs with free-range iguanas for company. Fresh-

off-the-boat fish perfectly grilled, fish fondue, crispy *accras*, and generous quantities of rum ready to flambé anything from succulent crayfish to bananas.
🕑 Closed Wed. 🅢 V

MARTINIQUE

🏨 CAP EST LAGOON
🍴 RESORT & SPA
$$$$–$$$$$
LE FRANÇOIS
TEL 0596/54 80 80
OR 800/735-2478
capest.com
A sense of Zen-like calm pervades this quiet, upscale beach resort set on the edge of a lagoon among palms and sea grape trees on the east coast. Vibrant creole colors juxtaposed with Asian-style simplicity, luxurious suites, a gorgeous pool and gardens, excellent cuisine as befits a Relais & Châteaux property.
ℹ️ 50 🅿️ 🛗 🏊 📺 📶 Free
🅢 All major cards

🏨 DOMAINE ST. AUBIN
🍴 $$$
PETITE RIVIÈRE SALÉE, LA TRINITÉ
TEL 0596/69 34 77
domaine-saint-aubin.com
Wonderful views and charming hosts put this rather remote restored plantation hotel on the map. Set in rolling hillside gardens, the fanciful Louisiana-style house has been furnished with antiques. Joelle Rosemain's French-Caribbean cooking is a treat.
ℹ️ 36 🅿️ 🛗 🏊 📶 Free
🅢 MC, V

🏨 HÔTEL BAKOUA
$$$
POINTE DU BOUT, LES TROIS-ÎLETS
TEL 0596/66 02 02
hotel-bakoua.fr
Attractive, well-equipped resort set on a bluff above a private beach. Comfortably appointed rooms with views. Tennis, water

sports, tour desk; golf nearby.
ℹ️ 138 🅿️ 🛗 🏊 📶 Free
🅢 All major cards

🏨 RÉSIDENCE OCÉANE
$
ANSE BONNEVILLE, RUE DU SURF, LA TRINITÉ
TEL 0596/58 73 73
residence-oceane.com
Off the beaten path in the Caravelle Nature Reserve, this quiet creole-style property is a few minutes' walk from a deserted surf beach. Studios with kitchenettes and sea views, complimentary French breakfast. Lots of steps and a short drive into Tartane for shops and restaurants.
ℹ️ 25 🅿️ 🛗 🏊 📶 Free
🅢 AE, V

🍴 LA TABLE DE MAMY NOUNOU
$$$–$$$$
HÔTEL LA CARAVELLE, TARTANE
TEL 0596/58 07 32
hotel-la-caravelle-martinique.com
Picturesque hotel-restaurant

🏨 Hotel ℹ️ No. of guest rooms 🍴 Restaurant 🕑 Open/Closed Hours 🅿️ Parking 🅢 Nonsmoking

clinging to a wooded hillside with breezy verandas and views. Innovative creole-influenced cuisine such as the seafood platter with cider and cinnamon cream sauce and delectable iced soufflés. Dinner reservations are essential.

🕒 Closed Tues. & Jun. & Sept. 💳 MC, V

🍴 LE TOULOULOU
$$–$$$
POINTE MARIN, STE.-ANNE
TEL 0596/76 73 27
Great beachfront spot for an authentic French creole dining experience. Generous *plateaux de fruits de mer* (seafood platters) piled with lobster, clams, and shrimp, classic *tarte aux pommes* to finish.

🕒 Closed Sun. p.m. & Mon. p.m. 💳 MC, V

🍴 LE ZANZIBAR
$$–$$$
11 BLVD. ALLÉGRE, LE MARIN
TEL 0596/74 08 46
Restaurant-lounge bar with an eclectic creole-Moroccan vibe and lovely views over the bay and marina. The cooking is similarly worldly, tuna tartare, chicken tagine, and even *moules-frites* (mussels and fries); fine Belgian beers.

🕒 Closed Sun. 💳 All major cards

🍴 RESTAURANT 1643
$–$$
ANSE LATOUCHE, CARBET
TEL 0596/78 17 81
restaurant1643.com
Pretty and historic creole cottage decked out in citrus hues with a shady terrace flanked by tropical flowers. Top-notch seafood, duck with foie gras, a huge meat brochette served with an array of flavorsome dips, followed by crème brûlée or a saucy little chocolate pudding.

🕒 Closed D Sun. & Mon. 💳 V

ST.-BARTHÉLEMY

🏨 EDEN ROCK
🍴 $$$$$
ST. JEAN
TEL 0590/29 79 99
OR U.S./CANADA 855/333-6762
edenrockhotel.com
St. Barts's first hotel has been stylishly developed and extended from its original hub, which appears to grow organically from a rocky promontory above the beach. Cool classic suites featuring natural wood or colorful silks, romantic boudoirs, and delectable cottages. Good restaurants.

🛏 34 rooms + 3 houses & villas 🅿 ❄ 🌊 📶 🛜 Free 💳 All major cards

🏨 HOTEL LE TOINY
$$$$$
ANSE DE TOINY
TEL 0590/27 88 88
OR 800/680-0832
www.letoiny.com
Superbly elegant and secluded Relais & Châteaux property, with a dozen spacious and beautifully decorated cottages boasting private pools, kitchenettes, and fitness equipment. Excellent restaurant (see **Le Gaïac**, this page).

🛏 15 🅿 ❄ 🌊 🛜 Free 💳 All major cards

🏨 NORMANDIE HOTEL
$$
ROUTE DE SALINE, LORIENT
TEL 0590/27 61 66
normandiehotelstbarts.com
Small, friendly B&B hotel a two-minute walk from the beach, restaurants, and shops. Lots of stylish contemporary glass block and a nautical nod to the 1930s art deco liner, the S.S. *Normandie*. In-room fridge and Wi-Fi, plunge pool in the tiny tropical garden.

🛏 8 🅿 ❄ 🌊 🛜 Free 💳 All major cards

🍴 LE GAÏAC
$$$$$
HOTEL LE TOINY, ANSE DE TOINY
TEL 0590/27 88 88
Small, chic, with sea views, Le Gaïac serves fine French-Caribbean cuisine. Black truffle spaghetti with parmesan, memorable lobster thermidor with lemongrass-scented vegetable risotto, and more. Reservations recommended.

🕒 Closed Oct. 💳 All major cards

🍴 EDDY'S
$$$
RUE SAMUEL FAHLBERG, GUSTAVIA
TEL 0590/27 54 17
Balinese teak, bamboo, and an explosion of greenery lend a Southeast Asian note to the decor, extending to the French-Caribbean-Asian menu. Fashionable spot for shrimp green curry, creole Colombo, and grilled fish.

🕒 Closed L & Sun. 💳 All major cards

🍴 LE REPAIRE
$$
RUE DE LA RÉPUBLIQUE, GUSTAVIA
TEL 590/27 72 48
A useful all-day pit stop opposite the waterfront serving a classic and varied brasserie menu with local influences, drinks and ice creams. Decent wine list; mussels and home-made fries on Thursdays.

💳 All major cards

■ WINDWARD ISLANDS

DOMINICA

🏨 PAPILLOTE RAINFOREST
🍴 RETREAT
$$
TRAFALGAR VALLEY
TEL 767/448-2287
papillote.dm

🚪 Elevator ❄ Air-conditioning 🏊 Indoor pool 🏊 Outdoor pool 🏋 Health club 🛜 Wi-Fi 💳 Credit cards

Neat rain forest inn (8 simple rooms) with tables on a leafy terrace hemmed in by greenery. The unpretentious menu is packed with favorite Caribbean staples, locally sourced seasonal fruits, and vegetables. Reservations recommended.

⬧ All major cards

🏨 FORT YOUNG
$–$$
ROSEAU
TEL 767/448-5000
OR U.S. 855/223-9519
fortyounghotel.com
Attractive rooms and spacious suites built around a pool deck nestled in the remains of a historic seafront fortress, plus a smart new ocean-view block down on the water. Good location, in-house tour desk.

🚪 73 🅿 🚭 ⛱ 📶 Free
⬧ All major cards

🏨 ANCHORAGE HOTEL & DIVE CENTRE
$
CASTLE COMFORT
TEL 767/448-2638 OR
U.S. 888/790-5264
anchoragehotel.dm
Small block of modern units with a splash of creole color and balconies overlooking the sea just south of Roseau. This is a great base for activities, with a PADI dive center and hiking trips, a squash court, plus helpful and friendly staff.

🚪 32 🚭 ⛱ 📶 Free
⬧ All major cards

🏨 PICARD BEACH COTTAGES
$
PICARD BEACH, PORTSMOUTH
TEL 767/445-5131 OR
U.S. 888/790-5264
picardbeachcottages.com
Simple rooms in quiet creole cottages on one of Dominica's better black-sand beaches. Private verandas and kitchenettes; lovely gardens on an old coconut plantation.

🚪 18 🅿 🚭 Some rooms
📶 Free ⬧ All major cards

SOMETHING SPECIAL

🏨 ZANDOLI INN
🍴 **$**
ROCHE CASSÉE, STOWE
TEL 767/446-3161
zandoli.com
A lovely little country inn balanced on cliffs 80 feet (24 m) above the ocean in the island's south. Fabulous views, delightful gardens with a plunge pool, and pretty guest rooms decked out in soothing blues and greens. Good food (and company) in the restaurant. Walking trails nearby. No children under 12.

🚪 5 🅿 ⛱ 📶 Free ⬧ MC, V

🍴 PALISADES
$$
FORT YOUNG HOTEL, ROSEAU
TEL 767/448-5000
fortyounghotel.com
The island's smartest restaurant overlooks Roseau Bay from its wraparound veranda. Lunchtime creole favorites include pumpkin and ginger soup, fish sandwiches, and spicy jerk chicken wraps; more classical fare in the evening.

⬧ All major cards

🍴 COCORICO CAFÉ
$–$$
BAYFRONT (AT KENNEDY AVE.), ROSEAU
TEL 767/449-8686
cocoricocafe.com
A French café set in a jauntily painted creole house, and a great spot in front of the ferry terminal to watch the world go by. Croissants for breakfast, homemade cake with morning coffee, and delicious filled baguettes, salads, crêpes, and spicy jerk chicken for lunch.

🕐 Closed D & Sun. (except when a cruise ship is in)
⬧ MC, V

🍴 8 CASTLE STREET
$
8 CASTLE STREET, ROSEAU
TEL 767/317-1703
Tucked away in a hidden courtyard, this is a fun find decked out in ramshackle style with recycled furnishings from old desks to cooper's barrels. Smiley waitstaff serve up generous fluffy omelets, salads, grills, and fish platters. Jazzy Sax & The City music night on Thursdays.

⬧ No credit cards

GRENADA

🏨 SANDALS LA SOURCE GRENADA RESORT & SPA
$$$$$
PINK GIN BEACH
TEL 473/444-2556
OR 888/527-0044
sandals.com
This luxurious, all-inclusive couples resort received a total makeover in 2015. Laid out in three themed villages, the top-of-the-line Italian Village features Butler Suites and striking Skypool Suites with infinity plunge pool on the balcony.

🚪 225 🅿 🚭 ⛱ 🎾 📶 Free
⬧ All major cards

🏨 SPICE ISLAND BEACH RESORT
$$$$$
GRAND ANSE
TEL 473/444-4258
OR 800/501-8603
spiceislandbeachresort.com
Elegant, family-run beachfront all-inclusive that combines Grenadian hospitality with impeccable service. Classical-contemporary decor in spacious suites (some have private pools and exercise facilities). Tennis and nonmotorized water sports.

🚪 66 🅿 🚭 ⛱ 🎾 📶 Free
⬧ All major cards

🏨 CALABASH HOTEL
$$$$–$$$$$
L'ANSE AUX ÉPINES

🏨 Hotel 🚪 No. of guest rooms 🍴 Restaurant 🕐 Open/Closed Hours 🅿 Parking ⬧ Nonsmoking

TEL 473/444-4334
OR U.S. 800/738-4752
calabashhotel.com
Tranquil and charming beach-front hotel with comfortable suites (some with small private pools) arranged in an arc of two-story garden cottages. Caring service includes breakfast prepared in your suite. Tennis and nonmotorized water sports; good food. An exclusive development of architect-designed villas lies to the west.

⬛ 30 suites, 5 villas 🄿 🅢 ⛱ 📺 📶 Free 🄲 All major cards

🏨 COYABA BEACH RESORT
$$$
GRAND ANSE
TEL 473/444-4129 OR
U.S./CANADA 855/626-9222
coyaba.com
Only palm trees and tropical gardens separate Coyaba's low-rise accommodations from Grenada's top beach. Plain but comfy guest rooms with splashes of tropical color, dining (meal plans available), pool bar, water-sports packages, transportation nearby.

⬛ 80 🄿 🅢 ⛱ 📺 📶 Free 🄲 All major cards

🏨 LA SAGESSE
$$
LA SAGESSE, ST. DAVID'S
TEL 473/444-6458
lasagesse.com
Off-the-beaten-path beach hideaway with simple, spacious rooms in a 1920s estate house, an oceanfront annex (including a suite and two duplexes), and two rooms in a cottage. Ceiling fans, verandas, good food.

⬛ 12 🄿 📶 Free in restaurant & some rooms 🄲 MC, V

🏨 GREEN ROOF INN
$–$$
HILLSBOROUGH, CARRIACOU
TEL 473/443-6399
greenroofinn.com
This unpretentious little

guesthouse on the island of Carriacou is an absolute charmer. Clean pastel shades and white linen in the guest rooms and a romantic white clapboard cottage hideaway with its own kitchenette. Fabulous views, beach access, friendly bar, and veranda restaurant. It's a 15–20 minute walk to town.

⬛ 5 rooms, 1 bungalow, 1 cottage 🄿 📶 Free 🄲 MC, V

🍴 RHODES RESTAURANT
$$$$
CALABASH HOTEL,
L'ANSE AUX ÉPINES
TEL 473/444-4334
calabashhotel.com
This elegant and pretty terrace dining room is a Caribbean outpost for acclaimed British chef Gary Rhodes. The seasonally inspired menu features local produce from jerk chicken with sweet pawpaw salad to Grenadian fish stew. Reservations are recommended.

🕑 Closed L 🄲 All major cards

🍴 COCONUT BEACH RESTAURANT
$$$
GRAND ANSE
TEL 473/444-4644
thecoconutbeachgrenada.com
Dine on the sand or inside the old wooden house. French creole specialties such as conch curry, lobster, or catch of the day in a variety of sauces.

🕑 Closed Tues. 🄲 All major cards

🍴 BB'S CRABBACK
$$–$$$
PROGRESS HOUSE, THE
CARENAGE, ST. GEORGE'S
TEL 473/435-7058
bbscrabbackrestaurant.com
Great waterfront views across the harbor below Fort George, and top-notch Caribbean cuisine. Callaloo soup, goat curry, the eponymous crab-backs (a local land crab), and

quantities of island vegetables and ground provisions.

🄲 MC, V

🍴 AQUARIUM
$$
TAMARIND BEACH,
POINT SALINES
TEL 473/444-1410
www.aquarium-grenada.com
Woodsy, open-air beach restaurant. Well-prepared world food from satay or pumpkin and ginger soup to snapper with a coriander-herb crust, callaloo canneloni, New Zealand lamb, and U.S. steaks. Sunday barbecues.

🕑 Closed Mon. 🄲 All major cards

🍴 BELMONT ESTATE
$$
BELMONT, ST. PATRICK
TEL 473/442-9524
belmontestate.net
It's worth making an around-island tour just to lunch at this organic farm-to-plate restaurant set in fruit groves. Feast from the mouthwatering buffet, sample the fresh goat cheese salad, scrumptious tropical juices, homemade ice creams, and to-die-for estate chocolate puddings.

🕑 Closed D & Sat. 🄲 MC, V

ST. LUCIA

🏨 ANSE CHASTANET RESORT
$$$$–$$$$$
SOUFRIÈRE
TEL 758/459-7000
OR 800/223-1108
ansechastanet.com
Set in a steep-sided beach cove down a bumpy track, this delightful small spa resort is wonderfully relaxing and a good dive center. Lovely rooms in octagonal gazebos with wraparound balconies, hillside or beachside suites, great views, tennis, yoga, restaurant.

⬛ 49 🄿 📶 Free 🄲 All major cards

🛗 Elevator 🅢 Air-conditioning 🏊 Indoor pool ⛱ Outdoor pool 📺 Health club 📶 Wi-Fi 🄲 Credit cards

TI KAYE RESORT & SPA
$$$–$$$$
ANSE LA RAYE
TEL 758/456-8101
tikaye.com
Grafted onto a wooded bluff above the beach between Castries and Soufrière, charming cottages and duplexes (great for families) in landscaped grounds. Hammocks on the balcony, net-draped beds, some private plunge pools. Super restaurant, beach bar-grill, diving.
🛏 33 🅿 ⛱ 📺 📶 Free
All major cards

MARIGOT BEACH CLUB & DIVE RESORT
$$–$$$
MARIGOT BAY
TEL 758/451-4974
marigotbeachclub.com
Delightful waterfront property that appeals to independent travelers. Studios and two- and three-bedroom villas with kitchenettes above Marigot Bay. Tiny beach, water sports, dive shop, sailing packages.
🛏 25 🅿 ⛱ 📺 📶 Free
All major cards

HARMONY SUITES
$$
RODNEY BAY
TEL 758/452-8756
OR U.S. 888/790-5264
harmonysuites.com
Small and friendly complex on the water minutes from Reduit Beach. Well-equipped standard suites and deluxe units, some kitchenettes. On-site bistro.
🛏 30 🅿 ⛱ 📺 📶 Free
All major cards

SOMETHING SPECIAL

RAINFOREST HIDEAWAY
$$$$$
MARIGOT BAY
TEL 758/451-4485
rainforesthideawaystlucia.com
Imagine a rustic-chic

waterfront dock set with tables, a champagne bar among the mangroves, and gentle jazz. The fusion dinner menu combines classical expertise with Caribbean flavors (think ravioli stuffed with ginger and coconut crab).
🕐 Closed L, Sun., Tues., & mid-May–Nov. 30
All major cards

COAL POT
$$$$
VIGIE COVE, CASTRIES
TEL 758/452-5566
coalpotrestaurant.com
The side road past the airport does not look promising, but Vigie Cove is a pretty spot and the Coal Pot's deck is right on the water. Creole-style fish is the main event, and you can choose your flavors from a range of spices, rubs, and sauces; steak is also popular. Love the fishy crockery, too!
🕐 Closed Sat. L & Sun.
All major cards

JACQUES WATERFRONT DINING
$$$
RODNEY BAY MARINA
TEL 758/458-1900
jacquesrestaurant.com
In a pleasantly breezy marina location, French patron-chef Jacques Rioux serves up fish and seafood including favorites such as octopus and conch in a curried coconut sauce. Excellent Sunday brunch.
All major cards

JARDIN CACAO
$$–$$$
FOND DOUX ESTATE, SOUFRIÈRE
TEL 758/459-7545
Sun-dappled, gingerbread-trimmed open-air restaurant surrounded by tropical greenery. At lunch, the generous creole buffet spread is laden with grilled fish, meaty stews, barbecue ribs and chicken,

rice 'n peas, vegetable fritters and more; à la carte in the evenings. Where possible this is plantation-to-plate dining.
MC, V

HUMMINGBIRD
$$
HUMMINGBIRD BEACH RESORT, SOUFRIÈRE
TEL 758/459-7232
hummingbirdbeachresort.com
Delightful garden restaurant with views of the Pitons and a reputation for creole cuisine. The signature seafood dish is dorado with local herbs, salads and sandwiches are available at lunchtime, and the vegetables are homegrown.
All major cards

ST. VINCENT & THE GRENADINES

BEQUIA

BEQUIA BEACH HOTEL
$$$$–$$$$$
FRIENDSHIP BEACH
TEL 784/458-1600
bequiabeach.com
Delectable upscale resort on one of Bequia's prettiest beaches. Breezy, gingerbread-trimmed, contemporary/colonial-style suites and villas. Lovely gardens, spa, fine dining (meal plans), charming staff.
🛏 41 rooms/suites, 7 villas
🅿 🅢 ⛱ 📺 📶 Free
All major cards

FIREFLY PLANTATION
$$$$–$$$$$
SPRING BAY
TEL 784/488-8414
fireflybequia.com
Idyllic rural retreat on a working plantation in the hills above Spring Bay. Romantic rooms with stone floors and gauzy drapes on four-posters; views over citrus orchards and coconut groves to the sea; hammocks, tennis, plantation tours; pavilion dining room on

the site of the 18th-century great house.

🛈 4 rooms, 1 cottage 🅿 ⛱ 🛜 Free 🃏 All major cards

🍴 GINGERBREAD
$$

PORT ELIZABETH
TEL 784/458-3800
Three dining options in one: The daytime Gingerbread Café does a great line in coffees, juices, and homemade cakes. Fresh seafood kebabs and chicken end up on the Gingerbread BBQ at lunch. Or there is the Gingerbread Restaurant, with bay views from the veranda and a lunch menu of pasta, salads, omelets. Callaloo and shrimp soup and curries in the evening.

🃏 All major cards

CANOUAN

🏨 CANOUAN RESORT & GRENADINES ESTATE VILLAS
$$$$$

TEL 784/458-8000
canouan.com
Peerless luxury resort set amphitheater-style around a pristine bay. Huge and elegant accommodations in single- and double-story villas, every amenity from personal golf carts and Fazio-designed golf course to kids' clubs and a luxurious spa.

🛈 156 ❄ ⛱ 🏋 🛜 Free 🃏 All major cards

MUSTIQUE

🏨 MUSTIQUE VILLA RENTALS
$$$$$

TEL 784/488-8500
mustique-island.com
There are 74 two- to nine-bedroom villa rentals on the island. All come with cook and maid. Meals can be taken at the 17-room Cotton House Hotel, and facilities on the

island include horseback riding, tennis, and diving.

🛈 74 villas 🃏 All major cards

ST. VINCENT

🏨 YOUNG ISLAND
$$$$–$$$$$

OPPOSITE VILLA
TEL 784/458-4826 OR
U.S. 800/223-1108
youngisland.com
A private island resort with pretty wood and stone cottages enfolded in tropical greenery. Patios and sea views, some small swimming pools. Tennis, water sports, yachting excursions, spa treatments.

🛈 30 🅿 ⛱ 🃏 All major cards

🏨 COBBLESTONE INN
🍴 $

BAY STREET, KINGSTOWN
TEL 784/458-4227
thecobblestoneinn.com
A really handy address if you're looking for a restaurant, a bar, or a room for the night in Kingstown. This old Georgian sugar warehouse has bars at street level and on the breezy rooftop, a good local restaurant (up three flights of stairs, but your reward for all that exercise is a tour of the building), and pleasant rooms.

🛈 26 rooms/suites 🛜 Free 🃏 All major cards

🏨 GRAND VIEW BEACH HOTEL
$

VILLA POINT
TEL 784/458-4811
grandviewhotel.com
Suitably grand views and very comfortable rooms in a turn-of-the-20th-century plantation house with a bright and airy modern wing on a cliff top promontory. The Grand View offers steps down to the beach, tennis, squash; friendly and helpful staff.

🛈 21 🅿 ❄ ⛱ 🏋 🛜 Free 🃏 All major cards

🍴 FRENCH VERANDAH RESTAURANT
$$$

MARINERS HOTEL,
VILLA BEACH
TEL 784/453-1111
marinershotel.com
Charming hotel-restaurant on the waterfront facing the twinkly lights of Young Island at night. The menu is long on fish and seafood, some local flavors such as callaloo and conch soup and stuffed crab backs, and indubitably French garlic snails and *steak-frites*. Good French wines.

🛈 20 🃏 All major cards

■ BARBADOS

🏨 COBBLERS COVE
🍴 $$$$$

SPEIGHTSTOWN, ST. PETER
TEL 246/422-2291 OR U.S./
CANADA 800/890-6060
cobblerscove.com
Small and elegant all-suite hotel. Lovely accommodations with balcony or terrace overlooking the tropical gardens, plus two fine luxury suites. Tennis, water sports, notable restaurant.

🛈 40 🅿 ❄ ⛱ 🛜 Free 🃏 All major cards

🏨 CORAL REEF CLUB
$$$$$

PORTERS, ST. JAMES
TEL 246/422-2372 OR
U.S. 800/223-1108
coralreefbarbados.com
Gracious family-owned operation with a faithful clientele. Accommodations in thoughtfully appointed garden cottages and more luxurious suites. Lovely grounds, tennis, water sports, good food.

🛈 88 🅿 ❄ ⛱ 🛜 Free 🃏 All major cards

⌂ BOUGAINVILLEA BEACH RESORT
$$$$
MAXWELL, CHRIST CHURCH
TEL 246/418-0990 OR
U.S./CANADA 800/495-1858
bougainvillearesort.com
Very spacious and comfortable
studios and one- or two-
bedroom suites with kitchenettes and waterfront balconies
or terraces. Dining, tennis, and
water sports are all available.
🛏 138 🅿 ⓢ ⛵ 📺 📶 Free
ⓢ All major cards

⌂ LITTLE ARCHES HOTEL
$$$$
ENTERPRISE BEACH,
CHRIST CHURCH
TEL 246/420-4689
littlearches.com
The arches lend a Spanish-
Moorish feel to this delightful
little adults-only boutique
hotel on a white-sand beach.
Spacious and attractive rooms/
suites, excellent fusion cuisine
rooftop restaurant, mini spa,
and chilled towels by the pool!
🛏 10 🅿 ⓢ ⛵ 📶 Free
ⓢ All major cards

⌂ SEA-U GUEST HOUSE
$$$
TENT BAY, BATHSHEBA,
ST. JOSEPH
TEL 246/433-9450
seaubarbados.com
Delightful B&B in a clapboard
Bajan inn above the Atlantic
coast. Romantic rooms/suites
with louvered shutters, wooden
floors, and mahogany or bam-
boo beds. Amazing homemade
breads for breakfast; dinner in
the gazebo restaurant.
🛏 9 🅿 ⓢ 📶 Free ⓢ MC, V

⌂ RADISSON AQUATICA RESORT
$$–$$$
AQUATIC GAP, CARLISLE BAY
TEL 246/426-6000
radisson.com
Glorious beachfront location

just south of Bridgetown close
to restaurants and transporta-
tion make this a great base
for local explorations. Warm
welcome, ocean-view rooms
with attractive contemporary
colonial furnishings, family
friendly, meal plans available.
🛏 124 rooms/suites 🅿 ⓢ ⛵
📺 📶 Free ⓢ All major cards

🍴 THE CLIFF
$$$$$
DERRICKS, ST. JAMES
TEL 246/432-1922
thecliffbarbados.com
A brace of theatrically lit
terraces carved into the lime-
stone sea cliffs and clientele
poised to sample some of the
finest cuisine in the region.
Combinations such as lightly
chargrilled tuna with coriander
cream sauce; impressive wines.
Reservations a must.
🕐 Closed L ⓢ All major cards

🍴 DAPHNE'S
$$$$$
PAYNE'S BAY, ST. JAMES
TEL 264/432-2731
daphnesbarbados.com
A Caribbean outpost for one
of London's exclusive restau-
rants. Flaming torches in the
courtyard, beachside dining,
and stylish modern Italian cui-
sine that's both delicious and
beautifully presented. Reserva-
tions advised.
🕐 Closed L ⓢ All major cards

🍴 CHAMPERS
$$$–$$$$$
SKEETES HILL, ROCKLEY,
CHRIST CHURCH
TEL 246/434-3463
champersrestaurant.com
Seafront dining on a rocky
bluff with panoramic veranda.
Popular for a special occasion,
the menu is a balanced mix
of classics and local flavors
(caramelized scallops, spiced
pork tenderloin) skillfully
prepared and presented.
Attentive service, good wine

list, excellent value prix fixe
menu ($$$).
🕐 Closed L Sat. ⓢ MC, V

🍴 ATLANTIS HOTEL RESTAURANT
$$
BATHSHEBA, ST. JOSEPH
TEL 246/433-9445
atlantishotelbarbados.com
The panoramic clifftop terrace
and dining room make this a
popular lunch stop on around-
island tours. Wednesday's set-
price West Indian buffet lunch
is a veritable feast, and the
Sunday brunch (reservations
advised) is an island institution.
🕐 Closed D Sun.
ⓢ All major cards

🍴 THE SEA CAT
$–$$
HARLCYNTH HOUSE, TRENTS,
ST. JAMES
TEL 246/422-6802
the-seacat-restaurant.letseat.at
The jaunty yellow and white
chattel house facade opens
onto a garden patio at this
friendly, affordable spot on the
Platinum Coast. Beer-batter
fish bites make a tasty starter
followed by Bajan spicy octopus
salad, blackened mahi or conch,
and sweet potato fries.
🕐 Closed Sun.–Mon. ⓢ MC

■ TRINIDAD & TOBAGO

TRINIDAD

⌂ ASA WRIGHT NATURE CENTRE & LODGE
$$
ARIMA
TEL 868/667-4655 OR
U.S./CANADA 800/426-7781
asawright.org
Simple lodgings at the famous
rain forest nature center.
Rooms with screened verandas
in garden cottages, a two-bed
cottage, or two large, airy
rooms in the main building. All

---

meals included; field trips extra.
🛈 25 🅿 📶 Free in main house
📵 All major cards

🏨 TRINIDAD HILTON
$$

LADY YOUNG RD., PORT OF SPAIN
TEL 868/624-3211
hiltoncaribbean.com
A reliable option on Queen's
Park Savannah, the Hilton combines polished service and good
facilities. Well-appointed rooms,
tennis, and entertainment.
🛈 412 🅿 🏊 🏋 📶 Free
📵 All major cards

🏨 MT. PLAISIR ESTATE
🍴 $

GRANDE RIVIERE
TEL 818/670-1868
mtplaisir.com
Remote, no-frills beach getaway
with a rain forest backdrop and
sea views. Rooms furnished by
local craftsmen (sleeping 4 to
6); turtle-watching and eco-
excursions; restaurant serves
local dishes including lobster,
fruit and vegetables from the
estate, and homemade bread.
🛈 13 🅿 📶 Free in
public areas & some rooms
📵 All major cards

🍴 APSARA
$$$–$$$$

LEVEL 1, 13 QUEEN'S PARK EAST,
BELMONT, PORT OF SPAIN
TEL 868/623-7659
apsaratt.com
A renovated colonial house
is the setting for impeccably
authentic northern Indian food
in stagy Indian surroundings.
Specialties from the tandoori
ovens include locally caught
lobster tails.
📵 All major cards

🍴 TIKI VILLAGE
$$–$$$

KAPOK HOTEL (8TH FLOOR),
16–18 COTTON HILL,
PORT OF SPAIN
TEL 868/622-5765

kapokhotel.com/dining
The great Trinidadian culinary
melting pot continues with this
popular Chinese and Polyne-
sian restaurant perched above
Queen's Park Savannah with
views over the city lights at
night. Sunday's lunchtime dim
sum brunch is very popular.
🕐 Closed D Mon.–Wed.
📵 All major cards

🍴 VENI MANGÉ
$–$$

67A ARIAPITA AVE.,
WOODBROOK, PORT OF SPAIN
TEL 868/624-4597
Funky lunch spot with colorful
local art on the walls. Nouvelle
Caribbean dining adds up to
great soups, creative seafood,
vegetarian options such as
black-eyed pea croquettes, and
soursop sorbet for dessert.
🕐 Closed D Mon., Tues.,
Thurs. & Sat.–Sun. all day
📵 All major cards

TOBAGO

🏨 VILLAS AT STONEHAVEN
$$$$–$$$$$

STONEHAVEN BAY, BLACK ROCK
TEL 868/639-0361
stonehavenvillas.com
Perfect for a quiet retreat or a
family gathering, this gated
villa estate is set back from the
coast close to the rain forest.
The light and spacious French
colonial-style villas feature
pretty fabrics, fully equipped
kitchens, private sundecks with
infinity pools, and glorious
views across tropical gardens
popular with birds from the
adjacent reserve. Dining; housekeeping; beach, golf, restaurants, and shops nearby.
🛈 14 🅿 🏊 📶 Free
📵 All major cards

🏨 KARIWAK VILLAGE
$$

CROWN POINT
TEL 868/639-8442
kariwak.com

A "holistic haven and hotel,"
Kariwak nurtures guests with
yoga, relaxation sessions, mas-
sage, and healthy food. Accommodations in garden rooms or
pool cabanas a ten-minute walk
from the beach. Daily shuttle to
Pigeon Point.
🛈 24 🅿 🏊 📶 Free
📵 All major cards

🍴 KARIWAK VILLAGE RESTAURANT
$$–$$$

KARIWAK VILLAGE,
CROWN POINT
TEL 868/639-8442
Alfresco dining in a nest of
palm-thatched tiki huts. Here
you'll get flavorful home cooking from seafood soup with
cumin and basil to scrumptious
nutmeg ice cream. Buffet and
band Friday and Saturday.
📵 All major cards

🍴 LA TARTARUGA
$–$$

BUCCOO BAY ROAD,
BUCCOO
TEL 868/639-0940
latartarugatobago.com
Italian specialties include homemade pasta, pizzas, authentic
antipasto, fish and rock lobsters,
and scrumptious desserts served
inside or on the deck. More than
200 Italian wines in the cellar.
🕐 Closed L & Sun.
📵 All major cards

🍴 CIAO CAFÉ
$

20 BURNETT STREET,
SCARBOROUGH
TEL 868/639-3001
A handy Italian café and gelat-
eria in downtown Scarborough.
Enjoy a break with a real cap-
puccino or espresso and a slice
of cheesecake, or choose from
20 different flavors of ice cream.
More substantial offerings
include lasagne al forno and
freshly made pizzas.
🕐 Closed Sun. L
📵 No credit cards

🛗 Elevator 🌀 Air-conditioning 🏊 Indoor pool 🏊 Outdoor pool 🏋 Health club 📶 Wi-Fi 📵 Credit cards

Shopping

If your idea of the perfect vacation is not complete without a spot of shopping, the Caribbean is for you. These diverse and colorful islands provide visitors with a wealth of opportunities to buy local crafts, jewelry, lightweight clothing, and the region's famous spices, coffee, and rum.

■ JAMAICA

Jamaica offers something for everyone, from hand-rolled cigars to elaborate wood carvings or duty-free goods. The roadside stalls and crafts markets' best-sellers are wood carvings, T-shirts, batik clothing, hammocks, shell craft, straw hats, bamboo items, and alabaster sculptures.

Almost every town has a market, usually with some craft items. However, for the widest range of straw goods, hats, and similar items, the best places to go are **Market Street** in Montego Bay, Negril's **Rutland Point** market, or the **Ochos Rios Craft Market** on Main Street. Bargaining over the price (or haggling) is the norm—never pay the first asking price. Avoid items made using tortoiseshell (from the endangered hawksbill turtle), black coral, or crocodile skins: Importing these into the United States is illegal.

For a more upscale shopping experience in Montego Bay, the **Half Moon Shopping Village** is a popular boutique shopping and dining destination, and there's the cute Old World **The Shoppes at Rose Hall** complex. In Ocho Rios cruise passengers gravitate to the duty-free malls on Main Street and convenient **Ocean Village**, while handsomely restored **Harmony Hall** showcases collectible artworks by local artists. Visitors to Kingston's **Devon House** can also enjoy a tempting selection of boutique-style craft and clothing stores.

Essential oils and body-care products make excellent souvenirs. Local spices are always a good buy, particularly food seasonings such as the spicy Pickapeppa sauces

or "jerk" sauces, and guava jelly. Blue Mountain coffee (or the less expensive High Mountain type), either pre-ground or as beans, is another good and easily transported souvenir. Premium Jamaican rums are widely available, as is the superb locally made Tia Maria coffee liqueur.

Duty-free or "in bond" shops carry items such as silverware, crystal, china, watches, jewelry, linens, and perfumes. Savings can be made, but check the purchase price at home before leaving. Last-minute buys and souvenirs are also available at the well-stocked duty-free shopping area in **Sangster International Airport.**

■ CAYMAN ISLANDS

On duty-free Grand Cayman, there's no sales tax, either, so considerable savings can be made on items such as linens, leather goods, designer clothes, crystal, porcelain, perfumes, watches, and camera equipment. Most shops are in George Town, but several malls have sprung up on West Bay Road, including the **West Shore Centre, Galleria Plaza, Coconut Place, The Strand,** and **The Falls. Camana Bay,** an upscale shopping, dining, and entertainment destination, also hosts a farmers market on Wednesdays, where you can find crafts and homemade island jellies and chutneys. In George Town itself, the **Anchorage Shopping Centre, Landmark,** and **Kirk Freeport Plaza** are some of the main outlets.

Local arts and crafts are worth seeking out in galleries such as **Pure Art** (S. Church St., tel

345/949-9133) and **Cayman Craft Market** (near the cruise-ship pier). Sea-salvaged coins from Spanish or Dutch treasure ships can be bought at **Mitzi's Fine Jewelry** (Bay Harbour Centre, tel 345/945-5014), and similar numismatic items are also available at **24 K-Mon Jewelers** (several locations, including The Falls, tel 345/949-1499). For an unusual underwater souvenir, take home a stunning print by world-famous underwater photographer **Cathy Church** (Sunset House Hotel, S. Church St., tel 345/949-7415).

The islands' biggest selling export item is rum cake made from a recipe reputedly more than 100 years old. Buy it at any one of the many outlets of the **Tortuga Rum Company,** which can be found in the island's major shopping centers.

■ TURKS & CAICOS ISLANDS

If you are planning to go shopping in the TCI, then head for the gateway island of Providenciales. Most of the shops here are in small malls along the Leeward Highway, such as **Ports of Call, La Petite Plaza, Salt Mills Plaza,** and in Grace Bay's **Regent Village.**

With no sales tax on the islands, you can buy duty-free goods such as jewelry, watches, perfumes, crystal, cameras, cigars, and liquor. The **Grand Turk Cruise Center** stocks a wide range of duty-free items. One of Provo's best known galleries, the **Bamboo Gallery** (Market Place), features paintings by local and Haitian artists, beaded jewelry, ceramics, and sculpture. Other craft and art outlets include **Anna's Art Gallery & Studio** (Salt Mills) and **Greensleeves** (Central Sq.). **Flavours of the Turks & Caicos Islands,** Regent Village, is a good source of Bambarra Rum, locally made teas, and seasonings. Handmade crafts, such as woven baskets from the Middle Caicos Co-operative, are on sale from National Trust shops on Providenciales and Grand Turk.

■ DOMINICAN REPUBLIC

Santo Domingo has several top-end malls, including **Acrópolis, Plaza Central,** and the **Malecón Center.** The main shopping streets are **Calle Duarte** and pedestrianized **Calle El Conde.** Most major resorts have shops selling summer attire, T-shirts, and swimwear. Crafts can be found in the main markets in every town. The biggest is **Mercado Modelo** in Santo Domingo, with a wide range of ceramics, straw hats, wood carvings, and naive Haitian art; Sosúa is also renowned for crafts shopping. Amber and blue larimar jewelry is also a popular buy. Local jeweler **Harrisons** (harrisons.com) is a reputable source with branches in most resorts. The Dominican Republic produces reasonably priced rum and cigars.

■ PUERTO RICO

Puerto Rico is not a duty-free island (sales tax is 5.5 percent), but there is no duty on items taken into the U.S., so you can find good prices on china, crystal, fashions, and crafts. All prices are in U.S. dollars. Old San Juan offers a variety of shops, especially for jewelry, leather, and clothes. Check out the factory outlet stores on Calle Cristo. There are also some fine art galleries.

Condado is known for its exclusive boutiques and fashion designer shops, which congregate around exclusive Avenida Ashford.

In the heart of the San Juan metropolitan area is **Plaza Las Américas,** Hato Rey, the largest shopping center in the Caribbean, with more than 300 stores.

Old San Juan has a number of souvenir and handicraft shops. For local arts and crafts buys, don't miss the excellent **Centro Nacional de Artes Populares y Artesanías** (Calle Cristo 253).

Popular gifts include *santos* (small carved saint figures), Carnival masks, and *mundillo*, handmade bobbin lace. Fine hammocks are still made here, and, of course, Puerto Rico is a major producer of rum and cigars.

■ VIRGIN ISLANDS

U.S. VIRGIN ISLANDS

ST. CROIX

Downtown **Christiansted** offers the best shopping on the island, centered on Strand, King, and Company Streets, and King's Alley Walk. The Walk offers boutiques and galleries, craft stalls selling coconut shell carvings, and jewelry stores, where the turquoise-colored gemstone larimar (found exclusively in the Caribbean) has been incorporated in pendants, rings, and bracelets. Cruzan Hook bracelets are a popular souvenir re-created by jeweler Sonya Hough at **Sonya Ltd.** (1 Company St.). You wear the hook facing your heart if it is taken, away from the heart if you are available.

Frederiksted's main shopping area is clustered near the cruise-ship pier, and offers a selection of specialty shops and art galleries displaying works by local artists.

You can watch artists work in the **St. Croix LEAP** woodwork studio (Mahogany Rd. Rte. 76), north of Frederiksted, and buy carvings on island hardwoods. The **Estate Whim Museum** gift shop has a good range of local crafts, condiments, books, and maps.

ST. JOHN

Shopping on St. John is low-key, but full of temptations. There are a few small boutiques and jewelers in **Wharfside Village,** close to the ferry dock. For more of a selection, head to **Mongoose Junction** (North Shore Rd.)—an open-air complex in the local plantation house–style. **R. & I. Patton Goldsmithing** sells Rudy and Irene's island-inspired designs in 14- to 18-karat gold and sterling silver, as well as authenticated antique Spanish coins set in rings and pendants.

Big Planet Adventurer Outfitters can outfit hikers and offers colorful swimwear and resortwear; find island artworks at **Bajo el Sol;** and **Fabric Mill** specializes in batik. Irresistible hand-painted cotton T-shirts and sweaters by local designer **Sloop Jones** are available from his studio/shop in the East End (off Hwy. 10).

ST. THOMAS

U.S. visitors to this Caribbean retail mecca can take advantage of a $1,600 duty-free allowance each on returning home, and families can pool their allowances for larger purchases. Any items actually made in the USVI do not count toward the duty-free exemption. Popular buys are fine crystal and china, electronics, jewelry, and perfume, sold in large stores on Dronningens Gade/Main Street and in Havensight Mall. Stores are generally open Monday to Saturday 9 a.m. to 5 p.m. If a cruise ship calls on a Sunday, some stores will open for at least part of the day.

In Charlotte Amalie a slew of boutiques are tucked in the narrow alleys leading down to the waterfront, where the eye-catching boutique **Local Color** does a fun line in pretty Jams World uncrushable sundresses as well as other cotton prints, straw hats, hand-painted T-shirts, and silver jewelry.

For great Caribbean crafts and souvenirs, check out the **Native Arts and Crafts Cooperative** (bottom of Tolbod Gade), piled high with locally produced items including wood carvings, costume dolls, and Taste of Paradise sauces and jellies. Also the **Caribbean Marketplace** in Havensight Mall.

Outside Charlotte Amalie, **Tillett Gardens** is an artisans' enclave with galleries, craft studios, a restaurant, and tame iguanas basking in the shade. At Red Hook, **The Color of Joy Art & Framing** (American Yacht Harbor) showcases owner Corinne van Rensselaer's vibrant watercolors and a selection of work by other local artists.

BRITISH VIRGIN ISLANDS

TORTOLA

Road Town's top souvenir stop has to be **Sunny Caribbee Spice Co.** on Main Street (also at Soper's Hole). This is condiment city, piled high with exotic fruit teas, preserves made from guava, papaya, and passion fruit, tamarind chutney, and jerk seasonings. The art gallery next door showcases Caribbean paintings, affordable prints, Haitian voodoo flags, and pottery.

You can purchase Pusser's rum and yachting-style casualwear at **Pusser's Company Store;** or take a stroll while searching for T-shirts and other small souvenirs at the colorful pastel-painted stalls behind the waterfront.

In the West End assorted boutiques and souvenir outlets at the **Soper's Hole Marina** provide retail therapy.

◼ DUTCH CARIBBEAN

ARUBA

Bargain hunters will find most of the big stores in Oranjestad's **Ports of Call Marketplace, Renaissance Marketplace, Royal Plaza Mall,** and along the main street, **Caya G.F. Betico Croes.** China, linens, electronic goods, perfumes, and designer clothes are all good buys. At Palm Beach the upscale **Paseo Herencia** mall is a magnet for style-conscious shoppers.

Jewelry is a popular buy, and **Gandelman Jewelers** outlets around town stock precious and semiprecious jewelry items, designer watches, Montblanc pens, Baccarat crystal, china, and leather accessories.

For arts and crafts, check out **Art & Tradition Handicrafts** (Caya G.F. Betico Croes 30 & Royal Plaza Mall). Also, the **Bonbini Festival** at Fort Zoutman every Tuesday evening.

CURAÇAO

Willemstad offers good deals on perfume, jewelry, china, cameras, and electronic goods. The major stores and boutiques are crowded into the Punda district around Breedestraat. On the Otrabanda side, close to the cruise terminal, **Gallery Kas Di Alma Blou** (the Blue House) is a popular stop with art lovers. The gallery occupies a 300-year-old plantation house with a pretty courtyard tea garden and also sells quality island crafts in the gift shop.

Out in the countryside, several *landhuizen,* including **Landhuis Jan Kok, Landhuis Groot Santa Martha,** and **Landhuis Bloemhof,** house arts and crafts galleries. Locally made soaps, soothing gels,

and skin-care products are on sale at the **Curaçao Aloe Plantation & Factory,** Groot St. Joris.

SABA

Mary Gertrude Johnson introduced the art of drawn threadwork, or Saban lace, to the island in the 1870s, and intricately embroidered linen tableware is sold in several **Windwardside** craft shops. Another local specialty is Saba Spice, a 75.5-proof rum flavored with cinnamon, cloves, nutmeg, orange peel, and brown sugar. For local artworks, look in at the **Peanut Gallery,** Lambee Plaza, next door to sister store **El Momo Folk Art.**

SINT MAARTEN/ ST.- MARTIN

Both Dutch and French sides of the island offer duty-free shopping and deals worth 15 to 30 percent on U.S. prices for perfumes, electronic goods, jewelry, china, crystal, linens, and fashions.

Philipsburg's **Front Street** shopping district boasts the widest array of goods. It is worth noting that the U.S. dollar prices on the Dutch side are likely to offer better savings than the euro deals on the French side.

For locally made souvenirs, check out the open-air **Philipsburg Market Place,** on Back Street. Also the boutiques, stores, and sidewalk cafés on Old Street.

Marigot is the island's fashion capital, with plenty of temptations to be found on rue de la République and on rue de la Liberté. The small mall in the smart **Marina Royale** is brimful with boutiques selling designer labels, and the fashion-conscious can take their pick from racks of elegant apparel from the high priests of the fashion scene. Imported French wines and gourmet canned foods or bonbons also make a great treat or gift to take home.

In Grand Case art lovers will find **Tropismes Gallery,** 107 Blvd. de Grand Case, one of the island's most high-profile art showcases.

■ LEEWARD ISLANDS

ANGUILLA

Black-belt shopaholics may suffer withdrawal symptoms on Anguilla. However, it does offer a couple interesting arts and crafts outlets. The **Savannah Gallery** in The Valley special- izes in Haitian paintings, tin carvings, fabulous sequined voodoo flags, and works by local photographers.

On Main Road West look for **Cheddie's Carving Studio,** where Cheddie Richardson exhibits his sculpture and limited-edition bronzes. His evocative wood carv- ings of dolphins, fish, birds, and human figures are fashioned from driftwood, mahogany, and walnut.

ANTIGUA

Downtown **St. John's** is this island's chief shopping district. **Heritage Quay** is packed with duty-free stores selling jewelry, designer fashions, perfumes, and gifts. On **Redcliffe Quay,** there are boutiques stocked with color- ful island fashions; Hans Smit sells his innovative and tempt- ingly affordable jewelry at **The Goldsmitty;** and **The Pottery Shop** displays Sarah Fuller's 100 percent Antiguan pieces created from local clays.

Outside St. John's, **Harmony Hall** on the east coast is a great place to check out local arts and crafts. Also **Rhythm of Blue,** English Harbour, where potter Nancy Nicholson displays her own dazzling blue ceramics alongside fine art, jewelry, and sculpture by

fellow local and regional artists (gal- lery open Nov.–May; studio visits by appointment). In Nelson's Dock- yard **Things Local** offers works by Carl Henry, one of Antigua's finest wood sculptors, who selects Anti- guan hardwoods such as mahogany and almond for his carvings.

MONTSERRAT

Not surprisingly, volcano-related souvenirs are popular on Mont- serrat. Stunning photographs of the Soufrière Hills volcano in its active phase sell at **Woolcock's Craft & Photo Gallery,** Brades; and look out for David Lea's DVD *The Price of Paradise* (Lea is the proprietor of Gingerbread Hill, p. 373), which charts the effect of the eruption on the island and its people. The **Oriole Gift Shop,** National Trust Museum, Little Bay, is a good source of island handicrafts, while philatelists can seek out the **Montserrat Phila- telic Bureau,** Government Build, Brades, for unusual and beautiful stamps. Last-minute purchases can be made at the well-stocked **Jus Lookin** craft and rum shop at Gerald's Airport.

ST. KITTS

Cruise-ship visitors to St. Kitts are greeted by the **Port Zante** shop- ping complex at the foot of the gangplank, complete with all the usual duty-free jewelry and booze stores. **Spencer Cameron Gallery** (10 Independence Square) show- cases a terrific array of works small and large by Caribbean artists, including owner Rosey Cameron, and Kittitian resident Kate Spen- cer's delectable silk art scarves. Call ahead to visit Kate's studio on the Rawlins Plantation (tel 869/669-7740). Also unique to the island, the **Caribelle Batik Fac- tory,** Old Road Town, welcomes visitors. Their comfy, loose-fitting

Hawaiian-style shirts, sundresses, and wraps are popular buys with travelers.

NEVIS

Charlestown's restored water- front district boasts a few small boutiques and souvenir outlets, as does the Cotton Ginnery building nearby, where **The Craft House** stocks a range of handcrafted local pottery, coconut and shell jewelry, and leather sandals. **Island Hopper,** on Main Street, carries Caribelle Batik's bright, casual clothing from St. Kitts.

The seasonal (Nov.–March) **Charlestown Gallery,** Cotton House Building (near the tourist office) is a not-for-profit showcase for local artists. Among the fine art, ceramics, and carvings, look for Deborah Tyrell's fun and funky Nevisian cloth art.

Stamp collectors can capture a little local color at the **Nevis Phila- telic Bureau,** in Lower Happy Hill Alley between the ferry berth and Main Street.

■ FRENCH ANTILLES

GUADELOUPE

Shopping is not a high priority in Guadeloupe, though French luxury goods at mainland prices can be tempting. Some **Pointe- à-Pitre** stores offer an extra 20 percent discount on purchases made with a credit card or trav- eler's checks.

The capital's main shopping streets are **rue Frébault, rue Schoelcher,** and **rue de Noziers,** and there are small, upscale bou- tiques in the **Centre St.-John Perse** mall by the cruise-ship terminal.

Rum is available from super- markets, the airport duty-free, or the **Musée du Rhum** in Bellevue. Gosier, Ste.-Anne, and St.-François all have handicrafts shops and stalls specializing in Caribbean arts and crafts, and souvenirs such as costume dolls dressed in bright Madras cotton.

MARTINIQUE

Fort-de-France is the style capital of the French Antilles, offering French luxury goods from designer fashions and perfumes to china and glass at prices lower than in mainland France. Some stores give an additional 20 percent discount for luxury purchases made with certain credit cards (always ask).

The best selection of boutiques is found along **rue Victor Hugo** and the grid of streets between **rue de la République** and **rue de la Liberté.** Jewelers on rue Lamartine and rue Isambert are an excellent hunting ground for Baccarat crystal, Limoges porcelain, and jewelry including the *chaîne forçat,* a gold "slave chain" necklace that puts the finishing touch to traditional creole costume. Madras cotton traditional costumes and frilly white shirts are sold at market stalls in most towns.

Beyond the capital, the bustling resort of Les Trois-Îlets is a good spot for art galleries and boutiques selling fashions and beachwear. Or stop by **Domaine Château Gaillard,** rte. des Trois-Îlets, which combines crafts studios with the island's biggest plant nursery and an on-site restaurant.

Martinican rum is among the Caribbean's finest, and the island's basketware, pottery, shell art, and patchwork are displayed in souvenir stores and galleries.

ST.- BARTHÉLEMY

St. Barts's duty-free status is a good excuse to indulge in some seriously upscale retail therapy. Cartier, Gucci, and Hermès all maintain outposts in **Gustavia,** alongside duty-free emporiums

such as **Carat,** on rue de la République. The upscale mall **Le Carré d'Or,** quai de la République, is a favorite shopping destination. French perfumes and cosmetics, jewelry, watches, and crystal are all popular buys.

Wine buffs can check out the impressive vintage selection at **Cellier du Gouverneur,** quai de la République.

Hollywood A-listers are known to stock up on island style at **Vanita Rosa,** rue Oscar II; and for up-to-the-minute French and Italian fashions, try **Stéphane & Bernard,** Gallerie Gréaux. Beyond Gustavia, the best of the rest can be found at the **Villa Créole** mall in St.-Jean.

◼ WINDWARD ISLANDS

DOMINICA

The island's Carib craftsmen are famous for their basketware made from l'arouma reeds. The intricate designs are fashioned in a combination of natural, brown, and black, and can be bought from roadside stalls in **Carib Territory,** or from one of Roseau's many crafts shops. There is a **Craft Market,** behind the Dominican Museum, which combines local crafts with a raft of souvenirs, and local artists, wood-carvers, and jewelers set up stalls along Bay Street when cruise ships are in port. Look out for island motifs such as parrots, dolphins, and butterflies. Haitian-born Louis Desiré is one of Dominica's leading sculptors in wood. His work can be found in the **Butterfly Boutique** at Papillote Wilderness Retreat.

Other Dominican products to look out for include the island's 100 percent Arabica coffee, Café Sisserou, bay rum and colognes from Dominica

Essential Oils & Spices, and Bello's pepper sauces, fruit syrups, and marmalades.

GRENADA

Cruise visitors will find the **Esplanade Mall** at the bottom of the gangplank and some good deals on spirits and perfumes in its duty-free stores, as well as Grenadian specialty exotic fruit jams and jellies. Spices are a great buy on Grenada. Mixed baskets of nutmeg, cinnamon, cloves, and bay rum leaves make popular gifts for cooks, or as souvenir potpourri. And don't forget delectable island-made gourmet **Bonbon Chocolates** from the Grenada Chocolate Company.

The **Carenage** boasts several small galleries and craft shops, and Young Street is home to **Yellow Poui Gallery** for local art; **Art Fabrik,** where you can watch the batik process in the courtyard factory; and crafts emporium **Tikal,** across the street.

Convenient for the southern beach hotels, **Grand Anse Shopping Centre** and **Spiceland Mall** have a good selection of gift shops and galleries selling Caribbean arts and crafts, including the excellent contemporary **Art and Soul Gallery,** and boutiques stocking island fashions. There is a local spice market, too, located between the main road and the beach.

ST. LUCIA

The waterfront **Castries craft market,** and the vendors' market across the street, offer T-shirts, handwoven straw goods, local pottery, and wood carvings.

For a more upscale shopping experience, the attractive open-air mall on the cruise-ship pier at **Pointe Seraphine** presides over a selection of duty-free stores, boutiques, and galleries, as does the larger **La Place Carenage** on the opposite side of the harbor.

Just outside Castries, at La Toc on the slopes of Morne Fortune, **Bagshaw Studios** has a factory shop. This local cottage industry specializes in colorful hand-printed clothing, good-quality T-shirts, and a range of pretty table linens adorned with parrots and tropical hibiscus and poinsettia flowers.

Farther up Morne Fortune, **Eudovic's Studio & Gallery** show-cases works by master wood-carver Vincent Joseph Eudovic and artists including his son Jallim. Eudovic Senior's stunning abstract pieces are displayed alongside more affordable souvenir items such as African-style masks and pineapple-shaped wall decorations symboliz-ing Caribbean hospitality. Purchases can be shipped home.

In the north of the island, bou-tiques, gift stores, and mini-marts can be found at **Gablewoods Mall,** Choc Bay, and the **Baywalk Mall,** in Rodney Bay Village.

ST. VINCENT & THE GRENADINES

There is duty-free shopping at the cruise terminal in **Kingstown,** as well as boutiques and souvenir outlets offering a selection of Caribbean crafts, spices, and gift ideas. Woven straw hats, mats, and baskets are Vincy specialties on sale around the island. For contemporary arts and crafts and a bite to eat, drop in at the **Little Gallery** housed in the eye-catching surroundings of the beachfront Grand View Grill in Villa.

On Bequia, **Noah's Arkade** at the Frangipani Hotel, Port Elizabeth, stocks a good range of island arts, crafts, and souvenir items. Bequia's boatbuilding heri-tage is celebrated in miniature at **Sargeant Brothers Model Boats,** Front Street. **The Oasis Art Gallery**

displays original works and *giclée* prints of colorful hummingbirds, mermaids, and ships at anchor in the bay by gallery curator L. D. Lucy, as well as her husband Prop's model boats that sail. Regular exhibitions showcase the talents of other local artists.

Farther afield, painter Julie Savage Lea displays her colorful island scenes at **Mango Art Studio,** Belmont (tel 784/455-4677); while **Claude Victorine's Art Studio,** Lower Bay (tel 784/458-3150), is a showcase for beautiful hand-painted silk cushion covers, scarves, and pareus.

■ BARBADOS

Bridgetown is a duty-free port offering savings of up to 30 to 40 percent off European and U.S. retail prices. The best of the tax-free action is on Broad Street, where the **Cave Shepherd** and **Harrisons** department stores, and the **DaCostas Mall** offer the widest selection of jewelry and watches, cameras, electronic goods, china, crystal, perfumes, and cosmetics. To make a duty-free purchase, take the immigra-tion slip issued on arrival in Barbados; most stores will deliver to the airport or hotel.

For Caribbean crafts and island fashions, check out the **Pelican Craft Centre,** near Bridgetown Harbour, and colorful **Chattel Village** shopping complexes in Holetown and St. Lawrence Gap. Holetown also boasts the **West Coast Mall,** while Speightstown has a duo of art galleries—**Man-go's Fine Art Gallery** and the **Gallery of Caribbean Art.**

A terrific range of decora-tive island pottery is on sale at **Earthworks,** Edgehill Heights, St. Thomas, where you can also watch the assortment of bowls, platters, mugs, and jugs being made and painted.

On the south coast shoppers head for **Hastings Plaza** and the **Quayside Centre** in Rockley.

The **Best of Barbados** boutiques around the island are a good source of quality local crafts, gourmet treats, and gifts.

■ TRINIDAD & TOBAGO

The lower end of **Frederick Street** in Port of Spain resembles a hectic international bazaar. Indian sari shops and boutiques spill out onto the sidewalk and street vendors hawk jewelry, leather goods, and the latest calypso, soca, and chutney CDs. Though "chutney" signifies East Indian music not a condiment when choosing a CD, adventur-ous gourmets might like to stock up on edible Trinidadian condi-ments, such as fiery hot pepper sauces, tamarind and mango chutneys, and Angostura bitters.

For a more upscale shop-ping experience, take a trip to **Ellerslie Plaza** in Maraval, and the **Market Shoppes,** with its boutiques, galleries, and craft shops attached to the Normandie Hotel (Nook Ave., St. Ann).

Tobago is somewhat limited on mainstream shopping, but there is no shortage of arts and crafts. The small shopping village at **Store Bay** offers a colorful array of batik and tie-dye beach-wear, T-shirts, straw hats, bead jewelry, pottery, and other crafts. Check out local galleries and stu-dios as you tour the island.

Sports & Activities

One of the best regions in the world for outdoor activities, the Caribbean offers superb diving, snorkeling, boating, and fishing in its turquoise waters, as well as golfing and rain forest hiking.

■ JAMAICA

Adventure & Sightseeing Tours

Jamaica's leading provider of soft adventures with outposts in Montego Bay/Negril and Ocho Rios/ Falmouth, **Chukka Adventure Tours** (tel 876/979-8500 or U.S. 877/424-8552, chukka.com) has close links with the cruise operators and offers activities ranging from rain forest zip-lining to visiting the Bob Marley Centre.

Boating

Day sails are available through a number of operators including **Dreamer Catamaran Cruises** (tel 876/979-0102, dreamer catamarans.com).

Diving & Water Sports

The best diving is off the north coast, on the edge of the Cayman Trench. PADI-certified **Jamaica Scuba Divers** (tel 876/381-1113, scuba-jamaica.com) offers a full range of dive services and will pick up from destinations along the coast to Ocho Rios. In Negril **Sun Divers Watersports**, Travellers Beach Resort (tel 876/405-6872, sundiversnegril.com) combines dive services with water sports, including parasailing and snorkeling.

Golf

Golfers flock to the north coast resort areas for the pick of Jamaica's dozen or so courses, many of which occupy spectacular sites. West of Montego Bay is the stunning championship course at the **Tryall Club,** Sandy Bay (tel 876/956-5681, tryall club.com); to the east, the White Witch course at **Rose Hall** (tel 876/632-7444,

whitewitchgolf.com). Golfers of all abilities can benefit from the golf academies at the Trent Jones Sr.–designed championship course **Golf at Half Moon,** Montego Bay (tel 876/953-2560, halfmoon. rockresorts.com); and **Runaway Bay Golf Club,** Jewel Runaway Bay Beach & Golf Resort (tel 876/972-7400, jewelresorts.com).

Horseback Tours

Riding excursions can be arranged through **Chukka** (see Adventure & Sightseeing Tours) and **Prospect Outback Adventures**, just outside Ocho Rios (tel 876/994-1058, prospectoutbackadventures.com). The **Half Moon Equestrian Centre** in Montego Bay (tel 876/953-2286, horseback ridingjamaica .com) offers beach rides and swimming with horses.

Sportfishing

Full- and half-day sportfishing charters are available from marinas along the north coast and from Port Antonio, or contact Falmouth's **Glistening Waters Marina** (tel 876/954-3229, glisteningwaters.com).

■ CAYMAN ISLANDS

Boat Trips

For nondivers who want to experience the wonders of the deep off Grand Cayman, the 48-passenger *Atlantis* **submarine**, S. Church Street, George Town (tel 345/949-7700, caymanislandssubmarines .com) is the solution. **Cayman Kayaks** (tel 345/926-4467, cayman kayaks.com) offers a brace of excellent tours, including the amazing night-time tour on a secret lagoon where bioluminescence blooms.

Diving

The Cayman Islands' superb dive sites are matched by well-equipped dive operators offering everything from snorkeling and basic tuition to highly sophisticated technical training.

Cayman Brac: **Reef Divers,** West End (tel 345/948-1642, reefdiverscaymanbrac.com).

Grand Cayman: **DiveTech,** Cobalt Coast Resort, Sea Fan Drive (tel 345/946-5658 or 888/946-5656, divetech.com); **Indepth Watersports** (tel 345/926-8604 or 866/476-2195, indepthwatersports.com); **Ocean Frontiers,** 344 C Austin Conolly Drive, East End (tel 345/947-7500 or 800/348-6096, ocean frontiers.com).

Little Cayman: **Reef Divers,** Little Cayman Reef Beach Resort (tel 345/948-1033, littlecayman .com); **Southern Cross Club** (tel 345/948-1099 or 800/899-2582, southerncrossclub.com).

Hiking

On Grand Cayman, there are regular guided tours of the National Trust's **Mastic Trail,** a 2-mile (3 km) woodland hike through old-growth forest (tel 345/749-1121, nationaltrust.org .ky). Guided hikes are also offered by butterfly and plant expert **Ann Stafford** (caymANNature.ky). On the sister islands, **Nature Cayman** (tel 345/948-2222, itsyoursto explore.com) provides free tours and information.

Sportfishing

Visitors seek out the Cayman Islands for deepwater game fish as well as for tarpon, bonefish, and reef fishing expeditions. The

Cayman Islands Angling Club (tel 345/945-3131, fishcayman .com) is a useful source of information and hosts an annual International Fishing Tournament (April). Full- and half-day fishing trips are available from charter boat operators such as **Bayside Watersports,** Morgan's Harbor (Grand Cayman, tel 345/949-3200, baysidewatersports.com); and **Captain Ron Ebanks,** Fly Fish Grand Cayman, Coconut Place, West Bay Road, Grand Cayman (tel 345/947-3146, flyfishgrand cayman.com).

■ TURKS & CAICOS ISLANDS

Adventure Tours

See sidebar page 91.

Diving & Snorkeling

The TCI offer world-class diving opportunities in the archipelago's calm, crystal clear waters. Recommended dive operators include:

Grand Turk: **Blue Water Divers** (tel 649/946-2432, grandturk scuba.com); **Oasis Divers** (tel 649/946-1128 or 800/892-3995, oasisdivers.com).

Providenciales: **Big Blue Unlimited** (tel 649/946-5034 or 649/231-6455, bigblueun limited.com); **Dive Provo** (tel 649/946-5040 or 800/234-7768, diveprovo.com); **Provo Turtle Divers** (tel 649/946-4232 or 800/833-1341, provoturtle divers.com).

Golf

Fringed with palm trees and studded with lakes, the **Provo Golf & Country Club** (Grace Bay, tel 649/246-5991 or U.S./Canada 877/218-9124, provogolfclub .com) is an 18-hole championship course.

■ DOMINICAN REPUBLIC

Adventure Tours & Hiking

Whether you want to hike, bike, horseback ride, or try your hand at white-water rafting, the island's two leading adventure tour operators should be able to help. Contact **Iguana Mama,** Cabarete (tel 809/571-0908, iguanamama .com); and **Rancho Baiguate,** Jarabacoa (tel 809/574-6890 or U.S./Canada 646/727-7783, ranchobaiguate.com).

Diving

Every major resort area has dive operators, including: **Dressel Divers,** Iberostar, Punta Cana (tel 809/221-1889, dresseldivers .com); **Las Galeras Divers,** Las Galeras (tel 809/538-0220, las-galeras-divers.com); **Neptuno Dive Center,** Juan Dolio (tel 829/578-4671, neptunodive .com); **Northern Coast Aquasports,** Sosúa (tel 809/571-1028, northerncoastdiving.com).

Golf

The Dominican Republic boasts around 18 championship courses and dozens more, mostly concentrated in the eastern Coconut Coast region. Try **Cocotal Golf & Country Club,** Playa Bavaró, Punta Cana (tel 809/687-4653, cocotalgolf.com); also the stunning oceanfront Corales and La Cana courses at **Puntacana Resort & Club** (tel 809/959-4653 or 1-888/442-2262, puntacana.com). On the north coast, the **Playa Dorada Golf Course,** Puerto Plata (tel 809/320-3472, playadoradagolf .com) is recommended. Southeast of Santo Domingo, **Casa de Campo** (tel 809/523-8115 or 800/336-5520, casadecampo .com.do) boasts three world-class courses designed by Pete Dye.

Sportfishing

Dozens of charter boats offering deep-sea fishing excursions occupy marinas along the east coast. Half- and full-day trips can be arranged through the Aquatic Center at **Puntacana Resort & Club,** Punta Cana (tel 809/959-2262, puntacana.com); also with the **Casa de Campo Marina,** La Romana (tel 809/523-8646, marinacasadecampo.com.do).

Water Sports

Cabarete is one of the world's top windsurfing and kiteboarding destinations. Well-equipped operators offering equipment rentals and tuition include **Cabarete Windsports Club** (tel 809/571-0784); **Laser Training Cabarete** (tel 809/571-0640, caribwind.com); **Kitexcite** (tel 809/981-0778, kitexcite.com); and **Laurel Eastman Kiteboarding** (tel 809/571-0564, laurel eastman.com).

■ PUERTO RICO

Adventure Tours & Hiking

Puerto Rico's mountainous rain forest is a playground for adrenaline junkies. **Toro Verde Nature Adventure Park,** Orocovis (tel 787/867-7020, toroverdepr .com) offers a ropes course, rappelling, and zip lines. For hiking, rappelling, and waterfall climbing, contact **Acampa Nature Adventure Tours** (tel 787/706-0695, acampapr.com); or **Rocaliza Adventure Tours** (tel 787/268-0101, rocaliza.com).

Diving

Puerto Rico's south coast has fantastic wall diving from La Parguera and Guánica in the southwest. Off the east coast, the idyllic islands of Vieques and Culebra are fringed with coral reefs, while the calm seas, mini-walls, and caverns around the mainland dive center of Fajardo create the perfect conditions for beginners. Contact local operators **Culebra Divers** (tel 787/742-0803, culebradivers.com); **Island Scuba**, Guánica (tel 787/309-6556, sanjuandiver.com); or **Sea Ventures Dive Centers**, Fajardo (tel 787/863-3483 or 800/739-3483, divepuertorico.com).

Golf

Puerto Rico has some 20 fine golf courses to choose from. The most talked about recent addition to the roster is the glorious **Royal Isabela Luxury Golf Course & Resort**, Isabela (tel 787/609-5888, royalisabela.com), a links-style course built into the challenging contours of an ocean-view plateau. The **Dorado Beach, A Ritz Carlton Reserve** (tel 787/626-1100 ext. 7209, ritzcarlton.com) has three courses, including Robert Trent Jones Sr.'s restored East Course. Meanwhile, Trent Jones Jr.'s environmentally friendly course at **Bahía Beach Golf Club,** Río Grande (tel 787/809-8920, bahiabeachpuertorico.com) has won an Audubon award; there are two stunning courses at the **Wyndham Río Mar Golf Club,** Río Grande (tel 787/888-7060 or 800/474-4627, wyndhamriomar .com), poised between the ocean and El Yunque; and the **Arthur Hills Golf Course** at the Waldorf Astoria El Conquistador, Fajardo (tel 787/863-6784, elconresort .com) is literally breathtaking with its 200-foot (61 m) elevation changes.

Sportfishing

Charter fishing boats are available year-round from harbors in San Juan, Fajardo, Humacao, and Mayagüez. The best fishing is from October to early March, when game fish are in season. However, the aptly named "Blue Marlin Alley" off the north coast sees plenty of migrating fish in summer. Half-day, full-day, or longer charters from **Bill Wraps Fishing Charters P.R.,** Fajardo (tel 787/364-4216, billwrapsfishingpr .com); and, just east of San Juan, **Caribbean Outfitters,** Carolina (tel 787/396-8346, fishingin puertorico.com).

■ VIRGIN ISLANDS

U.S. VIRGIN ISLANDS

ST. CROIX
Boating
Plenty of local operators offer day trips to Buck Island with lunch and snorkeling. Day and half-day boat trips with **Caribbean Sea Adventures** (tel 340/773-2628, caribbeanseaadventures.com) depart from the Christiansted waterfront; or sail off with Captain Dee of **Bilinda Charters** (tel 340/514-2270, sailbilinda.com).

Diving & Snorkeling
Sites appealing to divers of all skill levels include the Cane Bay Wall, a short wade from Cane Bay beach and home turf for the **Cane Bay Dive Shop** (tel 340/718-9913 or 800/338-3843, canebayscuba.com); **St. Croix SCUBA** (tel 340/773-5994 or 877/567-1367, stcroixscuba .com) have operations in both Christiansted and Frederiksted, and can take cruise visitors diving right off the Frederiksted pier.

Golf
Fine golf courses include the elegant Trent Jones Sr. course at the **Carambola Golf Club** (tel 340/778-5638, golfcarambola .com); and the scenic 18-hole course at the **Buccaneer Hotel** (tel 340/712-2144, thebuccaneer .com).

Horseback Riding
Just north of Frederiksted, experience beach rides and nature tours in the hills surrounding the Sprat Hall Plantation with **Paul and Jill's Equestrian Stables,** Creque Dam Rainforest Road/Rte. 58 (tel 340/772-2880, paulandjills.com).

Island Tours
Explore the island on a minibus tour with **St. Croix Safari Tours** (tel 340/773-6700, gotostcroix .com/guided-tours).

ST. JOHN
Boating
Hop aboard the *Fantasy* (tel 340/513-3212, daysailfantasy .com) for a day of swimming, snorkeling, fishing, and exploring the beaches of the national park; or take a little beach catamaran and a guide from **Sail Safaris** (tel 340/626-8181, sailsafaris.net) to neighboring islands.

Diving & Snorkeling
Snorkeling off St. John is as easy as wading off the beach (see sidebar p. 158). Divers will need transportation to the best sites, which lie a little farther offshore and in the BVI. Recommended local operators include **Cruz Bay Watersports** (tel 340/776-6234, cruzbaywatersports .com) and **Low Key Watersports** (tel 340/693-8999 or 800/835-7718, divelowkey.com).

Horseback Riding
Enjoy scenic 60- or 90-minute rides in the hills above the East End with views from **Carolina Corral** (tel 340/693-5778, horsesstjohn.com).

Kayaking
St. John's scalloped coastline is perfectly suited to kayaking

expeditions. Guided coastal tours and rentals from **Arawak Expeditions,** Cruz Bay (tel 340/693-8312, arawakexp.com).

ST. THOMAS
Boating
See sidebar page 153, for details of day sails to neighboring islands. Another option is a powerboat rental from **Nauti Nymph** (tel 340/775-5066, nautinymph.com).

Diving
Calm seas, excellent visibility, and superb reef and wreck diving make for a great dive break in the islands. Look for hotel dive packages. Independent operators include **Coki Dive Center** (tel 340/775-4220, cokidive.com) and **Red Hook Dive Center** (tel 340/777-3483, redhookdive center.com).

Golf
Fabulous views across the BVI from the north shore and a challenging 18-hole Fazio-designed course draw golfers to **Mahogany Run Golf Course,** Mahogany Run Road (tel 340/777-6250 or 800/253-7103 ext. 2; book tee times at mahoganyrungolf.com).

Sportfishing
St. Thomas lies about 20 miles (32 km) below the North Drop, famed for blue marlin fishing in the prime June through September season. Several outfits operate out of American Yacht Harbor at Red Hook. Contact **Marlin Prince** (tel 340/693-5929, marlinprince.com) or **Double Header Sportfishing,** Sapphire Beach Resort (tel 340/777-7317, doubleheader sportfishing.net).

BRITISH VIRGIN ISLANDS
Boating
Excursions from Tortola to Virgin Gorda or Norman Island, with lunch and snorkeling, can be booked through the catamaran *Aristocat* (tel 284/499-1249, aristocatcharters.com) or **Voyage Charters** (tel 410/956-6919, voyagecharters.com). You can captain your own powerboat or opt for an experienced local to do it for you with **TRC Boat Rentals & Charters,** East End, Tortola (tel 284/495-8025, trcboatingbvi.com).

Diving & Snorkeling
Superb diving and snorkeling opportunities abound in the Sir Francis Drake Channel. The BVI's top dive sites include the wreck of the R.M.S. *Rhone* off Salt Island, while snorkelers shouldn't miss The Baths on Virgin Gorda. Recommended local operators include **Blue Water Divers** (tel 284/494-2847, bluewaterdivers bvi.com); **BVI Scuba Co.** (tel 284/540-2222, bviscubaco .com); **Sail Caribbean Divers** (tel 284/495-1675, sailcaribbean divers.com); and **Jost van Dyke Scuba** (tel 284/495-0271, jost vandykescuba.com).

Windsurfing & Water Sports
Trellis Bay is Tortola's windsurfing center. Making the best of the BVI's steady 15-knot trade winds, **Boardsailing BVI Watersports** (tel 284/495-2447) rents out boards (tuition available and other water-sports equipment, including kayaks). On Virgin Gorda, **Blue Rush Water Sports,** Leverick Bay (tel 284/547-0583, bluerushwatersports.com), rents out dinghies, kayaks, waverunners, and paddleboards (some have LED lights on the bottom

for really cool night tours); they can also tutor the adventurous in flyboarding.

■ DUTCH CARIBBEAN

ARUBA
Diving & Snorkeling
Prime sites are found amid the calm waters of the protected western and southern coasts, and the 400-foot-long wreck of the *Antilla* is one of the largest in the Caribbean. Trips, refresher tuition, and PADI certification courses are available from **Red Sail Sports** (tel 297/586-1603 or U.S. 305/454-2538, redsailaruba .com). Also highly rated is the full-service **Mermaid Dive Center,** Eagle Beach (tel 297/587-4103, scubadivers-aruba.com).

Golf
Aruba's best golfing is the scenic Trent Jones Jr.–designed **Tierra del Sol,** Tierra del Sol Resort (tel 297/586-0978 ext. 224 or 866/978-5158, tierradelsol.com).

Guided Tours
Offering a range of excursions encompassing minibus tours, day sails, dive trips, and Jeep safaris, **De Palm Tours** (tel 297/522-4400, depalmtours.com) is Aruba's leading tour operator. ATV tours can be arranged through **Rancho Notorious** (see Horseback Riding p. 394).

Hiking
Hiking on Aruba means a trip to Arikok National Park (see p. 196). Check schedules for ranger-led tours, or contact former lead ranger Eddy Croes of **Nature Sensitive Tours** (tel 297/585-1594, naturesensitivetours.com). The best times to trek are early morning or late afternoon.

Horseback Riding

Horseback trails are a great way to explore the rugged *cunucu* backcountry. Saddle up with **Rancho Daimari** (tel 297/586-6284) or **Rancho Notorious** (tel 297/586-0508, rancho notorious.com).

Sportfishing

Mahi Mahi, Renaissance Marina, Oranjestad (tel 297/587-0538, aruba-mahimahi.com) has a small, well-equipped fleet; or let one-stop water-sports operator **Red Sail Sports,** Oranjestad (tel 297/586-1603 or U.S. 305/454-2538, redsailaruba.com) make the arrangements.

Water Sports

Palm Beach is Aruba's water-sports capital, where concessions offer a host of motorized and nonmotorized water activities. Windsurfing and kitesurfing are available through **Aruba Active Vacations,** Hadikurai Beach (tel 297/586-0989, aruba-active-vacations.com), and **Vela Aruba,** Palm Beach (tel 297/586-9000 or U.S. 800/223-5443, velawind surf.com).

BONAIRE

Diving & Snorkeling

Without doubt one of the world's most spectacular reef diving destinations, Bonaire is equipped to satisfy snorkelers and divers of all skill levels. Hotel/dive packages are available through such established operators as **Buddy Dive Resort** (tel 599/717-5080 or U.S./Canada 866/462-8339, buddydive.com) and **Captain Don's Habitat** (tel 599/717-8290 or U.S./Canada 800/327-6709, habitatbonaire .com). Or contact **Bonaire Dive & Adventure** (tel 599/717-2227, bonairediveandadventure.com), who also arrange kayaking and

mountain biking, as well as an excellent five-day Island Explorer package based around activities and tours of your choice.

Horseback Riding

Explore the island's back roads on horseback with **Horse Ranch Bonaire,** Kunuku Warahama (tel 599/786-2094, horseranch bonaire.com). The route passes the Pekelmeer flamingo habitat and ends with a horse-and-rider swim at Lac Bay.

Windsurfing & Kayaking

Breezy Bonaire is a great place to learn to windsurf; contact **Jibe City** (tel 599/717-5233, jibecity.com), which also rents kayaks. Coastal kayaking tours can be arranged through the **Mangrove Info Center,** Kaminda Lac (tel 599/780-5353, mangrovecenter.com) and **Bonaire Dive & Adventure** (see Diving & Snorkeling).

CURAÇAO

Adventure Tours & Hiking

See sidebar page 188.

Boating & Sportfishing

Half- or full-day snorkel and dive trips, sunset cruises, and deep-sea fishing charters can be booked with **Bounty Adventures** (tel 5999/767-9998, bounty adventures.com). The handsome 120-foot (37 m) 1931 sailing ship *Insulinde* (tel 5999/560-1340, insulinde.com) departs on afternoon snorkel and swim sails from the historic Willemstad waterfront, and makes occasional weekend trips to Bonaire and longer cruises to the San Blas islands off Panama.

Diving & Snorkeling

The best dive and snorkel sites lie off the protected leeward

coast. Conveniently located right on Seaquarium Beach, **Ocean Encounters,** Lions Dive & Beach Resort (tel 5999/461-8131, oceanencounters.com) is a one-stop dive shop offering dive trips to sites around the island, courses ranging from PADI certification to underwater photography, and a raft of water-sports activities.

SABA

Diving & Snorkeling

See sidebar page 184.

Hiking

For information about trails, guided walks, and hiking Mount Scenery, drop in at the **Saba Trail Shop,** Windwardside (tel 599/416-2630).

SINT EUSTATIUS

Diving, Snorkeling, & Hiking

The island's dive operations are centered on Gallows Bay. General information and divers' marine tags can be obtained from the **Statia National Parks Office,** Bay Road, Lower Town (tel 599/318-2884, statiapark.org), which also supplies details of hiking trails and Statia's Sea Turtle Conservation Program. For reservations, contact the **Golden Rock Dive Center** (tel 599/318-2964, goldenrockdive.com) and **Scubaqua Dive Center** (tel 599/318-5450, scubaqua.com).

SINT MAARTEN/ ST.-MARTIN

Bicycling & Kayaking

The island is not renowned for its sporting facilities, but on the Dutch side, **Tri-Sport,** Simson Baai (tel 721/545-4384, trisport sxm.com) arranges mountain bike and ocean kayak tours and bike and kayak rentals.

Boating & Sportfishing

Visiting the islands of St. Barts and Anguilla is a favorite pursuit either by ferry or on day-sail vessels. **Bluebeard Charters,** Simson Baai (tel 721/587-5935, bluebeard charters.com) visits Shoal Bay, Anguilla, and Prickly Pear Island aboard its 60-foot (18 m) catamaran; or circumnavigate the island with **Eagle Tours,** Philipsburg (tel 721/542-3323, sailingsxm.com). Sportfishing trips can be arranged with **Rudy's Deep Sea Fishing,** Simson Baai (tel 721/545-2177, rudysdeepseafishing.com).

Diving & Snorkeling

Several shops in Simpson Bay, Sint Maarten, provide instruction and equipment rental, including **Dive Safaris,** La Palapa Marina (tel 721/545-2401, divestmaarten .com). On the French side, **Octopus Diving,** Grand Case (cell 690/88 53 39 or U.S. 914/487-1315, octopusdiving.com) is an English-speaking operation offering snorkel tours and dive tuition for every level from try dives and discovery courses to more advanced PADI certification programs.

Horseback Riding

Nature trails, beach rides, and children's pony rides on Sint Maarten from **Seaside Nature Park,** Cay Bay (tel 721/544-5255, seasidenaturepark.com); on St.-Martin, contact **Bayside Riding Club** (Gallion Beach, tel 690/62 36 18, baysideranch.com).

◾ LEEWARD ISLANDS

ANGUILLA

Bicycling

Flat-as-a-pancake Anguilla provides some great off-road tracks in the undeveloped East End. A number of hotels and villas provide bikes free to guests; rentals

are available from **Exotic Plus** (tel 264/497-8803) and **Premier Mountain Bike** (tel 264/235-8931) in The Valley.

Diving & Snorkeling

Calm and exceptionally clear conditions, reefs, wreck dives, and abundant marine life tick all the boxes for divers and snorkelers at every level. Contact **Shoal Bay Scuba,** Shoal Bay (tel 264/235-1482, shoalbayscuba.com), and Rob Willsher at **Vigilant Divers,** The Valley (tel 264/235-4096, email vigilantdivers@gmail.com).

Golf

The 18-hole course at the **CuisinArt Golf Club** (tel 264/498-5602, cuisinartresort .com) combines magnificent views with eco-friendly credentials and course design from Greg Norman.

Horseback Riding

Riders of all abilities are welcome at **Seaside Stables,** Cove Bay (tel 264/235-3667, seasidestables anguilla.com). Beach rides last around one hour; longer by arrangement.

Sportfishing

The go-to guy for sportfishing off Anguilla is Garfield Richardson of **Garfield's Sea Tours** (tel 264/235-7902, gotcha-garfields -sea-tours-anguilla.com).

ANTIGUA & BARBUDA

Boating

See sidebar page 207.

Diving & Snorkeling

Antigua's best reef sites are off the sheltered south and west coasts. Dive operators around English Harbour include **Dockyard Divers** (tel 268/729-3040, dockyard-divers.com). On the

west coast, contact **Indigo Divers,** Jolly Harbour (tel 268/562-3483, indigo-divers.com); or **Jolly Dive,** Jolly Beach (tel 268/462-8305, jollydiveantigua.com). For snorkeling trips to Cades Reef, Green Island, and Bird Island, contact **Treasure Island Cruises** (tel 268/461-8675, treasureislandcruises.ag).

Eco- & Island Tours

A half-day eco-experience with **Paddles,** Seaton's Village (tel 268/720-4322, antigua paddles.com) includes kayaking through mangrove-lined waterways, bird-watching, and snorkeling in the North Sound Marine Park. Or launch into a full day of eco-discovery with **Adventure Antigua** (tel 268/726-6355, adventureantigua.com). For an around-island Jeep safari or a combination of safari and kayaking, contact **Tropical Adventures** (tel 268/480-1225, tropicalad .com), who can also whisk you off on a day trip to Barbuda.

Golf

Antigua's top golfing spot is the 18-hole championship course at the **Jolly Harbour Golf Club** (tel 268/462-7771 ext. 608, jollyharbourantigua.com/golf). Northeast of St. John's, there's another 18-hole course at the **Cedar Valley Golf Club** (tel 268/462-0161, cvgolfantigua .com).

Horseback Riding

Take a gentle hack up into the hills above English Harbour and down to the beach for a swim with **Spring Hill Riding Club,** Falmouth (tel 268/773-3139, antiguaequestrian.com).

Sportfishing

Head out to Antigua's Atlantic fishing grounds with **Nightwing**

Charters (tel 268/464-4665, fishantigua.com) and **Overdraft** (tel 268/720-4954, antiguafishing.com). Fly-fishing for bonefish is also possible.

Turtle-Watching

During the sea turtle nesting season (March–Nov.), female hawksbill, green, leatherback, and loggerhead turtles come ashore at night to lay their eggs on Antigua's beaches. Contact the **Environmental Awareness Group** (tel 268/462-6236, eagantigua .org) for turtle-watching.

MONTSERRAT
Diving, Snorkeling, & Kayaking

Montserrat's superb diving is one of the Caribbean's best kept secrets. Off the sheltered west coast, reef shelves forested with pristine corals teem with exotic fish and sea creatures. PADI-affiliated **Scuba Montserrat** (tel 664/491-7807, scubamontserrat .com) offers dive and snorkel trips, customized packages, and tuition, as well as extras like kayaking, and beach picnics.

Hiking & Bird-Watching

The **Montserrat Tourist Board** (tel 664/491-2230, visitmontserrat.com) and the **National Trust** (tel 664/491-3086, montserratnationaltrust.ms) can advise on routes and trail guide services, or contact **Scriber's Adventure Tours** (tel 664/492-2943, scribersadventures.com).

ST. KITTS & NEVIS
Boating & Snorkeling

The **Reggae Beach Bar & Grill,** Cockleshell Bay (tel 869/762-5050, reggaebeachbar.com) is the home of the **St. Kitts Sailing School,** which rents out ocean kayaks and snorkel equipment,

and can arrange private day-sail charters and deep-sea fishing. **Leeward Island Charters** (tel 869/465-7474, leewardislands charters.com) and **Blue Water Safaris** (tel 869/466-4933, bluewatersafaris.com) can also arrange cruises and snorkel trips.

Diving

Though not a major league dive destination, St. Kitts has plenty to entertain novice and more experienced divers. Local PADI-certified operators include **Dive St. Kitts** (tel 869/465-8914, divestkitts.com) and **Pro Divers** (tel 869/660-3483, prodivers stkitts.com). On Nevis, Oualie Beach is home to high-tech, PADI five-star outfit **Scuba Safaris** (tel 869/469-9518, divestkittsnevis.com).

Golf

Sandwiched between the Atlantic Ocean and the Caribbean Sea, the 18-hole course at the **Royal St. Kitts Golf Club** (tel 869/466-2700, royalstkittsgolfclub.com) provides challenges and views. On Nevis, there is an excellent 18-hole course at the **Four Seasons** (tel 869/469-1111, four seasons.com/nevis).

Hiking, Safari, & Heritage Tours

Lush rain forest hikes on St. Kitts and more strenuous treks up through areas of cloud forest to Mount Liamuiga's crater rim can be arranged through knowledgeable guide outfit **Greg's Safaris** (tel 869/465-4121, gregsafaris .com). Greg's Off-the-Beaten-Track 4WD safaris visit plantations and sugar mill ruins. Nevisian history is uncovered on eco-rambles with Lynnell Liburd of **Sunrise Tours** (tel 869/665-1959, nevisnaturetours.com), whose varied excursions include rain

forest hikes, village walks, and bird-watching. Michael Herbert of **Heb's Nature Tours** (tel 869/762-5119) leads treks to Nevis Peak.

Mountain Biking

For top-of-the-line bike rentals and tours from former windsurfing champ Winston Crooke, contact **Wheel World Cycle Shop** (tel 869/469-9682, bikenevis.com).

■ FRENCH ANTILLES

GUADELOUPE
Boating & Whale-Watching

For day sails from St.-François (Grande-Terre) to Marie-Galante, and Petite Terre in the Guadeloupean archipelago, contact **Paradoxe Croisières,** Marina St.-François (tel 0590/88 41 73, paradoxe-croisieres.com). Whale-watching cruises can be arranged in winter (Dec.–March) through **Les Heures Saines,** Plage de Malendure, Basse-Terre (tel 0590/98 86 63, heures-saines.gp).

Diving

The Cousteau Underwater Reserve surrounding Pigeon Island is the island's best dive destination, but also its busiest. Experienced operators **Les Heures Saines** (tel 0590/98 86 63, heures-saines.gp) are based at Bouillante and offer a variety of dive options, including night dives. **Plaisir Plongée Karukera** (tel 0590/98 82 43, ppk-plongee -guadeloupe.com) dispatches several dive boats a day to Îlet de Pigeon.

Hiking & Bicycling

Adventure tour specialist **Vert Intense** (tel 0590/99 34 73, vert-intense.com) offers guided trekking excursions into the national park (reservations essential). See also sidebar page 239. Grande-Terre offers gentler cycling. Bike and scooter rentals are widely available; details of tour operators and rental companies are available from local tourist offices.

Sportfishing

For day trips off the west coast of Basse-Terre, contact **Michel Pêche au Gros,** Bouillante (tel 0690/40 15 01).

ST.-BARTHÉLEMY
Boating

Conveniently encircled by protected harbors, St. Barts is one of the Caribbean's top sailing destinations (see sidebar p. 245). The Gustavia tourist office on the marina can advise on day-sail options and schedules, or check out two dockside operations: **Jicky Marine Service** (tel 0590/27 70 34, jickymarine.com) and **Ocean Must** (tel 0590/27 62 25, oceanmust.com), which offer a range of water activities.

Tours

Taxi tours are available from the dock in Gustavia; or inquire at the tourist office for details of their own minibus tour itineraries.

MARTINIQUE
Boating

Boating excursions from Pointe du Bout north to St.-Pierre, or down the coast for a view of the Rocher du Diamont, a buffet lunch, and a spot of snorkeling are a popular option with **Kata Mambo** (tel 0596/66 11 83, kata-mambo.com). Or head farther afield to St. Lucia with **Passion** (tel 0596/74 00 67, excursions-passion.com).

Diving & Snorkeling

Martinique's best reef sites are off the south coast; there's also good snorkeling off the beach at Anses d'Arlet. Contact **Alpha Plongée,** Anses d'Arlet (tel 0596/48 30 34, alphaplongee .com) and **Crazy Frog,** Anses d'Arlet (tel 0596/48 32 17, crazy .frog.free.fr). In the north of the island, **A Papa d'Lo** (tel 0696/50 13 68, apapadlo.net) is based in St.-Pierre, where the eruption of Mont Pelée in 1902 created a unique wreck dive site.

Golf

The l'Impératrice Joséphine course at the **Golf Country Club de la Martinique,** Les Trois-Îlets (tel 0596/52 04 13) is a glorious Trent Jones Sr.–designed 18-hole, 71-par challenge on the bayfront.

Hiking

There are 64 marked trails totaling around 300–400 miles (483–644 km) of hiking paths around the island. Information is available from the offices of the **Parc Naturel Régional de la Martinique,** 9 blvd. Général de Gaulle, Fort-de-France (tel 0596/64 42 59, pnr-martinique .com), or contact the **Bureau de la Randonnée et du Canyoning** (tel 0596/55 04 79, bureau -rando-martinique.com).

Horseback Riding

Ride through a plantation estate with **Ranch de Trenelle,** Rivière-Salée (tel 0696/83 41 68, ranch detrenelle.fr), or head inland and circle back to the beach with **Black Horse Ranch,** Les Trois-Îlets (tel 0696/31 73 00, ranch blackhorse.fr).

Mountain Biking

Cyclists looking to team up with a group for tours (full- and half-day

options), can contact **VT Tilt,** Les Trois-Îlets (tel 0596/66 01 01).

Water Sports

Hotels and concessions provide water-sports facilities on main tourist beaches. For windsurfing and kiteboarding, contact **Alizé Fun,** Ste.-Anne (tel 0696/91 71 06, alizefunkitemartinique.com); experienced windsurfers will find more challenging conditions on the Atlantic side, where the **Bliss École de Surf de Martinique,** Tartane (tel 0596/58 00 96, surf-martinique.com) offers rentals and tuition.

◼ WINDWARD ISLANDS

DOMINICA
Diving & Snorkeling

A top-ten entry on any list of the world's best dive destinations, Dominica has two main dive areas, both off the sheltered west coast. The must-do site is the southern Scotts Head/Soufrière Bay Marine Reserve, ranged around a submarine crater. Snorkelers can also get their fill of exotic marine life at the reserve's Champagne Reef. Contact **Anchorage Whale Watch & Dive Centre** (tel 767/448-2638 or U.S. 888/790-5264, anchoragehotel.dm) and **Dive Dominica** (tel 767/448-2188, divedominica.com), both based at Castle Comfort. To the north, there are some fine dive sites in Cabrits Marine Park and midway down the coast at Mero; contact **Cabrits Dive Centre,** Portsmouth (tel 767/445-3010, cabritsdive .com).

Hiking & Tours

Intrepid hikers are spoiled for choice in Dominica's mountainous and densely forested interior. For longer treks a local guide is strongly recommended. Completed in 2011, the **Waitukubuli National Trail** (waitukubulitrail .com) is the jewel in the crown of Dominican hiking: A 115-mile (185 km) transisland hiking path, it is divided into 14 sections that can be hiked in part or in total (allow at least a week). Guides can be arranged in Roseau through the **Forestry Department,** Botanical Gardens (tel 767/266-3817), and the tourist office, **Discover Dominica,** Valley Road (tel 767/448-2045, discoverdominica.com).

Part of the **Anchorage Whale Watch & Dive Centre** (see Diving p. 397), **Dominica Tours** (experience-dominica.com) offers a raft of island and heritage tours, hiking, birding, and whale-watching excursions. Or contact **Ken's Hinterland Adventure Tours** (tel 767/448-1660 or U.S. 866/880-0508, khattstours.com).

Whale-Watching

See sidebar page 268.

GRENADA & CARRIACOU

Boating

Grenada is a hub for yacht charters and boat trips. Around-island excursions, snorkeling, and sunset cruises are available from **Carib Cats** (tel 473/444-3222), **First Impressions** (tel 473/440-3678, catamaran charteringcom), and **Shadowfax** (tel 473/437-3737, banana boattoursgrenada.com). One of the region's leading yacht charter brokers, **Horizon Yacht Charters** (tel 473/439-1002 or U.S. 866/463-7245, horizon yachtcharters.com), supplies

crewed and bareboat charters, and teaches ASA sailing courses.

Diving & Snorkeling

Grenada's 50 dive sites line the protected Caribbean coast, with the best underwater scenery found in the southwest Marine Protected Area. Carriacou, which translates as "land of reefs," also has some superb diving and snorkeling. In Grenada contact **Aquanauts** (tel 473/444-1126, aquanautsgrenada.com), **Dive Grenada** (tel 473/444-1092, divegrenada.com), and **Eco Dive** (tel 473/444-7777, ecodiveand trek.com). On Carriacou contact **Arawak Divers** (tel 473/443-6906, arawakdivers.com), **Deefer Diving** (tel 473/443-7882, deefer diving.com), and **Lumbadive** (tel 473/443-8566, lumbadive.com).

Hiking

See sidebar page 294.

Sportfishing

Grenada's sportfishing fraternity heads out into the Atlantic in search of marlin, sailfish, dorado, tuna, and wahoo. Contact **First Impressions** (tel 473/440-3678, catamaranchartering.com) and **True Blue Sportfishing** (tel 473/407-4688, yesaye.com).

Tours

Sightseeing tours and rain forest hikes can be arranged through **Henry's Yacht Services & Tours** (tel 473/444-5313, henrysafari .com), or there's Jeep tours, mountain biking, and river tubing with aptly named **Adventure Tours** (tel 473/444-5337, adventuregrenada.com).

Whale-Watching

Day-sail operators **First Impressions** (tel 473/440-3678, cata maranchartering.com) also offer

dolphin- and whale-watching excursions throughout the year. Winter (Dec.–April) is high season for whale sightings.

ST. LUCIA

Boating

Picture-perfect St. Lucia is a glorious backdrop for a day sail, and the most picturesque views of the famous Pitons can be enjoyed aboard a sailboat traveling down the coast from Castries to Soufrière. **Endless Summer** (tel 758/450-8651, stluciaboat tours.com) and **Sea Spray Cruises** (tel 758/452-8644 or U.S. 321/220-9423, seaspray cruises.com) run catamaran trips with sightseeing shore excursions included, and sunset cruises are popular. Sea Spray also operates a replica pirate ship, *Black Magic,* for fun-packed family days out. Based in Soufrière, **Mystic Man Tours** (tel 758/459-7783, mysticmantours.com) offers a full range of day and evening sails, whale-watching, sportfishing, and snorkeling excursions.

Plenty of crewed and bareboat charter operations work out of the busy Rodney Bay and Marigot Bay marinas. One of the largest and most experienced operators is **The Moorings,** Rodney Bay (tel 758/285-1270 or U.S. 888/952-8420, moorings .com). **Sunsail** (tel 758/285-1270 or 877/936-2793, sunsail.com) runs flotilla holidays in both St. Lucia and the BVI for less confident (or more gregarious) yachtsmen as well as individual charters.

Diving & Snorkeling

St. Lucia's underwater scenery is every bit as impressive as its terrestrial landscape. Snorkelers can access the reefs straight off the beach at Anse Chastanet, where **Scuba St. Lucia** (tel 758/459-7755 or 800/223-1108, scubastlucia.com) offers tuition, beach and boat dives, and snorkel excursions in Scotts Head/Soufrière Bay Marine Park. For dive adventures off the northwest coast and snorkeling around Pigeon Island, **Scuba Steve's Diving,** Rodney Bay Marina (tel 758/450-9433, scuba stevesdiving.com), promises a range of marine life.

Golf

So far, St. Lucia has just one 18-hole golf course, the **St. Lucia Golf & Country Club,** Rodney Bay (tel 758/450-8523, stlucia golf.com), set in the private Cap Estate on the northern tip of the island. There's also an attractive 9-hole course at the **Sandals Regency La Toc Golf Resort & Spa,** Castries (tel 758/452-3081, sandals.com).

Hiking

See sidebar page 276.

Horseback Riding

Mosey through rolling farmland to Pigeon Island National Landmark on a trail ride with **Trim's National Riding Academy,** Gros Islet (tel 758/450-8273, trims ridingstlucia.com).

Sportfishing

Full- and half-day charters on well-equipped craft depart from the Vigie Marina in Castries. Contact **Captain Mike's** (tel 758/452-7044, captmikes .com), a third-generation family operation; and **Hackshaw's Boat Charters** (tel 758/453-0553, hackshaws.com).

ST. VINCENT & THE GRENADINES

Boating

The must-do day sail on St. Vincent is a trip around the northern tip of the island to the Falls of Baleine. Boat trips to the falls, and down the Grenadines to Tobago Cays and Mustique, are offered by **Fantasea Tours** (tel 784/457-4477, fantaseatours.com) and the Bequia-based and hand-built schooner *The Friendship Rose* (tel 784/457-3739, friendshiprose .com). **Sea Breeze Nature Tours** (tel 784/458-4969, seabreeze naturetours.com) pioneered whale- and dolphin-watching off the island.

The Grenadine Islands are a magnet for sailors and there are numerous operations offering crewed and bareboat charters. Family-run **Barefoot Yacht Charters** (tel 784/456-9526, barefoot yachts.com) also operates a sailing school. Charter brokers **The Moorings** (tel 784/482-0653 or U.S. 888/952-8420, moorings .com) has bases on neighboring St. Lucia and Grenada, as well as St. Maarten and the BVI, allowing for one-way voyages.

Diving & Snorkeling

For an expert introduction to local marine life, you can't beat an outing with dive master Bill Tewes of **Dive St. Vincent** (tel 784/457-4928, divestvincent .com). **Indigo Dive** (tel 784/493-9494, indigodive.com) also offers lessons, cruises, and snorkel tours. Some of the best snorkeling around the island is found at Chateaubelair and Buccament Bay, or take a day sail (see Boating) to reach less accessible sites.

For diving and snorkeling in Bequia, contact **Dive Bequia** (tel 784/458-3504, divebequia .com). Farther down the islands **Canouan Scuba Center,** Canouan (tel 784/532-8073 or U.S. 917/796-1100, canouandivecenter.com), and **Grenadines Dive,** Union Island (tel 784/458-8138, grenadinesdive .com), also run dive and snorkel trips to Tobago Cays.

Golf

The pint-size Grenadine Island of Canouan is a somewhat unlikely location for the glorious **Grenadines Estate Golf Club** (tel 784/458-8000, canouan.com /golf), a challenging, 18-hole Jim Fazio creation carved into the undulating shoreline.

Hiking & Tours

See sidebar page 280.

■ BARBADOS

Boating

A number of day-sail vessels ply the west coast offering excursions with lunch, a snorkel stop, and a sea turtle encounter. For daily departures from Bridgetown, contact **Cool Runnings** (tel 246/436-0911, coolrunningsbarbados.com), **El Tigre** (tel 246/417-7245, eltigrecruises.com), and **Tiami Catamaran Cruises** (tel 246/430-0900, tiamicatamaran cruises.com). Call ahead to make reservations, and check schedules for sunset cruises.

Diving & Snorkeling

Along the west coast from Maycocks Bay down through the Platinum Coast to Carlisle Bay, south of Bridgetown, the sea is calm and visibility is excellent. Well-established dive operations offering single dives, packages, and PADI-certification courses include **Barbados Blue,** Carlisle Bay, St. Michael (tel 246/434-5764, divebarbados blue.com); **High-tide Watersports,** Holetown, St. James (tel 246/432-0931 or 800/970-0016, divehightide.com); and **The Dive Shop Ltd.,** Carlisle Bay, St. Michael (tel 246/426-9947 or U.S. 866/978-6983, divebds.com).

Golf

Barbados's most prestigious pay-as-you-play course is the Country Club course at **Sandy Lane,** Paynes Bay, St. James (tel 246/444-2500, sandylane.com /golf). Sandy Lane's intimate and attractive par-36 Old Nine course is also open to visitors. Two exceptional guest-only courses in St. James are the **Apes Hill Club** (tel 246/432-4500, apeshillclub.com) and the **Royal Westmoreland** (tel 246/419-7242, royalwest moreland.com). On the south coast, the **Barbados Golf Club,** Durants, Christ Church (tel 246/428-8463, barbadosgolf club.com) welcomes visitors. The popular and very sociable **Rockley Golf Club,** Rockley, Christ Church (tel 246/435-7873, rockleygolf club.com) has a surprisingly challenging nine-hole parkland course.

Sportfishing

Half- and full-day boat charters from Bridgetown's Careenage provide a choice of coastal and deep-sea fishing expeditions. The high season for billfish is December through April. Contact **Predator Sportfishing,** Bridgetown (tel 246/230-1845, fishbarbados .com). Fishing trips with several other local operators, such as **Billfisher III** (tel 246/431-0741), can be arranged in advance.

Tours

Island Safari (tel 246/429-5337, islandsafari.bb) pioneered 4WD adventure tours that take in the sights from clifftop lookouts and off-road forest trails to beaches. They also offer catamaran excursions with snorkeling and turtle encounters.

Walks

The **Barbados National Trust** (tel 246/426-2421, barbados nationaltrust.org) organizes the free Hike Barbados Sunday fun walk program. The guided walks depart at 6 a.m. and 3:30 p.m. (call ahead for details).

Water Sports

Water-sports facilities are widely available from hotels and beach concessions on the Caribbean coast. Along the south coast, breezy Silver Sands Beach is the hub of the local windsurfing and kiteboarding scene. Experienced surfers come for the big Atlantic swells that thunder onto the east coast December through April. **Barbados Surf Trips** (tel 246/255-3509, surf barbados.com) offers tuition, rentals, tips, and customized surfing packages.

■ TRINIDAD & TOBAGO

Diving & Snorkeling

Trinidad's proximity to the Orinoco Delta hampers underwater visibility. Most divers head for Tobago and its pristine reefs, where visibility is excellent. Snorkelers can just step off the beach along the Caribbean coast. For more experienced divers, the excitement lies farther north around Charlotteville and Speyside, where the Japanese Gardens and Aquarium off Batteaux Bay are world-class dives. Dive operators in Speyside include **Blue Waters Diving** (tel 868/660-5445, bluewatersinn.com) and **Tobago Dive Experience** (tel 868/660-4888). For diving off the south coast, contact **R & Sea Divers,** Crown Point (tel 868/639-8120, rseadivers.com).

Golf

Set in the smart residential suburbs of Port of Spain, Trinidad's finest golfing is found at **St. Andrews Golf Club,** Maraval (tel 868/629-0066, golftrinidad .com). On Tobago, **Mt. Irvine Bay Resort Golf Club**'s (tel 868/639-8871, mtirvine.com) once lovely old hillside course is currently looking very unkempt (2016), but golfers can enjoy a round at the PGA-designed **Tobago Plantations Golf Club** (tel 868/660-8740, magdalenagrand .com), which rolls down to the mangrove-lined shore.

Guided Tours

Wildlife photographer Stephen Broadbridge of **Caribbean Discovery Tours** (tel 868/624-7281, caribbeandiscoverytours.com) offers a wide range of eco- and island discovery tours; or contact **Kalloos** (tel 868/622-9073, kalloos.com) for taxi tours and trips to Caroni, Asa Wright, and Tobago.

On Tobago, **Peter Cox Nature Tours** (tel 868/751-5822, tobago naturetours.com) leads birding and sightseeing tours and visits to Scarborough market, or contact **Yes Tourism** (tel 868/357-0064, yes-tourism.com) for island tours and side trips to Trinidad.

Turtle-Watching

For turtle-watching in Trinidad, see sidebar page 324. On Tobago contact **Peter Cox Nature Tours** (tel 868/751-5822, tobago naturetours.com).

INDEX

ILLUSTRATIONS CREDITS

National Geographic

TRAVELER
The Caribbean: Ports of Call & Beyond

Since 1888, the National Geographic Society has funded more than 12,000 research, exploration, and preservation projects around the world. National Geographic Partners distributes a portion of the funds it receives from your purchase to National Geographic Society to support programs including the conservation of animals and their habitats.

National Geographic Partners
1145 17th Street NW
Washington, DC 20036-4688 USA

Become a member of National Geographic and activate your benefits today at natgeo.com/jointoday.

For information about special discounts for bulk purchases, please contact National Geographic Books Special Sales: specialsales@natgeo.com

For rights or permissions inquiries, please contact National Geographic Books Subsidiary Rights: bookrights@natgeo.com

ISBN: 978-1-4262-1709-8

The information in this book has been carefully checked and to the best of our knowledge is accurate. However, details are subject to change, and the publisher cannot be responsible for such changes, or for errors or omissions. Assessments of sites, hotels, and restaurants are based on the author's subjective opinions, which do not necessarily reflect the publisher's opinion.

Printed in Hong Kong

16/THK/1

THE COMPLETE TRAVEL EXPERIENCE

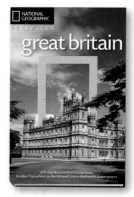

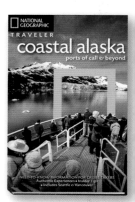

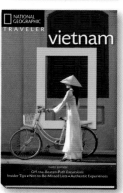

With more than 75 destinations around the globe; available wherever
books are sold and at www.shopng.com/travelerguides

TRIPS
natgeoexpeditions.com

MAGAZINE

for iPhone®,
iPod touch®,
and iPad®

APPS

NATIONAL
GEOGRAPHIC